TRUCKING

Tractor-Trailer Driver Handbook

THOMSON
★
DELMAR LEARNING

Australia   Canada   Mexico   Singapore   Spain   United Kingdom   United States

Trucking: Tractor-Trailer Driver Handbook

Business Unit Executive Director:
Susan L. Simpfenderfer

Executive Production Manager:
Wendy A. Troeger

Executive Marketing Manager:
Donna J. Lewis

Developmental Editor:
Patricia Gillivan

Cover Design:
John Orozco

Channel Manager:
Wendy E. Mapstone

NOTICE TO THE READER

Contents

Chapter One

An Introduction to Trucking   1.1

Chapter Two

Control Systems   2.1

Chapter Three

Hours of Service   3.1

Chapter Four

Vehicle Inspection   4.1

Chapter Five

Vehicle Systems   5.1

Chapter Six

Basic Control   6.1

Chapter Seven

Shifting   7.1

Chapter Eight

Backing   8.1

Chapter Nine

Coupling and Uncoupling   9.1

Chapter Ten

Visual Search **10.1**

Chapter Eleven

Communication **11.1**

Chapter Twelve

Space Management **12.1**

Chapter Thirteen

Speed Management **13.1**

Chapter Fourteen

Night Driving   14.1

Chapter Fifteen

Extreme Driving Conditions   15.1

Chapter Sixteen

Hazard Awareness   16.1

Chapter Twenty-One

Sliding Fifth Wheels and Tandem Axles   21.1

Chapter Twenty-Two

Special Rigs   22.1

Chapter Twenty-Three

Preventive Maintenance and Servicing   23.1

Chapter Twenty-Four

Recognizing and Reporting Malfunctions   24.1

Chapter Twenty-Five

Handling Cargo   25.1

Chapter Twenty-Six

Cargo Documentation   26.1

Chapter Twenty-Seven

Personal Health and Safety   27.1

Chapter Twenty-Eight

Trip Planning   28.1

Chapter Twenty-Nine

Public Relations and Employer-Employee Relations 29.1

Preface

Training and retention of skilled tractor-trailer drivers are among the foremost challenges of the trucking industry. The Professional Truck Driver Institute, Inc. and Delmar Learning have produced *Trucking: Tractor-Trailer Driver Handbook* to help prepare professional truck drivers for entry-level positions in the industry. This book meets the standards established by the Federal Highway Administration's Model Curriculum (Proposed Minimum Standards for Training Tractor-Trailer Drivers). It also matches the standards of the certification program established by the Professional Truck Driver Institute, Inc.

Professional driver training schools, motor carriers, and individual instructors will find that *Trucking: Tractor-Trailer Driver Handbook* readily meets their needs in the classroom and on the driving course. It has been revised and designed to ultimately provide the trucking industry in the 21st century with professional drivers who are knowledgeable, proficient in their jobs, dedicated to safety, and skillful in every aspect of their profession.

Trucking: Tractor-Trailer Driver Handbook addresses the knowledge needed by professional drivers as well as the procedures that, with practice, will enable the student to become skilled in every aspect of professional driving. Safety practices are emphasized.

Professional drivers are entrusted with valuable cargoes and operate costly equipment on a daily basis. Additionally, they represent the industry to shippers, receivers, and the public. Therefore, this book stresses the important traits necessary for professional drivers to present the best possible image for the industry and emphasizes the behavior that characterizes true professionals in every situation.

SUPPLEMENTS

Used in conjunction with the textbook, the following supplements provide a comprehensive, turnkey curriculum for tractor-trailer driver training.

Trucking: Tractor-Trailer Driver Course Management Guide on CD-ROM. The Course Management Guide includes the following components:

- **Computerized Test Bank**—500 multiple choice, true/false, matching, and fill-in-the-blank questions that the instructor can customize to meet individual course needs.
- **Instructor's Manual**—chapter objectives, overview, outline, and answers to review questions in the textbook.
- **Teacher's Resource Materials**—transparency masters and sample lesson plans.

Trucking: Tractor-Trailer Driver Handbook/Workbook Instructor's Manual. A print version of the Instructor's Manual can be purchased separately.

Trucking: Tractor-Trailer Driver Handbook/Workbook Transparency Masters. A print version of the transparency masters can be purchased separately.

Trucking: Tractor-Trailer Driver PowerPoint Presentation. The PowerPoint Presentation has been updated and includes Chapter 19, Passive Railroad Crossings. Each chapter of the book is conveniently organized into a single classroom presentation.

Trucking: Tractor-Trailer Driver Web Tutor. *Web Tutor* is a content-rich, web-based teaching and learning aid that reinforces and clarifies concepts covered in the textbook. *Web Tutor* helps instructors organize their courses and students maximize their understanding. It includes a course calendar, chat, e-mail, and threaded discussions. Instructors can monitor student progress and participation, and students receive immediate feedback when they take chapter quizzes.

ACKNOWLEDGMENTS

Many individuals made the development and publication of this book possible. Special thanks to Alice Adams who took the numerous revision plans, updated the content, and produced an easy-to-read manuscript. PTDI and Delmar Learning would also like to thank the following reviewers who provided suggestions for revising and updating the content, and reviewed the manuscript:

Christopher Antonik Delaware Technical and Community College, Georgetown, Delaware

Richard Campbell CDL Masters, Jacksonville, Florida

Alan Coldwell SAGE Technical Services, Post Falls, Idaho

Christopher J. Couty, Sr. Safety Solutions, Plaquemine, Louisiana

Darrell Creel Albuquerque Technical Vocational Institute, Albuquerque, New Mexico

Willy Eriksen Western Pacific Truck School of Oregon, Portland, Oregon

Vardis Gaus Albuquerque Technical Vocational Institute, Albuquerque, New Mexico

Lew Grill SAGE Technical Services, Billings, Montana

Don Hess John Wood Community College, Quincy, Illinois

Joseph M. Kishur, Jr. Mesalands Community College, Tucumcari, New Mexico

Michael McCombs Great West Casualty Company, Boise, Idaho

David Money Liberty Mutual Insurance Company, Wilbraham, Massachusetts

Charles J. Mosqueda Wichita Area Technical College Commercial Driver Education, Wichita, Kansas

Van O'Neal Houston Community College Northeast Commercial Truck Driving Center, Houston, Texas

Tony Pepitone Commercial Driver Training Inc., West Babylon, New York

Lana Pierce Tennessee Technology Center at Nashville, Nashville, Tennessee

Kim Richardson KRTS Transportation Specialists, Inc., Caledonia, Ontario Canada

Denny Shollenberger All-State Career Schools, Lester, Pennsylvania

Tom Waite McFatter Technical Center, Davie, Florida

Thank you also to:

Freightliner Trucks, a division of Freightliner LLC. Freightliner LLC is a division of Daimler Chrysler Company.

Operation Lifesaver, Inc.

Peterbilt/Rush Truck Center, Houston, Texas

Chapter One

An Introduction to Trucking

FROM NOW ON. . .

ONLY THE BEST
WILL DRIVE!

OBJECTIVES

When you have completed this chapter, you should be able to:

- Have a working knowledge of trucking

- Explain why the trucking industry is vital to our nation's economy

- Explain the rules and regulations under which the industry operates

- Understand the main systems and parts of tractor-trailers

- Describe the professionalism drivers should demonstrate

KEY TERMS

Cab-over-engine tractor (COE)

Combination vehicle

Commercial Driver's License (CDL)

Commercial Motor Vehicle (CMV)

Commercial Motor Vehicle Safety Act of 1986 (CMVSA/86)

Common carrier

Contract carrier

Conventional tractors

Department of Motor Vehicles (DMV)

Drive axle

Duals

18-wheeler

Environmental Protection Agency (EPA)

Federal Motor Carrier Safety Administration (FMCSA)

Federal Motor Carrier Safety Regulations (FMCSR)

For-hire carrier

Full trailer

Gross Vehicle Weight Rating (GVWR)

Hazardous Materials Regulations

Interstate carriers

Intrastate carriers

Motor Carrier Safety Assistance Program (MCSAP)

Motor carriers

National Transportation Safety Board (NTSB)

Nuclear Regulatory Commission (NRC)

Occupational Safety and Health Administration (OSHA)

Office of Hazardous Materials Transportation (OHMT)

Private carrier

Pusher axle

Research and Special Programs Administration (RSPA)

Rocky Mountain double

Semitrailer

Standard double

Straight truck

Tag axle

Tandem

Tandem axle tractor

Tractor

Trailer

Truck tractor

Turnpike double

Twin screws

U.S. Department of Transportation (U.S. DOT)

INTRODUCTION

Those professionals who drive tractor-trailers over this nation's roads and highways are vital members of a major service industry.

It has been said, "If you have it, a truck brought it"—and this, in a nutshell, captures the true importance of professional drivers. An entire nation's economy depends on the legions of professional drivers who move freight over our highways each day. Without professional drivers and the trucking industry, no city, no neighborhood, no family, and no individual in the United States could enjoy the comforts and quality of life available today.

Figure **1-1** Trucks transport most goods in this country.

Figure **1-2** Professional truck drivers are vital to our economy.

Trucks transport almost everything we eat, wear, use, or need—from origin to final destination (see Figure 1-1). The needs of families, business, industry, farms, the medical community, government, and education are served by trucks that haul farm products from the field to the processing plant and then to the market. Trucks also move crude oil from the oil field to the refinery or from barges to petrochemical plants and then from petrochem plants to service stations or homes. Professional drivers transport raw materials like coal, ore, and chemicals from mines to processing plants and from plants to manufacturers and finally to the retail market.

This country's two-million-plus fleet of tractor-trailers hauls three out of every four tons of goods in this country each year. This means 735 billion ton-miles of freight are carried over the road by professional drivers every year (one ton-mile equals one ton of goods carried one mile).

More than eight million Americans work in the trucking industry, including drivers, dock workers, dispatchers, safety directors, administrative support and sales personnel. And almost 13 percent of all Americans depend on employment within the trucking industry—more than 33 million people.

"If you have it, a truck brought it" is a true statement. It is also true that without the efforts of a professional truck driver, you would not have even the basic necessities of life (Figure 1-2).

THE U.S. TRUCKING INDUSTRY

The trucking industry has become an essential part of America's economy. The lives of every citizen of every age are affected by professional drivers moving freight from one point to another across the city, across the state, and across the nation.

Tightly regulated by federal and state laws and regulations (Figure 1-3), U.S. **motor carriers** attempt to employ drivers that are not only skilled and safe operators but also professional in their attitudes and approach to every job. In addition, carriers of every size continually work to improve safety in the workplace as well as driver safety on the nation's streets and highways. Many companies annually reward drivers earning safe driving records for their professional performance.

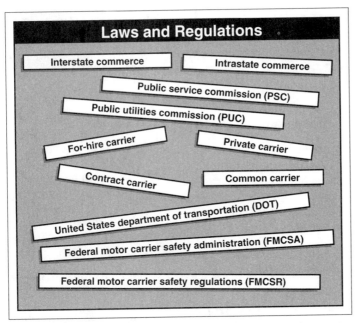

Figure **1-3** The trucking industry is regulated by federal and state laws and regulations.

America's trucking industry has evolved over more than 100 years of service and is divided into two distinct categories of operation. Carriers that operate within the borders of one state are known as **intrastate carriers** and are subject to that particular state's rules and regulations.

Carriers that move cargoes from one state to another are known as **interstate carriers** and are subject to federal regulations administered by the **U.S. Department of Transportation (U.S. DOT)** as well as the regulations of the state in which they operate. State regulations are generally the same as federal regulations but states often impose their own cargo size and weight rules as well as insurance requirements.

Carriers can be classified as **for-hire carriers** and **private carriers. For-hire carriers** are companies that haul cargo for their clients by truck. **Private carriers** are corporations that transport their own goods with their own fleet of trucks. For-hire carriers can further be divided into two groups: **common carriers** and **contract carriers.**

Common carriers are motor carriers that offer services to all individuals and businesses.

Contract carriers are motor carriers that are under contract to transport the freight of a customer. The contract sets the rates and other terms of service.

Any common carrier transporting cargo by truck in interstate or foreign commerce must first receive authority to operate from the DOT. That carrier must also file its rates with the DOT. Contract carriers and private carriers do not have to file rates.

HOW THE TRUCKING INDUSTRY IS REGULATED

More than 80,000 various government entities regulate the trucking industry. These include federal, state, county, and city authorities. State governments, including counties, cities, towns, and villages, regulate routes, speed limits, truck loading, and parking zones. State laws also regulate commerce within each state.

KNOW YOUR STATE REGULATIONS

1. What is the speed limit for commercial vehicles on interstate highways? County and local roads?

2. What is the maximum weight limit for a combination of vehicles such as a tractor-semitrailer? Straight truck pulling a trailer?

3. Who should you contact for an overweight or oversize vehicle?

4. What is the maximum legal length for a combination truck and single trailer? Double trailers, if allowed? Triples?

5. What is the maximum vehicle height allowed without a permit?

6. What is the maximum width allowed for a commercial vehicle?

7. How far can rearview mirrors extend from the side of the vehicle?

8. How far can a load extend from the vehicle?

9. How many hours can you legally drive?

10. How many hours can you legally be on duty?

11. If your vehicle is involved in an accident, what must you do?

12. What items do you need to bring to the licensing office to apply for your CDL?

13. Which commercial drivers need a CDL?

14. What class of CDL will you need?

15. Do experienced commercial drivers with a good driving record need to take the CDL knowledge (written) and skill (driving) tests to get their new CDL? Can you obtain a waiver?

16. What type of CDL endorsements do you need?

17. What group of drivers are exempted by state law from having to obtain a CDL?

Figure **1-4** Professional drivers must know and obey the laws in the states where they travel.

Federal Regulations

Federal laws regulate commerce that crosses state lines. Interstate trucking operations are regulated principally by the DOT.

State Regulations

Every state in the United States regulates motor carriers and has established vehicle laws. Each state's **Department of Motor Vehicles (DMV)** usually assist in making these laws, which usually (1) decide maximum loads trucks may carry; (2) decide maximum length, width, and weight of **Commercial Motor Vehicles (CMVs);** (3) license drivers, including the testing required to issue the **Commercial Driver's License (CDL);** (4) collect road and fuel taxes; and (5) set minimum insurance requirements.

Professional drivers must know and obey all federal regulations and must know and obey the laws in the states they travel (see Figure 1-4).

FEDERAL REGULATING AGENCIES

U.S. Department of Transportation

All U.S. motor carriers operating in interstate or foreign commerce must follow the **Federal Motor Carrier Safety Regulations (FMCSR)** and the **Hazardous Materials Regulations** of the U.S. DOT.

Through the **Motor Carrier Safety Assistance Program (MCSAP),** most states put these federal regulations into effect.

Most of these regulations probably also apply to intrastate commerce, which means they apply to all commercial motor vehicles (CMVs) with a **gross vehicle weight rating (GVWR)** more than 10,000 pounds. They also apply to any vehicle hauling hazardous cargo requiring placards.

In 1935, the Motor Carrier Act was passed by the U.S. Congress. The Motor Carrier Act created the Bureau of Motor Carriers of the Interstate Commerce Commission. The Interstate Commerce Commission was charged with the responsibility to develop and enforce safety regulations in the trucking industry. The safety regulations developed by the Interstate Commerce Commission constitute the FMCSR.

Despite extensive deregulation of the trucking industry through the 1980s and the transfer of licensing and monitoring of professional truck drivers to the states, the FMCSR remain the sole safety standard by which professional truck drivers and motor carriers are required to follow in the operation of commercial motor vehicles.

Federal Motor Carrier Safety Regulations apply to trucks and buses used by common carriers, contract carriers, and private motor carriers for interstate or foreign commerce. These regulations define:

- Insurance requirements
- CDL regulations
- Driver qualifications
- Driving rules
- Hours of service
- How to report accidents
- How to inspect, repair, and maintain CMVs
- Parts and accessories for safe operation
- Hazardous materials regulations

The Federal Motor Carrier Safety Administration (FMCSA) issues and enforces the FMCSR.

The **Research and Special Programs Administration (RSPA) Office of Hazardous Materials Transportation (OHMT)** classifies hazardous materials. It also sets standards for shipping containers, shipping documents, marking and labeling, and placarding (see Figure 1-5).

Hazardous material is also regulated by the **Environmental Protection Agency (EPA),** the **Nuclear Regulatory Commission (NRC),** and the **Occupational Safety and Health Administration (OSHA).**

The **National Transportation Safety Board (NTSB)** investigates accidents and offers solutions to prevent future accidents. At this time, because of an increased emphasis on safety and security in all American industries, new laws and regulations are being decided. However, one of the

Figure **1-5** Placards help fire and emergency personnel identify dangerous cargo in the event of an accident or spill.

most up to date listings of rules and regulations for the trucking industry may be found on the Internet at http://www.fmcsa.dot.gov. (See Chapter 20 for more information on the trucking industry's involvement in homeland security.)

Carriers not regulated by the DOT include intrastate carriers and private carriers that do not infringe on the definition of for-hire carriers.

THE COMMERCIAL MOTOR VEHICLE SAFETY ACT OF 1986

Before passage of the **Commercial Motor Vehicle Safety Act of 1986 (CMVSA/86),** drivers who were clearly unfit to drive were allowed to continue to do so. The CMVSA/86 ensures that all CMV drivers are qualified and prevents drivers from having more than one CDL. The CMVSA/86 also disqualifies drivers from driving if they commit certain traffic law violations. The CMVSA/86 applies to:

- Interstate drivers and carriers
- Intrastate drivers and carriers
- Drivers of CMVs with a GVWR of more than 26,000 pounds
- Drivers of vehicles carrying 16 or more passengers, including the driver
- Drivers of any vehicles transporting hazardous materials requiring placards

The CMVSA/86 states that employers shall not employ any driver of a CMV who has more than one CDL; whose CDL has been suspended, revoked, or canceled; or who has been disqualified from driving under the FMCSR. The CMVSA/86 requires that drivers have only one CDL; notify their employer and the state that issued the CDL within 30 days of a conviction for any traffic violation, except parking violations; and provide every employer with information about all driving jobs held during the past 10 years.

The FMCSR requires drivers to notify their employers at once if their CDL is suspended, revoked, or canceled, even though the CMVSA/86 does not require this.

COMMERCIAL MOTOR VEHICLES

As a professional driver, you may be required to drive any number of commercial motor vehicles. To acquaint you with the various types of CMVs on the road today, the following terms and descriptions will introduce an assortment of these vehicles.

Truck Tractors

A **truck tractor** or **tractor** is used to pull one or more vehicles. Tractors may pull semitrailers, tankers, flatbeds, lowboys, car haulers, and other types of vehicles. The tractor is built to carry only part of the load of the vehicle it pulls.

Tractors usually come in two cab styles. A **conventional tractor** houses the engine under the tractor's hood and provides a smoother ride because the driver sits between the front wheels and the rear wheels (see Figure 1-6). The conventional cab's longer wheelbase makes maneuvering in tight spaces more difficult.

Cab-over-engine (COE) tractor has a flat face with the engine beneath the cab (see Figure 1-7). The cab

Figure **1-6** A conventional tractor with the engine under the hood.

Figure **1-7** The cab-over-engine
tractor has a flat face with the engine
beneath the cab.

Figure **1-8** A two-axle truck with a single
drive axle.

and driver are situated over the front wheels, providing a firmer ride, and visibility may be greater because the hood does not block any part of the forward view. The COE's shorter wheelbase can pull a longer trailer and remain within legal length and weight limits.

Both **straight trucks** (single-unit vehicles with engine, cab, and cargo compartment all on the same frame) and **truck tractors** have a front axle and one or more rear axles. The front axle is the steering axle. The rear axle that is powered is called the **drive axle.**

A truck or tractor with only one axle in the rear is called a two-axle truck with a single drive axle (see Figure 1-8). The wheelbase of the single-drive-axle tractor is usually shorter, which allows easier turning in small spaces, but the shorter wheelbase also limits the amount of weight the truck can carry.

To carry heavier loads, another axle must be added to lengthen the wheelbase. The two axles are called a **tandem.** A **tandem axle tractor** usually has two drive axles (also called **twin screws**). Twin screws give the truck more traction in slippery or extreme conditions.

A driveshaft runs between the differential of the front drive axle and the differential of the rear drive axle. Many twin screws also have a differential lock to spread power evenly to each axle. The lock is engaged only in slippery conditions and at low speeds.

Some tandems have only one drive axle. The nondriven axle can be a **tag axle** (mounted behind the drive axle) or a **pusher axle** (mounted ahead of the drive axle).

Wheels with tires mounted in pairs on each end of the axle are called **duals.** A single-drive-axle tractor with dual rear wheels has six wheels with tires (see Figure 1-9). A tandem tractor with dual wheels on the rear axles has 10 wheels (see Figure 1-10). Some fleets use the "super single"

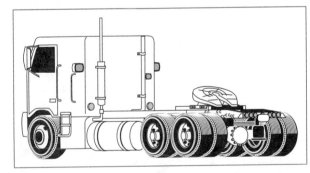

Figure **1-9** Typical tractor configuration.

Figure **1-10** Typical tractor-trailer rig.

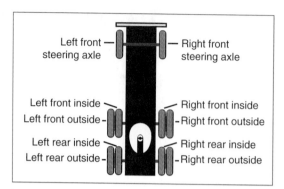

Figure **1-11** Tractor wheel identification.

instead of duals. The super single is a large single tire that has less rolling resistance than duals, resulting in better fuel economy.

Each wheel on a tractor is identified in Figure 1-11. If you have to report a tire problem to your dispatcher, use these IDs. Be sure to call each wheel by its proper name.

TRAILERS

A **trailer** is a vehicle built for hauling cargo. It has one or more axles and two or more wheels. There are two types of trailers: **full trailers** and **semitrailers.** A **full trailer** is built so that no part of its weight rests on the vehicle pulling it. A full trailer is fully supported by its own axles. It can be pulled by a straight truck or a truck tractor. Full trailers are often used as the second trailer in a double-trailer rig. They can also be used as the second and third trailers in a triple-trailer rig (see Figure 1-12).

Figure **1-12** A full trailer is designed so that no part of its weight rests on the vehicle pulling it.

The front of the **semitrailer** rests on the fifth wheel of the tractor. The fifth wheel is a plate mounted over the rear axle of the tractor (see Figure 1-13). It has locking jaws in the center into which the trailer's kingpin fits. This couples the units together. The fifth wheel is the pivot point between the tractor and the trailer. It bears the weight of the front of the semitrailer (see Figure 1-14).

A semitrailer can be made into a full trailer by coupling it to the fifth wheel on a converter dolly (see Figure 1-15). The dolly is hooked to the rear of another trailer. When you put a dolly on a semitrailer, it becomes a full trailer. There are many different types of semitrailers. Some of them are shown in Figure 1-16.

When a trailer is added to a tractor or a straight truck, it is called a **combination vehicle** or combination rig. Some of the many types of combination vehicles are shown in Figure 1-17. Combination rigs can have different types of wheel and axle arrangements.

Figure **1-13** A semitrailer has axles only at the rear of the trailer. The front of the trailer is supported by the tractor.

Figure **1-14**   Fifth wheel.

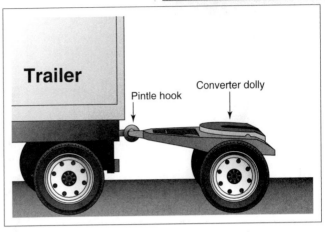

Figure **1-15**   A semitrailer is made into a full trailer by coupling it to the fifth wheel on a converter dolly.

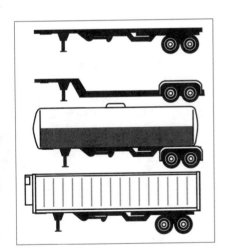

Figure **1-16**   Different types of semitrailers.

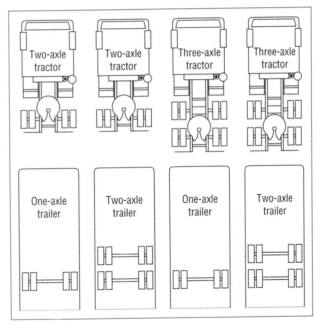

Figure **1-17**   Combination vehicles.

Other types of combination vehicles include the following:

Rocky Mountain double: This rig has double trailers. The truck has three axles. The 40- to 45-foot semitrailer has tandem axles. Then there is a single-axle dolly and a 27- to 28-foot single-axle semitrailer. There are a total of seven axles on this rig. It is not legal in some states.

Standard double: A single-axle tractor pulling a 28-foot semitrailer and a 28-foot trailer. These are not legal in some states.

Turnpike double: A tandem axle tractor pulling a 48-foot semitrailer and a 48-foot trailer. These are not legal in some states.

18-wheeler: The most familiar combination rig. The tractor has 10 wheels. The semitrailer has eight wheels. There are five axles on an 18-wheeler.

Figure **1-18** One way drivers show their professionalism is in how they handle the paperwork required in their jobs.

BECOMING A PROFESSIONAL

Professional truck drivers who are successful always drive responsibly and act in a professional manner. They also know their jobs and are responsible for each detail; maintain clean, dependable vehicles; have a positive attitude; practice safety at all times; make responsible, independent judgments when necessary; are accountable for their driving and their actions; and know and understand the equipment they use.

Why is truck driving a profession requiring professionals?

- It requires specialized knowledge, specific skills and attitudes that result from intense preparation, training, and experience.
- It is based on a specialized body of knowledge, regulations, practices, and procedures.
- It requires that all driver personnel meet the requirements for the profession through licensing, physical examination, and other testing.

Professionals in any field are expected to take action and make independent judgments based on their knowledge, skill, and experience—in any situation and to the best of their ability. Professional drivers are accountable for their behaviors on the road, while handling cargo, in their interactions with customers and coworkers, and in their handling of required paperwork (see Figure 1-18). In every instance, professional drivers are expected to conduct business in an ethical manner and in every way be committed to the public good.

Today's motor carriers work in a competitive environment where profit margins continue to shrink. Carriers want drivers who perform in a manner that is not only professional but also efficient. They entrust expensive equipment and valuable cargoes to the driver's care. Carriers also know that drivers present the company's corporate image to their clients and to the public both on the road and in public places, such as roadside parks, truckstops, and destination locations.

Competent, safe, courteous, and responsible drivers are invaluable to a company and a credit to the industry. Drivers who become a hazard or a liability will have short careers in this vital service industry.

During the aftermath of the terrorist attacks on the World Trade Center in New York City and the Pentagon in Washington, truck drivers became the lifeline for America. In this emergency situation, the entire country and the U.S. business community relied on professional drivers to keep the wheels of commerce turning—drivers with strong personal values, above-average commitment to their industry, and a can-do attitude in the face of tragedy.

Professional tractor-trailer drivers must also rank above average in the following areas:

Physical and mental abilities: Meets government, industry, and company standards.

Skill: Is qualified by training, experience, and desire to operate specific vehicle types (tractor-trailer, tankers, and so on).

Safety standards: Understands and practices safe driving methods, obeys the law, knows more and is safer in all highway situations than the average driver, and concentrates constantly on the highway environment, reading clues and working to avoid hazards or accidents.

Tolerance and courtesy: Can accept negative traffic behaviors and blatant road rage from other drivers without becoming involved or attempting to get even, cooperates with other road users at all times, and communicates regularly with dispatchers.

Efficiency: Delivers cargo on time and works courteously with others while obeying laws and regulations, recognizes that a carrier cannot be successful unless schedules are met, and does everything possible to use fuel efficiently.

Knowledge: Knows government regulations and follows industry requirements for driving and handling cargo.

Professional drivers understand that *they are the trucking industry* in the eyes of their customers and the motoring public. They know they must always perform at higher skill levels than the average drivers—and they also realize that driving well is not enough. They must also conduct themselves in a courteous manner and practice the highest levels of safety, on the road, at the dock, and wherever they drive (see Figure 1-19). Finally, professional drivers know they must continually improve their skills and their knowledge of the equipment they use and the technology that supports their industry.

Ensuring responsible professional drivers throughout this nation's transportation industry is critical to improving highway safety. And, as carriers hire the next generation of drivers, they continue to look for those individuals—men and women—who will represent the best of the profession—drivers who consistently employ good judgment, common sense, and courtesy in every situation.

SAFETY

Safety is the professional driver's highest priority.

The ultimate goal of the U.S. transportation industry is to move cargo from one point to another without damage to the equipment or cargo and without injury to the driver or those

Figure **1-19** Professional drivers are always courteous.

around him or her. Unsafe vehicles and unsafe driving threaten the economic well-being of the trucking industry as well as the nation as a whole.

Professional driving can be one of the most dangerous and demanding jobs in transportation today. And because it is demanding to constantly meet the highest levels of safety standards, professional drivers today not only must know their vehicles and be highly skilled in every task but must also be constantly aware of their environment.

Accidents happen in the blink of an eye, and professional drivers must be constantly on guard, reading clues—from other drivers, road conditions, weather conditions, and their own vehicles—so they can avoid hazards and difficult maneuvering situations.

Professional drivers must always think ahead and look ahead to avoid hazards. They must use common sense, always work at the highest level of alertness, and have the training and experience it takes to avoid costly and dangerous situations.

TRAINING AND INSTRUCTION

A driver must be prepared. The more driving skill he or she gains while in training, the less there is to be learned on the job. Formal training is valuable when learning to drive any vehicle, but the value increases with the size of the vehicle.

Safe driving is more likely to occur when drivers understand their personal strengths and weaknesses, when drivers understand the capabilities and limitations of their vehicles, when instruction has been given for both good and bad driving conditions (see Figure 1-20), and when drivers have been taught to look for and identify potential hazards.

Looking for and identifying possible hazards is very important because most emergencies do not appear in a split second; rather, they grow gradually. Drivers can be taught to *see hazards* before they have grown into full-scale problems. Drivers can then take steps to reduce the threat.

Figure **1-20** Professional drivers are trained to drive safely in good and bad weather.

Of course, there are some emergencies that do happen quickly. These may be due to the road conditions, traffic, or unsafe actions of others. In these cases, drivers must know how to analyze the situation and decide the best course of action. Here again, training can be a major factor in how well the driver performs.

CMV drivers tend to have more accidents in the first few months they drive. This may be due to a lack of training or experience. If training includes experience and experience reduces accidents, then better training of tractor-trailer drivers can reduce the accident rate on our highways.

Truck drivers who perform in a professional manner can improve overall highway safety, promote courtesy on the road, and in general provide better highway conditions for all drivers. They are an asset to their employers and are regarded with respect by all others.

Chapter Two
Control Systems

Vehicle Controls

Vehicle Instruments

OBJECTIVES

When you have completed this chapter, you should be able to:

- Describe engine controls, primary vehicle controls, and secondary vehicle controls

- Name, locate, and describe the function of the controls for the following:

Starting the engine	Accelerating
Shutting down the engine	Braking
Shifting	Parking

- Locate the controls for lights, signals, and comfort

- Understand the importance of using seatbelts

- Describe the acceptable operating range for the fuel, oil, air, cooling, exhaust, and electrical systems

- Discuss how checking these systems often can help you spot problems early

- Understand the function of warning devices

KEY TERMS

Accelerator pedal

Air brake application gauge

Air pressure gauge

Ammeter

Antilock brakes

Auxiliary starter button

Axle temperature gauge

Brake controls

Clutch brake

Clutch pedal

Computerized idle timer

Coolant level alarm

Coolant temperature gauge

Coolant temperature warning

Cruise control

Differential warning

Electric retarder

Emergency engine stop control

Engine brake

Engine controls

Engine oil temperature gauge

Engine stop control knob

Exhaust brake

Exhaust pyrometer gauge

Foot brake control valve

Fuel gauge

Gear box temperature gauge

Hydraulic retarder

Interaxle differential lock control

Low air pressure warning alarm

Odometer

Oil level alarm

Oil pressure gauge

Parking brake control valve

Primary vehicle controls

Pyrometer warning

Seatbelts

Secondary vehicle controls

Speedometer

Splitter valve

Steering wheel

Tachometer

Trailer air supply valve

Trailer brake control valve

Trailer emergency relay valve

Transmission control

Voltmeter

INTRODUCTION

If you've ever seen the cockpit of an airplane, you know that there is a vast difference between the console of an aircraft and the dashboard of your personal vehicle. Because the workload of a big rig is much different than that of a smaller truck or an automobile, the controls and instrumentation are also different (see Figure 2-1).

The objective of this chapter is to introduce the basic controls and their functions found in tractors and straight trucks today.

VEHICLE CONTROLS

Let's begin with the basics and build from there. There are three basic types of controls found on big

Figure **2-1**   A typical tractor control console.

rigs: **engine controls,** which start the engine and shut it down; **primary vehicle controls,** which provide the driver with control of the vehicle; and **secondary vehicle controls,** which assist the driver with vision, communication, comfort, and safety but do not affect the vehicle's power.

Engine Controls

Engine controls start the engine and shut it down. Engine controls do not control movement. They are similar in most vehicles. Differences in these controls depend on the type of engine, the fuel used, and the starter mechanism.

Engine Control Switch

The engine control switch starts the engine. This switch is much like a gate through which an electrical current must pass before the engine cranks. The switch must be in the "on" position for the engine to start.

Starter Button

Some trucks also have a starter button. To start the engine in this type of vehicle, turn the key to the "on" position and push the starter button.

Other Engine Controls

Other controls that relate to starting or stopping the engine include the following:

Auxiliary starter button.   Available on some cab-over-engine (COE) models. It lets you to start the engine with the cab tilted.

Engine stop control knob.   Used in some diesel engines to shut off the engine. You pull the knob out and hold it until engine stops.

Computerized idle timer.   A function of the engine's electronic controls, it will shut down the engine in a prescribed amount of time after the truck has come to a halt.

Emergency engine stop control.   Shuts down the engine. Use this control in emergency situations only. Many companies insist that it be reset by a mechanic after each use.

Cruise control.   Available in most newer vehicles. It enables you to maintain a constant speed without having to depress the accelerator (see Figure 2-2).

Figure **2-2** Cruise control is available in most newer trucks.

Figure **2-3** The professional driver needs to know where all of the controls are and how to operate them.

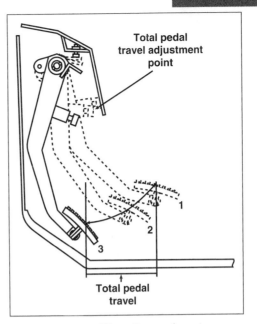

Figure **2-4** The three basic clutch pedal positions are (1) engaged, (2) free play, and (3) disengaged.

Primary Vehicle Controls

The primary vehicle controls do exactly what their name implies—they allow the driver to control the vehicle. Primary vehicle controls include the clutch pedal, transmission control, accelerator pedal, steering wheel, and brake control. As a professional driver, you must know not only where these controls are found in the cab of a truck but also how to operate them (see Figure 2-3).

Clutch Pedal

To start the engine or shift gears, you must use the clutch pedal. There are three basic pedal positions (see Figure 2-4):

1. **Disengaged:** The pedal is pushed within 2 inches of the floor. When the pedal is in this position, the engine and drive train are separated. The clutch must be disengaged to start the engine and shift gears.
2. **Free play:** This is the amount of pedal movement possible at the top of the stroke without engaging or disengaging the clutch. It should be between 1/2 and 2-1/2 inches.
3. **Engaged:** The pedal is fully released. The driver is not applying any pressure. The word *engaged* means the engine and drive train are connected and moving together.

The clutch pedal also passes through a transition distance when the clutch is engaging or disengaging.

Clutch brake. Most transmissions use a **clutch brake** (see Figure 2-5). It stops or controls the speed of the transmission input shaft and countershaft. The clutch brake is used to engage only the first gear or the reverse gear when the vehicle is stopped. It works when the pedal is within 1 or 2 inches of the floor, depending on its adjustment.

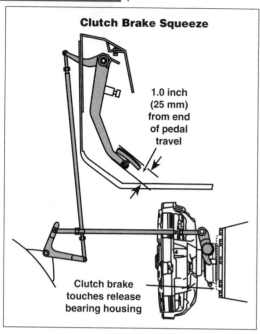

Figure **2-5** Mechanics of the clutch brake.

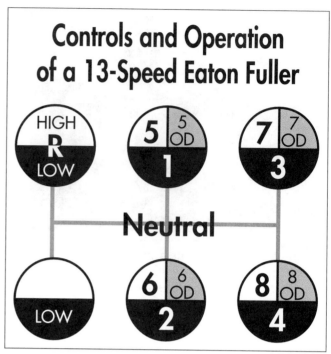

Figure **2-6** Diagram of a manual transmission.

Transmission Controls

Transmission controls vary with different types of transmissions. Many tractors have a manual transmission with both a clutch and a gear lever. All gear changes are controlled by the driver. Some tractors have semiautomatic transmissions, which include a clutch and gear lever, but some of the gear changes are controlled by an on-board computer. A few trucks have fully automatic transmissions with just a gear lever and no clutch. All gear changes are controlled by hydraulics or by an on-board computer.

Controls on a typical manual transmission gear lever. A range change lever on the front of the lever allows you to switch between ranges. The lever is in the down position for the low range (usually the bottom four or five gears) and in the up position for the high range (the top four or five gears).

Splitter valve. Some transmissions, such as the 13-speed and 18-speed Eaton Fuller, use a **splitter valve** to split gears into direct or overdrive (see Figure 2-6). The valve is controlled with a button on the top of the gear shift knob.

Automatic Transmissions

More commercial motor vehicles today are equipped with automatic transmissions. Some companies have added these vehicles to their fleets to encourage male-female partners to drive in teams.

The following are some basic suggestions for driving tractors or trucks with automatic transmissions. For the purposes of this instruction, the Eaton Fuller Automated Mechanical Transmission is used.

Proper start-up.   To start a truck or tractor equipped with an automatic transmission, the following steps are suggested by the manufacturer:

1. Make sure the shifter is in neutral ("N") and the parking brake is set.
2. Depress the clutch pedal and turn the ignition key to "on."
3. Wait for the service light on the shifter to go out and a solid "N" appears on the gear display.
4. Start the engine and let out the clutch pedal to register proper input speed. If the proper input speed is not registered, the transmission will not shift into the initial starting gear.

Selecting the starting gear.   Once the engine has been properly started, the next step is to select the starting gear. These steps are suggested:

1. Select "D," "H" for Manual mode, or "L" for Low mode.
2. Depress the clutch pedal. A solid number on the gear display indicates that the gear is fully engaged. If flashing down arrows appear on the gear display, this indicates the input shaft has not slowed down enough to get into gear.
3. Continue to depress the clutch pedal until the down arrows are off. If down arrows are off and the gear number continues to flash slowly, let up on the clutch pedal to fully engage the gear.
4. Depending on how your vehicle is programmed, you can select different starting gears while in "D" or "H" (Manual) by using the up and down buttons. Remember to choose the correct starting gear for your load and grade.
5. Let out clutch.

Available gears.   The following gears can be used:

"H" = Manual Mode

1. Can be selected while moving or from a stop.
2. Must use the up and down buttons to shift.
3. Shifter will "beep" if shift cannot be completed because of engine RPM (revolutions per minute) and road speed.

"L" = Low Mode

1. Can be selected while moving or from a stop.
2. Selecting "Low" from a stop engages and maintains first gear.
3. Selecting "Low" while moving will allow for downshifts only, and downshifts will be performed at a higher RPM.

"R" = Reverse Mode

1. Selecting Reverse from Neutral will engage Low Reverse, and an "R" will appear on the gear display.
2. Transmission models with multiple reverses must use the up and down arrows to select other reverse gears. Remember to select the proper reverse gear for your load and grade condition.
3. All reverse gears can only be engaged at less than 2 miles per hour.

Proper Shut-Down Procedure

1. Remember to depress the clutch when stopping the vehicle.
2. Before shutting the vehicle off, you must select Neutral on the shifter and make sure a solid "N" is on the gear display.
3. Turn the key off, release the clutch pedal, and set the parking brake.

Note: It is very important that you *do not* shut the truck off or stall the engine while the transmission is in gear. This will cause the transmission to lock in gear, and the engine will not restart.

Tips for drivers: Automatic transmissions. The following general suggestions are provided by Eaton Fuller regarding the Automated Mechanical Transmission:

1. The clutch is needed only at start-up, when selecting a starting gear, and when stopping. "D," "H," or "L" can be selected at any speed.
2. When first starting the engine after changing loads, AutoShift needs to adapt to the changing conditions of the vehicle. If the transmission holds a gear while in "D," simply push the "up" button, and the shift will be completed. This may have to be done several times before the transmission "remembers."
3. "H" should be used whenever you want to control the shifts, such as moving around the yard, going up a grade, or in poor traction situations.
4. "L" should be used anytime you want to maximize the engine brake, such as going down a long grade or when coming to a stop.
5. The service light will come on and go off during power-up. If the service light comes on and stays on or comes on while you are driving, the transmission (AutoShift) has detected a fault in the system. Note the conditions when this occurs—hot/cold, wet/dry, on a grade/flat terrain—and get the vehicle to a service facility. Some faults prevent the transmission from shifting into other gears.

Other Controls

The accelerator controls the amount of fuel entering the combustion chamber.

Accelerator pedal.   Controls the vehicle's road speed (mph). Push the pedal down to increase speed and ease off to reduce speed.

Steering wheel.   Used to steer the rig. The steering wheel is 6 to 12 inches larger across (diameter) than on a car. The larger size gives the turning leverage needed to control big rigs.

Brake controls.   Used to slow or stop the rig. Learning how to use the brake controls is very important. You will learn how to use the following controls:

- **Foot brake control valve** (also called foot valve or treadle valve): This valve operates the service brakes on both the tractor and the trailer. When pushed in, it supplies air pressure to all tractor and trailer service brake chambers on the rig (see Figure 2-7).
- **Trailer brake control valve** (also called hand valve, trolley valve, or independent trailer brake): Operates the service brakes on the

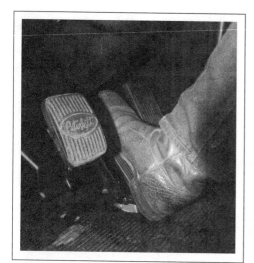

Figure **2-7** The foot brake control valve operates service brakes on both the tractor and the trailer.

Figure **2-8** Trailer air supply valve.

trailer only. This hand brake is used only in special situations and should not be used to hold the rig when parked.

- **Parking brake control valve:** A flip switch or push-pull knob that lets the driver put on the parking brake. The parking brake should be put on only after the rig is stopped.

- **Trailer air supply valve:** In the open position, it provides air to the trailer brakes. In the closed position, it shuts off the air supply to the trailer. It is closed, or pulled out, when there is no trailer. Never use this valve as a parking brake. If you do so, loss of air will occur (see Figure 2-8).

When the air supply drops to 20 to 45 pounds per square inch (psi), the valve closes automatically. This stops the flow of air and protects the tractor's air supply. The trailer air supply valve triggers the emergency relay valve that puts on the trailer brakes.

- **Trailer emergency relay valve.** Activates when the air supply is lost, as with severed air line(s) or diaphragm failure. The spring brake will remain locked/parked until the chambers are caged with a caging tool and/or air supply lines are replaced or repaired and the air supply is restored.

Other primary controls found on some rigs include the:

Antilock brakes.   As of March 1, 1997, all new tractors must be fitted with an antilock braking system (ABS). The system is largely invisible from the cab, except for a warning lamp to tell you if the system is malfunctioning.

The ABS is designed to maintain vehicle stability while braking by preventing the wheels from locking and losing traction. Sensors at the wheels detect impending lockup and electronically release and reapply the brakes so that traction is maintained. The whole process occurs in split seconds—much faster than you could physically pump the brakes. The most important thing to know about driving with ABS is to always hit the brakes and *hold* them. *Do not pump them.* Even though it may take longer to stop, ABS will prevent more accidents because it allows you to stay in control and steer around objects. Without ABS, wheels are more likely to lock which may result in loss of control of the vehicle.

Engine brakes and retarders.   Slow the rig without using the service brake system. They keep the rig operating at a reasonable speed. There are four basic types of auxiliary brakes or speed retarders.

Figure **2-9** Engine brake.

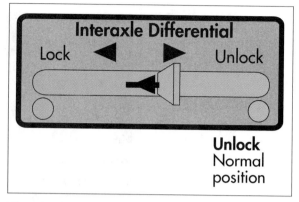

Figure **2-10** Interaxle differential in the normal position.

Note: Many cities restrict the use of retarders because of noise.

1. **Exhaust brake:** Simplest form of retarder. It keeps the exhaust gases from escaping. The exhaust brake builds up back pressure in the engine. This keeps it from increasing speed. It is controlled by an on/off switch in the cab or automatically by a switch on the accelerator or clutch pedal.

2. **Engine brake** (see Figure 2-9): Most widely used type of retarder. It alters valve timing and turns the engine into an air compressor. The engine brake can be operated by hand with a switch on the dash or automatically when the foot is removed from the accelerator pedal.

3. **Hydraulic retarder:** A type of drive line retarder mounted on the drive line between the engine and the flywheel or between the transmission and drive axles. It reduces speed by directing a flow of oil against the stator vanes. The retarder can be turned on by hand with a lever in the cab or automatically by an accelerator switch on the floor.

4. **Electric retarder:** Uses electromagnets to slow the rotors attached to the drive train. The driver turns it on or off with a switch in the cab.

Interaxle differential lock control (also known as the power divider). Locks and unlocks rear tandem axles. Unlocked, the axles turn independently of one another on a dry surface (see Figure 2-10). In the locked position, power to the axles is equalized to help keep the wheels without traction from spinning. This position is used on slippery roads. The control should be locked before the wheels begin to spin.

Secondary Vehicle Controls

These controls do not affect the rig's power or movement. They have other jobs; they help drivers:

- Vision:
    - Lights
    - Windshield wipers
    - Defroster
- Communication:
    - Horns
    - Radios
    - Lights (headlights, brake lights, four-way flashers)
- Comfort:
    - Seat position
    - Air vents
    - Air conditioner
    - Heater
- Safety:
    - Seatbelts
    - Door locks

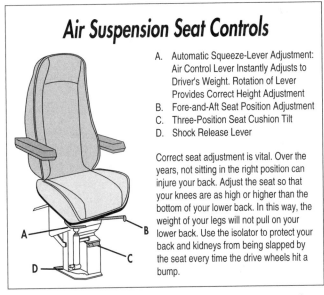

Air Suspension Seat Controls

A. Automatic Squeeze-Lever Adjustment: Air Control Lever Instantly Adjusts to Driver's Weight. Rotation of Lever Provides Correct Height Adjustment
B. Fore-and-Aft Seat Position Adjustment
C. Three-Position Seat Cushion Tilt
D. Shock Release Lever

Correct seat adjustment is vital. Over the years, not sitting in the right position can injure your back. Adjust the seat so that your knees are as high or higher than the bottom of your lower back. In this way, the weight of your legs will not pull on your lower back. Use the isolator to protect your back and kidneys from being slapped by the seat every time the drive wheels hit a bump.

Figure **2-11** An example of driver comfort controls.

Many of these controls are similar to those found in cars (e.g., the switches for the lights and windshield wipers). Others are found only on tractor-trailers (see Figure 2-11). The number and function of the secondary controls vary with the design of the truck.

Other controls not related to driving include those for the hydraulic cab tilt operation and fifth-wheel lock assembly.

Seatbelts and Seatbelt Laws

In a recent study of accidents involving commercial vehicles, the National Transportation Safety Board (NTSB) found that 92.3 percent of drivers killed in crashes had safety **seatbelts** available but were not using them.

Forty-nine states (all except New Hampshire) and the District of Columbia have mandatory seatbelt laws. In most states, these laws cover front-seat occupants only, although belt laws in 14 jurisdictions (Alaska, California, District of Columbia, Kentucky, Maine, Massachusetts, Montana, Nevada, Oregon, Rhode Island, Utah, Vermont, Washington, and Wyoming) cover all rear-seat occupants, too.

Most trucks are now fitted with full lap and shoulder belts. Although they will not prevent all injuries and fatalities, seatbelts can greatly improve a driver's chances of survival.

If a shoulder belt is uncomfortable because of the action of the suspended seat, get a special locking clip to keep the belt from constantly tightening. Most carriers are safety conscious enough to encourage drivers who wear seatbelts and discipline those who do not.

FMCSR Section 392.16 requires commercial drivers to use seatbelts whenever they are driving:

A commercial motor vehicle which has a seat belt assembly installed at the driver's seat shall not be driven unless the driver has properly restrained himself/herself with the seat belt assembly.

VEHICLE INSTRUMENTS

As you scan a tractor dashboard, you will see a number of gauges and meters. These are included to keep you informed about the condition of your rig and its parts. They will also warn you of possible problems and help you avoid major difficulties.

As you learn the skills and attitudes of a professional driver, you will find the following to be very important:

● Understand the function and purpose of each instrument.
● Understand the information each instrument provides. For example, temperature and pressure gauges can indicate improper or unsafe operating conditions that will ultimately damage your rig.
● Take action to correct a problem when an improper reading is registered on one or several of the gauges.
● Know when your rig has reached the correct range of operation. For example, a professional driver will know the correct readings needed for air pressure, oil pressure, and water temperature.

Your vehicle's instruments are divided into two types: basic instruments, or devices that monitor basic operations of the rig's various systems, and warning devices, or warning lights and buzzers found in most commercial motor vehicles to tell when certain levels, pressures, or temperatures have reached a danger point.

Basic Instruments

Speedometer

Displays road speed in miles and kilometers per hour. FMCSR 393.82 requires each commercial motor vehicle have a speedometer that is operational (see Figure 2-12).

Odometer

Indicates how many miles or kilometers the rig has been driven (see Figure 2-12).

Tachometer

Displays engine speed in RPM (see Figure 2-12). The tachometer is a guide that indicates when to shift gears and assists the driver in using the engine and transmission effectively during acceleration and deceleration.

Fuel Gauge

Indicates how much fuel is in the fuel tanks (see Figure 2-13). Since the gauge is not always accurate, a driver should check the tanks visually before each trip and at all stops.

Voltmeter

Measures the voltage output of the battery (see Figure 2-14). The meter needle should be between 13.0 and 14.5 volts during normal operation. The operator's

Figure **2-12** Speedometer.

Figure **2-13** Fuel gauge.

Figure **2-14** Voltmeter.

manual will tell you if the reading should be different for your rig. Higher-than-normal voltage may boil away battery fluids and shorten the battery's life.

Ammeter

Measures how much the battery is being charged or discharged. Under normal operating conditions, the ammeter should read:

Engine off—zero

Engine starts—needle jumps to the charge side and flutters

Engine warmed—reading drops back to zero or slightly on the charged side

A consistently high reading indicates the battery may be ready to fail. Continuous discharge means the battery is not receiving a charge from the alternator or generator.

A number of things can cause these readings:

- The battery needs fluid.
- The voltage regulator is not working properly.
- A bare wire is causing a short circuit.
- The alternator is defective.
- There are loose or worn belts.

Air Pressure Gauge

The air brake system is activated by air pressure. The air pressure gauge indicates the amount of pressure in the tanks (see Figure 2-15). Air pressure should start building as soon as the engine starts and continue until the maximum pressure is reached. This is usually 120 psi. In normal operation, when the air pressure drops to 90 psi, the air compressor will automatically build it back to 120 psi. The air compressor governor controls this operation.

If the air pressure drops to 60 psi while driving, the low pressure warning alarm light will turn on. At 20 to 45 psi, the tractor protection valve will close and shut off the air supply to the trailer. Shutting off the air to the trailer triggers the emergency relay valve, which puts on the trailer brakes.

Low air pressure can result from air leaks, failure of the compressor or compressor governor control, broken or kinked air lines, or an open air tank petcock.

If you have a loss of air pressure, stop your rig at once. Locate the source of the problem and get it repaired. *Do not operate your rig without enough air pressure.*

Oil Pressure Gauge

Metal engine parts that rub against each other create friction (heat). A thin film of oil between these parts prevents overheating and excessive wear. The lubrication system provides the oil, and the oil pressure gauge indicates the oil pressure within the system (see Figure 2-16).

If pressure is lost, it means there is not enough lubrication in the system. In this case, the engine can be destroyed in a short period of time. Oil pressure should register within seconds after the engine is started. It should then rise slowly to the normal operating range. The normal range will depend on the type of vehicle and

Figure **2-15** Air pressure gauge.

Figure **2-16** Oil pressure gauge. Idling = 5 to 20 psi. Operating = 35 to 75 psi. Low, dropping, fluctuating—STOP IMMEDIATELY! Without oil, the engine can be destroyed rapidly.

the engine RPM. You should stop and check oil level if pressure does not register or if it fluctuates rapidly when starting or a loss in pressure occurs.

A number of things can cause low oil pressure, including not enough oil, oil leaks, and oil pump failure.

An adequate oil level with no leaks suggests a problem with the oil pump or a clogged oil line or filter.

Other Types of Gauges

The number and types of gauges found on vehicles will vary. The only gauges required by law are the speedometer and air pressure gauge.

Air brake application gauge.   This indicates, in psi, the amount of air pressure used when the brake pedal or hand valve is applied.

Coolant temperature gauge.   This gauge shows the temperature of the coolant in the engine block. The cooling system protects engine parts against destruction from the heat created by the burning of fuel in the combustion chamber, rapid movement, and friction. The normal operating range is 170° to 195° or the safe range indicated by the operator's manual (see Figure 2-17).

If the gauge registers above the normal range, the engine may be overheating. Shut down the engine at once. Overheating can be caused by:

- Not enough engine oil
- A loose or broken fan belt or malfunctioning fan clutch or control
- A blocked radiator—either from the inside or from the outside
- A broken thermostat, coolant pump, or radiator shutter
- A severe load on the engine (attempting to pull too much or pull too hard)
- The winter front may need to be removed

Engine oil temperature gauge.   This gauge indicates the temperature of the engine oil. The normal operating temperature for engine oil is 180° to 225°. This is 20° to 60° higher than the coolant temperature (see Figure 2-18).

High oil temperature causes the oil to thin (because of reduced viscosity). This decreases the oil pressure. Engine oil temperatures, however, can run as high as 250° to 265° for a short period without damaging the engine. However, never operate the engine above the safe operating range.

Exhaust pyrometer gauge.   This gauge indicates the temperature of the gases in the exhaust manifold. If the gases are too hot, they can damage the turbocharger. Maximum safe operating temperatures may be shown on the pyrometer name plate or listed in the operator's manual.

Gear box temperature gauge.   This gauge shows the temperature of the lubricant in the transmission. The normal reading is 150° to 200°. A high reading may indicate a low oil level.

Axle temperature gauge.   This gauge shows the temperature of the lubricant in the front and rear drive axles. The normal reading is 150° to 200°. This

Figure **2-17** Water temperature gauge. Normal temperature is 170° to 195°, depending on the engine model.

Figure **2-18** Engine oil temperature gauge. Normal temperature is 180° to 225° and loaded is 250° to 265°.

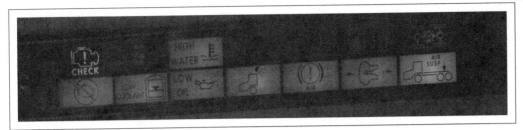

Figure **2-19** Warning lights indicate potential problems.

reading does not vary when the rig is loaded. Higher readings, up to 230° to 250°, are acceptable for short periods. The readings for both drive axles should be within 10° of each other. Readings above the normal range can mean bad bearings or a flat tire. The forward rear axle in a twin screw will run hotter than the rear axle.

Warning Devices

Most commercial motor vehicles have warning lights and buzzers to tell when the fuel, air pressure, or temperature has reached a danger point. Some warning lights are on the dash. They will buzz or flash when there is a problem. Immediately stop your rig when any warning devices sound or light up (see Figure 2-19).

You should become familiar with the following warning lights or buzzers:

- **Low air pressure warning alarm:** Sounds or lights when there is low pressure in the air brake system
- **Coolant level alarm:** Lights when the coolant level starts dropping, indicating a probable leak
- **Oil level alarm:** Lights when the oil level becomes too low for normal operation
- **Coolant temperature warning:** Lights when the temperature is too high
- **Pyrometer warning:** Lights when exhaust temperatures are too high
- **Differential warning:** Flashes when the interaxle differential is in the *locked* position

Chapter Three
Hours of Service

OBJECTIVES

When you have completed this chapter, you should be able to:

● Record your time and activities while on the road

● Make entries in a logbook and know what information must be included

● Compute on-duty hours and required rest stops while on the road

KEY TERMS

Carrier's Time Record
Driver's Daily Log, or
    (Driver's log)
Driving time
Hours of service
Off-duty time

On-duty time
Principal place
    of business
Sleeper berth
Sleeper berth
    time

INTRODUCTION

Sixty years ago, federal laws were developed to regulate the number of hours a driver could spend on the clock and behind the wheel. As a professional driver, you have the daily responsibility of maneuvering up to 40 tons of loaded equipment in all types of demanding weather and traffic conditions.

In order to perform your job in a timely and safe manner, you will need to know how to manage your time behind the wheel as well as how to record the activities required to successfully transport freight from origin to destination.

And yes—there is far more to professional driving than simply driving the truck.

Numerous studies over the years have indicated the human body must have regular rest as well as nutrition, exercise, and hydration in order to function at its best. All of us have been guilty of pushing ourselves beyond human limits at times. However, if we push too hard, the result is being unable to complete the task because of a lack of strength or sheer exhaustion.

Like airline pilots, professional drivers have strict limitations on their hours behind the wheel as well as specific guidelines for rest between trips. Federal guidelines determine the maximum number of hours you may drive and specify hours of rest needed before you may get behind the wheel again.

As of early 2002, the Federal Motor Carrier Safety Administration had not completed the revision of hours of service for professional truck drivers and bus drivers. Two years prior, FMCSA's proposed new regulations met with strong criticism from carriers, shippers, drivers, and safety groups. For more information on the proposed changes to the hours-of-service regulations, go to http://www.fmcsa.dot.gov/hos.

EXISTING REGULATIONS

The laws that currently govern maximum time on duty are found in Part 395 of the Federal Motor Carrier Safety Regulations (FMCSR). These may be found on the Internet at http://www.fmcsr.org. The professional driver must know and comply with these regulations at all times.

As they are currently written, the **Hours-of-Service** (time-on-duty) regulations apply to anyone driving a commercial motor vehicle that has a GVWR of 10,000 lbs. or more; transports more than 15 persons, including the driver; or transports cargo requiring hazardous materials placards.

Until further changes are made, no driver shall drive more than 10 hours after having eight hours off duty. The only exception to this rule is when the driver is delayed by adverse driving conditions, such as snow, fog, or unusual road conditions (see Figure 3-1).

Figure **3-1**   In adverse driving conditions, drivers may exceed hours-of-service rules to reach a safe place.

DEFINITIONS

On-duty time: The time the driver begins work or must be ready to go to work until the time he or she is relieved from work of any kind. On-duty time includes all time spent:

- Working or waiting to be dispatched at your terminal or a shipper's facility
- Inspecting, servicing, or getting your tractor or trailer ready
- Driving or in the cab except for sleeper berth time
- Loading or unloading cargo or supervising the loading or unloading
- Obtaining shipping documents
- Performing required duties at an accident involving your rig
- Repairing your rig or staying with it while repairs are being made
- Doing any work for pay for a carrier
- Performing any compensated work for any non–motor carrier

Off-duty time: Any time during which the driver is relieved of all on-duty time responsibilities.

Driving time: All time spent at the controls of your tractor.

Seven consecutive days: Seven days in a row beginning on any day at a given time.

Eight consecutive days: Eight days in a row beginning on any day at a given time.

Twenty-four-hour period: Twenty-four hours in a row beginning at a time set by the carrier.

Regularly employed driver: A driver who works for one motor carrier for any 7 consecutive days.

Sleeper berth: A berth in the tractor cab in which the driver can sleep. Its size and other specifications are determined by law.

Driver-salesman: A driver who also sells products or provides services to the customer. An example is a beverage or baked goods delivery person. The driver works within 100 miles of his or her home terminal and spends at least half of his or her time selling or taking orders for restocking products.

Multiple stops: Several stops in the same village, city, or town that can be entered as one stop.

Principal place of business: The main office of the carrier where all records are kept.

MAXIMUM DRIVING AND ON-DUTY TIME

Federal laws provide that no carrier shall require or permit a driver to drive:

- more than 10 hours after having 8 hours off duty,
- after being on duty for 15 hours following 8 hours off duty,
- after being on duty for 60 hours in any 7 consecutive days if the carrier does not operate every day of the week, or
- after being on duty for 70 hours in any 8 consecutive days if the carrier operates every day of the week.

These same regulations apply to an owner/operator. The laws say no commercial driver can drive more than the specified hours. Section 395.3 of the FMCSR provides for exceptions to the rules for maximum hours in certain cases.

Travel Time

If an employer requires a driver to travel, even though he or she is not driving, the time must be counted as on-duty time unless the driver is given 8 consecutive hours off duty when he or she arrives at the destination. Then the travel time will be counted as off-duty time.

Adverse Driving Conditions

Snow, sleet, fog, icy pavement, and unusual road or traffic conditions may prevent the driver from completing his or her scheduled run in the 10 hours allowed by law. In such cases, the driver is allowed, by law, to drive for 2 hours more to reach the original destination or a safe place to park the rig. Adverse driving conditions must be noted on the driver's log to show the reason for the extra driving time.

RECORD OF DUTY STATUS

There are only two ways permitted by federal law to record a driver's duty status. The status must be noted in the **Driver's Daily Log** or the **Carrier's Time Record.**
     The Carrier's Time Record may be used only when:

- The driver operates within a 100-mile radius of his or her home terminal.
- The driver reports back to his or her home terminal and was not on duty more than 12 hours.
- The driver has at least 8 hours off duty after each 12 hours on duty.
- The driver does not drive more than 10 hours following 8 hours off.
- For 6 months, the carrier prepares and maintains records showing the time drivers go on duty and go off duty, the total hours per day, and the preceding 7-day record for new or part-time drivers.

     The form shown in Figure 3-2 is used for first-time or intermittent drivers.

```
HOURS OF SERVICE RECORD FOR FIRST TIME OR INTERMITTENT DRIVERS

Name (Print)_____
              First         Middle        Last

              DAY    TOTAL TIME ON DUTY
               1       _____
               2       _____
               3       _____
               4       _____
               5       _____
               6       _____
               7       _____
              _____
                  TOTAL _____
     I hereby certify that the information contained heron is true to
     the best of my knowledge and belief, and that my last period of
     release from duty was from

     _____  to  _____
         (Hour/Date)                 (Hour/Date)

        Signature _____ Date _____
```

Figure **3-2** Typical hours-of-service form for first-time or intermittent drivers.

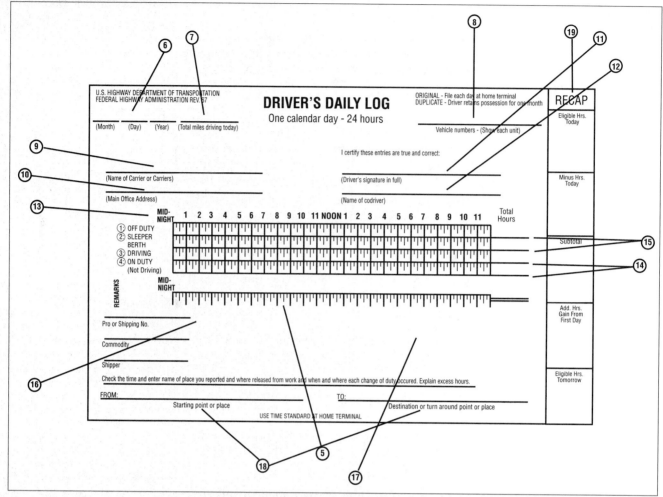

Figure 3-3 Typical page from a Driver's Daily Log. There are many types of Driver's Daily Log forms. Ask your carrier which type they would prefer you to use.

The Driver's Daily Log is the most commonly used record of duty status for drivers. Other than pickup and delivery operations, most tractor-trailers are driven over 100 miles from their home terminal.

Federal laws require every carrier to make sure each driver records, in duplicate, his or her duty status for all 24-hour periods. This information must be recorded on the specified form.

The form shown in Figure 3-3 shows the entries the driver must make on the daily log. The correct blanks in which to make the entries are identified by the number of the duty status or other information that is required.

Duty status must be recorded as:

1. Off-duty, or OFF.
2. Sleeper berth, or SB (if a sleeper berth is used).
3. Driving, or D.
4. On-duty, not driving, or ON.
5. Each change of duty status must show the name of the nearest city, town, or village and the state abbreviation in the Remarks section.

The form must also show the following:

6. Date by month, day, and year.
7. Number of miles driven each day.

8. Tractor and trailer number or license plate number.

9. Name of the carrier or carriers: when you drive for more than one carrier in a 24-hour period, you must show the names of all carriers and the time you started and finished work for each.

10. Address of the carrier's main office.

11. Driver's signature on certification.

12. Name of the codriver (if there is one).

13. Starting time for the 24-hour period.

14. Total hours in each on-duty status.

15. Total hours of duty status: line 14 + line 15 must = 24.

16. Shipping document number or the name of the shipper and the product.

17. When noting the city and state where the change of duty status took place, include such information as adverse weather or emergency conditions in the Remarks section.

18. On some Driver's Daily Log forms, the starting point and final delivery, or turnaround, point may be entered. If the run is a turnaround back to the original terminal, enter the name of the most distant point and then the words *and return.*

19. Although it is not required by law, it is a good idea, and often company policy, for a driver to complete the Recap section of the Driver's Daily Log. List the number of hours remaining on duty and state whether you will be driving. Figure 3-4 shows how one type of recap may be completed.

Recap

1	2	3	4	5	RECORD OF TIME WORKED	1	2	3	4	5
	DAILY TOTAL DUTY & DR. HRS.						DAILY TOTAL DUTY & DR. HRS.			
LAST SEVEN CONSECUTIVE DAYS IN PRECEDING MONTH		8 DAYS – 70 HOURS			DRIVER:	LAST SIX CONSECUTIVE DAYS IN PRECEDING MONTH	10	7 DAYS – 60 HOURS		
				HOURS AVAILABLE FOR ON-DUTY TIME NEXT DAY (70 MINUS) (COL. 4) ▼	MONTH:		10			HOURS AVAILABLE FOR ON-DUTY TIME NEXT DAY (60 MINUS) (COL. 4) ▼
		TOTAL ON-DUTY HOURS LAST 8 DAYS	TOTAL ON-DUTY HOURS LAST 7 DAYS		BOOK NUMBER:		15	TOTAL ON-DUTY HOURS LAST 7 DAYS	TOTAL ON-DUTY HOURS LAST 6 DAYS	
							4			
							15			
							0			
1					INSTRUCTIONS	1	0	54	44	16
2					This form is designed for use in maintaining a running record of a driver's time on-duty each day. It may be used equally well for drivers working on a midnight-to-midnight or noon-to-noon basis and, by using the proper chart, for drivers eligible to work 60 hours in 7 consecutive days or 70 hours in 8 consecutive days. The person using the chart can also determine the time that a driver has available for work the next day in compliance with the Hours of Service Regulations of the Department of Transportation.	2	10 1/2	54 1/2	44 1/2	15 1/2
3						3	10 3/4	45 1/4	40 1/4	19 3/4
4						4	10 1/2	50 3/4	46 3/4	13 1/4
5						5	10	56 3/4	41 3/4	18 1/4
6						6	3 1/4	45	45	15
7					In keeping the record, be sure to use the proper chart. For a driver working 70 hours in 8 consecutive days, use the chart on the left. For a driver working 60 hours in 7 consecutive days, use the chart on the right.	7				
8						8				
9					Column 1 of each section lists days of the month, 1-31 inclusive, plus the last days of the preceding month that must be counted.	9				
10						10				
11					In column 2 of the proper section enter the time on-duty for the day, (the total of Line 3, Driving, and Line 4, On-Duty Not Driving of the Drivers Daily Log). If the driver does not work on any day, enter a "0" for that day and compute other figures in accordance with the instructions below, as though he had worked.	11				
12						12				
13						13				
14						14				

Figure **3-4** A form used to recap a week of driver activity. Be sure to follow the instructions on the form because different logbook designs may present the recap in a slightly different manner.

Driver's Daily Log Entries

The Driver's Daily Log is his or her personal record of duty status and the time worked for each employer. If the driver was paid for work for a noncarrier, he or she must also record this as on-duty time.

All entries must:

- Be made only by the driver.
- Be legible.
- Be current to the last change of duty status.
- Be made using the time zone of the driver's home terminal; for example, a driver on a run to New York from his or her home terminal in California will make all entries using Pacific Standard Time. If the return run starts at 7:00 A.M. out of New York, he or she will enter the time as 4:00 A.M. Carriers with multiple terminals assign a home terminal to each driver.
- Be certified as correct by the driver's signature
- Be made on the correct section of the grid: a solid line will mark every 24-hour period
- Be readable on the duplicate copy: press hard to make sure

According to the FMCSA, it is now acceptable to use electronic programs, such as Driver's Daily Log, to record duty status as long as the computer-generated printout includes the minimum information required by Part 395.8 of the FMCSR and must be formatted in accordance with the rules. In addition, the driver must:

- Print the log at the completion of each day and sign it. Note that the driver's signature cannot be electronic; the driver must physically sign the log after printing it.
- Be able to print the log for the current 24-hour period on demand.
- Maintain a copy of printed and signed logs for the previous 7 consecutive days and have it available for inspection at the request of an enforcement officer.

Recording Your Duty Status

Two or more consecutive 24-hour periods off duty may be recorded on one daily log. **Sleeper berth time** is only the time spent resting in an approved type of **sleeper berth.** Time spent sleeping on the seat or while sitting in the cab cannot be counted as sleeper berth time. All time spent at the controls of the rig must be counted as driving time. Changes in duty status must be recorded to the nearest 1/4 hour. The driver must have daily logs for the previous 7 days.

All daily logs must be kept by the driver for seven days; turned in to the carrier within 13 days, either in person or by mail; and kept temporarily at the home terminal by the carrier. Then they should be kept at the carrier's main office for at least 6 months from the date on the log.

The Driver's Daily Log shown in Figure 3-5 shows entries made by a driver on a midnight-to-midnight run from Richmond, Virginia, to Newark, New Jersey. Notice how the 24-hour period contains a solid line made by the entries.

Schedule

6:00 A.M.–7:15 A.M.: Driver reported for work at his home terminal in Richmond, VA, and helped load his trailer.

7:15 A.M.–7:30 A.M.: Picked up the shipping documents and did the pretrip inspection.

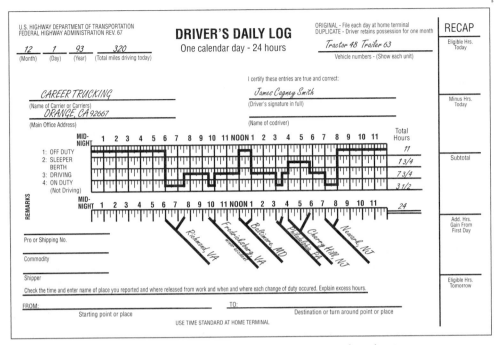

Figure **3-5** Daily log showing entries for a midnight-to-midnight run.

7:30 A.M.: Driver got behind the wheel and began driving.

9:30 A.M.–10:00 A.M.: Driver was in minor accident near Fredricksburg, VA. Filed police report.

12:00 noon: Driver arrived at the company's terminal in Baltimore, MD. Was relieved from duty to go to lunch while repairs were made to his tractor. The driver returned to the terminal at 1:00 P.M. and resumed his trip.

3:00 P.M.–3:30 P.M.: Made deliveries to 2 locations in Philadelphia, PA.

4:00 P.M.: Stopped at rest area in Cherry Hill, NJ.

4:00 P.M.–5:45 P.M.: Slept in sleeper berth.

5:45 P.M.: Started driving again.

7:00 P.M.: Arrived at Newark, NJ, terminal. Parked rig and went to driver's room to complete paperwork.

7:00 P.M.–8:00 P.M.: Driver completed daily log, vehicle condition report, and insurance report on the accident.

8:00 P.M.: Driver went off duty.

DRIVER DECLARED OUT OF SERVICE

A driver may be declared out of service (see Figure 3-6) by any agent of the Federal Highway Administration (FHWA) for either of the following reasons:

- The driver has been on duty too many hours.
- The driver does not have daily logs for the previous 7 days.

Out of Service

Figure **3-6** A driver declared out of service loses time, money, and often a job.

Note: A driver who has not completed the log for the current day and the day before, but has logs for the previous six days, may be given a chance to bring his logs up to date without being declared out of service.

If a driver is declared out of service because of too many hours on duty, he or she cannot drive until they have been off duty long enough to be eligible to legally drive again.

If the driver is declared out of service for not having the daily logs, he or she may not drive until they have been off duty for 8 hours in a row and can legally drive again.

PENALTIES

Drivers who make false entries on their Daily Logs, do not prepare a Daily Log, or drive more than the allowable hours are subject to heavy fines and/or being declared out of service by an agent of the FHWA.

The driver may also face delays in delivering their cargo. If a driver has driven too long, he or she can have an accident. As a result of this accident, both the driver and the carrier may face civil and criminal liability.

Carriers who do not keep proper records on all their drivers are also subject to heavy fines and civil liability if there is an accident because the driver violated the regulations.

A current log that is neat and readable means the driver has a professional attitude about knowing and obeying the trucking laws.

Chapter Four
Vehicle Inspection

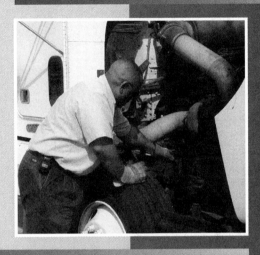

OBJECTIVES

When you have completed this chapter, you should be able to:

- Describe a routine to use for thorough and complete pretrip inspection

- Recognize damaged, loose, or missing parts and system leaks

- Explain the importance of correcting malfunctions before starting your trip

- Understand and use federal and state regulations for inspection

- Explain the steps for enroute and posttrip inspections

KEY TERMS

Air reservoir

Brakes

Cargo compartment doors

Coupling system

En route inspection

Exhaust system

Federal Motor Carrier Safety Regulations (FMCSR)

Fifth wheel

FMCSR, Part 396, Inspection, Repair and Maintenance of Motor Vehicles

FMCSR 396.9 (c) Motor Vehicle Declared Out-of-Service

Four-way flashers

Frame

Free play

Inspection routine

Instruments and gauges

Posttrip inspection

Pretrip inspection

Rims

Signal (or identification) lights

Spare tire

Splash guards (mud flaps)

Steering system

Steering wheel lash (play)

Suspension system

Tarp

Tires

Trailer hand valve brake

Vehicle Condition Report (VCR)

Wheels

INTRODUCTION

A large and increasingly complex vehicle, today's tractor-trailer rig requires consistent maintenance and experienced drivers for optimum performance. Each of the rig's systems must be regularly inspected to ensure that each part remains intact and in good condition. Fluid levels must be constantly checked and refilled when necessary. Routine maintenance must be thoroughly and expertly performed. However, the most critical key to rig performance is the driver's timely, step-by-step pretrip and posttrip inspection.

The focus of this chapter is to emphasize the critical nature of these inspections and to provide an efficient routine for you to follow each time you inspect your rig.

PRETRIP, EN ROUTE, AND POSTTRIP INSPECTIONS

The skills of a professional driver can first be measured in the thoroughness of each of his or her inspection routines (see Figure 4-1). And while the priority of all tractor-trailer inspections is safety and the safe operation of the rig, inspections also provide the driver with information about the rig, including:

- Systems or parts that are working properly
- Systems or parts that are not working properly
- Parts that have been damaged or are loose or missing
- Systems or parts on the verge of failing
- Systems or parts in danger of failing or malfunctioning

Goal of Inspection

- **Goals**
  - To identify
    - A part or system that is malfunctioning or has already failed (or is missing)
    - A part or system that is in imminent danger of failing or malfunctioning
    - A part or system that is all right or is functioning properly
    - The legal requirements for various parts or system conditions
- **Driver Responsibility**
  - Safety of vehicle and cargo
  - Vehicle inspection
- **Types of Inspection**
  - Pretrip
  - Enroute
  - Posttrip
- **Basic Reasons**
  - Safety
  - Economy
  - Public relations
  - Legality
- **Three Elements of a Good Inspection**
  - Knowing what to look for
  - Having a consistent way of looking for it
  - Being able to report findings in a technically accurate way so that the mechanics will be able to identify and repair the problems

Figure **4-1** The pretrip, en route, and posttrip inspections are pivotal to the performance of the rig and to the efficiency and effectiveness of the professional driver.

By law, each rig must meet certain performance standards, and meeting these standards is the responsibility of professional drivers and their regular safety inspections of the rigs they drive (see Figure 4-2).

Professional drivers are responsible for three types of vehicle inspections:

- **The pretrip inspection:** A systematic parts and systems check done before each trip, including how cargo is loaded and/or tied down.

- **The en route inspection:** A systematic check of the rig's controls, instruments while driving, and other critical items, such as couplings, cargo tie-downs, tires, and wheels, at each stop.

  - **The posttrip inspection:** A thorough check of the rig at the end of the trip and a written **vehicle condition report (VCR)**, listing any defect noted during operation and inspection. These reports are required by law and by company policy.

Vehicle condition inspections are important for a variety of reasons, including safety, economy, driver's peace of mind, legal reasons, and public relations.

Safety is the leading—and most obvious—benefit each time a thorough inspection is done, but inspections also help avoid mechanical defects, malfunctions that could lead to an accident, or costly delays due to breakdowns.

Skipped or sloppy inspections are also costly for other reasons. Maintenance costs rise, small problems evolve into major repairs, and systems that are not properly maintained can shorten the work

Figure **4-2** Professional drivers are responsible for making regular safety inspections of the vehicles they drive.

life of any vehicle. Careless or skipped inspections can also result in higher fuel costs, high breakdown rate, and expensive out-of-service fines.

Federal and state laws require certain types of commercial vehicle inspections by approved inspectors. Many states have trained inspection teams that travel their highways, stopping tractor-trailer rigs and performing complete inspections. If a rig does not meet basic inspection standards, you will be put out of service, and your company will be fined and possibly monitored for future inspection violations.

The bottom line is that the trucking industry has spent time and thousands of dollars building goodwill among the general public. The individual professional driver can add to this public relations effort with careful vehicle inspections and attention to any problems with a rig as they arise. Accidents or traffic tie-ups caused by poorly maintained equipment take away from the positive public image carriers and trucking associations have worked to establish. A thorough inspection also cuts down on public ill will toward truckers by cutting down on exhaust smoke and noise and may improve the rig's appearance.

Several carriers are so aware of the importance of positive public relations that they spend thousands of dollars every year in regular truck washes and crisp, clean uniforms for their driver personnel.

Are inspections important enough to do the best job possible each time you inspect your rig? The answer is a resounding "Yes!"

WHAT MAKES A GOOD INSPECTION GREAT?

Ask any professional driver, and they'll tell you that learning to conduct a thorough vehicle inspection will not only make your job easier but may save your life and the lives of others.

In fact, most drivers will tell you that learning how to perform a thorough inspection is the first thing they learned before going over-the-road. Said one veteran, "You can only do a good inspection if you have the knowledge, first of all, but you also have to have the desire to do it right the first time, and you have to commit to the effort it takes to thoroughly inspect your rig before, during, and after every trip. Plus, you have to know what you're doing, what to look for every inch of the way—and you have to understand why you're doing the inspection and what's in it for you."

As you learn to perform inspections of tractor-trailer rigs, you should:

- Learn and follow a regular routine. By using the same routine each time you perform an inspection, you will cover the rig, front to rear, without missing any critical points.
- Know what you're looking for.
- Report any problems so mechanics can easily identify and repair the rig.

WHAT TO LOOK FOR DURING A RIG INSPECTION

The major reasons for performing regular inspections of your rig are, as stated earlier, (1) to maintain the rig properly, (2) to make operation of the rig as safe as possible, (3) to minimize breakdowns, (4) to maintain good public relations, and (5) to make your life easier.

As a professional driver—and in order to make a thorough inspection—you need to know:

- If a system or part is working properly
- When a system or part is in danger of failure or malfunction
- The difference between major and minor defects
- Defects and problems that make your rig illegal and could cause it to be put out of service during a roadside inspection by federal or state inspectors

To understand what state and federal inspectors look for when they perform roadside inspections, look at **Federal Motor Carrier Safety Regulations (FMCSR), Part 396, Inspection, Repair and Maintenance of Motor Vehicles.**

By law, all professional drivers must also know the requirements of the **FMCSR 396.9(c), Motor Vehicle Declared Out-of-Service.** This regulation prevents any driver from driving a commercial motor vehicle that is out of repair and *imminently hazardous to operate.* Safety defects considered imminently hazardous include:

- A defective steering system
- Brake shoes that are missing or do not work
- Cracked brake drums
- Serious air loss in the brake system
- Missing lights or ones that do not work
- Bad tires
- Cracked wheels, ones that have been welded, or ones that have missing lug nuts
- Fuel system leaks
- Cargo not properly secured
- A defective coupling system

This same regulation also states that a motor carrier cannot require or permit a driver to operate a vehicle that has not been regularly inspected or maintained.

Fluid Leaks

Figure **4-3** Check fluid levels during each inspection.

You may have previous experience with fluid leaks—as in going out to your personal vehicle and finding pools of leaking fluid on the driveway or the ground under it. And, as you also may know, serious engine damage or breakdowns can occur because of loss of fluids, like coolant or lubricants.

During every inspection—pretrip, en route or posttrip—always check every fluid level, including oil, coolant, battery, and fuel (see Figure 4-3). Also check for signs of fluid loss under the vehicle, and while you are driving, keep a constant eye on the gauges that monitor these vital fluids.

Bad Tires

Like every other American traveler, you have certainly driven down a highway and seen the remains of blown or damaged 18-wheeler tires. Tire defects increase the chances of a blowout and can make any big rig dangerously difficult to handle. Federal regulations forbid professional truckers to drive with faulty tires (see FMCSR 393.75).

Figure **4-4**   Carefully inspect each tire.

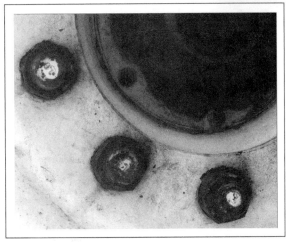

Figure **4-5**   Check for rust around the lug nut holes as well as rust trails and loose or missing lugs.

Careful inspections of each wheel and tire will make blowouts less likely and may prevent accidents as well as costly downtime (see Figure 4-4). When inspecting tires, look for tires that are flat, underinflated, or have leaks you can hear; tires that are badly worn, cut, or damaged in any way; tires that are not matching, such as radials and bias-ply tires or tires of various sizes used on the same rig; tires that touch other tires or parts of the rig.

Wheels and Rims

Defective **wheels** or **rims** can cause a tire to come off and cause a serious accident. Look for:

- Dented or damaged rims or cracks starting at the lug nut holes; these can cause tires to lose air pressure or come off the rim in a turn.
- Rust trails indicating a loose wheel (see Figure 4-5).
- Missing clamps, spacers, studs, or lugs.
- Unevenly tightened lugs (see Figure 4-6); this can cause the wheel to wobble. Wobble causes vibration and early tire failure.
- Mismatched, bent, or cracked lock rings.
- Welded wheels or rims; these may be weak and unsafe.
- Loose rims that can spin and cut valve stems when the driver puts on the brakes.
- Rims that have already spun. Most open-well wheels have safety catches to protect the valve stem. If the lug wedges are against them, check them for damage or have them checked.

Figure **4-6** Check for unevenly tightened lugs.

Braking Systems Inspection

You must be able to control slowing and stopping to drive a rig safely. To do so, your **brakes** must be in top shape.

Air Pressure

You should not hear any air leaks. The sound of air coming from any part of the air brake system means the system is defective and can be dangerous.

To check for air brake system pressure loss (leaks), follow these steps:

1. Set the brakes (parking and trailer), start the engine, and let air pressure build until the system is fully charged—about 125 pounds per square inch (psi).
2. Turn off the engine, chock the wheels, and release the parking brake and trailer brakes (puts air into the spring brake system). After the initial air pressure drop (about 10–15 psi), apply firm pressure (about 90 psi) to the service brake pedal (puts air into the remainder of the system). Hold this for one minute.
3. Watch your air pressure gauge. The air pressure should not drop more than
   a. 3 psi in 1 minute for tractor,
   b. 4 psi in 1 minute for a tractor and trailer, or
   c. 6 psi in 1 minute for a tractor and three trailers.

Air leaks that can be heard or are more than the amounts listed here should be repaired before the truck or combination is driven because they are unsafe and violate safety regulations.

Brake Lines

You should not hear any air leaks. You should check for air lines that are:

- not secured properly;
- hardened or swollen;
- chafed or worn so that the fabric or steel braid is visible;
- cut or cracked;
- crimped, pinched, or in any way restricted; or
- taped or not spliced right.

Air Reservoir

The **air reservoir**(s) (see Figure 4-7) must be properly attached to the rig. They must be bled each day to remove moisture. A good time to bleed them is during the pretrip or posttrip inspection.

Brake Adjustment

Adjustment procedures are covered in a later chapter.

Note: Many trucks have air dryers. These may or may not have automatic drain valves.

Steering System Inspection

At all times and in all situations, the professional driver should be in control of his or her rig. Lack of this control may be the result of poor maintenance or system malfunction. The **steering system,** for example, provides some of the driver's most immediate control over the direction of a rig, and defects in this system create unsafe situations.

Steering system defects may affect total control of the vehicle and the higher the speed the vehicle is traveling when steering system problems occur, the more these problems will affect your rig and your possibility of escaping without an accident.

When conducting pretrip, en route, or posttrip inspections of your vehicle, look for:

- Bent, loose, or broken parts, such as the steering column, steering gear box, tie rods, Pitman arm, and drag link
- Missing nuts, bolts, cotter keys, or other securing devices
- Damaged hoses and pumps
- Proper fluid level in the power steering reservoir (see Figure 4-8)

Figure **4-8** Check the fluid level in the power steering reservoir.

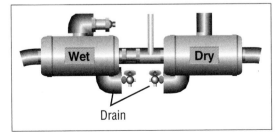

Figure **4-7** The air reservoirs should be bled each day.

Figure **4-9**   Check the steering wheel for looseness.

Table **4-1**   Parameters for Steering Wheel Lash (FMSCA 393.209).

Steering Wheel Diameter	Manual Steering System	Power Steering System
16 inches or less	2 inches	4-1/2 inches
18 inches	2-1/4 inches	4-3/4 inches
20 inches	2-1/2 inches	5-1/4 inches
22 inches	2-3/4 inches	5-3/4 inches

- Air and fluid leaks
- Check the steering wheel for **Steering wheel lash,** or looseness or **play,** in the steering wheel's movement (see Figure 4-9). For power steering, if there is more than 5-3/4 inches of play, the rig should be placed out of service. Table 4-1 will help you determine whether there's too much play in the steering wheel.

Suspension System Inspection

The **suspension system** supports the rig's load and maintains axle attachment and alignment. Failure can have tragic results. Check for:

- Cracked or broken torque arms and U-bolts.
- Hangers that let the axle move from its proper position.
- Missing or broken leaves in a spring leaf cluster: The rig will be put out of service if one-fourth or more of them are missing. Any broken or missing leaves can be dangerous.
- Leaking or faulty shock absorbers.
- Cracked or broken spring hangers.
- Missing or damaged spring hangers or other axle positioning parts.
- Damaged or leaking air suspension systems.
- Broken leaves or leaves that have shifted and are touching the tires, wheels, frame, or body in multileaf springs.

- Missing or broken torque rods.
- Loose, cracked, broken, or missing frame members.

Exhaust System Inspection

Faulty **exhaust systems** can lead to noxious fumes in the cab or sleeper berth. Look for:

- Loose, broken, or missing exhaust pipes, mufflers, tailpipes, or vertical stacks
- Loose, broken, or failing clamps, bolts, nuts, or mounting brackets
- Exhaust system parts in contact with fuel system parts, tires, wiring, or other parts of the rig
- Exhaust system parts that leak in an area where the airstream will carry the fumes into the cab or sleeper
- Black soot around the coupling (indicates exhaust leaks)

Coupling System Inspection

Failure of the **coupling system** (upper or lower **fifth wheel**) can cause cargo damage or serious accidents. Check for:

- Too much slack in the fifth-wheel locking mechanism
- Cracks or breaks in any part of the fifth-wheel assembly
- Bent, broken, or missing parts of the locking mechanism (see Figure 4-10)
- Missing pins or other defects in the slide mechanism of the sliding fifth wheel (see Figure 4-11)
- Bent, cracked, or very worn kingpins

Figure **4-10** Check the coupling system locking mechanism for bent, broken, or missing parts.

Figure **4-11** A dry fifth wheel.

- Missing U-bolts, cracked or broken welds, or other defects in the fifth-wheel mounting devices(s) (see Figure 4-12)
- More than 3/8 inch horizontal movement between the pivot bracket pin and bracket
- Pivot bracket pin missing or not secured

Cargo Inspection

Cargo must be checked to make sure it cannot move in transit. Unsecured cargo often causes accidents. Cargo handling is covered in detail in a later chapter.

STEPS TO A PRETRIP INSPECTION

You have a moral, professional, and legal duty to your employer, other motorists, and yourself to conduct a thorough pretrip inspection of any rig you drive. It takes much longer to learn how to perform a quality pretrip inspection than it takes to do one. After a lot of practice, you will be able to do a thorough inspection in less than 15 minutes.

The secret to making an efficient and accurate inspection is to learn a step-by-step **inspection routine.** If you inspect your rig the same way each time, you will do it more quickly and will not be as likely to forget to check a key part (see Figure 4-13).

Note: Many companies have specific policies on vehicle inspection. Some carriers require drivers to conduct a more extensive inspection. Some carriers prohibit certain checks. All drivers must establish a procedure that is consistent with company policy.

Figure **4-12** Check for defects in the fifth-wheel mounting devices.

Seven-Step Pre-Trip Inspection Checklist

1. Approach vehicle — look for leaks
2. Check under hood or cab
3. Start engine and check inside cab
4. Check headlights
5. Conduct walk around
6. Check signal lights
7. Check air brake system

Figure **4-13** The secret to an accurate and efficient inspection is to learn a step-by-step routine.

Step 1: Approach the Vehicle

While walking toward the rig, look for signs of damage. Also look for anything that may be in the way when you try to move the vehicle. As you approach the rig, look at the following items:

Vehicle posture. A truck sagging to one side may mean flat tires, overloading, shifted cargo, or suspension problems.

Cargo. Make sure the trailer or **cargo compartment doors** are closed and properly fastened. On flatbed trailers and other open cargo compartments, make sure the cargo is not hanging over the side and that restraints can stand 1-1/2 times any pressure from the load (see Figure 4-14).

Figure **4-14** Check the cargo and restraints.

Figure **4-15** Check under the hood or cab.

Damaged, loose, or missing parts. Look for cracked glass, dents, or missing parts such as fenders, mud flaps, and lights. Check for loose parts, such as a fuel tank hanging with unsecured straps.

Leaks. Glance under the truck for puddles of fresh oil, engine coolant, grease, or fuel. Check for other signs of leakage.

Area around vehicle. Look for anything that may be damaged by the rig or will damage it as you drive away. Include objects on the ground, such as glass or boards with nails. Look up for low-hanging branches, electric or telephone wires, and any other overhead objects that may be hit by the tractor or trailer.

Step 2: Check Under the Hood or Cab

Check the engine compartment to make sure the vehicle has been properly serviced (see Figure 4-15). Look for signs of damage or possible problems with the engine, steering mechanism, and suspension system. Most conventional tractor-trailer hoods are equipped with safety latches of one kind or another. These are intended to keep the hood from falling onto a person while he or she is checking beneath the cab. The cab-over-engine (COE) tractor, however, has a hydraulic system with a safety latch that drops into place when the cab is jacked up to the service position. It is important for drivers to use the latches and then to remember to undo them before lowering the hood or cab to avoid breaking or damaging them.

If the latches are not used, a hood or cab can have the appearance of being safely open, only to fall suddenly on the driver, causing severe injury or even death.

Fluid levels. Check the crankcase oil, radiator coolant, battery fluid, windshield washer fluid, and any other fluids, such as automatic transmission fluid and engine oil in the makeup reservoir. Make sure all fluids are at the right levels before starting the engine.

Leaks.   Look for leaks of oil, water, or hydraulic fluid in the engine compartment. Check around the entire compartment for any grease, soot, or other signs of fluid leaks. Inspect the exhaust manifold for signs of leakage. If your vehicle's main air tanks are under the hood or cab, listen carefully for the sound of leaking air.

Electrical system.   Make sure the battery is secured and the terminals are not corroded. Check for loose electrical wires. Check the insulation to make sure it is not cracked or worn through. If your rig has spark plugs, check for secure electrical connections.

Belts and pulleys.   Inspect the alternator, air compressor, and water pump belts for cracks or frays. Test the belts for tension and slippage. If you can slide a belt over a pulley, it is too loose and should be tightened or replaced.

Coolant system.   Check the radiator and its shroud and shutters to make sure it is structurally sound and free of dents or other damage. (Newer systems have thermostatic fans that eliminate shutters.) Make sure all parts of the coolant system are properly secured. Check the hoses for cracks or breaks. Inspect the fan for missing blades. Look for hanging wires or hoses that can catch on the blades (see Figure 4-16).

Steering system.   Check the steering linkage and gear box closely. Make sure they are secure. Look for signs of wear, such as paint that has been rubbed off. If the rig has power steering, make sure the power steering lines are securely connected and there are no leaks. Check fluid levels.

Braking system.   Look for cracked brake drums, missing brake shoes, and missing or disconnected brake hoses and slack adjusters. If the rig has air brakes, make sure the air intake screen (if there is one) is not clogged with dirt, leaves, or other de-

Figure **4-16** Inspect the fan.

Figure **4-17** Check the suspension system.

Figure **4-18** Check the exhaust system.

bris. Open the air tank petcocks and drain the tanks. Check for oil contamination. Be sure to close the petcocks when you are through.

Suspension system. Check the U-bolts, spring pins, spring brackets, and torque arms for cracks, bends, or missing bolts (see Figure 4-17). Check the axles for signs of rubbing. If the truck has adjustable axles, make sure all locking pins are in the proper position and fully engaged. Make sure the safety clamps holding the locking pins are securely in place. Look for cracks in the truck's frame and cross members. Check the whole suspension system for rust or shiny spots that may indicate excessive wear. Look at all leaf springs for missing, out of place, or broken leaves. Leaves sticking out from a leaf spring may touch the tires, rims, or frame. Look for leaking or defective shock absorbers. If the rig has an air suspension system, make sure the air bags are not damaged or leaking.

Exhaust system. Examine the muffler. Be sure it is securely connected and has no holes or large dents or is crushed (see Figure 4-18). Make sure all lines and hoses connected to the system are securely fastened. Report all damage found before your trip. Be sure the fuel and electric lines will not come too close to any part of the exhaust system that gets hot.

Hood or cab. When you have finished the under-the-hood checks, lower and latch the hood or cab. Make sure all fastenings are secure.

Step 3: Start the Engine and Check Inside the Cab

After checking the engine compartment, get into the cab and prepare to start the engine. You are not yet ready to move the vehicle. This part of the inspection is to make sure the cab and all controls and instruments are in good working order.

Vehicle entry.   Check to see that the ladder, grab handle, and door handles are secure and free of oil, grease, or ice. Make sure the door opens and closes freely and latches securely.

Emergency and safety equipment.   Be sure you have all the required emergency and safety equipment. Always have a fully charged and mounted fire extinguisher and at least three reflective triangles (see Figure 4-19). Store them properly to prevent breakage.

Mirrors and glass.   Clean all window glass before you drive. Check for cracks and breaks. Dirty windshields and windows interfere with vision, especially at night. Make sure the windshield wipers work. Run your hand along the wiper blades to feel for worn spots (see Figure 4-20). The rubber should be soft and pliable. Make sure mirrors are securely mounted (see Figure 4-21). Check them for cracks. Adjust the seat to a driving position that is right for you. Then check the mirrors and adjust them as needed.

Engine start-up.   Make sure the parking brake is on and the transmission is in neutral for starting the engine. Start the engine at zero throttle. Do not crank over 15 seconds. Listen for unusual noises from the engine and exhaust system (knocking, pinging, skipping, and so on). Let the engine idle.

Instruments and gauges.   With the engine running, check to see that all instruments and gauges are working. Be sure the major systems are within proper limits. Look at:

- **Oil pressure gauge:** It should begin to register a few seconds after engine start-up and gradually rise to the normal range.
- **Ammeter/voltmeter:** The needle should jump, flutter, and then register "charge" or "+."
- **Coolant temperature gauge:** It should gradually rise to the normal operating range.
- **Warning lights:** The oil, coolant, and generator warning lights should go out almost as soon as the engine is started.

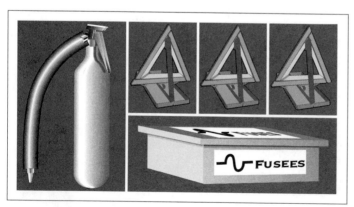

Figure **4-19**   Required by law, each truck should have a fire extinguisher, reflective triangles, and spare fuses.

Figure **4-20**   Check the windshield wiper blades.

Figure **4-21**   Make sure the mirrors are securely mounted.

- **Low air pressure warning buzzer:** The buzzer or alarm should sound until the air pressure builds to about 60 psi. At this point, the buzzer or alarm should stop.
- **Air pressure gauge:** Pressure should build steadily. Check the time needed for the pressure to build from 85 to 100 psi. If it is within 45 seconds, the buildup is OK. Note: The buildup could take longer with oversized air tanks.
- **Air pressure governor cut off:** Pressure buildup should stop between 115 and 125 psi. If the buildup stops below or above that range, adjustments are necessary.

Note: In trucks with electronically controlled engines, the needles on all gauges will make a full sweep right after the engine is turned on. This is a self-check function to ensure all gauges are working.

Primary controls.   With the engine still running, check the vehicle's main controls:

- **Steering mechanism:** Check steering for free play, or "lash." Open the cab door and lean out so you can see the left front tire of the truck. While watching the tire, turn the wheel until the tire starts to move. Refer to Table 4-1 for unsafe levels of free play for manual and power steering wheels.
- **Clutch:** Depress the clutch until you feel a little resistance. For most clutches, 1 to 2 inches of free play is normal. Too much or too little free play can cause hard shifting, gear clashing, and clutch or transmission damage.

- **Transmission:** With the clutch depressed, check to see that the transmission lets you shift freely from neutral into the other gears.
- **Accelerator and brake pedals:** Check both pedals for looseness or sticking. Be sure there is no dirt buildup underneath.

Secondary controls. Check the controls for the:

- Defroster
- Fan
- Horn
- Interior lights
- Turn signal
- High-beam indicator

- Heater and air conditioner
- Lanyard to the air horn
- Windshield washers and wipers
- Dash lights
- Four-way flashers
- Steering tilt

They should all be in working order.

Cab housekeeping. Make sure all cab parts are where they belong. Check the dashboard knobs, rubber pedal covers, and door handles. Everything in the cab should be in place and properly secured. Make sure nothing limits your vision or movement. Remove papers, cans, and trash. Loose trash in the cab can get under the accelerator, brake, or clutch pedals and become a hazard.

Prepare to leave the cab. When the air pressure has built to the governor cutout pressure, turn off the engine. If the engine shutoff is the pull-out type, leave it in the pulled out position until you start the engine again. Put the rig into the lowest forward gear. Set the parking brake. Turn on the low-beam headlights and **four-way flashers.** Remove the starter switch key and place it in your pocket to keep someone else from moving the rig while you are making the outside inspections.

Step 4: Check the Lights and Mirrors

After you get out of the cab, go to the front of the rig. Check the:

- Low-beam headlights: Do they work? Are they aligned? (see Figure 4-22)
- Four-way flashers: Do both work?

Reach into the cab and switch the lights to high beam:

- Do they work?
- Are they aligned?

Inspect the mirrors:

- Are they clean?
- Adjust the mirrors if necessary.

Step 5: Conduct a Walk-Around Inspection

Go back to the cab. Turn off the headlights and four-way flashers. Turn on the right turn signal. Leave the cab and start a walk-around inspection.

The walk-around inspection is a 14-point routine (see Figure 4-23). During this part of the pretrip inspection, you will be looking at vehicle parts that are outside the cab.

Figure **4-22** Check the headlights.

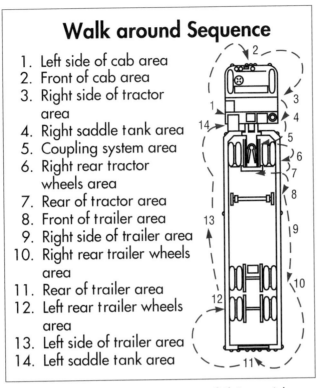

Walk around Sequence

1. Left side of cab area
2. Front of cab area
3. Right side of tractor area
4. Right saddle tank area
5. Coupling system area
6. Right rear tractor wheels area
7. Rear of tractor area
8. Front of trailer area
9. Right side of trailer area
10. Right rear trailer wheels area
11. Rear of trailer area
12. Left rear trailer wheels area
13. Left side of trailer area
14. Left saddle tank area

Figure **4-23** Make a copy of this guide and use it as a guide when performing inspections.

Note: In some states, such as Kansas, the driver is expected to perform the walk-around sequence beginning on the left side of the vehicle and proceeding along the left side to the rear of the vehicle and then to the right side. This is done so the driver is facing traffic, ensuring his or her safety. Be sure to check your state's requirements for performing the walk-around inspection.

Left Side of the Cab

How does it look in general? Check the:

- **Driver's door glass, latches, and lock.**
- **Left front wheel and rim:** Check for damage. A bent or damaged rim can make a tire lose pressure or separate from the wheel. If the rims have more than one piece, they are under extreme pressure and can explode from the wheel if damaged, mismatched, or not mounted properly. Always have experts adjust them for you. Such adjustments are regulated by standards set by the Occupational Safety and Health Administration (OSHA).

  Check for improperly mounted tires. Loose or missing lugs put too much stress on the other lugs. They could break off and cause the wheel to come off. Look for a rust trail around the lugs. This tells you the lug nuts may be loose. Use a lug wrench to check the lugs. Look for signs of lubricant leaking from the wheel seals. Lost lubricant can cause a wheel to lock up. Check the hub oil level.

- **Left front tire:** Check the:
  - Air pressure

- Tread (should be no less than 4/32 inch; see Figure 4-24)
- General condition

Low tire pressure makes the rig hard to handle. It can increase the chance of a blowout or tire fire. It also reduces tire life. Always check the tire air pressure with a gauge.

Bald or worn tires can cause a blowout or make the rig hard to stop and difficult to handle. If the road surface is wet, driving on worn treads causes the rig to hydroplane. Cuts, separated treads, bulges, and missing or broken valve stems may cause tire failure. Remove any objects, such as stones, nails, and glass, that have become wedged in the tread.

- **Left front brake:** Check the condition of the:
  - Brake drum
  - Hoses
  - Shoes (if they can be seen) (linings should not be less than 1/4 inch)
- **Air tanks:**
  - Drain
- **Left front suspension:** Check the condition of the:
  - Springs and spring hangers/shock absorbers
  - U-bolts
- **Shock absorbers:** Look for:
  - Leaks
  - Defects

Front of Cab

Check the condition of the:

- Front axle
- Steering system: no loose, worn, bent, or damaged parts (test the steering mechanism for looseness)

Make sure the license plates are on tightly. Check that all legally required inspection stickers, tax plates, decals, and so on are in place.

Check the condition of the windshield. Make sure it is clean and undamaged. Check the windshield wiper arms for proper spring tension. Check the wiper blades for damage and be sure they are attached correctly.

Check the parking, clearance, and ID lights to be sure they are:

- clean,
- the right color (amber in front; red in rear), and
- all in working order.

Make sure all reflectors are clean and not damaged. Check the right turn signal light to be sure it is:

- clean,
- the right color (amber in front; red in rear), and
- in working order.

Figure **4-24** Tire with good tread (no less than 4/32 inch).

Right Side of Cab

Check all items on the right side of the cab that you checked on the left side. If your tractor has a COE, check the cab tilt mechanism to be sure it is in working order. Check all primary and safety locks. Make sure they are engaged.

Right Saddle Tank Area

Check the:

- **Right fuel tank(s):** The tank(s) should be in good condition and securely mounted. The fuel crossover line should be secure. The tanks should be full of fuel and the caps firmly in place.
- **Rear of engine:** No leaks should be detected.
- **Transmission:** No leaks should be seen.
- **Drive shaft:** Check how it looks in general. Is it in position and secured both on the front and on the rear?
- **Exhaust system:** Are the brackets, pipes, and other parts secure and free of leaks? Be sure no fuel lines, air lines, or wires are in contact with exhaust parts. Look for soot, fluids, or burned areas, indicating leaks.
- **Frame and cross members:** Look for bends and cracks in the parts of the frame you can see.
- **Air lines and electrical wiring:** Be sure they are secure and will not snag or rub against anything.
- **Spare tire carrier and rack:** Make sure they are sturdy, strong enough to carry the load, and not damaged.
- **Spare tire and wheel:** They should be firmly mounted in the rack. Make sure they are in good condition. Check the tire to be sure it is the right type and size and is properly inflated.

Coupling System

Inspect the following:

- **Lower fifth wheel:** Is it properly lubricated? Is it firmly mounted to the frame? Are any parts missing or damaged? You should see no space between the upper and lower fifth wheels. Be sure the locking jaws are securely fastened around the shank of the kingpin. Never leave them around the head of the kingpin. The release arm must be properly seated, and the safety latch/lock must be engaged.
- **Upper fifth wheel, or apron:** The guide plate should be firmly mounted on the trailer frame. The kingpin should not be worn, bent, rusted, or damaged.
- **Air and electrical lines to the trailer:** These lines should be in good condition (see Figure 4-25). Be sure they will not get tangled, snag, or rub against anything. They should not be oily, greasy, or damaged. The air lines must be properly connected to glad hands. Glad hands are air hose connections between the tractor and trailer. Be sure there are no leaks. Electrical lines should be firmly seated and locked in place.
- **Sliding fifth wheel** (if your rig has one): The sliding fifth wheel should not be worn or damaged. Make sure there are no missing parts. It should be properly lubricated. All lock pins should be there and locked in place. If it is air powered, make sure there are no air leaks. The fifth wheel should not be too far forward. If it is, the trailer could hit the cab, tractor frame, or landing gear during turns.

WARNING!

Whenever checking the coupling of a tractor-trailer or inspecting the kingpin of the trailer and the jaws of the fifth wheel, be sure to remove the ignition key from the tractor and chock at least one set of wheels of the trailer and one set of wheels of the tractor before crawling under the tractor-trailer to physically check the coupling.

Figure **4-25** Check the air lines to the trailer.

Right Rear Tractor Wheels Area

Inspect the following parts:

- **Dual wheels and rims:** All wheels and rims should be on and in good condition. Spacers, studs, clamps, or lugs should not be missing, bent, or broken.
- **Dual tires:** All tires should be properly inflated with the valve stems and caps in good condition. There should be no cuts, bulges, or serious tread wear. Tires should not rub each other. Make sure nothing is stuck between them. All tires should be the same type and size. Check for any leaks from the wheel bearings.
- **Suspension:** Make sure the springs, spring hangers, shackles, and U-bolts are in good shape. Check the torque rod arms, bushings, and shock absorbers to be sure they are OK.
- **Brakes:** Inspect all brake chambers to make sure everything is connected and in good working order. Where you can see them, check the brake drums for cracks and signs of rust or wear. Be sure brake shoes (see Figure 4-26) are evenly adjusted. If they are not, the vehicle will pull to the side during braking.

Check the slack adjusters on disc S-cam brakes. Park on level ground. Chock the wheels. Turn off the parking brakes so you can move the slack adjusters. Wear gloves. Pull hard on each adjuster you can reach. It should not move more than 1 inch where the push rod attaches to it. Adjust them or have them adjusted if they move more than 1 inch. Too much brake slack can make the rig hard to stop.

Rear of Tractor

- The frame and cross members should not be:
  - bent,

Figure **4-26** Brake shoes.

- cracked,
- damaged, or
- missing.
- All **lights and reflectors** should be:
  - the proper color,
  - clean,
  - in good condition, and
  - working.
- **License plates** should be:
  - clean,
  - firmly mounted, and
  - not expired.
- All **splash guards** should be:
  - present,
  - properly attached, and
  - not rubbing the tires.
- **Air and electrical lines** should be:
  - secured,
  - not damaged, and
  - not rubbing against anything.

Front Area of the Trailer

- The **license/registration holder** should be:
  - in place and contain the current registration and
  - firmly mounted with the cover closed.
- The **header board** should be:
  - securely mounted and
  - not damaged.
- **Canvas or tarp carrier** (if your rig has one) should be:
  - securely mounted,
  - damage free, and
  - tarps should be secured in the carrier.
- **Clearance and ID lights** should be:
  - the proper color,
  - clean,
  - in good condition, and
  - in working order.

Reflectors and reflective tape should also be clean and damage free.

Right Side of Trailer

The following items should be inspected:

- **Front trailer support (landing gear or dolly):** This device should be fully raised with no parts bent, damaged, or missing (see Figure 4-27). The crank handle

Figure **4-27** Landing gear.

should be present, properly secured, and in low gear if possible. If the crank handle is power operated, there should be no air or hydraulic leaks.

- **Spare tire carrier or rack:** It should be strong enough to carry the load. Make sure it is in good condition.
- **Spare tires and wheels:** Make sure the rack is secure. The spare tires and wheels should be in good condition. They should be the right size and inflated.
- **Lights and reflectors:** Trailer side clearance lights and reflectors should be:
  - clean,
  - the proper color (amber in front and red in rear),
  - in good condition, and
  - in working order.
- **Frame and body:** The frame and cross members should be:
  - free of bends,
  - free of cracks and traces of rust,
  - free of damage, and
  - in place with no missing cross members.
- **Cargo:** The cargo should be properly blocked, braced, tied, and chained. Side boards and stakes should be strong, properly mounted, and free of damage. Canvas or tarps should be properly lashed down to prevent water damage, tearing, blowing about, or blocking the view from the rear-view mirrors. Side doors should be securely latched with the security seals in place.

Right Rear Trailer Wheel Area

The following areas should be inspected:

- **Dual tires and rims:** Spacers, studs, clamps, or lugs should not be bent, broken, or missing. The tires should be properly inflated with valve stems and caps in good condition. They should be free of cuts, bulges, and serious tread wear and should not rub together. Check to be sure nothing is stuck between the dual tires. Tires should be the same size and type.
- **Tandem axles:** If the rig has sliding axles, check their position and alignment. Also check for damaged, worn, or missing parts. All locks should be present, in place, and secured. Air lines should be checked for cracks, cuts, crimping, and other damage. Be sure they are not tangled, dragging, or rubbing against anything.
- **Suspension:** The springs, spring hangers, shackles, U-bolts, torque rod arms, bushings, and shock absorbers should be in good condition.
- **Brakes:** Inspect all brake chambers. Make sure everything is connected and in good working order. Where you can see them, check the brake drums for cracks, rust, and wear. The brake shoes should be evenly adjusted. Uneven adjustment can cause the vehicle to pull to the side during braking.

Check the slack adjusters on disc and S-cam brakes (see Figure 4-28). Park on level ground. Chock the wheels. Turn off the parking brakes so you can move the slack adjusters. Wear gloves. Pull hard on each adjuster you can reach. It should not move more than 1 inch where the push rod attaches to it. Adjust them or have them adjusted if they move more. Too much brake slack can make the rig hard to stop.

Also check the spring brakes (if your rig has them). Drain the moisture from the air reservoir and close the petcock.

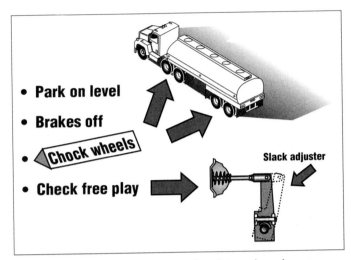

- Park on level
- Brakes off
- Chock wheels
- Check free play

Slack adjuster

Figure **4-28** Steps required to check manual slack adjusters.

Rear of Trailer

Inspect the following items:

- **Lights and reflectors:** The rear clearance lights, ID lights, taillights, license plate lights, and right rear turn signal lights should be clean, in good condition, and the appropriate color.
- **ICC underride prevention bumper:** This should be present and sound.
- **License plates:** They should be in place, current, clean, and securely fastened.
- **Splash guards:** These should be properly attached and undamaged.
- **Cargo:** See that cargo is properly blocked, braced, tied, or chained. Tailboards should be up and properly secured. End gates should be free of damage and secured in the stake pockets. Canvas or tarps should be properly lashed down to prevent water damage, tearing, or blowing about. Make sure the rear-view mirrors and rear lights are not blocked. The rear door should be securely locked with the required security seals in place.

Left Rear Trailer Wheel Area

Inspect the same things that you did on the right side except the air tank.

Left Side of Trailer

Inspect it in the same way you inspected the right side.

Left Saddle Tank Area

Check the same items that you did on the right side tank area except the spare tire. Also check the:

- **Battery box:** See that it is firmly mounted to the vehicle and its cover is in place.
- **Battery:** (if not mounted in engine compartment): Be sure it will not move and the case is not broken or leaking. The fluid should be at the proper level.

All caps should be tight. The vents in all cell caps should be free of anything that could block the escape of gases.

Step 6: Check the Signal Lights

- Return to the cab.
- Turn off all lights.
- Walk around the vehicle.
- Check the left front and rear of the tractor.
- Check the left rear trailer turn **signal lights.** Make sure they are:
  - clean,
  - the right color, and
  - in working order.
- Check tractor and trailer stop lights.

Step 7: Check the Air Brake System

- Return to the cab.
- Turn off all the lights.
- Make sure you have all trip manifests, permits, and required documents.
- Secure all loose articles in the cab so they will not be in the way while you are driving the rig.
- Fasten your seatbelt!

Note: The air brake system check is sometimes combined with the air loss check and the cab check.

Now you are ready to test the air brake system. Be sure to check all the following items.

Low-Pressure Alarm and/or Light

Start *"fanning"* off the air pressure by rapidly applying and releasing the treadle valve. At approximately 60 pounds of pressure, the low air pressure warning alarm should sound and/or the light should go on.

Tractor Protection Valve

Continue to fan off the air pressure. Emergency spring brakes should apply at no less than 20 pounds and no more than 45 pounds. This action must cause the trailer brakes to lock up. If they do not, there is a defect in the system.

Air Pressure Buildup

With the engine at operating rpm, the pressure should build from 85 to 100 psi within 45 seconds in dual air systems. If the air tanks are larger than minimum, buildup time can be longer and still be safe. In single air systems, pressure should build from 50 to 90 psi within 3 minutes with the engine idling at 600 to 900 rpm.

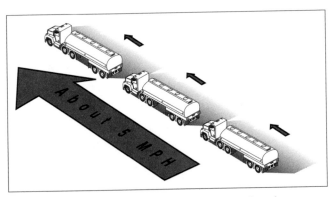

Figure **4-29** Testing the service brakes.

Parking and Trailer Hand Valve Brakes

1. Set (lock) the tractor spring brakes and release the trailer spring brakes. Then tug against the brakes.
2. Set the trailer spring brakes and release the tractor spring brakes. Then tug.
3. Release all spring brakes, apply the trailer hand valve, and tug against the trailer service brakes.
4. Move the truck forward, disengage the clutch, apply the service pedal, and stop evenly.

Too Much Slack in the Fifth Wheel

Put on the trailer brakes. Now, carefully and very gently, rock the tractor in first and reverse gears. Feel and listen for too much slack in the kingpin locking jaws. If there seems to be too much slack, check it out! Also be sure the clutch is working correctly during this procedure.

Brake System Balance and Adjustment

While still in an off-street area, build the vehicle speed up to 5 to 7 mph. Put on the service brakes sharply (see Figure 4-29). Note if the rig is *pulling* to one side or the other. If the stopping rate or adjustment of the brakes does not *feel* right, get it checked out right away. Do not drive the rig until you are certain the service brakes are working right.

EN ROUTE AND POSTTRIP INSPECTIONS

En Route Inspection

These specific en route driver inspections are required by the Federal Motor Carrier Safety Regulations (FMCSR).

FMCSR 392.9 (b) (2) on En Route Inspections

You must examine the cargo and its securing devices within the first 25 miles of a trip. Make adjustments as needed to maintain a secure load. Continue making periodic exams of the cargo. Resecure as needed. This requirement does not apply to a sealed trailer.

C A U T I O N :

If the trailer is empty, it is possible to pull it with the brakes locked. This causes undue wear. It can also be pulled out from under the trailer if the fifth wheel is not latched properly.

Figure **4-30** Conduct a walk-around inspection every 150 miles or 3 hours (whichever comes first) during a trip.

FMCSR 397.17

If you are hauling hazardous material and your vehicle has dual tires on any axle, you must check the tires before beginning a trip and each time you stop during a trip. You should identify and take off overheated tires at once to prevent a fire and identify and repair or correct tires with not enough air pressure.

One of your major jobs as a driver is to know and understand your instrument readings. This should be done every few minutes while driving.

Conduct walk-around safety inspections (see Figure 4-30) every 150 miles or every 3 hours (whichever comes first). Check the:

- **Tires:** Check the air pressure and whether they are getting too hot.
- **Brakes:** Check the adjustment and temperature.
- **Cargo:** Check doors and whether the cargo is still secure.
- **Coupling device:** Check to be sure it is still firmly attached. Turn off the engine, remove the key from the ignition, and chock one set of wheels of the tractor and trailer before crawling under the tractor-trailer to check the coupling.
- **Lights:** Check the vehicle lights before sunset and at every stop while driving at night.

Posttrip Inspection

After the trip, you will be required to do the following:

- Drain the moisture from the air tanks and fill the fuel tanks as instructed by your employer.

- Identify any problems found during the en route inspection, such as unusual noises, vibrations.
- Inspect the rig to further identify or locate these problems and to discover any developing problems.
- Identify or diagnose the source of problems (this is covered in detail in Chapter 24).
- Complete an accurate vehicle inspection report.

Reporting Findings

Inspections have no meaning unless you take action. As a driver, you are required to:

- Report findings to your supervisor and/or maintenance department as your company policy directs
- Report to the mechanics any problems you find
- Prepare an accurate, written report (required by law) for each rig driven during each day or work shift

VEHICLE INSPECTION REPORT

A written vehicle inspection report at the end of a trip is required by law for companies in interstate or foreign commerce (FMCSR 396.11). The report must cover the following parts:

- Service brakes, including trailer brake connections
- Parking brake
- Steering mechanism
- Lights and reflectors
- Windshield wipers
- Rear-view mirrors
- Wheels and rims
- Tires
- Horn
- Coupling devices
- Emergency equipment

The U.S. Department of Transportation has prepared a recommended Vehicle Condition Report (VCR). There are several versions of this report (see Figure 4-31). All serve as the record of what the driver finds during inspection of the rig.

The law requires that one copy of the report be kept in the company files for at least 3 months. Another copy must be kept in the vehicle until the next VCR is made. This will tell the next driver about defects or problems. The items should be repaired by this time. As a driver, you must, by law, review the previous driver's report and sign it.

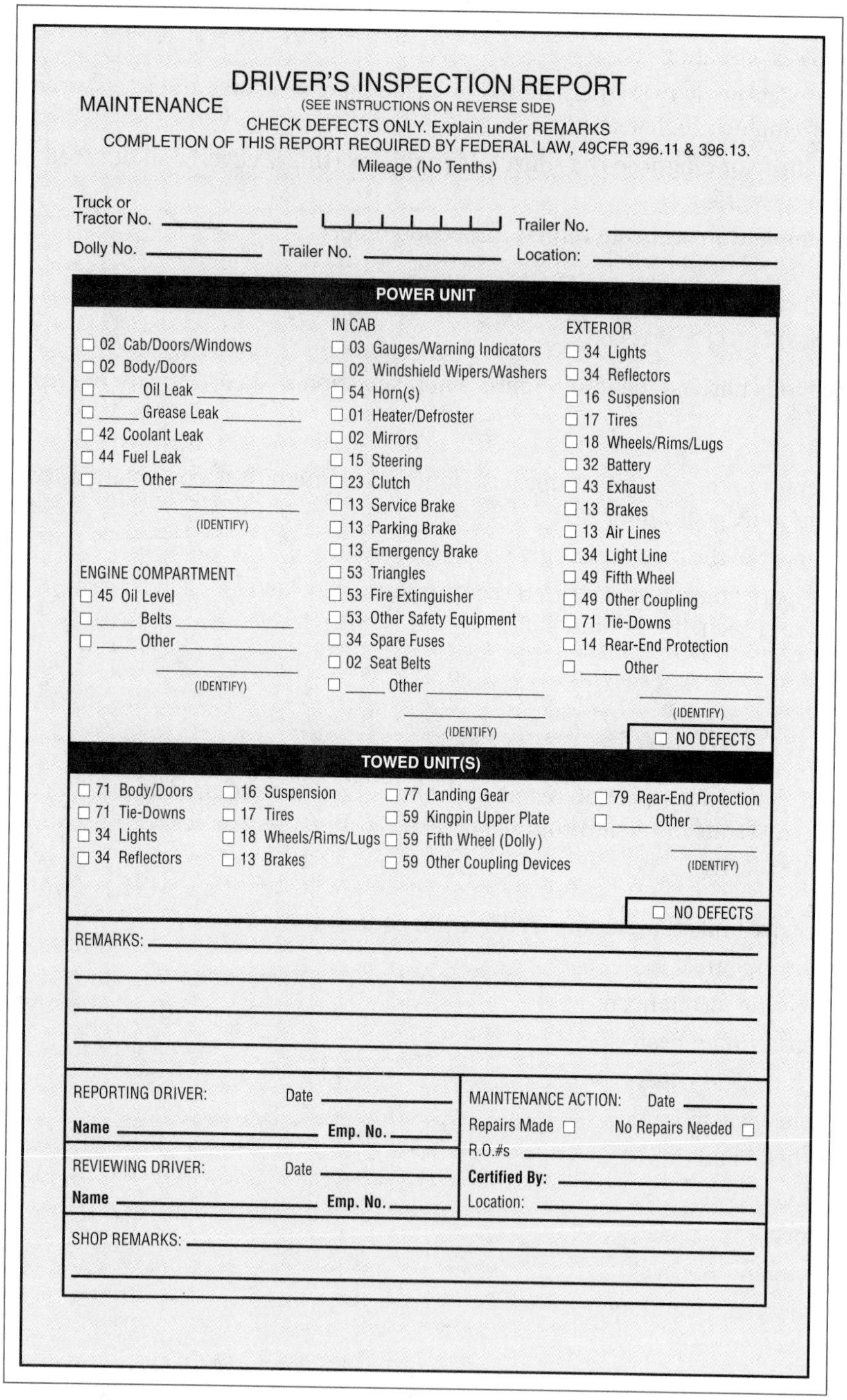

DRIVER'S INSPECTION REPORT

MAINTENANCE (SEE INSTRUCTIONS ON REVERSE SIDE)
CHECK DEFECTS ONLY. Explain under REMARKS
COMPLETION OF THIS REPORT REQUIRED BY FEDERAL LAW, 49CFR 396.11 & 396.13.
Mileage (No Tenths)

Truck or
Tractor No. _____ |__|__|__|__|__|__| Trailer No. _____
Dolly No. _____ Trailer No. _____ Location: _____

POWER UNIT

IN CAB
☐ 02 Cab/Doors/Windows
☐ 02 Body/Doors
☐ ___ Oil Leak ___
☐ ___ Grease Leak ___
☐ 42 Coolant Leak
☐ 44 Fuel Leak
☐ ___ Other ___
_____
(IDENTIFY)

ENGINE COMPARTMENT
☐ 45 Oil Level
☐ ___ Belts ___
☐ ___ Other ___
_____
(IDENTIFY)

☐ 03 Gauges/Warning Indicators
☐ 02 Windshield Wipers/Washers
☐ 54 Horn(s)
☐ 01 Heater/Defroster
☐ 02 Mirrors
☐ 15 Steering
☐ 23 Clutch
☐ 13 Service Brake
☐ 13 Parking Brake
☐ 13 Emergency Brake
☐ 53 Triangles
☐ 53 Fire Extinguisher
☐ 53 Other Safety Equipment
☐ 34 Spare Fuses
☐ 02 Seat Belts
☐ ___ Other ___
_____
(IDENTIFY)

EXTERIOR
☐ 34 Lights
☐ 34 Reflectors
☐ 16 Suspension
☐ 17 Tires
☐ 18 Wheels/Rims/Lugs
☐ 32 Battery
☐ 43 Exhaust
☐ 13 Brakes
☐ 13 Air Lines
☐ 34 Light Line
☐ 49 Fifth Wheel
☐ 49 Other Coupling
☐ 71 Tie-Downs
☐ 14 Rear-End Protection
☐ ___ Other ___
_____
(IDENTIFY)
☐ NO DEFECTS

TOWED UNIT(S)

☐ 71 Body/Doors
☐ 71 Tie-Downs
☐ 34 Lights
☐ 34 Reflectors

☐ 16 Suspension
☐ 17 Tires
☐ 18 Wheels/Rims/Lugs
☐ 13 Brakes

☐ 77 Landing Gear
☐ 59 Kingpin Upper Plate
☐ 59 Fifth Wheel (Dolly)
☐ 59 Other Coupling Devices

☐ 79 Rear-End Protection
☐ ___ Other ___
_____
(IDENTIFY)
☐ NO DEFECTS

REMARKS: _____
_____
_____
_____

REPORTING DRIVER: Date _____
Name _____ Emp. No. _____
REVIEWING DRIVER: Date _____
Name _____ Emp. No. _____

MAINTENANCE ACTION: Date _____
Repairs Made ☐ No Repairs Needed ☐
R.O.#s
Certified By: _____
Location: _____

SHOP REMARKS: _____
_____

Figure **4-31** Example of a driver's inspection report.

Chapter Five
Vehicle Systems

OBJECTIVES

When you have completed this chapter, you should be able to:

- Describe and explain the function and relationship of the different vehicle systems

- Locate and explain how the frame, axles, wheels and their parts, engine, drive train, and brakes operate

- Understand the relationship of the previously listed systems

KEY TERMS

Air application pressure
    gauge
Air bag suspension
    system
Air brake system
Air intake system
Air power steering
    system
Air pressure gauge
Air reservoirs
Ammeter
Antilock braking system
Axles
Battery
Belted bias tires
Bias-ply tires
Braking system
Bypass system
Cable-operated clutch
    control
Camber
Carrier bearings
Caster
Centrifugal filter
Charging circuit
Clutch
Combination
    bypass/full-flow
    system
Compressor
Conventional converter
    dolly
Converter dollies
Converter dolly axle
Coolant
Cooling system
Coupling system
Cranking circuit
Crankshaft bearings
Dead axle
Diesel engines
Diesel fuel
Differential
Dipstick
Direct clutch control

Disc brakes
Disc wheel
Drag link
Drain cocks
Drive pinion gear
Drive shaft
Drive train
Drum brakes
Electrical system
Emergency relay valve
Engine block
Exhaust system
Fan belt
Fifth wheel
Filler neck
Fixed-mount fifth wheel
Frame
Frameless construction
Fuel filters
Fuel system
Fuel system heater
Fuel tank
Full-flow system
Gasoline engine
Generators and
    alternators
Glad hands
Governor
Hydraulic power
    steering system
Ignition circuit
Independent trailer
    brake
Inserts
Interaxle differential
Internal combustion
    engine
Jifflox converter dolly
Kingpin
Leaf spring suspension
    system
Lift axle
Live axle
Low-pressure warning
    signal

Lubrication system
Lug tread
Multiple axle assembly
Oil filters
Oil pan
One-way check valve
Ordinary trailer axle
Parking brakes
Pitman arm
Power steering
Pusher tandem
Pyrometer
Quick-release valve
Radial tires
Radiator
Radiator cap
Relay valve
Rib tread
Ring gear
Safety valves
Service brakes
Shock absorbers
Single drive axles
Sliding (adjustable) fifth wheel
Sliding tandem
Spider gears
Splines
Spoke wheel

Steering arm
Steering gear box
Steering shaft
Steering system
Steering wheel
Supply/emergency brakes
Suspension system
Tag tandem
Tandem axles
Thermostat
Tie rod
Tire tread
Tractor parking valve
Tractor protection system
Tractor steering axle
Transmission
Treadle valve
Tri-drive axles
Twin screw
Universal joints
Variable-load suspension (VLS) axle
Voltage regulator
Voltmeter
Water jacket
Wristpins

INTRODUCTION

A tractor-trailer is made up of many parts and systems. Just as the human body has a system to circulate blood through its organs, the tractor of your rig has a system to send oil through its parts. Each system must do its part if the truck is to work efficiently (see Figure 5-1).

This chapter will explain and discuss:

- The reason for each of the rig's systems
- The function of the system's major parts
- The relationship of the system to safety and economy of operation

FRAME, SUSPENSION SYSTEM, AND AXLES
Frame

Many van trailers and cargo tanks are of **frameless construction**, which means that the exterior of the van or truck, instead of the frame, is the weight-carrying part.

Figure **5-1** Cutaway view of a truck and its systems.

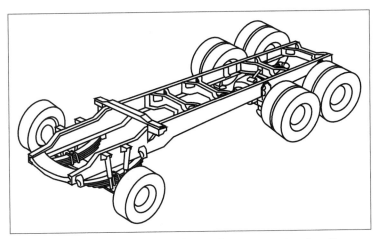

Figure **5-2** The frame includes two steel rails that run the length of the vehicle.

On many other tractors and trailers, however, the **frame** is the backbone of the truck tractor and many trailers. Engine mounts are attached to the frame to hold the engine in place. The body is connected to and strengthened by the frame. The frame is the unit through which the axles and wheels are connected to the suspension system.

The frame includes two steel rails that run the entire length of the vehicle. Lightweight tractors may have aluminum rails (see Figure 5-2). Tractors that haul oversized or overweight loads usually have extra strength steel rails. Cross members connect the two rails and provide strength and support to the frame.

Suspension System

The **suspension system** supports, distributes, and carries the weight of the truck. This system is made up of springs and spring hangers. The front and rear axles are attached to it, and the frame rests on it. As the ground changes, the system allows the axles to move up and down independently without seriously affecting the cargo. By securing the suspension system at several points along the frame, the stress of road shocks can be evenly distributed.

How strong and durable the system must be is determined by the weight and type of cargo the rig will transport. A good suspension system should be able to support the load and transmit full engine or braking power to the chassis frame.

The suspension system should hold the axles securely to ensure correct driveline alignment. It should also cushion the ride for the driver and cargo, whether the trailer is empty or loaded. Ready access to the system makes it easy to maintain.

There are two main types of suspension systems: a **leaf spring suspension system** consists of narrow metal strips of varying lengths that are bolted together and attached to frame hangers. Heavy duty systems commonly use the "stack," or "multileaf," spring. The tapered leaf spring is used on lighter-weight, tandem axle vehicles. An **air bag suspension system** uses bags of air placed between the axle and the frame. Widely used on trailers, air bag suspension is also used on truck tractors.

Note: Many trucks use a combination of the spring and air suspension systems.

Leaf spring suspension systems are used for deadening shocks, but the air bag suspension is becoming increasingly popular because loaded and empty vehicles differ little in their ride, and these systems provide a smooth ride and decrease damage to both rig and cargo.

Air pressure for the air suspension system comes from the tractor's air compressor. Some systems have valves, allowing the driver to adjust air pressure for specific loads. Frame height can also be changed for different loads.

There are more tandem suspensions now that most states have increased the legal gross weight limits. One popular system uses both leaf spring suspension and air pressure suspension. The combination results in a sturdy yet smooth ride. It can be installed on a single-axle, dual-axle, or three-axle setup.

While combining the two systems reduces many common air cushion problems, some trouble spots continue to need attention. Leaks and other problems can occur around the leveling valves and linkage. Loads with a high center of gravity are unstable and rock easily. The leaf springs help improve these situations.

Shock absorbers reduce the motion of the vehicle body as the wheels move over uneven surfaces (see Figure 5-3). They are usually needed in the independent coil and air bag suspension systems.

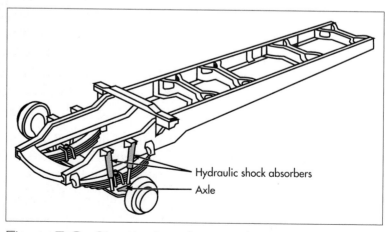

Figure **5-3** Shock absorbers reduce the motion of the vehicle as the wheels move over uneven surfaces.

A shock absorber operates like a piston in a cylinder with a hole in it. Since liquid is almost impossible to compress, liquid is forced through the tiny hole as the shock is compressed. The liquid resists the pressure and smooths out the ride.

Axles

Axles connect the wheels to the rest of the trailer-tractor. They also support the weight of the vehicle and its cargo. Different axles perform different functions. While all axles support the weight of the vehicle, each type of axle performs a special function.

The front tractor axle connects the steering mechanism and brakes. The tractor drive axle transfers power from the engine and drive train to the wheels. Along with trailer axles, it also serves as a connecting point for the brakes.

All axles fall into two types: dead and live.

Dead Axles

A **dead axle** is not powered. It receives, or houses, the wheel; supports vehicle weight; and provides a place to connect steering mechanisms and brake components (see Figure 5-4).

Most dead axles are straight, but some have a drop-center design that allows space for the drive shaft (see Figure 5-5). Some are I-beam construction, while others consist of a hollow tube or box.

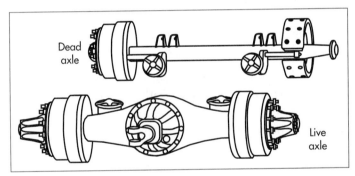

Figure **5-4** There are two types of axles: live and dead.

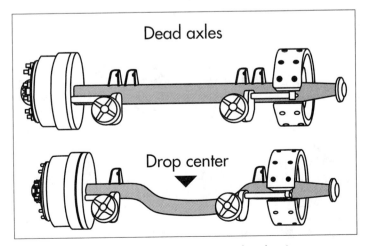

Figure **5-5** The drop-center axle design allows space for the drive shaft.

There are several types of dead axles, including the following:

- **Ordinary trailer axle:** Connects the trailer wheels to the trailer body.
- **Tractor steering axle:** Supports and steers the front end of the tractor. The front wheel assemblies at each end of the axle turn. The axle does not turn.
- **Converter dolly axle:** Attaches to the front end of the trailer. This axle steers the second trailer in a set of doubles. The entire axle turns for steering.
- **Multiple axle assembly:** Two or more dead axles together. They spread the rig's weight over more axles. This reduces the amount of weight on any one axle.
- **Lift axle:** When a vehicle is loaded and the lift axle is in the lowered position, tire and axle wear is reduced on the other axles because the weight of the vehicle and its load is distributed over more axles.
- **Variable-load suspension (VLS) axle:** Allows adjustment of the weight carried by each axle. One type uses air or hydraulic suspension. The other type has springs.
- **Sliding tandem:** Used on semitrailers. Allows the trailer axles to be moved forward and backward on a track. Weight can be transferred back and forth between the tractor and trailer. When the axle is moved backward, more weight is placed on the tractor.

Live Axles

A **live axle** is powered. It supports the vehicle's weight, sends power to the wheels, and is hollow.

Because the live axle is hollow, the gears and axles can transmit power through this space to the wheels. Examples of live axles include the following:

- **Single drive axles:** Found on the rear of the tractor.
- **Tandem axles:** Two axles that work together. There are three types of tandem axles:
  1. **Twin screw:** Both axles are powered (see Figure 5-6).

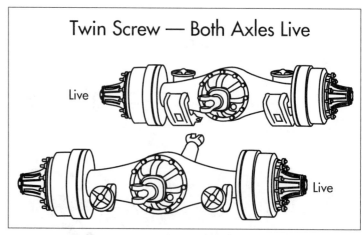

Figure **5-6** There are three types of tandem axles: twin screw, pusher tandem, and tag tandem.

2. **Pusher tandem:** The rear axle is powered (live), and the forward axle is not powered (dead). The forward axle must have a drop center so the drive shaft can be attached to the live axle.

3. **Tag tandem:** The forward axle is live and the rear axle is dead. The dead axle "tags" along behind the live axle.

- **Tri-drive axles:** Three axles in the same assembly. They are used where a load-carrying advantage is needed.

ENGINES

This chapter will not go into great detail about the many types of engines and how they work. If you want that information, you should take a mechanic's training course. However, tractor-trailer drivers should know something about how engines operate and the types of engines commonly used in trucking (see Figure 5-7).

The engines on truck tractors are **internal combustion engines.** The engines may be gasoline or diesel (two-stroke cycle or four-stroke cycle).

An internal combustion engine burns fuel inside itself, within enclosed chambers. These chambers are called cylinders. The cylinders are the heart of the engine. They are where power is generated to turn the wheels that run the tractor and pull the trailer.

The basic parts of the engine are the block, cylinders, pistons, connecting rods, and crank shaft.

Think of an **engine block** as a large block of steel with holes, or cylinders, drilled into it. Think of a cylinder as a coffee can. One end of the can is sealed shut. The other end is open. A plunger (piston) fits snugly against the cylinder wall, but it can move up and down the wall. When fuel burns within the cylinder (combustion), it creates the expansion that forcefully moves the piston.

A rod attached to the piston moves with it. Since the rod is connected to a crank, it turns the crank. Therefore, the up-and-down movement of the piston is converted into the circular motion of the crankshaft.

This circular or rotary motion is the force that is applied to the wheels to move the vehicle.

Fuel alone will not power an internal combustion engine. In the case of the **gasoline engine** (used on most cars and smaller vehicles), fuel (gasoline) must be

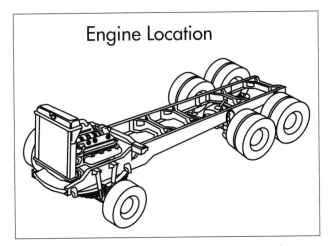

Figure **5-7** Engines come in many types to perform various tasks.

mixed with air when it is sent to the cylinders for burning. This mixing takes place in the carburetor. A mass of pressurized air is forced over a thin jet of gasoline. This breaks the fuel into a mist, or vapor, of very small droplets and air.

Today, almost all tractors have **diesel engines.** Diesel engines do not have carburetors. They have fuel injectors to supply fuel to the cylinders. The air intake system supplies the air to the cylinders.

Other differences between gasoline and diesel engines are:

- In a gasoline engine, the fuel/air mixture is ignited by an electrical spark from a spark plug.
- In a diesel engine, the extreme compression of the fuel/air mixture in the cylinder by the piston squeezes it so much that the diesel fuel ignites.

No matter what type of engine the tractor has, the fuel/air mixture is burned in the cylinders. After burning has expanded it, the burned fuel is forced out of the cylinder through exhaust valves and manifolds.

FUEL SYSTEM

The **fuel system** sends fuel to the engine. It regulates the amount of fuel that is sent and the how often it is injected into the cylinders. The basic components of the fuel system are the injector, a tank containing fuel, and an engine-driven pump.

The pump moves the fuel from the tank, through the filtering system, and into the injector. Usually the pump delivers more fuel than is needed, so there is a pipe to return the extra fuel to the tank.

Just before the fuel reaches the injector, a filter cleans it. Even a small speck of dirt can ruin an injector, so the fuel can never be too clean. Because dirt can do so much damage to the engine and its operation, there is often another filter between the tank and the pump.

The injector must figure just the right amount of fuel and inject it into the cylinder at exactly the right time and at the right pressure. The amount of fuel needed varies because of power needs. Most new engines use electronic controls to do this. Obviously, electronics are more efficient than the old mechanical controls.

Fuel Tank

The **fuel tank** is a container that holds fuel. Sometimes larger trucks have two tanks, one of which is strapped to each side of the frame. On straight trucks, a single tank may be placed behind the cab. If a straight truck has more than one tank, the fuel lines are joined with a Y or an I type connection.

Fuel tanks are vented to maintain equal pressure on the inside and outside. The vent hole is usually in the filter pipe cap or at the top of the tank.

The fuel cap area must be kept clean at all times. The fuel filter cap and the neck of the tank should be completely clean before removing the cap. If the tank is under the chassis, use *great care* when cleaning the cap to keep dirt from getting into the fuel system.

Fuel Filters

Filters in the fuel system clean the fuel as it goes from the entry tube of the tank, through the tank and fuel lines, and into the injectors. A coarse filter is the first dirt block. A finer filter is next. Finally, a filter/water separator protects the injector jets and engine from water, rust, and other contaminants. This filter is the most important one because water can seriously harm the fuel system. Rust and corrosion destroy engine parts. This is important to remember.

Fuel System Heaters

Trucks driven in cold weather should have **fuel system heaters.** Many kinds of heaters are available:

- Some units heat the fuel in the tank.
- In-line units heat the fuel when it is going from the tank to the injector system.
- Filter heaters heat the filters, which then heat the fuel as it passes through the injection system.

When a truck is driven in severely cold weather, all three types of full system heaters may be needed. Chemicals are also used to help the fuel flow in cold and sub-zero weather. The chemicals prevent the fuel from jelling and keep wax crystals from forming. Some chemicals even clean the injectors and improve the fuel.

Diesel Fuel

Diesel fuel has an advantage over gasoline. It has a low vaporizing rate, and it does not create an explosive air fuel mixture when it is accidentally spilled or leaked. This can be very important when hauling highly volatile fluids or explosives.

The "cetane number" is an indicator of diesel fuel quality. It indicates the amount of time needed for the fuel to ignite the hot air in the combustion chamber of the cylinder. Cetane numbers generally range from 30 to 60. The higher the number, the faster the fuel mixture will ignite.

If the cetane number is too low, the engine will be difficult to start. It will knock, and there may be puffs of white smoke from the exhaust. This is often seen during the warm-up period and during light road operation. If it continues, harmful deposits can collect in the cylinders.

A negative characteristic of diesel fuel is that it creates wax crystals in cold weather. These crystals make starting and operating the engine difficult. If too many crystals collect, the engine will not start. Lower-density fuel is less likely to crystallize or jell in cold weather.

AIR INTAKE AND EXHAUST SYSTEMS

The air intake and exhaust systems are another vital element of the diesel engine. A lot of fresh air is needed and must be easily available for use in the engine's air supply system (see Figure 5-8).

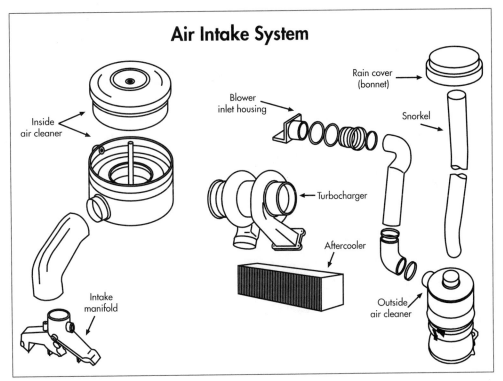

Air Intake System

Inside air cleaner

Intake manifold

Blower inlet housing

Turbocharger

Aftercooler

Rain cover (bonnet)

Snorkel

Outside air cleaner

Figure **5-8**   Fresh air is vital for use in the engine's air supply system.

Air Intake System

The **air intake system** delivers fresh air to the cylinders. An air cleaner removes dirt, dust, and water from the fresh air. Air cleaners must be kept clean for the engine to operate at its best. If the weather is dusty or rainy, you may have to check the cleaners each day.

The clean air flows into the air intake manifold. The manifold is simply a pipe with an equal number of outlets and cylinders. Each outlet from the manifold is an intake port for a cylinder. Valves regulate the flow of air into the cylinders. The cylinders act as combustion chambers.

Exhaust System

After combustion (burning), the **exhaust system** expels used gases. Exhaust valves open in each cylinder. A stroke of the piston expels the used gases through ports in the exhaust manifold. The gases pass through the exhaust pipe and a muffler. The muffler quiets the noise. The gases are discharged from the vehicle through a vertical stack or tail pipe. A vertical exhaust stack has a movable rain cap that opens to let the gases escape and closes to keep the rain out.

Pyrometer

Some instrument panels have a **pyrometer** that measures the temperature of exhaust gases. This gauge lets the driver know how hot the exhaust gas is. The temperature may be anywhere from 600° to 1,000°F. The normal operating range varies from truck to truck, so you must learn the normal range for your truck.

You must be careful the temperature of the gas does not get too high. This is especially important on mountain roads or long grades. If the exhaust temperature gets too high, you can damage the engine. An exhaust temperature that is too hot usually results from lugging the engine because the driver did not downshift when needed or the engine is receiving too much fuel. Take your foot off the accelerator if the engine begins to lug or the pyrometer temperature does not drop. Shift the transmission.

LUBRICATION SYSTEM

The **lubrication system** distributes oil to the parts of the engine. The film of oil between the moving parts keeps them from rubbing together. Instead, they ride or slide on the oil. This reduces the friction between the surface of the parts (see Figure 5-9). When you keep friction to a minimum, you increase engine efficiency and increase engine part life.

A lot of heat is created by the rapid movement of parts. With the oil film present, some of the heat is absorbed into the oil instead of into the metal parts. The flowing oil carries the heat away. This helps keep the engine operating at a safe temperature.

Oil also cleans the engine. As it flows through the engine, it collects bits of dirt, carbon, and even worn metal. The biggest particles settle to the bottom of the oil pan. The smaller ones are filtered out.

Another vital function of the oil is to prevent the loss of pressure between the pistons and cylinder walls. When pressure is lost, power is also lost.

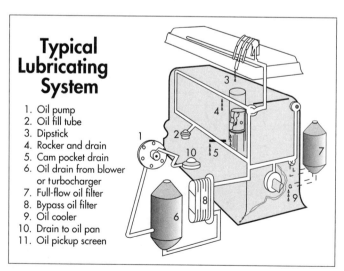

Typical Lubricating System

1. Oil pump
2. Oil fill tube
3. Dipstick
4. Rocker and drain
5. Cam pocket drain
6. Oil drain from blower or turbocharger
7. Full-flow oil filter
8. Bypass oil filter
9. Oil cooler
10. Drain to oil pan
11. Oil pickup screen

Figure **5-9** The lubricating system distributes oil to parts of the engine to reduce the wear and tear caused by friction.

When there is an oil film between these parts, the force of combustion delivers a firm push against the piston. This sends the maximum amount of power to the drive shaft and the wheels. Without an oil seal, a great deal of power would be lost.

Oil also protects engine parts from corrosion, wear, and rust. It coats the surfaces that do not move and protects them from rust. When rust collects, it flakes off and damages other parts of the engine.

Finally, engine oil absorbs shocks. It forms a cushion between surfaces that are subjected to shocks. For example, each time ignition occurs in the combustion chamber, a sudden force hits the piston. This, in turn, sends the force through a wrist pin, connecting rod, and crankshaft. The oil helps absorb the shock to these parts as well as reduce noise and wear.

Operation and Parts of the Lubrication System

Bolted to the bottom of the engine is a container, or reservoir, called the **oil pan.** When lubricating oil is poured into the engine, it flows down to the oil pan. When the engine is operating, oil is pumped, under pressure, from the pan to all the vital friction and pressure points of the engine.

Vital friction and pressure points include the following:

- The **crankshaft bearings** (sometimes called the main bearings): These bearings are inserts between the crankshaft and its holder, the crankcase.
- **Wristpins:** These are used to fasten the connecting rods to the pistons
- **Inserts** (or bearings): This is where the connecting rods are joined to the crankshaft.

Oil is not pumped directly to many engine parts that need lubrication. Instead, they get oil by the "splash method." The bearings and many other rapidly moving engine parts throw off oil. With the constant motion, a fine oily mist reaches those parts not included in the pressure line of the system. The area between the pistons and cylinder walls is lubricated in this way.

Oil Changes

You must drain the old oil before you change or add new oil. You cannot tell the quality of the oil by its color or feeling it with your fingers. Detergents have been added to prevent or slow the corrosion of the bearings and formation of sludge and deposits in the engine. These additives may cover up the "feel" of dirty oil. It is better to follow the manufacturer's recommendations for changing the oil as well as for what oil to use.

Oil Filters

Another way of prolonging the life of the oil and the life of the engine is by carefully filtering the oil. As the oil circulates and does its work of cooling the engine and reducing friction between moving parts, it collects foreign matter and holds it in suspension. Such grit, dirt, small bits of metal, and so on must be removed before they damage the engine. **Oil filters** strain out the impurities.

There are several different types of oil filtering systems: full-flow system, bypass system, and a combination full flow/bypass system.

In a **full-flow system,** all oil leaving the oil pump passes through an oil filter. The filter uses what is called a "one-pass method." All contaminants, dirt, and floating particles must be filtered out during this one trip through the filter.

Because the filter must remove all the floating material, it often becomes clogged. Then the flow of oil to the engine is restricted. A valve opens to let the oil flow. Even though impurities may be carried to the engine, keeping oil from the bearings would create more damage.

The **bypass** (or part-flow) **system** filters a small amount (about 10 percent) of the oil flow. It is normally used along with the full-flow system. It filters the excess oil that does not go through the bearings but is normally returned to the oil pan. The flow of oil through the bypass filter is controlled by an opening.

The **combination bypass/full-flow system** is the best type of filtration system. Oil from the full-flow filter goes to the bearings. Oil from the bypass filter returns to the oil pan.

The thorough cleaning of the full-flow system is combined with the added protection of the bypass system. As a result, the oil and filters last longer because there is less contamination. The longer life of the oil and filters cuts costs.

Centrifugal Filter

This is a type of bypass filter. The oil entering the permanent housing spins the filter at high speed, forcing the dirt and particles out of the oil for more efficient cleaning of the oil. It is used in addition to the other oil filters.

Dipstick

A **dipstick** is a stick-like device found in the engine block that indicates the oil level in the engine. The dipstick is housed in a shaft at the side of the engine. The dipstick itself is marked with a gauge in increments—usually "low" or "add" marks— although this varies from manufacturer to manufacturer.

To accurately measure the oil level with the dipstick, with the engine off, remove it from its housing. Because the dipstick could be hot, be sure to always wear gloves when checking oil levels. Next, wipe it thoroughly with a utility rag.

Insert the clean dipstick back into the shaft where it is housed (see Figure 5-10). Then withdraw it again, and the level of the oil will be indicated on the stick with an oily film and will indicate if an appropriate amount of oil exists within the engine.

If the oil level is at the "low" or "add" mark, add oil before driving the rig again. Be sure to follow the manufacturer's recommendations to use the proper oil for the truck you are driving.

Figure **5-10** Use the dipstick to measure the oil level.

If the oil mark is too high on the dipstick or you notice a light foam, check immediately for a possible cooling leak.

COOLING SYSTEM

Heat is the basis of the internal combustion engine. However, intense heat can quickly destroy an engine. The **cooling system** keeps the temperature down (see Figure 5-11).

The engine is cooled by coolant that circulates through the engine block and cylinder head. Remember, we said to think about the block as a solid block of steel into which large holes (cylinders) were drilled. The block is actually a lot more complex than that. In addition to the cylinder holes, the block is honeycombed with a channel that comes very close to all the cylinders. This channel is called the **water jacket.**

Coolant flows through the jacket. It picks up heat as it goes. The channel then takes the coolant to the radiator. In the radiator, the coolant flows through small, thin walled tubes that are surrounded by air. The coolant is cooled in the tubes.

Then it is pulled into the pump and forced back into the engine. When the coolant enters the water jacket, the process is repeated and the coolant is again cooled.

The **filler neck** is located in the upper tank of the radiator. A **radiator cap** is placed at the top of the filler neck. To the side of the filler neck is an overflow tube that allows excess water or pressure to escape the radiator.

It is important to keep the radiator filled with the proper amount of coolant. Too much coolant will flow out when too much pressure is built inside the radiator. If pressure is excessive, the pressure raises the radiator cap, attached to the filler neck with a spring-loaded seal. At this point, the excess coolant and water will boil out and into the overflow tube (coolant is about half antifreeze and half water). When the pressure drops, the spring-loaded cap falls back into place and stops the flow of coolant.

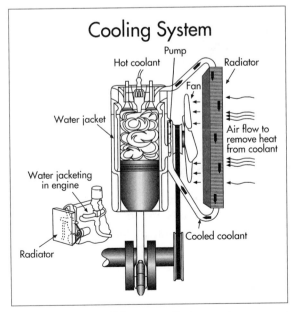

Figure **5-11** The cooling system regulates the heat in an internal combustion engine.

Note: The pressure cap will allow the coolant to reach a higher-than-usual boiling point. For this reason, the cap needs to be tested at each preventive maintenance check.

In addition to the filler neck, the water jacket, radiator, fan, and water pump, the cooling system also includes a thermostat and the coolant.

Note: Water should not be used in the cooling system because, used alone, it can cause rust or other damage to the system and engine. It seldom has the correct pH (acid-alkaline balance). Commercial antifreeze cools better and should be changed every year.

Coolant is a fluid, usually water and antifreeze, that circulates within the system. It absorbs heat from the engine and takes it to the radiator for cooling. The coolant then returns to the engine to repeat the process.

The coolant should always be carefully selected according to the manufacturer's specs for the type of engine and conditions through which the truck will travel.

The **thermostat** is a valve in the water jacket located at the point where the coolant leaves the engine. Until the engine runs long enough to heat the coolant, the thermostat is closed. When the engine reaches operating temperature (usually about 180°F), the thermostat opens to let the coolant go to the radiator for cooling.

The **radiator** is the largest part to be found in the cooling system of any engine and consists of upper and lower tanks, a core, an overflow tube, connections for water hoses, and a filler cap. The radiator's coolant retains heat as it travels through the block and then releases this heat into the air.

The radiator cap is located at the top of the radiator. It keeps the coolant from overflowing. The cap also maintains pressure on the coolant. The pressure is important because the higher the pressure, the higher the boiling point of the coolant. A leaking radiator cap can cause the entire cooling system to operate improperly. Most engines now have separate coolant reservoirs to check coolant levels. They are see-through and easy to open so that coolant can be added.

The **fan belt** is a belt from the engine that drives the fan. The belt must be checked for slack. Pull on the belt to see if it is too loose. Also look for any cracks or worn spots on the belt. It should be tightened or replaced as needed. The fan must work properly at all times. This is very important in stop-and-go driving or when the truck is idling. A shroud or cowling usually surrounds the fan to protect it and direct the airflow. Many engines have fan clutches or viscous drives that disengage the fan when it is not needed.

CAUTION:

Do not remove fill at reservoir.

ELECTRICAL SYSTEM

The **electrical system** is very complex on a tractor-trailer. For more detailed information than this book provides, read a manual on electrical systems.

The four parts of the electrical system follow:

1. Charging circuit
2. Cranking circuit
3. Ignition circuit
4. Lighting and accessory circuit

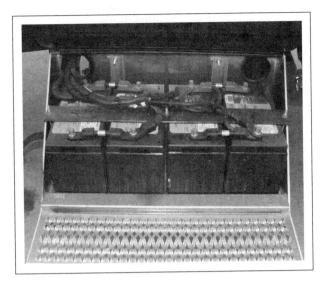

Figure **5-12** Batteries.

Charging Circuit

The **charging circuit** produces electricity to keep the battery charged and run the electrical circuits. The parts of the charging circuit are:

- Battery (see Figure 5-12)
- Alternator or generator
- Voltage regulator
- Ammeter or voltmeter
- Electrical wires
- Battery cables

Battery.   Creates (through chemical reactions) or receives and stores electrical energy. This is the energy that activates the starter. It is a backup source of electricity for a number of accessories when the alternator cannot keep up with electrical needs.

   The battery has two posts—positive and negative—through which electricity flows. The negative post and electrical parts are attached to the vehicle frame. Electricity travels from the positive post through wires to the electrical equipment, on to the frame, and back through the negative post to the battery.

Generators and alternators.   Devices that recharge the battery when it loses electricity. They create electricity that can be used by the battery and electrical system. Most systems today use alternators. In either case, the device is run by a fan belt that receives its power from the engine crankshaft.

   In other words, when the engine is running, the alternator (or generator) is creating electricity. Through an automatic control system, the electricity used for operating, except starting the engine, is provided by the alternator or generator.

   In summary, the battery provides the energy to start the engine and is a backup for extra energy when needed. The alternator or generator furnishes all other electricity.

Ammeter. A gauge on the instrument panel that shows the current output of the alternator. It indicates whether the battery is being charged by the alternator or is discharging.

Voltmeter. Gives an overview of the charging system. It tells the state of charge of the battery and whether the charging system is keeping up with the demands for electricity. It can warn of battery, alternator, or regulator failures, a loose and slipping fan belt, and broken, loose, or corroded wires and cables.

Voltage regulator. Controls the voltage produced by the alternator or generator. The regulator keeps the battery voltage from getting too high. This prevents the battery from overcharging and boiling off the battery fluid. It also keeps the other electrical parts from burning themselves out.

Cranking Circuit

The **cranking circuit** sends electricity from the battery to a small starter motor (see Figure 5-13). This starter motor is connected to a large disc (flywheel) by a gear. The disc turns the crankshaft and starts the engine. All a driver needs to know is that activating the starter switch puts this process in motion. A few trucks still have air starters that use compressed air instead of electricity to crank the engine.

Ignition Circuit

In a gasoline engine, the **ignition circuit** provides the sparks for each cylinder to ignite the fuel/air mixture. An ignition circuit is not needed for diesel trucks because the compression of the air ignites the fuel.

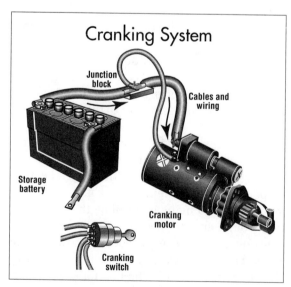

Figure **5-13** The cranking circuit sends electricity from the battery to a small starter motor.

Lighting and Accessory Circuits

The lighting and accessory circuits send electricity to:

- **Lights:**

  Headlights

  Taillights

  Turn signals

  Running lights

- **Horns**
- **Instrument lights:**

  Speedometer

  Odometer

  Gauges and so on.

- **Windshield cleaners:**

  Wipers

  Washers

DRIVE TRAIN

The **drive train** takes the power generated by the engine and applies it to the tractor's drive wheels. As the wheels turn, the rig moves. The drive train has five main parts:

- Clutch (see Figure 5-14)
- Transmission

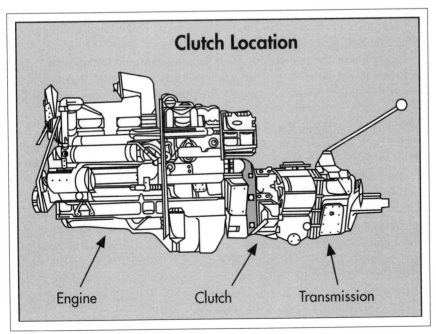

Clutch Location

Engine   Clutch   Transmission

Figure **5-14**   The clutch connects or disconnects the engine from the rest of the power train.

- Drive shaft
- Universal joints
- Differential

They perform four basic functions:

1. Connect the engine (source of power) to and disconnect it from the drive train
2. Modify the torque (twist) and engine speed (rpm) produced by the engine to let the vehicle operate at its best
3. Carry the power of the engine to the rear axle and drive wheels
4. Change the direction of the torque, or twist, to propel the rear wheels

The simple explanations that follow show what happens when you put various parts of the power train into action with your pedals and levers. Remember again, this is not a complete explanation. It is simply an overview.

Clutch

The driver uses the **clutch** to connect or disconnect the engine from the rest of the power train (see Figure 5-15). One of the primary jobs of the clutch is to help the driver easily shift gears.

The main parts of the clutch include:

- Clutch housing
- Flywheel
- Clutch disc or discs
- Pressure plate
- Release assembly
- Controls

On most trucks there are three plates that can be engaged (pressed together) or disengaged (pulled apart). The middle plate, or clutch disc, is the "driven member." It is connected to a shaft leading to the transmission. The other two plates are "driving members." They connect to the engine.

A spring forces the two driving members toward each other, squeezing them against the middle plate until they all turn together as one unit. When the plates are together, the clutch is "engaged." When the plates are apart, the clutch is "disengaged."

The engine flywheel is the first driving member. It has a smooth surface where it squeezes the driven plate. The other driving member is called the pressure plate. It is made of heavy cast iron that is smooth on one side. It is fastened to the cover, which is bolted to the flywheel so they can all turn together. This disc can slide toward and away from the driven plate.

The driven plate, or clutch disc, is a flat disc of steel with a friction facing on each side. The plate is fastened by grooves or slots called **splines** to a shaft connected to the transmission. The disc fits into the grooves on the shaft so that the plate and shaft turn together and the plate can slide backward and forward on the shaft.

The clutch disc is softer than the other plates, and because of this, it will be worn out before damage can occur to other parts of the drive train. When a clutch "goes out," it is usually the clutch disc that must be replaced.

To prevent excessive wear or damage, clutches should be adjusted, and they have an access hole to permit this adjustment.

The Clutch in Action

1. When the driver pushes down on the clutch pedal, it disengages the clutch so the gears can be shifted.
2. When the clutch is depressed, this activates the clutch release assembly, and it separates the pressure plate from the clutch plate. When this happens, the power from the engine is separated from the transmission.
3. After the driver shifts gears, the clutch pedal is released, forcing the pressure plate against the clutch plate, which is pressed against the flywheel.
4. When this happens, all three parts rotate as one unit, and the engine's power is now being transmitted by the clutch to the transmission gears.
5. The gears cannot be shifted when there is power on the gears.

There are two types of mechanical clutches: **direct clutch control** consists of a manually operated assembly made of levers, rods, and springs connecting the pedal to the clutch release mechanism. Conventional tractors often use such a clutch. The **cable-operated clutch control** uses a cable to replace part of the linkage. Cab-over-engine tractors sometimes use a cable-operated clutch control because it is several feet from the clutch to the pedal and the cable provides a way for the linkage to flex when the pedal tilts up with the cab.

TRANSMISSION

The **transmission** is a case, or box, of gears located behind the clutch. The case is usually fastened to the clutch housing. The clutch and transmission look like an extension of the engine.

The transmission adjusts the power generated by the engine so it provides the right speed and torque for the job. For example, when the loaded rig moves from a stopped position, a great deal of power is needed.

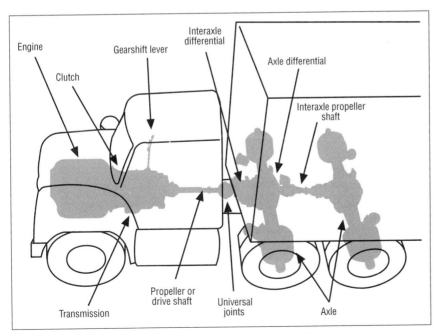

Figure **5-15** The main components of the drive train.

The driver adjusts the gears in the transmission to provide the needed combination of power, torque, and speed. The transmission then sends, or transmits, the power from its source, the engine, to the drive, or powered, axles. This is the power that propels the vehicle.

The gears in the transmission help control the speed and power of the vehicle. The engine can be kept at a relatively constant speed. The rig, however, can be moved either slowly or rapidly with much the same power output. Once under way, the vehicle needs less power to keep it going than it needed to start it rolling. Gears make all this possible.

You need to understand two basic, related facts when selecting gears:

1. More torque, or power, means less speed.
2. More speed means less torque.

In other words, as the gears increase torque, they decrease speed at about the same rate. This means the driver can change the ratio between the engine and the drive wheels to get either more speed or more torque. The lower the gear, the more torque or power. The higher the gear, the more speed.

Types of Transmissions

There are many types of transmissions. They may have the following:

●   Different numbers of forward speeds
●   One or more shift levers
●   Single or multiple gear housings
●   Single or dual drive axles
●   Different types of gear selector switches
●   Manual, power-assisted, or auxiliary units
●   Different combinations of main transmissions and variable-speed rear ends

We will not go into detail about the many possible combinations and why they are needed. However, new drivers should be aware that operating the transmission correctly is an important part of learning to drive a tractor-trailer.

DRIVE SHAFTS AND UNIVERSAL JOINTS

Behind the transmission is a propeller called the **drive shaft.** The drive shaft is a steel shaft that runs from the transmission to the rear of the vehicle. Usually the drive shaft is hollow. On trucks with a long wheelbase, **carrier bearings** join two drive shafts. It is in a metal casting mounted on a cross member between the two drive shafts.

At each end (front and rear) of the shaft are the **universal joints,** or U-joints. They are called universal joints because they can move in almost any direction. They are usually made of two U-shaped pieces set at right angles to one another and fastened together by cross arms of equal length. As the drive shaft spins, it transfers, or carries, the twisting motion back to the rear axle. The U-joints let the drive shaft change its angle of operation.

The U-shaped pieces (yokes) pivot on the arms of the cross. Since there are two pivots, the shaft can be at an angle and still transmit power. The U-joints do not have to be in a straight line. This is very important because they become somewhat misaligned with each bump in the road. The rear axle moves up and down with the wheels, while the transmission does not move as much. The U-joints let the propeller shaft turn even though its two ends are shifting in relation to one another.

DIFFERENTIAL

There are two types of differentials on trucks today: the differential and the interaxle differential. The **differential** divides the drive axle in half, allowing each half to spin independently. This gear mechanism performs two specific tasks. It transmits power from the drive shaft to the axles. And because it divides the drive axle into two independent halves, each axle half may turn at a different speed. This allows each wheel to rotate independently, which facilitates cornering. When a truck maneuvers around a corner, the outside wheel must rotate faster than the inside wheel. If your truck were not equipped with a differential, you would drag at least one set of tires—and wear them out faster—each time your truck turned a corner.

Some people believe the differential divides the vehicle's drive power equally among all the wheels, but this is not true. And the differential does not send all the engine's torque to the wheels with the most traction. Both of these misconceptions are widespread. A differential *does* send all the power to the wheels with the least traction.

There are several types of differentials, but we want to focus on the major components of the typical differential: the **drive pinion gear,** the **ring gear,** and four **spider gears.** All these components are housed in an enclosed differential case mounted at the center of the drive axle housing.

The drive pinion gear is connected to the end of the drive shaft and drives the ring gear. Attached to the ring gear are four spider gears, meshing with gears on the ends of the drive axle halves. Each of the spider gears can rotate freely, and each axle gear meshes with all four spider gears. This accomplishes the transfer of power from the ring gear through the spider gears and into the drive axle halves.

The pinion and ring gears accomplish two jobs:

1. They turn the force, or torque, of the pinion shaft at right angles so that wheels can turn and drive the vehicle.
2. They can reduce speed and increase torque because the pinion gear is much smaller than the ring gear.

If your truck is traveling in a straight line down the highway and both wheels are turning at the same speed, the drive pinions are rotating with the spider gears. However, when the truck maneuvers through a turn, the inside wheels slow, and as one axle half begins spinning at a lower speed than the other, the spider gears begin rotating, allowing the axle halves to spin at different speeds to accommodate the turn without scrubbing your tires.

The second type of differential—the **interaxle differential**—divides the two axles and allows each to turn independently of the other. The interaxle differential is used on tandem rear-drive axle trucks and is sometimes called a power divider.

The interaxle differential is just another differential: It does the same thing the differential does but between two axles rather than two axle halves. This differential is necessary because the front and rear axles rotate at different speeds at times, just as the two axle halves do. In these cases, the interaxle differential compensates for slippage and mismatched tires between axles and corner, and it improves traction when trying to couple to a loaded trailer.

What is the main difference between the differential and the interaxle differential? The interaxle differential should be used on slippery roads and should remain unlocked at all times on normal roads in good weather. However, on slippery highways, locking the interaxle differential will provide double the traction because it sends power to each axle.

As soon as you get back traction, the interaxle differential should be returned to the Unlock position. Be sure to let up on the accelerator to interrupt torque to the wheels when shifting between the locked and unlocked positions.

Driving on dry pavement with the interaxle differential in the locked position is not recommended. Switch immediately to Unlock when you are back on a good surface.

BRAKING SYSTEM

Of the numerous systems required to operate a rig safely and efficiently, the **braking system** is one of the most important. For obvious reasons—such as stopping the rig as quickly as necessary—the braking system should be kept in top shape so the driver, the load he or she is carrying, and other roadway users are kept out of harm's way.

A truck's braking system consists of three elements: **service brakes,** which normally are used to slow down or stop the vehicle; **supply emergency brakes,** which slow or stop the rig if the service brake system fails; and **parking brakes,** which are used to hold the rig in place when it is parked.

There are two types of foundation brakes used in the service brake system: **drum brakes** and **disc brakes.**

Drum brakes.   This brake is a metal cylinder that looks something like a drum. It is bolted to each end of the axle (see Figure 5-16). The drum rotates with the turning wheels. To stop the vehicle, the brake shoe linings are forced against the inside surface of the brake drums. This creates the friction that slows or stops the rig when enough friction is created. Friction creates heat. When too much heat is created, the drums expand out away from the shoe lining. This causes brake fade, and the truck is hard or impossible to stop.

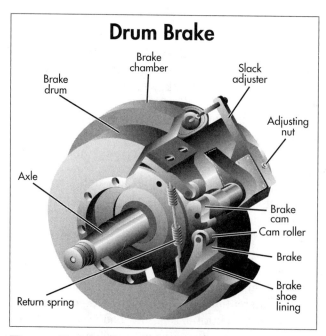

Figure **5-16** Drum brakes look like a drum bolted to each end of the axle.

Disc brakes. A modern disc brake system usually has a fixed disc attached to the inside of the wheel. It rotates with the wheel. This circular part is flat and made of steel that is machined on both sides. To slow down or stop, the linings are squeezed against each side of the disc. This looks something like a wide-jawed vice closing quickly on a spinning disk. It creates the friction that slows or stops the rig.

Air Brake Systems

Air is compressible; that is, it can be squeezed into a smaller space than it normally occupies. The smaller the space into which it is forced, the more resistance, or pressure, it can exert (see Figure 5-17).

In an **air brake system,** this pressure is used to increase the braking force. The compressed air can multiply the force of mechanical braking many times.

A number of parts make up the air brake system:

- Compressor
- Governor
- Air reservoirs
- Brake chambers
- One-way check valve
- Safety valves
- Drain cocks
- Air pressure gauge
- Low-pressure warning signal
- Air application pressure gauge

- Treadle valve
- Independent trailer brake
- Tractor parking valve
- Tractor protection system
- Glad hands
- Quick-release valve
- Relay valve
- Emergency relay valve

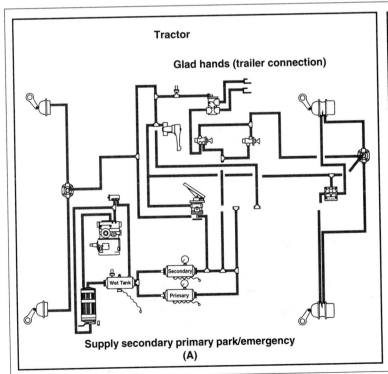

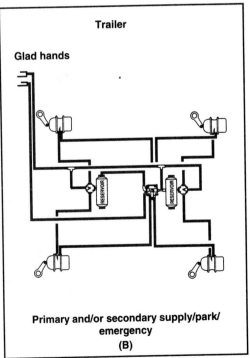

Figure **5-17** (A) Schematic of tractor's air brake system; (B) schematic of trailer's air brake system.

Compressor. Squeezes the air into a smaller space. This increases the force the air exerts. Compressors operate in different ways. They may use belts and pulleys or shafts and gears, but they are always run by the engine. When the engine runs, they run.

Even though the compressor runs with the engine on, it is not always pumping. The compressor pumps, or compresses, air until the pressure of the air in the reservoir reaches around 125 pounds per square inch (psi). Then it stops pumping until it is needed again.

Governor. Regulates the air compressor to maintain the desired pressure. As the pressure approaches 125 psi, the inlet valves are held open. This releases air. When the pressure drops below 100 psi, the governor closes the inlet valve to let the compressor build up again.

Air reservoirs. Hold the compressed air supply. There are three tanks: wet tank, dry tank, and trailer reservoir.

The size of the tank varies, depending on how many tanks there are and the size of the brake chambers. The wet tank receives the hot moist air from the compressor and delivers it to the dry tank. The trailer reservoir is near the trailer brake chambers. Compressed air held in this tank is ready for both normal and emergency use (see Figure 5-18).

One-way check valve. Prevents air from flowing back into the compressor from the reservoirs. When air flows back, the brakes do not work. This valve is located between the compressor and the wet tanks on the tractor. If two of the valves are used, the second one is located between the wet and dry tanks.

Safety valves. Keep the air pressure from rising to a dangerous level. One valve is placed in each air tank. It usually opens and releases air when the pressure reaches 150 psi. This lowers the pressure in the system.

After the safety valve has been activated, the governor will need servicing. This is a job for a qualified mechanic. Never attempt to adjust the governor yourself.

Drain cocks. Drain moisture from the air brake system reservoirs. Air becomes hot when it is squeezed by the compressor. When it reaches a reservoir, it expands, cools, and releases moisture. This moisture condenses in the tank. If the moisture is not removed, it damages the system.

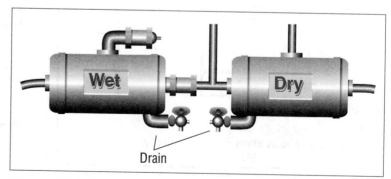

Figure **5-18** Air reservoirs hold the compressed air supply for the air brake system.

Drain this moisture each day. Drive your rig onto a level surface. Chock the wheels to keep the rig from rolling. Be sure to allow all of the air to escape so the moisture can drain out. Some trucks also have air dryers to remove moisture. These should also be drained regularly.

Note: Drain the wet tank first to avoid drawing moisture further into the air system and other tanks.

Air pressure gauge.   Tells how much air pressure is in the system in pounds per square inch (psi). This gauge is found on the instrument panel. The normal operating range is 90 to 120 psi.

Low-pressure warning signal.   Tells the driver the air pressure has dropped below 60 psi. A red warning light will turn on, a buzzer will sound, or both will happen.
   If one of these signals activates, stop at once—60 psi is still enough air pressure to put on the brakes. If you do not stop at once, you may lose more pressure, and the spring brakes will apply between 20 and 40 psi. The cause of the low air pressure must be fixed before you go on.

Air application pressure gauge.   Shows the amount of air pressure being applied to the brakes. When the brakes are not in use, the gauge will read 0 psi (see Figure 5-19).

Treadle valve.   Controls the air that operates the brakes. It is also called the foot brake. The further down the pedal is pushed, the more air is sent into the system. Letting up on the pedal releases the brakes by letting the air exhaust from the brakes.

Independent trailer brake.   A hand valve that regulates the airflow to only the trailer unit and puts on the brakes. It is usually called the trolley valve and is normally on the right side of the steering column.

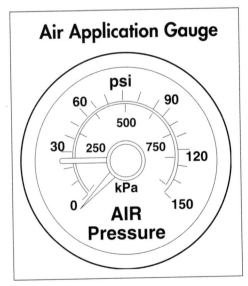

Figure **5-19**   The air application gauge shows the amount of air pressure applied to the air brakes.

Figure **5-20** Braking control panel.

Tractor parking valve.   A round blue knob you can push in to release the tractor parking brake. You pull it out to put on the parking brake. It also operates the spring brakes.

Tractor protection system.   Secures the tractor's air pressure if the trailer should break away from the tractor and snap the air lines. The tractor protection system is made up of two valves: the tractor protection valve and the emergency valve.

The tractor protection valve is closed by the driver to keep air from going out of the tractor. When it is pulled, it sets the tractor's spring brake. When it is pushed, it supplies air to the maxichamber to compress the spring and release the brakes (see Figure 5-20).

Glad hands.   Connect the service and emergency air lines of the tractor to the trailer. The connections are secure when the glad hands lock. An O-ring seals the coupling to prevent air loss. Because it is important to keep the O-ring damage free, check for dirt and sand before connecting the air lines.

When the air lines are unhooked, they should be sealed to keep dirt out. Covers, protection plates, or dead-end (dummy) couplers may be used. They will keep the air lines from dropping down onto the drive shaft and being torn off. You will have much less risk of brake failure if you keep the air lines clean.

Quick-release valve.   Allows the brakes to release swiftly. When you remove your foot from the brakes, air escapes from the chambers into the atmosphere. This quickly releases the brake shoes regardless of the distance between the foot valve and the brake chamber.

Relay valve.   Makes up for brake lag on a long-wheelbase vehicle. When you brake, the distance between the brake pedal and the brake chambers is a factor. The greater this distance, the longer it takes before the brakes apply. This means the rear trailer brakes will not apply as soon as the tractor brakes. The relay valve speeds up the action of the trailer brakes.

Emergency relay valve.   Relays air from the trailer air tank to the brake chambers. If there is a break in the lines between the tractor and trailer, the valve sends air from the trailer reservoir to the brake chambers.

This is part of the emergency brake system and activates automatically. You can also put on the trailer brakes in an emergency with the cab-mounted emergency valve. The emergency relay valve can also help release the trailer brakes quickly.

Operation of the Air Brake System

The one-way check valve is between the compressor and wet tank. The compressor pumps pressurized air to the wet tank, where most of the moisture is removed. The air then passes through the one-way check valve to the dry reservoir.

When the driver puts on the foot brake, the air flows through the service air lines to the front and rear tractor brake chambers. At the same time, air is sent through the tractor protection valve to the trailer brake chambers.

When the brake pedal is released, air escapes through the foot valve, or relay valve, in the tractor and through the quick-release, or relay valve, in the trailer.

Antilock Braking System

An **antilock braking system** (ABS) is an electronic control system that prevents wheels from locking, thus avoiding jackknifing and loss of vehicle stability, according to a spokesperson from Eaton ABS.

These relatively new antilock braking systems work when special ABS sensors monitor wheel speed at a rate of 100 times per second. If the system detects that any wheel is overbraking for conditions, the electronic control unit signals a modulator valve to reduce braking forces on that wheel until the threat of a skid is eliminated. It is important to maintain a safe following distance because of the greater stopping distance required as a result of reduced braking forces.

Tips for Driving Trucks Equipped with ABS

1. Do not brake any differently to slow or stop an ABS-equipped vehicle. When necessary, ABS will automatically modulate braking. This means the driver should maintain brake pressure in all situations.
2. Do not "pump" the brakes. ABS will control braking for the driver.
3. Do not take unnecessary risks. ABS cannot substitute for safe driving practices. Cautious driving, such as maintaining adequate distances from the vehicle ahead, is key to any safe operation.

What Else Should You Know about ABS?

The ABS warning lamp is typically located on the dashboard or instrument cluster, although its location will vary. Check the vehicle operator's manual for details.

ABS is functioning properly if the warning lamp comes on for approximately 3 seconds and then turns off. The lamp should remain off during vehicle operation.

If the lamp remains on during operation, ABS may not be operating. The vehicle will retain normal braking, although without the benefits of ABS. Have the vehicle serviced as soon as possible to restore ABS operation.

It is also important to have the lamp bulb and power source for ABS truck, tractor, and buses inspected if the warning lamp does not come on at ignition.

For trailers with full-time powered ABS (usually obtaining power over the blue line of the J560 connector), the trailer ABS warning lamp will function just like the tractor ABC warning lamp.

Each time the brakes are applied, the warning lamp will come on for approximately 3 seconds before turning off. If the lamp remains on during braking, ABS may not be working. The vehicle will retain normal braking, although without the benefits of ABS. Have the trailer serviced as soon as possible.

Spring Brake System

Many vehicles with air brakes also have spring brakes, which serve as dependable parking or emergency brake systems. The brakes are applied or released by using a control in the cab or are automatically activated when air pressure falls below 20 to 40 psi.

MIXING OLD AND NEW EQUIPMENT

One problem you will face as a driver is the mix of equipment that does not work well together. Some trailers built before 1975 are still in operation. The brake application time for most of these older trailers is much slower than for current tractors. Some new tractors have air-operated disc brakes, so the problem is even worse. You must know what equipment you are operating so that it can be handled properly.

Suppose you have a tractor with ABS but not so with your trailer. What can you expect? Experts say if only your tractor is equipped with ABS, use your mirrors to watch your trailer during emergency braking, applying your brakes whenever necessary to keep your vehicle in its lane. Tractor ABS will help prevent jackknifing but will not keep your trailer from swinging out of your lane.

If only your trailer has ABS, maintain control by applying brakes as necessary to keep your entire rig in your lane of traffic. However, even though the trailer ABS helps prevent trailer swing, it will not prevent tractor jackknife.

The bottom line is that ABS has added new horizons of safety for America's professional drivers and the nation's highways. Yet systems have been known to fail, and no professional driver should ever push the limits thinking that new technology will automatically correct any carelessness or lack of skills on the part of the driver.

WHEELS

There are two types of wheels: spoke and disc.

Spoke Wheel

Usually called a "Dayton," the **spoke wheel** is made of two pieces. It is more difficult to balance spoke wheels and align the tires and rims. Also, the lug nuts must be checked often for tightness.

Disc Wheel

The **disc wheel**, commonly called a "Budd," is made of aluminum or high-tensile steel. Alignment is simpler because these wheels can be fastened together with 6 to 10 wheel studs.

MOUNTING SYSTEMS

Two types of wheel mounting systems are used: stud piloted and hub piloted. A stud piloted system uses the studs on the wheel hub to guide and center the wheel. A hub piloted system uses the wheel hub itself to guide and center the wheel during mounting. The two types of mounting systems cannot be intermixed.

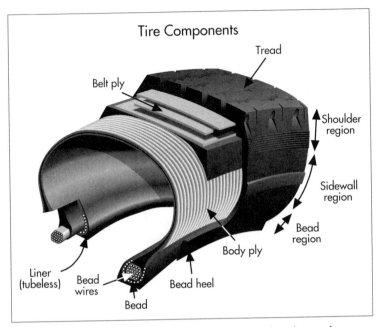

Figure **5-21** Components of standard truck tires.

Wheels are fastened by two methods: ball-seat nuts and flange nuts. Ball-seat nuts clamp the wheel on by seating in a tapered part of the stud hole. Flange nuts clamp onto a flat surface and provide more even clamping torque. These two types cannot be interchanged.

TIRES

There are three types of tires: radial, bias ply, and bias belted.

See Figure 5-21 to learn the various tire components.

Radial Tires

On **radial tires,** the body ply cords run across the tire perpendicular to the tread. There are also belt plies around the tire, parallel to the tread along the part that makes contact with the road. These hold the body ply cords tight and provide sturdiness for the tread (see Figure 5-22).

Radial tires cost more to buy than other tires, but they have a number of advantages. Radial treads last 40 to 100 percent longer. Because more of the surface of radials comes in contact with the road, they provide greater traction and also give better fuel mileage.

Bias-Ply Tires

Bias-ply tires have body cords running across the tire at an angle. There may also be breakers, or narrow plies, just under the tread that angle like the ply cords (see Figure 5-23).

Belted Bias Tires

Belted bias tires have body ply cords that run across the tread at an angle. The belt plies run around the tire under the tread (see Figure 5-24).

Radial
Body cords run perpendicular across the tread, belt piles run circumferentially around the tire under the tread.

Figure **5-22** Cross section of a radial tire.

Bias ply
Body cords run diagonally across the tread.

Figure **5-23** Cross section of a bias-ply tire.

Belted Bias
Body cords run diagonally across the tread. Belt piles run circumferentially around the tire under the tread.

Figure **5-24** Cross section of a belted bias tire.

Mixing Radial and Bias-Ply Tires

In general, it is best not to use radial and bias-ply tires together. Tires should be the same size and of the same type. To save money, however, you may use radial and bias-ply tires on the same vehicle if you carefully follow the manufacturer's guidelines.

The recommendation for combining radial and bias-ply tires applies to tractor wheels with a 20-inch or larger rim and 15-inch trailer tires only.

Note: NEVER put tires of different size or construction on the same axle. NEVER mix radial and bias tires on a tandem drive assembly.

Tire Tubes

Truck tires may or may not have tubes. Both radial and bias-ply tires can operate with tubes. Tubes can be used only with multipiece wheels, however.

In tires that have tubes, the tube fits between the tire and the rim. The air that keeps the tire inflated and supports the vehicle is held in the tube.

Tubeless tires are mounted on single-piece wheels. The tire itself holds the air that supports the rig. The advantages of using tubeless tires are:

- The wheels are much lighter.
- The tires run cooler.
- They are more efficient.

The wheels are also lighter because the parts of the multipiece wheel (flap, side ring, and lock ring) are not needed.

Figure **5-25**   A tire with rib tread.

TREAD DESIGN AND WHEEL POSITION

For highway use, there are two truck **tire tread** designs: rib and lug.

Rib tread.   Grooves in the tire tread run parallel to the sidewalls. Tires with a rib-type tread can be used anywhere on the rig and are designed for highway speed. These "all-position" tires are recommended for the front wheels on tractors and large straight trucks for high-speed, long-haul service. These tires help the driver maintain control of the vehicle and avoid skids. Be careful when choosing tires. There is a tire made for trailer use only that looks like the all-position tire (see Figure 5-25).

Lug tread.   Deep grooves in the tire shoulders run perpendicular to the sidewalls. These tires are best for the drive wheels. In high-torque road service, they wear better and have greater traction. They also have higher rolling resistance than the rib types. If you do not operate in cold areas, it may be wiser to use rib tires on the drive wheels for greater fuel efficiency (see Figure 5-26).

NORMAL TIRE INFLATION

Tires must be inflated correctly for the rig to perform at its best (see Figure 5-27). For the right number of pounds per square inch (psi), refer to the truck's owner manual and Federal Tire Regulations FMCSR 393.75.

Figure **5-26**   A tire with lug tread.

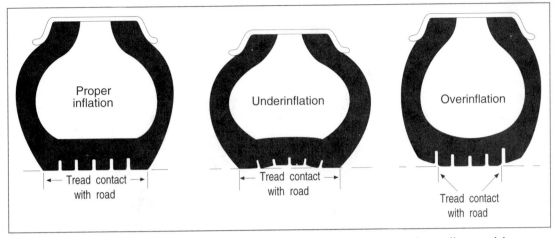

Figure **5-27** Properly inflated tires make a rig easier to handle and have a longer road life than under- or overinflated tires.

Pressure should be checked with an accurate gauge at least once a week. For a true reading of tire pressure, check when the tire is cool. Inspect the tires thoroughly and check the pressure with an accurate tire gauge. Driving causes the tires to heat and increase the pressure. The pressure in sizes 9R22.5 tubeless or 8.25R230 and smaller tube-type tires may increase by as much as 10 psi. Sizes 10R22.5 tubeless and 9.00R20 and larger tube-type tires may increase approximately 15 psi.

If you test your tires after they have been used and they show less than these increases, inflate them to the proper pressure. If the pressure of the heated tires is more than the recommended pressure, do not release any air. Wait until the tires cool. Check them again, then correct the pressure if you need to.

When you inflate tires, keep in mind the maximum pressure for the load you will be carrying. Do not exceed the rim or wheel rating. Check the pressure in new tires after 24 hours of operation to get an accurate reading. Always replace the valve stem caps to maintain a tight air seal and keep dirt and moisture out.

If tire pressure increases more than 10 to 15 psi during normal operation, the tires may be underinflated, the rig may be overloaded, the tires may not be the right size, or the rig may have been speeding. The increase may also be any combination of these causes. Correct the cause of the increase.

Underinflation

Underinflation increases tread wear and reduces tire life. When the temperature increases in an underinflated tire, it can cause the tread to separate from the body or belt ply of the tire. Also, the tire can flex excessively. As a soft tire travels over the road, this flexing builds up heat. Heat weakens the body cords. If it continues, the body cord deteriorates and may catch fire from the high internal temperature.

Tires that are underinflated can make the rig very hard to control. This can be dangerous at any time but especially in extreme conditions and emergencies.

If you are driving on duals and one is underinflated or flat, a fire can result. Because it is overloaded, the other tire may also fail. Both of these are very dangerous conditions.

Note: Radial tires at the correct pressure can show a bulge on the side that may make them appear to be underinflated. Check them to be sure the pressure does not get too low and cause too much wear.

Figure **5-28** Check tire temperature often.

Overinflation

Overinflation can damage tires and create hazards. It can also greatly reduce the stopping efficiency of an empty or lightly loaded rig. Rigid tires are damaged more easily by roadway objects. Roadway shock is not absorbed as well. This can cause stress and rim failure.

How Heat Affects Tire Rubber

A tire can become very, very hot during long-distance, high-speed driving. This can happen very easily during hot weather or when the tire is underinflated. Check the temperature often (every 2 hours or 100 miles in hot weather) to prevent problems (see Figure 5-28).

Internal friction heats the tire. When it reaches the combustion point, a tire can burst into flame. This usually happens in a dual assembly when one of the tires is underinflated. Often, just after the rig stops, the tire explodes. Such fires are very hard to control and extinguish.

Tire temperatures must also be checked for other reasons. As the tire's temperature passes 250°F, components weaken and the rubber softens. Tires can be more easily damaged if they rub against a curb, railroad track, or pit rail guide at the terminal dock.

Matching and Spacing Duals

If two tires of different diameters are put together, the larger tire may bulge at the sides. This happens because it is carrying more than its share of the load. The smaller tire may wear unevenly because it does not contact the road properly. The tread can then separate.

With some tire types, there may be a difference in diameter even if they have equal inflation pressures. There can be 1/4-inch difference in diameter for an 8.25

cross-section 9.22.5 or smaller tubeless tire. For a 9.00 cross-section 10.22.5 or larger tubeless tire, there can be a 1/2-inch difference.

To get true dual diameter readings, you should measure the tires with a steel pi tape 24 hours after they are inflated. If you measure them while they are on the rig, use a string gauge, straight edge, tire caliper, or large square.

To be on the safe side, keep the differences in diameter to less than 1/4 inch no matter what the size of the tires. Keep the space between the tires at the recommended distance to keep the tires from rubbing together.

Tread Life

Because conditions vary, no one can predict the life of the tire tread exactly. Quality of the tire, how the vehicle was handled, tire inflation, load distribution, and care of the tire will all affect the life of the tread.

The average tread life for any tire on the market today has been calculated. This is good information for the driver because it serves as a guide. If the driver shifts gears smoothly and is generally responsible, he or she may be able to get greater-than-average tread wear. On the other hand, the driver can cut tread wear in half by speeding or braking sharply.

Note: Tire wear depends on the type of operation, whether it is a light or heavy load, the type and grade of the tire, and the road surface.

STEERING SYSTEMS

To control your rig, the **steering system** must be working properly. There are a number of parts that must be checked often to ensure smooth operation (see Figure 5-29).

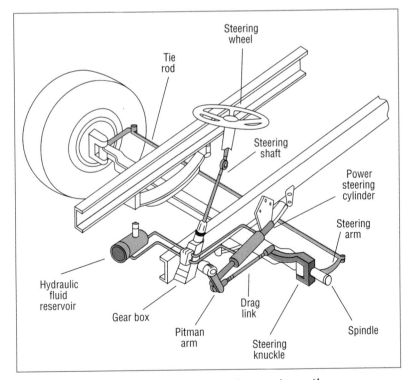

Figure **5-29** The steering system gives the professional driver control of his or her rig.

- **Steering wheel:** Connected to the steering shaft and controls the direction of the vehicle.
- **Steering shaft:** Connects the steering wheel to the steering gear box.
- **Steering gear box:** Transfers the turning of the steering shaft to the Pitman arm.
- **Pitman arm:** Connected to and moves the drag link.
- **Drag link:** Transfers movement from the Pitman arm to the left steering arm.
- **Steering arm:** The one on the right side attaches the tie rod to the wheels. The one on the left side is attached to the drag link.
- **Tie rod:** Connects the front wheels together and adjusts their operating angle.

Proper placement of the parts is known as *correct steering geometry.* All these parts must be correctly aligned, or the rig will be hard to steer. A rig that is hard to steer can be dangerous.

Wheel Alignment

The following alignment features on the front end of the rig are built in by the manufacturer. They may be changed as needed.

Caster. The amount the axle kingpin is tilted backward at the top. It is measured in degrees. The axle should have a positive caster. That is, it should tilt forward. When set in this manner, the vehicle has a natural tendency to go straight. It will also recover from turns more quickly. Positive caster makes steering easier.

Camber. The amount the front wheels are tilted outward at the top. It is best for trucks to have positive camber. The distance between the tires is greater at the top than at the bottom. With this kind of setting, the loaded truck tends to straighten the tires in relation to the road surface.

Other tendencies of alignment can result from wear and damage. Most noticeable are toe-in and toe-out:

- **Toe-in:** The amount the front wheels are closer together at the front than they are at the rear.
- **Toe-out:** The amount the front wheels are farther apart at the front than they are at the rear.

Power Steering

Power steering allows the driver to control the tractor with less effort and stress. This is a particular advantage when you have a blowout. In that instance, you can maintain control of the rig and have the ability to slowly lift your foot off the accelerator.

There are two types of power steering systems: the **hydraulic power steering system,** which uses fluid to make steering easier, and the **air power steering system,** which uses the force of air.

COUPLING SYSTEMS

The **coupling system** connects the tractor to the trailer (see Figure 5-30). Coupling systems have two main parts: the **fifth wheel** and the trailer **kingpin.**

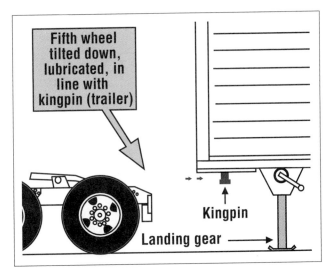

Figure **5-30** The coupling system includes the tractor's fifth wheel and the trailer's kingpin.

Figure **5-31** A fifth wheel.

Correctly coupling the tractor to the trailer with a single 2-inch kingpin is one of the biggest responsibilities a driver of big rigs has.

Fifth Wheel

The fifth wheel is not really a wheel. It is a flat disk on the tractor. The kingpin of the trailer fits into and is held by the fifth wheel. The linking of the fifth wheel and kingpin lets the tractor pull the trailer (see Figure 5-31).

Because of the type of coupling, some sideways, or lateral, motion of the rig is possible. Moving the tractor "pulls" the trailer along. When the tractor turns, it moves somewhat independently of the trailer. The trailer follows the tractor but along a different path of travel.

The trailer receives from the tractor stability, support, and direction of movement.

At the same time, the trailer enjoys some independent sideways movement. This lets the whole rig make turns better.

There are several fifth-wheel options a tractor may have to make it easier to couple and uncouple. All the following help cut down on wear to the fifth wheel and kingpin:

- Approach rails
- Tapered frames
- Complex locking mechanisms that remove excess movement between the kingpin and fifth wheel

There are different types of fifth-wheel styles. Which type you use will depend on the kind of cargo you are carrying.

Fixed-mount type.   The most common type. A fixed-mount fifth wheel is secured in a fixed position behind the cab. It has three parts: top, or base, plate; bracket sub-assemblies; and frame mounting members.

The top plate includes the locking mechanism and bears much of the stress of coupling. The bracket subassemblies hold the top plate in place. The frame mounting members are usually structural steel angles bolted to the fifth wheel.

Sliding (adjustable) type.   Slides backward and forward. It can be locked into place to adapt to different loads. It greatly increases the flexibility of the total rig. The sliding fifth wheel, or slider, helps the trucking industry conform to state laws regarding the length of vehicles and distribution of weight over the axles. This would not be possible with a permanent, or fixed-mount, fifth-wheel assembly.

Sliding fifth wheels may be locked in place in one of two ways:

1. Pins fit into matching holes in the slider track and hold it in place.
2. A plunger fits into a row of slotted holes in the base to keep it from moving.

The slider can be adjusted by hand or automatically. To adjust it by hand, the driver moves the pins or plunger himself and then adjusts the fifth wheel by moving it forward or backward.

When it is done automatically, an air-activated control in the cab unlocks the locking device. The driver sets the trailer brakes and moves the tractor forward or backward until the fifth wheel is in the correct position.

Fifth-Wheel Slack Adjusters

The slack adjuster on a fifth wheel adjusts the kingpin locking mechanism so it will fit snugly around the kingpin. Slack adjusters are used on most mechanical locking mechanisms. Compression locking mechanisms reduce problems with slack.

Kingpins

Kingpins are attached to the upper fifth-wheel plate, which is underneath the front of the trailer. The kingpin is usually a 2-inch steel pin that is locked into the jaws of the fifth wheel to couple the tractor to the trailer. It is made of high-strength steel and will usually last as long as the trailer.

OTHER COUPLING DEVICES

There are other devices that are often used when coupling a truck to a tractor and, after a trailer has been uncoupled, to support the front of the trailer. The purpose of each part is explained in the section that follows.

CAUTION:

Kingpins have different settings. Some are 28 inches, some are 30 inches, and some are 36 inches. Make sure your fifth wheel is set back, or the trailer may drop the pinsetting and the trailer could be pushed into the tractor.

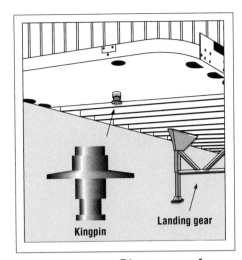

Figure **5-32** Close-up of a trailer's kingpin and landing gear. Different kingpin settings affect the hookup.

Converter Dolly

There are two types of **converter dollies: conventional dolly** and **Jifflox** (or universal) **converter dolly.** A conventional converter dolly is used to change semi-trailers into full trailers. The dolly becomes the front axle of the trailer. A Jifflox converter dolly, used in the eastern United States, is hooked behind the axle of a single axle tractor. This converts it to a tandem axle tractor. The tractor then can pull a loaded trailer.

Both dolly types are similar and include the same parts, including a fifth wheel, drawbar and eye, safety chains, air hose, and electrical cable connections.

Trailer Landing Gear

When it is not coupled to a tractor, a trailer needs support for its front end. The landing gear supports the trailer when it is not attached to a tractor (see Figure 5-32). It also moves the front of the trailer up and down as needed. The landing gear is usually hand cranked and may have either wheels or skid feet. Landing gears will not resist pressure from the side, front, or rear. They are only a means of stationary support for the trailer.

Chapter Six
Basic Control

Definitions

Diesel Engine

Putting the Vehicle into
Motion—and Stopping

Backing in a Straight Line

Turning the Vehicle

Range Practice

OBJECTIVES

When you have completed this chapter, you should be able to:

- Explain the routines for starting, warming up, cooling down, and shutting off two-cycle and four-cycle diesel engines

- Show how to safely test the trailer hookup

- Explain the proper way to put a rig into motion

- Describe the correct way to stop a rig

- Describe skills needed to back a rig in a straight line

- Explain the correct procedures for making right and left turns

- Define off-tracking

KEY TERMS

Buttonhook turn
Control routines
Cool-down period
Engine shutdown
Four-cycle diesel engine
Idling

Jug handle turn
Off-tracking
Starting routine
Two-cycle diesel engine
Warm-up

INTRODUCTION

Professional driving is much more than simply driving a truck down the highway. As you will learn in this and other chapters, professional driving means you have mastered a number of basic and advanced skills.

Reading about these skills—the whys and why nots—is the first step in becoming a skilled driver. And after you have read about them, you will want to practice what you have learned on the driving range or with a driver trainer.

Keep in mind that this is just the beginning. If you speak to any experienced driver, he or she will tell you that professional driving is something you continue to learn—that you continually build on basic skills and become more masterful in all the tasks involved in operating a big rig.

Professional drivers will also tell you that becoming a driving professional means spending a lot of time polishing the skills and knowledge you gain in the classroom. Getting the feel of basic control from this chapter and the learning activities at the end of the chapter will prepare you for the driving range and for driving on the road.

DEFINITIONS

Like any other profession, the transportation industry's professional drivers know and understand the meanings of certain terms that may be found only in this profession. Knowing some of these terms now will help as you work through this chapter. All the definitions you need may be found in the glossary at the back of the book.

- **Starting routine:** The steps used to start the engine.
- **Warm-up:** The period of time after starting the engine and before moving the vehicle. During this time, the engine will warm up. Gauges in the vehicle will show you when the engine is operating within the manufacturer's specified range.
- **Engine shutdown:** The period of time after stopping the rig until the engine is turned off. Shutting down the engine requires a cooling off period to prevent damage to engines with turbochargers.
- **Control routines:** These vary according to engine time, so be sure to note the differences in routines used for two-cycle and four-cycle diesel engines.

Note: As a professional driver, you need to know the kind of engine your rig will have and the basic operating procedures for that engine. If you are not knowledgeable of these procedures for specific engines, it is possible to seriously damage the engine. Learn as much as you can about all types of engines for commercial motor vehicles.

DIESEL ENGINE

Before starting the engine, you should always check the trailer coupling. How to check the coupling is described in detail in a later section.

Two-Cycle Diesel Engine

Always start a **two-cycle diesel engine** in this way:

1. Put on the parking brake.
2. Place the Stop and Emergency Stop controls in the Run position (if your rig has them).
3. Make sure the transmission is in neutral. Depress the clutch pedal (prevents the starting motor from turning the transmission gears).
4. Turn on the switch-key.
5. Operate the starter. If the engine does not start in 15 to 20 seconds, turn off the starter. Allow it to cool for at least 1 minute. Then try again. The reason for allowing it to cool is that trucks start on 24 volts and then drop to 12 volts. The extra volts can overheat or burn out the starter.
6. Control the engine speed with the foot throttle until it is running smoothly.
7. During warm-up, the engine should never be run at a higher revolutions per minute (rpm) than is needed to keep it running. Turbocharged engines should not be run at a higher rpm until the engine oil pressure has built up and stabilized. Until the engine has reached this point, there is not enough oil at the turbocharger bearings to meet the lubrication needs of higher speeds.
8. Check the instruments for system malfunctions.

Four-Cycle Diesel Engine

The start-up routine for a **four-cycle diesel engine** is as follows:

1. Apply the parking brake.
2. Release the throttle. Depress the clutch pedal. Make sure the transmission is in neutral.
3. Turn on the switch-key.
4. Operate the starter.
5. Crank for 3 or 4 seconds.
6. Check the instruments.
7. Warm up the engine.
8. During warm-up, the engine should never be run at a higher rpm than is needed to keep it running. Turbocharged engines should not be run at a higher rpm until engine oil pressure has built up and stabilized. Until the engine has reached this point, there is not enough oil at the turbocharger bearings to meet the lubrication needs of higher speeds.

Fuel-Efficient Starting

Keep these points in mind when starting an engine to save fuel:

- Pumping the throttle is a waste of fuel. It will only flood the engine.
- Rapidly revving the engine wastes fuel.

Engine Warm-Up for Operating at Low rpm

Warming up an engine:

- Allows the engine to reach a beginning operating temperature.
- Circulates oil.
- Reaches a favorable clearance between moving parts. This occurs at operating temperature.
- Builds the oil pressure to the proper level.
- Coats the cylinder walls with a film of oil.
- Lubricates the bearings.
- Increases the coolant temperature. This may not show on the gauge.
- Heats the oil to the proper temperature.
- Builds up air pressure.

Fuel-Efficient Warm-Up

While warming up, do not idle the engine any more than needed. Keep the rpms low and the speed under 30 mph. The owner's manual will tell you the idling time. Idling time should be kept to a few minutes. Many rigs warm up best while moving at slow speeds. Keep the speed to 30 mph or less until the engine is warm. Use creeping speed when first moving to lubricate the dry wheel, transmission, and rear end bearings. Use extra care in cold weather.

Results of Not Warming Up

Rapid acceleration or over revving before the engine is warm causes crankshaft and bearing damage, turbocharger bearing damage from lack of lubrication, and damage to most parts that have not been properly lubricated.

Normal Instrument Readings

When the instrument readings reach normal levels, it is safe to drive your rig at cruising speed. Check the operator's manual for the proper oil pressure, air pressure, coolant temperature, oil temperature, and voltmeter or ammeter readings. These vary with the rig.

Engine Shutdown

The steps in engine shutdown vary from one type of truck to another. The basic steps in turning off a diesel engine are:

1. Depress the clutch.
2. Shift to neutral and release the clutch.
3. Cool the engine.
4. Turn off the switch-key.
5. If the engine has a stop control, move it to the off position. The fuel flow is now cut off from the fuel injectors.

Cool-Down Period

In diesel engines, the **cool-down period** is the key step. It is as important as the warm-up. During the cool-down, the engine idles for up to 5 minutes, coolant and oil flow at reduced temperatures, and the turbocharger cools down (watch the pyrometer).

The cool-down period varies according to the manufacturer's specifications, type of trip completed (a longer period is needed for high-speed, long-haul trips), and type of load that was pulled: heavy versus empty (hot, overworked engines require longer periods).

Note: The cool-down period is a good time to exit the cab and perform a posttrip inspection. On returning to the cab, the temperature should be reduced to an acceptable level.

Excessive Idling

Too much **idling** wastes fuel and causes wear and tear on a truck's engine. When idling, the vehicle is getting zero miles per gallon—and idling can waste as much as one gallon of fuel in an hour. It can also clog fuel injectors, and because the engine may not be hot enough for complete combustion, the unburned fuel results in harmful deposits.

Today's engines do not require more than 5 minutes of idling. Studies have found that 1 hour of idling causes the same amount of engine wear as 2 hours of driving. The typical over-the-road truck idles 800 hours over its lifetime, equivalent to driving 64,000 additional miles.

PUTTING THE VEHICLE INTO MOTION— AND STOPPING

Moving a tractor-trailer rig differs from moving an automobile. Professional drivers are expected to have more specific skills and more expertise to move a rig—from testing the tractor-trailer's coupling to putting the vehicle into motion and, finally, bringing it to a stop.

Since most professional drivers will drive vehicles equipped with manual transmissions, this text covers procedures to be used with manual transmissions. When you operate a vehicle equipped with an automatic transmission, follow the manufacturer's recommendations.

Step 1: Testing the Trailer Hookup

Each time the trailer is hooked up, a test of the coupling must be made. This test is different for a vehicle with independent trailer brake control compared to the test for a vehicle that does not have the control.

Testing the Trailer Hookup with Independent Brake Control (Trolley or Hand Valve)

1. Depress the clutch.
2. Shift into the lowest forward gear.
3. Apply the independent trailer brakes (trolley or hand valve).
4. Release the clutch to the friction point.
5. Pull gently forward against the locked trailer brakes.
6. Depress the clutch.
7. Repeat the entire procedure to ensure proper coupling.

This routine also shows whether the trailer brakes are in working order.

Testing the Trailer Hookup without Independent Brake Control (Trolley or Hand Valve)

1. Depress the clutch.
2. Shift into the lowest forward gear.
3. Apply the trailer air supply (red) valve. Pull out to apply.
4. Release the clutch to the friction point.
5. Gently pull forward against the locked trailer brakes.
6. Depress the clutch.
7. Repeat the entire procedure to ensure proper coupling.

Step 2: Putting the Tractor-Trailer into Motion

Moving the rig smoothly and with ease is a skill that comes from much practice—and there is no substitute for practice (see Figure 6-1). To move a rig, follow these steps:

1. Push in the clutch all the way (activating the clutch brake).
2. Shift to the lowest forward gear.
3. Release parking brakes and slowly engage (let out) the clutch while slightly depressing the accelerator.
4. When the vehicle starts to move, slowly increase engine rpms to increase the rig's speed.
5. When the vehicle is in motion with the clutch fully engaged, take your foot off the clutch and prepare to shift to another gear or stop.

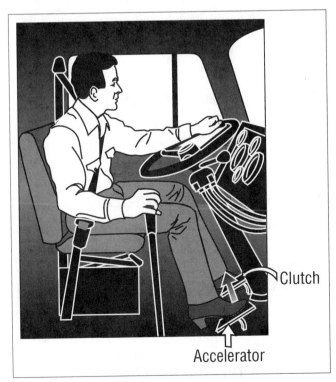

Clutch

Accelerator

Figure **6-1** Basic vehicle maneuvers require skill and coordination between the use of the accelerator and the clutch.

- Engage the clutch *slowly* to avoid slippage.
- When starting on an upgrade, shift into lowest forward gear, slowly release the clutch, and as the clutch engages, slowly accelerate and release the parking and trailer brakes.
- Allow for brake lag.

Step 3: Stopping the Tractor-Trailer

Stopping a big rig smoothly is also a skill learned from much practice behind the wheel. To stop a rig, follow these steps:

1. Push the brake pedal down.
2. Control the pressure so the rig comes to a smooth, safe stop.
3. Downshift as you stop. Do not coast to a stop.
4. If you are driving a manual transmission, do not push in the clutch until the engine rpm is almost to idle.
5. When you have stopped, select a low gear.

Note: Never coast to a stop in neutral or by holding the clutch down. Always downshift to a stop.

If you have stopped properly, there should be no nose rebound or bouncing of the cab.

Note: Since many professional drivers are behind the wheels of vehicles equipped with a manual transmission, this section addresses procedures used with manual transmissions. However, if you are operating a vehicle equipped with an automatic transmission, follow the manufacturer's recommendations for best practices.

BACKING IN A STRAIGHT LINE

Backing is a difficult maneuver and is covered in detail in a later chapter. Only basic information is presented here, but it should help prepare you for straight-line backing.

Step 1: Position the Vehicle Properly

Move forward until the tractor and trailer are aligned and the front (steering) wheels are straight.

Step 2: Speed Control

Shift to reverse gear. Back as slowly as you can using idle speed. Do not ride the clutch or brake pedals.

Step 3: Check behind Your Rig

Use both mirrors to constantly check behind the rig while backing. Be aware and careful of pedestrians. In later exercises, you will need to guard against backing into any object. Keep doors closed.

Step 4: Steering

The best way to keep your vehicle on course is not to oversteer. To correct drifting (when your tractor and your trailer get out of alignment and "drift" in different directions), turn the steering wheel toward the drift as soon as it occurs. If you catch the drift right away, a very slight movement will correct it. Little drifts need small corrections. Big drifts need big corrections.

Use the push-pull method to keep the trailer in a straight line. When the trailer gets bigger in the mirror, push the steering wheel toward that mirror. Immediately pull the steering wheel back to straighten the rig out. The biggest error in using the push-pull method is not returning the wheel to a straight position. This must be done as soon as you correct the drift.

Step 5: Pull up and Start Again if Too Far Out of Position

If your rig is getting too far out of alignment, remember it is easier to correct a drift moving forward than moving backward. Stop and pull forward to realign the tractor and trailer. Then continue backing.

TURNING THE VEHICLE

This section describes basic turning maneuvers (see Figure 6-2). Detailed instruction will be given in a later chapter.

A few basics to keep in mind when turning your vehicle are to know your vehicle, to allow for off-tracking, and to plan your turn in advance.

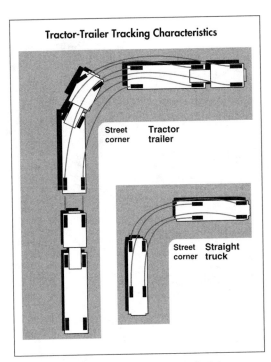

Tractor-Trailer Tracking Characteristics

Street corner   Tractor trailer

Street corner   Straight truck

Figure **6-2** Professional drivers know their rigs and how they will respond to each maneuver.

Off-Tracking

What exactly is **off-tracking?** It happens when you turn. The rear wheels do not follow the same path as the front wheels. They follow a shorter path than the front wheels. The more distance between the front wheels and the rear wheels and the sharper the turn, the more the rear wheels off-track. Keep off-tracking in mind when making turns or taking curves (see Figure 6-3).

Off-Tracking in Tractor-Trailer Rigs

Two key factors determine the off-tracking of a trailer: the distance between the kingpin and the rear trailer wheels and the amount of sideway drag of the rear tires.

The greater the distance between the kingpin and the rear trailer wheels, the more the off-tracking. For single-axle trailers, measure the distance from the center of the kingpin to the center of the rear axle. For tandem axle trailers, measure the distance from the center of the kingpin to the center point between the axles.

Sideway drag of the rear tires increases with the number of tires. The more sideway drag, the more off-tracking. Tandem axles have more sideway drag and greater off-tracking than does a single rear axle (see Figure 6-4).

Right Turns

Most right turns are tighter than the turning radius of your truck (see Figure 6-5). To make it safely around the corner without hitting a curb or other object, you will need to use more traffic lanes than you would in a car. At the same time, you do not want to obstruct traffic.

Off-Tracking Vehicle Path

- Truck width
- Outside tractor tire path
- Off-tracking
- Wheel or turning track width
- Outermost point of truck
- Inside trailer tire path
- Swept path

Figure **6-3** In off-tracking, the rear wheels of the rig do not follow the same path as the front wheels.

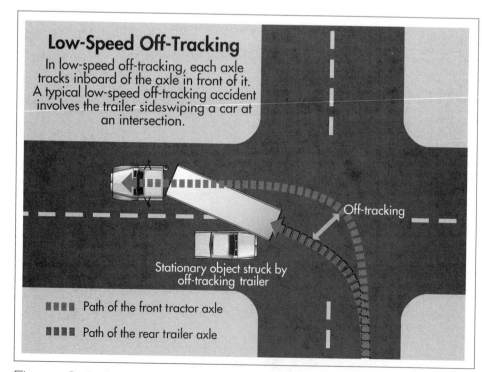

Low-Speed Off-Tracking

In low-speed off-tracking, each axle tracks inboard of the axle in front of it. A typical low-speed off-tracking accident involves the trailer sideswiping a car at an intersection.

Off-tracking

Stationary object struck by off-tracking trailer

▪▪▪▪ Path of the front tractor axle

▪▪▪▪ Path of the rear trailer axle

Figure **6-4** In low-speed off-tracking, each axle tracks inside the path of the axle in front of it.

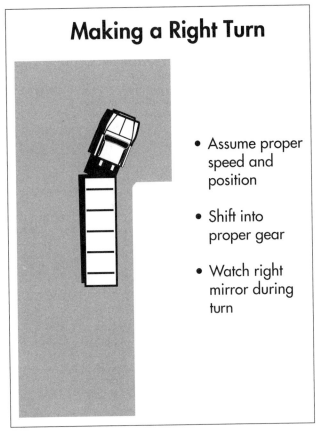

Making a Right Turn

- Assume proper speed and position

- Shift into proper gear

- Watch right mirror during turn

Figure **6-5** Right-turn maneuvers are tighter than the turn radius of your truck.

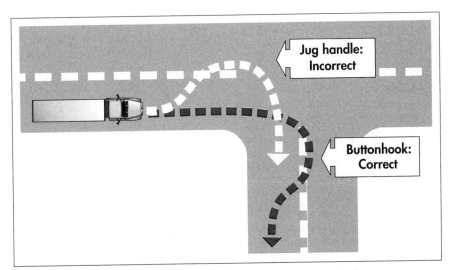

Jug handle: Incorrect

Buttonhook: Correct

Figure **6-6** Jug handle turns are sloppy and dangerous ways to make right turns.

Do not make the turn if you cannot clear the corner using the available space. Choose a different route. Sometimes you can continue straight ahead for another block and then make three left turns to get to the street you want.

Figure 6-6 shows two possible ways to make a right turn. One of them is a good method. The other is not.

A **jug handle turn** is a common but sloppy and dangerous way to make a right turn for the following reasons:

● Little, if any, real advantage is gained because the trailer tires do not have time to move away from the curb.

● If you signal right but move left, you confuse traffic. Someone behind you may even try to squeeze between the trailer and the curb.

A **buttonhook turn** will let you clear the corner without these problems (see Figure 6-7). You use the extra space in front of you in this manner:

1. Approach the intersection in the right lane.
2. If the lane width allows, position your truck about 4 or 5 feet from the curb. You want as much space on the right as you can have without letting a car slip in.
3. Turn on your right-turn signal.
4. Scan the intersection. Watch for a break in cross traffic.
5. Proceed straight ahead until the trailer tires will clear the corner in a hard right turn.
6. Turn hard to the right.
7. Finish the turn in the right lane.
8. Cancel your turn signal.

Plan ahead as you enter a turn to make the turn properly. Your plan should include signaling what you plan to do in advance, adjusting your speed, shifting into the proper gear, and postioning your rig properly.

Note: Regardless of the difficulty of the turn, you must always yield to motorists and pedestrians.

Signal in Advance

You must warn traffic that you plan to turn. Signal early enough that other drivers will not be in your way when you need to turn.

Figure **6-7**
Buttonhook turns allow safe right-turn maneuvers.

Adjust Your Speed

Adjust your speed as you approach the intersection or turning point. This enables you to speed up slightly as you make the turn.

Shift Gears

Slow down and shift into the proper gear before entering the turn. Then you will be able to complete the turn in the same gear. In this way, you can keep both hands on the steering wheel during the turn (see Figure 6-8).

Get into the Proper Position

You must pull your rig farther into the intersection than you would your personal vehicle. By doing this, you will not run over the curb during the turn due to

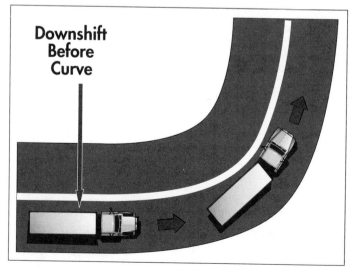

Figure **6-8** Planning ahead means shifting into the proper gear before a turn or curve.

off-tracking. A good rule of thumb for a right turn is to pull about one-half the length of the rig past the corner point of the intersection before beginning the turn. Keep the vehicle wheels straight before turning.

Making the Turn

Turn the steering wheel to the right and speed up slightly for a smooth turn. Watch the right mirror carefully for the position of the trailer wheels and other traffic.

As you finish the turn, turn the steering wheel back to the left to straighten the wheels.

Errors in Making Right Turns

Common major errors in making right turns include:

- Approaching the intersection too fast
- Not downshifting before the turn
- Shifting gears while turning
- Not allowing for off-tracking of the trailer
- Not getting far enough into the intersection before making the turn

Left Turns

Plan ahead for a left turn just as you would for a right turn (see Figure 6-9). Follow these steps:

1. Slow down as you approach the intersection.
2. Put the rig into the right gear for the turn.

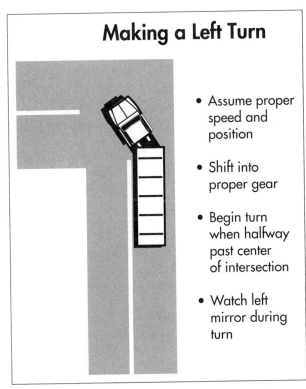

Making a Left Turn

- Assume proper speed and position
- Shift into proper gear
- Begin turn when halfway past center of intersection
- Watch left mirror during turn

Figure **6-9** Making a left turn requires planning and practice.

3. Keep your wheels straight.
4. Be as far to the right in the left-turn lane as you can.
5. Watch the left mirror during the turn.
6. After turning, turn the steering wheel back to the right to straighten the wheels.

Errors in Making Left Turns

Common errors in making left turns include approaching the intersection too fast and shifting gears while turning.

Highway Curves

Position yourself carefully for highway curves (see Figure 6-10). For right curves, keep the front of your vehicle toward the center of the lane. If you do not, the rear of the trailer may run off the road during the turn. For left curves, keep the tractor as close to the outer (right) edge of the lane as you can. This will keep the trailer from running over the center line.

RANGE PRACTICE

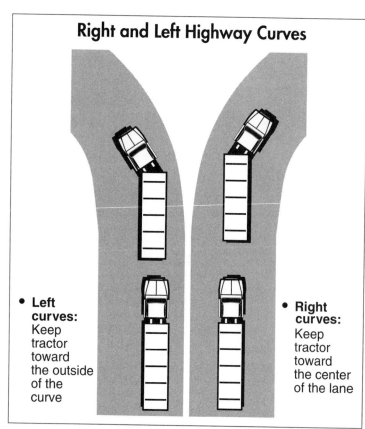

Right and Left Highway Curves

• **Left curves:** Keep tractor toward the outside of the curve

• **Right curves:** Keep tractor toward the center of the lane

Figure **6-10** Maneuvering highway curves requires planning and correctly positioning your vehicle in the traffic lane.

After you have learned the correct methods of operating and maneuvering your rig, your instructor may take you out for driving range practice. You will be expected:

● Start, warm up, and shut down the engine as directed by the manufacturer.
● Put the rig into motion and accelerate smoothly.
● Come to a smooth stop.
● Back in a straight line.
● Make turns correctly from the proper position.

To meet these goals, you will need other skills, including the following:

● Coordinated use of the accelerator and clutch
● The proper way to put on air brakes
● Coordinated use of all controls needed to drive forward or back in a straight line
● Understanding off-tracking, or the path the trailer will take as the entire rig takes curves or makes turns

All these driving skills can be mastered as you practice on the range. Using care in operating your rig will bring you success as a driver and profit to your company.

Chapter Seven
Shifting

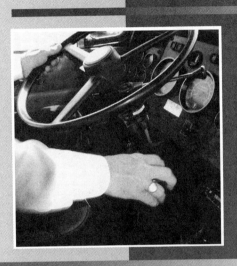

FROM NOW ON. . .

ONLY THE BEST
WILL DRIVE!

OBJECTIVES

When you have completed this chapter, you should be able to:

- Describe basic gear shifting patterns

- Understand shift patterns for major types of transmissions

- Demonstrate methods of shifting through the gears of all major types of conventional transmissions

- Demonstrate double-clutching and timing the shift for a smooth and fuel-efficient performance

- Know how to select proper gears for speed and road conditions

- Discuss shifting with automatic and semiautomatic transmissions

- Understand procedures to operate electronic synchronized and nonsynchronized transmissions

- Know how to use the instruments and controls in order to shift gears properly

- Be aware of common shifting errors and results of these errrors

- Demonstrate how to use hands, feet, sight, and hearing to obtain the best performance in shifting

- Know how improper use of the clutch and transmission can damage a rig

KEY TERMS

Accelerator
Automatic transmission
Clutch
Clutch brake
Double-clutching
Downshifting
Eaton Fuller Nine Speed
Eaton Fuller Super Ten
Eaton Fuller Thirteen
   Speed
Eaton Fuller Top 2
Gearshift lever
Governor
Lugging

Manual transmission
Nonsynchronized
   transmission
Progressive shifting
Rockwell Engine
   Synchro Shift (ESS)
Rockwell Ten Speed
Semiautomatic
   transmission
Spicer AutoMate-2
Spicer Pro-Shift Seven
   Speed
Synchronizing Skills
Tachometer
Upshifting

INTRODUCTION

Many professional driving students will admit that shifting gears looks to be the most difficult of all the new skills they have to learn.

Common sense tells you that shifting gears in a commercial motor vehicle could be more difficult than shifting gears in your personal vehicle. However, like most professional driving skills, shifting can become less intimidating and less difficult with practice.

This section provides clear definitions, good hands-on knowledge of the skill, and learning activities to help you increase and improve your skills behind the wheel.

This chapter introduces you to the differences in shifting patterns. It explains clutch and accelerator control and how to coordinate hands, eyes, feet, sound, and feel to handle the various transmissions found in today's tractor-trailer rigs.

This information and your time on the driving range or behind the wheel will help you master the skills you need. What you learn from the information here will serve as a handy reference later.

More important, however, you will understand that proper gearing evolves from learning, behind-the-wheel practice, and your instructor answering any and all questions you may have.

SHIFT CONTROLS

The controls used in shifting a **manual transmission** are the **accelerator, gearshift lever,** and **clutch** (see Figure 7-1).

The **accelerator** controls the flow of fuel to the engine. An increase or decrease in the amount of fuel to the engine determines the rpm at which the engine operates. Not new information? Of course not. But it is important to remember because engine speed and shifting are closely related.

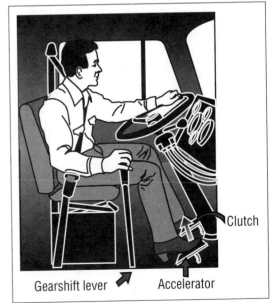

Figure **7-1** Controls used to shift with a manual transmission are the accelerator, gearshift lever, and clutch.

7.3

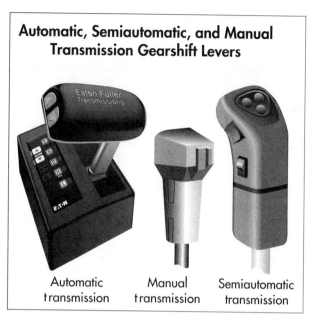

Figure **7-2** Gearshift levers come in a variety of shapes and sizes.

The **gearshift lever** selects a gear and determines how the engine speed is transferred into road speed. For example, at a specific engine speed, placing the transmission in a low gear will provide a lot of power from the engine but does not impact road speed. Why? In a low gear, the power of the engine can be multiplied 10 to 15 times. In a high gear, a high road speed can be attained, but actual available power is reduced.

The clutch connects or disconnects the transmission and engine. It makes shifting gears possible. When the driver pushes down the clutch pedal, the engine is disconnected (disengaged) from the transmission, and the gears may be safely shifted (see Figure 7-2).

If the idea of "engaged" and "disengaged" is hard to understand, think of it as with people. Engaged people are together. If the engagement is broken, they are disengaged, or separated.

COORDINATION OF CONTROLS

Operation of the controls requires coordination and careful timing. We know pushing down the clutch pedal separates the engine from the transmission. We know, too, it is safe to shift gears only when the engine and transmission are separated.

Knowing how to coordinate the clutch pedal and the gearshift lever is a required skill. First depress the clutch, then shift gears.

Lack of coordination of the accelerator and clutch pedal can cause revving of the engine. When this happens, engine speed increases before the transmission is engaged. If there is not enough acceleration when engaging the clutch again, the momentum can push the tractor and damage the drive line components. If you are on a slippery surface, this can cause you to skid or lose control of the rig.

WHEN TO SHIFT

Gears can be shifted either up or down, depending on driving conditions and needs. The following section explains when to upshift and when to downshift.

Figure **7-3** When driving up or down a hill, downshifting one or more gears gives more power to the engine and prevents "lugging," or overstraining, the engine.

Upshifting

A vehicle requires more power to start moving than to keep moving. This may sound like a "no brainer," but it is important to know and remember! Low gears provide a great deal of power but little speed. Thus, select low gear to get the rig in motion. And always select the lowest gear needed to move the vehicle without slipping the clutch or jerking the vehicle.

As the speed increases, shift to a higher gear to gain more speed. The purpose of **upshifting** is to allow the rig to gain speed. Power to the wheels decreases as the speed increases, but less power is needed to maintain speed.

Downshifting

Downshifting is a useful tool for the professional driver. When you are slowing down or going down a hill, downshifting acts as a braking force to slow the vehicle. You can also use downshifting to provide more power to the drive wheels when slowing, driving at a slower speed, or accelerating (see Figure 7-3).

Downshifting too early can result in the vehicle having too much speed for the next lower gear. This can cause the engine to rev beyond its operating range and strain its parts. Downshifting too early may also prevent rapid acceleration if needed.

AIDS TO SHIFTING

The speedometer, tachometer, and governor are all useful or, in some cases, necessary tools for shifting.

Speedometer

While speed ranges vary with the type of transmission, there is a range of road speeds to correspond to every gear. A driver must learn the speed ranges for his or her specific rig and then upshift or downshift as needed.

When the top of a speed range is reached for a given gear, the driver has to up-shift. When the bottom of a speed range is reached for a gear, downshifting is necessary.

Tachometer

The **tachometer** displays the engine speed in revolutions per minute (rpm). Just as there is a road speed range for each gear, there is an rpm range for each gear. Up-shifting and downshifting should be coordinated with rpm ranges the same as it is with road speed ranges (see Figure 7-4).

Governor

The **governor** prevents the engine from revving too much while downshifting. It also reduces the fuel supply to the engine when the maximum rpm is reached. In to-day's electronic engines, this is controlled by a computer chip or module.

Clutch Brake

A clutch has three phases: free play, working, and **clutch brake.**

The clutch brake stops the gears from turning. To engage it, push the clutch pedal all the way to the floor. It prevents the gears from clashing when shifting into

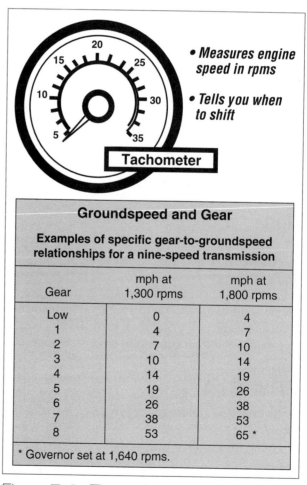

- **Measures engine speed in rpms**
- **Tells you when to shift**

Tachometer

Groundspeed and Gear		
Examples of specific gear-to-groundspeed relationships for a nine-speed transmission		
Gear	mph at 1,300 rpms	mph at 1,800 rpms
Low	0	4
1	4	7
2	7	10
3	10	14
4	14	19
5	19	26
6	26	38
7	38	53
8	53	65 *
* Governor set at 1,640 rpms.		

Figure **7-4** The tachometer indicates engine speed in rpms.

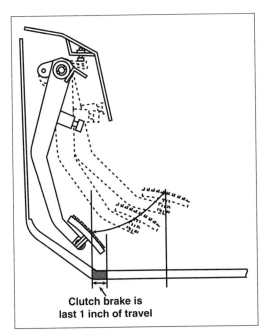

**Clutch brake is
last 1 inch of travel**

Figure **7-5** The clutch brake
stops gears from turning.

low or reverse. **Use the clutch brake only when the vehicle is completely stopped** (see Figure 7-5).

NONSYNCHRONIZED TRANSMISSIONS

Nonsynchronized transmissions are those that require "synchronizing," or bringing to the same speed, the teeth of the driving gear and the driven gear. When this is done properly, there is no grinding or clashing of the gears.

Double-clutching is a skill used by professional drivers to control the engine rpm and to shift gears smoothly. Here are the steps to double-clutching and shifting in the simplest form, beginning with upshifting.

Upshifting

1. Simultaneously take your foot off the accelerator, push the clutch pedal down, and move the gearshift lever to neutral.
2. Release the clutch pedal, engaging the clutch.
3. Allow the engine to reach the rpm required for the next gear. Move the gearshift lever to the next higher gear.
4. Push the clutch down again and move the gearshift lever to the next higher gear at the same time.
5. Simultaneously release the clutch pedal, engaging the clutch and transmission, and accelerate.

Note: The clutch should be pushed down 2 to 3 inches, or just past the free play. It is not necessary to push the clutch all the way to the floor as you would in your personal vehicle.

Downshifting

1. Simultaneously take your foot off the accelerator, push the clutch down, and move the gearshift lever to neutral.
2. Release the clutch.
3. Accelerate enough to match the engine rpm with the road speed. This avoids clashing gears.
4. Push down the clutch and at the same time shift to the next lower gear.
5. Simultaneously release the clutch pedal and accelerate.

Be sure to maintain correct engine speed throughout this procedure.

Synchronizing Skills

Although depressing/engaging the clutch twice on each shift is a big part of handling a nonsynchronized transmission, it is not the main shifting event. The key skill—the one requiring special shifting—is **synchronizing** (bringing to the same speed) the teeth of the mating gears (driving and driven gears). When gears are synchronized, there is no grinding or clashing of the gears.

There are actually three ways to determine engine speed: by reading the tachometer, by listening to the rpm, and by estimating the speed of the rig. It is true: Some drivers think they are using engine rpm to tell them when to shift when, in fact, they are using their sense of the rpm themselves.

A veteran driver in a nonsynchronized transmission rig uses his or her sense of rpm to know when to shift and needs three basic skills to properly shift this type of rig, including the ability to identify engine rpm, knowing the correct rpm the engine should be turning, and the ability to bring the engine to the correct rpm for each task.

How does the driver control the tooth speed of the driving gear?

1. After depressing clutch, shift into neutral.
2. Release the clutch. This allows engine rpm to drop on upshift or speed up on downshift. This also adjusts the tooth speed of next driving gear to the speed rpm of engine

How does the driver know how much to increase or decrease engine speed? First, always read the manufacturer's recommendations. A rule of thumb is that when changing gears, change the rpm by 25 percent, or about 500 rpm, although some transmissions differ from this rule.

Note: As long as shifts are started at the same rpm, synchronizing rpm will be the same for each shift—which makes shifts a matter of timing and coordination.

What about the synchronizing rpm in more complex shifts? Shifts may be started at various rpm, which means that the rpm to synchronize the next gear will also vary. On upgrades, rigs lose speed during shifts, so start to shift a little earlier than you would on flat ground. On downgrades, speed increases.

Note: Any change in vehicle speed occurring during shifting will affect synchronizing rpm. Experience and practice will teach new drivers to deal with each variation.

In addition to upshifting and downshifting, a third shifting skill is required for a nonsynchronized transmission. This is when a vehicle is rolling in neutral and the driver must get the transmission into proper gear. This is usually worked out by either mathematics or a sense or feel of matching the mph with the gear or rpm as necessary. In general, however, there is only one possible gear for each possible mph. Most drivers use their sense of feel, feeling the speed, recalling where the stick should be, and then simply putting the stick in front of that gear position. This process is known by many names, including picking a gear, hunting a gear, finding a gear, and hitting a gear.

How is it done? Here are the steps:

1. Think how the engine should feel at that speed at that gear.
2. With the clutch engaged, throttle up or down.
3. Push the stick lightly against the gear you think is correct (faster 5 higher, slower 5 lower) until it goes in without excessive grinding.

It may drop right into gear, but if it does not, work the throttle and feel how changing the engine rpm changes the stick vibrations:

1. If rpm is too high, the grinding noise will be high pitched.
2. If rpm is too low, the grinding noise will be deep and hollow.
3. When the engine is close to the proper rpm, stick vibrations are larger and farther apart.
4. When the correct rpm is reached, the stick will begin to fall into gear, so disengage the clutch and push the stick into place.
5. Release the clutch and speed up.

Finding the synchronizing rpm under all possible shifting conditions is needed to handle a nonsynchronized transmission.

Some Additional Information about Shifting

● When using the engine to lower the speed of the rig, the range selector should be shifted to the next lower range. If vehicle exceeds maximum speed for next lower gear, use the service brakes to reduce speed.

Key Elements of Shifting

Accelerator: Controls fuel to engine

Clutch: Controls connection between engine and transmission

Gear shift lever: Allows driver to select gears in transmission

- Match engine speed (rpm) to road speed

- Shift smoothly to avoid clashing gears

- Shift by the tachometer
  — Upshift when engine rpms approach top of manufacturer-recommended rpms
  — Avoid overspeeding

  — Downshift when engine speed approaches low range of manufacturer-recommended rpms

  — Avoid lugging

- Variety of rpm/gear shift patterns

- Learn rpm/shift pattern of vehicle you drive

Figure **7-6** Proper shifting is a sign of a skilled driver.

Summary of Shifting Skills

Good shifting technique is a sign of a professional driver (see Figure 7-6). Skills include:

● Good timing and coordination
● Shifting without forcing, raking, or grinding the gears
● Never riding the clutch pedal
● Always using the clutch to shift
● Selecting the proper gear for the best fuel economy
● Anticipating changes in terrain or traffic

A driver needs to know:

● What gear he or she is in at any given time.
● The top mph and rpm for each gear.

- Downshifting at too high a speed causes damage to internal gears.
- Automatic transmissions have a longer "coast down" time than manual transmissions, which means you will need to slow down earlier or use the service brakes until the downshift occurs.
- Always know what gear your transmission is in.
- Know the top mph and maximum/minimum rpm for each gear.
- Become able to anticipate changes in terrain or traffic and know what gear you will need next.

What happens if you shift into too low a gear by mistake? You will know immediately because you will hear the engine running too fast. This can damage the clutch, engine, transmission, or drive shaft, and it can cause you to lose control of the vehicle.

What is **lugging,** and what can happen if it occurs? Lugging occurs when the driver fails to downshift when the engine speed starts to fall below the normal operating range. In this condition, the tractor produces too little power and begins struggling, or lugging. This type of strain can cause engine overheating, damage to the drive train, and stress on most of the rig's systems. It can also shorten the life of all drive train components.

What is **progressive shifting?** Progressive shifting means shifting before you reach the maximum rpm for the gear the rig is in. Progressive shifting allows you to take the most advantage of the engine's power and save fuel at the same time. It is recommended that all drivers learn this technique, which is explained in Figure 7-7.

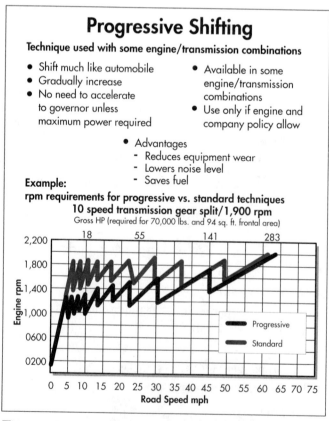

Figure **7-7** Progressive shifting allows the driver to take full advantage of the engine's power.

Note: Newer computer engines are usually set up for progressive shifting. When you accelerate, the engine will "flatten out" at a lower rpm. When you feel this no-power mode, or flattening out, select the next higher gear.

Shifting Procedures

When upshifting, shift when the engine reaches cruising rpm instead of the maximum rpm set by the governor or computer. In power gears, shift at the lowest rpm possible without lugging the engine.

When downshifting, shift as soon as the rpm reaches peak torque (1,300 rpm on most engines—check the operator's manual)

Progressive shifting is advised by many companies because it reduces equipment wear, lowers the noise level, saves fuel, and allows smoother shifts.

SHIFTING PATTERNS AND PROCEDURES

In this section, we look at the shift patterns of common transmissions: *Spicer Pro-Shift Seven Speed, Eaton Fuller Nine Speed, Eaton Fuller Super Ten, Rockwell Ten Speed,* and *Eaton Fuller Thirteen Speed.*

Spicer Pro-Shift Seven Speed

The **Spicer Pro-Shift Seven Speed** is a constant mesh (nonsynchronized) twin-countershaft transmission with a single-range operation.

Shift Pattern

The Spicer Pro-Shift Seven Speed transmission uses a simple no-repeat shift pattern, starting first at the bottom left and working up through the gears to seventh at the bottom right (see Figure 7-8). No range selectors or splitters are needed for any of the shifts.

Shifting Procedures

Upshifting:

- Depress the clutch.
- Move the gear down and the shift lever as far left as possible for first gear.
- To shift to second, double-clutch, move the lever up and slightly to the right.
- Shift up through the next five gears using the normal double clutching and following the standard "H" pattern.

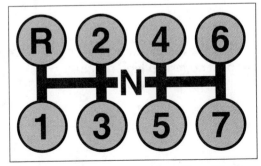

Figure **7-8** The Spicer Pro-Shift Seven Speed shift pattern.

Downshifting:

- Shift from seventh to sixth by double-clutching, moving the lever straight forward, and matching the engine speed to the road speed before shifting.
- Use the same procedure for all further downshifts, following the "H" pattern back down to first.

Eaton Fuller Nine Speed

The **Eaton Fuller Nine Speed** is a constant mesh (nonsynchronized) twin-countershaft transmission with high- and low-range operation.

Shift Pattern

Low range has five forward gears: low through fourth gear. To use high range, lift the range control lever. High range has four more gears (fifth through eighth). The shifting sequence is commonly known as the double-H pattern (see Figure 7-9). When the trailer is empty or lightly loaded, start in first at the top left, then straight back to second, up and right to third, and straight back to fourth. To engage fifth, flip up the range lever and move the lever back to where you started in first. Then you go through the "H" pattern again for the top three gears.

Shifting Procedures

Upshifting:

- Depress the clutch.
- Make sure the range lever is down (low range).
- Move the gear lever to first gear (use low gear only if you are starting from a steep grade with a heavy load).
- Shift up through fourth gear using normal double clutching.
- To shift from fourth to fifth, lift the range control lever up before moving the gear lever.

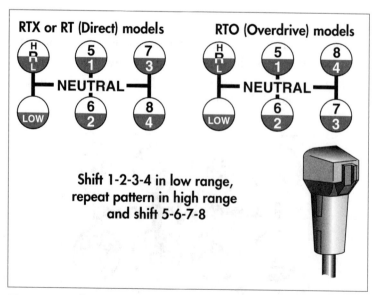

Figure **7-9** The Eaton Fuller Nine-Speed controls and shift pattern.

- As the gear lever passes through neutral, the transmission pneumatically (with air assist) shifts to high range.
- Shift from fifth to eighth using normal double clutching.

Downshifting:

- Shift down from eighth to fifth using normal double clutching and engine and road speed matching.
- To shift down from fifth to fourth, push the range lever down before moving the gear lever.
- As the gear lever passes through neutral, the transmission pneumatically shifts to low range.
- Shift down from fourth to first using normal double clutching and engine and road speed matching.

Eaton Fuller Super Ten

The **Eaton Fuller Super Ten** (Figure 7-10) is a constant mesh (nonsynchronized) twin-countershaft transmission with a low-inertia design and auto-range actuation to make shifting easier. With low-inertia technology, the main shaft is disconnected from the back box during compound shifts. Drivers can preselect all button shifts up and down, helping to speed shifts and reducing misshifts.

Shift Pattern

Unlike other dual range transmissions, the Super Ten does not have a range change lever. Instead, you just have five gear positions that you split, reducing gear lever movements by half. For example, you start in first gear at the bottom left. Then you preselect the next gear with a splitter button. To engage the gear, all you need to do is release the throttle to break torque and then accelerate again when you are in gear. You only need to move the gear lever from second to third, fourth to fifth, sixth to seventh, and eighth to ninth.

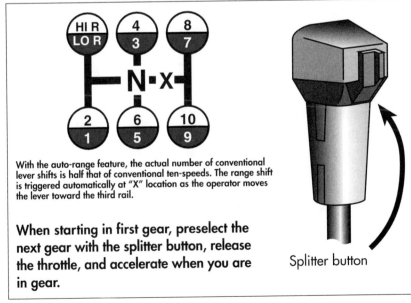

With the auto-range feature, the actual number of conventional lever shifts is half that of conventional ten-speeds. The range shift is triggered automatically at "X" location as the operator moves the lever toward the third rail.

When starting in first gear, preselect the next gear with the splitter button, release the throttle, and accelerate when you are in gear.

Splitter button

Figure **7-10**   Controls and operation of the Eaton Fuller Super Ten.

Shifting Procedures

Upshifting:

● Depress the clutch.
● Move the gear lever to first gear.
● To make a splitter shift (first to second, third to fourth, fifth to sixth, seventh to eighth, or ninth to tenth), move the splitter button forward, take your foot off the throttle, wait a few seconds for the gear to engage, and then accelerate.
● To make a lever shift (second to third, fourth to fifth, sixth to seventh, or eighth to ninth), move the splitter button back, double-clutch, and make a normal shift.

Downshifting:

● To make a splitter shift down (tenth to ninth, eighth to seventh, sixth to fifth, fourth to third, or second to first), simply move the splitter button back and whenever you are ready, release the throttle, wait a few seconds for the gear to engage, and accelerate again.
● To make a lever shift down one gear, move the splitter button forward, double-clutch, match the engine rpm to road speed, and make the shift.

Rockwell Ten Speed

The **Rockwell Ten Speed** is a constant mesh (nonsynchronized) twin-countershaft transmission with high- and low-range operation.

Shift Pattern

Low range has five forward gears: first through fifth gear. To use high range, you lift the range control lever. High range has five more gears—sixth through tenth (see Figure 7-11). You start in first at the bottom left, then up and slightly to the right for second, and through the normal "H" pattern to fifth. To engage sixth, flip up the range lever and move the lever back to the bottom left where you started in first. Then you repeat the "H" pattern again for the top four gears.

Shifting Procedures

Upshifting:

● Depress the clutch.
● Make sure the range lever is down (low range).
● Move the gear lever to first gear at the bottom left.
● Shift up through fifth gear using normal double clutching.
● To shift from fifth to sixth, lift the range control lever up before moving the gear lever.
● As the gear lever passes through neutral, the transmission pneumatically (with air assist) shifts to high range.
● Shift from sixth to tenth using normal double clutching.

Downshifting:

● Shift down from tenth to sixth using normal double clutching and engine and road speed matching.

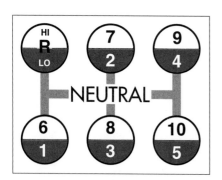

Figure **7-11** The Rockwell Ten Speed shift pattern.

- To shift down from sixth to fifth, push the range lever down before moving the gear lever.
- As the gear lever passes through neutral, the transmission pneumatically shifts to low range.
- Shift down from fifth to first using normal double clutching and engine and road speed matching.

Eaton Fuller Thirteen Speed

The **Eaton Fuller Thirteen Speed** is a constant mesh (nonsynchronized) twin-countershaft transmission with high- and low-range operation as well as a splitter on high-range gears.

Shift Pattern

The transmission has five gears in low range, including a low over low gear. High range has four direct ratios as well as another four overdrive ratios. Overdrive can be engaged in high range with a splitter switch. The shift pattern is the basic double H. You start in first at the top left (see Figure 7-12), then move through the "H" to fourth, flip the range lever up, move to fifth, and repeat the pattern.

Shifting Procedures

Upshifting:

- Depress the clutch.
- Make sure the range lever is down (low range).

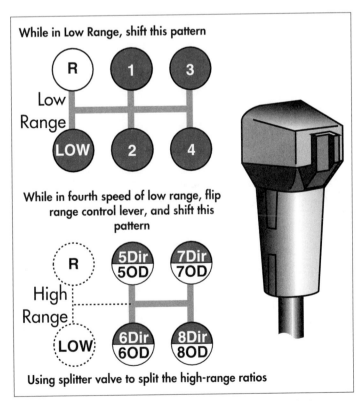

Figure **7-12** Controls and operation of the Eaton Fuller Thirteen Speed.

- Move the gear lever to first gear (use low-low only if you are starting from a steep grade with a heavy load).
- Shift up through fourth gear using normal double clutching.
- To shift from fourth to fifth, lift the range control lever up before moving the gear lever.
- As the gear lever passes through neutral, the transmission pneumatically shifts to high range.
- Shift from fifth through eighth using normal double clutching.
- To split a gear in high range (go from direct to overdrive), flip the splitter switch, release the accelerator, depress and release the clutch, and accelerate again.
- To shift from overdrive to direct drive in the next higher gear, move the gear lever into the next gear and flip the splitter switch just before your foot has come off the clutch.

Downshifting:

- To split down from overdrive to direct in the same gear, flip the splitter switch, release the accelerator, depress and release the clutch, and accelerate again.
- To shift down from direct in one gear to overdrive in the next lower gear, flip the splitter switch to overdrive and make a normal downshift.
- To shift from fifth direct to fourth, push the range lever down, double-clutch, and make a normal downshift.

SHIFTING SEMIAUTOMATIC TRANSMISSIONS

Some newer, **semiautomatic transmissions** use electronic controls to help you shift. They are essentially manual transmissions, with a clutch and a similar-looking gear lever, but some of the gears are automated. In this section, we look at the operation and shift patterns of three types: the Eaton Fuller Top 2, the Spicer AutoMate-2, and the Rockwell Engine Synchro Shift.

Eaton Fuller Top 2

The **Eaton Fuller Top 2** uses the control module of an electronically controlled engine to automatically change the top two gears. It comes in two versions: the Super Ten Top 2 (a 10-speed) and the Super Thirteen Top 2 (a 13-speed). Both are twin-countershaft nonsynchronized transmissions with low-inertia technology that disconnects the back box during compound shifts.

Shift Pattern

The Super Ten Top 2 (see Figure 7-13) has the same shift pattern as the standard Super Ten and the Super Thirteen Top 2 has the same change pattern as the Eaton Fuller Thirteen Speed. With both transmissions, the top gear position is marked A. Once the gear lever is in this position, all upshifts and downshifts between the top two gears are automatic.

Shifting Procedure

- Both transmissions are operated as normal nonsynchronized transmissions in all gears but the top two.
- Automatic mode can only be engaged when the vehicle is traveling over 40 mph.

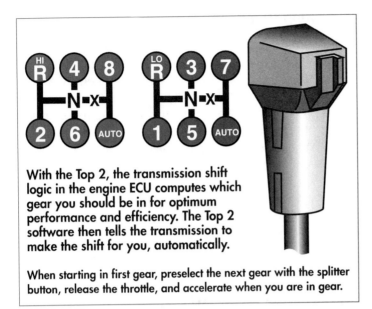

With the Top 2, the transmission shift logic in the engine ECU computes which gear you should be in for optimum performance and efficiency. The Top 2 software then tells the transmission to make the shift for you, automatically.

When starting in first gear, preselect the next gear with the splitter button, release the throttle, and accelerate when you are in gear.

Figure **7-13** Controls and operation of the Eaton Fuller Super Ten Top 2.

- With the Super Ten Top 2, you change normally to eighth, then double-clutch and move into the "A" position.
- With the Super Thirteen Top 2, you shift normally to eleventh, then double-clutch and move into "A".
- While in the "A" position, the engine and transmission work together to change, up or down, when needed. When a shift point is reached, the engine speed automatically changes to match road speed and the change is made— all without driver input.
- You can delay an upshift by applying more throttle or delay a downshift by easing off the throttle.
- With the engine brake on, the electronic controls automatically extend governed engine speed by 200 rpm to help maintain the lower gear on a downgrade.

Spicer AutoMate-2

The **Spicer AutoMate-2** is a 10-speed transmission that uses electronic controls on the transmission to automatically change the top two gears. It is available in direct-drive and overdrive versions.

Shift Pattern

The AutoMate-2 has a familiar 10-speed shifting pattern. First gear is at the bottom left, second is up and to the middle, third straight down, and so on. When you reach fifth, you flip the range lever up and come back to the bottom left, then up and to the middle for seventh, and straight down for eighth. The letter A is where ninth would normally be. Once the lever is moved to that position, the transmission automatically senses road and engine speed and changes up to tenth and back down to ninth when necessary.

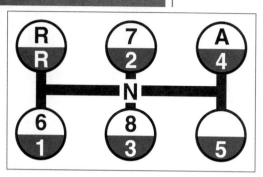

Figure **7-14** The Spicer AutoMate-2 shift pattern.

Shifting Procedure

- The AutoMate-2 is operated as a normal nonsynchronized transmission in the bottom eight gears. You first use the clutch and then change up or down by manually matching the road and engine speeds (see Figure 7-14).

- The truck must be traveling over 38 mph to engage the automatic mode.

- When you reach eighth gear, double-clutch and move to the A mode.

- No driver input is needed to change gears in ninth and tenth. The transmission automatically senses when a change is needed, adjusts the engine speed (no matter where the driver has the throttle), and makes the change.

- Upshifts in the A mode can be delayed by applying more throttle, and downshifts can be delayed by easing off the throttle.

Rockwell Engine Synchro Shift

The **Rockwell Engine Synchro Shift (ESS)** uses engine electronic controls to automatically synchronize the engine speed to road speed during shifts in all gears. The system reads the input and output speeds of the transmission, the neutral position of the gear lever, and the position of a special shift intent switch on the side of the gear knob. The engine controller processes the information and sends a message to the fuel control system to automatically increase or decrease the engine speed to synchronize with the road speed during shifting. In essence, it turns a nonsynchronized box into a synchronized one. The driver has the option of turning the system off and operating the transmission as a fully manual box.

Shift Pattern

ESS is fitted to either the Rockwell Nine Speed or the Rockwell Ten Speed manual transmissions. It allows the driver to move through the standard shifting pattern. Both transmissions are nonsynchronized boxes with range-change shift patterns (see Figure 7-15).

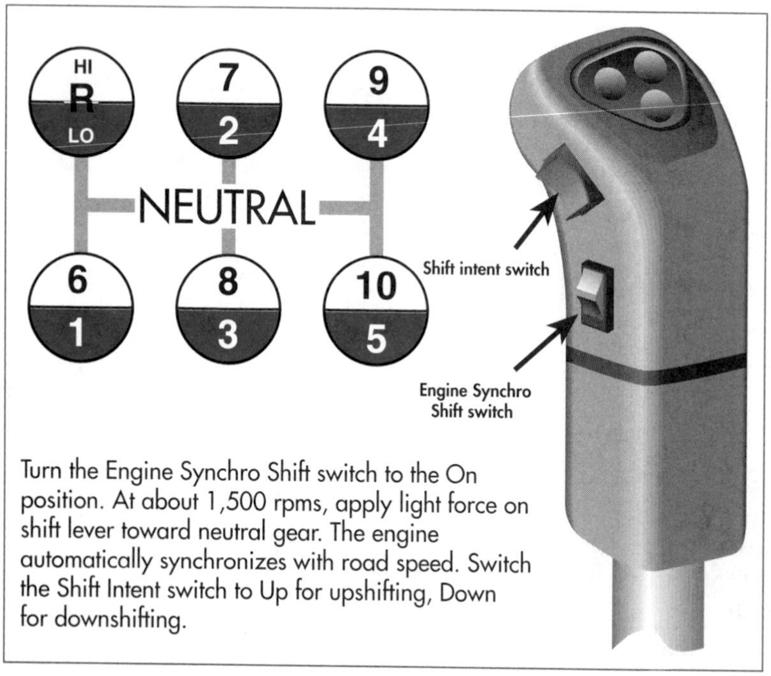

Shifting Procedure

- Starting out, the driver turns the ESS switch on the side of the gear knob to the On position.

- The clutch pedal is depressed, first gear is selected, and the clutch is released. After that, the clutch only needs to be used again when coming to a complete stop.

- To shift up, the driver puts the Shift Intent switch on the side of the gear knob in the up position.

- At the appropriate engine speed (around 1,500 rpm), the driver applies light force on the shift lever toward neutral while in gear. The transmission should allow a shift to neutral.

Turn the Engine Synchro Shift switch to the On position. At about 1,500 rpms, apply light force on shift lever toward neutral gear. The engine automatically synchronizes with road speed. Switch the Shift Intent switch to Up for upshifting, Down for downshifting.

Shift intent switch

Engine Synchro Shift switch

Figure **7-15** Controls and shift patterns for the Rockwell Engine Synchro Shift.

- The engine automatically synchronizes with the road speed and allows the driver to move to the next gear without touching the throttle or the clutch.
- Downshifting is similar, except you put the shift intent switch in the Down position before making the shift. The engine automatically increases its speed to match the road speed for a smooth shift.
- While in the ESS mode, the range control function is automated, so the driver does not have to flip from low to high or high to low.
- Any time the driver uses the clutch while the truck is moving or turns the ESS switch off, the transmission reverts back to fully manual operation, and the driver must use the clutch and throttle to shift gears.

SHIFTING FULLY AUTOMATIC TRANSMISSIONS

Fully **automatic transmissions** use a torque converter instead of a clutch to transfer power. These converters provide a fluid coupling instead of the hard frictional coupling a clutch provides. Newer transmissions may also have lockup functions that lock the converter mechanically when the transmission is in top gear. This provides a more solid coupling and helps improve fuel mileage.

Many automatic transmissions use a lever to change gears (see Figure 7-16), but some newer models with electronic controls use buttons instead. To select a gear position on these models, simply push a button instead of moving a lever.

Range Selector Positions

Neutral (N)

Neutral is used for starting, standing, and parking the vehicle. The parking brake should be set when the vehicle is standing or parked. Never coast in neutral because transmission damage and loss of control of the rig can result.

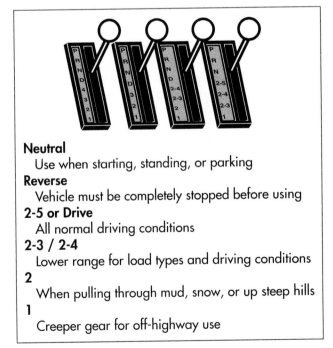

Neutral
Use when starting, standing, or parking
Reverse
Vehicle must be completely stopped before using
2-5 or Drive
All normal driving conditions
2-3 / 2-4
Lower range for load types and driving conditions
2
When pulling through mud, snow, or up steep hills
1
Creeper gear for off-highway use

Figure **7-16** Controls and shift procedures for a fully automatic transmission.

Reverse (R)

Reverse is used to back the rig. There is one gear in the reverse range. The vehicle must be stopped (no movement) before shifting into reverse. A reverse warning signal sounds when the gear is placed in reverse.

2-5 or Drive

This position is used for all normal driving conditions. It starts in second and shifts up to third, fourth, and fifth as you accelerate. Downshifting is automatic as your speed slows.

2-3/2-4 Lower Range

Some road, cargo, or traffic conditions make it desirable to restrict automatic shifting to the lower range. Low ranges provide greater engine braking. When the need for this range is over, shift back to high range (Drive or 2-5).

2/Low Gear

This gear is used for pulling through mud and snow or driving up a steep grade. It provides the most engine braking power. The lower ranges (2-3/2-4) will not upshift above the highest gear selected unless the engine governor speed for that gear is exceeded.

1/Creeper Gear

For off-highway use. Provides the greatest traction. You should never make a full power shift from creeper gear to a higher range.

Upshifting and Downshifting with an Automatic Transmission

Upshifting using the accelerator:

- The pressure of the foot on the accelerator pedal influences automatic shifting.
- When the accelerator is fully depressed, the transmission automatically shifts up to the recommended speed of the engine.
- When partly depressed, upshifts occur sooner at a lesser engine speed.
- Either method provides the accurate shift spacing and control needed for maximum performance.

Downshifting:

- Occurs automatically.
- The transmission prevents downshifting when the engine speed is too high.

Chapter Eight
Backing

Backing Principles and Rules

Basic Backing Maneuvers

OBJECTIVES

When you have completed this chapter, you should be able to:

- Describe procedures for backing and parking

- Prepare for backing maneuvers

- Explain the principles of reverse steering when backing an articulated vehicle

- Avoid the hazards of backing

- Understand the importance of using a helper during backing maneuvers

- Explain why drivers should avoid unnecessary backing and blind-side backing

KEY TERMS

Alley dock
Maneuver
Parallel parking

Pivot point
Straight-line backing

INTRODUCTION

Backing a 48-foot (or longer) trailer into position without any problems is a satisfying accomplishment. It also is a skill you must develop if you drive a rig.

BACKING PRINCIPLES AND RULES

There are, however, principles and rules you should know before you get into the cab and try to back a vehicle on your own. This chapter contains some of the information you need to know. Studying it will help you master this very necessary skill.

Steering Principles

Proper backing is important for safe and efficient operation of a tractor-trailer. Unless enough time and attention are devoted to mastering this skill, maneuvering the rig can be very difficult.

Most people feel comfortable backing a car. A car has two axles. In most cars, the front axle is used for steering, and the rear axle has fixed wheels that cannot steer. They simply follow the direction the car is headed.

The techniques involved in backing a tractor-trailer are much different. Backing is more complicated because the rig is made up of two units. The tractor steers both vehicles. The trailer, with its fixed wheels, depends on the tractor for direction. In other words, the tractor steers the trailer (see Figure 8-1).

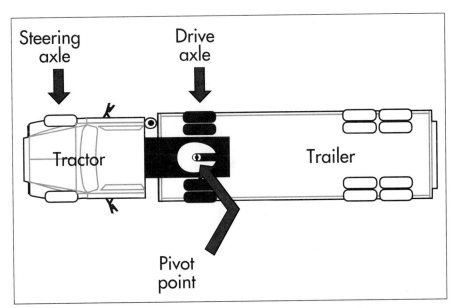

Figure **8-1** To learn backing techniques, new drivers should first be familiar with the parts of their rig involved in backing.

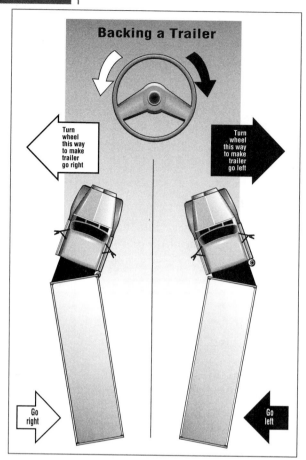

Figure **8-2** When the tractor moves in one direction when backing, the trailer moves in the opposite direction.

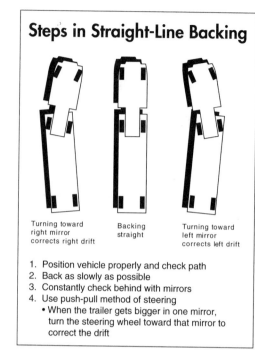

Figure **8-3** Backing in a straight line is the easiest of all backing maneuvers.

The rear tractor axle becomes the trailer's steering axle. In backing, when the tractor moves in one direction, the front of the trailer moves in the same direction. This forces the rear of the trailer in the opposite direction. When you turn the steering wheel to the right, the rear of the trailer goes to the left. When you turn the steering wheel to the left, the rear of the trailer goes to the right (see Figure 8-2).

Straight-line backing is the easiest backing **maneuver** to perform with a tractor-trailer and is also the basis of all other backing maneuvers. The point where the trailer is connected to the tractor becomes the pivot point for the vehicle (see Figure 8-3).

A **pivot point** (or point of articulation) is extremely sensitive to movement (refer again to Figure 8-1). For example, if the tractor and trailer are exactly aligned and you hold the steering wheel so the wheels are pointing straight ahead and parallel to the sides of the rig when you begin to move back, the whole unit will rarely, if ever, move in a straight line. Usually, the trailer will start to drift left or right as soon as you start backing.

The key to backing your rig in a straight line is to recognize what direction the trailer is drifting and make the necessary adjustments immediately. You must use *both* outside rearview mirrors to guide you in making these steering adjustments.

Before backing, make sure your mirrors are properly adjusted. Get out and look (GOAL) to avoid an accident. Once you release the clutch and begin backing, try rolling at a continuous, slow, safe speed until you complete the maneuver or need to reposition.

When the trailer is directly behind you, aligned and straight, the picture you see in both mirrors will be the same (see Figure 8-4). When the trailer starts to drift, the pictures will begin to change. If the trailer starts drifting to the right, you will start seeing more of the trailer in your right mirror and less of the trailer in your left mirror.

To correct the drift, turn the top of the steering wheel toward the drift. In this case, turn the steering wheel to the right. It takes very little movement of the steering wheel to correct a drift if you adjust early. Do not oversteer and overcorrect.

When the trailer begins to respond to the correction, begin turning the wheel in the opposite direction to remove the initial corrrection. Depending on the length of the trailer, it takes 8 to 12 feet for the trailer to respond. Shorter trailers react faster than longer trailers.

The key is to be patient. Think your moves through carefully. If you find the trailer has gone too far out of line, pull forward and position the rig for another try.

General Rules for Backing Safely

Because you cannot see directly behind your vehicle, backing is always dangerous. Common sense dictates that you avoid backing whenever possible. For example, when you park the rig, try to park so you will be able to pull forward when you leave.

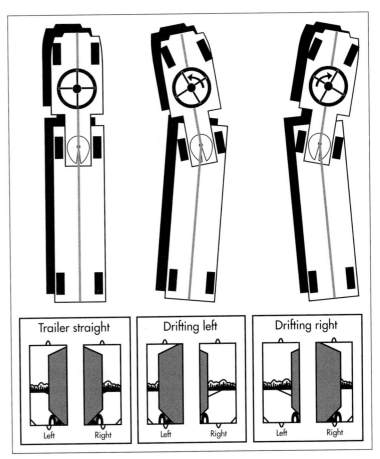

Figure **8-4** Use your mirrors to watch for and correct trailer drift when backing.

Even though you can reduce the need to back by planning ahead, almost everyone who drives a tractor-trailer will have to back it at times. When you do have to back, there are a few simple rules that will help you do it safely:

- Inspect your intended path
- Use a helper to signal your path.
- Back and turn toward the driver's side whenever possible.
- Use your four-way flashers and horn during the backing maneuver.
- Always watch your mirrors.

Inspect Your Intended Path

Whether you will be backing in a straight line or backing and turning, inspect the line of travel you intend to take before you begin. Get out and walk around the

Figure **8-5** Whenever possible, use a helper when backing.

vehicle. Check the clearance of the path your vehicle will make. Make sure the road, parking, or docking areas will be able to support your vehicle. Look for low clearances, such as wires and roof overhangs. Check for debris in your path, other parked vehicles, or any potential hazards that may be moving into your path, such as, fork trucks, people, and yard jockeys. Is your path sloped down to the dock? Is it into an enclosed area? Get a mental picture before you start backing.

Use a Helper

Use a helper when you have to back (see Figure 8-5). You cannot see behind the vehicle, and there are blind spots in the mirrors. A helper is always needed for blind-side backing. The helper should stand near the back and to the side of the vehicle so that the driver has a clear view of the helper's directions and the helper will not accidentally be run over by the truck.

Hearing a helper's spoken directions is sometimes difficult. Before you begin backing, work out a set of hand signals that you both understand. Agree on signals for directions such as "turn," "more turn," "less turn," "back," "clearance," "forward," and "stop." Remember, even though a helper is used, the driver is always responsible for any problems.

Back and Turn toward the Driver's Side

When you have to back and turn, try to back toward the driver's side of the vehicle. You will have a better view of what you are doing. You will also avoid the dangers of backing to your blind side.

If you back toward the driver's side, you can watch the rear of the vehicle by looking out the side window and by using your left mirror. In a tractor with a box trailer, you can see only the side of the trailer in the right mirror during blind-side backing. Do not become focused on one mirror. Always use both mirrors and scan back and forth several times while backing.

Avoid backing into the street if possible. Back into an alley instead so that you can drive out forward. If you must back into the street, driver-side backing lets you block off the whole street and protect other drivers who might otherwise try to pull around you before you get into position. Do *not* drive into an alley. Backing into it is safer. Whenever possible, get someone to watch your blindside. Other vehicles and people may try to get around you.

When you know that you will have to back, plan ahead so you can use driver-side backing. This may mean going around the block to put your vehicle in the correct position. The added safety and ease of operation, however, is worth the extra time and effort.

Use Your Four-Way Flashers and Horn

When you have inspected your intended backing path, get back into your cab and turn on your four-way flashers. If your truck is not equipped with a backup alarm, blow your air horn two or three times and then start backing. Check both mirrors and the front of the tractor constantly.

General Backing Rules

The four general rules for backing your vehicle are:

- Start in the proper position.
- Back slowly.
- Constantly check behind your vehicle.
- Start over when necessary.

Start in the Proper Position

The most important maneuver in backing is starting with the proper setup (Figure 8–6). The instructor will illustrate this in the classroom and demonstrate it on the backing range.

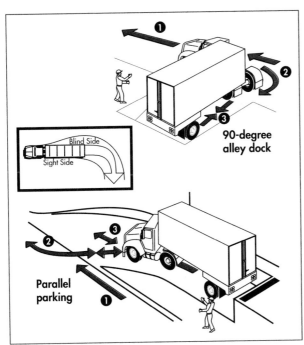

Figure **8-6** Examples of backing maneuvers. 1, set up; 2, back in, pullout; 3, straighten and adjust.

You must position your rig before beginning to back. Reach the right position by moving forward. When you think the vehicle is in the right spot, stop and secure it. Get out and check your position from front, rear and both sides. Try to limit the distance of the pull-up. The farther you pull up, the farther you must back up.

Back Slowly

Use the lowest reverse gear and back slowly. Be patient. If possible, stay off the accelerator and avoid riding the clutch.

Constantly Check behind the Vehicle

Backing a tractor-trailer is done with mirrors. You should know what the trailer looks like in the mirrors at all times. Use both mirrors and do not become focused on one mirror and use minimal steering correction. It takes 8 to 12 feet for the tractor to react to the driver's direction. Be patient. Go slowly.

Start Over When Necessary

If the trailer gets out of position, pull forward and start over. It is better to pull forward and try again instead of continuing to back from the wrong position.

BASIC BACKING MANEUVERS

Following are some basic backing maneuvers professional drivers need to know:

- Straight-line backing
- Alley dock
- Parallel parking

Straight-Line Backing

The key to backing a tractor-trailer in a straight line is to recognize which way the trailer is drifting and make adjustments to correct it immediately. Be sure the tractor is directly in front of the trailer before starting to back. Back slowly in the lowest possible gear. Visualize a straight line as the trailer's path.

Alley Dock

1. Pull forward, in a straight line, near the parking space. You should be about 3 to 5 feet out from other parked vehicles. When the front of the trailer is in line with the left side of the parking space, turn hard to the right (see Figure 8-7).
2. While continuing to move forward at a speed of about 3 to 5 miles an hour, when the tractor is at the 12 o'clock position, straight away from the parking space, turn to the left.
3. Keep moving this foward position until the trailer is near a 45-degree angle. When the tractor is at a slight angle to the left of the trailer and the parking space can be seen from the driver's window, straighten the steering tires and stop.
4. Set your brakes and get out of the cab. Your tractor tandem should be about 12 to 15 feet in front of the left side of the parking space. Be sure the steer-

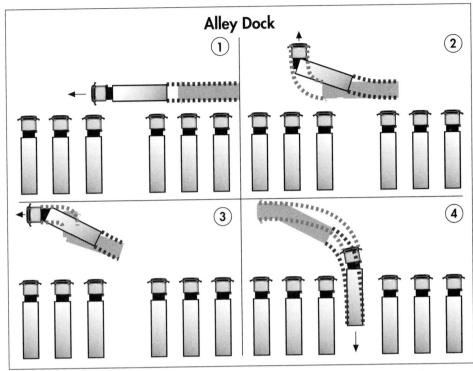

Figure **8-7** When alley docking a rig, turn hard to the right when the front of the trailer is in line with the left side of the parking space.

ing tires are straight. Get back in the cab and start backing. Straighten out the rig as you enter the space and watch the direction of the rear tandem. Correct drift as needed. Check for drift by using side mirrors.

Note: Check *both* mirrors for room on each side. Do not rely on just one mirror.

Straight-Line Parking

1. Pull forward in a straight line near the parking space. You should be about 3 to 5 feet out from the parked vehicles. Stop when your line of sight is in the middle of the parking space. Look out your right window for a reference point that is within a line of sight and even with the middle of the parking space (see Figure 8-8).
2. Continue moving forward. When the front of the trailer is in line with the left side of the parking space, turn hard to the right. Keep turning to the right until the tractor is headed toward the 2 o'clock position. Turn the steering tires straight.
3. Keep moving forward. When you see the right side of the parking space in your right convex mirror, turn back to the reference point.
4. Straighten the steering tires and pull forward until the rig is in front of the parking space. Set your brakes and get out of the cab. Be sure the trailer is directly behind the tractor. The rig should be directly in front of the parking space. Get back in the cab and start backing.

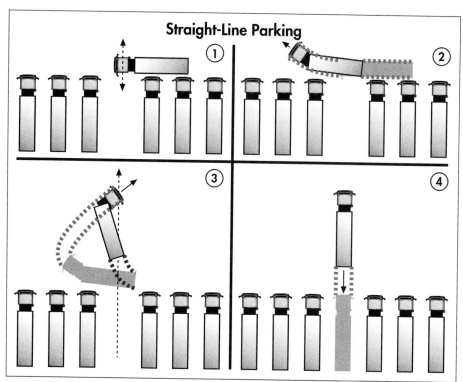

Figure **8-8** Before beginning a straight-line parking maneuver, pull the rig forward about 3 to 5 feet from other parked vehicles.

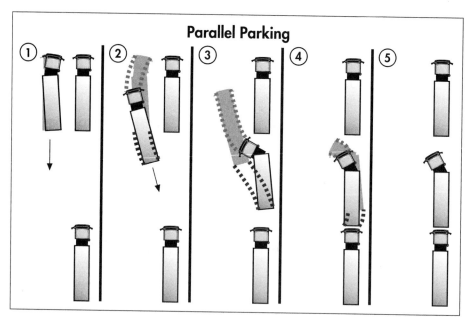

Figure **8-9** When parallel parking, pull the rig 2 to 3 feet from other parked vehicles.

Parallel Parking

1. You should be about 2 to 3 feet out from the other parked vehicles. Pull forward, in a straight line, near the parking space. Stop when the rear tandem axles of the trailer are about 8 feet in front of the parking space (see Figure 8-9).

2. Set your brakes and get out of the cab. Be sure your rig is in a straight line 2 to 3 feet away from other parked vehicles. Check to be sure the rear tandem axles of the rig are 8 feet in front of the parking space.

3. Get back in the cab and start backing with the steering wheel turned to the left. The angle between the left side of the tractor is about 12 to 15 degrees away from the front of the trailer.

4. Turn hard to the right and continue backing until the tractor and the trailer are in a straight line. The middle of the rig should be in the parking space (see position #2 in Figure 8-9). Continue backing until the front of the trailer is even with the front of the parking space (see position #3 in Figure 8-9).

5. Turn hard to the right and continue backing until the trailer is parallel inside the parking space. The tractor should be at an 85- to 90-degree angle to the left. Leave the tractor in this position. This will make it easier for you to exit the space.

Chapter Nine
Coupling and Uncoupling

Step-by-Step Coupling
Procedures

Step-by-Step Uncoupling
Procedures

FROM NOW ON. . .

ONLY THE BEST
WILL DRIVE!

OBJECTIVES

When you have completed this chapter, you should be able to:

- Demonstrate the correct way to couple a tractor with a trailer

- Demonstrate the proper way to uncouple a rig

- Describe the controls used when coupling or uncoupling

- Explain the hazards of coupling and uncoupling improperly

9.2

KEY TERMS

Chock
Coupling
Fifth wheel
Glad hand
Kingpin
Kingpin setting

Landing gear
Retention groove
Tractor
Trailer
Trailer air supply valve
Uncoupling

INTRODUCTION

A **tractor** and **trailer** are two separate units until they are brought together and joined, or coupled. It is the driver's responsibility to couple the tractor and trailer correctly for any trip. This chapter discusses how to couple and uncouple a rig safely in a step-by-step sequence.

Coupling is a basic skill to be mastered by the professional driver operating any tractor-trailer rig. FMCSR require all drivers to be qualified in this operation.

The best way to learn coupling is by using a 15-step approach that protects you and others from injury and your vehicle and cargo from damage. Trying to couple or uncouple a rig without knowing this sequence can be dangerous.

Typical hazards in coupling or **uncoupling** a rig include the following (see also Figure 9-1):

- When the tractor is not secured, brake lines can be damaged.
- When trailer brakes are not functioning, the trailer can be pushed into an obstruction.
- When the ground is not firm for uncoupling, the trailer can fall and become damaged.
- When trailer wheels are not chocked, the trailer may roll or be pushed into an obstruction and damaged.
- When climbing on the tractor during coupling, the driver could fall because of slippery surfaces.
- If the driver works under an unsupported trailer (no jackstand or tractor under the trailer's nose), he or she could be injured if the landing gear collapses and the trailer drops to the ground.
- The kingpin may be too shallow, or the tractor may be too long. Damage may result to the tractor, trailer, or landing gear.

Coupling and Uncoupling Hazards

Vehicle

Hazard	Result
• Tractor not secured	• Damage to brake lines
• Trailer brakes not functioning	• Trailer pushed into obstruction
• Jaws not securely fastened	• Trailer breaks loose on the road
• Ground not firm for uncoupling	• Trailer falls and is damaged
• Trailer wheels not chocked	• Is pushed or rolls into obstruction

Driver

Hazard	Result
• Climbing on tractor	• Falls from slippery surface
• Working under unsupported trailer (no jackstand or tractor under trailer nose)	• Injury when landing gear collapses and trailer drops to the ground

Figure **9-1** Coupling or uncoupling a rig without the proper skills can be dangerous.

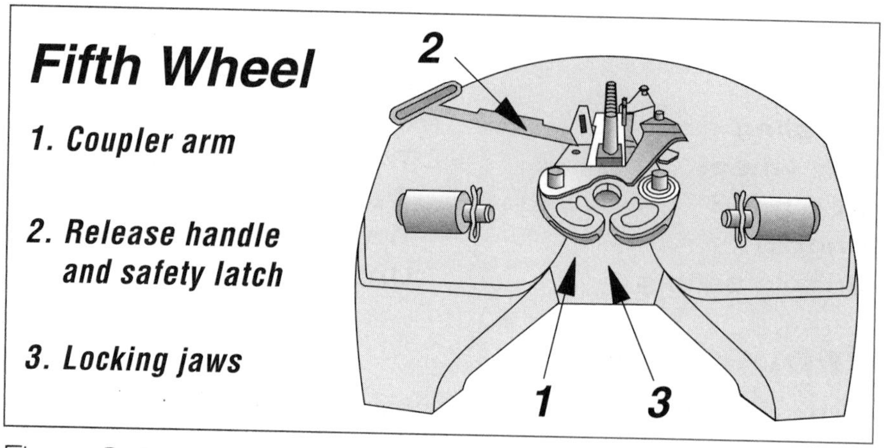

Fifth Wheel

1. **Coupler arm**

2. **Release handle and safety latch**

3. **Locking jaws**

Figure **9-2** Major parts of the fifth wheel.

STEP-BY-STEP COUPLING PROCEDURES

Step 1: Inspect the Fifth Wheel

When inspecting the **fifth wheel** (see Figure 9-2), you should check for damaged or missing parts as well as the mounting of the fifth wheel on the tractor to be certain it is secure and not damaged.

The fifth wheel must always have a coating of grease applied to the **retention groove** (see Figure 9-3) to ensure smooth movement when the trailer is being turned.

Also check:

- The fifth wheel is in position for coupling and tilted down toward the rear of the tractor.
- The jaws are open.
- The safety release handle is in the automatic lock position.
- The slider locks are in place.
- The fifth wheel position will allow coupling without allowing the rear end of the tractor to strike the landing gear.

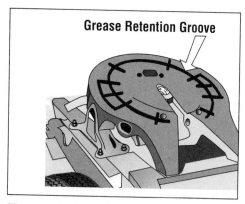

Grease Retention Groove

Figure **9-3** The fifth wheel must always have a coating of grease in the retention groove to ensure smooth movement.

Step 2: Inspect the Area and Chock the Trailer Wheels

Be sure the area is clear. Then **chock** the trailer wheels. Check the cargo to be sure it will not move when the trailer is coupled to the tractor.

Step 3: Position the Tractor

The tractor should be placed squarely in front of the trailer. Do not back the tractor at an angle. The wrong approach by the tractor can push the trailer backward or sideways. This can break the **landing gear** and cause the trailer to fall (see Figure 9-4).

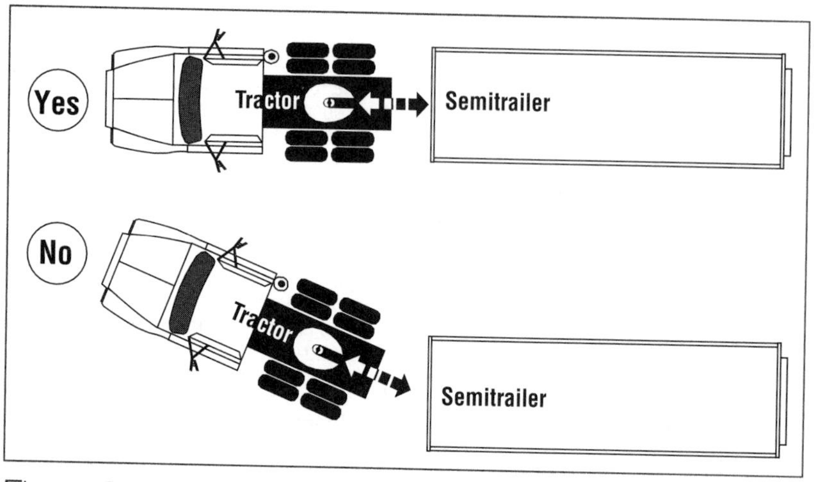

Yes Tractor Semitrailer

No Tractor Semitrailer

Figure **9-4** The tractor should be placed squarely in front of the trailer for coupling—not at an angle.

Figure **9-5** Proper positioning of the tractor
and trailer to begin coupling.

To be sure the tractor and trailer line up properly, use the outside edge of your
drive axle tires and the edge of the trailer as guide points. The tractor, outside edge
of the drive axle tires, and edge of the trailer should form a straight line if the trailer
is 96 inches (8 feet) wide. With many of today's trailers being 102 inches (8-1/2
feet) wide, the tractor drive axle tires should be approximately 1-1/2 to 3 inches inside the outside edge of the trailer (see Figure 9-5).

Note: Pulling up directly in front of the trailer for coupling is the preferred
method, but in some situations you may have to back in at an angle to the trailer. Do
not hesitate to exit the cab as many times as necessary to site the throat of the fifth
wheel with the kingpin.

Step 4: Back Slowly until the Fifth Wheel Just Touches the Trailer

Back slowly toward the nose of
the trailer and stop just before
the fifth wheel reaches the
trailer. You should be close
enough to hook up the air lines
and to compare the fifth-wheel
height with the trailer height.

Step 5: Secure the Tractor

Shift into neutral. Put on the tractor parking brake. Exit the cab.

C A U T I O N :

*If you are unfamiliar with the
truck and trailer, stop and exit
the truck to check the
distance from the trailer (see
Figure 9-6).*

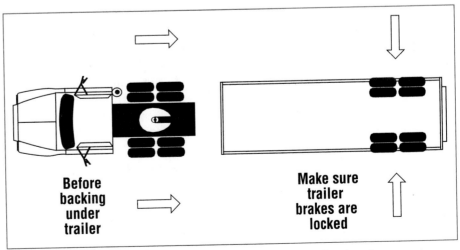

Figure **9-6** Always check to make sure trailer brakes are
locked before attempting the coupling procedure.

Figure **9-7** Inspect the height of the trailer nose compared to the fifth wheel. The nose should be slightly higher than the back of the fifth wheel.

Figure **9-8** Adjust the height of the trailer.

Step 6: Check the Trailer Height

Inspect the height of the trailer nose compared to the fifth wheel. The nose should be slightly higher than the back of the fifth wheel. To couple properly, the nose of the trailer should touch the middle of the fifth wheel (see Figure 9-7).

To adjust the height of the trailer, crank the landing gear up or down. If the tractor has an adjustable air suspension, you can adjust the fifth wheel to the correct height to couple with the trailer. If the trailer is too low, the tractor may hit and damage it. If the trailer is too high, it may ride up and over the fifth wheel and into the rear of the cab (see Figure 9-8).

Step 7: Connect the Air Lines (If the Trailer is Not Equipped with Spring Brakes)

When the height of the trailer is correct, you are ready to connect the tractor's air lines to the trailer. There are two air lines running from the tractor to the trailer. They are called the Service and Emergency air lines. Normally, one will be stamped "Service" and the other "Emergency." **Glad hands** connect the air lines (see Figure 9-9).

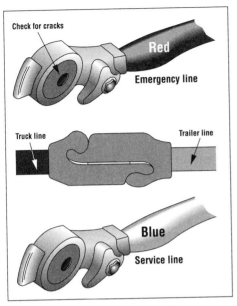

Figure **9-9** Connect the
service and emergency air
lines.

Figure **9-10** After the air lines are
connected, get back into the cab
and push in the red trailer air supply
valve to supply air to the trailer
brakes.

Sometimes the air lines are coded differently. They may be color coded (red for emergency and blue or black for service) or shape coded (round glad hands for the emergency air line and square glad hands for the service air line).

For the brakes to work properly, the air lines must be connected correctly. Match the plug to the connector. Do not force it if it does not fit. Sometimes the tractor's connectors and the trailer's connectors do not match. Use a converter if necessary. Firmly seat the plug in the receptacle. Put on the safety catch, or latch, to keep them from accidentally separating.

Step 8: Supply Air to the Trailer

After the air lines have been connected and secured (see Figure 9-10), get back into the cab. With the truck engine off, push in the red **trailer air supply valve** to supply the trailer brakes with air. Listen for escaping air. If you hear a leak or if the air pressure gauge registers excessive loss of air, correct the problem. You will notice air leaking if you have connected the air lines incorrectly.

Step 9: Release the Tractor Parking Brake and Put on the Trailer Brake

You are now ready to back the tractor under the trailer:

- Start the truck engine.
- Put truck into gear.
- Release the tractor parking brake (yellow valve).
- If the trailer is not equipped with spring brakes, pull out the trailer air supply valve (red) to apply the trailer brakes.

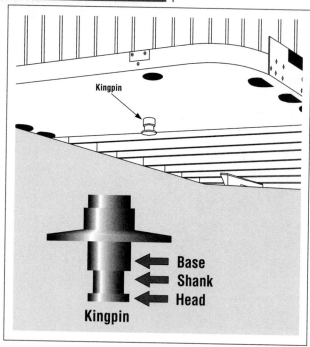

Figure **9-11** Parts of the kingpin. Note that the kingpin can be set at different lengths.

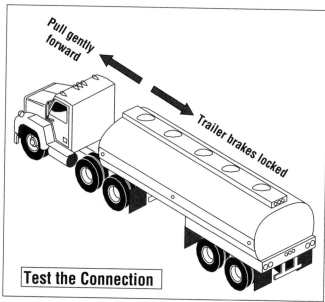

Figure **9-12** Test the hookup by gently pulling the tractor forward in low gear while the trailer hand brake is on.

Step 10: Back Under the Trailer

Using the lowest reverse gear, back the tractor slowly under the trailer. Stop when you feel or hear the **kingpin** lock into the fifth wheel (see Figure 9-11).

Do not hit the kingpin too hard. This could bend the kingpin, buckle the upper plate, jump the pin (the kingpin over the fifth wheel causes the trailer to hit the tractor), push the trailer away, or damage cargo in the trailer.

Step 11: Test the Connection

Test the hookup by pulling the tractor gently forward in low gear while the trailer hand brake is on (see Figure 9-12). As soon as resistance to forward motion is felt, disengage the clutch. Accelerate just enough to keep the engine from stalling. Then test the connection again.

Step 12: Secure the Vehicle

When you are sure of a solid hookup, apply the parking brake. Turn off the engine, put key in pocket, and get out of the cab.

Step 13: Inspect the Coupling

You will now need to go under the trailer and use a flashlight to get a good look at the coupling. Check that the following are done:

- Fifth-wheel jaws have engaged the shank of the kingpin and not the head. If the jaws are closed around the head, the trailer will bounce the kingpin out of the jaws.

- Jaws are closed and locked (see Figure 9-13). The safety catch is over the locking lever.
- Upper fifth-wheel plate is in full contact with the lower trailer plate. There should be no gap between the trailer apron and the fifth-wheel plate. If there is a space between the two, stop and fix the problem before doing anything else. The space may be due to uneven ground surface. Move the rig to flat ground and check again.

Step 14: Connect the Electrical Cord, Then Check the Air Lines

Plug the electrical cord into the trailer. Then fasten the safety catch. Be sure neither the electrical cord nor the air lines are damaged. These lines must not hit any moving parts of the rig.

Step 15: Raise the Landing Gear

You are now ready to raise the landing gear (see Figure 9-14). Most crank handles have a low speed and a high speed. Use the low speed to start raising the landing gear. Switch to high speed when the trailer weight is off the landing gear. Keep on cranking until the landing gear is fully raised.

STEP-BY-STEP UNCOUPLING PROCEDURES

Step 1: Position the Vehicle

To prepare for uncoupling, place the tractor directly in line with the trailer on level ground. This is to keep from damaging the landing gear when pulling the tractor from under the trailer.

Make sure the surface where you plan to uncouple the trailer will support the rig and is level.

Figure **9-13** After chocking one set of tractor and trailer wheels and removing the key from the ignition, check the coupling.

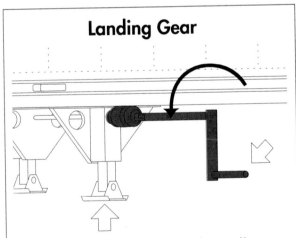

Landing Gear

- Check clearance between rear of tractor frame and/or mudflaps and landing gear.
- Use low range to begin raising landing gear.
- Once free of weight, switch to high gear.
- Crank until fully raised.
- Safely secure crank in holder in low gear.
- Check clearance between top of tractor drive wheels and nose of trailer.

Figure **9-14** Raise the landing gear.

WARNING!

Never drive your rig with the landing gear partly raised. It can catch on railroad tracks, dips in the road, and so on. Make sure the crank handle is safely secured to prevent damage to other vehicles or injury to pedestrians. Remove the wheel chocks and store them.

Note: Blacktop will soften in hot weather, making the surface unstable.

Step 2: Secure the Vehicle

Place the tractor protection valve in the emergency position. This cuts off the air supply between the tractor and trailer. Make sure you have backed tightly against the pin. If not, it will bind and not release properly. Put on the tractor parking brake. Exit the cab.

Step 3: Lower the Landing Gear

Inspect landing gear for rust and damage. Then lower the landing gear until both supports touch the ground. If one touches the ground but not the other, find a more level location to drop the trailer. Crank until you see the trailer begin to rise off the fifth wheel.

Step 4: Disconnect and Store the Air Lines and Electrical Cable

Carefully disconnect the air lines and electrical cable. Place the air line glad hands on the dummy couplers behind the cab. Hang the electrical cable down to avoid moisture on the plug and store in its holder. Secure the lines against snagging, cuts, scrapes, or other damage.

Step 5: Release the Fifth-Wheel Latch

To release the fifth wheel, raise the release handle lock pin and pull to the open position. On a single axle tractor, this is usually not hard. On tandem axle tractors, however, the release handle is sometimes hard to reach. If it is hard to reach, use a pull handle or hook.

Step 6: Lower the Air Bags

If your truck has air suspension, lower the air bags to prevent the end of the tractor from popping up when later pulling clear.

Step 7: Pull the Tractor Partly Clear of the Trailer

Get back in the cab and release the parking brake, leaving the tractor protection valve in the set position. Pull the tractor forward until the fifth wheel begins to clear the trailer apron plate. Stop the tractor while its frame is still under the trailer. This will keep the trailer from falling if the landing gear collapses or sinks.

Step 8: Secure the Tractor

Put on the tractor parking brakes. Exit the cab.

Step 9: Inspect the Trailer Supports

Be sure the landing gear is supporting the trailer and is not damaged.

Step 10: Pull the Tractor Clear of the Trailer

Release the parking brake. Check the area ahead of the tractor and pull the tractor slowly away from the trailer. Uncoupling is now safely completed.

Step 11: Reinflate the Air Suspension System

After pulling the tractor away from the trailer, reinflate the air bags.

Note: Use the following memory aid (LAPP) to help you remember how to start the uncoupling procedure:

L—Lower **l**anding gear

A—**A**irlines and electrical lines disconnected

P—**P**ull and release arm or release **p**in

PROCEDURAL STEPS AND CHECKLISTS

The following lists are included to give you a handy reference.

Coupling Procedures Checklist

1. Inspect the fifth wheel
   - Check for damage, missing parts, and proper lubrication.
   - Check mounting.
     - _____ Is it tilted down toward the rear of the tractor?
     - _____ Are the jaws open?
     - _____ Is the safety release handle in the automatic lock position?
     - _____ Check the position of the slider.
     - _____ Check the **kingpin setting.**
2. Inspect the area and chock the wheels
   - Be sure the area is clear.
   - Chock the trailer wheels to keep the rig from rolling.
   - Check the cargo. Be sure it will not move when the trailer is coupled to the tractor.
3. Position the tractor
   - Place the tractor squarely in front of the trailer, not at an angle.
   - Use the outside edge of the drive axle tires and the edge of the trailer as reference points.
   - Check the alignment by looking down the side of the trailer. The tractor, outside edge of the drive axles, and the edge of the trailer should form a straight line.
   - Make a final check with both mirrors to be sure the tractor and trailer are aligned.
4. Back slowly
   - Stop when the lower plate of the fifth wheel just touches the trailer.
   - Back slowly. Do not jar the trailer.

5. Secure the tractor
   - Apply the tractor parking brake.
   - Climb out of the cab.
6. Check the trailer height
   - Inspect the height of the trailer nose in relation to the fifth wheel.
   - The nose of the trailer should be slightly higher than the midpoint of the fifth wheel.
   - For proper coupling, the nose of the trailer should touch the middle of the fifth wheel.
7. Connect the air lines
   - Connect the service air line from the tractor to the service glad hand on the left side of the trailer.
   - Connect the emergency air line from the tractor to the emergency glad hand on the right side of the trailer.
8. Supply air to the trailer
   - With the truck engine off, push in the red trailer supply valve
   - Check the system for signs of excessive air loss.
9. Release the tractor parking brake and apply the trailer brake
   - Release the parking brake, allowing the tractor to move.
   - Put on the trailer brake to hold the trailer in place.
10. Back under the trailer
    - Use the lowest reverse gear to back the tractor slowly under the trailer.
    - Stop when you feel or hear the kingpin lock into the fifth wheel.
11. Test the connection
    - In low gear, pull the tractor forward gently while keeping the trailer hand brake applied.
    - As soon as resistance is felt, quickly disengage the clutch. Then test it again.
12. Secure the vehicle
    - Put on the parking brake.
    - Climb out of the cab.
13. Inspect the coupling
    - Chock a set of wheels on the tractor and trailer and remove the ignition key.
    - Using a flashlight, go under the trailer.
    - Check to see if the fifth wheel-jaws have closed around the shank of the kingpin.
    - See if the upper fifth-wheel plate is in full contact with the lower trailer plate.
    - Make sure the jaws are closed and locked and the safety catch is over the locking lever.
14. Raise the landing gear
    - Use the crank handle at low speed, and start raising the landing gear.
    - As soon as the trailer weight is off the landing gear, switch to high speed and continue cranking until the landing gear is fully raised.
15. Connect the electrical cord and check the air lines
    - Plug the electrical cord into the trailer.
    - Then fasten the safety catch.
    - Be sure neither the electrical cord nor the air lines are damaged.
    - Be sure these lines will not hit any moving parts of the rig.

Uncoupling Procedures Checklist

1. Position the vehicle
   - Position the tractor directly in line with the trailer.
   - Make sure the surface where you will uncouple the trailer is level and capable of supporting the rig.
2. Secure the vehicle
   - Place the tractor protection valve in the emergency position.
   - Apply the tractor parking brake.
   - Climb out of the cab.
3. Lower the landing gear
   - Lower the landing gear until both supports touch the ground.
   - Continue cranking until you see the trailer begin to rise off the fifth wheel.
4. Disconnect and store air lines and electrical cable
   - Secure the air lines against snagging, cuts, scrapes, or other damage.
   - Hang the electrical cable down to avoid moisture on the plug.
5. Release the fifth-wheel latch
   - Raise the release handle lock pin and pull the release handle to the open position.
   - If you cannot reach the release handle, use a pull handle or hook.
6. Pull the tractor partly clear of the trailer
   - Return to the cab.
   - Pull the tractor forward and stop while its frame is still under the trailer.
7. Secure the tractor
   - Apply the tractor parking brake.
   - Leave the cab.
8. Inspect the trailer supports
   - Check the landing gear for damage.
   - Make sure it is supporting the trailer. Check the surface.
9. Pull the tractor clear of the trailer
   - Get in the cab. Release the parking brake.
   - Drive the tractor slowly away from the trailer.

Chapter Ten
Visual Search

The Driver's View

Focusing on the Road
Ahead

What You Need to Know
about Scanning and the
Visual Search

Mirrors

OBJECTIVES

When you have completed the chapter, you should be able to:

● Look ahead and scan the environment

● Explain the different types of mirrors, their adjustments, and how to use them

● Describe the truck driver's responsibilities to other drivers

● Know the importance of using a standard visual search while driving

KEY TERMS

Bail-out areas

Convex mirror

External environment

Eye lead time

Fender mirror

Field of view

Internal environment

Plane mirror

Point of reference

Scanning

Systematic seeing

INTRODUCTION

To become a safe and efficient driver, it is important to learn how to be constantly aware of the environment: what is going on around your rig at all times. Sound strange? Keep reading!

Imagine having a view of your rig from a few hundred feet above. Notice the space on all sides of the rig—front, back, sides, and top. This is the **external environment:** the environment you will constantly need to see, hear, feel, and sense when driving.

There is also an **interior environment:** the environment in the cab of the tractor and one in which the driver must be constantly aware of the conditions in which he or she has to work.

Why is the interior environment important? Because the cab's environment has a great impact on how the driver feels, how quickly the driver is fatigued, and how well the driver can react to factors on the outside of the cab. Is the temperature too hot or too cold? Are there exhaust fumes filtering into the cab? Is the clatter of the CB distracting? Is music too loud or too chaotic? All these factors impact how you drive.

And one more thing: These environments change every second your rig is rolling. Therefore, you are constantly adjusting your awareness of what is around you.

As you read through this chapter, you will learn what you need to know to be constantly aware of your environment and how to respond and drive through each situation.

THE DRIVER'S VIEW

Think about what you are able to see when you are behind the wheel of a big rig. The view from the tractor's cab is much different from the view you have when you are behind the wheel of your personal vehicle.

Obviously, you can see a greater distance ahead because you are sitting higher—above the traffic. In some cases, you can see over the traffic, which is to your advantage (see Figure 10-1).

On the flip side, you cannot see as well to the sides and rear of your rig as you can when you are driving your personal vehicle. In the cab of a tractor, it is difficult to see the right side of the tractor-trailer and along the drive wheels on both sides. And when you are sitting behind the wheel of a big rig, it is also difficult to see smaller vehicles.

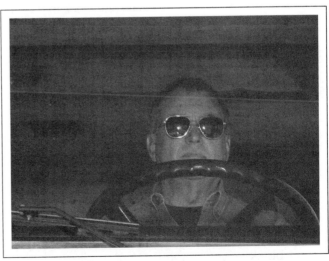

Figure **10-1** There are advantages and disadvantages to the driver's view from a truck.

Ultimately, the driver must be able to get a clear, complete, and accurate picture of the outside environment. Of course, there are existing blind spots that cannot be eliminated unless the driver does a vehicle walk-around before getting into the truck and makes the needed adjustments.

For example, blind spots exist in the front of the tractor and at the rear of the trailer. To be eliminated, these must be observed and cleared by the driver just as he or she would make sure the direction the truck is going is clear before staring the engine.

To find out what is happening around you in traffic, you must use your senses of sight, sound, and smell. Pay attention to movement, balance, and the *feel* of things through observation, experience with the vehicle and driving skill.

Sight is the most important sense in driving. It is your best source of information about the traffic scene. Seeing what is there, however, is not enough. You must also understand what you see and apply what you *sense* to the driving situation. To know what you see quickly and correctly, you must use a visual search pattern, or routine. This is called **systematic seeing** or **scanning.** It helps you know: what to look at, what to look for, and where to look.

Look ahead to where you intend to travel. Search the traffic scene ahead of the rig and to the sides. Use your mirrors to see to the rear.

FOCUSING ON THE ROAD AHEAD

While most of this discussion may seem obvious to you, it is important to explore the various responsibilities of a professional driver as he or she takes to the road.

Without question, looking up the highway as well as watching the road directly ahead and to the back and sides of your rig makes you aware of the environment around the truck. Steering toward an imaginary target or a reference point in the center of your lane of travel keeps you in your lane and aware of any possible problems up ahead. Having a target will keep you and your vehicle centered in the lane you are traveling.

Veteran truckers will tell you that a good rule of thumb is to have a target at least the distance you will travel in the next 12 to 15 seconds. Another name for this is **eye lead time.** In city driving, 12 seconds equals about one block ahead. On the open highway, 12 seconds ahead is about a quarter mile. If you cannot look ahead one block in the city or a quarter mile on the highway, slow down and be extra alert.

Looking this far ahead will give you time to do the following:

- Identify any problems ahead.
- Prepare for these problems.
- Decide how you can drive defensively to avoid the problem.
- Check anything that could keep you from making any changes in speed, direction, lane, and so on.
- Take the right action to keep you and others around you safe.

Looking ahead 12 to 15 seconds and having enough visual lead time will allow you time to respond efficiently and safely, save fuel, and save time because you will have fewer close calls, near misses, or accidents (see Figure 10-2).

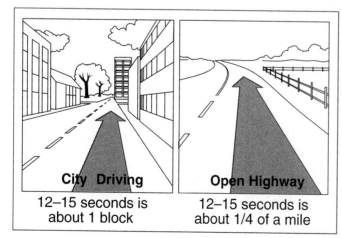

Figure 10-2 Looking down the road gives the driver time to avoid hazards.

- **Safety:** By looking ahead, you will see hazards early enough to avoid them.
- **Fuel:** By looking 12 to 15 seconds ahead, you can adjust smoothly and avoid quick speed adjustments, which will require less fuel.
- **Time:** Spotting situations early will help you avoid being trapped behind turning vehicles, getting stuck in the wrong lane, or missing your exit.

WHAT YOU NEED TO KNOW ABOUT SCANNING AND THE VISUAL SEARCH

While it is important to have 12 to 15 seconds of visual lead time as you drive, be careful not to spend all your time staring at the roadway ahead. Why? Because it is also important to know what is going on around your rig—to the sides, the back, and even on top of your rig.

Once you have chosen a reference point on the road ahead, make a visual search and scan around the rest of your rig. The routine is this: Look 12 to 15 seconds ahead of the rig and on both sides of the roadway ahead. Now quickly look away from your reference point ahead and scan both sides and in back of the rig before returning to the reference point. This process should occur every 6 to 8 seconds.

Let's review the routine:

1. Pick a reference point 12 to 15 seconds ahead and look at both sides of the road between your rig and that reference point.

2. Quickly look to either side—using your mirrors—and to the back of your rig before picking up the reference point.

When scanning, look for anything that can affect your travel path (see Figure 10-3):

- People—on foot and in cars
- Traffic signs
- Debris on the highway
- Signals
- Slick spots or chuck holes in the road
- Intersections
- Merging lanes
- Road shoulders

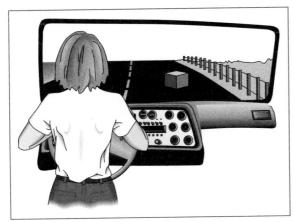

Figure **10-3** Visual scanning gives the driver time for defensive action.

- Construction zones
- School zones
- Stopped vehicles
- Emergency situations

And remember: As you scan, always look for **bail-out areas,** or places you can use to avoid a crash.

Once you become accustomed to the visual search and scanning pattern, you will also learn how to pick and choose what you look for, depending on traffic and your driving environment.

Scanning and Driving into Intersections

After stopping at an intersection, know how to look at this environment before moving into and across the traffic lanes. These general guidelines should help:

- Move your rig forward very slowly. Give other drivers a chance to see you. The slow, controlled speed will also let you stop again before pulling into the path of cross traffic.
- Look to the left, then to the right, and then straight ahead, then left again as you begin to move forward

The reason to use this order of scanning is that the first lane you cross carries traffic from the left. Until that lane is clear, you cannot move forward. If your search shows the right lane is also clear, you can safely begin to move forward. At this point, the second look to the left assures you there are no changes from that direction. You can now go through the intersection.

Finally, be aware of the blind spots created by the mirrors and the corner posts of your cab.

From your seat in the cab, you can see behind you only in your left and right side-view mirrors. Check these mirrors when you scan and search. It is very important to check them before you slow down, stop, or change lanes or direction.

Visual search is one of the most critical components of driver safety and efficiency. A systematic search begins with a walk around the vehicle every time it is driven, paying close attention to the space in front and to the rear of the vehicle.

The only way to avoid the hazards of front and rear blind spots is to first be aware that they are there. The driver sitting behind the steering wheel *always* has a blind spot directly in front of the vehicle that can range a distance of 30 to 50 feet. A blind spot existing directly behind a vehicle can range a distance of 200 feet.

An 8-foot-wide trailer multiplied by the 200-foot distance equals 1,600 square feet of blind space. So always begin a visual search before entering the vehicle.

Field of View

You will have the biggest **field of view** in the left mirror. The closer the mirror is to you, the larger the image. The larger the image, the bigger the field of view. Images will appear similar to those in the side view mirror of a car.

MIRRORS

There are two types of side mirrors, plane (flat) and convex (curved). The **plane mirror** gives the most accurate view of the rear of the trailer and the roadway behind. It does not give a wide view, and it can leave blind spots along the length of the rig (see Figure 10-4).

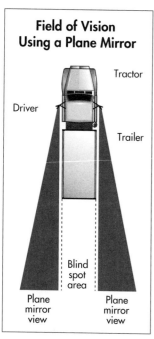

Figure **10-4** The plane mirror gives the driver the best view of the rear of the trailer and roadway behind, but it leaves blind spots.

Field of Vision Using a Convex Mirror

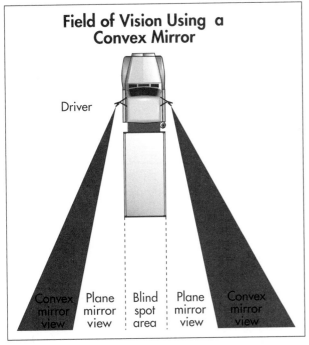

Figure **10-5**   Convex mirrors are curved to give a wide-angle view.

Combination of Plane/Convex Mirror

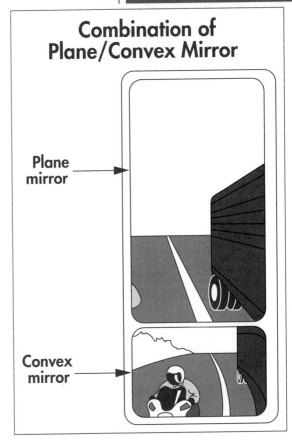

Figure **10-6**   Combination plane/convex mirrors provide the best rear and side vision.

Convex mirrors are curved to give you a wide-angle view. They are best used for side close-ups. You have a much wider field of view using convex mirrors than with a plain mirror (see Figure 10-5).

Convex mirrors eliminate most, but not all, of the blind area created by the plane mirror. The images you see, however, will be smaller and will appear farther away than they really are.

With plane mirrors, the blind areas are too large. Using only the convex mirror creates too much distortion. So, it is best to have both plain and convex mirrors. Many rigs have this combination because it gives drivers the best side and rear vision (see Figure 10-6).

Remember, though, that blind spots will still be there. Adjust your mirrors. Check both mirrors often. It is the only way to know if something is in a blind area.

A **fender mirror** is mounted on the fender of a regular long-nose tractor. It requires less eye movement, so you can have a better view of the road ahead.

Wide-angle (convex) fender mirrors let you see more when you are making right turns. This is helpful in a tight turn. The view of the road is similar to what you see with a convex side mirror, but there is less distortion (see Figure 10-7).

Adjusting Mirrors

Every driver should adjust both the left and the right mirror to get an accurate view of the sides and rear

Field of Vision While Making a Right Turn

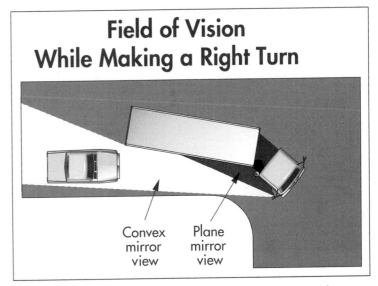

Figure **10-7**   The convex mirror gives a wider field of vision when making a right turn.

of the rig. All mirrors should be adjusted to show some part of the vehicle (trailer body, tires, and so on). This will give the driver a **point of reference** for judging the position of the other images. Adjust mirrors when the rig is straight for the best image.

Some rigs have motorized mirrors that allow you to adjust them from inside the cab. They can also be used to get a wider view when needed and then returned to the normal position.

Left-side mirrors. (Plane)   The inside, vertical edge of the mirror (about 3/4 to 1 inch) should show the trailer body. The remaining part will show what is beside and behind the trailer. The range of view to the side will be about 15 feet.

(Convex) The inside, vertical edge of the mirror should show part of the trailer. The top, horizontal edge should show a view overlapping that of the plane mirror by about five feet and going back to the end of the trailer.

Right-side mirrors. (Plane)   The inside, vertical edge of the mirror (about 3/4 to 1 inch) should reflect the trailer body. The rest will show what is on the side (for about 15 feet) and behind the trailer.

(Convex) The inside, vertical edge of the mirror should reflect part of the trailer. The top, horizontal edge should show a view overlapping that of the plane mirror by five feet and extend to the end of trailer.

Fender mirrors. The convex fender mirrors on both the right and the left side should be adjusted so you can see the trailer tires, curbs, and other objects when turning (see Figure 10-8).

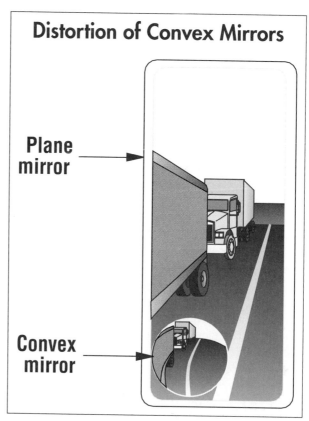

Figure **10-8** Be aware of the distortion of convex mirrors.

Seeing to the Rear

Checking your rig's mirrors is a part of scanning and searching. Be sure to check the security of your load as well as the tires for fire. In addition, your mirror checks can tell you if there are any hazards around your rig, what is beside or behind the rig that may be affected by a sudden move, and if your trailer has struck anything.

Using Mirrors When Making Changes

Before making any sudden changes in speed or direction, check the traffic behind you.

Changing lanes. Always use both the plane and the convex mirror when you change your path of travel. Be aware there are blind spots behind and to the sides of your rig. You may need to make many checks to be sure of the traffic situation. Remember, it takes longer to check to the rear when you are driving a rig than it does when you are driving a car. Properly checking the left mirrors takes almost 1 second. Checking those to the right side takes nearly 1-1/2 seconds.

Be sure it is safe to look away from the front of the rig before making the mirror checks. At 55 mph, you travel 80 feet in 1 second. Keep enough space between yourself and the vehicle in front of you. Do not take chances. If there is not enough space or time, delay the lane change (see Figure 10-9).

Turning corners. When coming to a corner where you want to turn, check your side-view mirrors before slowing down. Then check them again as you are turning. After completing the turn, check the mirrors to be sure that: your rig is not entangled with or dragging anything and that your rig has not damaged anything.

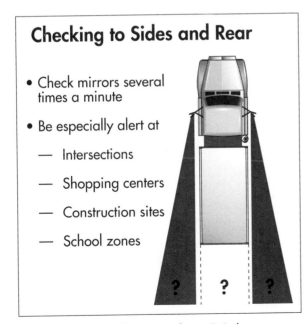

Checking to Sides and Rear

- Check mirrors several times a minute
- Be especially alert at
  - Intersections
  - Shopping centers
  - Construction sites
  - School zones

Figure **10-9** Remember, it takes longer to check the rear of the rig than it does to check the rear of your personal vehicle.

Chapter Eleven
Communication

Tell Your Intent
Signaling
Highway Communication

OBJECTIVES

When you have completed this chapter, you should be able to:

- Know and understand the importance of using signals to tell other highway users when you plan to change position in traffic

- Explain why good communication helps to avoid collisions and traffic violations

- Describe how to send and receive communications

KEY TERMS

Communication
Reflective triangle
Road rage

INTRODUCTION

Professional drivers realize that if their travel is to be safe and efficient, they must be in constant **communication** with others on the road. Does this mean the driver should communicate with everyone, using a cellular telephone or a CB radio? Absolutely not. But it does mean the professional driver must signal his or her next move through traffic and at the same time be alert to the messages coming from other drivers, pedestrians and cyclists. Remember to be patient with motorists and the sometimes poor decisions they make; after all, they are not professional drivers.

What is good communication on the highway? It is a skill developed by professionals that uses knowledge, foresight, experience, and an understanding of the driver's needs as well as the needs of others on the road. In its simplest form, communication on the highway is helping each other get down the road to get their jobs done.

How does good communication occur on the highway? In addition to using turn signals and emergency flashers when necessary, good communication also incorporates the horn and your speed—letting other highway users be aware of your presence, your position, and your intentions. But don't the drivers of those other vehicles automatically know when a big rig pulls behind them, in front of them, or beside them—because the rig is so big?

It may be difficult to believe, but some people do not know you are there because they are not paying close attention. They may be thinking about what they are going to have for dinner tonight or that sore tooth or a personal problem. They may be talking on the phone or listening intently to the music playing at that moment. Therefore, when you communicate your presence by letting others know where you are, you may be helping everyone avoid an accident down the road.

One more word before getting farther into this chapter: **Road rage** has become epidemic on America's highways today. Professional drivers tell of times they have seen or been involved in a dozen or more of these dangerous incidents during one trip. According to road rage psychologist Arnold Nerenberg, road rage occurs in North America as many as two billion times every year.

Road rage can be defined as anything from aggressive driving to criminal behavior or simply bad driving. One law enforcement officer defines road rage as "an event occurring when drivers are running out of time and running out of options." Another highway veteran calls road rage "a problem of sharing—conflict between the law-abiding road user and people who cut in and out, trying to beat the traffic."

Because road rage has surpassed epidemic proportions, professional drivers must be constantly aware of how his or her communication of their rig's presence or their intentions are perceived. Honking your horn too often, following too closely, or cutting off a driver at a ramp or turnoff may spike the opportunities for road rage.

So take care of how you communicate with others using the same roadway. Be aware of how important it is to let others know your whereabouts and your intentions and never "overdo" signals, flashing lights, speed, or other efforts to communicate your plans to maneuver your rig.

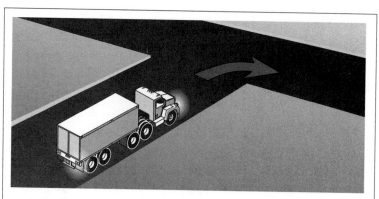

Signal early: Signal for some time before you turn. It is the best way to keep others from trying to pass you when it is not safe to pass.

Signal continuously: Do not cancel the signal until you have completed the turn.

Cancel your signal after you have turned: Turn off your signal if you do not have self-cancelling signals.

Figure **11-1** Using signals correctly communicates your next maneuver to others sharing the road.

TELL YOUR INTENT

You know where you are and what you are going to do. Others usually do not know what you are going to do unless you tell them. Remember the concern you felt when a bicyclist was in your lane on the highway? That concern is a good example of why it is important to tell your intentions to others.

To signal what you intend to do before you do it is important for all highway users, but there are some special rules for signaling when you drive a rig. The size of your rig, blind spots, and the space you need for turning mean you must do everything you can to help others know what you intend to do (see Figure 11-1).

SIGNALING

Signaling for Turns

There are three special rules to use when you signal before making a turn:

1. Signal early
2. Signal continuously
3. Cancel your signal

Signal early. The size of your rig makes it hard for you to see someone who is about to pass you or who may already be doing so. The best way to keep others from trying to pass when you are turning is to give advanced warning. Put on your turn signal early. The general rule of thumb is to turn on the signal one-half block before an intersection or about 500 feet on the open highway.

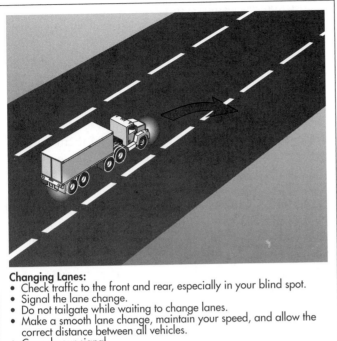

Changing Lanes:
- Check traffic to the front and rear, especially in your blind spot.
- Signal the lane change.
- Do not tailgate while waiting to change lanes.
- Make a smooth lane change, maintain your speed, and allow the correct distance between all vehicles.
- Cancel your signal.

Figure **11-2** Following these steps when changing lanes helps maintain roadway safety.

The FMCSR say you must signal at least 100 feet in advance. State laws vary from 100 to 500 feet. Keep in mind that the legal requirements are minimums—100 feet may not be far enough in advance for many conditions.

Signal continuously. You may find that after turning on your signal, you must stop and wait for a safe break in traffic. Keep the signal on. It tells everyone what you are going to do.

Cancel your signal. When you have completed the turn, cancel the signal. Do not cancel the signal until you have completed the turn. One good way to remember to cancel the signal is to connect it in your mind with the upshift. After completing a turn, speed up, cancel the signal, and upshift. Soon this routine will become a habit.

Signaling for Lane Changes

Lane changes need the same early signals as turns. They also need one more signal—the motion of your vehicle. Once you have started your lane change, pause for a few seconds as you enter the new lane. This will catch the attention of those who did not notice your earlier signal and will give them a chance to react (see Figure 11-2).

Slowing Down

Highway users expect vehicles ahead of them to keep moving. Any time you slow suddenly, give the driver behind you some warning. Communicate your intent. A few light taps on the brake pedal—enough to flash the brake lights without exhausting your air supply—should do the trick. Give a warning in any of the following situations:

Trouble ahead.   The size of your rig may make it impossible for drivers of vehicles that are following your rig to see around you.

Tight turns.   Few car drivers realize how hard it is to make a tight turn in a big rig. Often they are not prepared when a truck ahead of them slows to nearly a stop before starting a turn. Give them a warning using your signal ahead of the time you plan to make your turn.

Stopping on the road.   Unfortunately, truck drivers are sometimes forced to stop in a traffic lane when others may not be expecting it. It may be a case of having to unload cargo when there is no space at the curb. Sometimes it is at a railroad crossing. Maybe the driver is getting ready to back into a driveway, or it may be your rig just stopped running. In any case, the drivers that are following can be caught off guard. Give them a warning.

Driving slowly.   Sometimes drivers overtaking a slow vehicle do not know how quickly they are closing in on it. Often they are too close before they can react. If you are being slowed by hills or heavy cargo, tell other drivers by turning on your emergency flashers.

Laws regarding the use of flashers differ from state to state. Know the laws in your own state. Check on the laws of other states before driving through them.

Do Not Direct Traffic

Some truck drivers try to help other drivers by signaling when it is safe to pass. While they mean well, their judgment is poor. If there is another vehicle the truck driver did not see, this "help" can cause an accident (see Figure 11-3). The truck driver is then held liable, and this can be costly for the truck driver or his or her employer. Signaling others to pass is also illegal and dangerous. Signal only to tell others what *you* plan to do. Leave directing traffic to the police.

Overtaking Other Vehicles

Whenever you are overtaking another vehicle, a pedestrian, or a bicyclist, it is best to assume they do not see you. If they do not see you, there is also a chance they will suddenly move into your path. Tell them you are there with a light tap on the horn. Note we said *light tap.* At night, flashing your lights with the dimmer switch also works.

A light tap on your air horn is enough to tell others you are there. Avoid loud blasts of the horn that may startle them and cause them to swerve into your path. Loud blasts of the horn are for emergencies only. Use the electric horn in city traffic.

Signal any time you overtake and pass pedestrians or cyclists. Obviously, you cannot signal every time you overtake another vehicle, but it is a good idea to do it, especially

Avoid Guiding Others

DO NOT SIGNAL OTHERS TO PASS OR CROSS

Figure **11-3** Remember that your job is as a professional driver, not directing traffic.

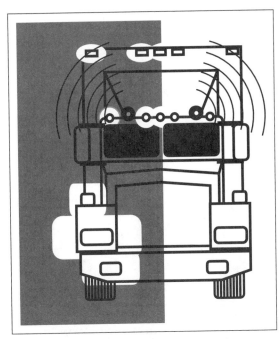

Figure **11-4** It is often difficult to see or be seen at dark or dusk.

when you approach a driver who is signaling a lane change or starting to pull into your path.

When It Is Hard to See

It is hard to see at dawn or dusk (see Figure 11-4), in rain or snow, on cloudy days, when driver is fatigued, and after a heavy meal.

A truck can be just as hard to see as any other vehicle. If you are having trouble spotting oncoming vehicles, you must assume other drivers are having a tough time seeing you. Turn on your lights. Use your headlights, not just ID or clearance lights. (Use your low beams. High beams can be as annoying in the day as at night.)

At the Side of the Road

Any time you pull off the road and stop, be sure to turn on your emergency flashers (see Figure 11-5). This is really important at night when a driver who has not seen you decides to pull off the road in the same spot. Do not trust your taillights to provide a warning. Many drivers have crashed into the rear of a parked truck simply because they were not warned properly.

If you are forced to stop on or near the road, you will need more than emergency flashers. Approaching drivers need advanced warning to get around you. Put out **reflective triangles** within 10 minutes (see Figure 11-6). For better safety at night, also use flares or fusees. Do not use flares or fusees if you are carrying hazardous cargo or there is spilled fuel.

Figure **11-5** Any time you pull your rig off the road, use your emergency flashers.

Figure **11-6** To signal a problem, use flares and reflective triangles before and after the rig.

Note: A fusee is a glowing flare used as a highway signal.

Place reflective triangles at the following locations if you must stop on an undivided highway:

- On the traffic side, 10 feet (4 paces) to the rear of the rig. This marks the location of the vehicle
- About 100 feet (40 paces) behind the rig on the shoulder or in the lane in which the rig is stopped to give overtaking drivers plenty of warning
- About 100 feet in front of the rig on the shoulder to give oncoming drivers plenty of warning

TIP

The law states triangles or other warning devices must be placed within 10 minutes of stopping.

If you must stop on a one-way or divided highway, place the triangles at the following locations:

- About 10 feet behind the rig. This will show approaching traffic the rig's location.
- About 100 feet behind the rig.
- About 200 feet (80 paces) behind the rig. This will give oncoming drivers plenty of warning there is a stopped rig.

Always place reflective triangles beyond a hill, curve, or anything that keeps drivers of overtaking vehicles from seeing your rig when they are 500 feet away.

If you have to double-park on a city street, triangles and flares are not practical. You must, however, turn on your emergency flashers so approaching drivers will know your rig is stopped.

Chapter Twelve
Space Management

OBJECTIVES

When you have completed this chapter, you should be able to:

- Explain the safest following distance for different conditions

- Show the importance of maintaining distance between your rig and other vehicles to be able to drive defensively

- Describe how to control your space

- Prevent the dangers of overhead obstructions

- Explain the correct procedure to make turns

- Manage space in intersections

KEY TERMS

Space management   **Tailgating**

INTRODUCTION

What does it take to become a professional driver in America's trucking industry? Some would say a citation-free, accident-free record. Others would say vehicles and cargoes reaching their destinations without incident or damage.

Obviously, both of these statements are true, but it takes more than a clean record and a well-handled load. In fact, a professional driver's highest achievement may be managing the space around his or her vehicle—at all times.

Veterans call space management "maintaining a cushion of air around the vehicle in every environment" (see Figure 12-1). For the purposes of this book, we'll call it **space management**—maintaining enough space around your rig to make every trip safe as you operate the rig economically and being considerate of other drivers.

THE IMPORTANCE OF SPACE MANAGEMENT

You need space all around your vehicle—in front, to the sides, and to the rear. When things go wrong on the road, space gives you time to adjust. Other vehicles will stop unexpectedly or turn in front of you. You may need space to change lanes, stop, or slow down. If, for instance, you must change lanes or swerve right or left, you will need to check your side-view mirrors. That takes time, and time requires space.

You need to be concerned with space in all directions—ahead, behind, to the sides, and even above and below. You also need to be aware of the space needed for turning, crossing roads, or entering traffic.

In order to have the space you need when something goes wrong, you need to manage space well at all times. While this is true for all road users, it is especially important for those who drive big rigs. They take up more space to begin with, and they need a great deal more space for stopping and turning.

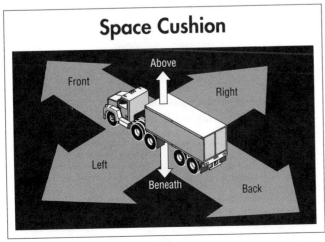

Figure **12-1** Space cushion.

SPACE AHEAD

Of all the space around your rig, the space ahead is the most important. This is the amount of space you need to stop your rig in any situation—and for any reason.

Experience and accident records indicate the vehicle most likely to be hit by a tractor-trailer rig is the one in front of it—and the most common cause of these collisions is that the rig has been following too closely.

If the vehicle ahead is lighter than your rig, it can stop faster and in less space. So, if the small sedan ahead suddenly puts on its brakes, it can stop before you have completed your braking process.

If that same small sedan begins to slow down and you—the driver of the rig that is following—do not notice it, by the time you realize what is happening and decide to put on your brakes, you have used up most or all of the space that separates your rig from that little sedan.

The lesson here is that if you are following too closely, you may not be able to avoid hitting the vehicle in front of you.

How Much Space Do You Need to Be Safe?

How much space should you put between your rig and the vehicle in front of you? A good rule of thumb is that you need 1 second for each 10 feet of your rig's length (see Figure 12-2). That means if you are driving a 40-foot rig, leave at least 4 seconds between your front bumper and the vehicle ahead of you. In a 60-foot rig, you will need 6 seconds of space between you and the vehicle traveling in front of yours (see Figure 12-3).

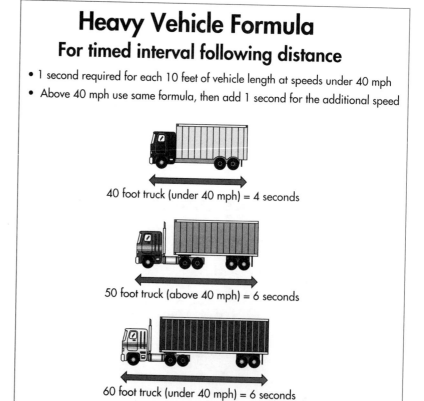

Heavy Vehicle Formula
For timed interval following distance

- 1 second required for each 10 feet of vehicle length at speeds under 40 mph
- Above 40 mph use same formula, then add 1 second for the additional speed

40 foot truck (under 40 mph) = 4 seconds

50 foot truck (above 40 mph) = 6 seconds

60 foot truck (under 40 mph) = 6 seconds

Figure **12-2** Determine adequate following distances based on the length of your rig.

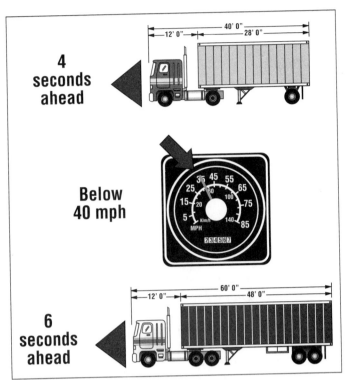

Figure **12-3** Adequate distance between your rig and the vehicle in front of you is measured in seconds.

To measure adequate following distance, note when the rear end of the vehicle ahead passes a marking on the road. Then count off the seconds, 1,001, 1,002, 1,003; and so on, until the front of your rig reaches the same spot. Compare your count with the rule of 1 second for every 10 feet of your rig's length.

If you are driving a 40-foot rig and count less than 4 seconds, you are following too closely. Drop back a bit. Then count again. Until you have at least 4 seconds of space between your rig and the vehicle you are following, you are in danger and so are all other road users near you.

For speeds above 40 mph, add 1 second to the basic amount of space needed.

Example: 50-foot rig traveling at 48 mph
- Basic amount of space needed—5 seconds (50/10 = 5)
- Above 40 mph—Add 1 second

Total following distance needed—6 seconds (5 rig length + 1 speed over 40 mph = 6)

For bad weather, poor visibility, or bad road conditions, you should add at least 1 more second.

Example: 60-foot rig with poor visibility traveling at 55 mph
- Basic amount of space needed—6 seconds (60/10 = 6)
- Above 40 mph—Add 1 second
- Poor visibility—Add 1 more second

Total following distance needed—8 seconds (6 rig length + 1 speed over 40 mph + 1 weather = 8)

The times listed here are the absolute minimums to ensure seeing time, thinking time, reacting time, and braking time.

SPACE BEHIND

As you know, you cannot completely control the space behind your rig. There are, however, a number of things you can do to control the space to the rear:

- Stay to the right
- Be careful when changing lanes
- Expect **tailgating**—when another vehicle follows you too closely to have adequate time to stop
- Respond safely to tailgaters

Stay to the right.   Sometimes going uphill or when a load is very heavy, a rig cannot keep up with traffic. At these times, it is best to use the special truck lanes or stay as far to the right as possible. However, in some states, driving on the shoulder is illegal.

When going uphill, do not try to pass a slower vehicle unless it can be done quickly. Being caught behind two trucks that are side by side is annoying to other drivers and could cause a case of road rage.

Changing lanes.   The length of a tractor-trailer makes it hard to judge whether a lane change can be made safely. Here are a few suggestions to make it easier to judge:

- When in doubt, leave plenty of space between you and other vehicles. Wait a little longer before pulling in front of the vehicle you have passed. On a multilane road, there is no need to rush your return to the right-hand lane (see Figure 12-4).
- Do not always trust the signals of other drivers. They may have the best intentions, but you really have no idea what they will do.

Anticipate tailgating.   In large vehicles, it is difficult to know when you are being tailgated. A good rule is to expect to be tailgated in the following situations:

- When you are traveling slowly: Drivers trapped behind slow-moving vehicles tend to edge up too close even though some states have minimum following distances.

Figure **12-4**   When changing lanes, leave plenty of space between your rig and other vehicles.

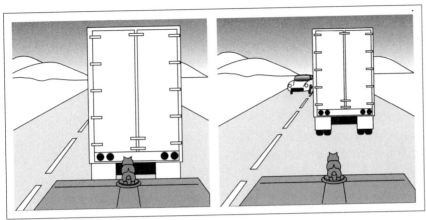

Figure **12-5** When being tailgated, the vehicle behind you has a reduced view of the road ahead.

- Bad weather: Many drivers follow large vehicles closely in bad weather, especially when visibility is poor.

Respond safely to tailgaters. If you find yourself being tailgated, these actions may help reduce the chance for an accident:

- Reduce your speed slowly. This may encourage the tailgater to pass you (see Figure 12-5).
- Avoid quick changes. If you have to slow down or turn, signal your intentions early and make the change very slowly.
- Increase your following distance. Create more space in front of your rig. This will help you avoid making sudden changes in speed or direction. It also makes it easier for a tailgater to get around you.
- Do not speed up. Tailgaters often tend to stay close, no matter how fast you go. It is better to be tailgated at a low speed than a high speed.
- Avoid tricks. Do not turn on your headlights or flash your brake lights to shake up the tailgater. You could make the situation worse by angering or confusing the driver following you.

SPACE TO THE SIDES

The wider your vehicle, the less space it has to the sides. To protect yourself on both sides, you need to manage space with care by keeping your rig centered in your lane. Avoid driving alongside others. Overtake and pass others carefully.

Staying Centered in the Lane

There is usually little more than a foot between the sides of your trailer and the edges of the lane in which you are driving. Keeping the rig centered is important for safety.

Keep as much space to the sides as possible. Concentrate on keeping your vehicle centered whenever you are meeting, passing, or being passed by another vehicle.

Do not move to the right simply because of an approaching vehicle. This may put you too close to the other side of your lane. While driving defensively, avoid any oncoming vehicles if they move over into your lane.

Visually scan your mirrors often to be sure your trailer has not drifted out of line. If it has, get in front of it and pull it back into the center of the lane.

Traveling Beside Others

Two dangerous situations can develop any time you travel alongside other vehicles:

1. Another driver may change lanes suddenly and turn directly into you.
2. You may need to change lanes and find there is no opening, so you are trapped in your present lane.

The best way to avoid either situation is not to "travel with the pack." Find an open spot where you have the road pretty much to yourself. There are times when traffic is so heavy you cannot find an open spot, and at these times you have no choice except to be alert and careful. If you have to travel near other vehicles, stay out of their blind spots. Drop back or pull forward so other drivers can see you.

SPACE OVERHEAD

Hitting overhead objects is a major cause of damage—both to rigs and damage done by them (see Figure 12-6). Make sure you have enough space above your rig at all times.

Most overhead collisions are with low-hanging wires, marquees, signs, and air-conditioning units. Check the heights of any overhead structures before driving under them. If there is any doubt about being able to pass under an object, slow down and drive very carefully. If any question remains, stop, get out, and check the clearance before continuing.

Do not rely entirely on posted heights at bridges and overpasses. Repaved roads or packed snow may reduce the clearance indicated by the signs.

The weight of your rig affects its height. The fact that you were able to drive under a bridge when you were fully loaded does not mean that you can do it on the return trip when your rig is empty or lightly loaded.

Sometimes your rig may tilt toward the side of the road because of a high crown or different levels of paving. When this occurs, you may not clear signs, trees, or other objects along the side of the road. If this is a problem, drive a little closer to the center of the road.

Figure **12-6** Hitting objects overhead is a major cause of damage.

Backing is often troublesome. Before you back into an area, get out and check any overhanging structures. Why? Because it is often not possible to see them while you are backing.

SPACE BELOW

Many drivers overlook the importance of maintaining adequate space beneath their rigs. That space can be "squeezed" when a vehicle is heavily loaded and the springs are compressed. When you are driving low-bed hauling equipment, there may not always be enough clearance beneath the rig.

The following situations may create space problems beneath your rig:

Railroad tracks.   Railroad tracks can extend inches above the surface of the road. This is often a problem on dirt roads and in unpaved yards where the surface around the tracks can wear away. Do not take the chance of getting hung up halfway across. Get out and measure the clearance.

Soft surfaces.   One way to lose clearance is to sink down until the truck frame is resting on the surface. Make sure any surface will hold the weight of your truck before driving onto that surface.

Shopping center parking lots.   Many parking lots are not made for large, heavy trucks. Look for signs indicating weight limits. If you have to make a shopping center delivery, check ahead to be sure the surface can handle your loaded rig.

Unpaved surfaces.   Many dirt surfaces will support your truck in good weather but not in bad weather. After a rainstorm, dirt can quickly turn to mud. Check before driving onto unpaved surfaces, especially if they are covered with grass or gravel. They may not be as firm as they look.

Excavated areas.   Excavated areas can be dangerous for big rigs. They may be covered over with planks that will not hold a truck. Sometimes they are filled in with loose dirt. Use care when you have to drive near road work or construction.

SPACE FOR TURNS

Having enough room on the sides of your rig when you turn is important (see Figure 12-7). Because of their wide turning radius and off-tracking, trucks frequently sideswipe other vehicles or run over objects during turns.

Right Turns

Because most right turns are tighter than the turning radius of your truck, you have to swing a little wide for a successful turn. Timing is a key factor. Stay to the right as long as possible if you have to swing out to the left for the turn. Otherwise, the driver of a vehicle following you may not realize you plan to turn and will try to move by you on the right. These steps can be useful:

- Approach the intersection in the right lane.
- Switch on your right turn signal at least 100 feet before turning.
- Swing left just as you approach the intersection (only if you need to).
- Turn sharply to the right.

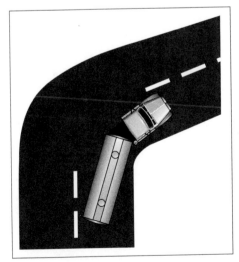

Figure **12-7** Having enough space to turn your rig is sometimes difficult.

Timing the left swing is critical. Wait until the last possible moment. You can keep people from passing on the right by staying to the right and using your trailer to block traffic. If you do this, by the time the trailer begins to move left, the tractor will be well into the turn and will keep anyone from passing.

If the turn is particularly sharp or difficult, swing out into the street you are about to enter. Watch your off-tracking to avoid running over the curb or a grassy area. Grassy areas often hide things, such as sprinkler heads. Return to the right lane as soon as possible. Remember, it is better to travel a few blocks further and make three left turns to get onto the street you want than to endanger others.

Left Turns

When you make a left turn, be sure you reach the center of the intersection before turning left. If you turn too soon, the side of the trailer, as it off-tracks, may hit an object or a vehicle waiting to enter the intersection.

Left turns from two lanes.   The choice of lanes is very important in a left turn. If there are two turning lanes, use the right lane. If you start in the left lane, you will have to swing out in order to make the turn. A driver on your right may not expect you to turn and may drive into the side of your rig. Keep traffic in the next lane on the sight side where you see it best. A vehicle to your right may be difficult to see.

SPACE TO CROSS OR ENTER TRAFFIC

New drivers often do not allow for the size and weight of their rigs when they cross or enter into traffic (see Figure 12-8). Remember these things:

- Because your rig accelerates slowly, it requires more space than a smaller, more responsive vehicle. Because of this, you need a much larger gap than a car does to cross or enter traffic.
- Acceleration varies with the weight of the vehicle. Allow more room and more time to accelerate if you have a heavy load.
- Before you start across a street, think about the length of the rig. Make sure there is enough space for you to clear the intersection completely.

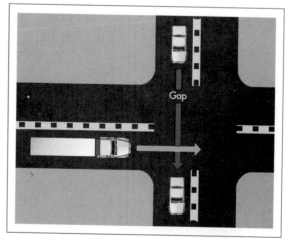

Figure **12-8** Keep the size and weight of your rig in mind when crossing an intersection.

Chapter Thirteen
Speed Management

FROM NOW ON. . .

ONLY THE BEST
WILL DRIVE!

OBJECTIVES

When you have completed this chapter, you should be able to:

- Explain the relationship of speed to stopping distance, hydroplaning, causes of accidents, the driver's ability to control the rig, and the rig's fuel economy

- Discuss the effect of speed on the rig's weight, the rig's center of gravity, and the rig's stability

- Show how the driver's available sight distance and the road surface conditions affect choosing a safe speed

KEY TERMS

Black ice
Center of gravity
Driver reaction distance
Field of vision
Gravity
Hydroplaning

Managing your speed
Speeding
Total stopping distance
Traction
Vehicle braking distance

INTRODUCTION

Speed limit laws, which date back to 1901, have traditionally been the responsibility of the states. Then, during the oil shortage of 1973, Congress directed the U.S. Department of Transportation to withhold highway funding from states that did not adopt a maximum speed limit of 55 mph.

The National Research Council attributed 4,000 fewer fatalities to the decreased speeds of 1974, compared with 1973, and estimated that returning the speed limit on rural portions of the interstate highway system to pre-1974 levels would result in 500 more fatalities annually, a 20 to 25 percent increase on these highways.

As concerns about fuel availability and costs faded, however, speeds began to gradually climb on U.S. highways, and by the mid-1980s a majority of the vehicles across the U.S. highway system were traveling at speeds that exceeded 55 mph. In 1987, Congress allowed states to increase speed levels on rural interstates to 65 mph.

In 1995, the National Highway System Designation Act repealed the maximum speed limit and allowed states to set their own speed limits. Many states quickly raised speed limits on both urban and rural interstates as well as limited-access roads. As of June 2000, 20 states had raised speed limits to 70 mph or higher on some of their roads.

As a professional driver, it is your job to know the speed limits of each of the states in which you travel, but more important, it is also your job to know the principles of speed management and how to adjust your speed to fit each traffic and road condition you encounter.

As the driver of a big rig, you must use not only your knowledge and skills as a professional driver but also your best judgment while in traffic. As any veteran will tell you, in this profession there is no place for cowboys or show-offs.

SPEED AND STOPPING DISTANCE

Speeding is defined as exceeding, or driving faster than, the legal or posted speed limit. You also speed when you drive too fast for current road, traffic and weather conditions. The second part of the definition—driving too fast for the conditions—is harder to specifically define but is just as important.

Managing speed is a big part of driving safely. The faster you go, the less time you have to react to what is happening around you. Conditions, as you know, can change in a split second.

The faster you go, the longer it will take you to stop. It takes over eight times more distance to stop at 50 than it does at 15 mph. Table 13-1 will give you an idea of the distance it takes to stop a tractor-trailer on dry pavement. Remember, the distances are not exact.

Table **13-1** Stopping Distances

Miles per Hour	How Far the Rig Will Travel in 1 Second	Driver Reaction Distance	Vehicle Braking Distance	Total Stopping Distance
15	22 ft.	17 ft.	29 ft.	46 ft.
30	44 ft.	33 ft.	115 ft.	148 ft.
45	66 ft.	50 ft.	260 ft.	310 ft.
50	73 ft.	55 ft.	320 ft.	375 ft.
55	81 ft.	61 ft.	390 ft.	451 ft.

The three distances are defined as follows:

- **Driver reaction distance:** The distance your rig travels during the time you identify a hazard to the time you apply the brakes.
- **Vehicle braking distance:** The distance your rig travels from the time you apply pressure to the brake pedal until the rig stops.
- **Total stopping distance:** The driver reaction distance plus the vehicle braking distance.

The weight of the rig as well as how well the brakes are working will affect the braking distance.

There is no speed that will always be a safe speed. Speed must be adjusted to the conditions. These conditions can and do change often during a trip—even a short one (see Figure 13-1).

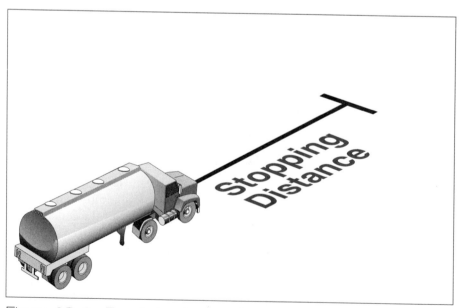

Figure **13-1** Empty trucks need greater stopping distances because an empty vehicle has less traction. The brakes, tires, springs, and shock absorbers on heavy vehicles are designed to work best when the vehicle is fully loaded.

Figure **13-2** The points of friction (traction) between the tires and road are small.

DRIVING ON VARIOUS ROAD SURFACES

To steer your rig or stop it, you need **traction.** Traction is created by the friction of tires making contact with the road (see Figure 13-2). Sometimes, it is defined as the "grip" of the tires on the road. Some road surfaces keep the tires from having good traction. When this occurs, you must slow down to maintain control of your rig. The sections that follow discuss some of these surfaces.

Slippery Surfaces

It takes longer to stop when the road surface is slippery. It is also harder to turn your rig. This is because the tires lose their grip on the road. If you are to control your rig, slow down when the road is slippery. This is called **managing your speed.**

If your rig has antilock brakes, do not expect to stop faster than with other brakes. All antilock brakes do is allow you to stay in control while braking your rig.

How much you slow down depends on the conditions. If the surface is wet, you need to reduce your speed by about one-fourth. If you are driving 55 mph, slow down to about 40 mph. On packed snow, reduce speed by about one-half. That means at 55 mph, you slow to about 28 mph.

If the surface is icy, you will need to cut back speed by about two-thirds. At 55 mph, you should slow to about 18 mph. Table 13-2 tells, generally, safe driving speeds in different kinds of weather conditions.

Identifying Slippery Surfaces

Sometimes it is hard to know if a road is slippery. Certain clues can help you identify bad spots. When you see any of the following, slow down.

Table **13-2** Safe Driving Speeds

Normal Driving Speed	Driving in Rain	Driving in Snow	Driving on Ice
55 mph	40 mph	28 mph	18 mph
50 mph	35 mph	25 mph	17 mph
45 mph	33 mph	23 mph	15 mph
40 mph	30 mph	20 mph	13 mph

Figure **13-3** Icy, wet roads pose hazards to drivers.

Shaded area.   When the sun begins to melt the ice and snow, the shaded areas of the road stay icy long after the open areas are clear. Examples are around bridges and trees.

Bridges.   Because air can circulate over and under bridges, these structures tend to freeze more quickly than other parts of the road. Be very careful when the temperature is right around 32°F. When the ice begins to melt, bridges will be wet and even more slippery.

Black ice.   A thin layer of ice clear enough to let you see the road beneath is called **black ice.** This condition makes the road look wet. Any time the temperatures outdoors are below freezing and the road looks wet, watch out for black ice. Another way of detecting black ice is to watch tire spray. If it disappears when the weather is cold enough, you may be on black ice (see Figure 13-3).

On rainy days when the temperature is near or below freezing, look for ice beginning to form on your vehicle. An easy way to check for ice is to open the window and feel the front of the mirror. If you feel ice, the road surface is probably getting icy, too. Ice buildup on the antennas of other vehicles is another sign to watch for.

Just after rain begins.   When rain begins to fall after a period of dry weather, it mixes with dirt, grit, oil, and other road particles, which makes the road surface very slippery. For the first 15 minutes of rain, the road will be very slippery. On hot days, this is a problem on asphalt roads because the oil tends to rise to the surface. This is called "bleeding tar." As the rain continues, the mixture is washed away. In heavily forested areas, when there are leaves on the road, they tend to be very slippery—even after the rain has stopped—from the oil and water trapped between them and the surface of the road.

Hydroplaning

When water and slush collect on the roadway, your wheels may lose contact with the road's surface. This loss of traction is called **hydroplaning.** It is much like waterskiing. A thin film of water separates the tires from the road, and your rig simply slides along on top of the water. Under these conditions, you lose much of your ability to steer, brake, or control the rig.

Figure **13-4** When your rig hydroplanes, do not brake but gradually lower speed.

Your rig can hydroplane on even a very thin layer of water. Usually it occurs at higher speeds, but it can happen at speeds below 30 mph. This will depend on how much water is on the road and the condition of your tires (see Figure 13-4).

TAKING CURVES SAFELY

Center of Gravity

All drivers must adjust their speed to the conditions of the road and the weather. This becomes more important when you are driving a big rig. How the weight of the load is distributed also makes a difference in controlling your rig in extreme conditions.

How high your **center of gravity** is will determine your speed when you take curves (see Figure 13-5). One layer of crates of equal weight will keep the center of gravity lower than the same number of crates stacked on top of each other in an 8-foot stack. The higher the load is stacked, the higher the center of gravity. The higher the center of gravity, the more likely the rig will be to tip over during turns (see Figure 13-6). How the load is secured is also important. A shifting load can cause serious control problems for the driver.

Adjusting Your Speed

Taking a curve too fast can cause you to lose control. This happens in one of two ways:

1. The wheels lose traction and continue straight ahead. This is a skid.
2. The wheels may keep their traction, but momentum will not allow the rig to turn. This can cause a rollover.

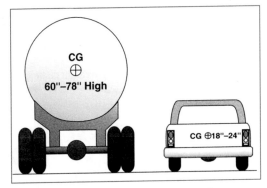

Figure **13-5** Your center of gravity helps determine safe speeds on curves.

Figure **13-6** The higher the center of gravity, the more likely your rig will tip over during turns.

Braking as you maneuver through a curve is dangerous because the wheels can lock. Instead of braking, slow to a safe speed before entering a curve. Ease off the accelerator or downshift. If you downshift, slow down enough before you shift to be in the bottom of a usable engine rpm (revolutions per minute) when you shift. This will allow you to speed up when you need to. You can then speed up slightly in the curve. This will help keep your rig stable. When you are through the curve, bring your rig back up to speed.

Note: When approaching a curve, watch your speedometer as you slow down to a safe speed. After driving at high speeds for a long period of time, your body may be fooled into thinking you have slowed down enough, but you may still be traveling at too high a speed for the curve.

DRIVING ON HILLS
Adjusting Your Speed

Gravity affects speed on upgrades and downgrades. On upgrades, your rig is working against gravity. To maintain speed, you must increase pressure on the accelerator.

Going downhill, your vehicle is working with gravity to increase your speed. You must be careful to slow your rig to a safe speed to keep it under control. This will be discussed in detail in a later chapter.

CAUTION:

The speeds posted for curves are the safe speeds for cars in good weather. To be safe, drive your truck slower than the posted curve speed.

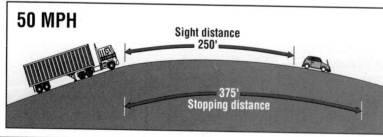

Effect of Speed on Sight Distance

40 MPH
Sight distance 250'
Stopping distance 250'

50 MPH
Sight distance 250'
375' Stopping distance

Figure **13-7** Your field of vision often requires adjustments in your speed.

HOW FAR CAN YOU SEE?

How far you can see and your **field of vision** also require speed adjustments. You must adjust your speed to how far you can see ahead of your rig. Driving at 45 mph, you will need 310 feet to stop your rig. If, because of fog or rain, you can see ahead only 100 feet, you are in a dangerous situation. Imagine a stalled vehicle on the road just beyond the limit of your vision! A general guideline is that you should always be able to stop within the distance you can see ahead (see Figure 13-7).

Night Driving

You can apply the same general guideline to night driving. Low beams let you see about 250 feet ahead. If you drive faster than 40 mph at night with low beams, you will not be able to stop in time to keep from hitting something that suddenly appears on the road in front of you (see Figure 13-8).

Bad Weather

Heavy rain, sleet, snow, fog, and smog can reduce your visibility a great deal. Poor weather conditions can limit what you see ahead to a very few feet. You must slow

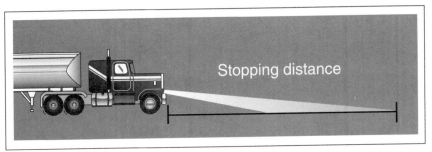

Figure **13-8** Low beams allow you to see about 250 feet ahead.

down as much as you need to drive safely. Remember, when it is hard for you to see other vehicles, other drivers are having trouble seeing you.

Speed and the Field of Vision

Your field of vision includes everything you can see (front and both sides) while looking straight ahead. The faster you go, the less you can see to the sides. As your speed increases, your field of vision decreases.

In order to see something clearly, you must stop your eyes from moving and fix them on the object you want to see. Try this experiment: Look in a mirror and try to see your eyeballs move. That's right! You can see them only when they stop moving.

Remember this when you are looking for cross traffic or at the scene around you. Moving eyes do not see clearly. You cannot react to what you do not see. You cannot see an object if you are not looking at it. Fix your eyes where you want to see.

SPEED AND TRAFFIC

The safest speed in traffic is usually the same speed as other vehicles (see Figure 13-9). Accidents happen more often when vehicles are traveling at different rates of speed. As a general rule, it is best to blend with other traffic. Adjust your speed to match that of others while still obeying traffic laws. Some drivers try to save time by speeding. This never pays because speeding is risky and often leads to accidents, and when there is other traffic, you usually cannot save more than a couple of minutes in an hour of driving. It simply is not worth the extra risk to speed.

The following may occur if you drive faster than the other traffic:

● You will have to pass many other vehicles (each time you change lanes to pass, there is risk of an accident).

● You will tire from driving faster.

● You will be more likely to attract the attention of the police or highway patrol.

● You will waste fuel and increase the wear on your brakes (going with the flow is not only safer but also easier and cheaper).

Figure **13-9** Continual visual search makes your driving a rig safe and efficient.

Chapter Fourteen
Night Driving

Photo copyright
© TruckShots

Night Driving Factors

Night Driving Procedures

Night Driving Adjustments

OBJECTIVES

When you have completed this chapter, you should be able to:

- Show how varying amounts of light affects your ability to see

- Describe how and when to use high-beam headlights

- Know the three factors that most affect night driving: the driver, the road, and the rig

- Get your rig ready for night driving

- Explain how headlight glare interferes with the vision of other drivers

- Describe factors affecting night vision

- Show how sunglasses help night vision

KEY TERMS

Auxiliary lights
Fatigue
Glare
Overdriving

Sight distance
Turn signal lights
Vision

INTRODUCTION

Night driving problems require special attention by the driver and change the following:

- Inspection routines
- Scan and search
- Communication
- Speed control
- Space management

This chapter discusses how to meet the special demands of night driving.

NIGHT DRIVING FACTORS

Your vision at night is less because there is less light. In order to see possible hazards, you must be closer to them. Not being aware of this simple fact causes more than one-half of all traffic accidents occuring at night. Four factors contribute to the night driving problem: driver, road, vehicle, and weather.

The Driver

As a beginning tractor-trailer driver, you should be aware of factors affecting your driving at night. These factors include **vision, glare, fatigue,** and lack of experience.

Vision

Your eyes need time to adjust to the change between daylight and darkness. But, even after they adjust, your eyes cannot see as well at night as they can during the day. Objects are harder to make out. You cannot see as well to the sides. The bottom line to this: You have limited vision at night.

Glare

Glare from oncoming headlights and other lights often causes temporary blindness and, as you may realize, recovering from glare takes time. Unfortunately, while your eyes recover, you and your rig continue moving along the road.

Fatigue

Fatigue is always a concern when you drive, but more so at night. Why? Because you do not see as clearly when you are tired, and, as you become less alert and are slower to see hazards, you do not react as quickly (see Figure 14-1).

Figure **14-1** The more hours you drive, the more fatigue you experience.

Lack of Experience

Lack of experience driving a rig and the problems of reduced vision, glare, and fatigue add up to the fact that new drivers have higher nighttime accident rates than more experienced drivers. In view of these facts, you must learn how to adjust your speed, space management, and driving techniques to night conditions as soon as possible.

Road Conditions Affecting Night Driving

These five road conditions can affect night driving:

1. Low-level light at night
2. Changes in levels of light
3. How well you know the road
4. Other road users
5. Drivers who are under the influence of alcohol or drugs

Low-level light at night.   Lighting on two-lane roads depends on headlights. Headlights are useful for a short and narrow path directly ahead of your vehicle. However, it is useful to remember that headlight beams do not bend around corners.

Changes in levels of light.   You must continually adjust your eyes to different types and degrees of light. Flashing lights distract as much as they illuminate, and traffic signals are hard to see against a background of other lights in towns and cities. Going through a business district in the rain, for example, can be very difficult because of the extra glare. Your rig may also need extra stopping distance.

How well you know the road.   If you are driving at night, you need to be extra alert on roads you have never driven during the day. Do not take even familiar roads for granted. Your view of the road will not be the same at night, so situations on the same road will also change.

Other road users.   Other road users, generally, cannot be easily seen at night. They include pedestrians, joggers, bicyclists, and animals. All are hazards, and you must be on alert for all of them.

Drivers who are under the influence.   It is always possible to meet a driver on the road who is under the influence of drugs or alcohol. Your chance of meeting one increases after sundown. Keep this in mind when driving past roadside taverns and similar businesses, such as liquor stores, strip clubs, or ballrooms.

Driving Your Vehicle at Night

As a driver, you must be sure your rig is safe for night driving (see Figure 14-2). Be sure to check the following:

- Headlights
- Auxiliary lights
- Turn signals
- Windshield

1. Headlights
2. Side-marker lights
3. Side reflectors
4. Turn signal lights
4a. Turn signal lights (optional location)
5. Identification lights
6. Clearance lights

Figure **14-2** Your rig should be equipped with the proper tools to make driving at night less difficult.

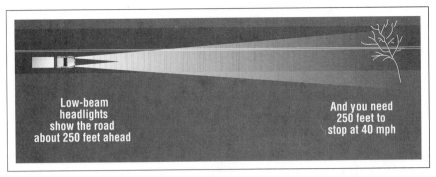

Low-beam headlights show the road about 250 feet ahead

And you need 250 feet to stop at 40 mph

Figure **14-3** Never overdrive your headlights or sight distance.

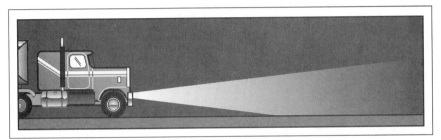

Figure **14-4** Slow down so you can stop in the distance you see ahead.

- Side windows
- Rear-view mirrors

Headlights. Your tractor's headlights are your best source of light on the road after sundown. They are also the main sign to other road users of your rig's location. Be sure your headlights are clean and properly adjusted at all times.

The distance you can see ahead is much less at night than during the day. Low beam headlights light a path about 250 feet ahead of your rig (less than the length of a football field). High beams light 350 to 500 feet.

Your **sight distance** is limited to the range your headlights provide. You must drive at a speed that will allow you to stop within your sight distance. If your speed is greater than this, you are **overdriving** your headlights (see Figure 14-3). Driving within your headlight or sight distance is your best bet for avoiding accidents with objects or other road users (see Figure 14-4).

Auxiliary lights. When all lights are working, big rigs can be easily seen by other highway users (see Figure 14-5). The following **auxiliary lights** must be clean and working:

- Reflectors
- Marker lights
- Clearance lights

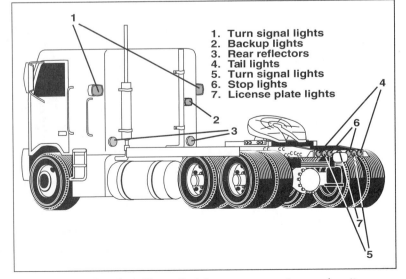

1. Turn signal lights
2. Backup lights
3. Rear reflectors
4. Tail lights
5. Turn signal lights
6. Stop lights
7. License plate lights

Figure **14-5** Auxiliary lights on your rig make it easier for others to see you at night.

Figure **14-6** Turn signals assist in communicating with other roadway users at night.

- Taillights
- ID lights
- Brake lights

Turn signals. How well you can communicate with other road users depends on your turn signals (see Figure 14-6). **Turn signal lights** that are not working or are dirty do not let you tell your intent. This increases the risk of an accident.

Windshield. A clean windshield is a must for safe driving (see Figure 14-7). Even a clean windshield shuts out 5 percent of the available light. Dirty windshields can block light and also cut your ability to see and relate to traffic. Clean the inside and outside of the windshield so you can see as well as possible.

Figure **14-7** A clean windshield and wipers that function are a must for safe driving at night.

Mirrors. Mirrors help you see what is going on around you. Unless you can see the other vehicles, you cannot relate to the other road users. Be sure to keep your mirrors clean and properly adjusted at all times (see Figure 14-8).

NIGHT DRIVING PROCEDURES

Before you attempt to drive at night, you must prepare yourself and your rig. If you wear glasses, be sure they are clean. Dirty or scratched glasses increase the effects of glare. Do not wear sunglasses at night. Wear sunglasses during the day, when you must also drive that night, to help your night vision because your eyes will need less time to adjust to the darkness.

Plan your route. Know where the rest stops are. Think ahead to known hazards along your route. Know the locations for unlighted areas, exit ramps, and construction areas and keep your eyes open for new changes.

Check all lights on the rig during your pretrip inspection. Clean or replace them as needed.

Do Not Blind Other Drivers

Headlight glare from oncoming and following vehicles can be a problem on the highway at night. The FMCSR state that a driver must dim his or her headlights 500 feet before encountering an oncoming vehicle. This regulation meets all state laws as well, plus it is also common sense to be considerate. If your lights make it hard for an oncoming driver to see, you and your rig are in danger.

Dim your headlights before they impair the vision of other drivers. Although not required by the FMCSR, you should also dim your headlights 200 feet before overtaking another vehicle. In addition to helping others, this action complies with most state laws.

Figure **14-8** Your mirrors add to your visual field.

Avoid Blinding Yourself

Keep the inside of the cab as dark as possible. Adjust the instrument panel lights to a low level, yet be sure they are bright enough to be read easily. Keep the dome light off! The brighter the inside of the cab, the harder it is to see outside.

Use high-beam headlights when it is safe and legal to do so. Many drivers make it a habit to always drive with low beams on. This seriously cuts down their vision. Most nighttime accidents happen because a driver cannot see. Always try to give yourself the best night vision (see Figure 14-9).

Take advantage of headlights from the vehicles ahead to spot hazards, and let road signs and reflectors act as visual guides.

NIGHT DRIVING ADJUSTMENTS

Some basic daytime driving techniques must be modified for nighttime driving.

Communicating. Make sure you signal to reduce speed, stop, or turn in time. It is wise to signal earlier

Use high beams when safe and legal to do so

Figure **14-9** Use high beams when they will not impact visual fields on oncoming drivers.

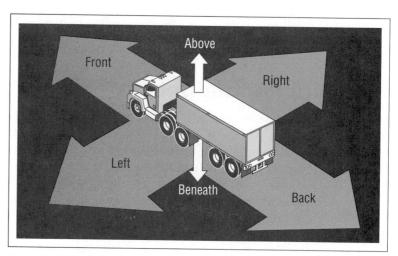

Figure **14-10** Managing the space around your rig is more crucial at night.

than you would during daytime conditions. Check to be sure your taillights, backup lights, and turn signal lights are in working order.

Signal your presence since eye contact is not always possible at night. Light use of the horn can be helpful, and do not hurt the vision of others by using your headlights to signal.

Space. Since you cannot see as well or as far at night, you need more time to react to events around your rig. Get the needed time by increasing the space around your rig (see Figure 14-10). Increase your following distance at night by at least 1 second more than the normal daytime following distance (review Chapter 12).

Speed. Adjust your rig's speed to keep the stopping distance within the sight distance. Do not overdrive your headlights. The lower speed is needed to keep from hitting objects when they suddenly come into view. If you do not adjust your speed to nighttime conditions, you will have too little time and too little space to safely react to hazards (see Figure 14-11).

Figure **14-11** Appropriate speeds keep stopping distance within your sight distance.

Chapter Fifteen
Extreme Driving Conditions

FROM NOW ON. . .

ONLY THE BEST
WILL DRIVE!

OBJECTIVES

When you have completed this chapter, you should be able to:

- Recognize conditions that reduce traction, such as rain, snow, ice, and mud

- Realize the effects of rain, snow, and ice on your ability to control your rig

- Understand the causes of skidding and jackknifing and how to avoid them

- Show the effects of ice, snow, water, mud, and debris on the rig's brakes

- Perform hot weather driving procedures

- Demonstrate the best ways of driving in the mountains

KEY TERMS

Arrester beds

Auxiliary brakes

Bleeding tar

Chain control area

Combination ramp and arrester bed

Electric retarders

Emergency equipment

Engine brakes

Escape ramp

Exhaust brakes

Extreme driving conditions

Gravity ramp

Hydraulic retarders

Jackknife

Sand pile

Skidding

Speed retarders

Tire chains

Traction

Visibility

INTRODUCTION

The words **extreme driving conditions** are easy to say—you have probably heard or used them yourself. But what do they really mean? "Extreme" means "the worst." The term refers to the most difficult driving conditions: when it is cold, wet, dry, hot, windy, snowing, or foggy. Driving in mountain ranges is also considered an extreme driving condition.

No one can learn how to drive in all these conditions by reading a book or sitting in a classroom. On the other hand, you can learn many useful facts and tips by studying this chapter. Since you may be driving a rig in all these conditions, continue reading very carefully.

EXTREME WEATHER

Knowing the rig's parts, systems, and how they work is critical when you drive in extreme weather conditions. Less traction and poor visibility are two major safety hazards. Less traction increases the stopping distance and decreases the driver's ability to control the rig. Reduced visibility means you will not see hazards as quickly, and you will have less time to respond.

Vehicle Checks

You must be sure both you and your rig are ready before you drive in extreme weather conditions. Make a regular thorough pretrip inspection (see Figure 15-1). This pretrip inspection should include the following items.

Coolant level and antifreeze concentration. Make sure the cooling system is full. A low coolant level affects the operation of the heater and defroster. If the coolant level is very low, the engine will not perform as well as it should. The antifreeze concentration should be checked with a tester (see vehicle or company specs).

Heating equipment. A badly heated cab can reduce your job efficiency. Be sure to check the heater hose for wear and the controls and fans. The operator's manual will tell you how to operate them. Check the window defrosters. Include the heaters for the mirrors, battery box, and fuel tanks in your check.

**Special Extreme Weather Checklist
for Pretrip Inspection**

- Coolant and antifreeze
- Heater/defroster
- Wipers/washers
- Tires
- Chains
- Brakes
- Lights and reflectors
- Windows and mirrors
- Hand and toe holds
- Radiator shutters and winterfronts
- Exposed wiring and air lines
- Fuel tank
- Engine and exhaust systems
- Coupling devices
- Interaxle differential lock
- Emergency equipment
- Weather reports and road conditions

Figure **15-1** Extreme weather conditions will change your pretrip inspection priorities.

Wipers/washers. Check the washer reservoir for cracks, collapsed areas, and loose clamps. Make sure it is full and the fluid is not frozen. In the winter, add antifreeze to the reservoir and make sure the washers work.

Test the condition of the rubber blades on the wipers. They should operate at the manufacturer's recommended arm pressure. The wrong pressure will let the blades slide over the snow instead of sweeping it off your windshield.

Tires. Check all tire mountings. Look for any flaws on the sidewalls or tread. Check the air pressure with a gauge (see Figure 15-2). Are all tires inflated properly? Check the tread depth also. Do you have at least 4/32-inch tread in every major groove on the front wheels and at least 2/32-inch tread on the other wheels? The tires must have enough traction to easily push the rig over wet pavement or through snow.

Chains. Nobody likes to use tire chains, but you must be prepared. Carry the correct number of properly fitting chains and extra cross-links. Watch for broken hooks, worn or broken cross-links, and bent or broken side chains. (Tire chains are covered in greater detail later in this chapter.)

Figure **15-2** Check tire air pressure with a gauge.

Brakes.   Check the brake balance. The brakes should all apply pressure equally and at the same time. If one wheel stops turning before the others, it may cause a skid or handling problems. Check the adjustment and take up the slack, if needed.

Check the brake linings for ice. Ice can cut the braking power and cause the shoes to freeze to the brake drums. Keep trailer brakes released when parked.

Finally, drain the moisture from both the tractor and trailer air tanks. Water in the air lines can cause the brakes to freeze. If your rig has other moisture controls such as spitter valves or alcohol evaporators, check to be sure that they are operating properly.

Lights and reflectors.   Be sure they are not dirty, muddy, salty, icy, or snowy. Check often during a trip. How well you can see, and others can see you, depends on how clean the lenses are.

Hand and toe holds.   You can enter and leave the cab much more safely if you keep the hand and toe holds free of ice and snow. If you need to, use a brush to clean them before getting out of the cab.

Radiator shutters and winterfront.   Remove the ice from the radiator shutters. Ice can keep the shutters from opening and cause the engine to overheat. Keep a close check on the engine temperature when driving. If the engine overheats, you may need to adjust the shutters and winterfront to maintain proper operating temperature. Close them if the engine is too cold. Open them if it gets too hot.

Winterfronts that have to be checked are not recommended for engines with air-to-air aftercoolers. Some winterfronts must have air flow through to the automatic fan activator sensor.

Exposed wiring and air lines.   Be sure all wiring and lines are properly supported. Remove any ice or snow before and during a trip. Snow and ice buildup can cause the lines to sag and snag on the tire chains.

Figure **15-3**   Fill the fuel tank before you start your trip.

Fuel tank.   Make sure the fuel tank is full before you begin a trip (see Figure 15-3). If extreme weather is expected, top off the tank frequently. If you do not, you can run out of fuel and be stranded without power.

Beware of low-quality fuel. It can freeze (jell) in the fuel lines and filters. It is wise to fill the tank at the end of a trip to reduce the buildup of moisture, and it is also best to drain water from the bottom of fuel tanks. Ice buildup on a crossover line can freeze or break the fuel line between tanks.

Engine and exhaust systems.   The exhaust connections must be tight to keep carbon monoxide or other dangerous gases from leaking into the rig.

Coupling devices.   Make sure the fifth wheel is coated with a winter-grade lubricant to prevent binding. This will also help steering on slippery roads. Double-check the locking mechanism whenever you stop or every 300 miles.

Interaxle differential lock (if your rig has one).   Check the operator's manual for proper operation of the interaxle differential lock. If it is air operated, check for water in the air lines when you are stopped (see Figure 15-4).

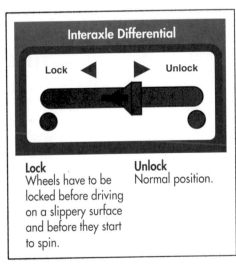

Figure **15-4**   If your rig has an interaxle differential lock, operate it according to directions in the owner's manual.

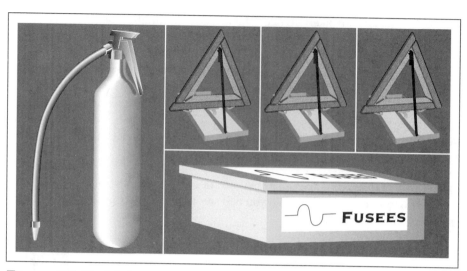

Figure **15-5** Make sure you have all necessary emergency equipment before you start your trip.

Emergency equipment. Driving in the winter without proper clothing and **emergency equipment** can be deadly. You also need drinking water, extra food, medicine (as needed), hats, boots, gloves, extra pants, and proper outerwear on hand in case you are stranded in extreme weather. You should also have a windshield scraper, snow brush, flashlight, fusees (road flares), and a small folding shovel (available through army surplus stores) (see Figure 15-5).

Weather reports and road conditions. Drivers should keep informed of the latest weather and road conditions. The National Weather Radio Service broadcasts on 162.40 to 162.55 MHz. They constantly update weather forecasts from many locations around the country. Be alert. Conditions often change quickly, so plan your route accordingly.

TIRE CHAINS

Tire chains are a must for driving in many areas. Chains increase traction by as much as 500 percent. They can be the difference between driving and not driving. Chains improve the pulling power of the drive wheels when going uphill, and when going downhill, they improve the trailer wheel braking. They also help prevent stalls, skids, and jackknifes.

Mount your chains at the first sign of slippery conditions. To continue driving without them is to take the chance of skidding, damaging your rig, or getting stuck. Check individual state laws and regulations regarding the use of tire chains.

Using Chains

Chains are most effective in heavy, wet snow. If you drive on a heavy ice accumulation or in freezing rain on top of snow, you will probably need reinforced chains (see the section "How Chains Are Made"). Conventional chains provide little traction. In light snow, chains do not help traction much, but they do provide some stability for the rig. Most chains are not effective on glare ice, or black ice.

Installing Your Chains

Do not hesitate to install your chains. Once you have learned how, it is pretty easy. A few guidelines will help:

- Properly installed chains should be snug, not rigid.
- Chains are designed to "creep," or move. This prevents tire damage.
- Tighten your chains after driving 5 miles. This will keep them from slapping against the trailer or catching on the suspension.

Be careful when you put on your chains. When you are outside the rig, other drivers may not see you, or they see you and may put on their brakes but slide into you. Remember that slow-moving vehicles, even with chains, are very quiet in the snow. New snowfall absorbs sounds. There is danger also from your own rig. Hot tires melt snow. The surface can get quite slippery and cause your rig to slide sideways when it is parked.

When getting ready to put on chains, you should:

- Pull well off the road.
- Park on a level, solid surface.
- Be careful; footing can be slippery.
- Work facing traffic.
- Plan where to go if there is an out-of-control vehicle or one whose path suggests the driver may not see you.
- Make sure your own rig does not slide into you.
- Be sure you put on the chains right-side out.

How Chains Are Made

Cross chains go across the tread of the tire and provide traction (see Figure 15-6). Side chains go around the tires in the same direction as the sidewalls. They hold the cross chains. The cross chains are made with two types of links. One type is an ordinary, or conventional, link (see Figure 15-7). The other type is a reinforced link. This link has V-lugs or cleats welded to cross links to improve the chain's grip.

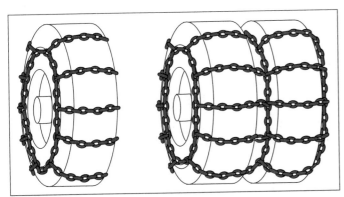

Figure **15-6** Chains are made for single tires or to go over dual wheels.

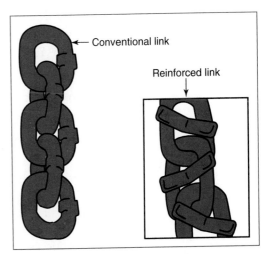

Figure **15-7** Standard or reinforced chains can assist when driving on ice or snow.

Chains may be single and made to go over a single tire. The chain is used on the outside tire of dual wheels. Double chains are made to go over a complete set of duals.

When to Use Your Chains

Many mountain states have rules for using chains in certain kinds of weather. Some states require that chains be carried in the truck during certain months. Drivers should know the rules of the states in which they operate. These rules may be obtained from state departments of motor vehicles.

Many states have laws that say where the chains must be installed on the rig. In some western states, the locations may vary from one part of the state to another. Again, it is the driver's duty to know the regulations.

You may enter a **chain control area.** This is simply a highway area on which it is illegal to drive without chains. Checkpoints usually are set up ahead of chain control areas. Trucks are stopped and checked to see that the proper number of chains are on board. If not, the inspectors will not let the rig into the chain control area. It is the driver's duty to be prepared.

"Chains advised" means it is your choice. Be careful in these areas because there can be large fines if you spin out or cause an accident and do not have chains.

STARTING YOUR ENGINE IN COLD WEATHER

In the winter, all engines are harder to start. The lower the temperature, the harder engines are to get started. Big rigs are no exception. There are, however, a number of devices that can be very helpful:

- Special starting substances, like ether or an ether-based fluid
- Glow plugs
- Preheaters

Ether.   Ether has a very low flash point. It ignites easily even at subzero temperatures. Since it is such a high energy fuel, using ether has some drawbacks. If not used properly or used too often, ether can damage the engine by cracking cylinder heads, breaking pistons, or snapping connecting rods. Also, ether is highly flammable. If you should spill any on your clothes, change as soon as possible. Stay away from open flames, matches, cigarettes, or hot exhaust pipes and heaters. They could easily cause your clothing to ignite.

Ether is packaged in a number of forms:

- Aerosol spray cans
- Pressurized cylinders
- Driver-controlled injection systems
- Capsules

These can be applied both manually (by hand) and automatically.

Capsules, aerosol sprays, and pressurized cylinders are used manually. One advantage of using a capsule is that only one person is needed to start the engine. The capsule is placed in a special holder attached to the air cleaner. Each capsule provides one start. Do not place it in the air cleaner. It could be sucked into the engine and could cause engine damage.

Aerosol sprays or pressurized cylinders require two people to start the engine. One person sprays ether into a rag hung in front of the air cleaner. The other starts the engine. It takes *very little* ether to start the engine. Be careful. Too much spray may cause a flashback fire or engine damage.

Automatic injection systems need only the driver to start the engine. Ether is put into the engine in one of two ways: The driver turns on a switch in the cab, and ether is injected into the engine, or ether is injected into the engine automatically when the engine is started.

Because the amount of ether is regulated, there is no danger of injecting too much ether. Do not use this system with glow plugs or preheaters.

Glow plugs.   Glow plugs are simply electric heating elements that warm the air coming into the engine from the air intake. They can be mounted in the intake manifold or in each combustion chamber. On diesel engines, they are sometimes located in a precombustion chamber.

Before operating a glow plug, consult the operator's manual and/or the instrument panel for instructions. The plug may need a pump that is hand-primed to spray the fuel into the combustion chamber.

Glow plugs raise the temperature in the combustion chamber. It is the hot compressed air that ignites the fuel. This usually takes about 60 seconds. *Never* use ether and glow plugs at the same time.

Preheaters.   Preheaters keep the engine warm while parked for the night. There are two types: in-block and immersion.

Most of the preheaters used on truck tractors are the in-block type. They fit into the freeze plug holes in the lower water jacket. The other end of the preheaters heat the coolant to approximately 160°F, which is near normal operating temperature. The coolant circulates through the engine and keeps it warm (see Figure 15-8).

The immersion type of preheater is used on off-highway construction vehicles and mining equipment.

Figure **15-8** Preheaters heat coolant to approximately 160°F. The coolant circulates throughout the engine and keeps it warm.

When you use a preheater, you do not need a warm-up period. You can use normal starting procedures. In extremely cold areas, heaters are often used with battery box heaters, oil sump heaters, and fuel heaters. Do not use a preheater without instruction. Consult your company's maintenance staff for further instructions.

An Engine That Will Not Start

If your engine will not start when you use starting aids, check to be sure the engine is getting fuel.

To check for fuel, look at the exhaust stack while you crank the engine. If no vapor or smoke is visible, the engine is not getting fuel. Do not keep on cranking the engine. This will not start the engine. It will only run down the battery. Check the fuel tank and fuel lines to be sure they are not blocked by ice or gelled fuel. Also check the fuel tank vent.

Never crank the engine more than 15 seconds at a time. If the engine is getting fuel and still will not start, check the electrical system. If the rig has an electrical starter, remember the battery does not operate at full capacity in cold weather. The battery must be in the best possible condition. Check for the following:

- Corrosion on the terminals
- Loose connections
- Cracks in the cables
- Moisture in the cables

If the rig has an air starter, the engine will not start unless there is an air supply. If there is no air, the air supply can be restored from another tractor or an air compressor. Check the operator's manual for the best way to do this.

BAD WEATHER OPERATING HAZARDS

There are two major hazards when driving in bad weather (see Figure 15-9): less **visibility** and less **traction**.

PRIMARY HAZARDS

Reduced visibility

Reduced traction

- Road surface
    - Different surfaces, different degrees of traction
    - Be aware of changing conditions
- Speed
    - Speed magnifies mistakes
    - Determine the speed at which the wheels roll without spinning
    - Adjust speed to changing road surfaces and conditions

Figure **15-9**   The two major driving hazards in bad weather are lower visibility and less traction.

Less Visibility

When ice and snow build up on windows and mirrors, you do not see as well. When this happens, you must stop often to clean the windows and mirrors. Do not drive with your side or rearview mirrors blocked. All lights and reflectors also should be free of ice, snow, and mud. Stop and clean them when you need to. Some states will issue a citation for a dirty windshield.

Even when your windows, lights, and reflectors are clean, your visibility is sometimes limited by rain, snow, or fog. Slow down and drive very carefully (see Chapter 13).

Sometimes visibility is almost zero. This happens at night in heavy snow, a downpour of rain, or dense fog. Driving is not safe in these conditions. Stop. Wait until you can see better before continuing.

Less Traction

Remember, traction is the grip, or friction, of the tires on the road. Different surfaces have different amounts of traction. Some states use an asphalt mix for roads that reduces spray and hydroplaning when wet. If there is ice or packed snow, about 80 percent of the traction is lost.

Slick roads—due to rain, sleet, ice, or snow—will cause drive wheels to spin easily. This often results in less traction and therefore less control of the rig. As you drive, be aware of changing conditions. To check traction, put on your brakes periodically.

Proper tire inflation, tread, and weight on the drive wheels provides better traction and better control of your rig.

Speed is another factor in traction. As the rig's speed increases, traction decreases. When traction is poor for any reason, slow down until you have the rig well under control.

If the road is wet, reduce your speed by one-fourth. This means if you are driving 55 mph, slow down to about 40. On packed snow, reduce your speed by 50 percent. At 55 mph, slow to about 27. On icy surfaces, cut down to about one-third of your normal speed. At 55 mph, slow to about 18 (see Figure 15-10).

Remember, these are general guidelines. Exact speeds will vary with the conditions. The following are also factors in determining a safe speed:

- Weight of the rig
- Type of rig
- Condition of the tires
- Type of road surface
- Temperature
- Type of snow or ice

Black ice is so clear that you can see the road surface under the ice. This makes it very hard to spot. It usually occurs on bridges, beneath overpasses, in dips in the road (where water collects), in shaded areas, and on the lower sides of banked curves.

Black ice is also very hard to spot at night. If a driver is not aware of the black ice, it can be very dangerous. When you are driving

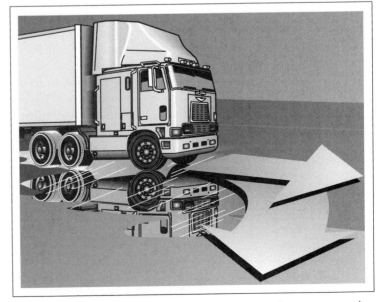

Figure **15-10** On icy surfaces, cut down speed by one-third or more.

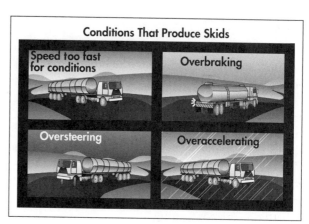

Figure **15-11**   The four basic causes of skids.

in near-freezing rain, feel for ice along the front of a mirror. If ice is there, there also may be ice on the road. When in doubt, check your traction by putting on the brakes gently to see if the vehicle skids. Before you perform this check, be sure no one is behind you.

Skidding

Skidding happens when a rig's tires lose traction on the road. There are four basic causes of skids (see Figure 15-11):

1. Driving too fast
2. Overacceleration
3. Overbraking
4. Oversteering

Driving too fast for the road conditions causes most of the serious skids. Drivers who adjust their driving to the conditions do not overaccelerate and do not have to overbrake or oversteer because of too much speed.

Overacceleration puts too much power to the drive wheels. This causes the tires to spin and may cause a skid.

Overbraking means braking too hard for the surface conditions. Excessive use of the service brakes is one cause of overbraking. Suddenly releasing the accelerator also can cause a braking effect that throws the rig into a skid. Skids also can be caused by using the engine brake incorrectly or downshifting to a gear lower than the speed requires.

Drivers overbrake when they drive too fast for the conditions, do not look far enough ahead, or do not leave enough following distance.

Oversteering occurs when a driver tries to go around a turn too fast and turns the steering wheel too quickly. The drive wheels want to continue to move straight ahead. Then there is too little grip between the tires and road. The result is a skidding trailer and a tractor-trailer jackknife.

Jackknifing

When the drive wheels lock up, they cause the tractor or trailer to skid. This skid can result in a **jackknife.** Be careful not to make things worse by putting on the brakes in a skid (see Figure 15-12).

SKIDDING AND JACKKNIFING

Causes

Overacceleration

Overbraking

Oversteering

Speed too fast for conditions

Figure **15-12** Four primary causes of skidding and jackknifing.

DRIVING IN BAD WEATHER

Professional drivers soon learn that trips over icy roads will take longer than driving the same distance under good road and weather conditions. In this section, discussion focuses on driving on slippery surfaces and the problem of wet brakes.

Driving on Slippery Surfaces

Follow these precautions on slippery surfaces:

- Start gently. At the beginning of the trip, take your time, getting a feel for the road. Do not hurry.
- Adjust turning and braking to the conditions. Make turns as gradually as possible. Do not brake any harder than you need to. Do not use the engine brake if possible (see Figure 15-13).
- Check your mirrors. Check the trailer when you brake to be sure it is not drifting to one side. You can prevent a jackknife by acting when there is still time to recover. At night, if your trailer's lights begin to show in the mirror, it may mean a jackknifing trailer.
- Adjust your speed to the conditions. Do not overtake and pass other vehicles unless you have to. Slow to a safe speed.
- Watch far enough ahead to flow with the traffic. This will help you avoid the need to change speeds quickly.
- Take curves and turns at slower speeds. Brake before curves. Be sure you are in the right gear before you enter a curve. Speed up slightly in the curve.
- As it gets warmer, ice melts and becomes more slippery. Slow down even more, if necessary.
- Avoid driving beside other vehicles. Stay out of packs. Leave your rig room for emergencies.
- Maintain longer following distance.
- When traffic looks congested ahead, fall back. Stop, if needed, and wait for traffic to thin out.
- Plan ahead for stops to avoid panic stopping.
- If your truck does not have antilock brakes, use controlled braking or stub braking to stop safely. If it

Figure **15-13** Caution: When your drive wheels have poor traction, the retarders may cause them to skid. Turn off your retarders when the road is wet, icy, or snow covered.

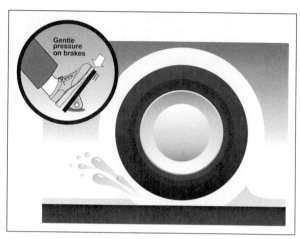

Figure **15-14** If your rig has antilock brakes, apply them and hold for safest stop.

does have antilock brakes, do *not* pump the brakes. Apply them hard and hold. This will provide the safest stop (see Figure 15-14).

Wet Brakes

When you drive in heavy rain or deep standing water, the brakes will get wet. Then the linings may slip on the drum or disc. This can cause uneven braking. The final result can be losing your brakes, wheel lockup, veering from one side of the lane to the other, or a jackknife.

It is best to avoid standing water. However, if you must drive through water, follow these steps:

1. Slow down.
2. Shift to a lower gear.
3. Place your left foot lightly on the brake.
4. Increase engine speed (revolutions per minute, or rpm).
5. Accelerate through the water

After you are out of the water, follow these steps:

1. Stay in the low gear.
2. Keep your left foot on the brake.
3. Increase the rpm to prevent stalling.
4. Keep a light pressure on the brakes for a short distance to dry them out.
5. Release the brakes.

Check to the rear of your rig to make sure no one is following too closely. Then make a test stop to be certain the brakes are working properly.

Summary: Operating in Bad Weather

All drivers and rigs have limits. As a tractor-trailer driver, one of your duties is to know these limits and adjust your driving to the changing conditions. The best way to prevent accidents in bad weather is to adjust your speed, braking, steering, and space cushion. When it is too dangerous to drive, stop and wait until the conditions improve and are safe to drive in again.

FREEING A STUCK VEHICLE

Avoid if possible

- Soft berm
- Deep snow
- Muddy road
- Slippery driving surface

When stuck

- Do not spin wheels
- Use traction aids
- Lock interaxle differential
- Place in higher gear
- Accelerate gradually

When using a tow truck,
remember:

- You are responsible for your vehicle and cargo
- You should maintain control
- You should hook the cable or chain to vehicle

Figure **15-15** Getting stuck can often be avoided by smart driving.

A Vehicle That Is Stuck

The best advice about a stuck vehicle is, Don't get stuck! You can often keep from getting stuck by smarter driving.

Stay away from situations that can cause a rig to get stuck, such as soft dirt on the roadside, deep snow, mud, and icy, slippery surfaces.

When in doubt, avoid any unknown or suspicious surface. Be alert when you leave the main road to make a delivery or when you pull off the road for rest, repair, or a vehicle check (see Figure 15-15).

Freeing Your Stuck Rig

To free your stuck rig, follow these steps:

1. Do not spin the drive wheels or rock back and forth. These actions will simply dig the vehicle in further. On ice, spinning the wheels will cause heat. This will warm the ice under the tires and reduce traction by about 50 percent.
2. Use traction aids. Dig under the front of the rig's wheels. Scatter sand or gravel in the path of the wheels. Lay loose chains in front of the wheels.
3. Lock the interaxle differential (if your rig has one).
4. Use a low gear, such as second or third gear. This will keep the wheels from spinning by reducing the force and applying it smoothly.

5. Start with the steering wheels straight ahead. If you have to start with the wheels turned, accelerate gently. Turn the steering wheel back and forth gently (less than an inch). This prepares a path for the wheels.

6. As you begin to move, accelerate smoothly and gently. Ease off the accelerator if you start to slide.

Towing

If your efforts to free your rig fail, call a tow truck. Remember that you are responsible for the equipment and cargo. You, not the tow truck driver, should supervise the operation. If the tow truck driver starts to do something you think is wrong or unsafe, stop him or her. Then correct the problem (see Figure 15-16).

Agree on the procedure before beginning the hookup or towing operation:

● In what direction will the tow truck pull?
● In what direction will you steer?
● When is the tow truck to stop?

The driver of the rig should signal the tow truck to stop. Agree on a signal, such as the horn or flashing lights.

It is best for you to hook the chain or cable yourself:

1. Pass it through the hole in the front bumper. Do not hook it to the bumper.

2. Attach the chain or cable to the tow hooks on the frame. If there are no hooks, fasten it to a solid portion of the frame. Be careful not to hook it around the steering tie rod or spring shackles.

3. From the rear, secure the cable or chain to the tow hooks or frame.

4. Leave enough slack in the cable or chain to keep the rig, once it is freed, from lurching into the tow truck.

5. The tow truck should accelerate gently.

6. When you have been pulled clear, signal the tow truck driver to stop.

7. Apply the tractor-trailer brakes. When the rig's brakes are applied, they will prevent the tractor-trailer from rear-ending the tow truck. Bring both the rig and the tow truck to a stop.

Figure **15-16** You, not the tow truck driver, should supervise any towing operation.

If Your Rig Breaks Down in a Remote Area

If your rig should break down or you are stranded in a remote area because of the weather, stay in the cab. Being out in the wind and cold can be dangerous. Put on extra clothing to stay warm. Do not try to walk for help. You may not make it. Stay with your rig so you can move it after it is freed.

If you must leave your rig, leave a note on the steering wheel telling the following:

- When you left
- Where you went
- When you think you will be back

If your engine will run, do not let exhaust fumes collect in the cab. Keep a window slightly open.

Smart drivers prepare for emergencies by carrying a supply of drinking water, candy bars, fruit, blankets, toilet paper, and extra clothing when bad weather is expected.

HOT WEATHER

In hot weather, you must be certain your rig is prepared for the worst. There are several areas that you must watch very carefully. They are as follows.

Vehicle Inspection

This is an important nondriving duty. You are the one who will be out there with the rig. If the heat becomes severe, you must deal with it. Be sure your rig and all the equipment can stand the heat. Check the following very carefully:

Tires. Check the mounting and inflation. If you are hauling hazmat, inspect them every 2 hours or 100 miles. If you are not hauling hazmat, inspect the tires every three hours or 150 miles. An increase of 10 to 15 pounds per square inch (psi) is common. Check the heat of the tire with the back of your hand, not the palm. If the pressure increase is more than 15 psi or if a tire becomes too hot to touch, stop driving. The tire could blow out or catch fire. Let it cool off. Never bleed air from tires when they are hot. Let them cool and then recheck the pressure (see Figure 15-17).

Engine lubrication. Oil helps cool the engine. Keep the oil at the proper level. Do not overfill. Check it before you start and often while driving. Check the oil temperature gauge regularly. Be familiar with the manufacturer's specs.

Figure **15-17** In hot weather, check tires, mounting, and inflation to guard against blowouts or fire.

Figure **15-18** In warm weather, check your water temperature gauge often.

Engine cooling system. Engines are big and powerful, but they also are delicate. They need heat to run, but too much heat can damage or ruin them quickly. The engine cooling system is vital to proper engine operation and should be kept full and clean. Watch your water temperature gauge (see Figure 15-18). Some types of engines tend to run warmer than others. Read your operator's manual to find the correct temperature for optimum engine operation.

Always carry extra coolant. If you must add coolant, let the engine cool. Then run the engine at high enough rpms to circulate the fluid. Very carefully remove the coolant reservoir cap with a heavy cloth. Keep your face and body clear because the coolant may spray. Add the new coolant slowly.

Engine belts. Check the belt tension. Then check the belts for cracking, fraying, or wear. Slipping belts can cause the fan or water pump to stop operating, which will result in an overheated engine. Carry a spare set or used belts to minimize delays.

Hoses. Check for cracks, fraying, and kinks. Be sure they do not collapse when the engine accelerates. The coolant must circulate freely to keep the engine operating at the right temperature.

DRIVING IN THE DESERT

Washes. Secondary roads often are built through dry riverbeds. In heavy rains, these roads, or washes, can flood very quickly. When it looks like rain, get to a main road as soon as possible.

Bleeding tar. Tar in roads often rises to the surface when it is very hot. Spots where tar is bleeding can become very slippery. Watch for them, and avoid them whenever possible.

High speeds. High speeds create additional heat for the tires and engine. Avoid continuous high-speed driving under hot, desert conditions. The heat cannot be disposed of by the engine cooling system, and tires simply have no way of giving off the heat.

Vehicle breakdown. If your rig breaks down in a remote area, do not leave it. Your body will not be able to stand the heat and sunlight. Body fluids are used up rapidly in the desert, and you will become dehydrated. You also can suffer sunstroke, so stay in the cab or sit under the trailer while you wait for help to come.

MOUNTAIN DRIVING

Mountain driving is different from other driving conditions. First of all, you and your rig must deal with gravity. Gravity is the force that pulls objects toward the center of the earth, and it changes normal driving patterns. It does not matter whether you are going uphill or down a grade. The pull of gravity is so severe you must adjust your driving. Failing to adjust can make your trip more difficult and more tiring. It can also damage your rig.

When you climb a grade, gravity adds to the weight of the load. This pulls the rig down. It will take more horsepower to move the rig. You cannot pass other vehicles as easily (see Figure 15-19).

When you go downhill, gravity pulls the rig toward the earth. This increases your momentum. If the grade is steep, gravity can pull the vehicle off the road on curves, bumps, or where there is loose gravel on the road.

Figure **15-19** In mountain driving, gravity requires adjustments in normal driving patterns.

Inspections

If your rig has air brakes, check the system carefully before driving in the mountains. Check the following:

- Compressor: Be sure it can maintain full reservoir pressure.
- Pressure drop when the brakes are fully applied: Be sure it is within the limits.
- Ice build-up on service or spring brakes.
- Slack adjusters: Check for correct adjustment.
- Air leaks: See if you can hear any. Check when the brakes are on and then again when they are off.
- Glad hands and air lines: Be sure they are secured.
- Brake drums: Check for overheating. Do not touch a drum. It can burn your hand. Hold the back of your hand close to the drum. Some heat is normal, but not a high temperature.
- Trailer supply valve: Be sure it is working.

When Driving on Upgrades

- **Shifting:** If the rpm falls, downshift to the next lower gear. Gravity will cut your speed during the downshift. Complete the shift quickly before the rpm reaches the bottom of the range. Downshift until you reach a gear that will maintain the rpm.
- **Position:** Drive on upgrades with patience. Move your rig to the far right or truck lane. Stay in this lane. Do not try to pass if you cannot do so quickly and safely. Remember, a slow uphill truck creates a negative reaction to our industry. Other drivers can lose patience and drive recklessly.

Note: Most states require the use of flashers under 40 mph.

- **Watch your gauges:** Pulling a heavy load up a long grade can cause overheating. Check the coolant and water temperature gauge often. Shift a few hundred rpms earlier than the lowest rpm for that gear. This will help compensate.

When Driving on Downgrades

Watch for signs showing the angle and length of the grade. These will help you decide on the correct speed for going downhill. Never go faster than the posted maximum safe speed. Talk with other drivers who have made the same downhill runs before. They can often offer helpful hints.

Because gravity plays a big part in mountain driving, you must allow for the pull of gravity on your rig when going downhill. Make sure your brakes are properly adjusted. Check your brakes before starting downhill. Check the traffic pattern in your mirrors, especially to the left and rear.

Downshift before you start down the hill. Never downshift while going downhill because if you try to downshift, you will not be able to get into a lower gear. You might not be able to shift at all. If that happens, you will lose all braking effect from the engine.

If you try to force an automatic transmission into a lower gear at a high speed, you can damage the transmission, and if you damage the transmission, you may lose all engine braking.

If you drive an older truck, a general rule is to use the same gear going downhill that you used going uphill. If you drive a newer truck, choose a lower gear because the truck is more streamlined and may have a more powerful engine.

CHECKLIST FOR MOUNTAIN DRIVING

Upgrades

- Downshift until you find a gear that will maintain rpms
- Position vehicle in right lane
- Do not pass

Downgrades

- Never downshift while descending
- Use a low gear
- Go slow
- Use close to rated engine speed to maximize drag
- Use snubbing method when braking

Figure **15-20** Knowing the skills required for safe and efficient mountain driving makes these trips easier.

When you are in the right gear, your engine will not race. Be sure your speed is not too fast for the total weight of the vehicle and cargo, length of the grade, steepness of the grade, road conditions, and weather.

Use your engine as the primary way to control your speed. The braking effect of the engine is the greatest when it is near the governed rpms and the transmission is in a lower gear. Save your brakes until you really need them. *Never* shift into neutral and coast. It is both illegal and unsafe to do so.

If you use your brakes too much, they may get hot and fade. Then you will have to apply them harder to get a braking effect. If you keep using them, they may fail completely, and then you will have no brakes (see Figure 15-20).

In an effort to determine the best way to brake when going down hills, the University of Michigan Transportation Research Institute (UMTRI) in cooperation with the National Highway Traffic Safety Administration (NHTSA) has performed experiments and has released these findings (March 1992):

The right way to go down long grades is to use a low gear and go slowly. Use close to rated engine speed to maximize drag. If you go slowly enough, the brakes will be able to get rid of enough heat so they will work as they should. The driver's most important consideration is to pick a control speed that is not too fast for the weight of the vehicle, the length of the grade, and the steepness of the grade.

Drivers who are unfamiliar with routes in mountainous regions need to select a low speed to be safe. . . . However, if the driver is not familiar with which grades are long ones, the driver needs to proceed with caution—perhaps at a low speed of no more than 20 mph . . .

To control speed going down a mountain, some people favor using a light, steady pressure to drag the brakes while others favor a series of snubs, each sufficient to slow the vehicle by approximately 6 mph in about 3 seconds. The snubbing strategy uses pressure over 20 psi for heavy trucks while the light drag may involve pressures under

10 psi. Tests have shown that either method will result in approximately the same average brake temperature at the bottom of the mountain as long as the same average speed is maintained. However, the snubbing method, due to the higher pressure involved, will aid in making each brake do its fair share of the work. Hence, the snubbing method will result in more uniform temperatures from brake to brake and thereby aid in preventing brakes from overheating.

Furthermore, light, steady pressure at highway speeds on short grades of roughly one mile in length can lead to problems with 'hot spotting' and drum cracking and fragmenting if the brake linings are new.

In summary, the most important considerations are to go slow enough and use the right gear. Remember that compared to a strategy based upon light pressure dragging, the snubbing strategy will aid in making each brake do its fair share of the work and reduce the tendency for hot-spotting and drum-cracking of new or recently relined brakes.

The American Association of Motor Vehicle Administrators (AAMVA) in their Model CDL Driver's Manual makes this recommendation:

Once the vehicle is in the proper low gear, the following is a proper braking technique:

1. *Apply the brakes just hard enough to feel a definite slowdown.*
2. *When your speed has been reduced to approximately 5 mph below your safe speed, release the brakes. The brake application should last for about three (3) seconds.*
3. *When your speed has increased to your safe speed, repeat steps 1 and 2.*

For example, if your safe speed is 40 mph, do not put on the brakes until you reach 40 mph. Then brake hard enough to reduce your speed to 35 mph. Release the brakes. Repeat this as often as you need to until you reach the end of the downgrade.

AUXILIARY BRAKES AND SPEED RETARDERS

Auxiliary brakes and **speed retarders** reduce the rig's speed without using the service brakes. This saves wear and tear on the brakes. The retarders help control the rig on long grades. They can often keep the rpms within a safe range. If they do not, the service brakes will also have to be used to keep the rig under control.

Types of Auxiliary Brakes and Speed Retarders

There are four basic types of auxiliary brakes and speed retarders: engine brakes, exhaust brakes, hydraulic retarders, and electric retarders.

Engine brakes (e.g., the Jake Brake) eliminate the engine's power stroke. They convert the engine to an air compressor for braking purposes. Fuel injection is stopped. The exhaust valves open. Compressed air is expelled and slows the piston movement.

Exhaust brakes (e.g., the Blue Ox) back exhaust gases into the engine to create the pressure (40–50 psi) that slows the piston movement. You often control engine and exhaust brakes with an on/off switch in the cab. Other types operate by an automatic switch that is turned on by releasing the accelerator pedal or turned off by depressing the clutch pedal. Some may have controls for the amount of retardation.

Hydraulic retarders (e.g., the Cat Brakesaver and Allison's Brake Preserver) are mounted between the engine and transmission. They use engine oil pumped against the stator, a fan-like device, or the cavity between the stator and the rotor to slow the rig.

Hydraulic retarders can be adjusted manually in the cab to different levels of operation. The higher they are turned up, the more effective they are. They also have a treadle valve and may have a clutch switch.

Electric retarders (e.g., the Jake ER Brake and Telma Retarder) are mounted in the drive line. They slow the drive shaft rotation with an electromagnet that can be turned on or off. There is no in-between setting. The Jacobs Jake ER Brake retarder has a four-position steering column switch and no throttle or clutch switch.

Operation and Control

Because these devices can be noisy, be sure you know where they are permitted. You will also need to know with which gears they may be used, the proper rpm for their use, and in what kind of weather you may use them.

Speed retarders are useful any time the service brakes are used continually, usually in the mountains or on long, downhill grades.

ESCAPE RAMPS

Escape ramps are designed to stop a vehicle safely without injuring people or damaging cargo (see Figure 15-21). They are built to stop a 50,000-pound GVW tractor-trailer traveling at 55 mph about 450 feet into the ramp. Stopping feels like a hard lock wheel stop on dry pavement.

Ramps either sink the rig in loose gravel or sand or send it up an incline. The grade may be up to 43 percent. Either way, damage to the rig and cargo is limited to minor scratches, nicks, lost battery covers, and so on.

How Ramps Work

At Rabbit Ear Pass, a 9,650-foot summit on U.S. Route 40 in Colorado, a 40,000-pound rig carrying steel beams was on a 7 percent downgrade when it had a

Figure **15-21** Escape ramps are available on mountain roads or continuous grades.

drivetrain failure. The brakes did not work. It was a runaway vehicle. The driver entered the escape ramp at 100 to 110 mph. The rig came to a stop 1,300 feet into the ramp. Both the driver and a passenger walked away unhurt. Damage to the rig was a dent in the cab and a missing battery cover. The total cost of the accident was $10 for two ramp markers and the price of a tow truck to free the rig.

The four basic types of escape ramps are the following:

- **Gravity:** These ramps have a loose material surface such as pea gravel. The grade is usually from 5 to 43 percent.
- **Sand piles:** These are mounds or ridges built high enough to drag the undercarriage of the rig. They are from 85 to 200 feet long.
- **Arrester beds:** These flat beds are masses of loose material, usually pea gravel, and range from 300 to 700 feet long.
- **Combination ramp and arrester bed:** These types rely on the loose surface material to stop the rig. They have a grade of 1.5 to 6.7 percent and are from 500 to 2,200 feet long.

If you find yourself having braking problems on a grade, remember the following:

- You can use an escape ramp.
- Try to enter the ramp squarely and not at an angle.
- You will most likely save your own life and maybe the lives of others.
- You will save your rig and its cargo.
- You may have to pay to have your rig towed back onto the highway.
- Know where escape ramps are located.
- If you are in any trouble, remember that things are not going to get better.
- When in doubt, use a ramp.
- You may not have another chance.
- Escape ramps save lives and cargo. Use them when you lose your brakes.

Chapter Sixteen
Hazard Awareness

FROM NOW ON. . .

ONLY THE BEST
WILL DRIVE!

OBJECTIVES

When the you have completed this chapter, you should be able to:

- Recognize possible hazards

- Determine when the road or the surroundings may be a danger

- Describe why a driver must always be alert to the changing scene

- Explain dangerous road conditions: slippery surfaces, uneven surfaces, curves, soft surfaces, and sloping roads

- Describe common highway threats to safety: debris, obstructions to visibility, and crosswinds

- Recognize clues that tell a driver when other road users may be a possible safety hazard

- Explain the importance of recognizing hazards early

KEY TERMS

Buttonhook

Centrifugal force

Clue

Conflict

Crosswind

Curvature

Hazard

Scene

Under the influence

INTRODUCTION

As a professional driver, you must have skills in a number of areas, but the majority of your skills are focused in two areas: your vehicle and dealing with the driving environment.

The driving environment includes the roadway and its condition, weather, buildings, people, signs, trees and animals. In order to operate safely at all times, you must be familiar with this environment and the possible changes that may occur as you drive from one area to another.

Some of what you will see along the roadway will be friendly, such as wide shoulders, emergency ramps, and climbing lanes. Some elements of the environment will be neutral, such as signs, stores, and homes along the roadway. Other elements will be dangerous, such as drunken or ill drivers in other vehicles, crosswinds on a mountain pass, heavy sleet or snow, tornadic winds, low bridges, wires, and trees.

The purpose of this chapter is to assist you in becoming aware of the driving environment and the clues it offers to help you drive safely. As a professional driver, part of your job is to recognize and interpret these clues so that you can adjust your driving and continue your trip in a safe, economical manner.

WHAT IS A HAZARD?

As you probably know, a **hazard** is any condition or road user (another vehicle and driver, cyclist, pedestrian, or animal) that could create a "possible" danger to you, your cargo, and your rig. "Possible" is the key word because these elements may or may not become a hazard and a danger on the road. Either way, you should be aware of the possibilities (see Figure 16-1).

Figure **16-1** Professional drivers need to be aware of their environment and recognize clues for possible hazards.

Figure **16-2** When you recognize a possible hazard, you can meneuver your vehicle to a safe place.

For example, the brake lights of the car ahead as it approaches an exit ramp could signal a possible danger. You do not know what that driver intends to do. Hitting the brake lights could signal that the driver does not know if this is the right exit or not. At the last minute, the driver of that vehicle could change his or her mind and veer back into your lane. If this happens, that vehicle is no longer a hazard. It is now a danger.

Why is it a danger? Because you will have to react—by either clearing the lane or using your brakes. What if there is not enough room in the next lane for you? What about the "slosh factor," or liquid surge, if you are driving a tanker (see Figure 16-2)?

This simple example zeros in on the whole idea of recognizing hazards. A driver who did not understand the vehicle was a hazard would not respond until it started to change lanes. The driver might then brake suddenly or change lanes. This could cause an accident.

LEARNING TO RECOGNIZE HAZARDS

Learning to recognize hazards is much like learning to read. In learning to read, we first see how letters look and sound. Later we can pick out whole words. Then the words fit together into sentences; now they mean something.

You can recognize hazards in much the same way. When driving, it is hard to see every detail. Drivers must learn to see and understand many **clues** and how they fit together in the changing **scene.** Hazards, when the clue is seen, will stand out. Then the driver can react correctly (see Figure 16-3).

Drivers learn these clues to hazards from their own experiences, close calls or accidents, other drivers' stories, and accident reports.

The rest of this chapter will help you benefit from what other drivers have learned by described hazards and pointing out clues.

In the situation presented earlier, the car's brake lights were a clue. The car ahead was slowing down or stopping. The driver sees the brake lights and either responds or prepares to respond. Seeing and knowing what the brake lights mean is recognizing a hazard. Though the vehicle is not a direct and obvious threat, the driver must understand it might become one (see Figure 16-4).

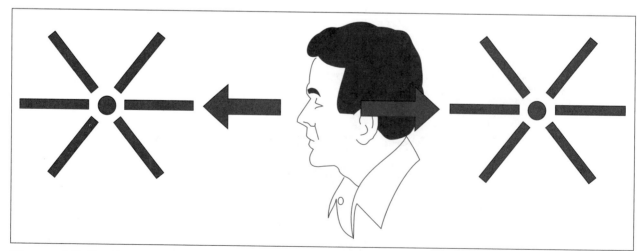

Figure **16-3** Drivers learn to recognize clues to possible hazards, interpret the clues, and react in a safe and responsible manner.

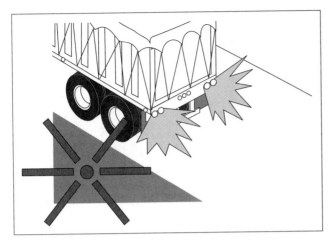

Figure **16-4** Seeing a vehicle's brake lights is a clue indicating a possible hazard.

Sources of Clues

Clues to hazards can be found around your rig in the driving environment. There are three types of clues: road conditions, appearance of other road users, and activities by other road users.

ROAD CONDITIONS

Road conditions are a major factor in tractor-trailer accidents because of:

1. Big rigs travel more miles and travel more in bad weather than do most cars. This exposes them to more danger.
2. Big rigs are less stable because of a higher center of gravity. This makes them tip over more easily.
3. Tractor-trailers require longer stopping distances than cars.

Road characteristics that can be hazardous to rigs include surface conditions, shape, and contour.

Road surfaces also may be hazardous if they are slippery, soft, sloping, uneven, or littered with debris.

Slippery Surface

Sometimes it is hard to tell if roads are slippery. The following sections describe some of these conditions (see Figure 16-5).

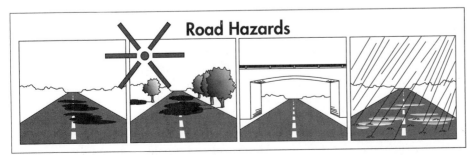

Figure **16-5** Road conditions signal possible hazards.

Figure **16-6** In wet weather, many surfaces become slick and dangerous.

Wet weather. In wet weather, many surfaces are more slippery than they look. Patches of oil dripped from vehicles are very slippery just after it starts to rain. Painted or paint-striped areas, railroad tracks, and construction plates can also be slippery (see Figure 16-6).

Cold weather. In cold weather, look out for black ice, shaded areas, and bridges.

Black ice is a thin, clear coating of ice that makes the road appear wet. Shaded areas can freeze in wet weather when the rest of the roadway is dry. Bridges, both the traveled surface and the roadway below, freeze more quickly than the rest of the road. Be extremely careful when cold weather, wet surfaces, bridges, and shade are combined.

Hot weather. In hot weather, oil may come to the surface of an asphalt road and make it slippery. When driving on an asphalt road, be very careful when it starts to rain. The water mixes with this surface oil and reduces traction, causing the surface to become very slippery until the oil is washed away (see Figure 16-7).

Figure **16-7** A slippery roadway requires more stopping distance for a big rig.

Soft Surfaces

Some surfaces will not bear the weight of a fully loaded rig. Some examples are asphalt, construction areas, and shoulders.

On very hot days, some asphalt roadways may become soft, and the truck may sink into it. In construction zones, surfaces that cover filled-in sewer trenches and septic tanks are seldom strong enough to hold a truck. Graded shoulders also may be very soft after heavy rains or when the snow thaws. In these conditions, there is a danger the rig may sink in or turn over.

Sloping Surfaces

The slope of the road can greatly affect a rig's handling. The force that pushes a vehicle off the road in a curve is called **centrifugal force** (see Figure 16-8). Proper banking of the curve helps overcome this force and keeps the vehicle from sliding off the road.

A curve that is not properly banked is a hazard. Your wheels are more likely to slide on the curve, so you must take the curve at a lower speed. Learn to recognize when a curve is not properly banked. Roads that are high in the middle and low on each side (high-crowned roads) are worse than flat roads. On curves, a wrong-way slope can cause severe front-end dip, front-wheel lockup, or loss of control.

Another hazard clue is pavement that drops off or slopes near the edge of the road. This dip can cause the top of the trailer to hit objects, such as signs or tree limbs that are near the road.

Figure **16-8** The force that attempts to push a vehicle off the road in a curve is centrifugal force.

Debris

No matter how large or small your vehicle may be, debris on the road is always a hazard. A small box may contain heavy material that can cause control problems or damage your rig. If a box does not move with the wind, think of it as a hazard. A pile of rags and paper or cloth sacks can also be a hazard. They may contain cement or another hard substance. If you hit them, you can damage tires, wheel rims, air lines, electrical lines, or fuel crossover lines.

Uneven Surfaces

Bumps in the road can hang up a low trailer and damage the undercarriage or tear off the dolly wheels. Try to avoid driving through puddles. They may disguise potholes filled with water that can cause you to lose control of your rig and cause damage.

Contour of the Road

The shape, or contour, of a road can create hazards. The most common problems result from curvature, restrictions to visibility, and crosswind areas (see Figure 16-9).

Figure **16-9** The shape or contour of the road can create a driving hazard.

Curvature. **Curvature** is the amount of curving the earth does in your line of sight. Trees, power lines, or buildings can be clues to a curving road before you reach them. Are they in a straight line? Do they go up and down toward the horizon?

Expressway ramps can be dangerous for all drivers, but they are worse for tractor-trailer drivers. Curving, downhill ramps are especially bad because the weight and high center of gravity of the rig work with the centrifugal force, pulling your rig to the outside of the curve to make holding onto the road harder (see Chapter 13).

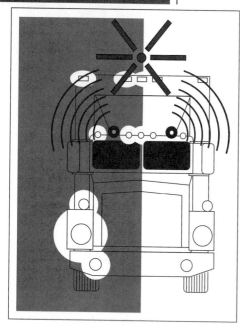

Figure **16-10** When approaching a tunnel during the day, take off your sunglasses and turn on your low beams.

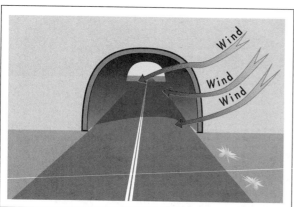

Figure **16-11** Crosswinds can come out of nowhere, so be prepared.

Restrictions to visibility. Many road characteristics restrict the driver's vision. Be prepared for these situations:

● At sunrise or sunset, you can be faced with extreme glare at the crest of a hill. It may help to lower your visor and put on sunglasses before you need them.

● At nighttime as you approach a hilltop, lights from the other side warn you of oncoming traffic. Be ready for headlight glare and protect yourself by looking to the right edge of the road.

● When approaching a tunnel in daylight, remember your eyes adjust slowly to changes in light. Take off your sunglasses before entering the tunnel. Put them back on after you leave the tunnel. Do the same when you enter a warehouse or dark alley on a sunny day (see Figure 16-10).

Crosswind areas. On windy days, you can be hit with a violent **crosswind** when moving from a protected area into an open area. A sudden crosswind can cause you to lose control of your rig. Look for the absence of trees, hills, or other protection when you come out into the open (see Figure 16-11).

APPEARANCE OF OTHER ROAD USERS

Drive defensively! While no driver can watch every move of every other road user, he or she can drive so that if the other driver makes a dumb or dangerous move, an accident can be avoided. Other drivers really are not bad drivers, but they are sometimes careless. It makes sense to watch for clues that tell you other road users may be ready to do something unexpected. As a big rig driver, you must be ready to deal with another driver's sudden change of speed or direction.

Among the clues you should watch for in other drivers are obstructed vision, distraction, confusion, slow travel, impatience, and impairment.

Obstructed Vision

People who cannot see the road well are a serious hazard to other drivers. This section discusses clues that identify drivers who may have obstructed vision.

Vehicles with limited visibility. Vans, loaded station wagons, and cars with obstructed rear windows are examples of some vehicles whose drivers may have limited ability to see the road around them. Drivers of rental trucks are often not familiar with their limited vision. Be alert for these drivers.

Sometimes vehicles are partly hidden by a blind intersection. You can see the other vehicle, but you know the other driver cannot see you. This is a defensive driving situation. Be alert!

A good example of this is when you enter an intersection with the intention of turning left. If oncoming traffic in the nearest lane is stopped to let you turn, you may not be able to see vehicles passing to the right of the stopped vehicles. They, of course, are a danger if you turn in front of them. And while the height of your cab can be helpful, it does not prevent other roadway users from being hidden from your view.

The vision of drivers of delivery trucks is sometimes blocked by packages or vehicle doors. Drivers of step vans, postal vehicles, and local delivery trucks may leave their vehicles in a hurry, often double-parking in the roadway. Watch out for these drivers.

Parked vehicles.   People in parked vehicles should always be considered a hazard. You never know when a driver may open a door and climb out in front of you. Watch for movement inside the vehicle. Parked vehicles may also move out into your lane of traffic unexpectedly.

When police units or emergency units are along the side of the road, move as far left as possible as soon as you can. Slow down if you can because anything can happen. Someone may even run out or be pushed into the traffic lanes.

Note: Some states, such as Kansas, will issue a citation for not moving far left.

Watch for:

- Brake and backup lights
- Exhaust gases
- A driver behind the wheel
- Turn signals
- Movement of the front wheel

Distraction

If a driver is looking at, thinking about, or reacting to anything else, he or she may not see your rig. This is a distracted driver (see Figure 16-12). A driver can attend to only those parts of the scene that he or she sees, hears, or senses. Therefore, you must help others see and pay attention to you and your rig. Following are some common clues that signal a distracted driver.

Lack of eye contact.   Road users who are looking elsewhere may not be aware of your rig and pull into your path. Always try to make eye contact with others. Even positive eye contact is no guarantee, however. Pedestrians or cyclists may assume you will yield or give them room. And remember that some states have pedestrian-right-of-way laws.

Talkers.   Drivers or pedestrians who are talking to another person or on a cell phone may not be aware of you and your rig. They are paying attention to the person to whom they are talking.

Distracted Drivers

Figure **16-12**   Cell phones, crying children, and driving an unfamiliar road can distract drivers.

Figure **16-13** Highway construction sites and workers around those sites often present a hazard.

Workers. Highway, construction, road repair, and utility workers often are not concerned about traffic. They may think someone else is directing the traffic. Delivery people may be distracted by their work, especially when they are loading and unloading. The presence of road repair equipment or delivery trucks is a clue for you to be alert (see Figure 16-13).

Vendors. A vendor's vehicle, such as an ice cream van or taco wagon, is a clue to a hazard. People seem to forget there is traffic when they deal with a neighborhood street vendor. They walk or run across streets and roads without paying attention to the other vehicles. Ice cream trucks and small children are also a very dangerous combination.

Objects appearing from the side. A ball or other object appearing in the street usually means a child is following. Be prepared to stop.

Disabled vehicle. A vehicle being worked on beside a road or street is always a hazard. Drivers changing a tire or tinkering with an engine are usually not thinking about traffic. Passengers often leave the vehicle to walk around or supervise. They, like the person working on the vehicle, tend to ignore traffic. Therefore, you must be on the alert when passing a breakdown on the roadway.

School bus. Slowing or stopped school buses almost always mean children are on the move. They may come out from in front of or behind the bus. From either side of the road, expect the unexpected, and know the state law concerning buses.

Toll booths. Always check ahead as well in your rearview mirors for pedestrians at toll booths. These may be drivers who have gotten out of their cars or toll booth employees. Often they do not realize the danger of walking near tractor-trailers.

Figure **16-14** Confused drivers present big hazards. Look for clues.

Confusion

Confused drivers often drive more slowly than the other traffic. They tend to stop or change direction without warning (see Figure 16-14). Clues that a driver may do something unexpected include:

- Cars topped with luggage
- Cars hauling a camping trailer
- Cars full of luggage or recreational gear
- Cars with out-of-state license plates
- Unexplainable actions, such as the car stopping in midblock, changing lanes for no apparent reason, or backup lights suddenly going on
- Hesitation, very slow driving, frequent braking, or stopping in the middle of an intersection
- Destination seeking: looking at street signs, maps, and house numbers

Slow Travel

Motorists who do not travel at the normal speed are a hazard. Sometimes it is hard to judge how fast you are closing in on or overtaking a vehicle. Following too closely can create a problem. Identifying a slow driver early can prevent an accident. Some clues to help identify slow moving vehicles include:

- Underpowered vehicles such as some subcompacts, recreational vehicles (RVs), or any vehicle towing a house trailer or other heavy load.
- Farm or construction machinery such as tractors and bulldozers.
- Mopeds.
- Vehicles with the slow-moving-vehicle symbol (orange triangle with red sides). At night the triangle may look like an orange blob.
- Vehicles signaling a turn: Turns into alleys or driveways may be very tight. Vehicles entering shopping centers may make sudden stops for pedestrians. Vehicles turning left may pause for oncoming traffic.

Impatience

Some impatient drivers view all trucks as slow moving. Because they do not want to be caught behind a tractor-trailer, they may recklessly try to get in front of it—at all costs. Watch for impatient drivers who overtake and pass you and then cut back over too quickly. They may even slow down after making the pass.

At intersections, be alert for drivers who pull out before it is safe. They are trying to avoid waiting until you and your rig pass through.

A commercial vehicle driver whose income depends on speed sometimes becomes impatient. They see you and your rig as getting in the way of their job. A taxi driver, messenger, or any worker who is behind schedule and in a hurry can be a hazard.

Impaired Drivers

While you may meet an impaired driver at any time, you are more likely to meet one late at night (see Figure 16-15). Two common forms of impairment are being **under the influence** of drugs or alcohol and fatigue.

Clues to a driver's being under the influence of alcohol or drugs are the following:

- Weaving across the lane(s)
- Running off the right side of the road
- Going over a curb while turning
- Stopping for a green light or sitting too long at a stop sign with no cross traffic in the vicinity
- Driving with the window open in cold weather
- Erratic speed: too fast, too slow, or changing from fast to slow often

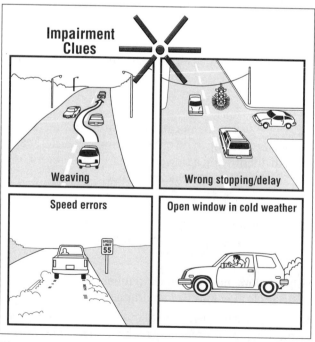

Figure **16-15** You are more likely to meet an impaired driver late at night.

- The driver talking to him- or herself
- Throwing material (lighted) out the window
- Acting unusually happy (false sense of well-being)

These clues may not mean that a driver is impaired, but your job is to be alert for such clues and drive your rig defensively. If the clues are strong enough, you may want to contact the authorities. Remember, however, that you are reporting only unusual or strange behavior! Do not suggest that the other driver may be impaired. Their strange driving could be a result of some other condition.

Drowsiness, or fatigue, like being under the influence, has a number of clues. Among them are weaving across lanes, running off the right side of the road, and slowing down and speeding up.

Remember, these clues may also mean something other than sleepiness, such as illness or other distress.

ACTIVITIES OF OTHER ROAD USERS

Any road user can be a hazard. Clues to hazards are often seen in their activities. Some examples are movement by the driver, movement of the vehicle, pedestrian and cyclist activities, and conflicts.

Movement by the Driver

Before doing something hazardous, a driver often makes some sudden movement of his or her body. Watch other drivers' heads, body, and vehicles.

Head movement. Looking to the side may mean the driver plans to change direction. Drivers usually look in the direction they are going to turn. A turn of the head, therefore, may warn of a possible turn of the vehicle. You may notice a driver looking at the rearview mirror. This may also indicate a lane change.

Body movement. Drivers often straighten up just before turning to brace themselves for the turn and to get better control of the steering wheel.

Vehicle movement. Drivers often edge across a lane in the direction of an intended turn. This sideways, or lateral, movement may be a clue for a lane change or turn.

As you know, big rig drivers, because of the length of their rigs, often make a **buttonhook** on tight right turns. That is, they swing out to the left to gain turning space before starting the right turn. Other drivers may do it too, especially older drivers. The key is to look out for buttonhooks. Do not try to pass a vehicle on the right that has swung out to the left just before an intersection.

Buses and Taxis

Passengers leaving buses may cross the roadway in front of or behind the bus. In many cases, they may not be able to see your rig, so it is up to you to watch for and protect them. A taxi that is reducing speed is a clue to possible danger. Drivers looking for passengers or following a passenger's directions often act in ways that create hazards. Slow movement, U-turns, quick stops, and changes in direction are common. Pass taxis carefully because passengers may leave a taxi from either side as soon as it stops. A pedestrian also may run out to catch a slow-moving taxi, so be prepared to stop quickly.

Figure **16-16** Never second-guess what a pedestrian will do.

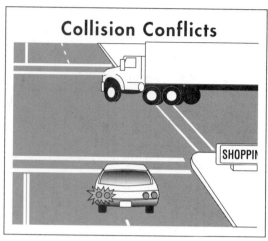

Figure **16-17** A conflict occurs when one vehicle is on a collision course with another vehicle or object.

Pedestrians and Cyclists

Pedestrians and cyclists can be a hazard for many reasons (see Figure 16-16): Watch for people on the sidewalk, shoulder of the road, or road itself.

- They may travel with their backs to traffic.
- In rainy weather, they often think about the rain.
- They are sometimes careless.
- Their clothing or something they are carrying can limit their vision. Examples are a hat pulled too low over their eyes or an umbrella.
- They may not realize where they are and move directly into your path.

Be aware that children are easily distracted. They tend to act without thinking or looking around. When kids are playing, they do not think about the traffic.

Emergency Areas

Accident scenes and hospital emergency areas are dangerous for all drivers because of curious lookie-lou's and rubberneckers. This is also true in slow-moving traffic. People become stressed out and try to see the reason for the delay, which distracts them from watching the road.

Conflicts

A **conflict** occurs when a vehicle is on a collision course with an object or another road user. The problems of other road users become your problems when you have to make a sudden change in direction or stop. Such actions can damage your rig or cargo. Being able to see and understand conflicts early is an advantage (see Figure 16-17). You can then plan what you will do and can often avoid the conflict.

Obstructions

A few examples of common obstructions are:

- The end of a lane
- A barricade

Figure **16-18** Whether on the open road or on a winding mountain road, alway be alert for obstructions.

- Slow-moving or stalled traffic
- A disabled vehicle
- An accident

Obstructions may be in your lane or another lane. If the obstruction is in your lane, you must see the hazard in time and avoid conflict with it. If the obstruction is in a lane going the same direction as yours or in an opposing lane, you must watch for other road users who may move into your path (see Figure 16-18).

Merging

Certain merge situations may force another vehicle into your path. Examples include a car that is entering a freeway, pulling out from a driveway or side street, and moving out of a parallel parking space.

Intersections

When streets or roads come together, conflicts can develop. Other road users may not stop or yield the right of way. They may be in your blind spot or hidden by shrubbery or buildings. Road users in conflict with you and your rig may come from the right, left, or the opposite direction. At times, you may even find yourself in conflict with more than one other road user.

Chapter Seventeen

Emergency Maneuvers

Avoiding Emergencies

Five Types of Emergency
Maneuvers

OBJECTIVES

When you have completed this chapter, you should be able to:

- Think ahead to avoid possible driving emergencies

- Show how driving past an emergency may be better than trying to stop

- Explain the reasons why leaving the road is safer than a head-on collision

- Describe the safest ways to make quick stops and quick turns off the road

- Describe the safe way to return to the highway

- Explain the safest ways of dealing with brake failure and blowouts

KEY TERMS

Air blockage

Antilock Braking
   System (ABS)

Blowout

Brake fade

Controlled braking

Countersteering

Defensive driving

Emergency stopping

Evasive steering

Handling brake failure

Off-road recovery

Secondary collision

Stab braking

INTRODUCTION

In an ideal road environment, vehicles of all types—cars, vans, trucks, motorcycles, buses, and bicycles—should maintain adequate space between themselves and other road users. This would not only be a safe environment for everyone but would also help each user avoid any problems. In reality, this will never happen.

Of course, when any of us slide behind the wheel of any vehicle, we can make mistakes and unknowingly create an emergency. This chapter has been included to help you prepare for, recognize, and respond to some possible emergency situations on the roadway. When you complete reading this chapter, you should know how to handle some difficult situations, maintain control of your rig, and avoid other road users through quick turns and changes in speed.

AVOIDING EMERGENCIES

The best way to handle an emergency is to avoid it. This sounds simple, but most emergencies happen when drivers make mistakes. These mistakes often create unsafe situations. If we do not practice **defensive driving**, accidents can occur.

Professional drivers reduce their chances of an accident by using the knowledge and skills offered in this book. They can recognize possible emergencies and react to them in order to avoid a problem.

There are a number of safe driving practices that will reduce your chances of an emergency (see Figure 17-1):

- Vehicle inspection
- Visual search
- Recognizing hazards
- Communication
- Speed management
- Space management
- Night driving skills and tactics
- Skill in driving during extreme operating conditions
- Maintaining good health
- Observing safety practices

An Indiana University study found that one-third of all vehicle accidents could have been avoided with the proper

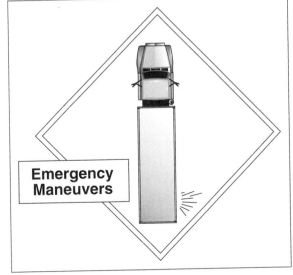

Figure **17-1** There are a number of skills that can help you reduce the chances of an emergency.

driving techniques. Though an escape route, or "out," was usually available, most drivers hit the brakes and let their vehicles skid out of control, according to the study. Panic braking is a result of habit. Drivers tend to put on the brakes any time there is an emergency or difficult situation.

FIVE TYPES OF EMERGENCY MANEUVERS

Five emergency maneuvers are reviewed in this section (see Figure 17-2):

1. **Evasive steering:** Steering out of an emergency situation
2. **Off-road recovery:** Using the roadside as an escape path and then safely returning to the highway
3. **Emergency stopping:** Stopping quickly while keeping the vehicle under control
4. **Handling brake failure:** Stopping the truck when the brakes fail
5. **Blowout:** Maintaining control when a front tire blows

Evasive Steering

Evasive steering is a safe way to get out of or avoid an emergency situation (see Figure 17-3). It reduces the chances of an accident, reduces the severity of the accident, and allows the use of possible escape routes.

Reducing the chance of an accident. You can usually turn a truck quicker than you can stop. Often you can turn far enough to avoid the emergency.

Reducing the severity of an accident. If evasive steering is used, any accident that occurs will probably be less severe than a head-on collision. With the size, weight, and height of a truck, a head-on or rear-end collision is likely to be fatal.

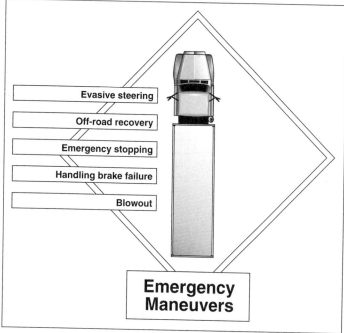

Figure **17-2** Five types of emergency maneuvers.

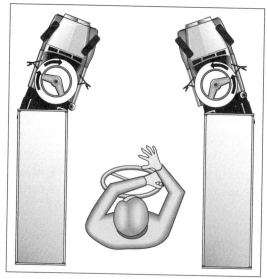

Figure **17-3** Evasive steering is a safe way to avoid an emergency situation.

Using possible escape routes. Another lane or the road shoulder are possible escape routes. If a lane is available, a quick lane change is often the best escape route. If there is not a lane available, the shoulder of the road is sometimes a suitable escape route.

If there is a choice between a collision and trying evasive action, trying to evade the collision is usually safer, but a sharp turn of the steering wheel can often cause a rollover. Using other evasive actions are usually safer.

If you are hauling a stable load and your rig has a low center of gravity, you have the best chance of avoiding an accident when using evasive action. Firm traction on the road or shoulder offers added safety.

General Procedures for Evasive Steering

- When you use evasive steering, turn the steering wheel as little as possible to avoid the emergency. Turn quickly. Be sure to use correct braking while you are turning. Countersteer when you have passed the emergency. **Countersteering** means turning back toward your intended path of travel.
- To turn as quickly as possible, hand-over-hand steering is best. Placing the hands in the 9:00 and 3:00 positions lets the wheel turn 180 degrees without releasing either hand. If you always drive with your hands in this position, you will be ready if a quick turn is needed. Remember, speed magnifies. The higher the speed, the less you turn the wheel.
- Brake before turning. If you can, avoid braking in a turn. Braking in a turn can cause the tractor and trailer wheels to lock up. By braking before the turn, a sharper turn can be made, and there is less chance of a rollover or jackknife.
- After making an evasive turn, be ready to countersteer at once. Do it smoothly to keep your rig from going out of the escape path or off the road. Timing is very important. Begin to countersteer as soon as the front of the trailer clears the obstacle.

Seatbelts. Almost every state has seatbelt laws, so you should always drive with them locked in place. When you turn the steering wheel of a rig quickly, you can slide out from under the wheel and lose control if you are not wearing a seatbelt. In fact, many **secondary collisions** occur when a driver swerves to avoid an emergency and slides out of the correct seating position. Because the driver is not able to countersteer, he or she loses control of the rig. Always wear your seatbelt.

Evasive Driving in Specific Situations

Different evasive techniques are used in different situations. Some of the most common situations are those that deal with an oncoming vehicle, a stopped vehicle, or a merging vehicle.

Oncoming vehicle. This is one of the most frightening emergencies (see Figure 17-4). Another vehicle comes toward you from the opposite direction. Driver error is nearly always the cause of this problem because the driver may be impaired, not paying attention, asleep, under the influence, ill, or simply reckless.

In any event, you must try to prevent a collision. The best move is usually to try to move to your right. A blast of your horn may startle the other driver into corrective action. Remember, leaving the road on the right is nearly always better than a head-on collision.

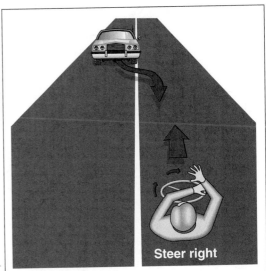

Steer right

Figure **17-4** An oncoming vehicle in your lane is one of the most frightening emergencies.

Steering to the left is usually a bad move. Why? Because the other driver may try to correct position by pulling back into their lane. Then you will still be on a collision course—but on the left side of the road.

Stopped vehicle. This situation usually happens in one of two ways:

1. You may be following the car ahead of you too closely, and they suddenly stop.
2. You may come over the top of a hill to find a stopped vehicle in your lane.

If this occurs, you can take three possible evasive actions:

Figure **17-5** The height of the cab lets you see the oncoming lane when maneuvering out of an emergency situation.

1. If the lane to your left is clear, you can turn into that lane and avoid the obstacle. This move is usually better than a swerve to the right; it prevents sideswiping a vehicle on your right. The height of the cab lets you see if the oncoming lane is clear (see Figure 17-5). This is one emergency situation in which it can be safe to turn left into an oncoming lane.
2. If you are driving along a clear shoulder with a good surface, you can swerve to the right. Sideswiping another vehicle on a shoulder is rare.
3. If you are in one of the middle lanes of a multilane road, move into whichever lane is clear. Otherwise, evade to the right. If there is a vehicle in the right lane, it is better to force it over than to force another vehicle into an oncoming lane.

Merging vehicle. An emergency situation involving a merging vehicle can develop in a number of ways (see Figure 17-6):

*   Another vehicle may try to change lanes and move into your lane.
*   Another vehicle may try to merge onto the highway without yielding to you.
*   A vehicle may pull out from a side street, driveway, or parking space.
*   Another road user, such as a pedestrian or cyclist, may enter the highway.

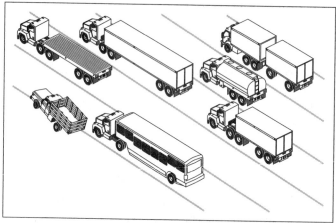

Figure **17-6** An accident waiting to happen: A merging vehicle in your lane.

Common sense tells you that blasting your air horn can—and usually does—startle the other driver. Sometimes, a blast on your horn will frighten the driver to the point that he or she will veer into your lane or stop suddenly. If this happens, you may be required to do more evasive steering to avoid the problem.

Some drivers think using the horn will annoy other drivers, and formal studies about driver behavior have found this to be true. However, in an emergency situation, annoying other drivers with your horn is better than a collision.

Stopping Instead of Evasive Steering

If there is enough space, a quick stop is always safer than an evasive turn because there is no risk of collision with a vehicle you did not see. Also, such a stop is not likely to cause a jackknife or rollover.

When evasive steering is not possible, braking is your only option. Even if you cannot bring your rig to a full stop, the impact of the collision will not be as hard, and both vehicles may have less damage. There will also be less chance of an injury or death. Activate your emergency flasher to warn traffic in the rear.

If your truck has antilock brakes, it will be possible to brake and make an evasive turn at the same time without losing control of your rig.

Off-Road Recovery

When the area beside the road provides the best escape path, it may be either the right shoulder of the road or the shoulder of the median strip.

Most drivers fear leaving the road (see Figure 17-7). This is because staying on the road is a strong habit. Some fear that the shoulder will not support their rig, or they may have heard of a crash when the roadside is used for evasive action. The truth is that most roadside crashes result from drivers being distracted or falling asleep. Keep in mind that many evasive actions are successful and avoid accidents but these incidents are never reported.

Sometimes drivers wait too long to leave the road. Successful **off-road recovery** often means the driver must leave the road at once. Most accidents that result from using the roadside are caused by the driver's poor technique. Generally, off-road recovery is safe when the roadside is wide enough and firm enough to handle the rig and the driver uses good judgment.

Off-Road Recovery Procedure

If you see the need to leave the road to avoid a collision, remember to brake before turning, avoid braking in the turn unless your rig has **antilock brakes,** and turn as little as possible.

You also need to think about whether the roadside is clear, when and how to countersteer, and how to handle the wheel drop that often happens as the wheels leave the road (see Figure 17-8).

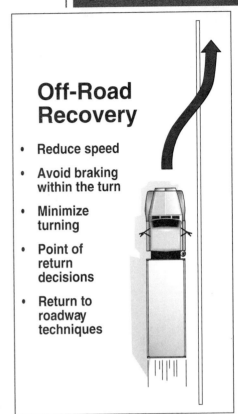

Off-Road Recovery

- **Reduce speed**
- **Avoid braking within the turn**
- **Minimize turning**
- **Point of return decisions**
- **Return to roadway techniques**

Figure **17-7** Most drivers try to avoid steering their rigs off the road.

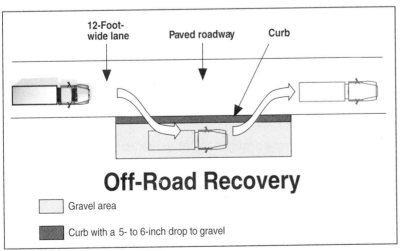

12-Foot-wide lane   Paved roadway   Curb

Off-Road Recovery

☐ Gravel area

▬ Curb with a 5- to 6-inch drop to gravel

Figure **17-8** Using good technique and skills can help avoid accidents in emergencies.

Brake before turning. When you plan to leave the road, slow down as much as you can. Use **controlled braking** or **stab braking** to keep control of your rig.

Avoid braking in the turn, unless your rig has antilock brakes. If you brake in a turn and the brakes lock, you may go into a skid. Control of your rig is very important when you enter the roadside.

Turn as little as possible. If possible, keep one set of wheels on the pavement. You will keep better control of the steering. Traction also is better on the pavement because gravel and dirt reduce your traction. Reduced traction causes skids. Turn as little as possible on the roadside. Maintain as straight a course as possible. Remember, each turn creates a chance for a skid.

Returning to the Highway

After leaving the road, drivers often try to return to the highway too quickly. You should grasp the wheel firmly and think about steering straight ahead. Stay on the roadside and allow the engine compression to stop the rig. Put on the brakes only when you have slowed enough to stop safely. Signal and check your mirrors before returning to the road.

If there is a telephone pole, sign, parked vehicle, or other obstacle in your path, stay off the road until your view is clear. Then turn back sharply onto the road.

Attempting a gradual return to the roadway may cause you to lose control of your rig and go into a skid. The skid may make your rig cross into an oncoming lane, jackknife, or roll over. Turning sharply lets you countersteer and decide the point where you will return to the road.

Countersteering

When you return to the road, countersteer (turn quickly away from the road). Countersteer as soon as the right front wheel rides up onto the surface of the road. Both turning back on the road and countersteering should be done as a single steering move.

When the Wheels Drop Off the Road

Wheels sometimes drop off the pavement when a rig is too close to the edge. Drivers often try to return at once. Do not do this. With one side of the rig on the pavement, controlling your rig is easy. Trying a quick return has caused many drivers to roll over or skid into oncoming traffic. Come to a complete stop before you attempt to return to the road.

Follow the same procedure as you do for an off-road recovery. If the path ahead is clear, let the vehicle slow to a complete stop. Then return to the road when it is safe.

Emergency Stopping

By using your brakes properly, you can maintain control of the rig and shorten the distance required for **emergency stopping.** There are two ways of braking, depending on your rig's braking system. If it does not have antilock brakes and you brake too much or too hard, you can lock the wheels and cause a skid. A skid can produce a jackknife in which the trailer may hit the tractor. Either the tractor or the trailer may then collide with other roadway users, trees, or buildings. If your rig has antilock brakes, hit them hard and hold down the pedal. The system's electronic controls will ensure the wheels do not lock.

If a vehicle pulls in front of you and you are going to overtake it quickly at your present speed, you can steer to the left or right (evasive steering) without braking in vehicles without antilock brakes or brake quickly.

If oncoming traffic and vehicles on the right prevent evasive steering, you have no choice but to brake quickly. For rigs without antilock brakes, either of two emergency braking techniques can be used: controlled braking or stab braking. Both can help prevent a skid or jackknife.

Controlled Braking

In controlled braking, put on the brakes with a steady pressure just short of wheel lockup (see Figure 17-9). The point of lockup differs among vehicles, and it is hard to find the exact point. Practice in your rig to find the lockup point. If you do not know where the lockup point is, stab braking is best.

Stab Braking

When you use stab braking, apply the brakes fully. Then release the pedal partly when the wheels lock. Put on the brakes again when the wheels start to roll. Repeat the stab braking sequence until you can safely stop or turn (see Figure 17-10). Never use this technique with antilock brakes.

Remember, putting on the brakes again before the wheels begin to roll can cause a skid. Stab braking provides maximum braking when the brakes are applied. It then avoids a skid when the brakes are released.

Handling Brake Failure

Well-maintained brake systems rarely fail completely. Several devices are designed for **handling brake failure** and preventing accidents. If you keep cool, you can usually bring your rig under control.

Stab Braking

Release after wheels lock up

Figure **17-10** In stab braking, apply brakes fully, release, and repeat.

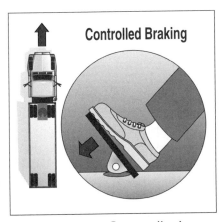

Figure **17-9** Controlled braking is when brakes are applied with steady pressure so they do not lock up.

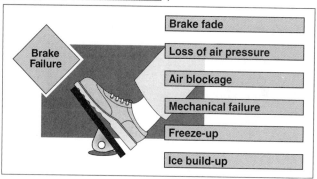

Figure **17-11** Well-maintained brake systems rarely fail. Those that do fail do so for these reasons.

Brakes usually fail because of loss of air pressure, air blockage, brake fade, or mechanical failure (see Figure 17-11).

Loss of Air Pressure

If a leak occurs in the air system, a warning buzzer will sound when the air pressure gets too low. When this happens, you should stop at once. If you do not stop, you may lose more air from the system. Then your brakes will fail, and you cannot stop your rig.

A built-in safety system automatically puts on the brakes when the air loss reaches a critical level. This happens while there is still enough air in the system to stop the rig. However, if the loss is too fast, the air supply may be used up before the rig is stopped.

The independent trailer brake valve will not put on the trailer brakes because they depend on the air system. If the rig has spring-loaded parking brakes, the brakes will come on automatically when the air pressure fails. They will generally stop the truck unless it is on a steep downgrade.

Air Blockage

Air blockage happens when air is kept from reaching the brakes. A common cause is water freezing in the air system.

Brake Fade

Brake fade occurs when the brakes overheat and lose their ability to stop the truck on a downgrade (see Figure 17-12).

Mechanical Failure

Some part in the braking system may not work. Usually, this will not affect all the brakes at the same time, and the rig can then be stopped.

WARNING!

Independent trailer brakes can fade to a point where they are ineffective.

Figure **17-12** When driving a long, steep downhill stretch, professional drivers should always be prepared for brake failure.

Procedures to Follow if the Brakes Fail

If your brakes fail, you must do two things: reduce speed as much as possible and find an escape path and follow it.

Reduce speed. If your rig is on a level surface, try to downshift. This will let the engine act as a brake to slow the rig. It also raises the revolutions per minute (rpm) and increases the air pressure. Keep downshifting until your rig is moving slowly enough that you can stop it with the spring-loaded parking brake. Do not downshift on a downgrade (see Chapter 15).

Find an escape path. Begin looking for an escape path at once. Do not wait to see if the rig can be stopped. If you do so, you may go past the only available escape path. Some safe escape paths include:

- A side road (particularly if it runs uphill)
- An open field (even though you may damage the undercarriage)
- A runaway vehicle escape ramp

Other Things to Do

Create drag. You may have to take other actions to slow down. Rubbing tires along the curb or your truck along a guardrail can help. In open country, you may be able to drive into heavy brush or small bushes. Remember, the main idea is to prevent serious damage to the rig or injury to yourself and others by avoiding a collision with other vehicles. Firm steering control is essential using this technique.

Inspect the brakes. After escaping the emergency, pull over to the side of the road. Do not return to the road until the brakes are working properly. This may require road service. Some drivers try to "nurse" the rig along to a repair station. This is a bad move and a dangerous risk because you may have another failure and be unable to avoid serious damage or injury. Vehicles equipped with spring-loaded brakes are designed to lock rather than freewheel.

Blowout

A **blowout** occurs when a tire suddenly loses air. This can happen because the tire may be worn to the point that it is too thin to hold air, have a crack in the tire casing, or be damaged from debris, potholes, curbs, nails, and so on.

You can prevent blowouts resulting from wear by careful pre-trip inspections and proper braking.

What Happens When a Tire Blows Out?

A front-tire blowout will cause steering problems so the rig will veer to the side (see Figure 17-13). A blowout to a rear tractor tire may produce a vibration in the cab. This can cause the rear of the tractor to pull in the direction of the air loss. Trailer tire blowouts can generally be identified by handling difficulties or by the sound of the tire blowing out. If it is an outside tire, you may be able to see it in your mirrors.

Front-Tire Blowout

If a front tire blows, you usually hear a loud bang. Remember, a tire can also deflate without a sound. Grasp the wheel tightly so it will not be jerked from your hands. You may have steering problems. You want to keep the rig from

Figure **17-13** A front-tire blowout will cause steering problems.

veering off to the side. Speed up to stop the side force and regain control. Then bring the vehicle to a gradual, controlled stop.

Having to grasp the wheel tightly in an emergency is one reason to hold the steering wheel at the 9:00 and 3:00 positions at all times. When holding the wheel at the 9:00 and 3:00 positions, the thumbs should be facing up. The force of a blowout can break a thumb wrapped around the wheel or under a wheel spoke.

By speeding up at once when you have a blowout, you help keep the rig moving in a straight line. Slow down gradually when you have the rig under control. Braking after a front-tire blowout is dangerous because it shifts weight to the front of the vehicle and makes steering more difficult (see Figure 17-14).

After the engine has slowed down the rig, it is safe to gently apply the brakes. You can then slowly pull off the road and brake gently to a stop.

Rear-Tire Blowout

A blowout of a tire on the rear of the tractor or trailer is not as dangerous as a blowout on a front wheel. You usually will not feel any pull on the steering wheel, but the truck may pull to the side of the flat. The trailer can also lean toward the side of the blown tire.

Front-tire blowout: Avoid braking

Figure **17-14** Braking after a front-tire blowout is dangerous because it shifts weight to the front of the vehicle, making it difficult to steer.

Do not brake at once. Let the rig slow down gradually. Then brake slowly and pull off the road before gently braking to a stop. Be sure to check inside and adjacent tires for damage.

The tire should be changed as soon as possible. Check for any damage the blown tire may have done. Check:

● The air lines and other parts
● The tire rim
● For fire
● For damage to other vehicles

Note: Remember, it is illegal to drive on a damaged tire or rim. If a rim or tire is damaged, have it fixed before driving further.

Chapter Eighteen
Skid Control and Recovery

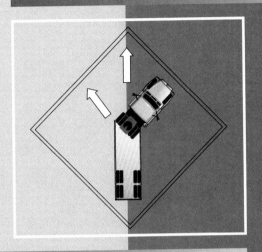

OBJECTIVES

When you have completed this chapter, you should be able to:

- Show how skid control can prevent accidents

- Explain vehicle control factors, including traction, wheel load, and force of motion

- Understand the causes of skidding

- Illustrate a tractor jackknife, front-wheel skid, and an all-wheel skid

- Explain recovery techniques

- Show why most skids can be prevented and can occur at any speed

- Describe the ways to recover from a skid if it is detected early and corrected properly

KEY TERMS

Antilock brake system (ABS)

Cable antijackknife devices

Centrifugal force

Countersteering

Drive-wheel skid

Fifth-wheel antijackknife devices

Force of motion

Jackknife

Oversteering

Power skid

Rolling traction

Sliding traction

Tire slides

Traction

Wheel load

Wheel lockup

INTRODUCTION

When any vehicle skids, the driver loses control. Skids occur when tires lose their grip on the road. What many people do not know is that drivers can prevent most skids, and, in fact, it is much easier to prevent a skid than to correct one.

Skids can occur because of one of the following four driver mistakes. The most common of the four is trying to quickly change speed (overacceleration). The next most common cause of a skid is trying to change direction too quickly (oversteering). Skids are also caused by overbraking, which is braking too hard and locking up the wheels or using the speed retarder when the road is slick. The most serious skids are caused by driving too fast. Most skids happen when the road is slippery due to rain, snow, and ice.

Loose material on the pavement, like gravel or wet leaves, can also make the road slippery and interfere with traction. Because most skids are caused by a sudden change in speed or direction, professional drivers must always be aware of the weather conditions and the road's surface and adjust their speeds based on these factors.

In this chapter, you'll learn how skids happen, how they can be prevented, and how to make corrections and recover control once your vehicle begins to skid.

Hands-on experience should be practiced only on a special driving range or skid pad (see Figure 18-1).

Figure **18-1** Skid control and recovery: Two important tools for the professional driver.

VEHICLE CONTROL FACTORS

When the vehicle control factors are not in balance, a skid will occur. Factors that affect control of the vehicle include **traction, wheel load,** and **force of motion.**

Figure **18-2** The points of friction (traction) between the tires and the road are small.

Traction

Traction is the "grip" between the tires and the road surface. It is the only contact the rig has with the road (see Figure 18-2). The points of friction, or "tire footprints," vary with tire size and pressure. Traction determines how much control the driver has over the rig. If the tires have good traction, the driver can speed up, steer, and stop properly. If there is poor traction, the driver cannot control the rig and the rig may go into a skid.

- When you speed up, traction between the tires and the pavement causes the vehicle to move.
- When you steer, the traction of the tires on the road surface resists the sideways (lateral) movement. This traction helps control the direction in which the rig will go.
- When you brake, the friction of the brake system slows the turning of the wheels. The traction of the tires against the pavement slows down the rig.

There are two types of traction. The first is **rolling traction,** or the friction of one surface rolling over another. The friction of a rolling tire moving over the road in the same direction the rig is moving is an example of rolling traction. The other is **sliding traction,** or the friction of one surface sliding across another. This occurs when other forces acting on surfaces are greater than the traction between them. This can happen whether the wheels are locked or turning.

Tires may slide in any direction when they lock up from too much braking. And too much **centrifugal** (outward) **force** may cause tires to slide sideways, even though the wheels are turning.

Wheel Load

Wheel load is the downward force of weight on a wheel. The greater the load on the wheel, the better the traction. Wheel load is determined by the weight of the vehicle plus the weight and distribution of the load.

Notably, while wheel load may increase the downward force and the amount of tread touching the pavement, wheel load may not actually improve the traction. For example, if there is ice or snow on the road surface, there is still a lack of adequate traction, and skidding can occur.

Some tractor-trailer drivers have the misconception that a heavier wheel load will guarantee better traction on slippery surfaces, but this is not true.

Force of Motion

The force of the motion of the rig is determined by the weight and speed of the rig. The heavier the rig and its load and the faster it travels, the greater the force.

To keep the rig under control, you must avoid skids as you drive. Remember, the major cause of skidding is a sudden change in either speed or direction.

Speed. A sudden change in speed can result from either too much braking or speeding up too fast. If the forces of motion are more than the traction of the tire against the pavement when you brake, the rig will skid instead of stopping. Make a conscious effort to periodically check your speed—do not trust your instincts.

Most people know that braking too hard will cause a skid. Not as many know that speeding up too fast increases the wheel speed to a point where the tires cannot provide traction. When this happens, a skid occurs. In some cases, such skids will simply be a spinning of the drive wheels. In more severe cases, the tractor may skid sideways or even **jackknife.**

Direction. Changing the direction of your steering too quickly can cause the rolling tires to lose their friction with the road surface. When this happens, the rig continues in the direction it is moving instead of changing to follow the direction of the steering wheel.

CAUSES OF SKIDS

To review, there are several reasons a truck will begin to skid, but the two basic causes are changes in speed and changes in direction (see Figure 18-3).

Change in Speed

Skids involving speed may be from braking or acceleration. Braking skids can result in **wheel lockup** and **tire slides.** Both of these conditions increase the rig's stopping distance and cause the driver to lose control.

Wheel Lockup

This happens because you put on the service brakes, exhaust brakes, or speed retarder too hard; downshift too much; or slow down suddenly. You lose control when the locked wheels slide and the rig skids out of control (see Figure 18-4). The skid may be straight ahead, sideways, or a jackknife. The unit will be out of control until you, the driver, correct the problem or a collision occurs.

Tire Slides

This occurs when the forces from weight and acceleration of the rig are greater than the tires' ability to maintain traction. Wheel lockups and tire slides increase the rig's stopping distance. Remember that sliding tires do not slow a vehicle as well as rolling tires.

Spinning tires occur when the force from acceleration on the drive wheels is more than the tires' ability to provide traction. The wheels spin, but the vehicle does not move. The spinning

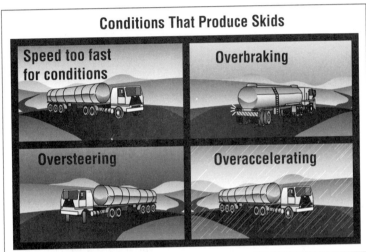

Conditions That Produce Skids

Speed too fast for conditions | Overbraking

Oversteering | Overaccelerating

Figure **18-3** All professional drivers need to understand common causes of skids.

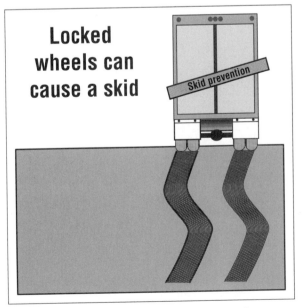

Locked wheels can cause a skid

Skid prevention

Figure **18-4** Wheels can lock when you apply brakes too hard, downshift too much, or suddenly slow down.

continues until the driver stops accelerating. The rear of the tractor may also move in a sideways spin. This is called a **power skid.**

Slowing down too fast may also cause a skid. If the rig has moved onto ice and the driver suddenly recognizes the problem, he or she may quickly react by removing their foot from the accelerator. This reaction may reduce the wheel speed too fast and cause a skid, so, if possible, slow down before reaching any icy spots on the road.

Change of Direction

When a vehicle makes a turn, centrifugal force makes it keep going in the same direction. As a result, the vehicle tends to slide outward in a turn.

If the rate of speed or the sharpness of the turn is too great, force exceeds traction. This causes the tires to skid sideways. A new driver may put on the brakes suddenly. Then the tires lock up, and this actually makes the skid worse because the driver has even less control.

PREVENTING SKIDS

In any situation, it is always better to prevent a skid than to try to recover once a skid occurs. Safe driving practices can help prevent skids. Here are a few tips to help you avoid skid situations:

- Adjust your speed on curves. This will reduce your chances of a cornering skid.
- Drive within your sight distance. This reduces the need for sudden stops and the possibility of a braking skid.
- Maintain enough following distance so you will not have to make a quick stop.
- Adjust your speed on slick surfaces.
- Check the backs of your mirrors for ice, which is an indicator of road conditions.
- Adjust your speed to the surface and weather conditions and to the curvature of the road.
- Avoid overbraking.
- Do not suddenly downshift.
- Inspect the air and brake systems before and during each trip. All wheels should start stopping at the same time. If the wheels do not brake evenly, a skid can result.
- Inspect tires, front-wheel alignment, and suspension system.
- Load cargo properly.

TRACTOR-TRAILER SKIDS

Tractor-trailer skids are grouped by what happens to the rig as a result of a skid. There are four major types of skids: trailer jackknife, tractor jackknife, front-wheel skid, and all-wheel skid.

Trailer Jackknife

A trailer jackknife is caused by too much braking or cornering. In either case, the trailer tires skid because they become locked. The force that locks them overcomes the traction with the surface of the road (see Figure 18-5).

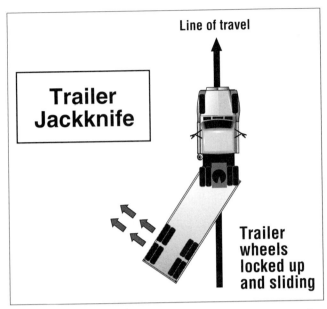

Figure **18-5** A trailer jackknife is caused
by excessive braking or sharp cornering.

Overbraking. A driver can overbrake by putting on the foot brake too hard or not using the trailer brake correctly. The trailer brake should not be used for stopping.

Sometimes, the driver is forced to use the brakes excessively because there is a mechanical problem, such as:

- A faulty air system that sends too much pressure to the trailer wheels
- Not adjusting the brakes on the trailer equally (called cam-over)
- Worn trailer brake linings that cause brake seizure
- A light trailer load

Excessive cornering. If a rig enters a curve too fast for the surface conditions, the tires may lose traction, causing the rig to jackknife or skid out of control. Always adjust your speed before you enter the curve.

A trailer jackknife can be prevented by adjusting speed to the surface conditions and curvature of the road. When entering curves, ease off the accelerator and then accelerate through the curve. This is done to ensure that the tractor pulls the trailer through the curve rather than having the trailer pushing the tractor through the curve. Inspect the air system and brake adjustments before and during each trip.

Tractor Jackknife

A tractor jackknife (also called a **drive-wheel skid**) occurs when the tractor drive wheels lose traction (see Figure 18-6). This happens because of wheel lockup, overacceleration, or trailer override.

When any of these three conditions occur, the drive wheels have less traction than the front wheels, so they try to overtake the front wheels. As a result, the

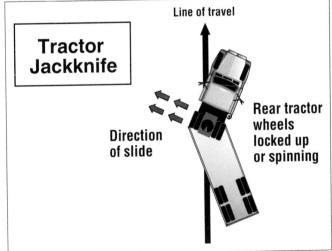

Figure **18-6** A tractor jackknife occurs when the tractor drive wheels lose traction.

rear of the tractor tends to swing out; as it does, the tractor pulls the trailer outward. Then the trailer pushes the tractor outward, and a jackknife results.

If a drive-wheel skid occurs on ice or snow, it can be easily managed by taking your foot off the accelerator. (If road conditions are very slippery, push in the clutch.) Otherwise, the engine will keep the wheels from rolling freely and regaining traction.

Wheel lockup.   Drive wheels can lock up for a number of reasons:
- Putting on the brakes too hard
- Downshifting on a slippery road surface
- Sudden release of the accelerator on a slippery surface
- Load imbalance (drive wheels too lightly loaded)
- Faulty brakes
- Poor tread on the drive tires

Over acceleration.   Too much pressure on the accelerator for the gear and vehicle speed can cause a power skid. A power skid is most likely to occur if you are driving on a slippery surface, your rig has an engine with high horsepower (high torque), or the trailer is heavily or improperly loaded.

Trailer override.   When you brake, the cargo may push the trailer against the tractor. This forces the tractor out of line and creates a jackknife. This condition is most likely to occur if the pavement is slippery, the trailer is not loaded properly, cargo is not distributed or secured correctly, or the rig is taking a curve or making a lane change.

The best way to prevent a tractor jackknife is to avoid overbraking, overaccelerating, or sudden downshifts; avoid sudden turns; inspect the brake system and tire tread regularly; and load the rig correctly and securely.

Front-Wheel Skid

Front-wheel skids happen when you lose front-wheel traction (see Figure 18-7). The rig continues to move forward, but you cannot steer it. The rig may slide sideways or fail to round a curve. Front-wheel skids can be caused by:

- Too big a load on the fifth wheel (this can also happen when the cargo is not loaded properly and shifts forward when you brake)
- Too much speed
- Not enough tread on the front tires
- Hydroplaning
- **Oversteering** in combination with any of the above
- Malfunction of the brake system
- Bad brake linings or other brake defects
- A dry fifth wheel

Front-wheel skids can be prevented by:

- Slowing down when driving on wet pavement
- Loading your cargo correctly
- Inspecting your tires, front-wheel alignment, and suspension system and correcting any problems you find
- Using good braking techniques

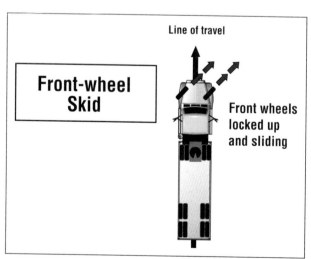

Line of travel

Front-wheel Skid

Front wheels locked up and sliding

Figure **18-7**   Front-wheel skids occur when your front wheels lose traction.

"Chopping the Wheel" to Prevent a Front-Wheel Skid

The technique known as "chopping the wheel" is especially useful as a preventive measure when you are driving on slick surfaces and have to make a sudden evasive steering maneuver or go around a tight corner. This technique uses very quick, short back-and-forth movements of the steering wheel and increases the amount of tire in contact with the road surface. This helps increase traction.

All-Wheel Skid

When all the wheels lock and do not roll, you lose traction. You stop rolling and start to slide. The rig usually continues in a straight line, but without traction, the driver loses control (see Figure 18-8).

The major causes of this kind of skid are excessive speed and overbraking on a slippery surface.

In cases of overbraking, one set of wheels generally locks up before the others. In some situations, even light brake pressure can cause lockup.

The best prevention for all-wheel skids is to allow plenty of stopping distance, control your speed, and not brake too much on slippery surfaces. If you must brake, use light, steady, or gentle braking to keep control of the rig.

Summary of Skid Prevention

Preventing skids was discussed earlier in this chapter. You learned that managing your speed and space, especially when driving in extreme conditions, is very important in helping you control your rig.

Most skids result from sudden changes in speed or direction. Overbraking and oversteering as well as fast acceleration or deceleration cause these sudden changes that often result in a skid. Avoid them.

Skidding usually occurs on slippery surfaces. To prevent this:

- Avoid quick braking or quick turns on slippery pavement.
- If you must turn or brake, do no more than you have to.

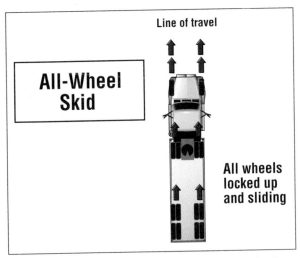

Line of travel

All-Wheel Skid

All wheels locked up and sliding

Figure **18-8** The major causes of all-wheel skids are excessive speed or overbraking on slick roads.

- When you must stop quickly, use controlled braking with antilock brakes or correct stab braking technique.
- Keep the brakes adjusted and balanced.

Reducing your speed and allowing more space is vital to safety when the road is slippery. It can prevent the need for quick turning or braking. If the pavement is wet, snowy, or icy, slow down and leave more following distance.

ANTIJACKKNIFE DEVICES

Antijackknife devices are made to restrict trailer swing and prevent damage. However, they do not prevent skidding. The two basic types of antijackknife devices are fifth-wheel devices and cable devices.

Fifth-wheel antijackknife devices are automatic and restrict the rotation of the kingpin. This prevents a collision between the trailer and the cab. They are mounted on the tractor and can be used with any kind of trailer.

Cable antijackknife devices are mounted on the trailer and connected to the tractor. They are activated by hard braking and keep the trailer and tractor in line. Their disadvantage is that using them conflicts with skid recovery. The hard braking prevents the use of controlled braking, and in some situations, cable devices may actually make a skid worse.

ANTILOCK BRAKES

Antilock brakes have become common equipment on tractors and trailers. The federal government has mandated them on all new tractors built after March 1, 1997, and on all new trailers built after March 1, 1998.

Antilock systems use electronic controls to read wheel speed and prevent the brakes from locking up the wheels under hard braking. This increases driver control during braking but does not necessarily shorten stopping distances. Also, if the tractor has antilock brakes and the trailer does not or vice versa, you need to apply the normal skid control procedures in this chapter to prevent jackknifing. Antilock brakes are most effective when you hit the brake pedal and hold it down.

Note: Since antilock brake systems lose their effectiveness with "pumping" the brakes, stab braking may not be the skid-recovery technique of choice. Why? Because stab braking actually reduces the effectiveness of antilock brakes and increases the braking power coming from the trailer. This situation sets up your rig for a trailer skid or the inability to come to a stop as soon as necessary.

SKID RECOVERY

Almost all tractor skids are corrected by the same techniques:

1. Disengage the clutch
2. Get off the brakes
3. Countersteer

Most skids happen when you try to change speed too quickly for the conditions. Remove your foot from the brake pedal to reduce skidding. Then you can more easily gain control of the direction the rig is going. Do not put on the independent trailer brake. If the trailer has started to jackknife, putting on the trailer brake can make it worse.

If overbraking resulted from downshifting, depress the clutch quickly, then use the foot brake for stab braking.

If overacceleration has been the cause of the skid, you should ease off the accelerator, then depress the clutch pedal to remove engine power from the drive wheels.

Corrective Steering

In a tractor jackknife, corrective steering is needed to put the tractor back on course (see Figure 18-9). Steer toward the direction the rear of the rig is moving. Steer in the line of travel as shown in Figures 18-6 to 18-8.

Oversteering. On a slippery surface when you lose control of your steering and traction, you must oversteer. Turn beyond the intended path of travel. You must do this because you have lost full traction. Unless you oversteer, you will not regain control of the rig.

Countersteering. When you try to correct a skid, little traction makes the rig slow to respond. As the vehicle resumes the correct course, the driver must countersteer early. Do this to avoid a new skid (see Figure 18-10). Continue countersteering until the rig is on a straight path. Each countersteering movement should get smaller until the rig is going straight again.

If a new skid happens because you countersteered too late, the rig may turn beyond the intended path and spin out. Although it may not spin out the first time you countersteer too late, each correction may make the situation worse until a spinout occurs.

Braking to a Stop

Once the vehicle is on a straight path, you can brake to a stop. It is best to brake lightly and steadily or gently. If the vehicle is equipped with antilock brakes, a light, steady application is preferred.

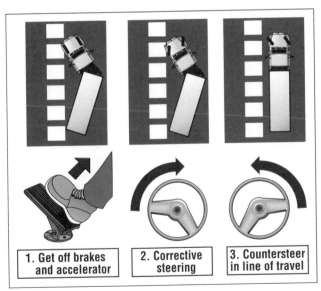

Figure **18-9** When a tractor jackknife occurs, corrective steering puts the tractor back on course.

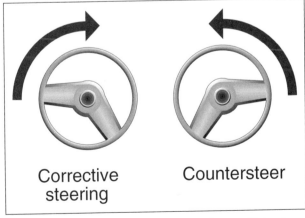

Figure **18-10** Countersteering will help you avoid a new skid.

Chapter Nineteen

Passive Railroad Crossings

Text and information provided by and reprinted with the permission of Operation Lifesaver, Inc. ("OLI"). More information about OLI and its highway rail grade crossing safety and railroad trespass prevention education programs is available at www.oli.org.

Operation Lifesaver

Active versus Passive Railroad Crossings

Engineering for Active Highway Rail-Grade Crossings

Engineering for Passive Warning Devices

Tips for Professional Drivers

OBJECTIVES

When you have completed this chapter, you should be able to:

- Identify active and passive railroad crossings

- Understand the dangers of active and passive railroad crossings

- Know how physical characteristics of crossings affect driver's visibility

- Know and explain the illusion created by a train's speed

- Identify behavior factors inhibiting a driver's field of vision

- Identify common driver distractions affecting safety at crossings

- Know and explain "best practices" for drivers at railroad crossings

- Know the rules and procedures associated with various loads and railroad crossings

KEY TERMS

Active railroad crossings
Crossbuck sign
Crossing gate
Highway rail-grade
crossing
Hump crossing sign

Passive railroad
crossings
Pavement markings
Tracks out of service sign
Yellow diamond-shaped
parallel track sign

INTRODUCTION

In 1972, the national average of collisions at **highway rail-grade crossings** exceeded 12,000 annually. Through the efforts of Operation Lifesaver, a non-profit safety education program begun in Idaho and now active in 49 states and the District of Columbia, this number has dropped by more than 70 percent.

According to available statistics, when motorists disregard signs, lights, bells, and gates at railroad crossings, a collision involving a vehicle and a train is 40 times more likely to result in a fatality than a collision involving another vehicle.

Today, every 120 minutes a collision occurs between a vehicle or a pedestrian and a train. In 2000, according to the Federal Railroad Administration, there were 3,500 collisions at highway rail-grade crossings in the United States. These collisions resulted in 425 deaths and 1,219 injuries. An additional 463 pedestrians died in 2000 because they were walking on or along tracks.

In 1998, the Federal Highway Administration proposed a new rule that would disqualify commercial vehicle drivers for grade-crossing violations. At that time, Federal Highway Administrator Kenneth R. Wykle explained, "This proposal will advance safety at railroad crossings by holding drivers and carriers accountable."

Grade-crossing laws and regulations vary from state to state, but under the new law, along with drivers, any employer who knowingly allows, permits, authorizes, or requires a driver to ignore or disobey warning signs or devices at a railroad crossing is subject to a fine of up to $10,000. Drivers disobeying or ignoring warning devices at railroad crossings also could be suspended for 60 days for a first offense and up to 120 days for subsequent convictions.

According to the FMCSA regulations (FMCSR 392.10), "Every motor vehicle shall, upon approaching any railroad grade crossing, make a full stop not more than 50 feet, nor less than 15 feet from the nearest rail of such railroad crossing, and shall not proceed until due caution has been taken to ascertain that the course is clear; except that a full stop need not be made at:

1. A street car crossing within a business or residence district of a municipality;
2. A railroad grade crossing where a police officer or a traffic control signal (not a railroad flashing signal) directs traffic to proceed;
3. An abandoned or exempted grade crossing which is clearly marked, as such by or with the consent of the proper state authority, when such marking can be read from the driver's position.

According to Operation Lifesaver, all such motor vehicles shall display a sign on the rear reading, "This Vehicle Stops at Railroad Crossings."

OPERATION LIFESAVER

Begun in Idaho in 1972, Operation Lifesaver came into being when the national average of collisions at highway rail-grade crossings exceeded 12,000 annually.

A nonprofit, nationwide public education program dedicated to ending crashes, injuries, and fatalities at intersections where roadways meet railways, Operation Lifesaver was originally a six-week public awareness campaign launched by the office of Idaho's Governor Cecil Andrus, the Idaho Peace Officers, and Union Pacific Railroad as a one-time, one-state initiative.

During the campaign's first year, Idaho's crossing-related fatalities dropped by 43 percent, and when the Operation Lifesaver campaign was adopted by Nebraska the next year, that state's collision rate was reduced by 26 percent.

Now in its 30th year, Operation Lifesaver programs are active in 49 states and the District of Columbia, and are credited with helping save 11,000 lives and preventing 54,000 injuries through its national outreach program. For more information on Operation Lifesaver, go to http://www.oli.org or contact the national office at 800-537-6224. See also Table 19-1.

Table **19-1** Highway Rail-Grade Crossing Collisions and Casualties at Public and Private Crossings for All Highway Users

Year	Collisions	Fatalities	Injuries
2000	3,502	425	1,219
1999	3,489	402	1,396
1998	3,508	431	1,303
1997	3,865	461	1,540
1996	4,257	488	1,610
1995	4,633	579	1,894
1994	4,979	615	1,961
1993	4,892	626	1,837
1992	4,910	579	1,969
1991	5,386	608	2,094
1990	5,713	698	2,407
1989	6,525	801	2,868
1988	6,615	689	2,589
1987	6,391	624	2,429
1986	6,396	616	2,458
1985	6,919	582	2,687
1984	7,281	649	2,910
1983	7,616	575	2,623
1982	7,748	607	2,637
1981	9,295	728	3,293

Source: Federal Railroad Administration. Available at http://www.oli.org.

Figure **19-1**   Active railroad crossing.

ACTIVE VERSUS PASSIVE RAILROAD CROSSINGS

An **active railroad crossing** usually attracts high traffic and is marked with the familiar white **crossbuck sign** with flashing lights or the crossbuck with flashing lights and a **crossing gate** (see Figure 19-1). These are active warning devices, which means that they activate only when a train is approaching the crossing or intersection.

Almost two-thirds of all railroad crossings in the United States, however, are **passive railroad crossings.** This typically means they are marked with advance warning signs, **pavement markings,** and crossbucks, but there are no gates and no flashing lights. Therefore, it is up to you—the professional driver—to look both ways and to make certain no train is coming before you proceed.

ENGINEERING FOR ACTIVE HIGHWAY RAIL-GRADE CROSSINGS

Over the past several decades, engineers have designed, tested, and implemented various technologies to help reduce the number of collisions, injuries, and fatalities at highway rail-grade crossings. Some of these technologies are being used today, but many other new ones are being tested, and some remain to be implemented.

The following is a brief overview of signage and technology that have been developed to help improve highway rail-grade crossing safety. Included is a preview of cutting-edge technologies for possible use in the future:

Crossbuck sign.   The crossbuck sign is one of the oldest warning devices. It is a white regulatory, X-shaped sign with the words "Railroad Crossing" in black lettering (see Figure 19-2). They are usually positioned alongside the highway prior to a railroad crossing.

Where possible, the crossbuck sign is located on the right-hand side of a public roadway on each approach to the highway rail-grade

Figure **19-2**   Crossbuck sign.

Figure **19-3** Hump crossing sign.

Figure **19-4** Advance warning sign.

crossing. The crossbuck sign is a passive yield sign to all vehicles approaching the crossing and is required at all public highway rail-grade crossings.

Hump crossing sign.   The **hump crossing sign** is a new sign warning drivers that their trucks may get hung up on the track (see Figure 19-3). Any truck's landing gear can get stuck. If you drive a lowboy, car carrier, or anything else low to the ground, you are at risk and should not proceed.

Advance warning sign.   The advance warning sign is a round yellow warning sign (minimum of 36 inches in diameter) with a black "X" and "RR" located alongside the highway in advance of the crossing (see Figure 19-4). It serves to alert the motorist that a crossing is ahead.

The advance warning sign is usually the first sign you see when approaching a highway rail-grade crossing. The distance of the sign from the track is dependent on the posted highway speed but should not be less than 100 feet in advance of the nearest rail. This distance will allow the vehicle's driver ample time to comprehend and react to the sign's message by slowing down, looking, listening, and being prepared to stop if a train is approaching.

The advance warning sign is used on each roadway in advance of every public highway rail-grade crossing except (1) on low-volume, low-speed roadways crossing minor spurs or other tracks that are infrequently used (2) in business districts where active highway rail-grade crossing traffic control devices are used, and (3) where physical conditions do not permit even a partially effective display of a sign.

Cantilevers.   These structures are sometimes used to locate the flashing light signals over one or more lanes of vehicular traffic. There are two slightly different uses of cantilevers related to the location of signals on the arm with respect to traffic lanes. Some states require the signals to be placed over the center of each lane. Other states mandate the signals be located to the right of the lane.

Standard structures are made with arm lengths up to 40 feet, and in some special designs, arm lengths of 50 feet or longer are possible. Cantilevers are being used in increasing numbers because several states have required roadside installation to be set back farther from the roadway surface.

Flashing light signals.   This is a regulatory device installed on a standard mast or cantilever that, when activated, displays red lights flashing alternately. The number of flashes per minute for each incandescent lamp is between 35 and 55. Each lamp is illuminated the same length of time. Flashing light signals indicate the approach of a train and require a complete stop by the professional driver.

When a train is approaching the highway rail grade, the flashing light signals are activated. These flashing signals are mandatory when gates are used to stop traffic at a highway rail-grade crossing. When both the gate and the flashing light signals are activated, the gate arm light nearest the tip is illuminated continuously, and the other two lights flash alternately in unison with the flashing light signals.

The typical flashing light signal assembly on a side of the roadway location includes a standard crossbuck sign and, where there is more than one track, an auxiliary "number of tracks" sign, all indicating a highway rail-grade crossing ahead (see Figure 19-5). A bell may be included in the assembly and will operate in conjunction with the flashing lights.

Highway rail intersection warning systems apply the "fail-safe principle" to activate the warning system when there are component failures or abnormal conditions in the system, such as a commercial AC power failure.

This is done by providing a source of standby power at the crossing. Storage batteries are the principal source of standby power for crossing warning systems, and because of the requirement that this standby power last as long as 48 hours (in some states), low-wattage bulbs must be used in the flashing light signals.

Flashing light signals are found at all types of public highway rail-grade crossings. They normally are placed to the right of the approaching highway traffic on all roadway approaches to a crossing.

Standard bell.   This device, when activated, provides an audible warning that may be used with flashing light signals and gates. A standard bell is most effective as a warning to pedestrians and bicyclists.

The standard bell is designed to ring loudly when a train is approaching to warn vehicles and people in the surrounding area. When used, the bell is usually mounted on top of one of the signal support masts. The bell is usually activated when the flashing light signals are operating. In some cases, the bell stops ringing when the lead end of the train reaches the crossing or when gate arms descend to within 10 degrees of the horizontal position.

A new technology being used by most railroads is the electronic bell, with a volume that can be adjusted to various levels, depending on the location.

Standard warning gate.   This device was first introduced in 1936 and is an active traffic control device used with flashing lights (see Figure 19-6). The device consists of a drive mechanism and a fully reflectorized red and white striped gate arm

Figure **19-5**
Typical flashing
light signal
assembly,
including
crossbuck and
number-of-tracks
signs.

Figure **19-6** Crossbuck, flashing
lights, and gate.

with lights. In the "down" position, these gates extend across the approaching lanes of highway traffic about 4 feet above the top of the pavement.

Gates can be made of aluminum, fiberglass, or wood. Fiberglass or aluminum gates are designed with a breakaway feature so that the gate is disengaged from the mechanism when struck. Gate lengths generally range between 24 and 40 feet.

The flashing light signal may be supported on the same post with the gate mechanism or separately mounted. In its normal upright position—when no train is approaching or occupying the crossing—the gate arm should be either vertical or almost vertical. A standard warning gate is normally accompanied by a crossbuck sign, flashing light signals, and other passive warning signs.

In determining the need for automatic gates, the following factors may be considered:

- Multiple mainline railroad tracks
- Multiple tracks where a train on or near the crossing can obscure the movement of another train approaching the crossing
- High-speed train operation combined with limited sight distance
- A combination of high speed and a moderately high volume of highway and railroad traffic
- Presence of school buses, transit buses, or farm vehicles in the traffic flow
- Presence of trucks carrying hazardous materials, particularly when the view down the track from a stopped vehicle is obstructed
- Continuance of accidents after installation of flashing lights
- Presence of passenger trains

Long-arm gate. This is structured the same as a standard gate assembly but with a longer arm. The reason for the longer arm is to reduce the driver's ability to drive around the gates.

Long-arm gates cover at least three-fourths of the roadway. A restriction on the use of long-arm gates would be a vertical constraint, such as overhead power lines. When these exist, articulated gates can be used instead of long-arm gates.

Four-quadrant gate. Compared to a standard gate assembly, four-quadrant gates have an additional pair of dual gate arms. These gate arms are lowered on each side of a bidirectional crossing. Potential gate violators are prevented from driving around the gates because the intersection is entirely sealed off.

Operating like the standard gate and the long-arm gate, four-quadrant gates restrict motorists from entering a highway rail-grade crossing by lowering the gate arm when the presence of a train is detected.

Four-quadrant gates are an integral part of the North Carolina Sealed Corridor Project between Raleigh and Charlotte. Their primary benefit is that they ensure that no crossing violations occur after the gate arms are lowered, unless the gate arms are penetrated.

Barrier gates. This is a fairly new warning gate technology that locks into a post when in the down position. This feature disallows vehicles from driving around them at a crossing.

Operating like standard gate assemblies, barrier gates have arms equipped with aluminum tubing containing three cables. When the gate arm is in the down position, its tip locks into a locking post, either all the way across the street or at a median in the street. When a vehicle attempts to drive through the gate, the cables grab it like a net to prevent it from attempting to cross. These cables are designed to catch a pickup truck traveling up to 50 mph and stop it with a soft landing, causing no harm to the driver or passengers.

Developed in 1997, there are currently only a few locations where barrier gates are being used.

Surfacing.   The highway rail-grade crossing surface usually consists of pavement or other highway and rail surface materials on the approaches and crossover points with the railroad track. As the vehicle moves across the highway rail-grade crossing, the material on which its tires roll is commonly referred to as a "crossing surface." This surface must carry the train or highway vehicle and transmit their wheel loads to the foundation structure.

Crossing surfaces today fall into two categories: monolithic and sectional. Monolithic crossings are those formed at the crossing and cannot be removed without destroying the surface. Typical monolithic crossings are made of asphalt, poured-in-place concrete, and cast-in-place rubber compounds.

Sectional crossings are those manufactured in sections or panels that are placed at the crossing and can be removed and reinstalled. Typical sectional crossing surfaces include treated timbers, reinforced concrete, steel, rubber, and high-density polyethylene.

The surface of the roadway at the crossing is an important aspect of highway rail-grade crossing. If the crossing surface is uneven, rough, or littered with exposed and protruding spikes, attention is on the surface rather than the warning signals.

Median barriers.   These consist of a prefabricated mountable island. The island is placed in the center of the roadway leading up to the highway rail-grade crossing.

Yellow and black reflectorized paddle delineators are mounted to the curb barrier, either on a rubber boot or in concrete. If the roadway is not wide enough to accommodate a median barrier, yellow and black tubular markers, mounted directly to the roadway's centerline, can be used.

Used at several crossings around the country, a key advantage to median barriers is that they are a proven low-cost investment with a high rate of safety return.

Intelligent Transportation Systems (ITS).   These are applications of electronics, communications, and information processing products and services used to solve surface transportation problems, such as safety problems at grade crossings.

ITS projects are developed with the following goals: to increase safety, to increase efficiency, to improve mobility, to increase productivity, and to conserve energy while improving the environment.

ITS projects have been implemented across the country in several metropolitan areas. Five of these demonstration projects are grade-crossing safety projects.

In Maryland's Timonium Road project, an active warning sign to alert motorists that a second train is approaching while they are stopped at a light-rail-grade crossing is being tested.

In San Antonio, Texas, that city's Advanced Warning to Avoid Railroad Delays (AWARD) system was designed to help motorists avoid delays due to railroads that cross freeway frontage roads. Radar and sensors at three grade crossings detect the presence of a train. The data are transmitted to San Antonio's areawide database and flow into traveler information services and the Transguide Traffic Management Center, in vehicle navigation units, kiosks, a Web page, and variable message signs. This information on roadway blockages allows drivers to select a different route to reach their destination.

At Mystic, Connecticut's, School Street crossing, which is part of the Amtrak high-speed rail corridor, four-quadrant gates, loop detectors, train control systems, video monitoring systems, operational tests, and prototype systems have been placed to improve safety.

The Illinois Department of Transportation is conducting a pilot study of advisory onboard vehicle warning systems at grade crossings. In the study, the driver's perception of these systems is being evaluated. Five crossings on Metra's Milwaukee North Line are being studied. Three hundred vehicles, including school buses, transit vehicles, municipal vehicles, and commercial vehicles, have been equipped with the warning system, which is a receiver activated by a transmitter at the crossing to provide advance warning to the driver of a train at the crossing.

In Minnesota, a project similar to that of Illinois is being tested—the viability of in-vehicle signing in school buses at grade crossings and the impact on driver behavior. Special crossbucks at five signalized crossings in Minnesota transmit signals that are received by "smart" license plates that, in turn, activate in-vehicle displays to warn of approaching trains at the crossings.

ENGINEERING FOR PASSIVE WARNING DEVICES

Exempt sign. This sign is placed in advance of and at a crossing authorized by state law or regulation to inform placarded hazardous materials, vehicles, buses, and other highway uses that a stop is not required, except when a signal, train crew member, or uniformed police officer indicates that a train, locomotive, or other railroad equipment is approaching the crossing (see Figure 19-7).

Yield sign. This sign assigns right-of-way. Vehicles controlled by a yield sign need to avoid interference with other vehicles, including trains, which are given the right-of-way.

Do Not Stop on Tracks sign. This is a black and white regulatory sign placed at a crossing when an engineering study or experience determines there is a high potential for vehicles stopping on the tracks (see Figure 19-8).

Stop sign. This is a red regulatory stop sign with lettering intended for use where motor vehicle traffic is required to stop. This sign can be added to the crossing, requiring all vehicles to come to a complete stop before crossing the railroad tracks.

Tracks Out of Service sign. A **Tracks Out of Service sign** is for use at a crossing in lieu of the crossbuck when a railroad track has been abandoned or its use discontinued (see Figure 19-9).

Figure **19-7** Exempt sign.

Figure **19-8** Do Not Stop on Tracks sign.

Figure **19-9** Tracks Out of Service sign.

Parallel track signs. **Yellow diamond-shaped parallel track signs** are located in roadways close to the railroad tracks to indicate the road ahead will cross tracks. These signs are intended to warn motorists making a turn that there is a highway rail-grade crossing immediately after the turn.

Low Ground Clearance warning sign. This new advance symbol sign for rail-grade crossings is a warning where conditions are sufficiently abrupt to create hang-ups of long-wheelbase vehicles or trailers with low ground clearance. Based on research conducted by the Federal Highway Administration, which tested the new sign with New York's professional driver population, the new Low Ground Clearance sign may be used at these special locations.

Multiple-track crossing signs. These signs indicate the number of tracks crossing the highway rail-grade crossing and will be placed on the post below the crossbuck.

RR lettering. These white letters are set into the surface of or applied to the pavement in advance of the crossing, which is for the purpose of advising, warning and guiding traffic (see Figure 19-10).

Figure **19-10**
Pavement
warning.

TIPS FOR PROFESSIONAL DRIVERS

"Always Expect a Train." Say this daily and every time you approach a rail crossing—active or passive.

Drivers should stay alert at places where the roadway crosses railroad tracks. These highway rail-grade crossings are a special kind of intersection—a highway rail intersection. Be aware that local and state laws may be more restrictive than the following reminders.

As a professional driver, you should expect a train to come through a highway rail-grade crossing at any time. You should also be aware that your slanted view of the track and a train's size and weight, combined with other factors, create an optical illusion. This makes it virtually impossible for you to judge the speed and distance of an oncoming train from the crossing—so do not try to beat the train across the tracks.

Many experts on rail-crossing safety say that drivers usually hit trains—or are hit by trains—within a 5-mile radius of their homes. Why? Because this is familiar territory, so it is easy for a driver to say, "I've never seen a train on these tracks. I'll just scoot across—no harm."

Stopping Safely at Highway Rail Intersections

At 80,000 pounds and pulling a 53-foot trailer, a typical rig on a level road with good surface conditions requires at least 14 seconds to clear a single track and more than 15 seconds to clear a double track.

Keeping this in mind, the following precautions are suggested when coming to a highway rail intersection:

- Stop no closer than 15 feet and no farther than 50 feet from the nearest rail, if required to stop.
- Never try to drive around lowered gates. If you suspect a signal malfunction, call local law enforcement, the railroad, 911, or the 1-800 number posted on or near the warning device or crossbuck.
- If there is a line of traffic at a traffic light and this causes your rig to stop on a railroad track, do not do it—even if you do not see a train coming. A good rule of thumb is to never stop on railroad tracks.

- Check for traffic behind you while stopping gradually. Use a pullout lane, if available.
- Turn on four-way flashers; leave on until following traffic has stopped safely.
- To better hear the train, roll down the window and turn off the stereo, CB, and fans.
- While stopped, look carefully in each direction for approaching trains, moving head and eyes to see around obstructions, such as mirrors and windshield pillars.
- If hauling hazmat, you are required to stop at all rail crossings. The law specifies a stopping point between 15 and 50 feet from the nearest rail.
- Never race a train to a crossing.
- If a train is stopped nearby, do not cross the tracks anyway. It is illegal and also dangerous. Many railroad crossings have multiple tracks, and you may not see another train, because of the stopped train, about to cross the intersection.

Resuming Travel

- Before resuming travel, make sure there is enough room on the other side of the tracks for the entire rig to clear the tracks, including any trailer overhang. (The train's overhang is at least 3 feet wider than the rails on both sides.)
- If you stopped in a pullout lane, signal and pull back onto the road when there is a safe gap in traffic. Expect traffic in other lanes to pass you.
- Use the highest gear, which will let you cross the tracks without shifting.
- If the red lights begin to flash after starting over tracks, *keep going.* Lights should begin flashing at least 20 seconds before the train arrives at the crossing.

When Stopping Is Not Required

In some states, when the crossing is controlled by standard traffic signals showing green when tracks are clear, stopping is not required. Other instances when you are not required to stop your rig at a railroad crossing are when the track is marked with signs showing Exempt, Abandoned, or Tracks Out of Service messages and when traffic is controlled by a flagperson or a police officer.

When You Are Always Required to Stop at a Highway Rail Intersection

- When transporting chlorine, whether or not placarded is required
- When driving any placarded vehicle carrying hazardous materials
- When driving a cargo tank used for hazardous materials, whether loaded or empty
- When transporting a Class 3 elevated temperature material in a cargo tank
- When transporting a hazardous material covered by a Department of Transportation (DOT) exemption (when shipping papers are marked "DOT-E" followed by an exemption number)

Special Situations

All professional drivers, no matter what their cargo, should be aware that certain rigs could get stuck on raised railroad crossings:

- Low-slung units, such as lowboys, car carriers, moving vans, and possum-belly livestock trailers
- Single-axle tractors pulling a long trailer with its landing gear set to accommodate a tandem axle tractor.

If You Get Stuck or Hung Up on Tracks

If you are crossing raised railroad tracks and your rig gets caught on the tracks, first get out of the truck and away from the tracks. Check signposts or signal housing at or near the crossing for emergency notification information. Then call 911 as soon as possible, giving the location of the crossing. To give emergency teams the best possible location, use all identifiable landmarks, especially the USDOT number (six numbers and a letter) if one is posted.

Train Facts to Remember

- A train traveling 55 mph travels 81 feet per second. Remember, too, that the train is 3 feet wider than the rails on each side.
- Trains cannot stop quickly. A fully loaded freight train of 100 cars, weighing approximately 6,000 tons and traveling 55 mph, requires a mile or more to stop after applying the brakes—the same distance as the length of 18 football fields.
- Passenger trains—either light rail or interstate—cannot stop quickly. When traveling 79 mph, they also require the distance of 18 football fields to come to a complete stop after emergency brakes are applied.
- If you are driving a vehicle equipped with a manual transmission, cross the track in a gear that will not require shifting until you are completely clear of the crossing—and that means remembering the train is 3 feet wider than the rails on each side.
- When stopped at the crossing, as you look down the track, you will experience an optical illusion. The train appears to be farther away and traveling more slowly than it really is. In reality, the train is going quite fast and is much closer than it appears. Do not misjudge either a train's speed or its distance. When in doubt, *wait* for the train to pass.

Chapter Twenty
Accident Procedures

Photo courtesy of ATA
Associates, Inc.

When an Accident Occurs

Accident Reporting

Giving First Aid

Fires and Fire Fighting

FROM NOW ON. . .

ONLY THE BEST
WILL DRIVE!

OBJECTIVES

When you have completed this chapter, you should be able to:

- Explain the correct procedures a driver should follow at an accident scene

- Detail the information needed for an accident report

- Know which subjects the driver should never discuss after an accident

- Outline the driver's responsibilities in an emergency

- Know how to protect the accident scene

- Describe types of fires and how to put them out

- Explain the special skills needed for a hazardous materials spill

- Know the special reports needed when hazardous materials are involved

KEY TERMS

Accident packet

Centers for Disease
  Control (CDC)

Chemical Transportation
  Emergency Center
  (CHEMTREC)

Class A fire

Class B fire

Class C fire

Class D fire

Emergency triangles

Fire extinguishers

First aid

Hazardous Materials
  Incident Report

National Response
  Center

U.S. Coast Guard
  National Response
  Center

INTRODUCTION

Like any major industry, accidents sometimes occur in the transport of cargo from point of origin to point of delivery. When an accident does occur—whatever the severity—the professional driver should know his or her responsibilities, including what to do immediately and what not to do.

The purpose of this chapter is to explain the professional driver's immediate responsibilities at the scene of the accident and how to protect equipment, cargo, and human life. Areas of discussion will include what you should do about your rig, how to report an accident, how to protect yourself and others, how to prevent a fire or control a fire if one ignites, what equipment to use, how to act safely, what you must do to stay within the law, and accident reporting.

WHEN AN ACCIDENT OCCURS

When an accident occurs, there are federal laws as well as company policies that will guide the professional driver, both at the scene and in reporting the incident. The professional driver should also know how his or her involvement in an accident will affect his or her driving record.

Steps to Take at the Scene of an Accident

Drivers should:

- Stop immediately
- Follow company procedures to the letter
- Protect the scene to prevent further accidents
- Notify proper authorities
- Remember that diesel fuel makes the road very slippery if spilled
- Provide reasonable assistance to injured persons
- Protect injured persons, not moving them unless they are in danger of additional injury (trained emergency personnel should move them, reducing the chance of further injury)

Get the following information from the other persons involved in the accident:

- Name and address of drivers
- Name and address of the motor carrier if any other commercial vehicles were involved

- Vehicle registration or license plate number
- Driver's license number and the state issuing it
- The name and address of their insurance company and the policy number

Give the following information to the other persons involved in the accident:

- Your name and address
- The name and address of your carrier
- Your vehicle registration or license plate number
- Your driver's license number and the state that issued it
- The name and address of the company insuring your rig and the policy number

Report the accident to your motor carrier as soon as possible.

You can expect to be tested for drugs or alcohol in your system after an accident. It is the driver's responsibility to be tested for drugs and alcohol if someone dies as a result of the accident, anyone is injured and must receive treatment, the vehicle is damaged so much it must be towed away, or the driver of the commercial motor vehicle receives a citation for a moving violation. Carriers must make sure their drivers know the rules for drug testing.

Common sense, the company's policy, and the law provide a sturdy guide for all drivers after an accident has occurred. Companies often provide guidelines for drivers after an accident (see Figure 20-1). These guidelines usually include:

1. Shut off engine and turn on four-way flashers.
2. Call for help—police and ambulance, if needed—and protect the injured from further injury.
3. Protect the scene to prevent further accidents.
4. Stay calm and courteous at all times.
5. Notify the company.
6. Remain on the scene until the company releases you to leave.
7. Provide required ID when requested.

Figure **20-1** The driver is responsible for the safety of others and for protecting the scene.

8. Collect facts: required ID of those involved, names/phone numbers of witnesses, and so on.

9. Say nothing about who is at fault. Do not offer to pay damages, and do not accept payment from anyone else involved.

10. Make sure any cargo that is spilled has been cleaned up before leaving the scene.

11. Check your rig to make sure it is in a condition to be driven again.

12. File a complete accident report when you arrive at your destination.

13. Expect a drug test.

If a commercial motor vehicle hits an unattended vehicle, the driver should stop and make a reasonable effort to locate the driver of the other vehicle. If he or she cannot be located, the driver must leave a note on the other vehicle where it will be easily seen. The note should contain the driver's name and address as well as the name and address of the carrier. Be sure to attach the note in such a way it will not blow away or fall off. Put it where the driver can see it easily. If it appears there was no note, you could be charged with hit-and-run.

Some drivers carry Polaroid-type cameras or disposable cameras with them so they can take photographs if they are in an accident. The photos a driver may take at the scene of an accident are not just for the purpose of showing damage to his or her rig. These photos are also important because they give accident reconstructionists a basis to begin their accident investigation.

Note: When taking photographs, focus on the vehicles, skid marks, damage to vehicles, and position of vehicles. It is not your job to take photos that may include pools of blood or bodies.

It is important to remember, however, that the driver should take photos of the accident scene only after they have completed protecting the scene, assisting those who may need help, and notifying the authorities as well as the company about the accident.

Accidents while Transporting Hazardous Materials

A driver who has a cargo of hazardous materials should be aware that any accident can be very dangerous. Always check the shipping papers in advance so that you know what class of hazardous material and the approximate amount you are hauling. The driver must make sure shipping papers for hazardous materials are within reach during the trip and can be read easily. Placards must either show the product's name or be empty. In 2001, slogans such as "Have a nice day" and "Drive safely" were outlawed.

If the driver of hazardous materials has an accident, he or she should:

- See if there are any leaks or cargo has spilled and assume it is hazardous material. Do not allow anyone to walk or drive through spills.

- Keep onlookers away (see Figure 20-2).

- Stay upwind of any spills. Do not allow anyone to eat, drink, or smoke in the area.

Figure **20-2** Keep onlookers away and stay upwind of any spills.

- Advise emergency responders there are hazardous materials and allow them to check the shipping papers. Always check to be sure they are legible when you accept the shipment.
- Set out warning devices to protect the scene.
- Notify local authorities. Be sure they understand the truck is transporting hazardous materials. Tell them the classes and quantities on board.
- Contact the motor carrier. Make sure the carrier also understands hazardous materials are involved and whether there has been a spill. If the accident is near water, inform the carrier.
- Follow the company's policy for what the driver is supposed to do at the accident scene.

ACCIDENT REPORTING

When a vehicle transporting hazardous materials is involved in an accident, additional reports must be made. Usually, the carrier handles these reports, based on the information given by the driver. The driver should not handle any of this reporting except when the driver is an owner/operator, the driver cannot contact the motor carrier for whom he or she is driving, the shipper's instructions require reporting by the driver, or authorities at the scene request the driver to make the report.

Emergency Procedures

Because the laws are constantly changing, always check with your employer before you begin a trip hauling hazardous material to learn what you must do if there is an accident or spill (see Figure 20-3). Some of the agencies you may need to notify are listed in the following paragraphs.

The **U.S. Coast Guard National Response Center** helps coordinate emergency forces in response to chemical hazards. Their number is 1-800-424-8802. The **Chemical Transportation Emergency Center (CHEMTREC)** can tell emergency personnel what they need to know to make the proper notifications (see

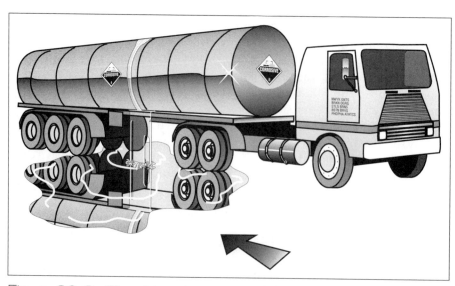

Figure **20-3** The driver is responsible for preventing further accidents or injury.

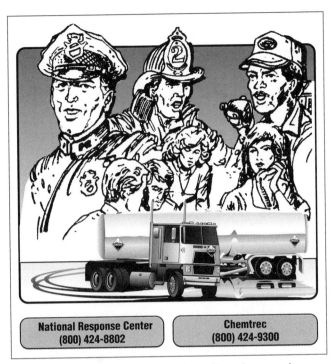

National Response Center
(800) 424-8802

Chemtrec
(800) 424-9300

Figure **20-4** If you are hauling hazardous material, you need to know and understand what these agencies do and what they cannot do.

Figure 20-4). Their 24-hour number is 1-800-424-9300 (emergency calls only). You can call 1-800-226-8200 for information.

If you call CHEMTREC, be sure to include:

- Your name and a call-back number
- The name of the motor carrier and the unit number
- The name of the consignee
- The name of the shipper or manufacturer
- A description of the accident scene

The **National Response Center** must be notified if there is an accident that results in the following:

- A fatality
- An injury requiring hospitalization
- Property damage of $50,000 or more
- Fire, breakage, spillage, or contamination from radioactive materials or etiologic (disease-causing) agents
- A situation presenting a continuous danger to life
- Discharge of a hazardous substance
- Public evacuation that lasts 1 hour or more
- A major transportation artery is closed or shut down for more than 1 hour

If the load is a disease-causing agent, then you should call the **Centers for Disease Control (CDC)** at 1-404-633-5313 or 1-202-267-2675.

For more specific information about reporting accidents involving hazardous materials, refer to CFR Section 171.15.

Federal laws also require filing a written **Hazardous Materials Incident Report** (Form 5800.1, Rev 6-89) for any unintended release of hazardous materials (with limited exceptions). The report must be filed within 30 days. The driver must report any such release and give the necessary information to the supervisor for preparing this report. For more specific information, refer to 49CFR Section 171.16.

How to Protect the Scene

The driver, or someone acting for him or her, warns oncoming traffic to prevent further accidents. To do this, a driver must know the types of warning devices that should be used to protect the scene, how to set up the warning devices quickly, and how to place the warning devices correctly.

Types of Warning Devices

Emergency triangles.   FMCSR 393.95 requires reflective **emergency triangles** to be carried on all current commercial vehicles (see Figure 20-5). The triangles are better warning devices because they can be used in the day or at night, are self-illuminating at night and have an orange border that is easy to see during the day, and can be used more than once. They can be used on any vehicle with any cargo.

Fusees.   Because of the danger of fire, fusees or other flame-producing warning devices cannot be used under certain conditions. Also, because of the fire hazard, fusees should not be used when flammable liquids or gases may be present.

Fusees or other warning devices or signals produced by a flame must not be used with:

- Any vehicle hauling Class A or Class B explosives (Explosives 1.1–1.3)
- Tanks used for flammable liquid or compressed gas (whether loaded or empty)
- Vehicles powered by compressed gas

Figure **20-5** Emergency triangles are required safety equipment on all rigs.

Figure **20-6** Fusees are ignited by striking the cap along the striker button on the side. Place your back to the wind and hold the fusee away from your body and clothing.

To give the red signal, fusees burn at a very high temperature. To light a fusee, read and follow the instructions printed on the fusee (see Figure 20-6). After they are lighted, molten material can drip and cause severe burns. When lighting or using a fusee, turn your back to the wind, point the lighted end away from yourself, and hold it at an angle that will keep the molten material from dripping. Although larger sizes are available, fusees generally have a 15-minute burning time.

When you use a fusee to signal by hand, hold the lighted end away and keep clear of any dripping molten material, avoid breathing the fumes, and do not look into the glare.

To put out a lighted fusee, press the burning end into dirt or rub it against a paved surface. Do not use water. Do not leave hot residue in the grass or anything else that will burn.

You must keep fusees dry or they cannot be lighted. They should be stored in a rack or container that is easy to reach from outside the cab.

Placing Warning Devices

The reason for using warning devices is to warn approaching vehicles of a problem and guide them around the scene. Properly placed warnings can be easily seen and do not confuse other motorists (see Figure 20-7).

When setting up triangles, it is best to walk well off the road and hold the triangle out in front of you so that approaching traffic can see it. This will make you more visible and help protect you from being hit by oncoming traffic.

When you stop your rig, follow these steps:

1. Turn on the four-way flashers as a warning to traffic.
2. While the flashers are on, put out the emergency warning devices. This should be done within 10 minutes after you stop.
3. After the warning devices are in place, turn off the four-way flashers to save the battery.
4. When you are ready to start again, turn on the warning flashers.
5. Pick up the emergency warning devices and put them in the cab.

Figure **20-7** Emergency triangles are placed to warn approaching traffic of a problem.

CAUTION

Do not jeopardize your own safety trying to retrieve emergency warning devices in heavy traffic. Triangles can be replaced; you cannot.

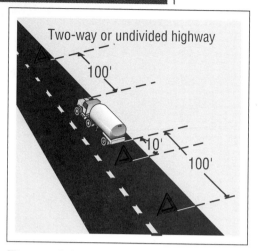

Figure **20-8** Placement of warning devices on a two-lane highway.

Always place flares or warning reflectors at least 100 feet from the accident or disabled vehicle. On a two-lane highway, place one device on the traffic side within 10 feet (4 paces) of the rear of the truck (see Figure 20-8), one device about 100 feet (40 paces) from the truck in the center of the traffic lane or shoulder where the truck is stopped, and one device 100 feet from the truck in the other direction.

On one-way or divided highways, place one device no more than 10 feet from the rear of the truck, one device 100 feet (40 paces) and one 200 feet (80 paces) from the truck toward the approaching traffic. Place them in the center of the lane or on the shoulder where the truck is stopped (see Figure 20-9).

In business or residential districts, use emergency devices when there is not enough light to give oncoming drivers a view of your truck from 500 feet away.

On a hill or curve, place the rearmost triangle at a point where oncoming motorists will receive adequate warning before coming on your truck (see Figure 20-10).

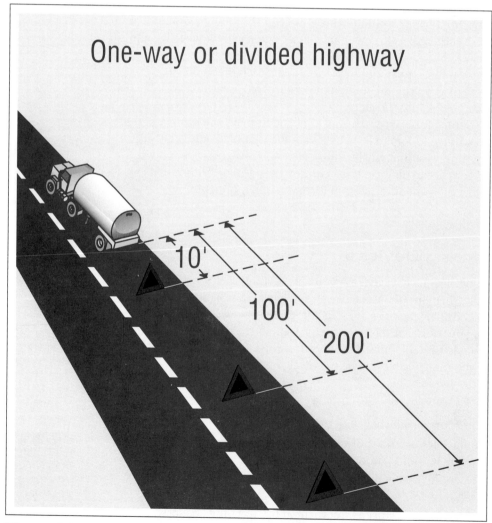

Figure **20-9** Placement of warning devices on a divided highway.

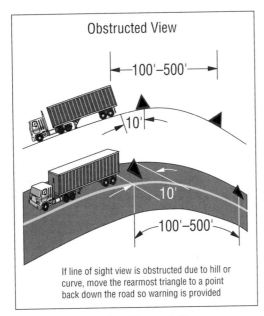

Obstructed View

←—100'–500'—→

10'

10'

←—100'–500'—→

If line of sight view is obstructed due to hill or curve, move the rearmost triangle to a point back down the road so warning is provided

Figure **20-10** On a hill or curve, warning devices are placed up to 500 feet from the accident site.

Handling the Accident Scene

If an accident occurs, it is your duty to call the police and ambulance (if necessary), protect the injured, conduct yourself properly, collect the facts, use accident packets, diagram the accident, identify witnesses, provide proper identification, and remain at the scene until all requirements are met.

Assist the Injured

After stopping and protecting the scene, your first priority is to help anyone who is injured. But beware—know your limitations:

- Do not try to do anything you are not trained to do.
- Do not move the injured unless they are in danger.
- Avoid doing anything that could bring additional liability.
- Insist that anyone who claims to be injured get medical help because a doctor's record is the best protection against future claims. If a person refuses treatment, be sure to report this fact.

Call an Ambulance

If it appears to be needed, call for an ambulance. Give the exact location of the accident. If you are not familiar with the area, ask others at the scene if they can help you determine the location. Use the CB emergency channel or a cellular phone or send someone to call for help if a phone is not available.

Conduct Yourself Properly

An accident can be a very emotional experience. Much depends on keeping your cool. Remain polite and calm even if others try to blame you. Do not debate right or wrong or admit in any way you are at fault. Remember, legal liability for what happened will be determined later (sometimes much later). What you do or say can affect the decision. Do not give or accept money. Do not sign any type of release form. The only paper you must sign is a traffic citation from a police officer.

ACCIDENT REPORT KIT

IN CASE OF ACCIDENT

- Stop and investigate IMMEDIATELY!
- Set out warning devices.
- Assist injured persons, but do NOT move if likely to cause further injury; call for medical assistance.
- Notify police, supervisor and insurance adjustor as instructed.
- Give your name, address, company name and address, vehicle registration number and exhibit operator's license to proper authorities.
- If there is no phone nearby, stop passerby and ask him to contact supervisor (use accident notification card)

- Secure names and addresses of witnesses or first persons at scene (use witness cards)
- If you strike an unattended vehicle and owner cannot be located, you MUST place your name and the address of the carrier securely on the vehicle.
- If the other driver admits his fault ask him to complete the exoneration card.
- Protect your vehicle from further damage and theft.
- Complete drivers report at accident scene.
- Comply with any required alcohol/drug test.
- Return the completed packet to your supervisor upon return to the terminal.

DRIVE SAFELY - IT MAKES GOOD SENSE!

Figure **20-11** Sample accident reporting kit (Courtesy of J. J. Keller & Associates, Inc.; www.jjkeller.com).

DRIVER _____

ACCIDENT DATA

Date _____ 19 ___ Time _____ □ A.M. □ P.M.

Place _____
(Town, City, State)

Roadway _____
(Rt. #, Street, Intersecting Hwys)

Landmark _____
(Near bridge, milepost, etc.)

DEATH AND INJURY

Persons Killed _____

Persons Injured _____

Was anyone taken away from scene for medical treatment_____ (Who & Where Taken)

INVESTIGATION

Was Accident Investigated by Police? _____

Department _____ Badge # _____

Officer _____

Citation Issued? _____

List persons cited or arrested & charges _____

YOUR VEHICLE

Were any mechanical defects apparent at the time of the accident?_____ Explain_____

Were you wearing safety belts? _____

VEHICLE NO. 2

Type _____ Make _____

Model _____ Year _____

Driver _____

Address _____

License # & State _____

Owner _____

Address _____

Phone _____ Insurance Co. _____

ACCIDENT DESCRIPTION

Explain in your own words what happened.

_____

Draw a diagram of accident using [1] as your vehicle, [2] as vehicle No. 2, etc.

Figure **20-12** Sample preliminary accident report form (Courtesy of J. J. Keller & Associates, Inc.; www.jjkeller.com).

Call the Company for Instructions

When you call your company for instructions:

- Tell them whether or not you are injured.
- Report any damage to the truck and cargo.
- Ask for help if it is needed. For example, you may need another rig or a crew to transfer the cargo.
- Be sure to tell them what your cargo is so that they can make any special arrangements if needed.
- Get instructions from your supervisor as to whether you should continue the trip or return to the terminal.

Most companies give drivers **accident packets** to help them handle their responsibilities at the scene of an accident (see Figure 20-11). Check for this packet during your pretrip inspection. Packets usually contain:

- Basic instructions for handling the scene of an accident
- Preliminary accident report or memo (see Figure 20-12)
- Witness cards (see Figure 20-13)

Draw a Diagram

If possible, photograph the scene before any of the vehicles are towed or moved. Draw a diagram of the scene showing the positions of the vehicles before, during, and after the accident (see Figure 20-14). Include a description of the damage to other vehicles and property and an estimated amount of property damage (if possible).

Witnesses and Witness Cards

Try to get witnesses who can verify the vehicles' positions, speed, use of turn signals, skid marks, and so on. Sometimes drivers of cars that were near you can verify your speed. If your company supplies an accident packet, use the witness cards from it to get names and addresses. If no one volunteers as a witness, write down the license plate numbers of possible witnesses. Note the addresses of nearby buildings from which someone may have seen the accident.

Remain at the Scene until Your Carrier Instructs You to Leave

Do not leave the scene until your carrier instructs you to leave. Be sure you have given all the required information to the authorities and to others involved in the accident. If there is a cargo spill, remove the unbroken packages as safely as possible. Clean up the contents of broken packages as soon as you can. If you are hauling hazardous material, you will need specialized cleanup. Do not handle the product unless you have been trained to do so and have the necessary special equipment.

Give your rig a pretrip type of inspection to see if it is safe to drive (see Figure 20-15). If it is not safe, call a mechanic to make repairs or a tow truck to remove the rig from the scene.

Legal Requirements

By law, every accident must be reported regardless of how bad it is. Leaving the scene of an accident is a major traffic violation. A conviction for leaving the scene of an accident while driving a commercial motor vehicle will result in losing your CDL for 1 year in addition to any other penalties imposed by state law.

The failure of a driver to report an accident to the motor carrier will almost always result in the driver's losing his or her job. The driver will also be subject to prosecution.

Importance of the Driver's Information

You must be very careful when you get information at the scene of the accident (see Figure 20-16). This information will affect everything that occurs as a result of the accident. Your information is needed by the company to prepare the required reports for the carrier's insurance company, state agencies, and the U.S. Department of Transportation (if required).

The driver's information is important to the company so they may determine their legal obligations. They also need to update the driver's

WITNESS CARD

Did you see the accident _____ Did anyone appear injured _____ Were you riding in a vehicle involved _____ Which one _____ Who do you think was responsible for the accident _____

Your Name _____

Address _____

_____

Phone

PLEASE RETURN THIS CARD TO THE DRIVER
Thank You!

© Copyright 1995 & Published By:
J. J. KELLER & ASSOCIATES, INC. - Neenah, WI 54957-0368

33F-3 / 131-F-2
Rev. 5/95
RM 5809

Figure **20-13** Sample witness card (Courtesy of J. J. Keller & Associates, Inc.; www.jjkeller.com).

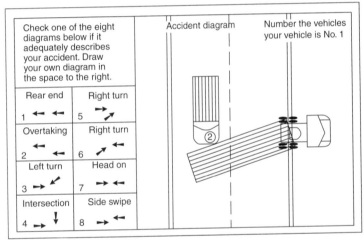

Figure **20-14** Include a diagram of the accident scene in your accident report.

Is your rig safe to drive?

Figure **20-15** Before leaving the accident scene, inspect your rig to ensure that it is safe to drive.

Sample Supervisor's Investigation Report

COMPANY	TERMINAL OR DIVISION
Safe Company Trucking	Tenth Street Terminal

DRIVER	TYPE OF VEHICLE IDENTIFYING NO.
M. Peachy	Single Truck

LOCATION OF ACCIDENT (Street, town, state)	DATE AND TIME OF ACCIDENT
Tenth Street Terminal Yard	February 6, 199X 8AM

NO. OF PERSONS INJURED AND EXTENT OF PROPERTY DAMAGE (Company and other)
No injuries.

Left rear fender (apx. $50.00 damage)

No damage to truck, bumper contacted car.

DESCRIPTION OF ACCIDENT (State in detail what occurred just before, and at the time of the accident)
Truck rolled away from loading dock, no chocks were placed at rear
wheels. Truck was not in gear, parking brake was not securely set.
(Truck brakes were out of adjustment.) Truck rolled apx. 10 feet and
struck rear fender of parked car in yard. Car was parked illegally
in yard.

UNSAFE CONDITION (Describe unsafe conditions such as faulty brake, light, etc. contributing to accident)

No chock blocks on truck.

Brakes out of adjustment.

UNSAFE ACT (Describe the unsafe action of driver as turning from wrong lane, speeding, failing to signal, etc.)

Brakes not secured when parked. Truck not in gear.

Car parked in truck area.

REMEDY (As a supervisor, what action have you taken or do you propose taking to prevent a repeat accident)

Check truck dock for chocks. Require chocks at loading dock and stops.

Driver issued warning. Keep private vehicles out of loading area.

SUPERVISOR	REVIEWED AND APPROVED BY	DATE REPORT PREPARED
R. Ray		February 8, 199X

(Use reverse side for sketch and additional detail)

Figure **20-16** The driver's information affects everything that occurs as a result of the accident.

record. They will also need the information to reach an equitable settlement if there are claims.

What the driver tells them may also be used to see if there are measures that can be taken to prevent similar accidents in the future. This information may also be used to assess the company's overall accident experience and trends in accidents.

Summary of Accident Reporting Requirements

Unless he or she is an owner/operator, the driver does not prepare the reports for the insurance company or state or federal agencies. However, the driver should understand the state and federal reporting requirements.

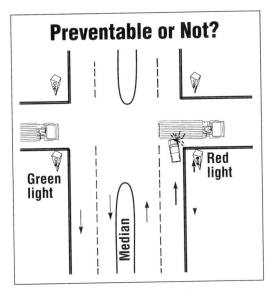

Figure **20-17** The trucking company usually decides whether the accident could have been prevented.

Federal requirements. A motor carrier operating in interstate or foreign commerce must report accidents to local authorities if they result in:

- A fatality
- An injury requiring treatment away from the scene
- Disabling damage to one or more vehicles requiring the vehicle to be towed from the scene

Local authorities are responsible for notifying the U.S. Department of Transportation (DOT). An accident does not have to be reported to the DOT if it involves only getting on or off of a vehicle or loading or unloading cargo unless the accident releases hazardous material. Then it must be reported.

State requirements. Every accident that results in a fatality or personal injury must be reported to state authorities. Each state has its own limit for reporting property damage accidents. The amounts range from $50 to $2,000. The driver involved in a property damage accident should be sure to check with the police about reporting requirements.

Accidents and the Professional Driver

Few things are more important to the professional truck driver than having a driving record that is free of accidents and violations, in either a CMV or a personal vehicle. The FMCSR requires interstate motor carriers to review the record of each driver every year. They must evaluate each driver's accident record and number of traffic violations.

Every accident costs the carrier money, even though the truck driver may not be to blame. If the driver is at fault in any way, the cost is much greater to the company.

Usually the trucking industry decides whether an accident could have been prevented (see Figure 20-17). This is more than just a question of whether the truck driver was issued a citation. They decide if the driver failed to take any action that could have prevented the accident.

Under trucking industry standards, an accident is considered preventable if the truck driver did anything that contributed to it or if the driver did not try to avoid it.

GIVING FIRST AID

First aid is immediate and temporary care given to a victim until professional help arrives. This overview will only be an introduction to first aid. To administer first aid, you should have more training such as the Red Cross course "Essential First Aid and CPR" so that you can be of help if needed in an emergency.

As a driver, your job at the scene of an accident is to stop and help. If help is already there, you do not need to stop. If you stop when you are not needed, you will only add to the congestion.

Limitations

A person's ability to help is limited by your company's policy and the state's laws for limits they place on you. Learn about each state's "good Samaritan" laws, which protect a person giving first aid. Learn also about each state's requirements for persons who are trained in first aid and cardiopulmonary resuscitation (CPR).

Basic Principles of First Aid

It is very important to stay calm. Do not move anyone who is injured unless there is danger to the person from fire, heavy traffic, or other serious threat. You should:

- Get help by calling police and ambulance.
- Keep onlookers back.
- Make the person(s) comfortable.
- Keep the injured person warm.
- Never give water or other liquids to an unconscious or partly conscious person.
- Talk calmly to the victim. Get the person's permission to help.
- Do not discuss the extent of injuries.

First Aid Summary

It is best to get training from the Red Cross or other agency before you need to give first aid. If you do have to give first aid, you should know your limits, know the state and federal laws for treating victims, and follow company policy.

FIRES AND FIRE FIGHTING

It is always better to prevent a fire instead of having to put one out. Ways to prevent fires and methods for putting them out will be explained in this section.

While fires occur in only a small percentage of truck accidents, such accidents usually cause deaths, severe injuries, and property damage. For this reason, drivers should know what types of fires they may encounter and how to safely deal with them (see Figure 20-18).

Knowing how to use a fire extinguisher effectively can assist a driver in saving someone's vehicle or controlling a fire long enough to rescue a trapped accident vic-

Figure **20-18**   Fires occur in only a small percentage of truck accidents.

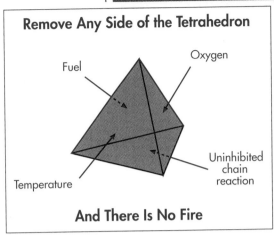

Remove Any Side of the Tetrahedron

Fuel

Oxygen

Temperature

Uninhibited chain reaction

And There Is No Fire

Figure **20-19**   If you remove one of the required elements, a fire will not burn.

tim. If a fire cannot be extinguished within 5 minutes with a fire extinguisher, the fire department or other authorities should be notified immediately.

To burn, a fire needs fuel, a source of heat, oxygen, and a chemical chain reaction.

If you remove one of these elements, there will be no fire (see Figure 20-19). You can put out a fire by cooling it to the point it will not burn. You can usually do this by putting water on it. You can also put out a fire by smothering it. This will cut off the supply of oxygen. You can do this with a gas or powder. The powder releases a gas when heated and smothers the flames. Certain agents, such as halon and some dry chemicals, extinguish the fire by interrupting the chain reaction.

Different types of fires must be put out using different methods. For example, using a stream of water on a burning liquid, or on a water-reactive hazardous material will make the situation worse. On other types of fires, such as a burning tire, water is needed to cool the burning material even though smothering may temporarily control visible flames.

There are different types of fires. They are divided into four classes: A, B, C, and D (see Figure 20-20).

Class A fire: A fire in ordinary combustibles, such as wood, paper, and cloth.

Class B fire: A fire in flammable or combustible liquids and gases, such as gasoline, diesel fuel, alcohol, paint, acetylene, and hydrogen.

Class C fire: A fire in live electrical equipment. You must put it out with something that does not conduct electricity. After the electricity is cut off, extinguishers suitable for Class A or Class B fires may be used.

Class D fire: A fire in combustible metals, such as magnesium and sodium. These fires can only be put out with special chemicals or powders.

Fire Extinguishers

Most **fire extinguishers** are marked by a letter and symbol to indicate the classes of fires for which they can be used. Every truck or truck-tractor with a gross vehicle

---

Classes of Fires

A. Wood, paper, ordinary combustibles
Extinguish by cooling and quenching
Use: water or dry chemicals

B. Gasoline, oil, grease, other greasy liquids
Extinguish by smothering, cooling, or heat-shielding
Use: carbon dioxide or dry chemicals

C. Electrical equipment fires
Extinguish with nonconducting agents:
Carbon dioxide or dry chemicals
Do not use water

D. Fire in combustible metals
Extinguish by using specialized extinguishing powders

Fire Extinguisher Type	For	Class of Fire
Regular dry chemical		B,C
Multipurpose dry chemical		A,B,C, or B,C
Purple-K dry chemical		D
KCL dry chemical		B,C
Dry powder special compound		D
Carbon dioxide (gas)		B,C
Halogenated agent (gas)		B,C
Water		A
Water with antifreeze		A
Water, loaded stream style		A,B
Foam		B, some use on A

Figure **20-20** Different types of fires require different fire extinguishers to be brought under control.

weight rating (GVWR) of 10,001 pounds or more must have a fire extinguisher. The extinguisher must be checked as part of the pretrip inspection.

If the vehicle is used for transporting hazardous material that requires placards, the extinguisher must have an Underwriter's Laboratory (UL) rating of 10B:C or more (see Figure 20-21). If the vehicle is not used for hazardous materials, an extinguisher with a UL rating of 5B:C may be used. The rating is usually shown near the UL certification on the extinguisher. If the rating also shows a 1A or 2A, it indicates the extinguisher can be used for fires of ordinary combustibles.

The extinguisher must be securely mounted so the driver can reach it easily. If the extinguisher is not in the driver's compartment (e.g., the luggage compartment of a sleeper cab), the outside of the vehicle should be marked showing its location. This is required by law in some states.

Every extinguisher has an instruction plate. The driver should read it to know how to operate the extinguisher in the event of a fire. Extinguishers for trucks are most effective for putting out small fires in their early stages. Because they do not hold a large quantity, the driver must plan how to use it to the best advantage. The stream range and discharge time are listed on the extinguisher. These vary, but generally they are as follows:

- **Stream range:** 5 to 12 feet
- **Discharge time:** Not less than 8 seconds

To put out a fire, aim the extinguisher at the base of the flames and spray back and forth in a sweeping motion. Be sure not to leave pockets of fire that may flash again later (see Figure 20-22).

The driver must not risk his or her personal safety trying to put out a fire. If the driver decides to fight the fire, he or she must be careful not to get surrounded and cut off by the flames. The driver should fight the fire with the wind at his or her back, if possible.

5 B:C or more

for hazmat 10 B:C or more

Figure **20-21** If a vehicle transports hazardous material, the fire extinguisher must have a UL rating of 10B:C or more.

Figure **20-22** To put out a fire, aim the extinguisher at the base of the flames and spray back and forth.

Additional Information about Truck Fires

If your tractor-trailer should catch fire, immediately drive it to the nearest safe place and stop. Stay as far away from buildings as possible. Get help as soon as you can. If the tractor can be unhooked from the trailer safely, do so. You may stop the spread of fire by doing this.

Tire fires.   Tire fires usually occur because the air pressure in the tire is too low. Tires that are low or flat flex too much. This causes heat build up inside the tire. When it gets hot enough, the surface will burst into flame. You can control the flames with a fire extinguisher, but large quantities of water must be poured on the tire to cool it down. Then the fire can be finally put out. Tires can easily reignite because heat builds up between the plies (see Figure 20-23).

These fires can be prevented by checking to be sure the tires are properly inflated. Tires can be checked best by using a truck tire gauge. It is the only way to be sure the air pressure is balanced for dual tires. Because of the dangerous cargo, drivers transporting hazardous materials are required to check the tires every 2 hours or after each 100 miles of travel.

Figure **20-23** Tire fires can be extinguished with a fire extinguisher and a large quantity of water.

Figure **20-24** In an accident, leaking fuel may be ignited by sparks from another source.

Cargo fires.   In a closed van, you may not know there is a cargo fire until smoke seeps out around the doors. To keep the fire smoldering instead of burning, keep the doors closed. This will limit the oxygen that can reach the fire.

Stop in a safe location and get help. Let the fire department open the cargo doors when they arrive. This will lessen the flare-up of fire. If you can safely do so, remove the undamaged cargo before firefighters put water on the fire.

Fuel fires.   In a serious accident, there is a great risk of fire if the fuel tank ruptures or a fuel line breaks. The leaking fuel may be ignited by sparks from the accident or another source (see Figure 20-24). The truck's fire extinguisher may not control a fire from a large fuel spill. Although diesel fuel does not burn as easily as gasoline, it will burn if it gets hot enough.

If you find any fuel leaks during a pretrip inspection, correct them before you start your trip. Be sure the caps are securely on fuel tanks. When you refuel, do not smoke or allow others around you to do so. Metal-to-metal contact must be maintained between the nozzle and the fill pipe.

Federal law says you cannot fill any fuel tank to more than 95 percent of its capacity. This will prevent spills when the fuel expands as it warms. If the cargo is hazardous material, a person must control the flow of fuel when the truck is being refueled.

Electrical fires.   Electrical fires can happen when the insulation on wiring is worn or frayed. If the bare wires touch each other or other metal parts of the truck, a fire can result. In an accident, damaged wiring can short-circuit and cause a fire. If you can safely disconnect the battery when there is an electrical fire, this will remove the source of heat.

Chapter Twenty-One

Sliding Fifth Wheels and Tandem Axles

OBJECTIVES

When you have completed this chapter, you should be able to:

- Describe the function of the sliding fifth wheel or trailer tandem axles

- Explain the concept of shifting weight between the tractor and trailer

- Explain the effects of the sliding fifth wheel or trailer tandem axles on overall length, maneuverability, and off-tracking

- Describe how to lock and unlock a sliding fifth wheel

- Explain the correct way to slide the fifth wheel of a tractor with a trailer attached

- Describe how to lock and unlock a sliding tandem axle

- Explain the correct way to slide the tandem axles of a trailer with a tractor attached

- Explain the hazards of sliding the fifth wheel or trailer tandem axles improperly

KEY TERMS

Air-operated release

Fixed (stationary) fifth
    wheel

Frame rails

Inner bridge

Lug control lever

Maneuverability

Manual release

Off-tracking

Outer bridge

Slide

Sliding fifth wheel

Sliding tandem axle

INTRODUCTION

Many tractor-trailers have a **sliding fifth wheel** on the tractor and **sliding tandem axles** on the trailer. Tractor-trailers can have either one or both of them.

The sliding fifth wheel can adjust the overall length of the tractor-trailer, adjust the turning radius of the vehicle, and adjust and balance the weight on each of the axles.

The sliding tandem axles on the trailer can adjust the off-tracking of the trailer, adjust the turning radius of the vehicle, and adjust and balance the weight on each of the axles on the trailer.

As you can see, wheels and axles have similar effects on both the tractor and the trailer. Their positions are important for the driver to understand if he or she wishes to safely and legally haul a load. Remember, the driver is responsible for the following:

- The legal gross vehicle weight of the vehicle
- The amount of weight per axle
- The overall length of the vehicle
- The rig's maneuverability and ability to turn safely, should state or local restrictions apply

The purpose of this chapter is to help you learn how to slide the fifth wheel and the trailer tandem axles. You will also learn some of the basic reasons for making these adjustments to a rig.

SHIFTING WEIGHT

When a trailer is coupled to a tractor, some of the weight of the trailer is transferred to the tractor through the connection with the fifth wheel (see Figure 21-1). If the freight is evenly distributed in the trailer, standard trailer axle and fifth-wheel settings will properly distribute the weight on each axle.

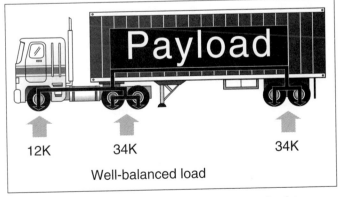

Figure **21-1** When a trailer is coupled to a tractor, some of the weight is transferred to the tractor.

Figure **21-2** Sliding tandems to the rear increases weight on the drive and steering axles.

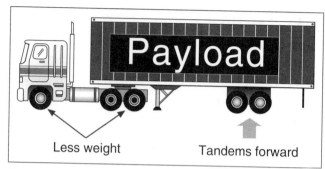

Figure **21-3** Sliding tandems forward shifts weight off the tractor.

Some trailers have sliding tandem axles to transfer weight to the tractor if the load in the trailer is not evenly distributed. The amount of weight transferred to the tractor can be adjusted by sliding the tandem axles on the trailer toward the rear. This will increase the amount of weight on the drive and steering axles of the tractor (see Figure 21-2).

By sliding the trailer tandems forward, you can shift weight off the tractor (see Figure 21-3). This causes the weight behind the trailer's tandem axles to actually tip the weight off the tractor. Shifting the weight decreases the amount of weight on the drive and steering axles of the tractor.

Figure **21-4** More weight on the steer axle makes the tractor more difficult to steer and maneuver.

Some tractors have a sliding fifth wheel. This can adjust the length of the tractor-trailer and balance, or shift, some of the weight from the trailer to between the steer axle and drive axles of the tractor.

By sliding the fifth wheel on the tractor forward, you can transfer weight to the steer axle and also shorten the overall length of the vehicle. If too much weight is shifted to the steer axle, the tractor will be hard to steer. It may also be harder to maneuver (see Figure 21-4). If you shift too much weight, the rig may also be overweight according to regulations on the steer axle. At night, your headlights will not be aimed properly, and you will not see as well.

If you slide the fifth wheel on the tractor toward the rear, you can reduce the amount of weight on the steer axle, but you will increase the total length of the tractor (see Figure 21-5). If too much weight is shifted off of the steer axle, the steering will feel light, and you will not have as much control over the steering. Shifting too much weight off the steer axle can also make the rig overweight on the drive axles. At night, your headlights will be aimed at the sky instead of on the road ahead.

Figure **21-5** Sliding the fifth wheel toward the rear increases total length of the tractor and reduces weight on the steer axle.

As you can see, the positions of the fifth wheel and the trailer tandem axles have a lot to do with the weight per axle and handling of the rig (see Figure 21-6).

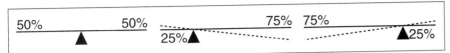

Figure **21-6** Distribution of weight has a teeter-totter effect.

THE BRIDGE FORMULA

To achieve the maximum legal weight on each axle, you will need to know the Bridge Formula. This is a national formula for axle spacings designed to protect the country's roads and bridges. All trucks operating on interstate highways and on some state highways must comply with this formula. Under the formula rules, tractors must have a minimum outer spread of 14 feet to scale the maximum 46,000 pounds (12,000 pounds on the steer axle, 34,000 pounds on the tandems). The outer spread is the distance between the center of the front axle and the center of the rearmost axle. This distance is not affected by sliding the fifth wheel forward or back. But two other distances are affected. These are the **inner bridge** (between the center of the rearmost tractor axle and the center of the leading trailer axle) and the **outer bridge** (between the center of the forward tractor tandem and the rearmost trailer axle). Sliding the fifth wheel or a trailer slider will change these distances and may affect your legal load-carrying capacity. For example, a five-axle tractor-trailer must have an outer bridge of at least 51 feet to haul the maximum allowable 80,000 pounds.

MANEUVERABILITY AND OFF-TRACKING

The **maneuverability** and **off-tracking** of the tractor-trailer are affected by the position of the trailer tandems and the position of the fifth wheel. When you slide the fifth wheel to the rear of the tractor, the overall length of the vehicle increases. The distance between the steer axle and the kingpin also increases along with the distance to the trailer tandem axles.

When you turn, the greater the distance between the steer axle and the pivot point (kingpin) of the trailer, the further the trailer will off-track. The swept path of the trailer will increase. You will need more space to make a turn (see Figure 21-7).

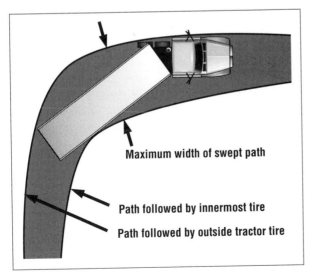

Figure **21-7** Off-tracking in a 90-degree turn.

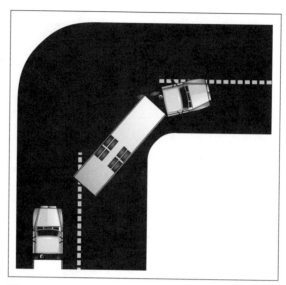

Figure **21-8** The sharper the turn, the more the rear wheels will off-track.

The position of the tandem axles of the trailer also affects off-tracking and the space needed to turn. When you slide the tandem axles all the way to the rear, the distance between the kingpin and the rear axle wheels increases. The overall length of the vehicle does not change, but the amount of space needed to turn increases.

When the tandem axles are all the way back, trailer off-tracking increases, and so does the swept path of the vehicle. The sharper the turn, the more the rear wheels will off-track (see Figure 21-8).

When you slide the tandem axles forward and the distance between the kingpin and the rear axles decreases, the rig is easier to maneuver. There is also less trailer off-tracking. This is very helpful when you are making deliveries. You must also be very careful when the tandem axles are all the way forward because there is a trailer overhang.

As you can see, the benefits of sliding the tandem axles forward when you drive in downtown traffic can be offset by the possible dangers of trailer overhang.

THE FIFTH WHEEL

There are two types of fifth wheels: **fixed (stationary)** and sliding.

A fixed, or stationary, fifth wheel is usually mounted directly on the **frame rails** of the tractor by a bracket assembly (see Figure 21-9). The bracket assembly allows the fifth wheel to rock up and down. The stationary fifth wheel is placed to get the best weight distribution between the tractor's steer axle and the drive axle(s) of a properly loaded trailer. Weight adjustments are made by sliding the tandem axles of the trailer.

Sliding fifth wheels are attached to sliding bracket assemblies (see Figure 21-10). The sliding bracket assemblies can be attached to a base that has a sliding rail assembly built into it. The base is then attached to the frame rails of the tractor. Sometimes the sliding rails are attached directly to the frame rails of the tractor. Then the fifth wheel and sliding bracket assembly are attached directly to them.

Figure **21-9** A fixed, or stationary, fifth wheel.

Figure **21-10** A sliding fifth wheel.

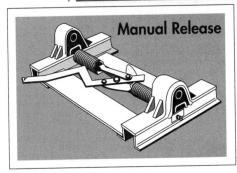

Figure **21-11** Manual release allows you to unlock the fifth wheel with a release handle.

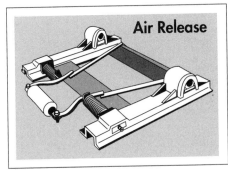

Figure **21-12** An air-operated release unlocks the fifth wheel by a release lever in the cab.

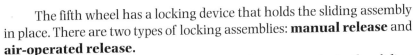

The fifth wheel has a locking device that holds the sliding assembly in place. There are two types of locking assemblies: **manual release** and **air-operated release.**

The manual release allows you to release, or unlock, the sliding mechanism by pushing or pulling a release handle. This release handle may be on the driver's side of the fifth wheel or directly in front of the fifth wheel. When the handle is pulled to the unlock position, the locking pins are released from the locking holes, or notches, on the mounting base or sliding rail assembly (see Figure 21-11).

The air-operated release lets you release the locking device on the sliding fifth wheel by moving the fifth-wheel release lever in the cab to the unlocked position. When the lever is in the unlocked position, air is forced against a piston on the fifth-wheel locking device. The piston forces the locking pins to release from the locking holes, or notches, on the mounting base or sliding rail assembly (see Figure 21-12).

SLIDING THE FIFTH WHEEL

Sliding the fifth wheel is not difficult. It should be done on a level surface, off the road, and away from hazards. The trailer must be properly connected to the locked fifth wheel and the kingpin locked into place. The air and electrical lines should be connected to the trailer. If the trailer has a sliding tandem axle, it should be locked into place. Be sure to set the tractor parking brake before getting out of the cab for any reason. This will keep the tractor from rolling away (see Figure 21-13).

Test the connection to the trailer by gently pulling forward with the trailer brake on. If you have just made the connection

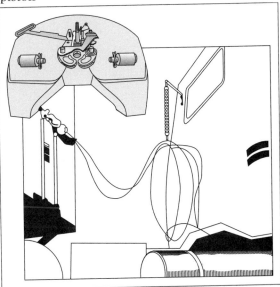

Figure **21-13** Preparation is required before sliding the fifth wheel.

TIP
To avoid damage, check the fifth-wheel position and trailer pin setting to make sure the trailer will not hit the cab when the fifth wheel is all the way forward or the landing gear when the fifth wheel is all the way back.

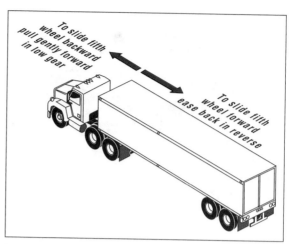

Figure **21-14** When sliding the fifth wheel, you may have some resistance from the sliding assembly.

to the trailer, look at the connection to make sure the fifth-wheel jaws are locked around the kingpin of the trailer. Then crank up the landing gear of the trailer.

The next step is to place the fifth-wheel release lever, or handle, in the unlocked position. Put on your trailer brakes either by pulling down your trailer brake hand valve (if you have one) or by pulling out the red trailer air supply valve. Release the tractor parking brake valve. Your tractor brakes are now released and your trailer brakes engaged. You are ready to slide the fifth wheel.

If you are going to slide the fifth wheel forward, put the tractor into reverse. If you want to slide the fifth wheel backward toward the rear of the tractor, use low gear. With the tractor in gear, ease the tractor forward or backward gently. You may have some resistance from the sliding assembly when you do this (see Figure 21-14).

If the fifth wheel has not been moved for quite some time, you may have what is called "binding." Look at the fifth-wheel locking pins first to be sure they have unlocked and that the fifth wheel is free to slide. Pressure on the pins may be holding them in place. If the pins appear to be stuck or binding, you can usually free them by gently rocking the tractor. Corrosion, dirt, or grime may have gotten into the mechanism, causing it to lock up. You may have to clean some of the road grime off the mechanism so it can work correctly. You may also want to lower the landing gear. It can help relieve binding and stress, allowing the fifth wheel to move easier.

Once you have moved the fifth wheel to where you want it, place the fifth-wheel release lever, or handle, in the locked position. With the trailer brakes still set, gently tug or push against the trailer. This will let the fifth-wheel locking pins or lugs seat themselves.

Set the tractor brakes. Look at the fifth-wheel slider to make sure it is properly locked into place. Now that you are done, remember you have just changed your overall length. This will make a difference in your ride, weight distribution, and maneuverability.

TRAILER TANDEM AXLES

Not all trailer axles are tandem axles. A light-duty trailer may have just one axle. In this case, the axle is usually stationary, or fixed. Trailers with a high-rated cargo carrying capacity usually have tandem axles. All trailer axles are attached to a suspension system and subframe (see Figure 21-15).

Trailer tandem axles can be grouped into two types: fixed (stationary) and sliding.

A fixed, or stationary, trailer tandem axle assembly includes the suspension and subframe. The assembly is usually mounted directly on the frame rails of the trailer. The stationary tandem axle assembly is placed to get the best weight distribution between the tractor and the trailer. Weight adjustments between the tractor and the trailer are then made by moving, or shifting, the load inside the trailer.

The sliding trailer tandem axle assembly is also mounted directly on the frame rails of the trailer. The difference is that the subframe assembly allows the trailer axles and suspension to slide, or move along, the frame rails of the trailer. The part of the subassembly that slides is called the tandem axle **slide.** There is one slide on each side of the trailer (see Figure 21-16).

You will notice there are evenly placed holes along the length of the slide. The holes are designed to seat four locking lugs or pins. These locking pins or lugs are attached to a lever, or handle, called the **lug control lever.** You engage the lug control lever manually. There is no cab control switch, as with an air-operated assembly. At the ends of the sliding rails there are stops that keep the assembly from coming apart when you slide the axles.

One-axle trailer   Tandem-axle trailer

Figure **21-15** Light-duty trailers may have only one axle, while trailers with high-rated carrying capacity usually have tandem axles.

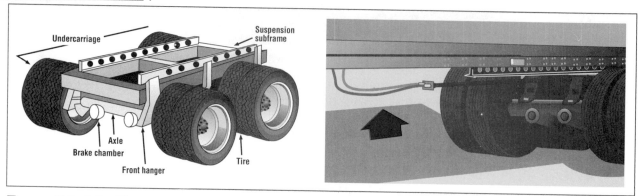

Figure **21-16** The part of the subassembly that slides is called the tandem axle slide.

Sliding the Trailer Tandem Axles

Sliding the trailer tandem axles is very similar to sliding the fifth wheel. This also should be done off the road, on a level surface, and away from hazards:

- The trailer must be properly connected to the fifth wheel.
- The kingpin should be locked into place.
- The air and electrical lines should be connected to the trailer.
- The sliding fifth wheel and the trailer's sliding tandem axle assembly must also be locked.

If you must get out of the cab for any reason, be sure to set the tractor parking brake. This will keep the tractor from rolling away. Now you are ready to test the connection to the trailer by gently pulling forward with the trailer brake in the on position. If you have just made the connection to the trailer, look at the connection to make sure the fifth-wheel jaws are locked around the kingpin of the trailer. Then raise the landing gear of the trailer.

The next step is to locate the pin or lug control lever. It is usually on the driver's side of the trailer and just in front of the trailer wheels. The lever is usually inside the lever guide that serves as a support. Some units have a safety pin or lock on the lever guide that keeps the lever from bouncing up and down while traveling (see Figure 21-17).

Figure **21-17** The pin or lug control lever is usually on the driver's side of the trailer, just in front of the trailer wheels.

Figure **21-18** Once you have unlocked the slides, make sure all four locking lugs are completely out of the holes in the slides.

You will note the lever controls four locking pins, two on each side of the trailer. Lift and pull this lever toward you until the grooves on the lever line up with the slot on the lever guide. Then slip the lever into the sideways slot. The slot will hold the lever in the unlocked position. Make sure the lever is firmly seated in the slot.

Now that you have unlocked the slides, it is important to make sure all four locking lugs are completely out of the holes in the slides (see Figure 21-18). Check the lugs on each side of the trailer. If any are not all the way out of the holes, you will have to repeat the unlocking procedure.

Get in the cab again. Engage the trailer brakes by either pulling down the trailer brake hand valve or by pulling out the red trailer air supply valve (see Figure 21-19). Release the tractor parking brake valve. You now have your tractor brakes released and your trailer brakes engaged. You are ready to slide the tandem axles. If you have wheel chocks, use them. They will keep your locked wheels from dragging along the pavement and scuffing the tires.

If you are going to slide the tandem axles forward, put the tractor into reverse. If you want to slide the tandem axles backward toward the rear of the trailer, use low gear. With the tractor in gear, ease the tractor forward or backward gently.

If the tandem axle assembly has not been moved for quite some time, the sliding assembly may resist (bind) when you do this. To let the assembly move freely, you will need to find out why it is binding.

Look at the locking pins first to be sure that they have unlocked and that the tandem axles are free to slide. There may be pressure on the pins holding them in place. If the pins appear to be stuck or binding, you can usually correct this problem by gently rocking the tractor against the trailer.

Corrosion, dirt, or grime may have worked their way into the slides themselves. This creates more friction and can cause them to lock up. You may have to clean some of the road grime off the slides so they will work properly.

Once you have moved the sliding tandem axle to the position where you want it, follow these steps:

1. Put on the parking brakes.
2. Climb out of the truck.
3. Release the lug control lever and place it into the locked position.
4. Get back in the tractor.
5. Release the tractor brakes.

Figure **21-19**
To the right of the driver on the control panel are two push-pull valves. The red knob on the button is called the trailer air supply valve. When this knob is pulled, only the trailer brakes are applied.

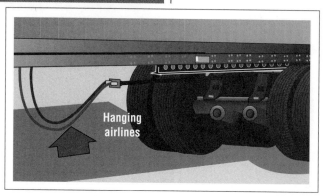

Figure **21-20** Once you have moved tandems forward, check to make sure air supply lines are not hanging down under the trailer.

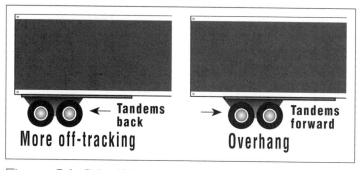

Figure **21-21** When you move the sliding tandem axle, you change axle dimensions and will have a difference in your ride, weight distribution, and maneuverability.

With the trailer brakes still set, gently tug or push against the trailer. This will let all four locking pins or lugs seat themselves. Set the tractor brakes and look at all four lugs or pins to be sure they are firmly seated through the holes in the tandem axle slides. Make sure the lug control lever has remained locked and is secured. If you have moved the tandems forward, make sure the air supply lines under the trailer are not hanging down. If they are hanging down, something along or in the road can damage or cut the lines (see Figure 21-20).

Now that you have moved the sliding tandem axle, remember you have just changed your axle dimensions. This will make a difference in your ride, weight distribution, and maneuverability (see Figure 21-21).

- If you moved the tandems forward, you now have an overhang that you must pay attention to on curves and turns.
- If you slid it toward the rear, your off-tracking will increase. You will have to compensate for this when maneuvering and turning.

Decide how you want to set up your rig for loading before it is actually loaded. It is easier to make adjustments on any empty unit than on a loaded one. Even though it may be difficult in the beginning, you need to become skilled at doing this.

TIP

A good way to learn is to keep a notebook on each customer. In it, describe how you set up your rig for the load, as well as directions for getting to the stop, their phone number and the person to talk to, the days and hours they ship, whether they are seasonal, and whether an appointment is needed. Then you will be able to set your rig before it is loaded because you have a diary of the loads you have already hauled.

How you adjust your fifth wheel and axles depends on a combination of factors. These include the following:

- Distribution of weight
- Overall length laws
- Legal axle weight limits
- Bridge weight laws
- Handling stability
- Maneuverability
- Preventing damage to the cargo

TIP

To prevent the trailer from sliding into the cab or the tandems from sliding out from under the trailer, be sure to check the fifth-wheel stop plates and the stop bars, welds, and brackets of the trailer slides to be sure they are intact.

QUICK REVIEW: MOVING THE SLIDING TANDEM AXLE

1. Make sure the tractor is properly coupled to the trailer.

2. Set the tractor brakes.

3. Lift and pull the lug (locking pin) control lever until the grooves slip into the sideways slot on the lever guide. This will disengage the locking pins/lugs.

4. Check to make sure all four lugs are retracted properly.

5. Set the trailer brakes by pulling out the red trailer air supply valve or pulling down the trailer brake hand valve.

6. Release the tractor brakes by pushing in the yellow parking brake valve.

7. Ease the tractor forward to slide the tandem backward. Ease the tractor backward to slide the tandem forward.

8. Reset the tractor brakes by pulling out the yellow parking brake valve.

9. Release the lug/pin control lever. Place it into the locked position.

10. Release the tractor brakes.

11. With the trailer brakes still set, gently tug or push against the trailer to seat the locking lugs.

12. Reset your tractor brakes.

13. Look at all four lugs/pins to make sure they are firmly seated through the holes in the tandem axle slides. Make sure the lug control lever has remained locked and is secured.

14. Inspect the trailer air supply lines for clearance under trailer. Be sure they are not hanging down.

Remember, you have just made changes to your tandem axle setting. This will affect the handling of the tractor-trailer.

Chapter
Twenty-Two
Special Rigs

OBJECTIVES

When you have completed this chapter, you should be able to:

- Identify common special rigs

- Understand the function, operating characteristics, size, special features, and hazards of special rigs

- Know the special skills and training needed to operate some rigs

- Know the hazards of operating a rig when not qualified

- Be aware of some of the types of cargos that are hauled

KEY TERMS

Articulation

Baffle

Belly mount

B-train

Bulkhead

Converter dolly

Double drop frame

Double trailer

Dry bulk tankers

Gooseneck

High center of gravity

Livestock transport
  trailer

Multiwheel low-bed
  trailer with jeep dolly

Nose mount

Outriggers

Overheight load

Overlength load

Oversized load

Overweight load

Overwidth load

Pole trailer

Refrigerated trailer

Rocky Mountain double

Single drop frame

Smoothbore tank

Standard double

Surging loads

Triple trailers

Turnpike double

Two-axle double drop
  low bed with
  outriggers

Two-axle float

INTRODUCTION

A special rig is any combination vehicle that differs from the standard tractor and 48- to 53-foot dry freight trailer van with five axles and 18 wheels. In this section, you will learn about the most common special rigs. We will describe many of these rigs. Their handling characteristics will be discussed in detail. The special skills and training needed by drivers will be noted (see Figure 22-1).

No one should drive any commercial vehicle without additional training. It is very important for drivers of all special rigs to receive training by either a school or an employer. The following information is intended only to familiarize you with the unusual nature and driving requirements associated with some special rigs.

You will learn about a wide variety of tractors and trailers. Among special rigs used widely today are those

- with more than one point of **articulation** (multiple articulation) (see Figure 22-2),
- that are **overlength, overheight, overwidth,** or **overweight,**
- with a very low vehicle-to-ground clearance,
- that have a high center of gravity when loaded,
- with load stability problems,
- that are used for special cargos, and
- that require special handling.

Note: The word *articulate* means consisting of segments separated by joints. A multiple-articulation rig is one that has several parts connected by joints. A typical tractor-trailer has just one joint. It connects the tractor to the trailer.

CAUTION:

Steering can be affected by dry fifth wheels on the tractor and dolly.

22.3

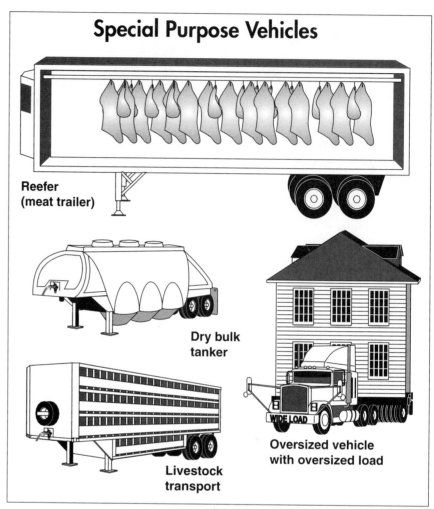

Figure **22-1** Special rigs are designed to haul specialized loads and require special driving skills.

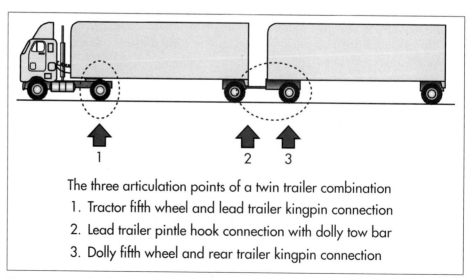

The three articulation points of a twin trailer combination
1. Tractor fifth wheel and lead trailer kingpin connection
2. Lead trailer pintle hook connection with dolly tow bar
3. Dolly fifth wheel and rear trailer kingpin connection

Figure **22-2** A typical tractor-trailer rig has one joint. Twin trailers have three articulation joints.

LONG COMBINATION VEHICLES

Rigs with more than one trailer are known as long combination vehicles. They include **double trailers, turnpike doubles, Rocky Mountain doubles, B-trains,** and **triple trailers.**

Twin Trailers

These rigs are also known as double-bottoms, doubles, or set of joints. There are two basic types of twin trailers: **standard doubles** and turnpike doubles.

Standard Doubles

Standard doubles use two semitrailers. The second trailer is converted into a full trailer by using a **converter dolly** (a set of wheels with a fifth wheel). The second semi couples with the fifth wheel of the converter. Most converters have a drawbar with one eye that connects to the pintle hook on the back of the first trailer. These are known as A-dollies. Some converters have a set of two parallel eyes that hook into two pintle hooks on the back of the first trailer. These are known as B-dollies. A rig with an A-dolly is also known as an A-train, and a rig with B-dollies can be called a C-train (see Figure 22-3).

Identifying Characteristics

Doubles have three points of articulation:

1. The first trailer kingpin and the fifth wheel.
2. The pintle hook and eye.
3. The converter dolly fifth wheel and the kingpin of the second trailer.

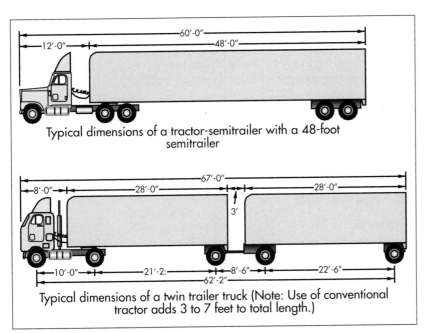

Typical dimensions of a tractor-semitrailer with a 48-foot semitrailer

Typical dimensions of a twin trailer truck (Note: Use of conventional tractor adds 3 to 7 feet to total length.)

Figure **22-3** Trailer lengths vary, and each combination requires special techniques in handling.

Figure **22-4** Steering a set of trailers should be smooth because jerking or whipping the steering wheel may cause the second trailer to overreact.

Other Major Characteristics

Trailer lengths vary from 26 to 28 feet with overall lengths from 65 to 75 feet. Trailers may be vans, flatbeds, tankers (used throughout the country), cargo or many other types.

Handling

Driving doubles requires some special handling techniques:

- Always hook the heavy trailer as the lead trailer.
- The driver must avoid backing. The vehicle is not designed for this maneuver.
- Steering must be smooth. Jerking or whipping the steering wheel may cause the second trailer to overreact (see Figure 22-4).
- Do not put on the brakes in a curve. This will cause the second trailer to dip.
- Be aware of the rig's greater length when passing other vehicles, changing lanes, or crossing intersections and railroad tracks.
- You cannot make tight turns with these closely coupled rigs.
- Be aware of bumps, potholes, and so on. This can cause the tops of the trailers to hit one another.
- Be aware of where your wheels are tracking. It is harder to stay in your lane when taking curves.

Special Requirements

A driver must have a Doubles/Triples Endorsement on his or her CDL. A driver also needs special knowledge and skills to safely drive double rigs. These rigs may be used in many states. Check the regulations for each state in which you will drive for the maximum allowed length and weight. Also check for needed permits and use requirements (see Figure 22-5).

During pretrip and en route inspections, the driver must inspect the drawbar and pintle hook articulation, safety chains, light cords, air line hookup, and valve positions with care. More difficult coupling and uncoupling procedures must also be mastered.

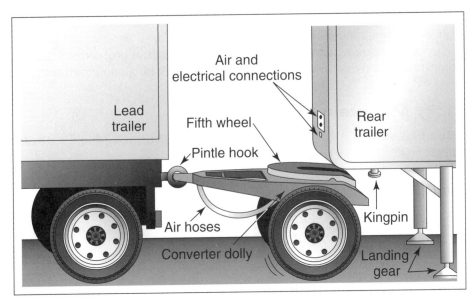

Figure **22-5** When driving doubles or triples, be knowledgeable of your rig and the special driving skills required as well as state laws and permits required.

Turnpike Doubles

Commonly used on turnpikes in eastern states, these are typically nine-axle rigs.

Identifying Characteristics

Trailer lengths: 40 to 48 feet.

Overall length of the rig: Over 100 feet.

Usually have high-powered engines and multiple-gear transmissions.

Other Major Characteristics and Handling

Same handling characteristics as standard doubles. Longer trailers require more room for manuevering.

> Trailer lengths: 26 to 28 feet may also be used.
>
> Overall length of the rig: Some states allow lengths of over 100 feet.
>
> The trailers may be vans, flatbeds, tankers (used mostly in the western states), or cargo (many types).

Special Requirements

A Doubles/Triples Endorsement is also required on the driver's CDL for these rigs. More knowledge and skills are needed for driving a turnpike double than for a standard double (see Figure 22-6).

Figure **22-6** Turnpike double: A three-axle tractor pulling two tandem axle semitrailers—nine axles in all.

If a special permit is held, turnpike doubles can be used on certain toll roads. For more information, see each state's regulations.

Inspection procedures are basically the same as for standard doubles. Toll road authorities sometimes require special, more demanding inspection routines.

Rocky Mountain Doubles

These are larger than standard doubles but smaller than turnpike doubles. The lead trailer is typically longer than the second trailer.

Identifying Characteristics

Trailer lengths: 40 to 53 feet for the semitrailer; 26 to 29 feet for the full trailer

Overall length: 80 to 100 feet

Other Major Characteristics and Handling

Same handling characteristics as standard doubles, but long lead trailer requires extra space for maneuvering.

The trailers may be vans, flatbeds, or tankers.

Special Requirements

A Doubles/Triples Endorsement is required in addition to the standard CDL. More knowledge and skills are needed for driving Rocky Mountain doubles than are needed for driving standard doubles.

Special permits are needed to operate them. They are most commonly permitted on limited access roads in western states and western Canada.

Inspection procedures are basically the same as for standard doubles.

B-Trains

A B-train is a rig with two semitrailers pulled by a tractor. The first trailer has two or three axles on the rear of the trailer body. The second or third axle extends beyond the rear of the trailer body and under the nose of the second semitrailer. A fifth wheel is mounted above the second axle. This removes the need for a converter. The second semitrailer couples to the first semi using the fifth wheel. This arrangement eliminates one point of articulation (see Figure 22-7).

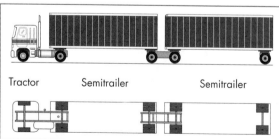

Tractor   Semitrailer   Semitrailer

Figure **22-7** A B-train is composed of a tractor towing two semitrailers. The towing trailers have an extended frame with a fifth wheel for attaching the next trailer made of a B-dolly and semitrailer.

Identifying Characteristics

Combinations with one tractor and one semitrailer have one point of articulation. Doubles have three. B-trains have two.

When a semitrailer has tandem axles, they are usually located all the way under the trailer. In B-train rigs, the second axle extends beyond the rear of the first semi.

Other Major Characteristics

The trailers and overall length vary depending on the state or province in which they are driven. For example, there may be two 40-foot trailers or one 40-foot and one 27-foot trailer. The trailers may be vans, tankers, flatbeds, dumps, and so on.

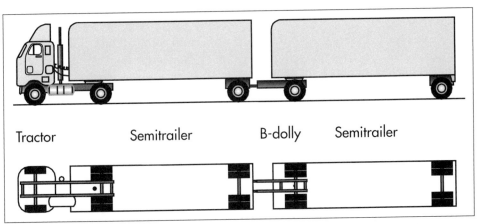

Tractor   Semitrailer   B-dolly   Semitrailer

Figure **22-8** A C-train is composed of a tractor-semitrailer towing one or more full trailers made of a B-dolly and semitrailer.

B-trains have been used in Canada for some time but now are also being seen in the United States. They carry many types of cargos.

In a C-train (see Figure 22-8), the rig includes a tractor, a semitrailer, a B-dolly and a second semitrailer.

Handling

In addition to the safe driving practices for regular combinations, there are a number of special handling points:

- Backing is difficult and should be avoided. However, B-trains are easier to back than doubles.
- Steer smoothly. Jerking or whipping the steering wheel causes the second trailer to overreact.
- The driver must be aware of the greater length when overtaking and passing other vehicles, lane changing, and crossing intersections.
- Must be aware of tracking to be able to stay in the lane through curves.

Special Requirements

Driving a B-train rig requires special training, skill, and knowledge. A Doubles/Triples Endorsement on the driver's CDL is needed. With special permits, these rigs may be driven on certain highways. For more information, see each state's regulations.

Triple Trailers

Other names for triple trailers are triples, triple headers, triple bottoms, or set of joints.

Description

Triple trailers are combination rigs that have three semitrailers pulled by a tractor. The second and third semis are converted to full trailers by converters. They are connected by drawbars and pintle hooks (see Figure 22-9).

Figure **22-9** Triples—or triple trailers.

Identifying Characteristics

Similar to doubles, there are a number of connection points. Triples have five: three kingpin and fifth-wheel connections and two eye and pintle hook connections. The length of each trailer is 26 to 28 feet.

Other Major Characteristics

These are also the same as for doubles.

Trailer lengths: 26 to 28 feet.

Overall length of the rig: Some states allow lengths up to 100 feet.

The trailers may be flatbeds, tankers, boxes (used mostly in the western states), or cargo (many types).

Special Requirements

Drivers of triples need skills that differ from those who drive doubles. They must also have better driving skills. Triples are operated in the far western states and Kansas and Oklahoma and need a special permit for certain highways. The driver must have a Doubles/Triples Endorsement on his or her CDL. Check each state's regulations regarding use of triples.

SPECIAL TRAILER TYPES

These trailer types are for oversized loads. They include lowboys, drop frames, flatbeds, and open-top vans.

They have many wheels and axles, depending on the vehicle, cargo weight, and state laws.

Many have **outriggers** to support the **oversized loads.** Converter dollies may be attached in the usual way or to the cargo itself to help distribute the weight over more axles and support longer loads.

These rigs haul many types of large, overweight loads:

- Equipment for power plants
- Nuclear reactors
- Industrial dryers
- Heavy construction equipment

Special Requirements

Special training, added skills, and knowledge are needed by the driver. The driver must have a Doubles/Triples Endorsement on his or her CDL. With special permits, these rigs may be operated on certain highways. For more information, see each state's laws.

Examples

Two-axle double drop low bed with outriggers. This rig has a double-top frame and two rear axles. Outriggers are attached to each side of the trailer. When they are extended, they support wider loads (see Figure 22-10).

Two-axle Double Drop Low Bed

Figure **22-10** Two-axle double drop low beds often use outriggers to support oversize loads.

Five-axle removable gooseneck low bed with detachable two-axle dolly. This low-bed frame has three rear trailer axles. A two-axle dolly is attached to the rear of the trailer. The detachable **gooseneck** lets the trailer rest on the ground when loading heavy equipment like bulldozers, front loaders, backhoes, and so on (see Figure 22-11).

Custom trailer and dolly for hauling large-diameter and long items. This rig has a drop frame and two rear axles (see Figure 22-12).

Two-axle float. This rig has a flatbed frame with two rear axles and no landing gear. It is used mostly in oil fields for hauling drilling equipment, pipes, and so on (see Figure 22-13).

Four-axle removable gooseneck low bed with outriggers. This rig has a low-bed frame, four rear trailer axles, and a detachable gooseneck. This allows the trailer to rest on the ground for loading heavy equipment like bulldozers and cranes. For wide loads, outriggers may be used (see Figure 22-14).

Multiwheel low-bed trailer with jeep dolly. This rig has a low-bed frame and two rear trailer axles (see Figure 22-15).

A two-axle dolly is attached to the trailer using the actual cargo. One end of the cargo rests on the dolly. The other end rests on the trailer.

Figure **22-11** Five-axle removable gooseneck, low bed with detachable two-axle dolly.

Figure **22-12** Custom trailer and dolly for hauling large-diameter and long commodities.

Figure **22-13** Two-axle float.

Figure **22-14** Four-axle removable gooseneck low bed with outriggers.

Figure **22-15** Multiwheel low bed trailer with jeep dolly.

A two-axle jeep dolly can be attached to the fifth wheel. The fifth wheel is between the tractor and trailer.

LOW-CLEARANCE VEHICLES

There are two types of low-clearance vehicles: drop deck and double drop deck (see Figure 22-16). The **double drop frame** drops close to the ground. The **single drop frame** drops about half the distance. Both drop far enough behind the kingpin plate to keep the tractor hookup from hitting the trailer drop. Be sure the fifth wheel is not too far forward. The tractor frame must not hit the trailer drop, and the rear wheel must not hit the trailer on sharp turns. Drop frames haul heavy, oversized cargoes or larger, space demanding loads such as van-type trailers on low beds.

Special Requirements

They are similar to other special rigs in their requirements of special training, added skills, and knowledge needed by the driver. With special permits, these rigs may be operated on certain highways. For more information, see each state's laws.

Double Drop Frame

Low beds are also known as flatbeds or lowboys. They haul heavy equipment such as bulldozers, cranes, and earth movers. They also haul oversized items, such as equipment for power plants, boilers, and generating stations. They may have as many as four axles and 24 wheels. These trailers can have bottom clearance problems at railroad crossings, curbs, and large potholes and require special skills for driving and maneuvering.

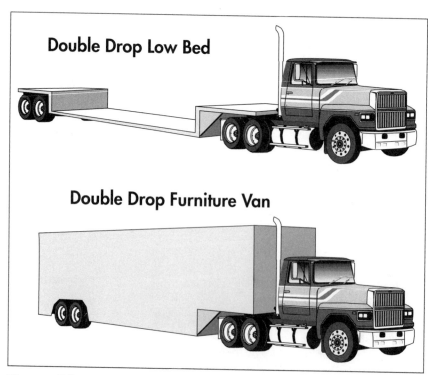

Double Drop Low Bed

Double Drop Furniture Van

Figure **22-16** Low-clearance vehicles.

Warehouse or furniture vans are the most commonly used vans in the household goods moving industry. The drop-in frame provides a greater load capacity. For instance, a drop of 27 inches gives an additional 3,000 cubic feet of cargo space. Generally, these vehicles are easier to load by hand because of the drop. However, the wheel housing can be a problem if a forklift is used.

Electronics vans were designed to handle delicate electronic equipment. They have air ride or soft ride suspension to protect fragile loads. Now they are also used to haul high-bulk, low-weight items such as clothing, potato chips, and plastics.

These vans have a smaller drop (21 inches) than a warehouse van. They have smaller wheels (15 inch), which make room for a flat floor with no wheel wells. The drawback to these vans is less space for the cargo. More heat buildup in the brake drums and tires also occurs.

Single Drop Frame

The low bed is also known as the flatbed. These can haul higher loads without going over the height limits set by law. Bottom clearance problems are not as bad as those of double drop frames (see Figure 22-17). These trailers can have many axles and wheels depending on type and weight of load.

Warehouse, furniture, or electronics vans can have either a single drop frame or double drop frame design.

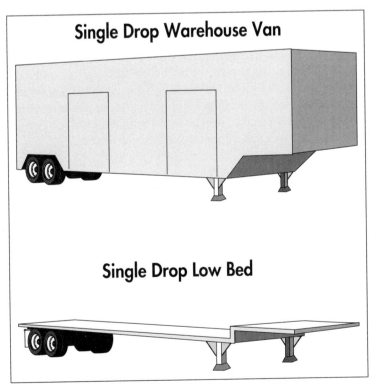

Figure **22-17** Low beds are designed to carry higher loads, and bottom clearance problems are not as frequent.

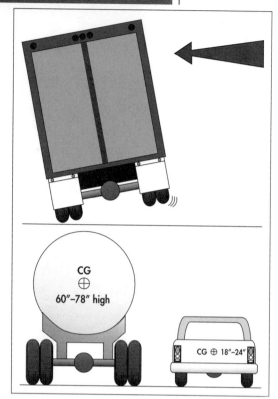

Figure **22-18** Trailers with high centers of gravity are more likely to roll over on a curve.

HIGH-CENTER-OF-GRAVITY VEHICLES

As the name suggests, the bulk of the weight of the cargo in these rigs is high in the load. The center of gravity, therefore, is farther from the road. This makes the trailer more likely to roll over when taking curves (see Figure 22-18).

Dry Bulk Tankers

The shape of the semitrailer varies but is usually cylindrical. It may be high at each end and slope to a center bottom discharge gate. Trailer lengths vary. The high center of gravity requires careful speed control, particularly on curves.

They are used to haul dry bulk cargo:

- Flour
- Sugar
- Powdered milk
- Ground limestone
- Cement
- Fly ash
- Plastic pellets

These rigs are usually loaded through openings in the top. They are unloaded by a blower from the tractor or through the bottom of the tanker.

Liquid Cargo Tankers

Milk tankers are rarely used for other cargoes. These smoothbore tanks do not have **baffles** or **bulkheads.** Their smooth linings must be kept very clean. These rigs can be difficult to handle because they must be driven with partial loads. As deliveries are made and the cargo is reduced, the handling characteristics change.

The smooth interior of the tanks and partial loads make driving very challenging. Drivers should accelerate slowly. Avoid braking in turns. Turn only at safe speeds. The greater the speed, the greater the force of the load.

Special Requirements

There are special requirements for drivers of liquid tankers. They

- must be familiar with the vehicle,
- must have experience with unstable loads,
- must know each state's requirements for road use and permits including those for transporting hazardous materials,
- must have a Tank Vehicles Endorsement on their CDLs, and
- must have a Hazardous Materials Endorsement on their CDLs if they are hauling hazardous materials.

Pretrip and en route inspections should include the standard semitrailer inspection. Check the tank for leaks. Also, check all hoses, valves, and fittings. Finally, a check of the emergency valve release is very important.

Figure **22-19** Livestock transport trailer.

Livestock Transport Trailer

These are semitrailers with either a flat floor or double drop frame design. They are used to carry live animals such as cattle, sheep, and hogs. Slots or holes in the sides allow the livestock to breathe. Many have side doors rather than rear ones. Some may have both (see Figure 22-19).

Characteristics

The length may vary between 27 feet and 45 feet. They carry a fixed tandem axle in the rear. These rigs can be changed to have two or three decks for smaller animals such as sheep or pigs. Some can be converted into dry freight vans for the backhaul (return trip).

Livestock trailers can have special handling problems. Live cargo shifts about and that changes the balance and stability. Drivers should drive at the speed that lets them keep the vehicle under control at all times. When braking, tap the brakes lightly to set the animals. Then slowly put on the brakes. Do not attempt to drive one of these rigs without proper training.

Special Requirements

The driver needs more knowledge and skill than for a regular rig. The driver is responsible for the cargo's health and safety. Road use and permits vary. See each state's requirements for transporting livestock.

Oversized vehicles sometimes carry loads with the cargo resting much higher on the trailer than normal. This raises the center of gravity. Any livestock transport that has two or three decks has a **high center of gravity** when loaded. The animals on the top level cause the high center of gravity.

UNSTABLE LOADS

The most common unstable loads are of two general types: liquid in tankers and livestock or carcasses such as dressed or processed meats ready for market (sometimes called swinging meat). It usually takes the first 100 to 200 miles of a trip for swinging meat to interlock and stabilize.

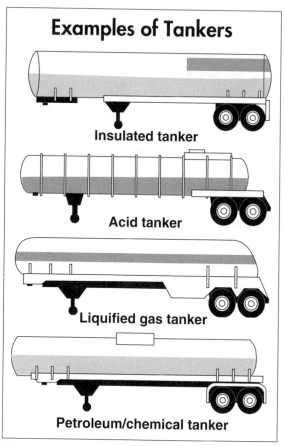

Examples of Tankers

Insulated tanker

Acid tanker

Liquified gas tanker

Petroleum/chemical tanker

Figure **22-20** Various types of liquid tankers.

Liquid Tanker

Liquid tankers are used to transport liquid cargo such as gasoline, asphalt, milk, orange juice, or liquefied gases. The tanker itself may be hot, cold, or pressurized. The type of tanker used will depend on the cargo it carries.

The semitrailers of these liquid tanker rigs are usually oval (most common), circular, or square shaped. The load/unload mechanism may or may not be connected to the tractor (see Figure 22-20).

The number and lengths of compartments vary. There may be one compartment or many. Some contain baffles (walls with holes to reduce surge) or bulkheads to prevent the liquid from surging front to back. Handling these vehicles can be very difficult. **Surging loads,** for example, create an unstable vehicle.

Petroleum or chemical tankers may have one to five compartments and may or may not have baffles. Their capacity can be as high as 9,500 gallons.

Acid tank rigs have a small diameter tank with outside stiffener rings and a variety of linings or baffles. They are sometimes insulated and can carry up to 6,000 gallons of liquid.

Liquefied gas tankers are designed for high pressure. They carry butane, propane, oxygen, hydrogen, and other gases in a liquid state.

Insulated tankers carry heated material. Steel tankers can carry materials as hot as 500°F (260°C). Aluminum ones can carry loads up to 400°F (204°C).

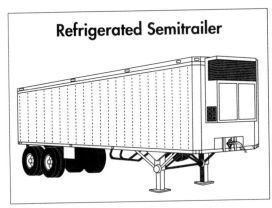

Figure **22-21** "Reefers" carry loads requiring controlled, cooler temperatures.

Refrigerated Trailer (Reefer)

There are two types of reefers: **nose mount** and **belly mount.** Nose mount trailers have the refrigeration unit at the upper front of the trailer. In belly mount trailers, the unit is under the trailer.

Both are box-type semitrailers. Some have racks or rails suspended from the roof. Beef, pork, and lamb are hung from these racks or rails. Others have separate compartments. Some cargo can be kept frozen while other cargo is only cooled. These units have slotted floors and canvas ducts in the ceiling to let air or gas circulate (see Figure 22-21).

Characteristics

Refrigeration units have their own engines. They may be powered by gasoline, diesel fuel, or liquefied petroleum gas. They also have their own fuel tanks. Generally, the floors, sides, and roofs are thickly insulated.

Refrigerated trailers, or reefers, that have rails attached to the trailer roof from which to hang meat present a special problem because the high-hanging meat raises the center of gravity.

 TIP It takes 100 to 200 miles for hanging meat to interlock and stabilize. Stepping on the brakes a few times will help to slide the hooks forward. Do this before adjusting the sliders for weight distribution.

Handling

Loosely packed, swinging meat loads create very dangerous stability problems. Swinging meat is more of a handling problem than sloshing liquid. Safe loading procedures are vital.

Special Requirements

These are similar to those of most other special rigs. Special training, added skills, and knowledge are needed by the driver. A Doubles/Triples Endorsement on the driver's CDL may also be needed. With special permits, these rigs may be operated on certain highways. For more information, see each state's laws.

Inspections should include a careful check of the trailer for holes in walls. Also check ceiling and floor ducts, doors and door gaskets, the fuel level of the reefer, and the reefer's engine coolant, oil, and refrigerant level. The driver should also monitor the operation of reefer unit.

SPECIAL CARGO VEHICLES

Any rig designed to haul one certain type of cargo is special. For example, a tanker designed to transport edible cargo should not carry any loads that cannot be eaten. Reefers cannot backhaul garbage or trash.

Pole Trailer

A **pole trailer** carries long, narrow cargo. A pole trailer can be telescoped, or made longer or shorter to fit the load. Cargo may be poles, timbers, logs, steel girders, or concrete beams (see Figure 22-22).

The load carrying bed is made of two U-shaped cradles (bunks) connected by a steel pole (reach). The reach is the part that can be lengthened or shortened. Some rigs do not have a reach. If this is the case, the load becomes the body. Sometimes a straight truck is used as the tractor and the front bunk of the trailer is mounted on the flatbed of the truck body.

Auto Transport Trailer

This rig hauls cars and pickup trucks. It can carry six full size cars or up to 10 sub-compacts. Sometimes another car is mounted on a rack above the tractor. A rear ramp that can be raised or lowered lets the cars be driven on and off the transport (see Figure 22-23).

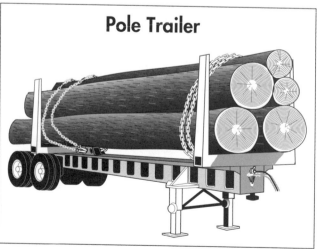

Figure **22-22** Pole trailers carry long narrow loads, such as logs, poles, timbers, girders, or concrete beams.

Figure **22-23** Auto transports can accommodate anywhere from six to ten cars.

SPECIAL HANDLING VEHICLES

These rigs have special handling problems because of visibility, location of the steering axle, and so on.

Low Cab Forward

The cab is in front of the engine on this small diesel used for city pickup and delivery work. A heavy-duty diesel may be used as a combination city and short distance haul rig (see Figure 22-24).

Snub Nose Tractor

The engine extends back into the cab in this otherwise conventional tractor. It is often used for close-clearance city work.

Yard Tractors

Sometimes known as a cab-beside-engine, this heavy duty diesel is most frequently used as a yard horse or goat. Its job is to shuttle, or transfer, trailers from one part of the yard to another (see Figure 22-25).

Dromedary Tractor

This is a tractor with a cargo body mounted just behind the cab and ahead of the fifth wheel. Its cargo space, or drom box, may be loaded from the rear or through side doors.

Figure **22-24** City pickup and delivery truck.

Figure **22-25** One model of a yard tractor.

Chapter Twenty-Three
Preventive Maintenance and Servicing

OBJECTIVES

When you have completed this chapter, you should be able to:

- Know and understand the different types of maintenance

- Know how to do various simple maintenance procedures

- Know your responsibilities in maintaining your rig

- Show dangers of certain types of maintenance

- Understand the inspection, repair, and maintenance requirements of the FMCSR

KEY TERMS

Air filter element

Air reservoir

Battery fluid

Circuit breaker

Coolant

Coolant filter

Federal Motor Carrier
   Safety Regulations
   (FMCSR)

Fuel filter

Fuse

Oil filter

Power steering fluid

Preventive maintenance

Routine servicing

Scheduled preventive
   maintenance

Unscheduled
   maintenance and
   repair

Vehicle Condition
   Report (VCR)

INTRODUCTION

A tractor-trailer that is well maintained will do its job much better and more efficiently than one that is neglected. To keep a rig in good shape, a driver must know how to inspect the vehicle and all its parts.

While some routine servicing tasks can be done by the driver, most service and repair work should be done by trained personnel. When someone who is trained for the job does the servicing, it costs less and takes less time. If someone who is not trained attempts to work on the rig, the work may not be done right and time is wasted (see Figure 23-1). This can result in accidents, injuries, or death.

A driver must know and understand what maintenance and repairs should be and what should not be part of his or her job.

This chapter has three goals:

1. To teach you the basic checks and servicing needed for the engine and vehicle (see Figure 23-2).
2. To show you how to perform some preventive maintenance and simple emergency repairs.
3. To show you that drivers are not expected to be mechanics. They should not try to do any maintenance or repair work unless they have been taught how to do it and have had experience repairing it under the guidance of a trained person.

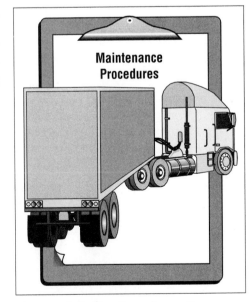

Figure **23-2** Good, routine maintenance eliminates downtime and other problems on the road.

Preventive Maintenance and Servicing

Figure **23-1** Maintenance is a must for high performance and efficiency.

PREVENTIVE MAINTENANCE

Preventive maintenance is the servicing done at regular intervals on a truck. By servicing the truck regularly, many costly emergency repairs can be avoided. Small problems can be fixed before they develop into big ones.

In many fleets, even the most routine maintenance is performed by the fleet's maintenance department, the dealer, an independent garage, or a truck leasing company. Drivers are not permitted to do any maintenance.

Other carriers, however, require drivers to perform certain minor maintenance tasks as part of their job. Independent owner/operators generally do more preventive maintenance than do drivers in larger companies. Owner/operators also have some work done by a garage or dealer.

TYPES OF MAINTENANCE

Maintenance includes **routine servicing, scheduled preventive maintenance,** and **unscheduled maintenance and repair.**

Routine Servicing

Routine servicing tasks can be done by drivers. These tasks often include the following:

- Adding fuel
- Adding oil
- Adding coolant
- Draining moisture from fuel and air systems

Scheduled Preventive Maintenance

Scheduled preventive maintenance is servicing that is based on time or mileage since the last scheduled maintenance (see Figure 23-3). Most fleets have a regular preventive maintenance schedule. This maintenance is often set up under four levels and is not performed by drivers (see Figure 23-4).

It is the driver's responsibility, though, to inform the shop of repairs that are needed or failures that occur between scheduled inspections.

Level A

15,000 to 25,000 miles; may be combined with level B service

Grease job

SCHEDULED PREVENTIVE MAINTENANCE

- Based on time or mileage or a combination of time miles
- Usually set up on four levels
  - Level A—Perhaps grease and oil change only
  - Level B—Same as A but more involved
  - Level C—All of A, plus B and an engine tune-up
  - Level D—All of A, B, and C plus a major overhaul of engine

Figure **23-3** Scheduled preventive maintenance is based on mileage since last scheduled maintenance.

Engine Compartment

Oil level 0

Coolant level 0

Power steering fluid 0

Water pump 0

Air compressor..0

Engine leaks 0

Alternator 0

Engine Start

Clutch/gearshift...0

Air buzzer sounds 0

Oil pressure builds..0

Ammeter/voltmeter 0

Air brake check 0

Steering play 0

Parking brake..0

Mirrors/windshield...0

Wipers...0

Lighting indicators..0

Horn(s)..0

Heater/defroster...0

Safety/emergency equipment 0

Figure **23-4** Partial preventive maintenance and servicing list.

Oil change

Filter change

Checking all fluid levels

Level B

If combined with level A, approximately every 15,000 miles; if not combined, typically every 25,000 miles

Includes all of level A

Inspection and maintenance of key components, such as lubricating water pump shaft

Level C

100,000 to 120,000 miles; many companies combine level C with the annual inspection

Includes all of level A and level B

Engine tune-up

Detailed inspection of all major components

Road test

Figure **23-5** Unscheduled maintenance and repairs require immediate attention and time.

Level D

500,000 to 750,000 miles unless the truck has a self-destruct decision

Includes all of levels A, B, and C

Complete overhaul of the engine

Rebuilding parts

Fuel pump

Alternator

Unscheduled Maintenance and Repair

Unscheduled maintenance and repair occurs when unexpected breakdowns or emergencies require immediate maintenance and includes the following (see Figure 23-5):

- Breakdowns on the road
- Repair of accident damage
- Problems listed in a driver's pretrip or posttrip inspection report

FEDERAL MOTOR VEHICLE INSPECTION AND MAINTENANCE REQUIREMENTS

All drivers must learn what the **Federal Motor Carrier Safety Regulations (FMCSR)** require and meet these requirements.

Part 392 and Part 396 of the FMCSR require drivers to do the following:

- Perform a pretrip inspection before operating a vehicle.
- Review the last daily vehicle inspection report.
- Sign the report to indicate they have reviewed it and confirm that a mechanic has completed any needed work on the rig.
- Perform en route inspections (see Section 392.9) after the vehicle has been driven for 3 hours or 150 miles, whichever occurs first. If the driver is hauling hazardous materials, see Part 397 for more requirements.
- Perform a posttrip inspection on:

Service brakes	Horn
Parking brakes	Windshield wipers
Steering mechanism	Rearview mirrors
Lights and reflectors	Coupling devices
Wheels and rims	Emergency equipment
Tires	

DAILY VEHICLE CONDITION REPORT

Results of the posttrip inspection must be entered on an official daily **Vehicle Condition Report (VCR)** form. The report must be completed even if no defects were found. The driver must make an accurate report of everything he or she finds. Then he or she must sign and date it. The report must then be delivered to the supervisor. Every day all drivers must complete this report for each vehicle they drive. Laws and these reports help the mechanics keep equipment in top condition (see Figure 23-6).

Vehicle Condition Report

Driver's Inspection Report

MAINTENANCE

(SEE INSTRUCTIONS ON REVERSE SIDE)
CHECK DEFECTS ONLY. Explain under REMARKS
COMPLETION OF THIS REPORT REQUIRED BY FEDERAL LAW, 49CFR 396.11 & 396.13.
Mileage (No Tenths)

Truck or
Tractor No. _____ |__|__|__|__|__|__| Trailer No. _____

Dolly No. _____ Trailer No. _____ Location: _____

POWER UNIT

	IN CAB	EXTERIOR
☐ 02 Cab/Doors/Windows	☐ 03 Gauges/Warning Indicators	☐ 34 Lights
☐ 02 Body/Doors	☐ 02 Windshield Wipers/Washers	☐ 34 Reflectors
☐ _____ Oil Leak _____	☐ 54 Horn(s)	☐ 16 Suspension
☐ _____ Grease Leak _____	☐ 01 Heater/Defroster	☐ 17 Tires
☐ 42 Coolant Leak	☐ 02 Mirrors	☐ 18 Wheels/Rims/Lugs
☐ 44 Fuel Leak	☐ 15 Steering	☐ 32 Battery
☐ _____ Other _____	☐ 23 Clutch	☐ 43 Exhaust
_____	☐ 13 Service Brake	☐ 13 Brakes
(IDENTIFY)	☐ 13 Parking Brake	☐ 13 Air Lines
	☐ 13 Emergency Brake	☐ 34 Light Line
ENGINE COMPARTMENT	☐ 53 Triangles	☐ 49 Fifth-Wheel
☐ 45 Oil Level	☐ 53 Fire Extinguisher	☐ 49 Other Coupling
☐ _____ Belts _____	☐ 53 Other Safety Equipment	☐ 71 Tie-Downs
☐ _____ Other _____	☐ 34 Spare Fuses	☐ 14 Rear-End Protection
	☐ 02 Seat Belts	☐ _____ Other _____
(IDENTIFY)	☐ _____ Other _____	(IDENTIFY)
	_____	
	(IDENTIFY)	☐ NO DEFECTS

TOWED UNIT(S)

☐ 71 Body/Doors	☐ 16 Suspension	☐ 77 Landing Gear	☐ 79 Rear-End Protection
☐ 71 Tie-Downs	☐ 17 Tires	☐ 59 Kingpin Upper Plate	☐ _____ Other _____
☐ 34 Lights	☐ 18 Wheels/Rims/Lugs	☐ 59 Fifth-Wheel (Dolly)	(IDENTIFY)
☐ 34 Reflectors	☐ 13 Brakes	☐ 59 Other Coupling Devices	☐ NO DEFECTS

REMARKS: _____
_____
_____
_____

REPORTING DRIVER: Date _____	MAINTENANCE ACTION: Date _____
Name _____ Emp. No. _____	Repairs Made ☐ No Repairs Needed ☐
	R.O.#s _____
REVIEWING DRIVER: Date _____	Certified By: _____
Name _____ Emp. No. _____	Location: _____

SHOP REMARKS: _____
_____

Figure **23-6**   Results of the posttrip inspection must be entered on an official VCR form.

TIP

Completing a thorough daily vehicle inspection is essential for safety and for preventing costly vehicle repairs. It also will help ensure that you do not receive out-of-service violations or fines.

Importance of Preventive Maintenance

Failure to perform preventive maintenance can increase the cost of operation. For example, breakdowns on the road may include these extra costs:

- Cargo transfer charges
- Late delivery charges
- Expensive road services (towing, out of town repair)
- Driver expenses (salary while not driving, living expenses)

Preventing part failure costs less than repairing or replacing a damaged part. Unscheduled maintenance disrupts the schedule of preventive maintenance for other parts and vehicles.

Operating Costs

Vehicles that are poorly maintained cost more to operate. For example, fuel costs are higher. A poorly tuned engine gets fewer miles per gallon and requires longer trip times.

A breakdown on the road can result in an accident. Of course, this adds to expenses and decreases trip efficiency. The extra costs can include repairing the damage, lost work time, medical expenses, and increase company insurance rates.

BASIC SERVICING AND ROUTINE MAINTENANCE

Drivers should understand and be able to perform basic servicing and routine maintenance. They should be able to:

- Inspect and change the engine fluids, certain filters, lights, and fuses
- Change a tire (change a wheel) in an emergency
- Drain the moisture from air reservoirs and the fuel system

Why should drivers learn basic servicing if they are going to work for a carrier that has a policy of not allowing drivers to do any servicing or adjustments to their trucks? A few good reasons are the following:

- If a mechanic is working on your rig and is doing something wrong, you should be able to recognize the error.
- If your rig breaks down at 2:00 a.m., it is −10°F, and you are 15 miles from the nearest telephone, you will be glad to have some basic mechanical knowledge.
- As a professional driver, you should know as much about your rig and its parts as possible. In this way, you can detect systems or parts that are in danger of failing.
- You may not always work for a carrier that does not permit the driver to do maintenance. You may go to work for one who expects the driver to do basic servicing.

CHECKING AND CHANGING ENGINE FLUIDS, FILTERS, LIGHTS, AND FUSES

This section will discuss the correct maintenance procedures for the following:

- Fuel tank, fuel level, and **fuel filter**
- Oil level and **oil filter**
- **Coolant** level and **coolant filter**
- **Battery fluid** level
- **Power steering fluid** level
- **Air filter element**
- Lights and bulbs
- **Fuses** and **circuit breakers**

Checking the Fuel Tank and Fuel Level

Fuel Tanks

1. Open the drain cocks on the bottom of the tanks, and drain out any water (see Figure 23-7).
2. Tighten all fuel tank mountings and brackets. Be careful not to tighten them so much you crush the tank. These systems are designed with some flexibility.
3. Check the seal in the fuel tank cap and check the breather hole.

Fuel Level

1. Park the rig on level ground.
2. Open the fuel tank cap.

Figure **23-7** Check the fuel level and drain out any water when you open the drain cocks on the fuel tanks.

3. Check the fuel level by looking at it.

4. Make sure the level matches the gauge reading in the cab.

Changing the Fuel Filter Element

1. Turn the fuel filter element counterclockwise until it comes off of the base. If you use a filter wrench, be sure to use it at the bottom of the filter so you will not crush the filter shell.

2. Discard the filter element according to Environmental Protection Agency (EPA) standards.

3. Clean the surface of the seal on the filter base. Be sure to always remove the old seal and use a new one.

4. Wipe up any fuel that spilled when you took off the filter.

5. Fill the new filter with clean fuel.

6. Coat the seal of the new filter with clean diesel fuel or engine oil.

7. Screw the filter onto the base until the seal touches the base.

8. Tighten the filter one-half turn.

9. Start the engine. Check for leaks.

Replacing the Filter

The following method of replacing the filter is general in nature. There are many types of fuel filter systems. To find the correct way to replace your filter, read the instructions on the filter.

1. Turn off the fuel supply from the fuel tanks.

2. Place a container under the filter.

3. Open the drain cock in the filter housing base.

4. Drain the filter.

5. Remove the filter body with the element. If you use a filter wrench, be sure to use it at the bottom of the filter so you will not crush the filter shell.

6. Discard the filter element according to EPA rules.

7. Clean the housing. Make sure the old filter came out.

8. Close the drain cock.

9. Install a new filter in the housing.

10. Fill the housing with clean fuel.

11. Install the filter housing containing the new filter element with a gasket. Always use a new seal. An old seal can leak.

12. Lubricate with fuel or engine oil and tighten.

13. Open the fuel line shutoff valve.

14. Start the engine.

15. Check for leaks.

Draining the Fuel Filter

To drain a fuel filter:

1. Locate the filter and water separator.

2. Remove the drain plug at the bottom of the filter.

3. Allow the water to drain.

4. Replace the drain plug.

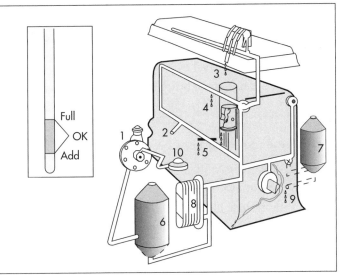

Typical Lubricating System

1. Oil from main gallery
2. Oil fill tube
3. Rocker and drain
4. Cam pocket drain
5. Oil drain from blower
   or turbocharger
6. Full-flow oil filter
7. Bypass oil filter
8. Oil cooler
9. Drain to oil pan
10. Oil pick-up screen

Full
OK
Add

Figure **23-8**   Be careful not to overfill when adding oil.

Checking the Oil Level

To check the level of the oil:

1. Park the vehicle on level ground.
2. Shut off the engine.
3. Wait a few minutes for the oil to drain down.
4. Find the dipstick.
5. Remove the dipstick.
6. Wipe it clean and replace it.
7. Pull it out again.
8. Check the oil level.

The level should be between the full and add marks. Do not overfill or drive when the oil level is below the add mark. Be careful not to overfill when you need to add oil (see Figure 23-8).

Changing the Oil Filter

Changing oil filters on a truck is a messy but important task. It is far harder than changing a car's filter. Like fuel systems, what is right for changing the filter on one system may be wrong for another type of system. *Change filters only after you have been trained and checked out by your supervisor or a mechanic.*

1. Remove the drain plug from the bottom of the filter housing.
2. Drain the oil.
3. Remove the filter housing that contains the filter element. Most filters today are one piece and disposable.
4. Discard the filter according to EPA standards.
5. Fill the new filter element with clean oil and install it.
6. Secure the housing.
7. Replace the drain plug.
8. Start the engine.

9. Check for leaks.
10. Turn off the engine.
11. Wait 10 minutes.
12. Check the oil level.
13. Add enough oil to bring it to the proper level on the dipstick.

Checking the Coolant Level

To check the coolant level:

1. Shut off the engine.
2. Wait until the engine is cool.
3. Put on thick cloth gloves to protect your hands.
4. Remove the radiator cap very carefully.

Turn the cap slowly to the first stop. Step back while pressure is released from the cooling system.

5. When all of the pressure has been released, press down on the cap and remove it.
6. Look at the level of the coolant.
7. Add coolant if needed. Check the operator's manual for specific instructions for your truck.

Many trucks now have sight glasses or see-through containers for checking the level of the coolant. If your rig has one, you will not need to go through the previous routine to check the level of the coolant. If the coolant level is too low, you simply add coolant to the reservoir.

Changing the Coolant Filter

To change the coolant filter, follow these steps:

1. Shut off the engine.
2. Wait until the engine is cool.
3. Put on thick cloth gloves. Do not handle a hot filter with your bare hands.
4. Turn the filter element counterclockwise to remove it.
5. Replace it with a new filter element and a new cover gasket.
6. Start the engine.
7. Check for leaks.

Storage Battery

Figure **23-9** Follow the safety rules when checking battery fluid.

Checking the Battery Fluid Level

You must be very careful when you are checking the level of the battery fluid. Follow these safety rules (see Figure 23-9).

1. Protect your eyes with goggles or glasses.
2. Protect your hands. Batteries contain acid that can severely burn you if it touches your skin.
3. Do not smoke. Batteries give off explosive gases.

Some batteries are maintenance free and do not need to have the level of the fluid checked. Others are not and must have the level of the fluid in the battery checked. To check the level of the fluid in the battery:

1. Open the battery caps.
2. Check the fluid level.
3. If the battery needs fluid, use distilled water.
4. Fill to the bottom of the split ring in the cell filler well.

Checking the Power Steering Fluid Level

With the engine running at normal operating temperature, turn the steering wheel back and forth several times to stabilize the fluid level. To check the fluid level:

1. Turn off the engine.
2. Remove the dipstick.
3. The fluid should be between the bottom of the dipstick and the full mark.
4. If fluid is needed, add enough to raise the level to the full mark. Do not overfill.

Changing the Air Filter Element

Dust, dirt, grease, or other grime can get into an engine when you change the air filter. Be careful to keep things as clean as you can.

On air cleaners with a restriction indicator, change the element or clean it when the indicator shows red. On trucks that have an air filter restriction gauge, consult a mechanic for information on when to change the element.

To change the air filter element, follow these steps:

1. Remove the end covering from the housing.
2. Make sure your hands are clean.
3. Remove the filter element.
4. Inspect the end cover and gasket surfaces for dents or possible air leaks.
5. Check the outlet tube to be sure it is clean and undamaged.
6. Check the filter element for wear.
7. Replace it if it is damaged.
8. If the filter is not damaged, clean with compressed air. Always blow the air in the opposite direction of the normal cleaner flow. Some filters should not be blown out. If your unit does not have an indicator or air filter restriction gauge, find out how often to replace it.
9. Wipe away any dirt in the filter housing.
10. Install the filter element.
11. Replace the end cover and secure it.

Always handle the filter element carefully to keep dirt from shaking loose onto the clean side of the filter system (see Figure 23-10).

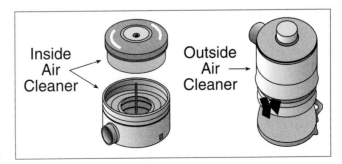

Figure **23-10** Always change the air filter carefully to avoid getting dirt on the clean filter.

Changing a Bulb in a Headlight or Clearance Light

To change a headlight bulb or a bulb in a clearance light, follow these steps:

1. Park the rig and turn off the engine.
2. Remove the trim ring from the burned-out light.
3. Unfasten the mounting screws.
4. Disconnect and remove the light from the socket. The bulb may be hot, so handle carefully.
5. Clean any dirt or bugs off of the socket area.
6. Plug in the new headlight bulb.
7. Test the light to see if it works properly.
8. Fasten the mounting screw.
9. Make sure the new light is clean.

Some lights have lenses that snap off to replace bulbs.

Note: Do not touch the headlight adjusting screws when you are changing the bulb.

Changing Fuses and Resetting Circuit Breakers

Fuses. Always use a fuse that is the right size and has the same amp rating as the fuse it replaces. To change a fuse, follow these steps:

1. Check the fuse and clip holder to be sure they are clean and do not have any burrs.
2. If the holder is dirty, touch up the contact points with a coarse cloth.
3. Gently but firmly snap the new fuse into the clip holder.
4. Make sure there is a good connection between the fuse ends and the clip holder.

Circuit breakers. To reset a circuit breaker, follow these steps:

1. Remove the circuit breaker cover panel.
2. Flip the circuit breaker switch back. This will reset it.
3. Replace the panel. (Some circuit breakers reset themselves.)

CHECKING THE AIR PRESSURE AND CHANGING TIRES

This section explains the correct way to check tire inflation pressure and change a flat or damaged tire and wheel assembly. Actually changing a tire (wheel)—removing it from the rim and installing a new one on the rim—is not taught in this book. *Only a trained mechanic with the proper tools and safety equipment should replace wheels.* Drivers, however, must know how to remove a flat tire and replace it with a spare tire in a roadside emergency.

Checking the Air Pressure

Check the air pressure when the tires are cool. Readings made when the tires are heated (during or immediately after a trip) do not give the correct pressure.

When the tires are cool, the correct way to check the pressure is to:

1. Remove the valve stem cap.
2. Place the air gauge over the valve stem opening.

3. Read the inflation pressure from the gauge.
4. Compare the tire's pressure with the correct pressure listed on the sidewall of the tire or in the operator's manual.
5. Replace the valve stem cap.

Changing a Tire

Drivers can learn the right way to change a tire from watching someone else do it. Changing a tire can be dangerous. If possible, it should be done by a trained professional. Remember, a driver should change tires only in an emergency (see Figure 23-11).

Drivers should, however, know what type of tire and wheel style their rig has. They should also know the manufacturer's specs for them. Drivers must understand great care is needed when handling an inflated tire/wheel assembly. Tires explode with great force.

To change a tire:

1. Park the rig on level ground.
2. Put on the parking brake.
3. Place the transmission in the lowest forward gear.
4. Chock the front tractor wheels.
5. Inspect the tires: check for overinflation, compare the side and lock rings, and check the seating of the inner tire (on duals).

Note: If the tire seems overinflated or the seating does not look normal, do not attempt to change the tire. Get the help of an expert.

6. Refer to the owner's manual for the correct way to place the jack.
7. Put a hardwood plank or block under the base of the jack, no matter what type of surface you have parked the rig on.

Figure **23-11** If possible, a damaged tire should be changed by a trained professional.

To remove the wheel/tire assembly:

1. Jack up the truck enough to remove the weight from the studs. Be sure to stand clear of the truck when you use a jack. The truck could slip and hurt you.
2. Loosen the wheel nuts.
3. Observe direction of rotation.
4. Examine the thread. On some wheels, the direction is indicated on the end of the stud ("R" means right, or clockwise; "L" means left, or counter-clockwise).
5. Stand to one side of the tire because parts of the wheel assembly can fly off and hurt you when the stud bolts are loosened.
6. Turn the wheel nuts by hand until they are flush with the end of the stud.
7. Loosen the clamp on cast-type wheels. Tap with a hammer. Do not remove the stud nuts until the clamp is free so it will not fly off the studs.
8. Remove the air lines from any wheels that have a tire pressure sensor. Cap the line and actuator.
9. Jack up the truck to let the tire clear the ground. Stand clear of the rig while raising the jack. The truck can slip off and severely hurt you.
10. Remove the wheel assembly by removing the wheel nuts and pulling the wheel from the hub.

DRAINING THE AIR RESERVOIRS

If your air tanks have drain valves, drain the **air reservoirs** as follows:

1. Park the truck on level ground.
2. Chock the wheels.
3. Open the drain cocks by twisting the valve on the bottom of the tank.
4. Allow all of the air pressure to escape. The air pressure gauge will read 0 psi. This will let the moisture drain out (see Figure 23-12).
5. Close the valve.

Note: Drain the wet tank first to prevent moisture from being drawn further into the air system and other tanks.

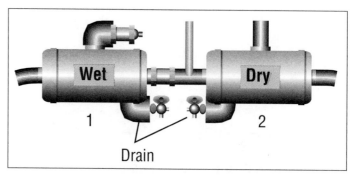

Figure **23-12** When air pressure gauge reads "0 psi," moisture will drain from air reservoirs.

ADJUSTING THE TRACTOR-TRAILER BRAKES

Some carriers require their drivers to make certain minor brake adjustments. Others do not. Because instruction in this area is lengthy and manufacturer specific, this book will not attempt to teach you how to adjust your brakes.

You should know, however, that many trucks and trailers now have automatic slack adjusters. But these still need to be checked regularly for proper adjustment.

Learn what your employer expects from you as a driver in adjusting the brakes. Learn what type of braking system your rig has. Remember, a person who is well trained for one type of braking system may not understand what is required for another system. Be sure the person who works on your brakes is qualified for the specific braking system on your rig. Brakes that have not been adjusted correctly can cause an accident.

Chapter Twenty-Four

Recognizing and Reporting Malfunctions

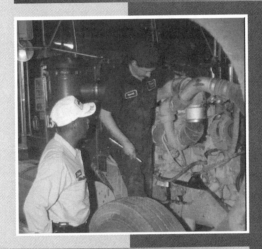

Diagnosing and Reporting
Malfunctions

Problem-Solving Exercises

Emergency Starting
Procedures

OBJECTIVES

When you have completed this chapter, you should be able to:

- Know when vehicle systems and parts are not working correctly

- Use the senses of sight, sound, feel, and smell to detect problems

- Define the driver's and the mechanic's responsibilities in vehicle maintenance

- Troubleshoot problems

- Discuss the importance of a driver being able to completely and accurately describe how the vehicle is functioning to maintenance personnel

- Explain to other drivers why they should not try to do any maintenance unless they are qualified

- Safely start a vehicle with a dead battery or without air pressure if it has an air starter

KEY TERMS

Air starter
Driver awareness
Federal Motor Carrier
   Safety Regulations
   (FMCSR)

Jump-starting
Maintenance policy
Malfunction
Troubleshoot
Vehicle Condition Report
   (VCR)

INTRODUCTION

Most tractor-trailer drivers are not expected to be mechanics. Most companies have a policy stating clearly what repairs and adjustments may and may not be done by drivers (see Figure 24-1). This chapter will help you understand what is generally expected of a driver. You also will learn about common mechanical problems: how to find them and what to do if they occur.

This chapter will show you ways to find out exactly what is causing the problem. After you find the cause, you will be shown what to do. In some cases, the correct action will be to adjust a part. In other cases, you will be told to move on to the nearest truck stop or call the company maintenance department for instructions.

You will learn how to use common sense and apply what you know. You will also learn to do only what you are capable of doing, be concerned about safety, follow company policies, and be concerned about yourself, others, your rig, and the cargo.

DIAGNOSING AND REPORTING MALFUNCTIONS

Many newer trucks have electronic controls that detect problems and sound buzzers or light up warning lights. From these warnings, drivers can often diagnose a problem. While you are not expected to become a mechanic, you should be knowledgeable enough of the various systems to find the source of a problem. This chapter will discuss how to gather information and report it to a mechanic. If this is done correctly, the mechanic can usually pinpoint the problem in the shop and come to the site with the proper tools and parts.

DRIVER RESPONSIBILITIES

- Know company maintenance policy
- Identify sources of problems
- Diagnose and fix simple problems when policy permits
- Report symptoms correctly

Figure **24-1** Knowing your exact responsibilities will make you more efficient and effective in your job.

DRIVER AWARENESS

A driver must be aware of his or her vehicle at all times: Be constantly alert

Use his or her senses:

Seeing	Feeling
Hearing	Smelling

Figure **24-2** Use your senses to detect danger signals given off by the vehicle's different systems.

Driver Awareness

Driver awareness is vital.

Drivers can be aware of the rig's condition at all times by using their senses (see Figure 24-2):

- Seeing
- Hearing
- Feeling
- Smelling

Look at the instrument gauges and exhaust smoke.

Look for fluid leaks, damaged tires, and missing wheel lugs.

Listen for unusual engine noises, air leaks, and any unusual noise.

Feel for vibrations, thumps, and swaying that is not natural for your truck.

Be aware when you smell diesel fuel, smoke, or burning rubber.

Report any of the symptoms to your service department. In some cases, you may be able to make an adjustment and cure the problem yourself.

By using these senses, you can notice a defect before it develops into a breakdown, a costly repair, or an accident.

Also, if you understand the electronic diagnostics on a truck, you may be able to help the mechanic pinpoint the problem to be repaired.

Early Detection of Malfunctions

By using your senses and noticing symptoms early, you can cut repair costs. Problems are found and fixed before major damage occurs. This means repairs will be minor and the vehicle will spend less time in the shop and the truck is being operated more efficiently. If you own the truck, you will be happy. If you work for a company, your carrier will be pleased with you (see Figure 24-3).

EARLY DETECTION OF MALFUNCTIONS

Early detection of malfunctions results in:

- Lower maintenance expense
- Minimum downtime
- Fewer accidents
- Longer vehicle life
- Lower operating cost

Figure **24-3** Using your senses and your experience can help head off major problems and damage.

When problems are noticed early and corrected, there is not as much of a chance for equipment to fail or accidents. The truck will probably also last longer. You may even avoid being stranded on the road.

Driver Responsibility

Your company should have a **maintenance policy,** and you should know what they expect of you. You will not have to be an expert, but you should be able to identify the sources of **malfunctions** and diagnose and fix simple problems.

How much you are allowed to do and what you do will depend on:

- Company maintenance policy
- Your knowledge and mechanical experience
- Whether the carrier has an approved repair service
- Your access to tools

Do not try to fix any problem unless you have been trained to do so.

Mechanic's Responsibility

The mechanic should:

- Learn about system failures from driver reports
- Diagnose the causes of the problems
- Correct the malfunctions
- Ensure that a problem or failure has been fixed before releasing the truck

Driver and Mechanic Joint Responsibility

Drivers and mechanics must work together if the company is to benefit. A driver can be very helpful to the mechanic by knowing the rig and reporting all problems—large or small—at once. The mechanic can make sure all problems are fixed as soon as possible. When drivers and mechanics work closely together, they can prevent serious damage to the equipment.

Troubleshooting

As a driver, you need to know:

- About your vehicle's systems
- Where the systems are located
- The parts of each system
- Where the parts are located
- How each system works
- How all systems work together

Understanding how a system works is the first step in realizing when it is not working properly or is in danger of failing. A vehicle will, in most cases, alert you to trouble by warning signals, such as:

- A sharp drop in fuel mileage
- Erratic gauge readings
- A temperature gauge reading that is too high or too low
- A thump, bump, whine, grind, or rattle

Figure **24-4** Detecting the beginnings of a problem can help avoid serious downtime.

If you know how your vehicle's systems work, you can notice the danger signals more easily, trace a problem to its source, report your findings to a qualified mechanic, or make the repair yourself if you are permitted (see Figure 24-4).

Detection of Problems

When you notice a symptom, stop the truck as soon as possible (or as soon as the seriousness of the problem dictates). Then think the problem through before starting to **troubleshoot.** Start with the most likely cause of the problem. Keep these points in mind:

- You are not a mechanic or a mechanical expert.
- You should not try to do the mechanic's job.
- If you cannot trace the problem and identify the exact source of the trouble—actually see the part that is broken or not working—do not try to guess.
- Carefully describe the problem when you report it. Report what was checked and what you found, observed, smelled, and so on. Include the "what," "when," and "where" and any other information you may have.

Reporting Requirements

Driver's job. If you find something wrong and are capable of and permitted to repair it, you should. If you cannot repair it, report the symptoms and findings to the maintenance department as soon as possible.

Written report. The **Federal Motor Carrier Safety Regulations (FMCSR)** requires drivers to submit a **Vehicle Condition Report (VCR)** for each trip or 24-hour period within a trip. Include any problems in this report. Drivers must also review previous VCRs to verify that all problems have been corrected before beginning the next use of the equipment.

Note: A VCR must be submitted for each power unit and each trailer and convertor used in a 24-hour day.

Oral report. It often helps to discuss the problem with the mechanic. This gives the mechanic a chance to ask questions about the written report and helps him or her understand the details of the problem.

Limitations. Remember, it is important to report only the facts about the symptoms and what your troubleshooting turned up. Guessing helps no one. The mechanic's job is to use the details you have given to solve the problem.

Vehicle Condition Report

Each company has its own VCR forms. The data the driver gives should be accurate so that the maintenance department can locate defects quickly and easily (see Figure 24-5). If there are no problems, your report should say so. If problems did occur, the driver should:

- Check the appropriate place on the form to show what system or part was involved
- Describe the symptoms and troubleshooting in as much detail as possible
- Discuss the problem with the mechanic, if company policy permits

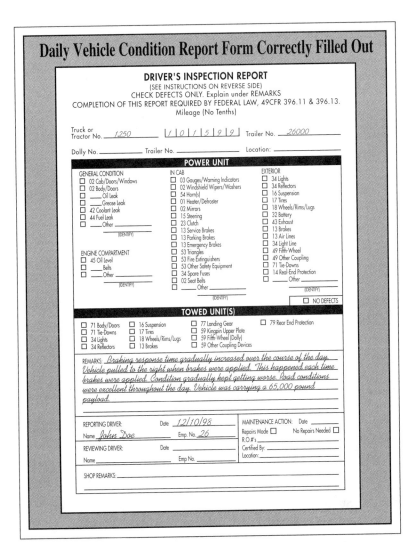

Figure **24-5** Daily VCR form correctly filled out.

Useful items for the remarks or comments section include:

● Symptoms

A description of the way the problem appears to the driver.

How did it start?

Did it start suddenly or gradually?

If it came on gradually, over what period of time? Several minutes, hours, days?

When did it appear?

● Conditions

What were the conditions when the symptoms occurred?

How long had you been driving?

Was the weather hot or cold?

What type of cargo and vehicle weight were you carrying?

How far did your troubleshooting go?

What did you find?

Did you repair or try to repair anything?

Example

A driver notices the braking response time is getting slower and the vehicle pulls to the right when the brakes are applied.

It came on gradually during the morning of the trip.

The weather was moderate.

The cargo was a max load of vegetables.

Troubleshooting consisted of checking the tires, suspension, and brakes.

Results:

Tire inflation OK.

No broken or bent springs, shock absorbers, and so on.

Must be the brakes or front-end alignment.

Called dispatcher for aid.

Told to bring truck in at once for servicing.

Troubleshooting Guide

You can find a Troubleshooting Guide in Appendix A. It is organized by sense; that is, IF YOU SEE, IF YOU HEAR, IF YOU FEEL, or IF YOU SMELL. It lists the systems that may be affected, what to look for, and what to do. Learn to relate the signals picked up by your senses with the kinds of problems they may indicate.

The following are examples of two signals or symptoms. One is something you can hear (a dull thud). The other is something you can see (gauge reading).

A dull thud.   Suppose you hear a dull thud in time with the turning of the wheels. What is causing the problem?

Possible systems involved	Possible cause
Tires	Flat tire
Wheels/rims/lugs	Loose wheel or tire lugs
	Rock between duals

Proper action

- Stop as soon as you can find a safe place.
- Decide what is the logical starting point for troubleshooting. Start with the simplest reason first. In this case, do you have a flat tire?

If this is not the reason—if the tire is not flat—you might need to tighten the lugs or remove a rock from between tires.

Note: Do not, for any reason, try to remove the tire from the rim.

Gauge reading.   Your ammeter shows a continuous maximum charge. Your signals are crossed (see Figure 24-6).

Possible systems involved	Possible cause
Electrical	Short circuit in wiring

Proper action

- Disconnect the battery terminal until the short is repaired by a mechanic.

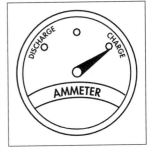

Figure **24-6**
Gauges often
indicate a problem.

PROBLEM-SOLVING EXERCISES

There are 12 problems presented in this section. After the instructor has set the scene, discuss and troubleshoot the following problems. Follow these three steps when solving the problem:

1. *Identify* the systems that may be involved.
2. *Trace* the problem toward its source.
3. *Decide* the best course of action.

Following the problems, the solutions are presented. The systems that may be causing the problem are identified. The possible source of the problem is noted. The best course of action is discussed. Compare these solutions with the class discussion. Was anything important overlooked?

Problem 1

Each time you stop, the tractor is bumped or pushed in the rear by the trailer.

Problem 2

Your mirrors are adjusted properly but you can see more of one side of the trailer than the other side (this is called trailer dog-tracking).

Problem 3

Your coolant temperature suddenly rises, and the oil pressure is falling fast.

Problem 4

The trailer sways too much when you make turns.

Problem 5

The low air warning buzzer keeps sounding for a split second at a time.

Problem 6

The circuit breaker for the trailer running lights keeps tripping.

Problem 7

When you make sharp turns on slippery road surfaces, the steering wheel is turned but the tractor continues moving straight ahead. In other words, the tractor does not turn fully in response to the turning of the steering wheel.

Problem 8

While coupling your tractor to the trailer, the tractor protection valve opens. There is a severe loss of air pressure.

Problem 9

You hear a loud snap or click when you start the truck from a dead stop.

Problem 10

You notice exhaust odor in the cab.

Problem 11

As you drive, you notice the ammeter registers discharge or there is a low reading on the voltmeter.

Problem 12

Excessive smoke is coming from the exhaust pipe.

Solutions

Problem 1.   Each time you stop, the tractor is bumped or pushed in the rear by the trailer.

Possible systems involved

- Trailer air brakes
- Coupling

Probable cause

- Slow timing of the trailer brakes (the driver cannot adjust the brake timing between the tractor and trailer)
- Air line connections between tractor and trailer
    - Loose glad hand connections
    - Worn or missing O-ring
- Air lines from glad hands to brake chambers
    - Holes or cracks in the line
    - Kinked hose

- Brake chambers
  - Air leaks
  - Slack adjuster
- Fifth-wheel locking mechanism loose
- Fifth-wheel slack adjuster needs adjusting
  - More than one-half inch of horizontal movement between the upper and lower halves will cause the unit to be put out of service.

Proper action

- Stop at the first safe place where you can pull the truck off the road.
- Check for the causes.
- If you can, move to the next truck stop or available telephone where you can call the maintenance department. Be sure all the details are correct.

Problem 2.   Your mirrors are adjusted properly but you can see more of one side of the trailer than the other side (this is called trailer dog-tracking) (see Figure 24-7).

Possible system involved

- Axles

Probable cause

- Tractor not aligned correctly
- Sliding tandems
  - Lock pins that hold the tandems in place are not in the holes. One may be in place but the other is not.
  - Lost pins
  - Pins are jarred loose
- Axles not aligned properly

Proper action

- Slow down at once.
- Find a safe place to pull off the road.
- Locate the problem areas.
- If you have sliding tandems:
  - Make sure the lock pins are in place in the holes opposite each other.
  - Replace the pins if they are gone.
  - Tighten the pins if they are loose.

Figure **24-7** Although your mirrors are adjusted properly, you can see more of one side of the trailer than the other.

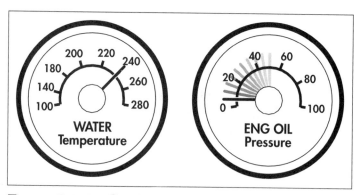

Figure **24-8** Coolant temperature is rising, and oil pressure is falling.

- If you have fixed tandems:
    - Get to the first available phone so you can call your maintenance department.

Problem 3. Your coolant temperature suddenly rises, and the oil pressure is falling fast (see Figure 24-8).

Possible system involved

- Lubrication

Probable cause

- Low oil level due to:
- Lost oil drain plug
    - Oil filter not properly secured or tightened
    - Broken oil line
    - Blown gasket

Proper action

- Pull off the road at once.
- Stop and turn off the engine.
- Check the engine oil level. CAUTION—the engine is very hot.
- Check all of the probable causes.
- Check for oil leaks in the engine compartment and under the truck.
    - Call your maintenance department for assistance. Be accurate.
    - Do not restart your engine!

Problem 4. The trailer sways too much when you make turns (see Figure 24-9).

Possible systems involved

- Suspension
- Tires

Probable cause

- Cargo has shifted
- Broken or loose shock absorbers

Figure **24-9** Excessive trailer sway may indicate that cargo has shifted.

- Broken or shifted spring or spring hanger
- Underinflated or flat tires

Proper action

- Slow down at once.
- Drive to first safe place and pull off the road.
- Check out the possible causes.
- If the cargo has shifted, move it back into position and secure it.
- If the problem is a shock absorber, go to the next truck stop and call your maintenance department.
- If the problem is a flat tire, call for help. Change it if you are permitted.

Problem 5. The low air warning buzzer keeps sounding for a split second at a time (see Figure 24-10).

Possible system involved

- Air brakes

Probable cause

- Severe air leak
- Loose compressor belt
- Ruptured air line
- Disconnected air line
- Petcock open on air reservoirs
- Malfunctioning compressor
- Loose glad hand connections
- Worn or missing O-ring on glad hand
- Blown brake chamber diaphragm

Proper action

- Stop at once.
- Park your rig.
- Locate the problem.
- Call for assistance.
- Correct the problem before resuming your trip.

Figure **24-10** A severe air leak or disconnected air line may cause periodic low air buzzer warnings.

Problem 6. The circuit breaker for the trailer running lights keeps tripping.

Possible system involved

● Electrical

Probable cause

● Exposed or hanging wire (the insulation may have worn off exposing the bare wire)
● Broken ground wire

Proper action

● Stop your truck at the first safe spot off the road.
● Turn engine off. Check out the problem.
● Repair the wire if you are permitted. You can splice a broken ground wire and tape it.
● Tape any bare exposed wire.
● Reset the circuit breaker.
● Drive to the first available truck stop and have the electrical system checked by a qualified mechanic. Taping is only a temporary repair!

Problem 7. When you make sharp turns on slippery road surfaces, the steering wheel is turned but the tractor continues moving straight ahead. In other words, the tractor does not turn fully in response to the turning of the steering wheel (see Figure 24-11).

Possible system involved

● Steering

Probable cause

● Steering axle too lightly loaded
● Fifth wheel needs grease
● Fifth wheel is iced up

Proper action

● Slow down at once and look for a safe place to pull off the road.
● Move the load to get more weight on the fifth wheel.
● If your truck has a sliding fifth wheel, move the fifth wheel forward.
● Grease the fifth wheel.

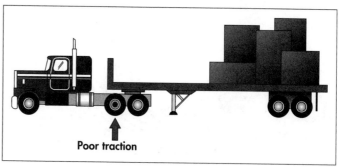

Figure **24-11** Poor traction may be caused by a lightly loaded steering axle.

- Remove ice from the fifth wheel.
- If the truck does not have a sliding fifth wheel but has sliding tandems on the trailer, move the tandems to the rear. This will put more weight on the fifth wheel by transferring weight to the steering axle.

Note: This is usually a problem on tandem axle tractors with a short wheelbase. The tandems are a short distance behind the steering wheel and tend to take control of the vehicle, preventing it from moving straight ahead.

Problem 8. While coupling your tractor to the trailer, the tractor protection valve opens. There is a severe loss of air pressure (see Figure 24-12).

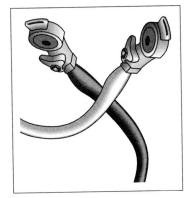

Figure **24-12**
Crossed air lines may cause a severe loss of air pressure.

Possible system involved

- Air brakes

Probable cause

- Glad hands are not seated properly or they have a bad O-ring.
- Air lines are crossed. The service line is connected to the emergency line, and the emergency line is connected to the service line.
- Trailer air tank petcock is open.
- Broken air lines

Proper action

- This problem must be found and corrected before you drive from the yard.

Problem 9. You hear a loud snap or click when you start the truck from a dead stop.

Possible system involved

- Drive train

Probable cause

- Loose universal joint
- Excessive wear on universal joint or differential

Proper action

- Be very careful when you put the truck into motion.
- Proceed to the nearest truck stop.
- Have the drive train checked by a qualified mechanic.

Problem 10. You notice exhaust odor in the cab.

Possible system involved

- Exhaust

Probable cause

- Loose connection in the exhaust system
- Cracked or broken exhaust pipe
- Leaking muffler

- Rusted exhaust system
- Cracked exhaust manifold

Proper action

- Open all the cab windows.
- Stop at the next truck stop.
- Have the exhaust system checked and repaired by a qualified mechanic as soon as possible.

Problem 11. As you drive, you notice the ammeter registers discharge or there is a low reading on the voltmeter.

Possible system involved

- Electrical

Probable cause

- Loose or broken alternator belt
- Loose wiring connection
- Burned-out generator or alternator
- Generator or alternator not adjusted right
- Defective voltage regulator

Proper action

- Do not shut off the engine.
- Pull off the road at the first safe spot.
- Look for any obvious cause.
    - Missing belt (keep hands away from any moving belts and pulleys)
    - Loose connections
    - Bare insulation or a worn wire
    - Short circuit in the wiring
- Go to the first available truck stop or area where expert mechanical assistance is available (see Figure 24-13).

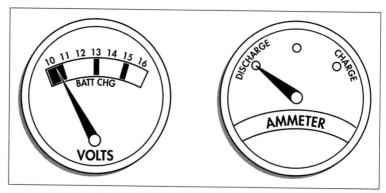

Figure **24-13** When ammeter registers discharge or there is a low reading on the voltmeter, go to the first available truck stop for a mechanic's assistance.

Figure **24-14** Smoke coming from the exhaust pipe may
signal a dirty air cleaner, an overfueled engine, or a frozen
turbine. Shut down immediately.

Problem 12. Excessive smoke is coming from the exhaust pipe.
Possible systems involved

- Exhaust
- Fuel
- Turbo malfunction

Probable cause

- Dirty air cleaner
- Poor-grade fuel
- Return fuel line is blocked, bent, or squeezed together
- Fuel pump malfunction
- Engine overfueled

Note: These are some of the most common causes. There are a number of other
possibilities (see Figure 24-14).

Proper action

- If you smell oil from the turbo, pull over in a safe spot and shut down
  immediately.
- Call your maintenance department for instructions.

Troubleshooting Summary

A good troubleshooter knows his or her vehicle and its systems, uses common
sense, is always aware when driving, knows the company maintenance policy, does
not attempt to make repairs for which he or she is not trained, and keeps good
records.

EMERGENCY STARTING PROCEDURES

In this section, you will learn the safe way to start a truck that has a dead battery.
If a truck has an air starting system and has lost air pressure, it will also have to be
manually started. The correct method is explained in this section as well (see Figure 24-15).

Figure **24-15** Safety is your top priority when starting a truck with a dead battery.

Jump-Starting Dead Batteries

There are three things to always remember when **jump-starting** a truck that has a dead battery:

1. Observe safety rules.
2. Prepare the truck.
3. Properly attach the jumper cables.

Observe Safety Rules

- Shield your eyes or wear safety goggles.
- Do not smoke.
- Make sure the batteries of both vehicles are negatively grounded and carry the same voltage (use a 12-volt battery to charge a 12-volt battery).
- Keep battery acid away from your skin and clothing.
- Never jump-start a battery if the battery fluid is frozen.

Prepare the Truck

- Align the vehicles so the jumper cables will reach without strain. Do not let the vehicles touch each other.
- Set the parking brake and chock the wheels.
- Shift into neutral.
- Add distilled water to the dead battery if needed.

Hook up the Cables Properly

- Clamp one cable to the positive (+) pole of the dead battery.
- Clamp the other end of the cable to the positive (+) pole of the booster battery.
- Connect the second cable to the negative (−) pole of the booster battery.
- Attach the other end of the cable to the stalled truck's frame, engine block, or other metal part as a ground.
- Start the booster truck—always start the "booster" vehicle first.
- Start the disabled truck.
- Remove the cables in reverse order.

Note: Do not attempt to jump-start a battery unless you are qualified to do so. Improperly connected cables can result in engine damage.

Starting Trucks That Have Air Starters

To start a truck that has an **air starter,** there are fewer safety precautions necessary. You should remember, though, that it is never a good idea to smoke when checking over or working on a vehicle (see Figure 24-16).

Prepare Vehicle

- Align the truck with the charged air supply.

Hook up the Air Line Properly

When you are using a compressor, follow these steps:

1. Hook up an air line from the compressor to the glad hand of the disabled truck's air reservoir.
2. Fill the reservoir.
3. Start the disabled tractor's engine.

Figure **24-16** It is never a good idea to smoke when working on a vehicle.

When you are using another tractor, supply the air in this way:

1. Hook up an air line from one reservoir to the other.
2. Start the booster tractor's engine.
3. Fill the empty air reservoir of the disabled truck.
4. Start the disabled tractor's engine.

Chapter Twenty-Five
Handling Cargo

OBJECTIVES

When you have completed this chapter, you should be able to:

- Know the importance of handling cargo correctly

- Specify the driver's responsibilities in handling cargo

- Outline the carrier's responsibilities in handling cargo

- Describe methods of containing and securing cargo

- Identify the federal and state regulations that control how cargo is shipped

- Explain distribution of weight when loading cargo

- Describe the special handling certain materials require

KEY TERMS

49 CFR Part 166
Axle weight
Block
Brace
Bulkhead
Cargo retainer bars
Center of gravity
Chemtrec
Combined axle weight
Drum truck
Dunnage
FMCSR Section 392.9
Forklift
Gross combination
  vehicle weight rating
  (GCVWR)

Gross vehicle weight
  (GVW)
Hand truck
Hazardous material
Hazardous material
  shipping papers
Hazardous Materials
  Endorsement
Headerboard
Individual wheel weight
National Response
  Center
Pallet jacks
Placards
Tank Vehicles
  Endorsement
Tie-downs
Weight distribution

INTRODUCTION

Professional truck drivers must have more skills and responsibilities than simply driving a truck down the highway. Being able to properly handle and load cargo that will avoid damage in transit is an equally important skill for professional drivers. And properly loaded cargo will add to the operating efficiency of any rig.

Freight that is improperly loaded not only presents the possibility of being damaged in transit but is also a danger to the driver and to others who use the highway. An overloaded truck or a load that is improperly secured presents an enormous threat to safety, on or off the highway, and because of this, the FMCSR has set specific methods for securing cargo as well as specific vehicle weight limits for rigs.

This chapter discusses the correct methods for loading cargo and distributing the weight of the load evenly over all axles. You also will learn the basics of general freight. Information about cargo requiring special handling, such as liquids in bulk, livestock, and unstable loads, can be found in Chapter 22.

Most states have adopted these federal regulations as their state laws through the Motor Carrier Safety Assistance Program (MCSAP). Therefore, enforcement of these laws is now the duty of both federal and state officials.

IMPORTANCE OF HANDLING CARGO PROPERLY

You are hired as a professional tractor-trailer driver to handle cargo for a carrier or shipper or consignee. Without a doubt, carrying goods safely and efficiently—and as cheaply and as quickly as possible—is the backbone of this nation's trucking industry.

Americans have learned to rely on trucks to carry goods from manufacturers to the retail consumer outlet in the shortest possible time. They also know these goods will have the best chance of arriving safely and in the best condition.

Figure **25-1** The driver's responsibility begins at the point of loading and ends at delivery.

Today's tractor-trailer rigs have been designed to safely carry maximum payloads. They are built of strong, lightweight materials. To make good use of this equipment, drivers know how to protect their vehicles—and the roads and bridges they use—from costly damage. This chapter provides information in this area as well.

The **FMCSR Section 392.9** states that no person shall drive a motor vehicle unless the vehicle's cargo is properly distributed and adequately secured. No company, by law, should allow or require you to drive your vehicle unless the cargo is properly distributed and adequately secured.

Your responsibility for that cargo begins at the point of loading and continues until it has been delivered (see Figure 25-1). In the interim, you should take all precautions to prevent any claims for loss, theft, or damage of this cargo.

Remember that the only protection you, as a driver, and your company have against liability for cargo claims is your professionalism and your skill as a professional. Remember too most preventable cargo claims result from inadequate concern or effort on the part of the driver.

New Cargo Securement Standard

In February 2001, the Federal Motor Carriers Safety Administration (FMCSA) developed new guidelines for how certain cargo is tied down on flatbeds and in van trailers, including the fact that carriers should use more than one method to tie down cargo.

A 1992 accident that killed four people in New York State pushed the FMCSA to develop new guidelines for **tie-downs.**

During the morning rush hour outside of Buffalo, a tractor-trailer struck the median barrier, causing the trailer's tie-down chains to snap. Four 20-ton steel coils shot off the trailer, crushing three cars. From March 1990 to July 1993, 11 people died in similar accidents.

The FMCSR standard, which requires carriers operating in the United States, Canada, and Mexico to meet certain goals, provides some flexibility as well. The proposed tie-down standard:

- Recommends proper tie-downs for all possible cargo that might be transported on semitrailers, including intermodal containers not covered by Canadian rules. The rules cover logs, dressed lumber, metal coils, paper rolls, concrete pipe, intermodal containers, automobiles, light trucks and vans, heavy vehicles, equipment and machinery, flattened or crushed vehicles, roll-on/roll-off containers, and boulders

- Eliminates rules that chains or webbing used to secure cargo attach to the truck bed at a specified angle
- Makes a distinction between direct and indirect methods of cargo tie-downs
- Stresses the importance of using friction between the cargo and trailer deck as a supplement to tie-downs
- Requires drivers to inspect the load within the first 50 miles of travel rather than the first 25 miles, as stated by previous rulings

A recommendation that manufacturers must label tie-down equipment with working load limits was also being considered to take the guesswork out of load securement.

Fundamentals about Cargo Securement

A tie-down is used to apply pressure and then lock the tension in place to prevent the cargo from slipping, shifting, or falling off any commercial vehicle with a **gross vehicle weight** of 10,000 pounds or more. The working load limit is the lowest load limit for tie-down components or their anchor points, whichever is least.

In selecting ways to immobilize cargo, such things as size, shape, strength, weight, and characteristics of the cargo must be considered. Carriers must ensure that all tie-down parts are in good working order, and drivers must conduct a pre-trip inspection to meet the regulations of the Commercial Vehicle Safety Alliance and must reexamine and make adjustments to the load in the first 50 miles of the trip and periodically thereafter. A containment system must be used to stop any loose parts from falling off the rig.

The sum of the working load limit from all tie-downs must be at least 50 percent of the cargo weight. The restraint force needed for a direct tie-down is calculated by taking one-half of the working load limit of each securement device connected between the vehicle and cargo plus the working load limit of each direct tie-down that is attached to the vehicle or connects the cargo and vehicle.

Minimum requirements to prevent shifting using indirect tie-downs:

- For an article 5 feet long or less or 1,100 pounds or lighter: one tie-down
- For an article 5 feet long or weighing more than 1,100 pounds: two tie-downs
- For an article between 5 and 10 feet: two tie-downs
- For an article longer than 10 feet: two tie-downs plus an extra device for each additional article to 10 feet in length

Cargo placed side by side and secured by crossover, indirect tie-downs must be placed in direct contact with each other or prevented from shifting toward each other during transit. Tie-down edges must be resistant to abrasion, cutting, or crushing.

Items with special tie-down requirements include logs, lumber (such as building material as well as packaged and dressed lumber), metal, coils, paper rolls, concrete pipes, intermodal containers, motor vehicles weighing 10,000 pounds or less, heavy vehicles, equipment and machinery such as big-rig trucks and tracker vehicles, flattened or crushed vehicles, roll-on/roll-off containers, and large boulders.

A vehicle's wall, floor, deck, tie-down, anchor points, **headerboard, bulkhead,** stakes, posts, mounting pockets, and overall structure must be strong enough to hold cargo in place over acceleration forces.

Current Working Load Limit Rules for Tie-Downs and Accessories (Source: North American Cargo Securement Standard)

Grade 3 Chain

Sizes (in inches)	Working Load Limit (in pounds)
1/4	1,300
5/16	1,900
3/8	2,650
7/16	3,500
1/2	4,500
5/8	6,900

Synthetic Webbing

Width	Working Load Limit
1 3/4	1,750
2	2,100
3	3,000
4	4,000

Wire Rope

Diameter	Working Load Limit
1/4	1,400
5/16	2,100
3/8	3,000
7/16	4,100
1/2	5,300
5/8	8,300
3/4	10,900
7/8	16,100
1	20,900

Manila Rope

Diameter	Working Load Limit
3/8	205
7/16	265
1/2	315
5/8	465
3/4	640
1	1,050

Synthetic Fiber Rope

Diameter	Working Load Limit
3/8	410
7/16	530
1/2	630
5/8	930
3/4	1,280
1	2,100

Steel Straping

Width and Thickness	Working Load Limit
1 1/4 × 0.029	1,190
1 1/4 × 0.031	1,190
1 1/4 × 0.035	1,190
1 1/4 × 0.050	1,690
1 1/4 × 0.057	1,925
2 × 0.044	2,650
2 × 0.050	2,650

Friction Mats

A friction mat placed on the deck or between cargo must provide resistance against forward movement equal to 50 percent of the weight of the cargo resting on it.

Wooden Restraints

Ash, beech, elm, hickory, hard sugar maple, and oak are used as **blocks, braces,** chocks, cradles, **dunnages,** and wedges to prevent rolling or as high-pressure restraints. The wood must be strong enough to withstand being split or crushed by the cargo or tie-down. Their working load limit is required to be 50 percent or greater than the weight of the material to stop it from moving forward.

THE SHIPPER'S RESPONSIBILITIES

Whether the shipper is the originator or the pass-through for a shipment, they are responsible for packing and loading the cargo in a manner that will ensure safe transportation. And, in keeping with this responsibility, the shipper is responsible for determining whether any protective devices are required to ensure safe transport of the shipment.

If the shipper is unsure of what is needed to protect a shipment, the driver can make suggestions for packaging and protective devices.

Once the driver has an opportunity to size up the load, and if the driver sees that the packaging or protective devices for any shipment are inadequate, the driver should call the driver manager or dispatcher for help in resolving the problem. Under no circumstances should you argue with the customer about how they have chosen to package or ship the merchandise.

The shipper is also responsible for counting the cargo as it is being loaded. Once the cargo is loaded, the shipper is responsible for signing the bill of lading.

One question the driver will have for any shipment is, "Do I load, or does the shipper load the cargo?" The answer is, "The shipper will load the cargo, and at the end of the trip, the consignee will unload unless the driver is instructed otherwise."

THE DRIVER'S RESPONSIBILITIES

Although many drivers do not load or supervise the loading of the trailers they pull, they are still responsible for checking to see that all cargoes are properly secured. They also must check to see that the cargo's weight is evenly distributed over all axles (see Figure 25-2).

When loading cargo, the driver is also responsible for:

- Preparing a bill of lading if one has not been provided by the shipper.
- Counting the cargo. The driver must make sure his or her count matches the shipper's count. Never assume a count is correct until you have counted the cargo yourself. If the bill of lading says there are 24 boxes in the shipment, the driver should count to make sure there are 24 boxes loaded and ready to ride.
- Inspecting the cargo. Do not assume that preloaded cargo is undamaged. If inspection is not possible, notify the safety department where you work.
- Recording the condition of the cargo. If the cargo is in perfect condition or if you see something that is less than perfect, record it on the bill of lading and then notify your safety department. When necessary, take photos of the shipment. An accurate description and photos of preexisting damage helps reduce your liability in the event of a claim.

How to Conduct a Visual Check of the Cargo

Checking a flatbed or open trailer or the quantities in each compartment of a cargo tank is fairly easy. But if an enclosed van has locking security seals, a more creative method is needed. Your check of your cargo should include:

- A visual check of the springs and tires of your truck for signs of overloading
- Checking for any sagging or bowing of the trailer—also a sign of an overload

Figure **25-2** The driver is required to see that all cargoes are properly loaded and secured.

- Awareness of whether you have adequate power to move the rig
- General handling characteristics
- Checking for any leaks that could indicate damaged cargo
- Figuring the weight of the load by adding all the weights shown on the shipping papers

If the trailer is an open type or a van without seals or restricted access, the driver is responsible for checking the load for:

- **Weight distribution** (are heavy items loaded close together?)
- Heavy freight loaded high in the trailer or positioned where it could fall on other cargo during transport
- Fragile or hazardous material
- Loose freight not properly secured by holding devices or dunnage (a filler material loaded into empty spaces to keep cargo from moving or falling)
- Materials that are not compatible
- Regulated or restricted materials

The driver is also responsible for checking all parts necessary for hauling, containing, and protecting cargo. These may include:

- Tailgates
- Tailboards
- Doors
- Headerboards
- Tarps

Securing the Cargo

It is the driver's responsibility to make sure the cargo is secured properly (see Figure 25-3). Some things to keep in mind when securing the cargo or checking to make certain it is secure are:

- Follow shipper's instructions for protecting cargo.
- Use your experience, judgment, and common sense in securing cargo.
- You are responsible for securing cargo in a manner that will avoid all damage during transit.
- Call your driver manager or safety department if you are unsure of the best way to secure certain types of shipments.
- Do not leave the shipper until required tarping is complete.
- Loads should remain tarped at all times until they are delivered to their final destination.

Additional Driver Responsibilities

Delivery of the cargo on time and in the same condition in which it was loaded is a major responsibility. To do this, avoid sudden stops and starts, and drive curves and on-ramps carefully.

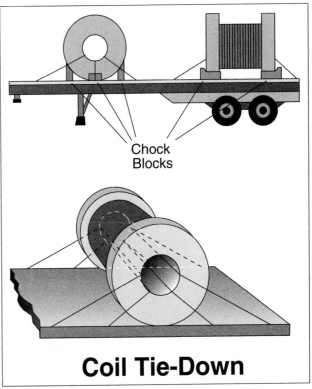

Chock Blocks

Coil Tie-Down

Figure **25-3** Cargo must be secured to prevent shifting or falling during transit.

Remember, you must stop within the first 50 miles of your trip and then every 3 hours or 150 miles thereafter to check your load and all securing devices. For security reasons, never discuss your cargo on your CB radio. Follow up on possible overages, shortages, or damage as soon as you become aware of it—and always notify your safety department.

Certain hazardous materials may need special equipment or protection from the weather as specified in **49 CFR Part 166.** Some states also require additional equipment to guard against falling cargo. Drivers of trucks hauling loose cargo in dump trailers, log and lumber trailers, or pole trailers should know all federal, state, and local requirements that apply.

THE CONSIGNEE'S RESPONSIBILITIES

The consignee, or the receiver, is responsible for unloading, counting, and inspecting cargo. They are then responsible for noting any overages, shortages, or damages on the delivery receipt. To signify that they have received the shipment, they must also sign your delivery receipt. Do not refuse to allow them to note any cargo damages, shortages, or overages on the delivery receipt.

THE DRIVER MANAGER'S RESPONSIBILITIES

The driver manager or safety department is responsible for instructing drivers in the use of protective devices to protect loaded cargo.

The customer will determine what devices are needed, and the driver manager will relay any required instructions to you prior to your departure.

Note: The driver is responsible for a nonsecured load whether or not the manager instructs the driver.

REGULATIONS

In order to load a tractor-trailer correctly or to inspect one that has already been loaded, you must know the regulations. All drivers are responsible for knowing and complying with federal, state, and local laws. Knowing the law helps promote safer operation of heavy trucks and tractor-trailers.

Federal Regulations

The FMCSR Section 392.9 protects a driver from driving a truck that is not correctly loaded or does not have the load secured properly. You cannot drive, and your company cannot make you drive, any truck unless:

- The cargo is properly distributed and secured as specified in Sections 393.100 to 393.106 of the FMCSR.
- Equipment, such as tailgates, tailboards, doors, tarps, and spare tires, are available and secured.
- The cargo is loaded so it does not interfere with the driver's vision, safety, or control of the truck.
- The driver has easy access to emergency equipment.
- The driver and passengers can readily get out of the cab, and no exits are blocked by cargo.

Except for trailers that have had the doors sealed or are loaded in such a way that you cannot see the load, the driver must do the following:

- Check the vehicle before driving it to be sure the cargo is properly distributed and secured, the vehicle components are secure, and the cargo does not interfere with operating safety.
- Check the cargo and adjust the securing devices within the first 50 miles of the trip.
- Check and adjust the cargo and securing devices when any of these conditions occur: change of duty status or completion of 3 hours or 150 miles of driving (whichever happens first).

State Regulations

As well as adopting federal regulations for safe handling of cargo, many states have their own laws. States regulate the gross weight of vehicles that travel their intrastate highways. A rig that never leaves a state must follow its regulations. The federal regulations set a gross vehicle weight for interstate hauling. The laws limit both the gross vehicle weight and the weight for each axle. Many states also require a cover on loose loads, such as sand, gravel, and crushed stone. This is to keep the cargo from blowing out and damaging cars or leaving debris on the highway. Know the laws of all the states in which you will drive.

SECURING CARGO

Federal regulations for protecting cargo from shifting or falling require specific methods of tie-down, blocking and bracing, and vehicle construction.

To keep cargo from falling or shifting, the law requires a trailer to have both sides and ends or enough tie-downs to hold the cargo in place. The following are specifics required to securing all types of cargoes.

Dunnage

Dunnage is often necessary to secure cargo in a trailer. It helps keep water-sensitive cargo from making contact with the trailer floor, and for this reason, it must be used on some specific loads, such as steel.

Be sure to inspect any dunnage you use for quality and make sure you have the means to secure the dunnage to the floor of the trailer. When using dunnage, place it in such a manner that it will support the total weight of the cargo you are securing. If you do, make sure it is properly tied down in the trailer when not in use.

Since dunnage is not always available at the shipper's location, it is a good idea to carry dunnage with you at all times.

Securement Devices

The FMCSR 393.102 (b) states the number of securement devices used to secure the cargo is determined by the weight of the cargo. This weight will include the weight of both individual items and the total weight of the shipment.

To determine the working load limit, make the following calculation. For example, a coil of steel weighs 36,000 pounds. To determine the number of straps needed for a secure tie-down, divide the working load limit of a 4-inch strap into 36,000. This will indicate you will need a minimum of nine straps to secure this cargo:

The working load limit of 5/16 chains is 4,700 pounds.
The working load limit of the 2-inch strap is 2,000 pounds.
The working load limit of the 4-inch strap is 4,000 pounds.

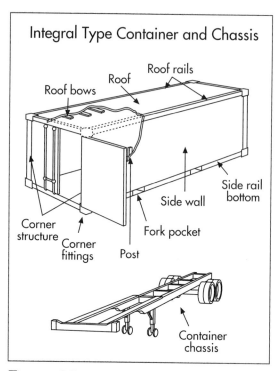

Figure **25-4** Intermodal cargo containers must be firmly locked onto the trailer's chassis.

Certain types of cargo—metal pipes, coils, bars, rods, sheets, slabs, and ingots—must have special tie-downs.

Intermodal cargo containers, like those taken from a ship and placed on a trailer, must be firmly locked to the trailer's chassis so they cannot move or accidentally come unfastened (see Figure 25-4).

Federal laws also specify the types of devices that may be used to tie down freight and will also specify the minimum strength of the devices. Devices that may be used are hooks and chains, binders, nylon and metal straps, ropes, and cables.

Remember: When only two chains are required on a coil, they must be crisscrossed through the eye of the coil.

Be sure you know the state laws for securing freight in those states you will be traveling. For example, Indiana requires three securing devices for every ten feet of bed space, and California requires three securing devices for every six feet of bed space.

Note: Using extra binders or straps may take more time, but the extra time may save someone's life—maybe your own.

Front-End Structures on Trailers

Federal laws require trailers to have a headerboard between the cargo and the driver. Van trailers satisfy this requirement if the front wall of the trailer is strong enough to protect the driver if the load shifts.

Flatbeds, log trailers, and similar types of trailers must have a headerboard or enough height and width to keep the cargo from shifting forward. The laws specify the strength requirements. Some tractors may have protective devices instead of a headerboard. Car carriers with vehicle tie-downs do not have to have headerboards.

Blocking and Bracing

Federal regulations set the standards for keeping loose cargo from moving (see Figure 25-5). Devices used to secure cargo include (see Figure 25-6):

- Blocking: Pieces of wood nailed to the floor
- Dunnage: Filler material, such as sheets of plywood, padding, inflatable bags, etc., used to fill voids in the load
- Bracing: Pieces cut to fit and nailed or otherwise secured
- **Cargo retainer bars**
- Built-in lockable bulkheads
- Use of freight to prevent movement of other freight
- Tie-downs
- Cargo netting
- Shrink-wrapped pallets

Handling Iron and Steel

When loading and hauling cargo of iron and steel, there are several points to keep in mind:

- **Vehicle weight:** It is not unusual for the total gross vehicle weight to be close to the legal limits. Be careful to distribute the load so your tandem weight is legal.
- **Chains:** Use the correct number of chains to secure the cargo. Plan on using at least one chain for every five feet of cargo. Never use one chain for a single coil or bundle, regardless of weight.
- **Edge protectors:** Use edge protectors to protect the cargo. Edge protectors are used to protect the steel from being gouged by the chain. There is no excuse for a cargo claim for neglecting to use edge protectors.

Action Load Locking Bars for Vans

Vertical load locking bars

Feet are mounted on 360° swivel ball joints

Blocked load prevents shifting

Horizontal load locking bars

Horizontal load locking hoops
(Slip over the ends of lock bars above)

Figure **25-5** Federal regulations set standards for securing cargo with various devices.

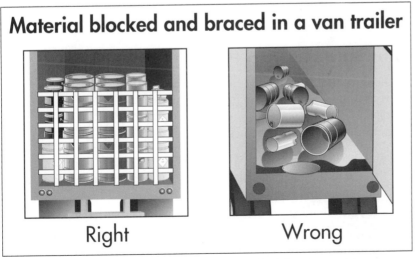

Material blocked and braced in a van trailer

Right   Wrong

Figure **25-6** Time taken to correctly block and brace cargo prior to departure will save valuable time later.

- **Dunnage and tarps:** Use dunnage and tarps to protect the cargo. It is extremely important to prevent steel from coming in contact with moisture and steel-to-steel contact. Dunnage helps protect the steel from those conditions. Always use dunnage to secure coils and beneath plate steel. (Coils on pallets do not require dunnage.)

Cargoes of Sheet and Plate Steel

Sheet and plate steel are sensitive to moisture and road contaminants and must be well protected during transit. To protect this form of steel, place dunnage at proper intervals to support the load and seal any leaks.

When working with sheet and plate steel, remember to leave a few gaps in the plastic or paper for ventilation. Then wrap the tarps around the load. Always protect steel in this order: paper, under tarp, and tarp over steel.

Place 2 × 4s to seal tarps to the trailer deck. Do not put nail holes in the tarps, as you are usually the one who will be responsible for repairing any tarps with nail holes.

Hauling Structural Steel

Structural steel will normally require only chains to secure the load. But it is recommended that you use edge protectors to guard against chain damage. You should also use enough 4 × 4 dunnage to support the load.

Remember: Use one chain for every 4,700 pounds of cargo and space chains so you are in compliance with the state laws along your route.

Loading and Hauling Coils

When transporting coils, it is required to block each coil to limit forward, rearward, or lateral movement. Use 4 × 4s as bracing blocks and connecting timbers for each coil.

Use 2 × 4 supporting blocks and connecting timbers, and use penny nails to secure the timber, driving them at an angle toward the coil. Also, make sure the coil is not resting on the trailer floor. Load coils with the eye toward the front and rear of the trailer, except when specified by the shipper or consignee.

The number of chains required to secure coils is determined by the total weight of the coil or coils. Use one chain or binder for every 4,700 pounds of weight. Never use only one chain on a single coil.

Determine the total number of chains needed by dividing the working load limit by the weight of the coil or coils—and always protect the coil as you would a steel plate: paper, under tarp, and over tarp.

Loading and Hauling Pipe

Some companies transport a wide range of pipe, including plastic, steel, concrete, and asbestos. Many companies encourage using the "belly-wrap" technique to secure the pipe.

The basic steps for using the belly-wrap are:

- Place a series of dunnage across the trailer.
- Directly behind the dunnage, place at least three chains across the trailer in the front, center, and rear.
- After the pipe is loaded, secure the load to the trailer with chains.

Remember, follow state laws regarding required distance between securing devices. If necessary, use chain softeners to protect pipe from chain damage.

- Wrap the front and rear belly chain around the cargo and secure the chains.
- Wrap and secure the center belly chain around the cargo.

Unloading Belly-Wrapped Pipe

When unloading belly-wrapped pipe, remove the load-securing chains, starting with the center chains. Release the belly-wrap chains, front and rear. After the load is secured by a **forklift,** crane, or loading equipment, release the center belly-wrap chain.

Handling Plastic Pipe

Plastic pipe is slippery and will shift frequently during transit if not properly secured.

Note: Do not depend on handling to secure any part of the load.

Carry extra dunnage and rope when dispatched for a load of plastic pipe. Protect the pipe from chain and rope damage. A smoke tarp is mandatory when transporting plastic or other lightweight, large-diameter pipe.

Pipe stakes are required when hauling heavy pipe in lengths of 20 or more feet. They may be required for plastic and fiberglass pipe as well. Generally, the shipper will not load pipe unless the required pipe stakes are in place.

Always check with your driver manager or dispatcher when dispatched to determine if pipe stakes are required. The dunnage required to separate layers of pipe should be required by the shipper.

Note: It is always a good idea to carry dunnage.

The FMCSR 393.103 requires that your tractor or trailer be equipped with a structure to prevent pipe from sliding forward into the cab area.

Tie-Down Devices

Several types of tie-down devices may be used to secure cargo. The load may need any one of these devices or a combination of several. It is important to choose the right type. It must be strong enough to hold the load in place. You also must be able to adjust it during transport (see Figure 25-7).

You must know how to keep the cargo from moving around or falling off. You should also know the working load limits for chains, cables, ropes, straps, and binders (see Figure 25-8 and Table 25-1). Never exceed the manufacturer's ratings. Federal laws require chains used as tie-downs to meet the specs set by the National Association of Chain Manufacturers. Hooks, binders, and connectors must be at least as strong as the chain required. Steel straps must also meet federal specs. Table 25-2 (page 25-18) shows the advantages and disadvantages of different types of tie-down devices.

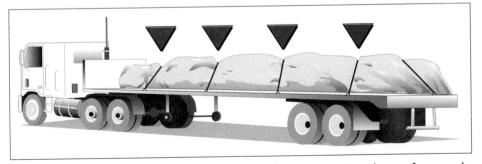

Figure **25-7** Cargo should have at least one tie-down for each 10 feet of cargo. Make sure you have enough tie-downs to meet this need. No matter how small the cargo is, there should be at least two tie-downs holding it.

Lever- or ratchet-type binders used with strong chains are the strongest and most easily adjusted means of securing cargo.

Ratchets and winches used with strong nylon strapping provide an adequate, easily adjustable cargo tie-down for loads such as lumber, gypsum board, plywood, or other cargo that can be damaged by chain tie-downs.

DOT OUT-OF-SERVICE CRITERIA FOR LOAD MANAGEMENT

The following are points covered by roadside inspectors regarding how cargoes are loaded and those loading errors that could cause a rig to be put out-of-service:

- Spare tire or portion of load/dunnage could fall from vehicle.

- Fitting for securing container to container chassis solely via corner fittings (for intermodal freight) is improperly latched.

- 25 percent or more of type/number of tie-downs required by FMCSR 393.102 are loose or missing.

- 25 percent or more of required type or number of tie-downs are defective.

- Chain is defective if working portion contains knot or damaged, deformed, or worn links. Clevis-type repair link, if as strong as original link, is okay.

- Wire rope is defective if working portion contains kinked, birdcaged, or pitted section; over three broken wires in any strand; over two broken wires at fitting; over 11 broken wires in any length measuring six times its diameter (e.g., with half-inch thick rope, more than 11 broken wires in any 3-inch section); repairs other than back or eye splice; or discoloration from heat or electric arc.

- Fiber rope is defective if working portion contains burned or melted fibers, except on heat-sealed ends; excessive wear, reducing diameter 20 percent; any repair (properly spliced lengths are not considered a repair); or ineffective (easily loosened) knot used for connection or repair.

- Synthetic webbing is defective if working portion contains a knot; more than 25 percent of stitches separated; broken or damaged hardware; any repair or splice; overt damage; severe abrasion; cumulative for entire working length of one strap, cuts, burns, or holes exceeding width of 3/4 inch for 4-inch-wide webbing, exceeding width of 5/6 inch for 3-inch-wide webbing, or exceeding width of 3/8 inch for 1 3/4-inch-wide or 2-inch-wide webbing. Multiple defects confined to one strand of a strap are not cumulative (just measure largest single defect in that strand).

- Load binders or fittings that obviously are cracked, worn, corroded, distorted, or discolored from heat or electric arc.

- Evidence of wire rope slipping through cable clamp.

- Anchor point on vehicle displays: distorted or cracked rails or supports, cracked weld, or damaged or worn floor rings.

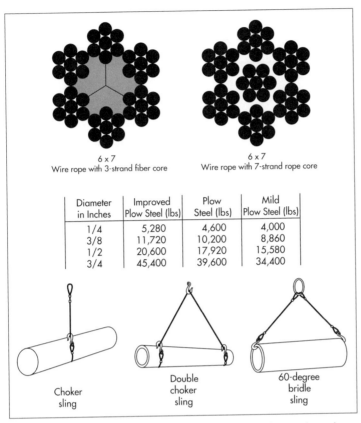

Figure **25-8** Approximate safe working loads for some types of wire ropes.

Table **25-1** Approximate Safe Working Loads for Various Fiber and Synthetic Ropes

Size in Inches (Diameter)	Manila (First Grade) (lbs)	Filament (Nylon) (lbs)	Filament (Dacron) (lbs)	Poly-ethylene (lbs)	Poly-propylene (lbs)
1/4	60	360	240	210	250
3/8	135	800	520	420	540
1/2	265	1,460	900	720	900
5/8	440	2,180	1,380	1,080	1,320
3/4	540	3,120	1,900	1,400	1,600
7/8	770	4,280	2,520	1,900	2,150

Note: Protect ropes from moisture, dragging in sand or grit, and from exposure to sunlight and chemicals. When not in use, they should be coiled and put in dark storage with good air circulation. If a wet rope becomes frozen, do not disturb it until completely thawed out, or frozen fibers will break when subjected to bending.

COVERING CARGO

There are two basic reasons for covering cargo: to protect the cargo and to prevent spills of loose cargo (see Figure 25-9).

Carriers use covers to protect the cargo because they:

- Keep metal from rusting
- Prevent damage to fiberboard containers

Table **25-2** Evaluation of Tie-Down Devices

Type	Advantages	Disadvantages
Nylon rope	Easily installed and adjusted	Stretches and becomes loose
Wire rope	Very strong	Difficult to handle
Web (nylon) straps	Strong, lightweight, easily adjusted	May become frayed or cut by sharp edges
	May be used with ratchet or winch assemblies	Sunlight rots nylon fiber
	Inexpensive and easy to store	May not be used to secure steel machinery or certain metal products
Steel straps	Good for securing boxes on pallets or wooden crates on vehicle	No means of adjustment during transport
		Vibration can cause failure
		Straps over 1 inch wide need two pairs of crimps
		May cut into cargo and become loose
Hooks and chains	Strong and durable	May damage cargo if too tight
	Readily available	Not of equal strength for rated load
	Hooks may be replaced and easily checked	
	Easily adjusted during transport	

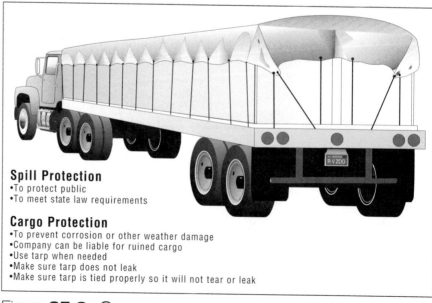

Spill Protection
• To protect public
• To meet state law requirements

Cargo Protection
• To prevent corrosion or other weather damage
• Company can be liable for ruined cargo
• Use tarp when needed
• Make sure tarp does not leak
• Make sure tarp is tied properly so it will not tear or leak

Figure **25-9** Cargo covers.

- Keep loads such as bagged cement from being destroyed
- Keep cargo that can absorb water from welting
- Cut down on claims for damaged freight

    Carriers want to keep cargo from spilling because:

- They want to protect both the company and the driver from liability for any injury or damage caused by spilled material.
- There are laws against littering.
- Many states have laws that require cargo covers.

Types of Coverings

The most common coverings are called tarpaulins, or tarps. There are many durable, lightweight materials that can be used for covering loads. The most common tarp materials are:

- Cotton canvas
- Rubberized or plastic coated canvas
- Nylon or other synthetic fabrics
- Polyethylene
- Vinyl
- Plastic coated paper with fiber plies

    For long hauls and continued use, a tarp should be of good quality and in good repair. Short trips or a one-time use may permit use of a less expensive tarp that is not as durable.

    You must store and maintain tarps that are used a lot to prolong their life. If tarps are not cared for, they may mildew and rot. If the tarp is a good one, it is expensive to replace.

    Federal laws require tarps to be properly tied down (see Figure 25-10). They cannot obscure the driver's vision or the lights on the vehicle. Always tie a tarp snugly in place. Ballooning or flapping in the wind can damage a loose tarp. Check tarp tie-downs often.

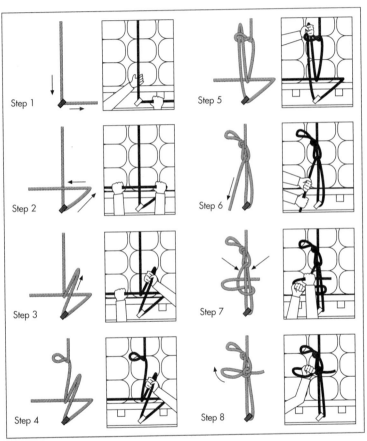

Figure **25-10** Trucker's draw hitch.

Tarps

Tarps will be needed to protect much of the cargo you haul. So be sure to have enough tarps to cover a load that measures 8 by 14 by 42 feet.

    Worn tarps or tarps with holes offer little or no protection. Make sure to inspect your tarps regularly and that they are functional.

    If you do not have enough tarps to protect your load, contact your driver manager. Remember, it is always better to buy protection with tarping than to pay a damage claim.

    Do not secure the edges of tarps to the outside of the trailer rub rail. This allows grime and moisture to get under the tarp.

Note: Loads of plastic pipe always require a smoke tarp covering the forward openings.

C A U T I O N :

Winds can be very dangerous when installing tarps, so always:

1. *Consider the wind direction.*
2. *Consider the strength of the wind or expected gusts.*
3. *Secure tarps in a sequence that minimizes risk.*
4. *Get help and avoid injury.*

Figure **25-11** When you accept freight, you become responsible for the safe delivery of that shipment.

ACCEPTING AND LOADING FREIGHT

When you accept freight for your trailer, you become responsible for safely delivering the load in good condition (see Figure 25-11). Always inspect cargo for:

- The condition of the packages
- Any leaking contents
- Broken palettes or torn shrinkwrap
- The proper container for the material
- Proper quantities as listed on the shipping documents
- Compatibility with the other freight
- Identification marks and addresses
- Weight: Will the rig be overweight?
- Identification of any hazardous materials
- Any packages marked glass or fragile

Bring any damage or inaccurate counts to the shipper's attention at once. Usually there is a company policy on accepting such shipments. Contact your supervisor when in doubt about accepting any shipment.

Loading Cargo

Always chock the trailer wheels, put the tractor in gear, and put on the parking brake while loading or unloading. If the loading dock has a dock lock, you may not need to use wheel chocks. Never attempt to load freight on your trailer without the proper tools. Some common tools for loading cargo are described in the sections that follow.

Figure **25-12** Operate only fork lifts on which you have been personally trained and certified. It is an OSHA (Occupational Safety and Health Administration) regulation.

Forklifts

Forklifts are used for loading pallets or heavy objects. Listed next are some basic rules for using forklifts (see Figure 25-12).

- Do not operate a forklift unless you are qualified to do so.
- Make sure the forklift is rated for the load.
- Check the overhead clearance.
- Operate the forklift carefully.
- Use dockboards when they are available to bridge between the loading dock and your trailer.
- Do not damage the freight with the forks.
- Do not raise it higher than you have to.
- Avoid tilting it. You might drop the freight.
- Do not damage the trailer.

Pallet Jacks

Pallet jacks are used for loading palletized cargo. They are similar to a forklift, only smaller. Use the same safety rules you would use if you were operating a forklift.

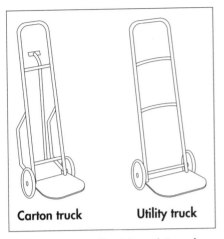

Figure **25-13** Hand trucks make carrying small loads easy.

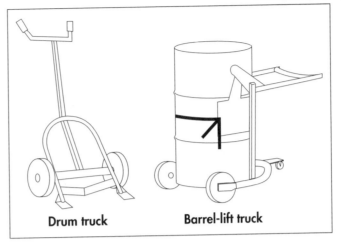

Figure **25-14** Use a drum truck to move a drum too heavy to handle.

Cranes and Hoists

Cranes and hoists are often used to load cargo. The following are some details you have to watch so you will not get hurt or the cargo will not be damaged:

- Check the load rating of winches, cables, chains, and so on.
- Never exceed the rated load.
- Do not stand under raised cargo.
- Provide protection in case the chain or cable breaks and whips around.
- Never drop freight roughly on your trailer.

Hand Trucks

Hand trucks are often used to carry small loads from the trailer to a storage area (see Figure 25-13). There are certain safety rules you must follow when using them:

- Never stack the boxes so high that they obstruct your vision.
- Do not stack the boxes so high that they can topple over.
- Use ramps or dockboards between the trailer and the dock.
- Never load an object that is too big for the hand truck.

Drum trucks. Never roll drums to load them. Use a **drum truck,** and secure the locking strap. Do not try to move a drum alone that is too heavy for you to handle (see Figure 25-14).

Levers. Use levers or Johnson bars to lift the edges of crates and so on. Use care so you will not damage the freight (see Figure 25-15).

Hand tools or hooks. Do not damage the outside packaging. Learn to identify fragile cargo. Use tools only for the purpose for which they were designed.

Note: For more information on proper lifting techniques, see Chapter 26.

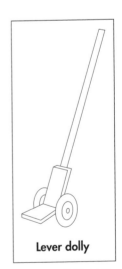

Lever dolly

Figure **25-15** Use a lever dolly to lift the edges of crates.

HAZARDOUS MATERIALS

Hazardous material is any material that may pose a risk to health, safety, or property while being transported. It is sometimes called "hazmat." Materials and substances that have been designated as hazardous are listed in Title 49 of the Code of Federal Regulations (49CFR). They should be handled and transported only by trained and qualified persons.

This section will teach you the basic requirements for transporting hazardous materials. If you are employed by a carrier to haul hazardous materials, they must provide additional training. In addition, you will have to obtain the **Hazardous Materials Endorsement** for your CDL (see Figure 25-16). If the hazardous material is carried in a tanker, you will also need the **Tank Vehicles Endorsement** on your CDL.

If you work for a carrier that does not haul hazardous materials, you must be able to identify such shipments so you will not accidentally load them.

Hazardous material is classified by hazard class. There are nine hazard classes. Some of the classes are further broken down into divisions. Each hazard class has requirements for labeling containers. The hazard classes are listed here.

Hazard Classes

Class 1: Explosives

Division 1.1   Explosives (with a mass explosion hazard)
Division 1.2   Explosives (with a projection hazard)
Division 1.3   Explosives (with predominantly a fire hazard)
Division 1.4   Explosives (with no significant blast hazard)
Division 1.5   Very insensitive explosives; blasting agents
Division 1.6   Extremely insensitive detonating substances

Class 2: Gases

Division 2.1   Flammable gas
Division 2.2   Nonflammable compressed gas
Division 2.3   Poison gas
Division 2.4   Corrosive gases (Canadian)

Figure **25-16** CDL with Hazardous Materials Endorsement.

Class 3: Flammable and combustible liquid

Class 4: Flammable solids; spontaneously combustible materials; dangerous when wet

Division 4.1   Flammable solid
Division 4.2   Spontaneously combustible material
Division 4.3   Dangerous when wet material

Class 5: Oxidizers and organic peroxide

Division 5.1   Oxidizer
Division 5.2   Organic peroxide

Class 6: Poisonous material and infectious substances

Division 6.1   Poisonous materials

Division 6.2   Infectious substance (etiologic agent)

Class 7: Radioactive material

Class 8: Corrosive material

Class 9: Miscellaneous hazardous material

Some hazardous materials, when they are packaged in small quantities, may be shipped as "consumer commodities" and are not required to display hazard class labels. Examples of "consumer commodities" are some paints, hair spray, drain cleaners, cleaning products, and all aerosols. Be alert for packages marked "Consumer Commodity ORM-D." Use care in handling and loading.

Some classes of hazardous material cannot be shipped together in the same vehicle. There are charts you can use as a guide when you load different classes of hazardous materials so you will not make a mistake.

For example, packages with a flammable solid label cannot legally be transported in the same vehicle with explosives. Packages with poison labels cannot be shipped in the same vehicle with food intended for humans or animals, unless they are packed in special containers.

Shipping Papers

Hazardous materials require special shipping papers. Items must be identified by the proper shipping name, hazard class, identification number, and packing group.

Hazardous material shipping papers must be in clear view and within the driver's reach when driving (see Figure 25-17). When the driver is not behind the wheel, the papers must be on the driver's seat or in the driver's door pouch. These papers may be inspected by officials at any time.

Carefully check shipping documents to see if any hazardous materials are in the shipment before you load freight. *Refuse to carry placarded loads of hazardous material if you do not have a Hazardous Materials Endorsement on your CDL (see Figure 25-18).*

Loading and Unloading

Federal laws require special handling for certain hazardous materials.

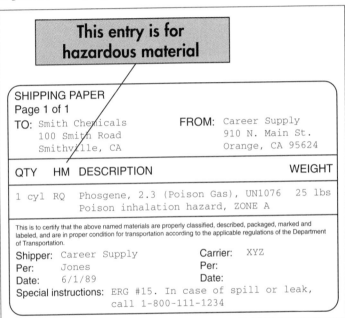

Figure **25-17** Hazardous material shipping papers must be within the driver's reach when driving.

Figure **25-18** Refuse to haul a hazmat load if you do not have the Hazardous Materials Endorsement on your CDL.

Figure **25-19** Hazardous materials must be properly marked, labeled, and loaded.

No smoking while loading or unloading explosives, flammable materials, or oxidizers. Keep anyone away who is smoking or carrying lighted smoking materials.

Tanks, barrels, drums, cylinders, or packages containing flammable liquid, compressed gas, corrosive materials, poisonous materials, or radioactive material must be secured so they cannot move while being transported. Valves and fittings must be protected from damage (see Figure 25-19).

Hazardous materials cannot be loaded into a trailer unless the parking brake is set. The truck must not move, so the wheels must be chocked. Do not use any tools to load or unload hazardous materials that may damage the containers.

Certain hazardous materials may not be transported in trailers with cargo heaters. If your trailer has a heater, check the regs before loading any hazmat.

The truck's engine must be shut off before you can load explosives or flammables. Explosives may not be transported in certain types of vehicles, such as doubles containing certain other hazardous materials. Check the inside of the trailer to be sure there are no nails or projections that can damage the containers of explosives.

Tightly close or cover packages and make sure they do not leak before hauling explosives, corrosives, oxidizing materials, or flammable solids. Batteries and corrosive acids must be specially stacked. Securely lock, box, and rack cylinders of compressed gas. Protect the valves from damage.

Trailers that have carried certain poisons or radioactive material must be thoroughly cleaned before they can be loaded with other freight.

Accidents or Spills

Whenever you have a spill of any hazardous material, federal regulations require you to make certain reports. Notify your supervisor at once if you have an accident involving a spill of hazardous materials. Follow the instructions your company gives you (see Figure 25-20). Keep on-lookers away. In some cases, you may even have to notify **CHEMTREC** or the **National Response Center.**

NATIONAL RESPONSE CENTER   CHEMTREC

Chemical Emergency

Figure **25-20** In case of accident or spill, follow company policy and instructions.

Figure **25-21** When refueling, be sure your engine is shut off—and do not smoke.

Figure **25-22** Federal laws specify when and where placards must be placed.

Refueling

When you refuel your truck, be sure the engine is shut off. Federal law says that it must be. Do not smoke. The person who fills the tank is to be in control of the nozzle or pump (see Figure 25-21).

Tires

When hauling hazmat in a trailer that has dual wheels, you must stop the truck in a safe place and check all tires at least once every two hours or after 100 miles of travel.

If you find an overheated tire, remove it and place it a safe distance from the truck. Inflate any tires that need it. Change any tire that is flat.

Placards

Federal laws specify when **placards** must be displayed on vehicles transporting hazardous materials (see Figure 25-22). They are 10 3/4 inches square and turned upright on a point in a diamond shape. The placards must be securely attached to all four sides of your vehicle and the hazard class or UN number readable from all four directions.

Shippers must furnish placards when they are needed, but you are responsible for putting them on your trailer. Check the shipping papers and package labels to determine if placards are required for the load.

Note: Placard holders must be empty when hazardous materials are not being transported. "Drive Safely" in a placard holder is illegal.

Driving

Certain highways are off limits if you are hauling hazardous materials. Often tunnels and bridges prohibit any vehicle loaded with these materials from using them.

Before you start a trip, make sure you will be permitted to travel on your intended route. It is your responsibility to obtain any needed permits. Avoid heavily populated areas, bridges, tunnels, and narrow streets and roads.

VEHICLE WEIGHT

Today's tractor-trailers are designed to safely, efficiently, and economically carry heavy payloads. The horsepower, gear ratios, and brake systems of these vehicles have improved greatly in recent years.

Increased use of the public highway system in America has made it more difficult for state and federal engineers and maintenance crews to keep up with the wear and tear on road surfaces and bridges. Very heavy wheel and axle loads can cause severe damage to deteriorating bridges and road surfaces (see Figure 25-23).

Cargo loads that exceed the manufacturer's weight limits for vehicles and tires can damage parts or even make new equipment unsafe:

- Tires may overheat and blow out.
- Springs, bearings, or the suspensions may break.
- Frames and couplers may break.
- The rig may not accelerate safely to operating speeds.
- Brake systems may fail.
- Steering control may be affected.

Figure **25-23**   Very heavy wheel and axle loads cause severe damage to roads and bridges.

Limits on the weight and size of vehicles vary from state to state. Federal guidelines and federal grant programs for highways have tried to make these state requirements uniform. Some states have lower limits than others. Check the regulations for each state you will drive through. Violations for the truck's being overweight are often expensive and can reflect on your driving record (see Figure 25-24).

Officials can detain an overweight vehicle. They may make the driver offload or redistribute the weight in addition to fining him or her. A rig that is detained for an overload results in great expense for the trucking company. It also means a late delivery to the customer.

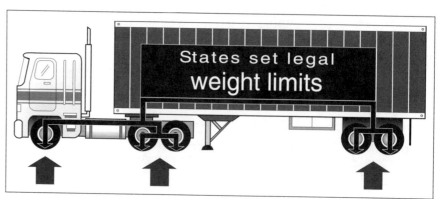

Figure **25-24**   Each state sets its own weight and length load limits.

Weights are usually checked in the following ways.

Individual wheel weight. **Individual wheel weight** is usually checked by state or local officials with a portable scale that measures the load on each wheel. Wheel weights are then checked against the permitted load for the tire.

Axle weight. **Axle weight** can also be checked with a portable scale. The weight of each wheel on an axle is recorded. The weights are then added to find the axle weight. At weigh stations, drive each set of axles on the scale to measure the axle weight.

Combined axle weight. Tandem or triple axles can have a different weight per axle than a single axle. To find the total **combined axle weight,** add the weights of all the axles. You can also find the total weight by driving the whole rig onto the scale platform.

Gross vehicle weight. **Gross vehicle weight (GVW)** is the total weight of a straight truck and load.

Gross combination vehicle weight rating. **Gross combination vehicle weight rating (GCVWR)** is the total weight of a tractor, trailer, and load. Local or state officials may check the GCVWR by weighing each wheel or axle individually and adding the total or by having you drive the entire rig onto the platform scale to be weighed as a unit.

There are more restrictions placed on short, heavy rigs for wheel, axle, and gross weights. The reason is because the total load is distributed over a shorter surface. This increases the stress placed on bridges and other highway structures. If you pull a heavy cargo in an intermodal container on a short trailer or chassis, you may exceed the weight limit for a bridge.

Some states are testing "smart" weigh stations that electronically weigh trucks that pass over a set of specially designed sensors.

Manufacturers' warranties and liabilities may be affected if you exceed the rated weight for each part. Limits include the following:

- **Tires:** Maximum load at specified inflation
- **Suspension system:** Maximum for spring assembly
- **Axle weight:** Rated weight for single or combination
- **Fifth wheel:** Maximum pull weight
- **GCVWR:** Recommended gross weight

DISTRIBUTION OF WEIGHT

If the weight is not distributed properly, the rig will be harder to handle. Distribution of weight on a tractor depends on the location of the fifth wheel:

- With a single rear axle, it should be slightly in front of the axle.
- With a tandem rear axle and a stationary fifth wheel, it should be slightly in front of the tandem center line.
- With a tandem rear axle and a sliding fifth wheel, the last notch of the slider adjustment should be just ahead of the tandem centerline.

With a movable fifth wheel, move it forward, and the load shifts more to the steering axle(s). Move it back, and the load shifts to the tractor drive axle(s).

You can make the rig handle differently by the way you distribute the weight. When the load is moved forward, the rig will handle better and give you better cornering. If too much weight is shifted forward, you can lose traction on the rear axles and have hard steering. When you move a load forward, be careful not to exceed the legal weight limits for the front axle.

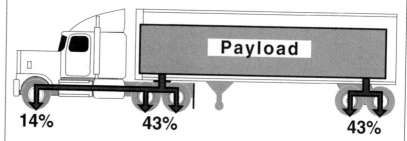

Weight Distribution on Tractor and Trailer

Payload

14%   43%   43%

Example of a Well-Balanced Load

Tractor
- Distribute weight properly over axles
- Weight distribution depends on position of fifth wheel
  - Single axle - slightly forward of centerline
  - Tandem axle
    - Stationary - just ahead of centerline
    - Sliding - last notch of slider adjustment
    - Fifth wheel moved forward
      - More of load shifted to front axle

Trailer
- Divide load evenly between front and rear
- Adjust load to meet axle weight limitations
  - Heavy freight on bottom
  - Properly distributed

Figure 25-25 It is the driver's responsibility to see that each load is balanced and weight is distributed evenly over all axles.

Figure 25-26 Too much weight on the steering wheel axle can damage the axle and tires and cause hard steering.

Weight shifted too far back causes light steering with poor control. It can also overload the drive axles (see Figure 25-25).

Distribution of weight in a trailer is just as important. Use care when you load the cargo. Distribute the weight as evenly as possible between the trailer's rear axle(s) and the tractor's drive axle(s) (see Figure 25-26). If you are pulling double trailers, center the weight on the converter dolly.

When you load the trailer be sure to:

- Find out the total weight of the cargo.
- Load half in the front and half in the rear (if possible).
- Spread the load evenly over the floor from side to side to prevent shifting.
- Keep heavy freight as low as possible. This will help to keep the vehicle's **center of gravity** low.
- Spread out any heavy cargo to prevent concentrated stress on the trailer floor (see Figure 25-27).

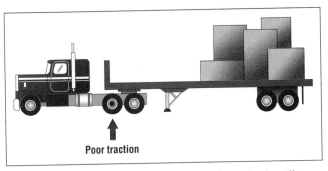

Figure **25-27** How cargo is loaded will impact the rig's overall traction.

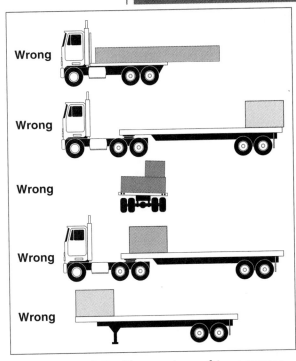

Figure **25-28** Examples of improper weight distribution.

- Do not load heavy objects where they can fall on other freight.
- Move the heavy freight as needed to keep the weight evenly distributed after part of the cargo has been unloaded (see Figure 25-28).
- The weight can be adjusted in trailers with sliding rear axles by moving the axle.
- Slide the axle forward to shift more weight to the trailer axle and off of the tractor drive axle.
- Slide to the rear position to shift the most weight to the tractor drive axle.

With sliding axles or fifth wheels, be aware of the Bridge Formula laws that dictate axle spacings. On interstate highways and on some state routes, you are required to have certain axle spacings to haul maximum allowable weights.

High Center of Gravity

Some vehicles have a high center of gravity (see Figure 25-29). This means the weight is carried high off the road. Such rigs are top heavy because they carry hanging loads, such as meat; tiered loads, such as livestock; or liquids in bulk, such as milk or gasoline.

They require special loading and driving techniques.

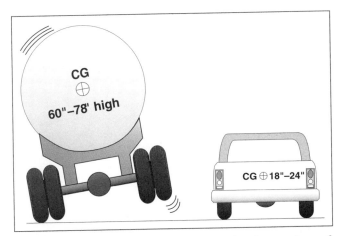

Figure **25-29** Vehicles with a high center of gravity, such as tankers, can easily turn over.

Chapter Twenty-Six

Cargo Documentation

OBJECTIVES

When you have completed this chapter, you should be able to:

- Check the shipping documents to verify the cargo and quantity to be shipped

- Check documents for compliance with the law

- Understand the legal terms of shipping contracts

- Explain how drivers can protect themselves and their companies from loss claims

- Specify how shipping document copies are to be distributed

- Explain what possession of the papers means

- Discuss the documentation and communication requirements for hazardous material shipments

KEY TERMS

Agent

Bill of lading

Collect-on-delivery
(COD) shipments

Common carrier

Connecting carrier

Contract carrier

Delivery (terminal) carrier

Delivery receipt

Detention time or
demurrage

Documentation

Dunnage and return

Exempt Commodity
Carrier

For-hire carrier

Freight bill

Freight broker

Freight forwarder

Hazardous materials
shipping paper

Hazardous waste
manifest

Helper service

Household goods bill of
lading

Identification (ID) number

Inside delivery

Interline carrier

Invoice

Labels

Manifest

Motor carrier (carrier)

Order notify bill of lading

Order notify shipment

Originating (pickup)
carrier

Packing slip

Placards

Prepaid shipments

Private carrier

Pro numbers

Receiver (consignee)

Residential delivery

Security seals

Shipper (consignor)

Storage and delay
charges

Straight bill of lading

Tailgate delivery

Through bill of lading

Transportation charges

Uniform straight bill of
lading

Warehouse receipt

INTRODUCTION

The **documentation** that accompanies shipments serves many purposes. Its most important use is to provide an accurate record of the cargo (see Figure 26-1). In some cases, it also serves as a contract for transportation services. As a professional driver, you must be able to understand the terms and content of the shipping documents and your legal responsibilities.

How important is your understanding of documentation?

If you do not understand how to properly prepare and handle the papers, you may be liable for civil or criminal penalties if there is cargo loss or shortages, damage your reputation as a professional tractor-trailer driver, be fired from your job, or endanger public health and safety by not properly communicating the dangers of hazardous materials cargo.

DEFINITION OF TERMS

To better understand certain words used by the shipper, carrier, or the person to whom the delivery is made, you will need to know specific terms and exactly what they mean. The following terms have special meanings when referring to the trucking industry:

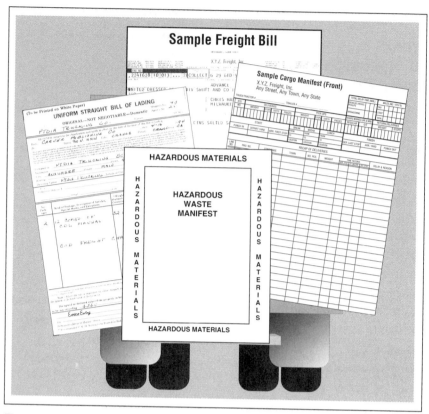

Figure **26-1** Documentation must be accurate because it often serves as a record of the cargo.

Shipper (consignor). The person or company who offers the goods for shipment.

Receiver (consignee). The person or company to whom the goods are being shipped or consigned.

Motor carrier (carrier). The person or company that is in the business of transporting goods. In this chapter, carrier may mean:

- **Private carrier**
- **For-hire carrier**
  - **Common carrier**
  - **Contract carrier**
  - **Exempt commodity carrier**

Freight broker. A person or company that arranges for transporting freight.

Freight forwarder. A person who gathers small shipments from various shippers and puts them together into larger shipments. These shipments then may go to a break-bulk facility where they are broken down for delivery to the consignees.

Originating (pickup) carrier. The carrier that first accepts the shipment from the shipper.

Connecting carrier. Any carrier that transports freight to an interchange location and then transfers the cargo to another company to continue the shipment.

Delivery (terminal) carrier. The carrier that delivers the shipment to the consignee.

Bill of lading. A written contract between the shipper and the carrier for transporting a shipment. The paper that identifies all freight in the shipment, the consignee, the delivery location, and the terms of the agreement.

Straight bill of lading. A contract that provides for delivery of a shipment to the consignee. The driver does not need to get a copy from the consignee when the goods are delivered.

Order notify bill of lading. A bill of lading that permits the shipper to collect payment before the shipment reaches the destination. The driver must pick up the consignee's copy of the bill of lading before he or she delivers the shipment.

Through bill of lading. A bill of lading used for shipments transported by more than one carrier that has a fixed rate for the service of all of the carriers.

Manifest. A list describing the entire shipment on the vehicle.

Packing slip. A detailed list of packed goods that is prepared by the shipper.

Freight bill. A bill submitted by a common carrier for transport services. The freight bill contains much of the same information as a bill of lading. A copy usually serves as a receipt for services when signed by the consignee.

Delivery receipt. A paper signed by the consignee or an agent of the consignee accepting the shipment from the driver. The driver keeps the receipt as proof of delivery.

Warehouse receipt. A receipt kept by the driver to prove the shipment was unloaded at a warehouse.

Agent. A person or company that acts as the official representative of another, such as a consignee's agent.

Hazardous materials shipping paper. A bill of lading that describes hazardous materials by the proper shipping name, hazard class, identification number, and the quantity being shipped. This form must be legible.

Hazardous waste manifest. A form (EPA-8700-22) that describes hazardous waste and identifies the shipper, carrier, and destination by name and by the identification numbers assigned by the Environmental Protection Agency. The shipper prepares, dates, and signs the manifest. All carriers of the shipment must sign the paper. It must also be signed by the consignee. The driver keeps a copy.

TRANSPORTATION CHARGES AND SERVICES

Transportation charges are the fees for transportation services. They may also include payment for the goods shipped (COD shipments). It is very important to understand the terminology about the charges and payment for services. You must understand all the terms of each agreement to protect yourself from liability and personal expense.

Usually the cost for the goods in the shipment is agreed on by the shipper and the customer before the shipment is offered for transport. Sometimes the carrier will also have to collect the payment for the goods being shipped and return this

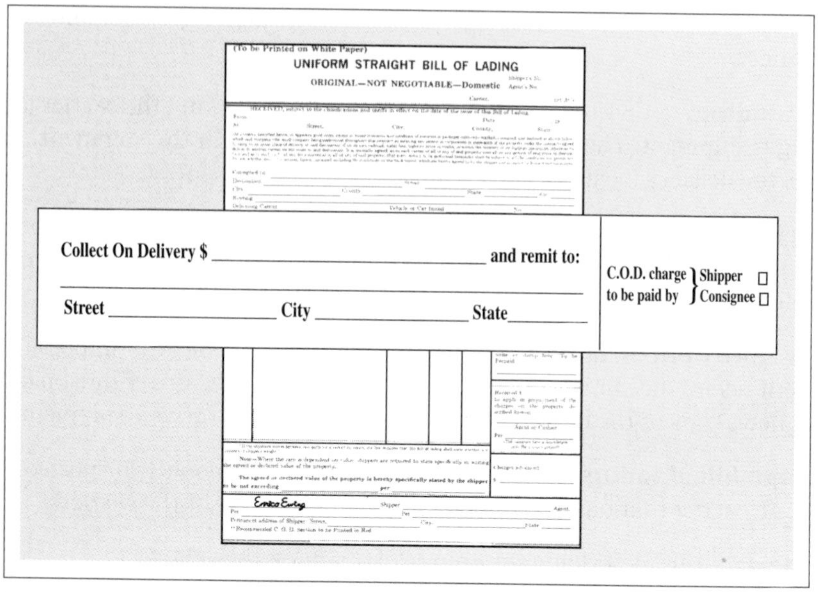
(To be Printed on White Paper)

UNIFORM STRAIGHT BILL OF LADING

ORIGINAL—NOT NEGOTIABLE—Domestic

Collect On Delivery $ ______ and remit to:

Street ______ City ______ State ______

C.O.D. charge to be paid by } Shipper ☐ Consignee ☐

Figure **26-2** On COD shipments, the driver must collect payment before the cargo is unloaded.

payment to the shipper. The shipper and carrier usually agree on the transportation charges before the freight is loaded.

Types of Payment

Prepaid. The transportation charges are paid at the shipping point.

COD. These are **collect-on-delivery shipments.** The driver must collect payment before the cargo can be unloaded (see Figure 26-2). The payment may be for the transportation charges only or also include the cost of the goods. A driver must know the company's policy for the types of payment that can be accepted, such as certified check, money order, or cash.

Note: You will not see a lot of COD shipments.

Order notify shipment. Payment for the goods is made when the driver gets a copy of the order notify bill of lading from the consignee. He or she must get the bill from the consignee before delivering the shipment.

In both prepaid and COD shipments, the bill must be signed and sent back to the carrier.

Transportation Rates

Charges for transportation are figured by multiplying the rate by the weight of the cargo and distance the load will be shipped. Rates are based on the value of the cargo and services performed by the carrier. It is important to understand that weights appearing on the freight bill may be true weights or an estimated weight of the cargo. If they are estimated, there could be a significant difference between the true and estimated weights—sometimes as much as 1,000 pounds.

The value of the cargo used for rate purposes is either the actual value of goods as shown on the bill of lading or the value shown on the bill of lading that is set by the shipper as the limit for carrier liability (see Figure 26-3).

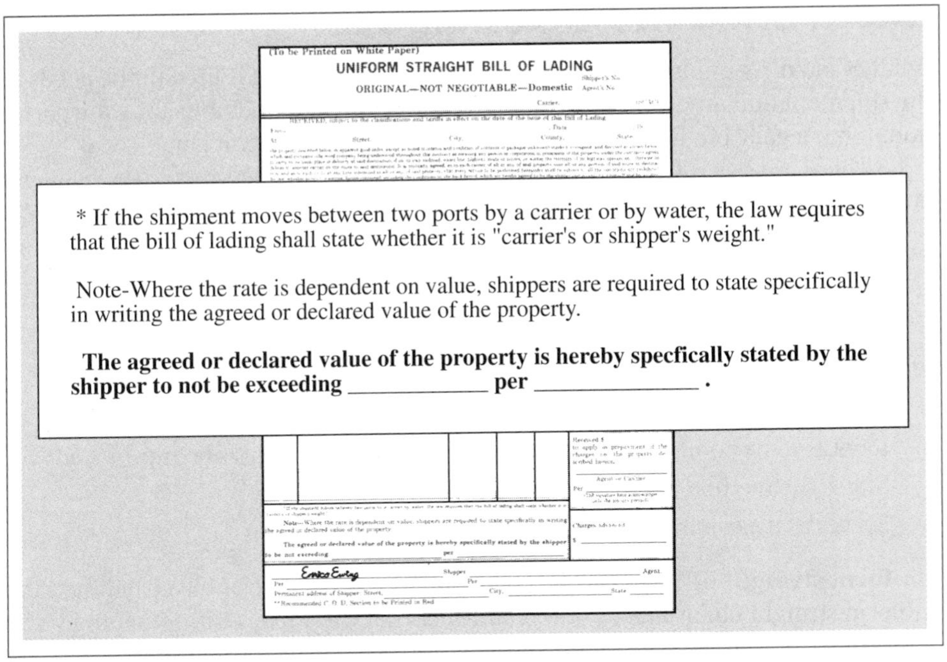
(To be Printed on White Paper)
UNIFORM STRAIGHT BILL OF LADING
ORIGINAL—NOT NEGOTIABLE—Domestic

* If the shipment moves between two ports by a carrier or by water, the law requires that the bill of lading shall state whether it is "carrier's or shipper's weight."

Note-Where the rate is dependent on value, shippers are required to state specifically in writing the agreed or declared value of the property.

The agreed or declared value of the property is hereby specfically stated by the shipper to not be exceeding ____________ per ______________ .

Figure **26-3** The value shown on the bill of lading limits the carrier's liability.

Services to be performed by the carrier are based on special handling requirements and tariffs. Tariffs are lists of services common carriers perform for the public and the rates charged for them.

Services and Surcharges

Rates for services and surcharges or additional charges are negotiated between the shipper and the carrier before the carrier accepts the shipment. Surcharges may include those for special services to be performed by the driver when delivery is made. You must know the meaning of the terms that describe certain services. The services should be clearly stated on the bill of lading.

Inside delivery. Indicates the freight is to be delivered inside instead of unloaded at the curb.

Tailgate delivery. The freight is unloaded and delivered at the tailgate (the back of the truck).

Helper service. A helper is to be provided for loading or unloading freight. The bill of lading specifies who will pay for the helper.

Residential delivery. The bill of lading will specify the address and method of collecting payment if the shipment is to a residence.

Dunnage and return. The weight of the dunnage will be listed on the bill of lading. If the shipper wishes it to be returned, this will be stated on the bill of lading.

Storage and delay charges. An additional amount to be paid to the carrier if a delivery is postponed by the consignee or shipper or a shipment must be stored before it can be delivered. These terms are stated in the bill of lading.

Detention time or demurrage. Detaining a vehicle beyond a given time. Payment is made to the carrier when delivery is delayed.

BASIC SHIPPING DOCUMENTS

A bill of lading is a contract between a shipper and a carrier. It lists all the goods in the shipment and any special handling requirements or conditions for transportation. It is a legally binding document that is regulated by federal law.

There are several different types of bills of lading, which serve the following purposes:

- Identifies the type and quantity of freight being shipped
- Shows the ownership of the goods
- States the value of the freight in case of loss or damage
- Establishes the rates and freight charges
- Serves as a legal contract
- Identifies the point of origin of the shipment and where it is being shipped
- States the method of payment for all charges
- Serves as a permanent record of the transaction

Uniform straight bill of lading.   The most common type of bill of lading is the uniform straight bill of lading. It is a contract that the parties cannot change. The goods must be delivered to the consignee or an authorized representative. There are usually three copies of the bill, distributed as follows:

- Copy 1 (original): Sent to the consignee
- Copy 2 (shipping order): Carrier copy
- Copy 3 (memorandum): Shipper copy

A uniform straight bill of lading (see Figure 26-4) will have the:

1. Motor carrier's name
2. Shipper's name
3. Date the goods were accepted by the carrier
4. The number of items in the shipment and a description of each
5. Condition of all packages or goods in the shipment
6. Space for the driver to note damage, shortages, or improper packing
7. Name of the consignee
8. Address to which the shipment is to be delivered
9. Routing, if more than one carrier will transport
10. Identification of connecting carriers, if any are necessary
11. Freight charges and the method of payment, such as COD or prepaid
12. Special handling or services
13. Signatures of the shipper and the driver as agents for the carrier. (The bill is not valid without signatures.)

Contract information will be detailed on the back of copy 2 in case the driver must check for specific duties on delivery.

Order notify bill of lading.   An order notify bill of lading is a special type of bill of lading. Ownership of the shipment can be transferred by the valid sale of this document. There will be three copies:

- Copy 1 (original): Yellow
- Copy 2 (shipping): Blue
- Copy 3 (memo): White

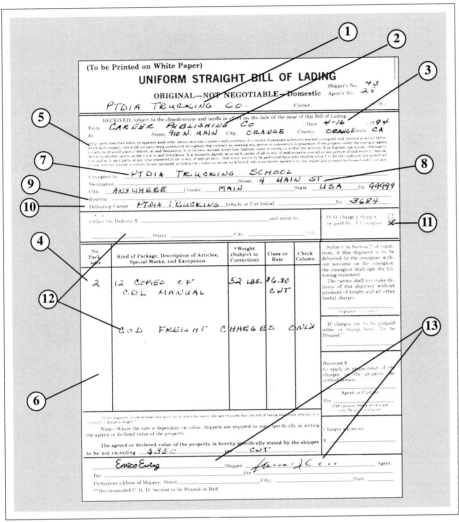

Figure **26-4** The uniform straight bill of lading must contain specific information about the shipment.

The information that describes the freight in the shipment will be the same as that needed for a uniform bill of lading.

The driver must check the back of the yellow page (original) to be sure it is signed by the shipper and any bank or financial institution that has paid the shipper.

If there is any question about the validity or proper preparation of the order notify bill of lading, contact the financial department or billing agent for your company.

The driver must not deliver any part of the shipment unless he or she has the original copy (copy 1) of the bill. After delivery, the original copy of the bill is given to the consignee. The holder of the order notify bill of lading is the legal owner of the freight.

Household goods bill of lading.   A **household goods bill of lading** is used by moving companies for their shipments. This type of bill serves as a legal contract between the shipper and the carrier. The household goods bill of lading lists the carrier and the customer. It is a combined bill of lading, freight bill, and record of the items in the shipment stating their appearance, their condition, and how they are packaged.

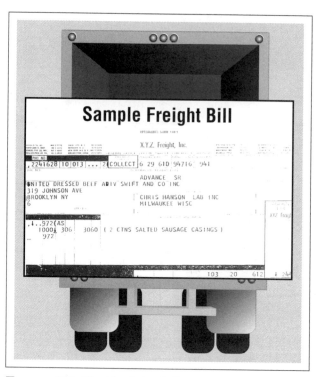

Figure **26-5** Freight bills are prepared by the carrier from the bill of lading.

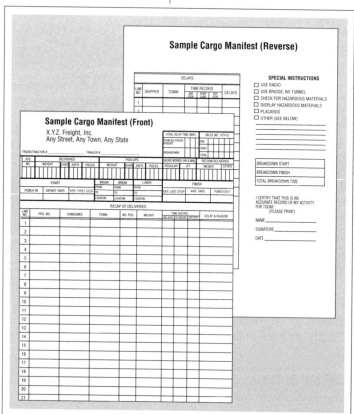

Figure **26-6** Drivers refer to cargo manifests as "pro bills" or "pro sheets" because the manifests list all freight bills.

Legal requirements for weighing a load with a household goods bill of lading differ from those for ordinary freight.

Freight bills. Freight bills are prepared by the carrier from the bill of lading (see Figure 26-5). Drivers are mostly concerned with copy 1, which serves as the delivery receipt copy. The driver must have the consignee sign the bill, showing that he or she accepts the shipment, before it can be unloaded.

The freight bill will tell the driver if the carrier charges are prepaid and there is a COD payment due on delivery.

Freight bills are usually preprinted with **pro numbers** (progressive numbers). The numbers are in front of the freight bill numbers. Often the driver will have to identify the bill by its pro number. Sometimes, drivers refer to cargo manifests as "pro bills" or "pro sheets" because the manifest lists all freight bills (see Figure 26-6).

Other Documents

Invoice. A bill from the shipper that lists the goods, prices, and total due. This may be mailed to the consignee, or the driver may have to give it to the consignee if it is a COD shipment.

Packing slip. A list of the total parts packaged in a shipment. The responsibility of opening packages and checking the contents against the packing slip belongs to the consignee.

DRIVER'S SIGNATURE AND RESPONSIBILITY

Your signature, as the driver, on a shipping document actually puts you and your company on the line. Never sign a shipping document unless you understand all terms and conditions completely. Be sure you compare all descriptions with the freight offered for loading.

Your signature on a bill of lading means:

- You and your company are legally responsible for fulfilling all the terms and conditions of the contract.
- You and your company agree to the methods and rates of payment for the services as stated.
- You and your company are responsible for delivering the articles in the quantities listed to the consignee, in good condition.
- You have inspected the shipment and found all items to be in good condition. The count is correct.
- You have noted any shortages, damages, or mistakes before signing the bill.

As a professional tractor-trailer driver, protect your reputation and your job by:

- Never taking the word of someone else for the freight count or the condition of the shipment. Always count the cargo yourself.
- Always observing the loading of cargo to ensure all pieces are loaded.
- Checking the descriptions on the packages against the bill of lading.
- Learning to quickly and correctly count palletized packages.
- Checking the address on the freight against the delivery address of the consignee to avoid loading the wrong cargo.
- Handling fragile goods properly when you load them. If they are loaded by others, watch out for rough handling and breakage.
- Never loading or permitting someone else to load leaking packages or drums. The leakage could damage other freight.
- Noting freight that is poorly packaged and could come out of the package during transport.
- Knowing the policies of your company for refusing damaged or incomplete shipments. If you accept these for shipment, it could result in freight claims.

PREVIOUSLY LOADED TRAILERS

Before signing a bill of lading for a shipment that was not loaded in your presence, inspect the load, if possible; check the bill of lading for incompatible freight, over-weight shipments, etc; and check the general appearance of the load for proper blocking and bracing.

If the trailer is sealed with a security seal or you cannot visually inspect it, make a note on the bill of lading "shipper's weight, load, and count." This releases you and your company from responsibility for any shortage or damage unless it is caused by an accident.

Figure **26-7** For trailers with security seals, record the serial number of the seal on all copies of the bill of lading.

Security Seals

For trailers that have been equipped with **security seals** by the shipper:

- Record the serial number of the seal on all copies of the bill of lading (see Figure 26-7).
- Note on the bill of lading "shipper's weight, load, and count."
- Check the seal to be sure it is properly locked. The serial number must match the number noted on the bill of lading.
- Have the consignee sign for the shipment on delivery before breaking the seal.
- If the seal is broken en route for inspection by enforcement officials, obtain their signature, badge number, and department and get a replacement seal.
- If the seal is broken en route by someone other than an enforcement official, notify your dispatcher or supervisor at once.

DELIVERY OF FREIGHT

When you deliver freight, remember you are responsible for the shipment until it is accepted by the consignee:

- Make sure delivery is to the proper consignee.
- Obtain the correct signature on freight bills, bills of lading, receipts, or other documents before you unload the shipment.
- Collect COD payments before unloading the cargo.
- Obtain the properly signed order notify bill of lading before you unload the shipment.
- Check to be sure the entire consignment is delivered.
- Any differences, shortages, or changes in the method of payment should be reported to your dispatcher or supervisor before you release the shipment to the consignee.
- Know your company policy on freight delivery problems.

INTERLINE FREIGHT

Pick up freight from an **interline carrier** in the same way you would from a shipper. Deliver freight to an interline carrier as if they were a consignee:

- Always inspect the shipment for damage or shortages.
- Compare the bill of lading with the freight.
- Do not sign freight bills, bills of lading, or receipts until you note any shortages or damages and they are signed by the interline carrier.
- Make sure you thoroughly understand any special services and the method of payment.
- Get signatures and receipts before you release the shipment to the connecting carrier.
- If there is an equipment interchange with the connecting carrier, know the policy of your company. Always follow the established procedures.

Remember, you are responsible not only for the freight but also for making sure the trailer is within legal limits. Check the weight of the shipment on the papers so you will not accept an overloaded trailer.

HAZARDOUS MATERIAL AND HAZARDOUS WASTE

Hazardous materials shipments must be specially labeled, prepared, handled, documented, and placarded.

Communication of hazards in transportation is vital to public health and safety (see Figure 26-8). If there is an accident or spill, police, fire, and emergency crews must be able to quickly recognize the presence of these materials.

As a professional driver, you must know how to recognize hazardous materials shipments and be aware of the dangers of each hazard class.

Shipper's Responsibilities

The shipper is required by federal law to:

- Train all employees involved in hazmat functions
- Identify all hazardous materials by hazard class
- Properly pack the material in the correct packaging
- Prepare the shipping papers, which list, in this order, the proper shipping name, hazard class, identification number, and packing group

Figure **26-8** All hazmat shipments must be specially labeled, prepared, handled, documented, and placarded.

- State the total quantity or volume of the material
- Properly label each package with the correct hazard class label if one is required
- Mark each package with the proper shipping name and identification number for the contents
- Provide placards for the carrier
- Provide the emergency response telephone number

Driver's Responsibilities

Drivers are required by federal law to be trained before they can accept shipments of hazardous materials. They may also need the hazardous materials endorsement on their CDL. A properly trained tractor-trailer driver has the ability as well as the legal responsibility to:

- Check the bill of lading for hazardous material cargo
- Make sure the shipping papers are complete and accurate
- Check the shipping papers to be sure the shipper's certification form is signed
- Check the packages for proper labeling and marking
- Check compatibility and segregation requirements for the materials
- Observe the special handling and loading requirements
- Properly placard the vehicle as required
- Comply with FMCSR

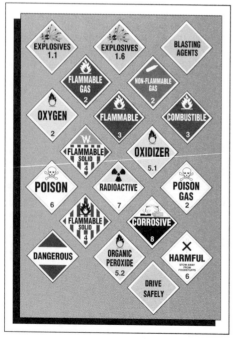

Figure **26-9** Placards must be displayed on each side of the vehicle.

Placards

Placards are diamond-shaped signs (10 3/4 inches on a side) that tell the hazard class of the shipment. They are similar in design to labels, except they are larger in size. They must be displayed on each side of the vehicle (see Figure 26-9). Placards communicate the hazard. From a safe distance, they tell others about the hazards aboard a trailer. This is important to emergency responders if the rig is in an accident or if there is a spill.

Because of changes in the hazardous materials regulations, two types of placards are being used by the trucking industry today.

Cargo tanks that have multiple compartments and are used for hauling hazardous material have special requirements for placards. When you haul these products, you must learn the special placarding regulations.

Placards must be visible on all four sides of the tractor-trailer and easily seen. Place them so the words and numbers are level and read from left to right. They must be at least three inches away from any other markings (see Figure 26-10).

Portable tanks and van trailers carrying bulk shipments that require placards and ID numbers must also have them on all four sides of the trailer.

The importance of placards to the safety of the driver, emergency responders, and the public is obvious. The driver has the legal responsibility to display the proper placards on the tractor and trailer when required and to remove them when hazardous materials are no longer aboard. Placards must remain on empty tank trucks and tank trailers until they are cleaned.

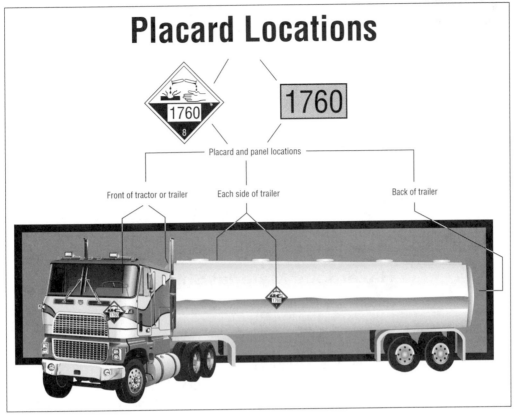

Placard Locations

1760

Placard and panel locations

Front of tractor or trailer

Each side of trailer

Back of trailer

Figure **26-10** Placards must be visible on all four sides of the tractor-trailer.

Labels

Labels and placards for each hazard class look very much alike (see Figure 26-11). Labels resemble small placards and must be placed on packages near the proper shipping name and identification number. You should have a chart that tells the proper color and format for each hazard class when you load freight. Some shipments of hazardous materials can be shipped as a consumer commodity, limited quantity, or small quantity and do not need labels on the package.

Federal laws require materials meeting the definition of more than one hazard class to display multiple labels.

As a professional driver, you must know the procedures for checking labels on packages.

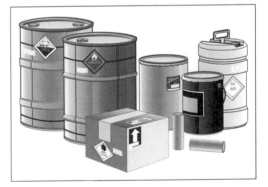

Figure **26-11** Labels and placards indicate the hazard class of each shipment.

Identification Numbers

All hazardous materials are identified by a four-digit **identification (ID) number.** The four-digit number is preceded by either the letters "UN" or "NA."

UN means the United Nations uses the number for that material worldwide. NA means that the number is used only in North America.

The ID number is used by emergency response crews and law enforcement to identify the material in the Emergency Response Guidebook so they can take the proper action at an accident.

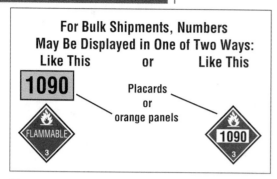

Figure **26-12** There are two ways of displaying numbers on bulk shipments.

ID numbers are required on all hazardous materials shipping papers. They must also be marked on all packages, along with the proper shipping name (see Figure 26-12).

ID numbers must be marked on two opposite sides of the following:

- Liquids: Bulk packaging with a capacity of over 118.9 gallons
- Solids: Bulk packaging weighing over 881.8 pounds
- Gases: Bulk packaging with over 1,000 pounds water capacity

ID numbers must be marked on all four sides of the following:

- Liquids: Bulk packaging with a capacity of over 1,000 gallons
- Solids: Bulk packaging of over 133.7 cubic feet

For bulk shipments, the numbers can be on orange panels with black numerals or on the required placard(s).

Hazardous Material Shipping Papers

Hazardous materials, when listed on shipping papers or bills of lading with other non-hazardous materials, must be clearly distinguished by one of the following methods:

- Listing the hazardous materials first on the paper
- Highlighting the entry
- Identifying the shipper with an "X" before the shipping name in the column titled HM (the letters "RQ" may be used instead of "X" if the shipment is a reportable quantity)
- Printing the entry in a contrasting color (see Figure 26-13)

When hauling both hazardous and nonhazardous materials together, the documents identifying the hazardous materials must be marked in one of the following ways:

- On top of all other papers
- Flagged with an easily recognized tab
- Enclosed in an envelope clearly marked "Hazardous Materials"

The shipping papers must be easy to see and find:

- When driving: Within the driver's reach with his seatbelt fastened
- Empty cab: Either on the driver's seat or in the pouch on the driver's door (see Figure 26-14)

The papers must be available for inspection by an official at any time.

Shipments must have emergency response information included. This information can be printed on the shipping papers or contained in another document attached to the shipping papers. The information should include the data about the material being shipped and an emergency response phone number.

Always remember to check all labels, markings, placards, and shipping papers to be sure they are correct. Any errors should be brought to the shipper's attention and corrected before the materials are loaded.

Because vehicles carrying hazardous materials cannot use certain highways, always check the shipping papers for special routing instructions (see Figure 26-15). If the driver plans the route, be sure to avoid restricted roads, bridges, tunnels, or heavily populated areas.

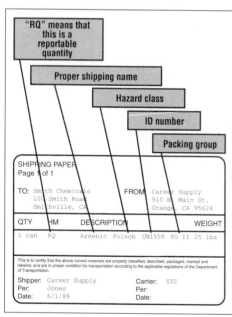

Figure **26-13** Hazmat shipping papers itemize the contents of a hazmat cargo and serve to inform drivers of any special handling requirements.

HAZARDOUS MATERIALS SHIPPING PAPERS

KEEP THIS ENVELOPE VISIBLE AND ACCESSIBLE

- While Drving - papers must be within driver's reach with seatbelt fastened.
- In Driver's Absence From Unit - Papers must be on driver's seat or in pouch on driver's door.

Date	Vehicle No.	Dispatched By	Classification of Hazardous Materials on Vehicle	Weight	Type of Placard	Applied By

IN CASE OF SPILL OR OTHER EMERGENCY CALL _____

Mark the location of each class of Hazardous Materials loaded
onto the vehicle on the Diagram below.
BEFORE GIVING TO DRIVER

DRIVER'S INSTRUCTIONS ON REVERSE SIDE OF ENVELOPE

Figure **26-14** Hazmat shipping papers must be within the driver's reach or on the driver's seat if the driver has left the truck.

HC

HAZARDOUS CARGO ROUTE

TO
395
SOUTHWEST
SOUTHEAST FREEWAY

HAZARDOUS CARGO PROHIBITED

Figure **26-15** Always check hazmat shipping papers for special routing instructions.

Chapter Twenty-Seven

Personal Health and Safety

FROM NOW ON. . .

ONLY THE BEST
WILL DRIVE!

OBJECTIVES

When you have completed this chapter, you should be able to:

- Understand why a truck driver's job demands good physical condition

- Describe the causes of and cures for fatigue

- Explain the FMCSR with regard to alcohol and drug use

- Describe the effects of fatigue and alcohol on the body

- Know the benefits of a good diet, exercise, and plenty of rest

- Identify danger zones for drivers and show how to use safety measures

- Describe how to lift objects safely

- Explain the value of the right protective gear in the prevention of injury

- Know and understand the causes of stress

- Show causes of accidents

KEY TERMS

Blood alcohol content (BAC)
Diet
Exercise
Fatigue
FMCSR 392.4

Judgment
Over-the-counter drugs
Perception
Prescription drugs
Stress

INTRODUCTION

As a professional driver, one of your greatest challenges will be staying healthy. This does not just mean eating the right **diet,** getting enough rest, getting **exercise** a few times a week, and avoiding **stress.** Staying healthy means doing all of this and anything else you can do to maintain good health, a positive outlook, and time for a satisfying career.

Today's drivers also need to avoid **fatigue** whenever possible, and professional drivers must avoid alcohol and drugs at all costs.

The FMCSR address alcohol, drugs, and fatigue, and you need to know what these laws say so that you keep your license and maintain your career and your paycheck.

The purpose of this chapter is to explain these laws and to give you information to help you be the best you can be behind the wheel, at home, and in all parts of your life.

PHYSICAL CONDITION

In order to be a professional driver, a person must pass a physical examination prescribed by the Department of Transportation (DOT) and get a certificate from a doctor every two years. This exam includes a vision test (see Figure 27-1).

Good vision is one of the most important physical requirements for driving. Being able to see well includes good side vision, color recognition, and night vision. Federal law says only that a driver must be able to see clearly, but night vision and glare recovery are also very important although not covered by federal laws. A driver must also hear well and have stamina.

A tractor-trailer driver must stay in shape to be able to drive safely and avoid the medical problems that could cause him or her to fail a physical exam. Plenty of rest and exercise are needed. Avoidance of drugs or drinking will help you be alert and in good health.

In 2000, the estimated life expectancy of a U.S. citizen was close to 74 years. That number, of course, depends on the health habits of the individual. A professional driver knows what has to be done to keep a truck running smoothly and to ensure a safe trip. Each part and each system contribute to keeping the vehicle operating safely (see Figure 27-2).

The same principle is true for the body. To keep the body healthy and running smoothly, the driver must have or else develop good eating habits, regular exercise, and the proper amount of sleep and must also have a plan to manage stress.

The Consequences of Poor Eating Habits

Meet Ralph. He has been a professional driver for 25 years. Driving was a second career for Ralph and helped him build a comfortable life for himself, his wife, and his two daughters.

Physical Requirements for Interstate Truckers

- Vision
  20/40 vision
  Peripheral vision—at least 70 degrees in each eye
  Distinguish red and green
  Eye check every 24 months

- Hearing
  Hear forced whisper at 5 feet

- Stamina
  To meet job requirements (e.g., loading and unloading)

- Disqualifications
  Loss of limb(s) or disease that limits limbs
  Chronic illness that seriously affects driving
  Examples:
  - Diabetes
  - Heart disease
  - Alcoholism

- Required physical examination
  Every 2 years
  At carrier's discretion
  After serious injury or illness

- Certification by physician
  Must be carried at all times
  As important as driver's license

Figure **27-1** Professional drivers are required to pass the DOT physical examination every 2 years.

Figure **27-2** Health habits make a difference in how you feel and how well you do your job.

Ralph has a new home, several acres of land, livestock, two daughters with college educations, and a couple of late-model vehicles in his driveway. Money is not a problem for Ralph and his family.

Several months ago, however, Ralph began noticing he was "running out of steam" before he could get home from his usual weekly trips. Often, he would have to stop in a roadside park and sleep a few hours just to make it home.

When Ralph was in high school, his friends called him "Skinny." A tour of duty in the military only built muscle. Today, Ralph is almost 60 years old and weighs 325 pounds.

His eating habits are not good. Many times he admits driving down the highway with a bag of chips, a bag of cookies, and a bag of candy, which he snacks on all day. By the time he stops for a meal, he is not hungry. When he is home, he and his wife usually go out to eat, and Mexican food is a favorite.

Ralph has never been one to go to the doctor, but his driver manager gave him the ultimatum—find out what is making you so tired, or plan to spend the rest of your career on the dock.

Ralph's doctor put it bluntly. He had developed diabetes, something all doctors look for if a patient is grossly overweight. Because of his weight, Ralph's heart was having to work so hard that he had developed congestive heart failure. And there were other problems as well.

After almost a month in the hospital and close to 3 months recuperating, Ralph is back in his truck, driving city pick-up and delivery (P&D) and he says he feels better than ever, thanks to a very strict low-fat, low-sodium diet; adding exercise to his daily routine; and taking medication after a balloon angioplasty and the insertion of a stent to open two of the major arteries to his heart.

"If I had known then when I know now, I'd never let myself gain the weight or abuse my diet," Ralph swears. "That doctor saved my life, and I plan to take better care of myself from now on."

Like Ralph, poor eating habits can be costly—and your poor eating habits can affect your alertness, reaction time, perception, overall driving ability, and health in later years.

The following are common poor eating habits:

- Eating foods high in fat content (an ounce of fat contains 2 1/2 times the calories as an ounce of protein or carbohydrates)
- Eating fried foods
- Eating breaded fried foods, such as fried fish and chicken-fried steak
- Eating gravies and sauces, as most have high fat content
- Eating too much salt
- Not eating enough vegetables and fruits
- Not eating enough foods high in fiber content
- Not drinking enough water (need 10 cups per day)
- Snacking on cookies and doughnuts

The following are suggestions for a good diet:

- Low fat. Many fast foods are high in fat and salt content
- About 2,000 calories per day for men and about 1,600 calories per day for women
- Follow the food guide pyramid
- Three to five servings of vegetables per day
- Two to four servings of fruit per day
- Six to nine servings of beans, cereal, rice, and pasta

- Two to three servings of milk, yogurt, and cheese
- Five to six ounces of meat

  Helpful hints for good nutrition:

- Reduce the amount of fast foods.
- Avoid fried foods.
- Eat roasted or baked meats.
- Remove the skin from chicken.
- Use nonfat spreads on breads and potatoes.
- Take a portable cooler or refrigerator on the road (more economical than restaurants). Breakfast from your cooler can include yogurt, banana, apple, and fruit juice. Snacks from your cooler can include fruit, such as apples, bananas, peaches, plums, grapes, and raisins; raw vegetables, such as celery, carrots, green or yellow squash, and bell peppers; low- or nonfat bagels; and diet drinks.
- Have a salad bar for one of your daily meals: eat vegetables and fruit; use nonfat dressings; avoid condiments, as they are often high in fat (potato and pasta salads are also high in fat). Many salad bars have baked potatoes and soups. Baked potatoes are a good choice (use nonfat dressing). Soups are another good choice, but avoid thick soups, such as chowder, because of the high fat content. Avoid desserts, as many are high in fat.

The Four Best Eating Habits

When you are out on the road, dealing with heavy traffic, careless four-wheelers, construction, and tight schedules, it is sometimes difficult to remember all this information about a good diet.

So if you will follow these four good eating habits, you will make a real positive impact on your health:

- No fast foods and not too much fat and salt
- No fried foods
- Breakfast and snacks from your cooler
- Salad bar for one meal each day

Exercise

To keep your body running as smoothly as your rig, you must have a total exercise program. A total exercise program consists of movement, strength training, and the development of flexibility.

Movement can be any activity that is done briskly. This includes walking, swimming, playing basketball, jumping rope, mowing the grass, hiking, playing golf, riding a stationary bike, or any number of other activities.

Rest

Truck drivers need to be alert and well rested. It is best for all drivers to avoid too much activity, parties, alcohol, and stressful situations during their off-duty time just before driving.

The FMCSR calls for 8 hours of rest before driving. Some people, of course, need more than 8 hours. Time off duty is not rest time if the driver has been partying, working hard around the house, and so on. Be sure to use your rest time resting.

Figure **27-3** Fatigue can be a
dangerous problem for professional
drivers.

FATIGUE

As a driver, you are responsible for your condition when you report for work. You
must do your best to stay rested. Fatigue can be a dangerous problem for truckers
(see Figure 27-3). It is the underlying cause of many accidents. Fatigue is often a
real problem for long-haul drivers who have irregular schedules.

Fatigue can be caused by:

- Lack of sleep
- Long, tedious tasks, such as long periods of driving
- Illness, even a cold
- Being out of shape or overweight
- Emotional problems
- A sleep disorder, such as sleep apnea
- Foods you eat

Fatigue usually occurs in the early morning hours, especially around 4:00
and 6:00. A fatigued driver loses some basic skills, such as **judgment,** the ability to
react, and **perception.**

Judgment. A fatigued driver will not recognize hazards and will tend to misjudge
clearances, gaps, and speed. He or she may not know how fast they are driving or be
able to judge the speed of others.

Ability to react. A fatigued driver may not be able to respond quickly to situations. He or she may not even realize they are reacting in slow motion.

Perception. A fatigued driver may distort the overall picture of the traffic situation. Depth perception is less accurate. He or she may misjudge speed and distance.
Normal reaction time is 3/4 of a second. If you are driving at 50 miles per hour, you
will travel 55 feet during that time. A driver who is fatigued may take a full second

to react. He or she will then travel 74 feet. Those 19 feet may make the difference in whether an accident can be avoided.

Fatigue can cause drivers to fall into "micro-sleeps." These are short unintended naps that may last only a second or so. Imagine what can happen if you are driving 30 miles per hour and you sleep for only 1/2 second. You will drive blind for 22 feet.

Fatigue also causes drivers to imagine they see hazards that really are not there: another vehicle, an animal, a tree or building, or even people. The driver then swerves to avoid the object and often loses control of the vehicle. This is a cause of many accidents.

Stress.   Stress increases the chance of fatigue. Causes of stress include:

- Tension on the job or at home
- Improper diet and lack of exercise
- Use of alcohol, cigarettes, or drugs
- Loneliness and boredom
- Worry
- Varied sleep patterns

How to Deal with Fatigue

The best way to deal with fatigue is to prevent it. If it does occur, you must recognize it and deal with it at once. You can cut the chances of fatigue if you get plenty of rest, eat the right foods, and get plenty of exercise. When you are on the road, try to remain active. If you become tired, stop and get some rest. Do not risk falling asleep at the wheel.

The major signs of fatigue are obvious. Your eyes get heavy and dull. Tired eyes mean a tired body and that fatigue is setting in. You may become cross and cranky. You may even feel unable or unwilling to do anything.

Fatigue and Myths

When you deal with fatigue, knowing what not to do is as important as knowing what to do. There are a number of things that have been guaranteed to ward off fatigue. Do not believe them. The most common myths are to:

- Open a window
- Turn up the radio
- Stop for something to eat
- Talk to someone
- Take a pill
- Have a drink
- Have a cup of coffee

Figure **27-4** The foods and beverages you consume each day contribute to fatigue.

Fresh air may actually lull a driver to sleep unless it is cold air. The sound of the radio may also lull you to sleep, even if it is loud. Eating a heavy meal actually increases the chances of falling asleep. Statistics show that many accidents occur roughly 30 minutes after a meal. After you eat, your body's circulatory system works hard to digest the food. This causes less blood to go to your brain, so it wants to rest (see Figure 27-4).

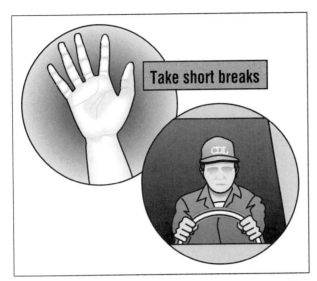

Figure **27-5** Short breaks or a nap will help ward off fatigue.

Pills do not halt fatigue. Nonprescription pills are illegal for drivers, and prescription medications should not be taken while on duty unless your doctor OKs it. Pills that keep you awake can be dangerous as they wear off.

It is against the law for a commercial driver to drink alcohol while on duty. Even if it were not illegal to drink and drive, alcohol is a "downer" and will put a driver to sleep. Though coffee may stimulate your system for a short period, it lets you down as it wears off. This increases your chances of falling asleep.

The Cure for Fatigue

So what should you do if you feel fatigue coming on? In a word, *sleep.* Sleep is the best solution. There is no substitute.

Pull off the road. Be sure you stop in a safe, legal place. Secure the vehicle properly. Get comfortable. Napping over the steering wheel is usually not helpful. Try to lie down and rest (see Figure 27-5).

If a nap does not rest you enough, stop driving. Pull into a rest stop or motel. Get the rest you need. Depending on your schedule, you may have to call your supervisor. If you are afraid you will be fired if you fail to keep up with your schedule, remember, it is better to lose your job than your life. It is even better to lose your job than to risk major losses because you fell asleep at the wheel.

Remember that air conditioning can help prevent fatigue. Keep the cab cool. Warm air can make you sleepy. Walk and stretch for a few minutes every so often.

ILLNESS

A person should not be on the road if they are ill or have an injury that interferes with their driving ability. Conditions that should keep a driver off the road include a heavy cold or allergy (these can cause drowsiness) and a painful, badly sprained ankle (this will prevent full movement of the foot).

FMCSR 392.3 states it is illegal to drive when impaired. Fatigue and illness are included as conditions that limit alertness and the ability to drive.

Table **27-1**   Myths and Truths about Alcohol.

Myth	Truth
Alcohol increases mental and physical ability.	Nonsense. It decreases both. A person under the influence of alcohol usually thinks he or she is doing better than they really are.
Some people can drink without being affected.	Not true. Any person who drinks is affected by alcohol. Some persons may be slower to show the effects because of greater body weight or experience.
If you eat a lot before drinking, you will not get drunk.	Not true. Food will slow down the absorption of alcohol, but it will not prevent it.
Coffee and fresh air will help a drinker sober up.	Not true. Only time will help a drinker sober up. Other methods just do not work.
Stick with beer—it is not as strong as wine or whiskey.	False. There is the same amount of alcohol in a 12-ounce glass of 5% beer, 5-ounce glass of 12% wine, or 1 1/2-ounce shot of 80-proof liquor.

ALCOHOL

We all know that drinking and driving is a serious problem. Each year, thousands of people are killed in accidents where a driver had been drinking.

There are a number of false beliefs about the use of alcohol. A person who believes these myths may be more likely to misuse alcohol. A few of the myths are shown in Table 27-1.

As a truck driver you should know how alcohol works in the human body, how alcohol affects your driving ability, the laws regarding the use of alcohol (FMCSR 392.5), and the legal, financial, and safety risks of drinking and driving.

How Alcohol Works

When a person drinks alcohol, it is rapidly absorbed into the bloodstream and carried directly to the brain, where it affects judgment, inhibitions, vision, coordination, and bodily functions. Unlike food, alcohol does not have to be digested before it is absorbed. The drinker can control the absorption rate by drinking slowly and spacing drinks. Having some food in the stomach will slow the absorption rate. See Figure 27-6.

The drinker cannot control the rate of elimination. Most of the alcohol (about 90 percent) is removed by the liver at the rate of about one drink per hour.

Alcohol collects in the bloodstream because it is absorbed faster than the drinker can get rid of it. The amount of alcohol in the bloodstream is measured as a percentage and is called the **blood alcohol content (BAC).**

The BAC is determined by the amount of alcohol consumed, the time it took to drink it, and the weight of the drinker.

Figure **27-6** All forms of alcohol have the same effect and can cause you to lose your CDL if you drink and drive.

Table **27-2** Effects of Alcohol as BAC Increases.

BAC	Effects
.01–.04	Judgment and inhibitions are slightly affected. Drinker is more relaxed, sociable, and talkative. Some risk if drinker drives.
.05–.09	Judgment, vision, and coordination are affected. Behavior changes. Drinker has false sense of security. Serious risk if drinker drives.
.10 and over (legal level of intoxication in most states)	Judgment, vision, and coordination are seriously affected. Drinker is not able to drive safely because of dangerously lessened abilities.

The faster you drink, the more alcohol your bloodstream absorbs. The more alcohol there is in your bloodstream, the higher your BAC. If there is food in your stomach, it will affect the BAC because it slows the absorption rate.

Alcohol and the Brain

As the BAC builds up, the brain's functions are affected more and more (see Table 27-2). The first parts of the brain to be affected are the higher-learning centers. These areas control judgment (common sense) and inhibition (control of your actions).

Muscle control, vision, and coordination are affected next. The drinker may feel he or she is performing very well when they are actually out of control.

Finally, bodily functions are affected. The drinker may even pass out.

As a person sobers up, the effects of alcohol disappear in the reverse order. Judgment is restored last.

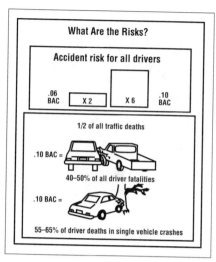

Figure **27-7** Alcohol risks for drivers.

Other Factors That Affect a Drinker

A person's mood, experience in drinking, tolerance of alcohol, and whether they are tired can affect the amount of influence alcohol will have on their body. If a person is angry or depressed, the alcohol may affect them more than usual.

People who usually do not drink generally have a very low tolerance for alcohol. They tend to show the effects quickly. Experienced or heavy drinkers may have a high tolerance. They may not appear to be affected, but they really are. If a person is tired, the effects of alcohol are quickly felt.

Alcohol and Driving

Alcohol has bad effects on judgment, vision, coordination, and reaction time. All are critical when driving, so there is an increased danger if you drink. Driving at the wrong speed, loss of lane control, and dangerous passing often happen (see Figure 27-7).

Sobering Up

The body requires about 1 hour to get rid of each drink. If you have more than one drink per hour, alcohol builds up in your system. Time is needed to clear the alcohol out of your system. There is no shortcut.

Alcohol and the Law

The alcohol regulations in FMCSR 392.5 state that:

- No person shall drink an intoxicating beverage or be under the influence of alcohol within 4 hours of going on duty.
- Driving while under the influence of alcohol is illegal.
- It is unlawful to drink any alcohol while on duty.
- A first violation can result in a 1-year disqualification. A second violation can result in a lifetime disqualification.

Figure **27-8** Use of alcohol or drugs can lead to traffic accidents, resulting in injury, death, or property damage. It can also lead to arrest, fines, jail sentences, and the end of a driving career.

Risks and penalties can be severe. Any time a vehicle is on the road, there is risk involved. If the driver is under the influence of alcohol, there is increased risk of accident and injury. Damage to the rig is more likely. Financial risks include fines and penalties, higher insurance rates, loss of license, jail sentence, and loss of job (see Figure 27-8).

DRUGS

Both legal and illegal drugs are common in our society. Many people take drugs under the direction of their doctors. Some individuals purchase **over-the-counter drugs** that can affect behavior. Tractor-trailer drivers must not take any substance that can bring on drowsiness or affect driving.

Every truck driver should realize that drugs, even those prescribed by a doctor, can have harmful effects on driving. One of the most common effects is drowsiness. Many cold and allergy over-the-counter remedies also have this side effect. Always check with your doctor before driving when using prescription drugs.

Some pills that are legally used to treat overweight people and severe cases of depression are misused by drivers to stay awake. They are nicknamed "bennies," "pep pills," or "copilots". They can increase alertness for a short period but can also cause headaches, dizziness, and agitation. Even worse, they may hide fatigue and keep a person from knowing how tired they are. In other words, if you take drugs, you may think you are alert and driving well when you really are not.

Also, it is often difficult to go without this type of drug. Fatigue is sometimes very severe, even overwhelming. A driver may have hallucinations, or visions, of something that is not there. Swerving into oncoming vehicles because of a vision is not uncommon.

Illegal Drugs

Some **prescription drugs** are sold illegally at or near truck stops. Marijuana, cocaine, heroine, LSD, and other illegal drugs are also widely available. Generally, people who buy drugs illegally have no idea what they are getting. Many times, they are contaminated, so the buyer cannot possibly know the side effects.

The best advice is to steer clear of drugs. Do not take chances. The risks are too great and the penalties too severe. Even if no accident occurs, the chance of losing your job, having a criminal record, being fined, or going to jail should be enough to cause any sensible trucker not to take illegal drugs.

Drugs and Alcohol

Combining drugs and alcohol can be very dangerous. The best policy is not to mix any drug with alcohol.

Tranquilizers and alcohol can, when used together, have multiple effects on the user. The combined effect of one pill plus one drink can be rapid and unpredictable. Blackout, rapid intoxication, and even death are possible. Again, read all labels carefully. If taking the drug and alcohol are listed as a bad mix, do not mix them.

The FMCSR and Drugs

The **FMCSR 392.4** prohibits driving while under the influence of any dangerous drug. These drugs include narcotics, morphine, heroin, codeine, and amphetamines.

The law does not prohibit possession and use of prescription drugs if a doctor has advised that it will not affect driving.

Drug Testing

As of January 1, 1996, all truck drivers must be tested for drugs.

Summary: Drugs and Alcohol

A professional driver is a safe driver. Anything that affects driving ability must not be used when driving. A driver who uses alcohol or drugs may be sued if an accident occurs. The driver's company can also be sued. A driver that uses drugs or alcohol can lose his or her job, reputation, and chance of future employment.

HAZARDS TO SAFETY

The need for safety equipment and safe practices while performing nondriving parts of the job cannot be stressed enough.

Many accidents and injuries happen while the trucker is working around the vehicle or with cargo. These nondriving accidents can be costly in a number of ways. They can even put the driver out of work because of an injury.

Safety Dress and Proper Equipment

Dressing properly for the job requires that the body be covered. Shorts, flip-flops, and T-shirts are not enough. Heavy denims offer the best protection. In cold weather, wear warm clothes.

Protect your hands.   Many hand injuries occur to truckers each year because there are so many hazards. Some of these hazards include sharp steel bands used to tie boxes and crates, nails, broken glass, and pointed wire; and irritating or corrosive chemicals.

Avoid wearing jewelry or rings because they can get snagged and cause serious injuries. Always wear gloves when handling cargo. Selecting the right gloves is important. Gloves should have a good gripping surface. Hazardous materials or

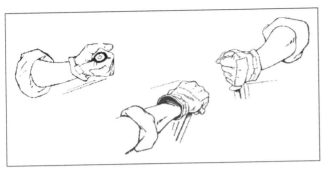

Figure **27-9** Protect your hands.

wastes usually require special gloves. Ordinary gloves may trap corrosives. Rubber or latex gloves do not (see Figure 27-9).

Protect your eyes. If you wear glasses, make sure they are shatterproof. Wear sunglasses to protect your eyes from glare. Be sure they are high quality and will filter out infrared rays. Protective goggles or a face shield are needed with some cargo. For example, goggles will protect your eyes when dealing with dust, flour, or cinders.

Protect your feet. Safety shoes protect your feet from falling objects. Steel-tipped shoes or work boots are best and required by some trucking companies. Do not wear sandals or tennis shoes.

Special Equipment

Some circumstances require special equipment. Special cargo like hazardous material or waste may mean you will need special equipment for protection. Find out what is needed and then use it properly. The special equipment needed may include the following:

- Hard hats to protect your head from chains and falling cargo at construction and delivery sites.
- Respirators to prevent being overcome by fumes when handling chemical loads and liquified chemicals. Some chemical loads require a self-contained breather (air supply). Find out what is needed. Take nothing for granted.
- Splash aprons to prevent liquids from splashing on your skin and causing burns.
- Goggles or a face shield to prevent severe eye damage from flying particles. Chemical face shields that have a splash guard may be needed for some acids or dangerous chemicals. Do not wear contact lenses. Fumes can get trapped under them and cause blindness.
- Dust masks to prevent respiratory problems when handling dry chemicals or similar loads. Some companies require drivers to be clean shaven with no facial hair so that dust masks and face shields will fit tightly.
- Shin guards that have heavy metal plates to protect the front of the leg and tips of the shoes from rolling steel bars.
- Special coveralls to protect the body from corrosives and other hazardous materials.
- Gas masks to protect from poisonous gases and other hazardous materials (see Figure 27-10).

Figure **27-10** Special cargoes require special protective equipment.

Danger Zones

There are many hazards when you work around a tractor-trailer or with cargo. A driver can be seriously injured if he or she falls, trips, or gets bumped. A driver must use care when exiting the cab or trailer. Most accidents in the vehicle and cargo danger zones can be avoided if the driver is aware of the possible dangers and is not careless. Using common sense is the best way to prevent these accidents.

Use great care when you are in the following five areas:

- Cab
- Coupling and uncoupling area
- Rear end of the trailer
- Cargo area
- Around the vehicle

You also must be very careful when cleaning your windshield.

The Cab

The height of the cab presents the greatest danger to the driver. Some cabs do not have handholds or steps. If there are handholds or steps, they may be slippery from fuel, oil, water, ice, or snow.

When getting in or out of the cab, look at the surfaces and always use the three-point stance (see Figure 27-11). Always enter and exit the cab facing the inside of the cab area. Smooth surfaces will be more slippery than ribbed surfaces. Be

Climb in safely
- **Look before climbing**
- **Watch for slippery surfaces, gloves and boots**
- **Use three-point contact**

Get out safely
- **Do not jump out of cab**

Figure **27-11** Getting in and out of the cab safely.

particularly careful of ice, grease, or oil on the surface or on your shoes. Check for grease or oil on your gloves. Then get a good hand grip.

Always keep a three-point contact with the vehicle when climbing into or out of the rig. A three-point contact means at least two hands and one foot or two feet and one hand in contact with the vehicle at all times. Do not jump down from the cab. Debris or a pothole could be in the landing area. Watch for stones. They too can cause you to sprain or turn your ankle.

Other injuries that can happen in and around the cab include:

- Injury from a falling hood while you are looking at or working on the engine. Be sure the hood (or raised cab in cab-over-engine) is properly secured and the safety locks or pins are in place.
- Thumb injuries from the steering wheel can occur if the wheel is not gripped properly. The hands should be on the outer edge in the 3:00 and 9:00 positions. If the truck hits a pothole or obstacle, the steering wheel can spin out of control. If the thumbs are between the spokes, they may be broken. The driver can then lose control of the vehicle.

Coupling and Uncoupling Area

The coupling/uncoupling area can be dangerous because of grease and oil (see Figure 27-12). If you have to stand on the vehicle to connect the air lines or electric cables, be careful of slippery surfaces such as the fuel tank or battery box. These are especially dangerous when they are wet or covered with ice, oil, or grease. If possible, use surfaces that have been treated with a rough material or have ribbed plates. Without proper precautions, pulling the release latch handle during coupling or uncoupling is dangerous because you may be thrown off balance and injure your back.

Rear of the Trailer

Open and close the swinging cargo door with great care to avoid injury or damaging the freight. When you open the door, remember the cargo may have moved and be resting against it. If it is, the door will pop open from the force of the cargo as soon as the latch is released. If that happens, you could be knocked down and have cargo fall on top of you. Be careful when it is windy. The doors can break your fingers and hands or knock you down.

Figure 27-12 The coupling and uncoupling area can be dangerous.

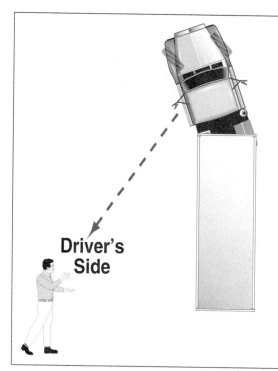

Walking backward is very dangerous. People have been hurt or killed when they were pinned between the rear of the trailer and the dock while guiding others. Stand off to the side when you are guiding someone who is backing up. Never stand directly behind the trailer.

Driver's Side

Figure **27-13** To avoid injury, stand to the side of the trailer when guiding a driver who is backing a rig.

Many drivers have been hurt closing the door because they stood on the trailer deck, grabbed the strap, and jumped to the ground. If the strap breaks or the driver loses hold of it, he or she may fall to the ground. If you add a length to the strap, you can pull it down while standing on the ground.

The power lift or elevating tailgate used for heavy cargo is another source of danger. Use common sense and care when you load or unload, and you will prevent serious problems. Keep your hands, feet, and cargo from the shearing, or pinching, areas. When loading with a liftgate, be sure the cargo is secure and will not fall off.

Other dangers at the rear of the trailer include:

- Slippery surface: You may slip and fall even if the surface is not slippery if your shoes have a slick sole or slippery substance on them.
- No handhold.
- Nails or splinters in the trailer floor: These can hurt the driver when he or she gets off.

Always use the proper handholds and steps when they are available. Also, wear gloves when getting off so you will not hurt your hands. Never jump down from a trailer.

You must also take care to avoid being pinned between the rear of the trailer and the loading dock when you are guiding a driver who is backing a rig to the dock (Figure 27-13).

Cargo Area

Various types of trailers and cargoes present different kinds of hazards. For instance, working with a tanker sometimes requires climbing to the top to hook or unhook dome covers. Flatbeds have no sides, so you can fall off while tying down the cargo. Open-top vans mean you may have to climb up the side to tie down the tarp cover.

Working inside a van is dangerous for many reasons:

- You may have to climb in, over, and around cargo to find a piece that is to be unloaded.
- You can be bruised or cut from nails or broken glass.
- You can bump into the sharp edges of cargo.
- Cargo can fall on you when you are climbing around.

Around the Vehicle

Damaged rigs can cause injury. Tears in the trailer skin and unrepaired damage to the fenders, bumpers, or hood can cut if you rub against or bump into them.

When working at night, a flashlight is a must. You cannot possibly couple or uncouple a rig or do a pretrip inspection without light.

Working under the rig is always dangerous. Make sure the vehicle cannot roll. Use wheel chocks when necessary. Be sure, too, that the keys are in your pocket so no one can hop in the rig and move it while you are underneath.

Cleaning Windshields

If possible, use an extension handle on the squeegee. Then you can stand on the ground instead of having to climb onto the tractor when you clean the windshield. If you must climb up to clean it, be careful of slippery surfaces. Keep both feet and one hand securely on the vehicle while cleaning the windshield.

Lifting

Many injuries occur when objects are not lifted properly or safely. All cargo handlers need to know how to safely and correctly lift to avoid back injury, hernia, or injuries to their hands or feet (see Figure 27-14).

The first rule in lifting is to not try to lift something if it is too heavy or not in a position to be moved. Get someone else to help you or use mechanical assistance. Also, before lifting anything, remember to protect your hands and feet.

The eight steps to safe lifting are:

1. Feet should be parted—one alongside and one behind the object.
2. Turn your forward foot in the direction of movement.
3. Keep your back straight.
4. Tuck in your chin.
5. Grip the object with your palm and fingers.
6. Tuck in your elbows and arms.
7. Put your body weight directly over your feet.
8. Avoid twisting (a common cause of back injuries).

To protect your hands, remember to use a good grip (a must for safe lifting), to use gloves that will help with

Figure **27-14** Use the correct techniques when lifting anything.

the grip and protect your hands, and to guard against pinching your hands in the cargo when lifting.

Most foot injuries result from dropped cargo. To protect your feet, be sure to wear safety shoes, keep your feet clear of the object being lifted in case it drops, and get a good grip and lift properly, which will reduce the chance of dropping the cargo.

Lifting with Others

When two or more persons lift cargo, working together is a must. They should all use the basic safe lifting techniques and safety precautions. Make sure each person has a good grip and can handle their share of the load. An unbalanced load is more likely to be dropped. If one person cannot hold up his or her share of the load, stop lifting and ease the item down. If you continue to lift, the load may drop and injure someone. And remember, be alert. Watch your fellow workers.

To safely lift cargo as a group, follow these guidelines:

- Get a comfortable hold on the object.
- Do not try to carry it too high.
- Carry freight the shortest distance possible.
- Talk to your partners. Let them know when you are going to put your end down. Never drop your end without warning.
- Choose a route before you start. Never climb over freight, cars, and so on.
- If two people are carrying an object, one may have to back up. Do not force this person to move too fast. Let them set the pace.
- Guide the person who is backing because they cannot see where they are going. Then follow their path.
- Beware of horseplay. It can cause tragedy.
- Keep your back as straight as possible.
- Lift the load with your legs.

ROADSIDE EMERGENCIES

When you must stop for an emergency, be careful. How, where, and under what conditions you stop your rig can make the difference between safety and serious problems.

There is great danger of being rear-ended if you park on the shoulder of the road. Pull off the road as far as possible. Look for a truck stop or rest area. Be especially alert when there is no breakdown lane or adequate area to stop. Rural roads and city streets do not have breakdown lanes.

Check before stopping. Be particularly careful in the dark when you cannot see the surface. Be sure the surface can support the rig. During or after heavy rain or snow, a road shoulder may be too soft to support it. A rig pulled onto a soft shoulder may get stuck or even roll over.

Stopping on Slippery Hills

Many drivers have been injured while checking a vehicle that is stuck on an icy or slippery hill or was spinning its wheels. Even after properly securing the vehicle (transmission in gear, emergency brake set, and wheels chocked), there is danger. A rig can slide downhill and roll over the driver. And remember, on a very slippery surface, both the wheels and the chocks may slide.

Get Out of the Cab Safely

Many drivers who have stopped properly in an emergency get hurt while leaving the cab. Do not jump out of the cab. Do not get out on the driver's side into the path of oncoming traffic. Remember, if you are not in a breakdown lane, there is great danger. Anything you do, such as jumping out, can increase the danger. Turn on the emergency flashers. After you get out of the cab, put out flares or triangles to warn other drivers of a problem.

Minor Repairs and Maintenance

Follow the guidelines for getting out of the cab safely when you install chains, change a tire, or make other roadside repairs. You should also make sure you are complying with company policies, face oncoming traffic, and be especially alert in wet or icy weather.

Cold metal.   When you stop to check your rig in freezing weather, your hands can freeze to cold metal. You may even rip your skin when you try to move them. Wear gloves to prevent this problem.

Hot tires.   You can be badly burned when checking hot tires. First, feel the heat without touching the tire and then slowly move your hand closer to the tire to touch it. Touching the sidewalls or tread with the palm of your hand can burn you before you can pull away your hand. Use the back of your hand. Your reflexes will pull away your hand more quickly in that position if the tire is too hot.

Live wires.   Bad storms sometimes knock down live electrical wires. They are very dangerous. If they land on your rig, do not try to get out of the cab. Do not move around in the cab or touch anything you are not already in contact with. Sit and wait for someone else to help. If you have a CB or a cell phone, call for help.

Avoiding Crime

In addition to driving hazards, truck drivers must be aware of and know how to avoid other problems. Among the other hazards you face are hijacking and robbery. You can best avoid them by knowing and following company policy. Be aware of crime areas and know which types of cargo are more likely to be targets.

Do not discuss your cargo or flash the shipping papers when you are carrying high-value cargo.

Do not set yourself up for crime. Do not carry a lot of cash. Stay away from dangerous areas. If something looks suspicious, use the CB radio to call for help.

Protect your truck by parking and securing it safely in a well-lighted area or rest stop. Never leave the truck unattended while the motor is running. Always close and lock all the doors when you leave. Drivers who leave their vehicles unsecured can be regarded as accomplices to crime and prosecuted.

Do not pick up hitchhikers. It is illegal (FMCSR). Finally, do not carry a gun. It is illegal without a permit, and a permit is valid only in the state in which it was issued.

CAUSES OF ACCIDENTS

Most over-the-road accidents are preventable. There are three main causes of traffic accidents: vehicle defects, road or weather conditions, and driver error.

Of the three, driver error is the main cause of most highway accidents.

Vehicle Defects

Mechanical defects, poor maintenance, and poor inspections are common causes of accidents. Parts that are failing or in danger of failing often do so while the rig is on the road. Parts also fail because they have been abused. Bad parts that are overlooked when the driver is inspecting the rig will eventually fail. Overloaded or improperly loaded vehicles can and do also lead to accidents.

Road or Weather Conditions

Slippery roads, poor visibility, lack of light (especially at dusk or dawn), and headlight glare can lead to accidents. Accidents can also be caused by poorly designed or maintained roads and signals. Examples are potholes, stop signs hidden by branches, and exit ramps that are too sharp for heavy-duty vehicles.

Driver Error

The major cause of accidents is driver error. Stress, both on and off duty, can lead to driver error. Staying in good condition is the responsibility of every professional driver.

The driver is the only person who can prevent an accident. By being aware of what is going on around the rig, thinking ahead, and using good judgment, the driver can adjust to problems before they happen. (See Figure 27-15) Statistics show that 80 to 90 percent of accidents involve one or more errors by the driver.

A driver's errors are usually caused by one or more underlying causes:

- Not being aware of what is happening
- Thinking of other things instead of the job at hand
- Driving while impaired (fatigued, ill, under medication, or under the influence of alcohol or drugs)
- Trying to make up lost time
- Emotional immaturity (showing off or being aggressive)
- Lack of technical knowledge of the vehicle
- Lack of driver training
- Failing to recognize personal limitations

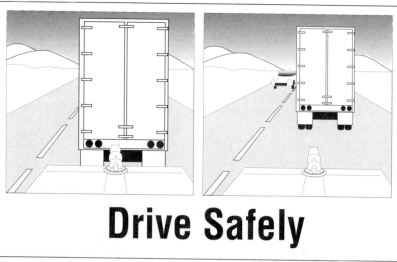

Drive Safely

Figure **27-15** Following too closely is one of many invitations to trouble.

Driving a tractor-trailer is a full-time job that takes all the driver's attention at all times. Nobody can drive a problem and a rig at the same time. It is up to the driver to park either the problem or the rig.

ON-DUTY AND OFF-DUTY JOB STRESS

Both the stresses of living and the job are often underlying causes for driver errors. Whatever the source, stress leads to fatigue, lack of attention, nervousness, poor physical and mental habits, and emotional breakdowns. This, in turn, leads to errors by drivers, which may cause accidents.

Job-related stress.   Normal job demands stress the driver physically, mentally, and emotionally. Any added stress increases the chance for driver error.

Among job conditions that can lead to physical, mental, and emotional fatigue are:

- Schedules that are always changing
- Frequent, short notices to report for a run
- Economic pressures
- Delays at the terminal and en route
- Poor layover conditions
- Physical demands of the job
- Over-the-road vibration
- Administrative duties

Changing schedules and short notices.   New drivers may have to fill in on short notice for sick or vacationing drivers or for unexpected runs. This can result in lack of sleep and not being able to look after personal affairs. This creates worry.

Economic pressures.   Demands to meet the schedule or lose their job lead to anxiety. Warning letters make matters worse. Trying to get in an extra trip during the week means driving longer hours, driving faster, and having less time off. Any existing physical or mental condition will get worse.

Delays.   Delays occur at the terminal waiting to be loaded or dispatched. Delays en route lead to hasty loading and unloading, driving too fast, and tailgating. The final result is added physical, mental, and emotional stress.

Poor layover conditions.   Noisy, uncomfortable hotels or truck stops often keep a driver from resting, relaxing, and eating properly. Loneliness encourages poor health habits. Poor health habits include:

- Not getting enough sleep
- Poor meals
- Too much drinking
- Watching television instead of resting
- Playing pinball and video games instead of sleeping

PHYSICAL DEMANDS OF THE JOB

Being a truck driver is a very demanding job. The driver needs to be in good physical condition. Some of the demands, which can be very tiring, are:

- The need to always pay attention to what is going on around him or her (looking and listening)

- Sitting up and steering an oversize wheel for long periods (a driver can become quite tired and uncomfortable as a result)
- Having to pay attention to the details of shifting, backing, and parking
- Nondriving tasks, such as inspecting the rig, handling cargo, and coupling and uncoupling the rig
- Loading and unloading cargo

Over-the-Road Vibration

Road vibration can drain a driver's physical strength and bring on physical problems. Noise levels can dull the driver's mind, making him or her feel very tired. Although today's trucks are more comfortable than ever before, they can still be noisier and rougher riding than cars, particularly on long-distance runs.

Administrative Duties

Federal, state, local, company, and union rules change often. Such changes create paperwork, such as filling out logs, trip reports, shipping papers, and mileage reports and keeping track of tolls.

Off-Duty Causes

Poor health habits, such as not eating the right foods, little or no exercise, and not enough rest, can all add to a driver's stress level. Even well-trained, experienced, and physically fit drivers are affected by personal problems. Worrying about what is happening also adds to stress and can make a driver perform badly.

Chapter Twenty-Eight
Trip Planning

OBJECTIVES

When you have completed this chapter, you should be able to:

- Explain how to locate the starting point and destination of a trip on a map

- Plan trip routes

- Choose alternate routes

- Estimate mileage and travel time

- Know how to obtain the necessary permits

- Describe the types of vehicles and cargos most likely to have routing restrictions or special requirements

- Explain where to get information about special requirements

- Describe how to plan for personal needs and expense money for trips

- Describe the different types of enforcement procedures

KEY TERMS

Atlas
Average speed formula
Designated System
Distance formula
Federal Bridge Formula
FMCSR 397
FMCSR 397.3
FMCSR 397.5
FMCSR 397.9
Fuel use tax
HMR 177.810
HMR 177.825
Inner bridge
International
  Registration Plan (IRP)
Interstate routes
Irregular route
Local pickup and
  delivery
Local truck routes
Long-distance transport
Meet and turn

National Network
National System of
  Interstate Highways
Open dispatch
Outer bridge
Over-the-road
Peddle run
Port of entry
Posted bridges
Regular route
Regular run
Relay run
Restricted routes
Roll and rest
Safe haven
Sleeper operations
State primary routes
Toll roads
Trip time formula
Turnaround
U.S. numbered routes
Weight distance tax

INTRODUCTION

As well as driving a rig safely, the professional driver must be able to read and understand maps, know the general size and weight laws, and understand registration and fuel tax requirements. Along with trip-planning skills, the driver must also be aware of the special regulations to be followed when planning a trip.

The driver must keep accurate records to show they have complied with the regulations for hours of service, cargo, fuel tax payments, and registration fees (see Figure 28-1).

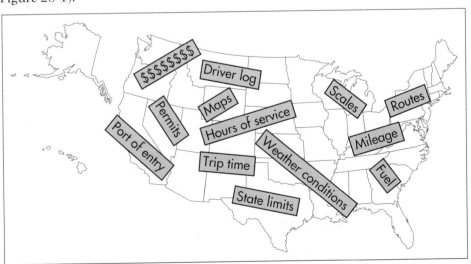

Figure **28-1** Trip planning requires skills as well as knowledge of regulations, restrictions, and registration fees.

As a professional driver, you should be able to estimate:

● Mileage from point of origin to destination
● Trip time
● Fuel requirements
● Personal financial needs

The driver may or may not be involved with these aspects of trip planning. Companies differ in what they require, depending on the type of operation, the size and type of carrier, length of haul, territory covered, and so on.

This chapter will help you understand the various steps for planning a trip. Knowing how to plan well will help you be a more responsible and efficient driver.

TYPES OF RUNS/ASSIGNMENTS

Various types of runs are made in the trucking industry. Some carriers operate only a single type of run. Other carriers operate many types. As a professional driver, you may or may not have a choice in the type of run you are assigned.

Many times, the driver will be given specific instructions about which routes to use. These instructions must be followed. In other cases, company management specifies the use of a particular route because it may be the best. Going off an assigned route without a good reason is a serious violation of company rules and may result in disciplinary measures.

Local Operations

Local pickup and delivery.   In typical **local pickup and delivery** operations, the driver operates in and around certain cities. He or she will usually be delivering freight to its final destination (the consignee) and picking up freight from shippers.

A local operation may represent the final step in delivering freight to its destination, after it has been brought into the area by a line-haul operation. Local P&D may also pick up freight that will be transported to a distant destination by another carrier. In other local operations, freight is moved between nearby points of origin and destinations.

The local driver must know the street system well so that pickups and deliveries can be made in the safest, quickest way. The local P&D driver must also know the local traffic patterns in order to avoid areas of congestion and delay whenever possible.

Peddle run.   A **peddle run** is a type of local pickup and delivery operation. Usually freight is hauled from the terminal to separate destinations in the nearby area. Peddle run drivers also pick up freight along the route and bring it back to the terminal. Because of frequent changes in the points to be served, drivers in this type of service may be asked to select their routes. Drivers should know how to select the safest and quickest route for each trip.

Shuttle operations.   In shuttle operations, some drivers move either empty or loaded trailers between nearby points, such as terminals to customer, drop yards to customer, railheads to customer, and vice versa. The number of trailers a driver moves during a single driving period will depend on the distances involved.

Long-Distance Transport

Long-distance transport involves moving cargo from a point of origin to one or more distant destinations (see Figure 28-2). Several types of operations fall within

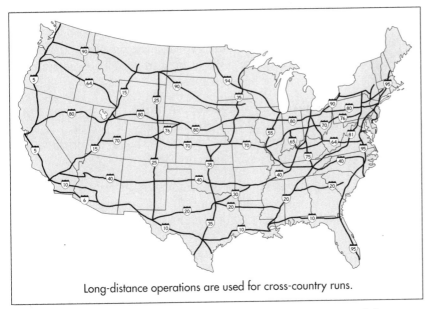

Long-distance operations are used for cross-country runs.

Figure **28-2** Long-distance operations are used for cross-country runs.

the general classification of a long-distance operation. In some cases, a long-distance driver may return to the home terminal at the end of about 10 hours of driving. In other cases, a driver may be on the road 2 days or more at a time. Brief descriptions of several types of long-distance operations follow:

Regular run.   In a **regular run,** the driver operates between the same points on each trip and may or may not have a regular starting and finishing time for each period of driving.

Open dispatch.   In **open dispatch,** the driver goes from the point of origin to a distant point. Depending on the driving time and the need to comply with hours-of-service limits, the driver may take another unit to an additional destination. After driving for 10 hours, the driver must rest. When the driver can legally drive again, he or she may be given a run heading toward the home terminal or may be dispatched to another point. The cycle may be repeated for several days before the driver returns home.

Regular route.   A **regular route** refers to line-haul transport between given origins and destinations using assigned highways. Most less-than-truckload (LTL) fleets are regular route operations.

Irregular route.   An **irregular route** describes long-distance transport between a combination of origin and destination points using any suitable route. This type of run is also called **over-the-road** trucking. Most truckload fleets are irregular route carriers. It is in this type of operation where the professional driver is most likely to be asked to select a route, but even in irregular route operations, management may set the routes to be used, and the driver must comply with these set routes.

Relay runs.   A **relay run** refers to a trip in which a driver drives for 10 hours and then goes off duty as prescribed by the hours-of-service laws. Another driver takes the unit on to the next point. This cycle may be repeated several times as the truck is driven from origin to final destination by several different drivers.

Figure **28-3** Drivers with sleeper rigs can save lodging costs on the road.

Meet and turn. **Meet and turn** is a relay run in which two drivers start toward each other from different points and meet at a chosen midpoint. At the meeting place, the drivers exchange complete units or only trailers. Then each driver goes back to his or her starting point.

Turnaround. In a **turnaround** run, a driver travels for about 5 hours to a destination and then returns to his or her home terminal. At the turnaround point, the driver may switch units or trailers for the return trip.

Roll and rest. In **roll and rest,** a single driver takes the truck from origin to destination in a roll-and-rest operation. At the end of each period of 10 hours of driving, the driver stops in a suitable location for the required off-duty time. The driver must plan the trip so there are suitable rest facilities at the intervals required by the hours-of-service regulations.

Sleeper operations. The driver of a rig that has a sleeper berth can accumulate the required off-duty time in two periods as long as neither period is less than 2 hours. To meet the requirements, the driver must use the sleeper berth. This is a special provision of the hours-of-service regulations. **Sleeper operations** may use a single driver or a two-driver team.

A single driver with a sleeper cab saves lodging costs on the road (see Figure 28-3). If the driver arrives early at an origin or destination, having a sleeper berth can let him or her get the required rest while waiting to load or unload.

Sleeper teams are also used when speedy service requires the unit to be on the road as much as possible or a second driver is needed for other reasons. In team operations, drivers usually exchange duties every 4 to 5 hours so one driver can rest while the other drives.

ROUTE SELECTION

There are many types of highways, and each type is coded on a map. If you understand this code, you will be able to know which are interstate highways, which are state highways, and which highways are country roads. The various types of highways are described in the following section. They are listed in the order of preference of use:

- Interstate routes
- Toll roads
- U.S. numbered routes
- State primary routes
- Other streets and highways

Interstate routes. **Interstate routes** are usually preferred because they separate opposing traffic, have limited access, and bypass many small communities. Although they are the safest type of highway, drivers must be aware that these popular and much-used highways can be snarled up by bad weather or traffic congestion, especially in urban areas. In selecting the interstates, drivers should note other available routes in case of a major traffic problem on the interstate. Drivers should also know about any "truck only" lanes on urban stretches of interstate highway.

Toll roads. Except for having to pay a toll, these **toll roads** are similar to the interstates. In many states, toll roads are part of the interstate system. The decision on whether to use a toll road must be based on many factors in addition to cost. Drivers should take into consideration:

- Differences in time and distance over alternate routes
- Terrain and traffic
- Road conditions
- The need to go through built-up areas
- The amount of stop-and-go driving
- Wear and tear on the equipment
- Fuel usage

U.S. numbered routes.   **U.S. numbered routes** are the major through routes. Those that parallel the interstates may be good alternatives in case of delays on the interstate because of weather or traffic.

State primary routes.   Within each state, **state primary routes** are the major routes. In some instances, a state primary route may be as good as or even better than a nearby U.S. numbered highway.

Other streets and highways.   Drivers often must use other types of roads to reach a loading or unloading point. In general, choose county roads or other routes designated by number or letter. These are the through routes set by the local authorities and are generally better than other local streets to safely handle truck traffic.

A driver should use extreme care when driving on local streets that are not designed for truck traffic. Avoid using side streets because they may have hazards such as low clearances, unsafe railroad crossings, poor road surfaces, sharp turns, and local restrictions.

Special Situations

It is not always possible to foresee every problem a driver may encounter. Drivers must learn to approach new situations carefully and use common sense. Some of the special situations you may find are **local truck routes, posted bridges,** and **restricted routes.**

Local truck routes.   Many cities and towns have designated routes for trucks. They are not always marked well, and if you do not stay on the route, you may get a ticket.

Posted bridges.   Many bridges have special weight restrictions. Do not cross a bridge if your rig's weight is more than the weight posted. Some fines are as much as $10,000 (see Figure 28-4).

Restricted routes.   One reason for prohibiting trucks on some roads is a long past history of accidents. Always heed posted prohibitions, even if it means driving on to a point where you can obtain information. If you do drive on the restricted road, you may get a ticket, be faced with a hazardous condition, or be unable to avoid an accident.

There are many ways to get the information or help you need. Here are some suggestions:

- Talk to other truck drivers or local residents about the conditions.
- Use local computer Web sites for route information and suggestions.
- If you are near a destination, stop and call the shipper or consignee for directions.

Figure **28-4** Never use a bridge if your rig is heavier than the posted weight.

- Stop and make inquiries about the local conditions at truck stops, service stations, firehouses, police stations, or other locations where there may be people who know the area.
- Look in a road atlas. Many have information on restricted routes, low clearances, and so on.
- Use a CB to ask any questions about the route.

MAP READING

Being able to read maps is important to the professional truck driver. Part of your job as a professional driver is to locate unfamiliar pickup and delivery points. Maps are a good investment because they offer the driver a chance to save time and miles. There are several types of maps: local or area map, state map, U.S. map, and **atlas.**

You may obtain maps from bookstores, drug stores, discount stores, auto clubs, filling stations, and truck stops.

Truck stops are the best place to get special atlases just for truckers. These have extra information on restricted routes, weigh stations, and so on.

Local or area map. A local or area map is useful for the local driver because it will show local streets. You can get local maps in bookstores and in many drug-stores, discount stores, and filling stations. Some show a single city, while other types may show one or two counties or a region. Because of the rapid growth in many urban areas, the driver should plan to obtain an updated map at least every other year.

State map. Often a free state map is available at border information centers and along the interstates. They are also for sale at other locations. When considering the purchase of a map, a driver should remember that maps covering several states or an entire region may not show the minor roads the driver will need to reach various destinations.

Atlas. A driver who expects to travel extensively should consider purchasing a trucking atlas. This special atlas contains maps of all the states, the Canadian provinces, and Mexico (in some cases), and maps of major cities. In addition to state, city, and area maps, these special atlases may include information about:

- The location of permanent scales
- Low underpasses
- Size and weight limits
- Fuel taxes
- Designated routes for the operation of twin trailers and 53/102 semitrailers or other specialized types of equipment
- State laws for access to the Designated Highway System
- Driving distances

The following pointers will help you when reading a map:

- In most cases, North is at the top of the map. Often it is also indicated by an arrow symbol with the letter "N" or a symbol showing all four points of the compass. In some cases, a map of a small area may be printed with North to one side. North will always be shown by some symbol.
- Read the key, or legend, that explains the symbols and colors used to show the interstates; federal, state, and local routes; rest areas; interchanges; distances; and other important features.
- Learn to figure the distance between points by adding the mileage figures shown along the route. Black numbers often refer to short distances between two black dots. Red numbers refer to longer distances between two red dots.

Many maps have mileage charts showing approximate distances between principal cities and towns. Many atlases have a special map showing distance and estimated driving times between principal cities. The driving times shown are usually for cars and light trucks. You should allow more time for driving a tractor-trailer.

Learn to use the grid coordinates to locate points on the map. Numbers are printed across the top and bottom of maps, and letters are printed down each side. Most maps also have an index. On a state map, the index will list names of cities, towns, and villages. On the map of a city or region, the index will list street names. In each case, the location will show a letter and a number, for example, C-6 or C6. To find the location, look down from 6 and across from C. The point will be near where the imaginary lines from the number and letter cross on the map.

CALCULATING TRAVEL TIME AND FUEL USAGE

Knowing how to figure the distance, your average speed, and trip time are required for trip planning. The driver who wants to keep track of the average speed and fuel usage may want to buy a calculator. The following formulas are used often by truck drivers for these calculations:

Distance = Speed multiplied by Time

50 mph $\times$ 9 hours = 450 miles

Average Speed = Distance divided by Time

450 miles/9 hours = 50 mph

Trip Time = Distance divided by Average Speed

450 miles/50 mph = 9 hours

Travel Time

Drivers must comply with the speed limits and hours of service. When a driver's log is checked, enforcement personnel will divide the miles driven by the number of hours of driving time to determine the average speed. This will tell them if the driver has been speeding.

Drivers and motor carriers may be required to document runs to show they can be made without violating the hours-of-service rules or the speed limits.

The distance that can be covered in 10 hours of driving will depend on the speed limits and other factors, such as heavy traffic, travel through urban areas, long upgrades, adverse weather, or anything that can reduce the safe operating speed.

Fuel Consumption

To figure the fuel consumption, follow these steps:

1. Fill the fuel tank and record the mileage shown on the odometer.
2. After driving, refill the tank and record the odometer mileage.
3. Record the amount of fuel put in the tank.
4. Subtract the odometer mileage at the first fill-up from the odometer mileage at the second fill-up. This will tell you the distance covered.
5. To determine the miles per gallon, divide the distance covered by the gallons of fuel used.

Example:

Odometer reading: First fill-up	65456
Odometer reading: second fill-up	65956
Gallons of fuel added	90

Distance covered = odometer reading at second fill-up (65956)

$\quad\quad\quad\quad$ − odometer reading at first fill-up (65456)

$\quad\quad\quad\quad$ = $\quad\quad\quad\quad$ 500 miles

Miles per gallon = $\dfrac{500 \text{ miles (distance covered)}}{90 \text{ gallons (fuel added)}}$ = 5.5 mpg

If a driver knows the capacity of the truck's fuel tank(s) and the average fuel mileage, he or she can figure the cruising range by multiplying the tank capacity by the miles per gallon:

Example:

Cruising range = Tank capacity × mpg

Tank capacity = 100 gallons

Miles per gallon = 5.5

Cruising range = 100 (gallons) × 5.5 (mpg) = 550 miles

The driver must be aware that under actual operating conditions, many factors can easily increase fuel usage. Some of these factors include:

- Prolonged idling
- Driving too fast
- Extended operation in low gears
- Stop-and-go driving
- Mountainous terrain
- Headwinds
- Low tire pressure
- Defects in the engine or fuel system

KEEPING RECORDS

A driver must always have all the up-to-date papers he or she needs while on duty. Each carrier has its own way of keeping records to meet the information needs of that carrier and to help drivers remain within the law. You must use the method your carrier specifies.

If the driver does not keep the records the carrier requires, both the driver and the carrier can be penalized. Not carrying the right papers or keeping necessary records may also cause delays in being paid.

The driver must have the following papers:

- Driver's license
- Medical certificate
- Driver's log
- Driver's inspection report

Law enforcement officers have the right to examine all these documents.

Driver's license. Your CDL must be the type required for the equipment you are driving. You must also have the proper endorsements. Federal law prohibits a truck driver from having more than one license.

Medical certificate. This must be current and valid. The driver must be in compliance of any special requirements, such as glasses, hearing aids, and so on.

Driver's log (record of duty status). The record must be correctly completed and kept up to date to the driver's last change of duty status. The driver must have the log for the current day and the 7 preceding days with him or her while on duty.

Driver's inspection report. The driver must keep a copy of the vehicle inspection report prepared by the previous driver and have a blank driver's inspection report available to prepare at the end of the trip or tour of duty.

The driver may also have other documents, including shipping papers and trip reports.

Shipping papers. There are many different forms that are used for this purpose (see Chapter 26).

Trip reports. Carriers usually develop the type of report that meets their needs. As a result, there are many types, and they provide different information. The following data are usually found on these reports:

- Name of driver
- Terminal

- Vehicle identification
- Departure time from terminal
- Routing instructions
- Address of each stop to deliver or pick up freight
- Times of arrival and departure for each stop
- Quantity of freight handled
- Time of return to terminal
- Space for remarks

Some trip reports have a space for the odometer reading when the driver crosses a state line or when going from origin to destination. Drivers must be very careful and accurate when noting these details. A driver must always comply with the carrier's rules when preparing a trip report.

On-Board Recorder

More and more carriers are now using on-board recording equipment. Some carriers use this equipment to show compliance with hours-of-service limits. If the carrier for which you work uses such devices, they will teach you how to use them properly.

Some trucks have recorders installed so the carrier can control how the truck is operated. Basic information recorded by these devices includes:

- Time the engine is running
- Whether the truck is stopped or moving
- Speed
- Miles driven

Personal Needs

The driver must be able to meet his or her personal needs during trips. These needs will include expenses he or she must meet while on the trip that will be reimbursed by the motor carrier, how the payment is to be made, what paperwork must be kept to prove the expense, and if there are forms to be filled out. These expenses and who is usually responsible are as follows:

Meals	Usually driver expense
Lodging	Usually carrier expense
Fuel	Carrier expense
En route repairs	Carrier expense
Tolls	Carrier expense if authorized
Permits	Carrier expense
Special fees	Carrier expense

Carriers handle their expense accounts in different ways. Some companies have accounts with fuel stops, motels, repair shops, and toll facilities and for permits. Others use Comchecks. Some carriers provide cash advances for these expenses. Always find out how your company handles expenses before you start on a trip. Keep copies of all receipts for your personal tax records. Retain logbooks to document your daily expenses for tax purposes.

Drivers should know the kind of weather they may find during the trip. They should know where there may be extreme weather conditions and carry the right kinds of clothes with them for any situation. Clothes for working outside the truck during bad weather should also be included. Many drivers also carry blankets, a sleeping bag, and an emergency supply of food in case they are stranded out in the middle of nowhere.

VEHICLE LICENSING AND PERMITS

Every vehicle must have a registration (license) plate (tag) in order to operate. Fees are paid each year and registration plates issued. The majority of trucks or truck or tractor combinations that weigh more than 26,000 pounds will be registered under the **International Registration Plan (IRP).**

The IRP is a registration agreement among the states and Canadian provinces based on the percentage of miles driven in each state or province. License fees are paid to each state or province in which the vehicle operates. A cab card is issued to the vehicle. This card states the IRP areas in which the vehicle can operate.

Usually, the carrier obtains the registration plate. The driver is responsible for keeping mileage records. The percentage of fees paid to each state depends on the number of miles driven in that state compared to the number of miles driven in all states and provinces.

If a truck that has IRP plates plans to operate in a state that is not shown on the IRP cab card, a trip permit must be obtained. The carrier is responsible for telling the driver how to obtain these permits. Permits are usually issued for a given period of time, ranging most often from 24 to 72 hours. Federal laws require all states to be members of IRP by Sepetember 30, 1996.

Fuel Use Tax

In order to operate legally in a state, a truck must be registered for **fuel use tax** purposes. When it is registered, a fuel tax decal will be issued and placed on the door of the tractor. The decal is evidence the vehicle is registered for fuel use tax purposes. The price of the decal varies considerably from state to state. The fuel use tax, itself, is paid quarterly by the carrier. The fuel tax registration law is usually enforced by the state revenue or taxation department.

The carrier pays the fuel tax in each state based on the number of miles driven in that state. If the carrier buys more fuel in a state than is needed to cover its fuel tax obligation, the carrier gets a tax credit. On the other hand, if not enough fuel is bought in a state, the carrier must pay more tax.

A driver must be sure he or she gets receipts for all fuel purchases and submits them to the carrier along with required record of miles operated. The information submitted by the driver forms the basis of the carrier's fuel tax report to each state.

Most fuel purchases automatically record information for the carrier's fuel tax report to each state.

Weight Distance Taxes

Some states have **weight distance taxes.** They are also called mileage taxes, ton-mile taxes, or axle taxes. These taxes are paid by the carrier and are based on the annual ton mileage (see Figure 28-5). The carrier must also file a quarterly report. States often require trucks to be registered for the weight distance tax. The carrier usually obtains a decal or number for the tractor. These taxes are enforced by the state's highway department or transportation department.

Mileage Control Sheet
(Speedometer Mileage Readings)

Destination _____

Date _____ Unit Nos._____

Driver _____

New Jersey
    Beginning   _____
    State Line OUT _____
    State Line IN   _____
    Ending   _____

New York
    State Line IN   _____
    State Line OUT _____

Connecticut
    State Line IN   _____
    State Line OUT _____

Pennsylvania
    State Line IN   _____
    State Line OUT _____

Figure **28-5** The mileage control sheet is used by the carrier to track its mileage taxes.

FEDERAL LENGTH AND WEIGHT LIMITS

The driver is responsible for staying within federal and state weight and length laws. All states must allow truck combinations of certain weights and lengths to operate on roadways that are part of the **National System of Interstate Highways.** This system is also known as the **Designated System** or **National Network.** Most of these highways are identified by the letter "I" and the number of the highway, such as "I80" or "I5." Many additional multilane, divided highways, such as the U.S. routes and turnpikes, are also part of this system.

In addition, states must allow federally authorized Surface Transportation Assistance Act (STAA) truck combinations to have access to terminals and facilities for food, fuel, repairs, and rest. States are allowed to determine the distance off the designated system these vehicles may travel for such purposes. The distances currently range from a limit of 1,500 feet off the New York State Thruway, for example, to unlimited access on state and local roads in Ohio.

Many state highways have requirements similar to the following federal weight and size limits, but it is always wise to check the applicable maps and charts for actual dimension limits.

Vehicle Weight

A maximum of 20,000 pounds may be carried on any one axle (except steer axles, which are allowed only 12,000 pounds) and 34,000 pounds on a tandem axle. An overall gross weight of 80,000 pounds is allowed on a typical five-axle tractor-trailer. The way the axles are spaced and the number of axles may lower the single and tandem axle limits. Rigs must also stay within weight-to-length limits based on the weight of groups of two or more adjacent (following) axles.

The **Federal Bridge Formula** is used to calculate permissable gross loads. Ideally, a typical 80,000-pound five-axle highway rig should get 12,000 pounds on the front axle and 34,000 pounds on each of the tandems. The tractor must have an outer spread (distance between the middle of the front axle and the middle of the rearmost axle) of at least 14 feet. The formula also requires minimum distances between the tractor and trailer axles (**inner** and **outer bridge**).

Vehicle Length

There is no limit on the overall length of a tractor-trailer on the interstates and designated highways. But some states do limit lengths. These are typically measured from the center of the trailer tandems. Pay special attention if the trailer is over 48 feet long. Some states may require a permit.

States cannot limit the length of trailers to less than 28 feet for doubles (semi-trailer and trailer). States must also continue to allow 28 1/2-feet double trailers if they were in operation before 1983.

No state can prohibit doubles on the interstate and Designated System. Longer doubles (more than 28 feet per trailer) and triple trailer combinations usually operate under special permits.

STATE LIMITS

Unless they are controlled by federal interstate law, weight and size limits vary from state to state. If a driver is not sure of a state's limits, he or she should find out about the limits before entering the state. Dispatchers usually have this information. So do most trucker atlases. The state police, highway patrol, departments of transportation, and state trucking associations can also provide accurate information.

When deciding whether a tractor-trailer is within limits, there are three key factors to be considered: vehicle weight, the number of axles, and vehicle length, height, and width.

Vehicle weight. Many state agencies provide color-coded maps (red, green, purple) that identify load maximums that can be carried on various roads. These maximums are generally based on the condition of the road and the weight that can be supported by the bridges. You can weigh your rig at fleet or shipper terminals, or you can use public scales at truck stops. Some public scales will certify the weight and even pay overweight fines if they are wrong (see Figure 28-6).

Number of axles. States have bridge laws that limit the maximum weight that may be carried. The laws are determined by the number of axles and the distance between them. While most states have adopted Federal Bridge Formula to determine axle weight limits and gross weight limits, some states have other means of figuring these limits.

Vehicle length. Vehicle length is regulated by both state and local governments. They also set the maximum load, length, and overhang (the distance beyond support of the load bed) that is permitted. The legal length may be set in terms of either overall length (from bumper to bumper) or trailer length.

Vehicle height and load. While some states permit vehicle heights of 14 1/2 feet, most restrict heights to 13 1/2 feet. This

Figure **28-6** Trucks are weighed on certified scales to be sure they are within legal limits.

Figure **28-7** Special permits often limit hours of operation and routes used.

limit includes the load. Overpasses on most interstates have clearances of 16 1/2 feet, but some are only 13 1/2 feet. Always check to make sure.

Special Permit Hauling

Loads that are larger than either the state or local laws allow need special permits. You can get these permits from state agencies and police departments. Typical loads that need these permits include machinery, buildings, and bridge construction girders.

Some permits limit hours of operation (e.g., before sundown, after sunup, or rush hours) and the routes to be used (see Figure 28-7). Permits may:

- Be limited to specific vehicles
- Require the use of special signs (e.g., oversize load)
- Require the use of escort vehicles both in front of and behind the load
- Require using special lights, such as rotating amber lights
- Specify the route to be followed

Drivers may have to submit their planned route before they can get a permit. If a detour or delay occurs, the driver may have to call the state or local agency that issued the permit to request a change in time or route.

HAZARDOUS MATERIAL

If you haul hazardous material, trip planning will be affected. First, you must know that the cargo is hazardous. Second, you must follow federal regulations for trip planning. Finally, you will need to know in advance which highways and facilities you may use and which ones restrict or prohibit hazardous materials. You may not use certain bridges or tunnels.

Federal regulations. You must obey **Section 397** of the FMCSR. These regulations deal with driving and parking vehicles that contain hazardous materials. You must understand and follow **Sections 397.3, 397.5,** and **397.7.**

FMCSR 397.3 requires all vehicles carrying hazardous materials to comply with state and local restrictions on routes and parking.

The **safe haven** regulation is FMCSR 397.5. It requires all vehicles carrying class A or class B explosives (explosives 1.1–1.3) to be attended at all times. They may be parked in a safe haven. A safe haven is an area approved in writing by local, state, or federal officials in which unattended vehicles carrying class A or class B explosives may be parked.

Parking with Division 1.1, 1.2, or 1.3 (Class A or B) Explosives

Never park with Division 1.1, 1.2, or 1.3 (class A or B) explosives within 5 feet of the traveled part of the road. Except for short periods of time needed for vehicle operation necessities (e.g., fueling), do not park within 300 feet of a bridge, tunnel, or building; a place where people gather; or an open fire. If you must park to do your job, do so only briefly.

Do not park on private property unless the owner is aware of the danger. Someone must always watch the parked vehicle. You may let someone else watch it for you only if your vehicle is on the shipper's property, on the carrier's property, or on the consignee's property. You are allowed to leave your vehicle unattended in a safe haven. Designation of authorized safe havens is usually made by local authorities.

FMCSR 397.9 controls the routes. Trips must be planned in the best interest of public safety, not for the operator's convenience.

Vehicles carrying hazardous materials must, when possible, operate over routes that do not go through or near heavily populated areas and should avoid tunnels, narrow streets, alleys, or places where crowds are assembled.

Loads of class A or class B explosives require a written trip plan. The carrier must submit the plan in advance. The driver must then follow the plan. In some cases, the driver prepares the plan for the carrier.

There are also specific regulations dealing with routing decisions in the Hazardous Materials Regulations. **HMR 177.810** requires drivers of vehicles containing hazardous materials to obey state and local laws for the use of tunnels.

Planning for trips and hauling radioactive material is controlled by **HMR 177.825.** There are detailed instructions for routing loads of radioactive materials. A written route plan must be submitted in advance for highway route-controlled quantities of radioactive materials.

ROADSIDE ENFORCEMENT

As well as the normal enforcement of traffic laws, there are three other types of controlling activities routinely carried on by states. Drivers need to be aware of scales, **ports of entry,** and roadside safety inspections (see Figures 28-8 and 28-9).

In many cases, these functions are carried out at a single location.

Scales

States usually enforce size and weight laws through a combination of permanent scales and the use of roving crews who have portable scales, or loadmeters. Permanent scales are often on the main highways at the state line. In some states, there are also scales at other key points. Not stopping at the

Figure **28-8** Be sure to obey all instructions at scales and ports of entry and during roadside inspections.

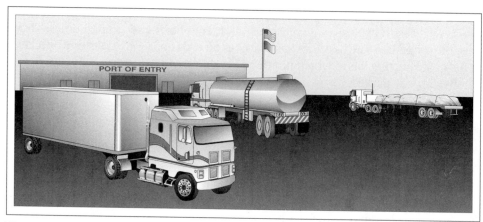

Figure **28-9** Observe all signs, follow instructions and have all paperwork ready for inspection at a port of entry.

scales is a serious offense and may result in a fine. Observe all signs, lights, and verbal commands when entering, weighing, and exiting the scales.

Ports of Entry

These are locations where the driver must stop and prove the carrier has authority to operate in the state. In some cases, the driver may have to buy permits or pay fees. Weighing may also be done at the port of entry. Do not pull onto the scales. Park near the scales and walk up to get your permit. Some states will fine you if you pull onto the scales without a permit. In some states, the driver's log will be checked for hours-of-service violations and are time-stamped by the person on duty.

Roadside Safety Inspections

These inspections are done at scales, ports of entry, or special safety inspection facilities or in a suitable safe area. The driver must show his or her license, medical certificate, driver's logs, and the shipping papers for the load. Inspectors have the authority to inspect the cargo, even if it is sealed. If a sealed load is inspected, a new seal will be put on by the inspector. The driver should record the identification number of the seal that is removed and the number of the new seal in his or her log.

The driver may be put out of service at once for certain violations. These include:

- Hours-of-service violations
- A vehicle so unsafe it is likely to be involved in an accident or breakdown
- Leaking hazardous material

At the end of a roadside inspection, the driver will be given a copy of the form filled out by the inspector. This form must be turned in to the carrier. If the driver will reach a company facility within 24 hours, the form may be turned in at that time. If not, the driver must mail the form to the carrier.

Chapter Twenty-Nine

Public Relations and Employer-Employee Relations

Public Relations

Customer Relations

Employer-Employee Relations

OBJECTIVES

When you have completed this chapter, you should be able to:

- Understand the importance of presenting a good image to the public
- Explain the results of presenting a bad public image
- Describe what is included in a good image for the industry
- Explain the importance of good relations with customers
- Follow the proper procedures for applying for a job as a truck driver
- Successfully participate in a job interview
- Understand reasons a driver candidate can be disqualified

KEY TERMS

Customer relations
Employer-employee relations
Public relations

INTRODUCTION

Public relations can be defined as how the general public thinks about or views a subject, an issue, or an industry.

Much of what the general public thinks about the trucking industry comes from how they see drivers behave on the road. Thoughtful and courteous tractor-trailer drivers create a positive impact on how the public views the entire industry. On the other hand, one careless or rude truck driver on the highway, in a truck stop, or in a roadside park can immediately create a poor image for the entire industry.

If you think about it, tractor-trailer drivers are the frontline public relations team for the carrier they represent and for all the people who work in the transportation industry. Professional drivers are the part of the industry the public sees most often, and the image they create is the image the general public remembers.

It is human nature for the memory of the public to be a short one. A four-wheeler driver may have seen a trucker risk his or her life to keep other highway users safe and may have had positive interactions with professional drivers on the highway for years. Then they may see a truck driver taking chances—perhaps repeatedly changing lanes in heavy traffic or cutting off other drivers on a freeway—and suddenly the positive image becomes a negative.

If the public does not like what they see, they will remember. Some may even complain to a lawmaker. The bottom line is that the industry will hear about it in ways that will hurt business and ways that will affect earnings and jobs.

This chapter discusses not only how professional drivers can create positive public relations but also the importance of good **employer-employee relations.** The chapter ends with a discussion about the professional driver's job search, qualifications, and recommendations for handling the job interview.

PUBLIC RELATIONS

How good the relations are between the trucking industry and the general public is often determined by how well truck drivers obey the laws and regulations meant to protect road users. Obeying the laws, being courteous, and using everyday common sense creates good public relations. This chapter discusses some common public relations problems along with the steps drivers can take to improve the image of the industry.

The Image of the Trucking Industry

The trucking industry operates under many state and federal laws and regulations. Most of the laws are made to protect the public. Some can be difficult for the industry, such as:

- High road use taxes
- Laws restricting vehicles from using certain roads
- Lower speed limits for heavy vehicles
- Hours-of-service rules that make it hard to get the rest you need when you need it

How the public feels about the trucking industry influences all laws that could affect the industry.

The public image of the trucking industry, whether it is accurate or not, sometimes results in letter-writing campaigns in which the public and media come out for or against the trucking industry. Complaints from the public create legislation that is unfavorable to the industry (e.g., higher use taxes or road restrictions) and less profit for the trucking industry. This often means a loss of jobs.

One driver's thoughtless performance can have a dramatic effect on the whole industry. The industry needs to be seen as a worthwhile profession. Courteous drivers who know and practice safe driving at all times can truly be seen by the public as the "knights of the road" (see Figure 29-1).

Figure **29-1** It is important to present a positive image to the public.

Contact with the Public

There are many chances for public contact. This contact can be either cooperative or abrasive and rude. Drivers must take great care that their conduct and actions create a good image in every situation (see Figure 29-2). All of us, whatever our positions, have to deal with difficulty and stress in our daily lives. The way truck drivers react to those situations creates the image for the industry and affects how the public feels.

Note: There is no excuse for road rage by a professional driver.

Every professional driver is responsible for maintaining a good image when driving. Drivers can do this by obeying the laws, making a good appearance, and sharing the road.

Obeying the law. Laws are meant to protect every citizen and visitor to this country. They should be obeyed at all times. When drivers obey the law, they project the image of a true professional. Obeying the law also cuts down on incidents that make life harder for your fellow drivers, the industry, and yourself.

Making a good appearance. A clean, neat driver looks like a professional and gains respect for the industry. Professional drivers also need to stay in top physical, mental, and emotional shape.

Professional drivers must be sure rigs are in top shape as well. A good pre-trip inspection may prevent an accident or breakdown. A clean, well-maintained vehicle makes the industry look good. Flapping tarps, spilling cargo, and dragging chains or rope say we belong to a shoddy industry.

Figure **29-2** Examples of bad public relations.

Sharing the road. Most conflicts with the public occur while sharing the road. Some actions that cause public resentment are:

- **Space related:** Following too closely or driving in packs that prevent others from passing.
- **Speed related:** Speeding and cutting in and out of traffic.
- **Going uphill:** Attempting to pass another truck without enough speed. As a result, two trucks block the flow of traffic. You could block an unmarked emergency or police vehicle. The same type of situation can occur when trucks do not keep to the right and pull over to allow other vehicles to pass. Be careful, and do not pull onto a soft shoulder. The rig could sink, turn over, or throw gravel at following vehicles.
- **Passing:** The truck driver cuts off other drivers or does not signal.
- **At intersections:** Do not try to bluff your way through intersections. Trucks are very large and can frighten some people so that they may react in a way that causes an accident. Other drivers do not always leave enough room for a tractor-trailer to turn. Keep cool and do not get mad. Do not jump the light on left turns. This can lead to the end of your career as a trucker. When a light turns from red to green, do not go until it is safe to do so. Be sure there are no emergency vehicles approaching.
- **Use of headlights:** Not dimming lights when meeting or following other vehicles is very dangerous. Shining high beams into vehicles ahead of you can confuse the driver and possibly cause an accident. Remember that the posted speed is the maximum you should drive. Remember, too, you are always creating an image.
- **Noise:** Using your air horn when it is not needed is irritating and often frightening. Mufflers that are damaged or not the right type create a lot of unnecessary noise.
- **Parking incorrectly:** When you block traffic unnecessarily, people may think it is deliberate. This reflects badly on the industry.

Improper actions by other drivers are often unsafe and frequently annoy truckers. Truckers must avoid trying to get even in any situation. Yelling, foul language, and obscene gestures accomplish nothing and may cause you to lose your job and hurt the image of the entire industry. Motorists sometimes report incidents to the company. The best policy is to act like a professional at all times. Remember, many of the trucks on the road today have a phone number painted on them that people may call to report both good and bad driving.

Make a habit of being clean and neatly dressed whenever you are on duty. Be courteous, polite, and helpful. Avoid arguments and be a good representative for the industry.

Even when you are off duty, you can often be identified by appearance or uniform. Loud, rowdy behavior in restaurants or other public places causes people to think of truck drivers as rude and badly behaved.

If company policy permits, you should help other road users whenever possible. Giving directions, assisting stranded motorists by directing help to them, and treating others properly will all pay off in good public relations for the industry.

CUSTOMER RELATIONS

Drivers *are* the company as far as the public is concerned. As a driver, how you act can lose or gain business for your company. The extra effort it takes to do a good job

Tips for Good Customer Relations

- Follow company procedures
- Do not argue or lose your temper
- Be courteous
- Be polite, honest, and helpful
- Always thank the customer

If you give that extra care,
you may get more business!

Remember... the driver has more
contact with customers than
any other person in the company

Figure **29-3** Good customer relations begin with drivers who conduct themselves professionally at all times.

is well worth it in the long run. Both you and the company will benefit from good **customer relations.** Remember: How you and your equipment look is important, and first impressions count.

All the factors that affect your image as seen by the public mean more when the public is a customer. The image you project is the customer's closest view of the company (see Figure 29-3).

Company rules and procedures were set up to improve and keep business. Follow the company policy for cargo and freight documentation and handling, dealing with customers, and dealing with freight problems.

Drivers who do not follow company policy give the company a bad reputation and can lose their jobs. If you have a problem, call your company. It is their job to help you.

A positive attitude is very important. Some signs of a positive attitude are:

- Promptness when picking up or delivering cargo
- Courtesy
- Politeness, helpfulness, and honesty at all times
- An easy manner (do not argue or allow yourself to be provoked)

EMPLOYER–EMPLOYEE RELATIONS

Before you read further, ask yourself this question: If you were running a trucking company, what kind of employees would you want to work for your firm?

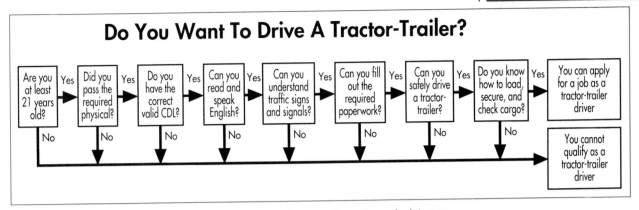

Figure **29-4** Basic job requirements for professional drivers.

Your answer, of course, is that you would want someone who works hard and is reliable, responsible, and dependable—in short, someone who will help your company make money.

This section discusses the requirements of a good employee. It also discusses attitudes and conduct as well as required skills.

Basic Job Requirements

A good attitude is a must for success in finding and holding any job. The general qualifications expected of a professional tractor-trailer driver are listed here. The driver must:

- Meet the requirements of federal law, including the medical qualifications and having the correct CDL
- Meet the employer's needs and qualifications as stated in the company policy
- Know about the trucking industry and have the attitudes and interests suited to its environment (see Figure 29-4)

Requirements of Federal Law

People who apply for professional tractor-trailer driving jobs must meet the U.S. Department of Transportation (DOT) qualifications as stated here:

- Be at least 21 years old (although 18-year-olds are allowed to drive intrastate)
- Be physically qualified (FMCSR 341.91)
- Have a valid CDL
- Be able to read and speak English (in some states, tests are administered by interpreters if a candidate's English is not strong enough)
- Understand traffic signs and signals
- Be able to fill out the required paperwork
- Be able to safely drive a tractor-trailer
- Know and use the correct methods for securing cargo
- Be able to determine if cargo is properly loaded and secured

Tractor-trailer drivers must also pass certain tests and be able to fill out the applications that are required:

- Fill out a job application that meets DOT requirement FMCSR 391.21 (carrier will supply the application)

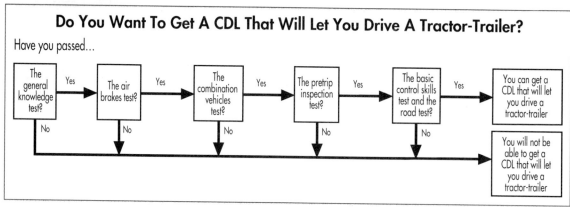

Figure **29-5** Requirements to earn a CDL.

- Take a written test and a road test given by the company (the DOT requires the company to keep the results on file)
- Have passed all the tests needed for their CDL:
  - General Knowledge Test
  - Air Brakes Test
  - Combination Vehicles Test
  - Pretrip Inspection Test
  - Basic Control Skills Test and Road Test

Drivers who operate double or triple trailer combinations or tankers or haul hazardous material must pass additional tests before they can drive these vehicles (see Figure 29-5).

Disqualifications

Under FMCSR 391.15, an applicant for a CDL that will let them drive a tractor-trailer must be disqualified for any of the following:

- Loss of license
- Operating a commercial motor vehicle (CMV) while under the influence of alcohol, amphetamines, or narcotics
- Transportation, possession, or unlawful use of a Schedule I drug
- Being in an accident that results in injury or death and leaving the scene
- Conviction of a felony involving the use of a commercial motor vehicle (see Figure 29-6)

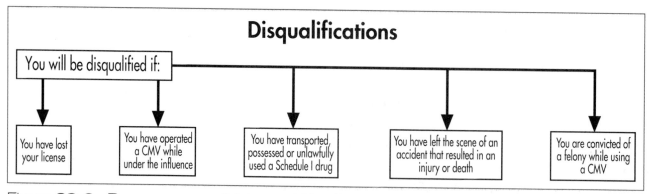

Figure **29-6** Reasons a candidate could be disqualified for a professional driver's job.

Note: As a CDL holder, you are subject to employment, random, and postaccident drug testing. Refusal means loss of license.

General Qualifications

Truck driver applicants should know something about the various types of vehicles used in the industry. They should also be informed about their systems and components. They should be able to speak the language of the industry as well as know how to fill out the required paperwork. A knowledge of state and local traffic regulations and laws must be demonstrated. This includes the basic hazardous materials requirements.

Being able to drive safely and learning to drive the employer's vehicles safely are *must skills*. The driver must also know how to handle cargo using the correct handling methods.

To qualify, an applicant must have a positive attitude toward the trucking industry, the employer, and the job.

He or she must also be willing to follow company policies regarding hours of work, safety rules, and public relations.

Finally, the candidate must have a personality that suits the job. This includes high job interest, maturity, safety awareness, enthusiasm, and a responsible nature.

Company Policy

Each company has its own policies. Company policy should be followed even if it differs from what you have learned in school or elsewhere. Find out what is expected during your job interview and then meet those expectations.

Most company policies have requirements that cover:

- Hours of work and benefits
- Basic work rules
  - Types of supervision
  - Requirements for advancement
  - Discipline including rules for dismissal
- Safety rules
  - Safety training
  - Safety meetings
  - Safe driving and cargo handling rules
- Vehicle inspection and maintenance requirements
  - Instructions
  - What is expected of the driver
  - Forms to be filled out
- Rules for trips
  - Driving rules for fuel economy
  - Where and when drivers can make fuel or rest stops
  - How drivers are to pay for fuel, food, and so on
  - Reimbursement policy for drivers
  - Use of credit cards
  - Cash advances
- Relations with the public and customers
  - Dress code
  - Conduct expected

- If there is any violation of federal, state, or local laws
- If you are not qualified
- If you will violate the hours-of-service regulations
- If the rig is unsafe to drive

Refuse to haul the load!

Figure **29-7**   No driver can be forced to work in violation of local, state, or federal law.

What Companies Cannot Require of a Driver

No driver can be required to work in violation of state, federal, or local regulations. Drivers must be provided with a safe place to work and a safe vehicle. No driver can be required to violate the hours-of-service regulations (see Figure 29-7).

Drivers and Company Policy

The more a driver applicant knows about a company, the easier it is to get a job interview and do well during the interview. The Internet may be a good source of information about a prospective employer. If possible, know the answers to the following questions in advance:

- Do you have the abilities the employer needs?
- If additional training is available, are you are willing to learn?
- Is this a place where you want to work?
- Are the hours, pay, and working conditions going to meet your needs?

Obviously, the greatest likelihood for success exists when the company and applicant agree on these needs. The job seeker should be aware that he or she will have to learn the company policies in depth and follow them.

Finally, a person's attitude is as important as their knowledge of company requirements. To review, the key attitudes you should have if you want to be successful on the job are:

- Loyalty
- Dependability
- Safety mindedness
- Honesty
- Enthusiasm
- Team player
- Good representative for your employer

Opportunities for Advancement

There are many types of jobs in the trucking industry. Many new drivers today start out driving tractor-trailers over the road for large fleets. But some start driving locally, perhaps in a smaller truck. They may even start as yard jockeys, dock hands, freight handlers, and truck washers before moving up to local deliveries with straight trucks. Then they may move on to intrastate work.

You can gain valuable experience at the local level. Picking up freight in the morning, making local deliveries and pickups all day, following dispatch instructions, and dealing with the shipping papers is good training for tractor-trailer drivers. This is the time to do a good job, show enthusiasm, and learn all you can. While you wait for a chance to get the driving job you want, the experience you gain and a good record will help you qualify for the over-the-road jobs that require more skill.

In trucking, advancement is usually from within. One type of advancement within the trucking industry is being promoted to the longer hauls that carry more valuable cargo or hazardous materials. Other positions are dispatcher, driver manager, terminal manager, or working in freight operations.

Applying for the Job

Generally, an applicant for a job as a tractor-trailer driver must fill out an application, give references for the employer to check, have a job interview, and be tested.

The application form is the first impression you make on the potential employer. If your application is neat, accurate, and honest, you will usually make a good impression on the employer. However, whether you meet their requirements is not always easy to tell from the application.

TIP Avoid leaving blank spaces in the application. Some trucking companies receive 100 applications per day. They do not have time to check incomplete applications.

For reference checks, you should have the names and addresses of previous employers. If there are "holes" or lapses in your work record, be prepared for questions about what you were doing during these periods. It is very important that you give an accurate account of your previous driving record. Be honest and truthful.

Next to the road test, the interview is the most important part in finding a job, and you have a chance to sell yourself. There are four key rules for a good job interview:

- Be prepared.
- Know how to act during the interview.
- End the interview well and thank the person for their time and consideration.
- Do not overstay your appointed time for the interview.

Preparing for the Interview

To prepare for the interview, do the following:

- Learn all you can about the company. Ask current and former employees and visit the corporate Web site.

- Be ready to ask intelligent questions, such as the following:
  - What are the company policies?
  - What are the chances for training?
  - Is there opportunity for advancement?
- Know your own abilities and limitations. Be realistic.
- Know whether you can you drive the kind of vehicle used in this job and handle the cargo.
- Know whether you will need extra training.
- Tell the truth—even if it is not always pretty.

Make sure you have all the necessary paperwork with you, including the correct license, endorsements, certifications, and letters of reference.

Be ready for the interview; be on time or a bit early. Visit the location a day or so before the interview so you will not get lost or be delayed. Dress neatly but ready to drive if you are asked to take a road test.

How to Act during the Interview

The interview is your chance to sell yourself. Be polite and courteous and do not smoke, even if you are invited to. When you are asked about your qualifications and experiences, present them clearly and honestly. Do not brag or stretch the truth. Be sure the interviewer knows what you have done in the past. Showing how your experiences and qualifications fit in with what the company needs is very important.

Most people are a little nervous before and during interviews. Do not let this bother you. Just try to relax and be yourself. Keep a positive attitude about the job. A good attitude is often what makes the difference in who gets the job.

Remember, the interviewer's job is to learn about you—to find out who you are and what you are like. Try to answer questions clearly but do not volunteer unnecessary information. Try to keep talk fixed on the job and why you are the best candidate.

Ask questions. Find out about the company. Do not wait until you get the job to find out you do not like it. If the interviewer does not tell you about conditions that are important to an employee, he or she expects you to ask. Do not hold back on any questions you have at this point.

End the Interview Well

Thank the interviewer for his or her time and interest. Show your interest in the company and the job and repeat how you can meet their needs. Ask how and when you will be informed of their decision.

You may not get the job. If you do not—and you think the company is a place where you want to work—you may choose to accept a job as a helper or dock worker as a place to begin.

Tests

Be prepared and well rested when you take the written and performance tests. To prepare for the written tests, study the regulations about safe driving practices, review the state driver handbook and FMCSR regulations (you can find these on the Internet), review the safe driving information and procedures learned in school.

Study the tests at the end of each chapter of this book to help you prepare.

Figure **29-8** The road test is the
most important part of applying
for a job.

The road test is a most important part of applying for a job (see Figure 29-8).
The test will probably include a pretrip inspection, coupling and uncoupling, backing, parking, and driving in traffic.

Be dressed and ready for the test. Ask about unfamiliar parts or accessories. If
you feel you are not qualified to drive the rig, do not drive. Do *not* take a risk with an
unfamiliar vehicle.

Physical Examination

You must have a current, valid doctor's certificate stating you have passed a physical examination and meet the minimum qualifications. If you have not had one, you
will need to have a physical exam. The company may also give its own physical.

Chapter Thirty

The Commercial Driver's License

FROM NOW ON. . .

ONLY THE BEST
WILL DRIVE!

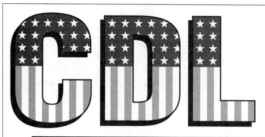

What commercial driver's license written knowledge tests will you need to pass?

It depends upon the type of commercial motor vehicle you drive and the cargo you haul. Here are some examples:

Straight truck
- Concrete mixer
- Dump truck
- Trash disposal
- Stake beds

- General knowledge test
- Air brakes test*

Straight truck

- General knowledge test
- Air brakes test*
- Hazardous materials test**

Straight truck with trailer

- General knowledge test
- Combination vehicles test
- Air brakes test*
- Hazardous materials test**

Double trailers

- General knowledge test
- Combination vehicles test
- Doubles/triples test
- Air brakes test*
- Hazardous materials test**

** If placards are required   * If so equipped

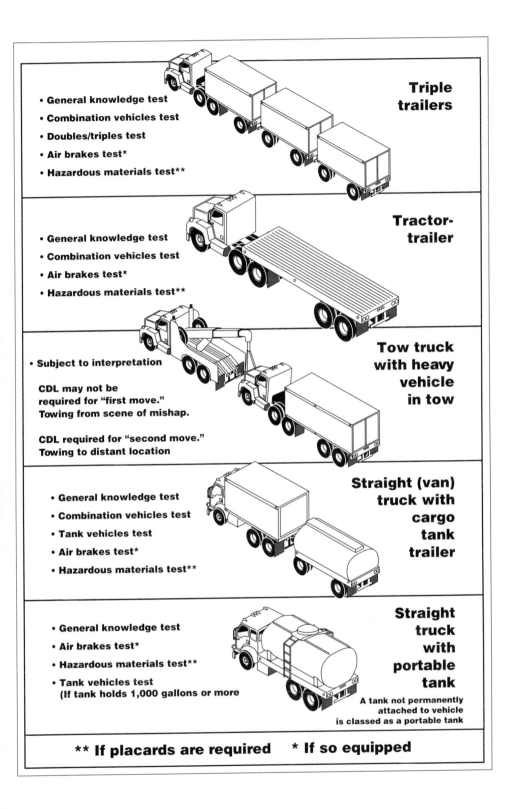

- General knowledge test
- Combination vehicles test
- Doubles/triples test
- Air brakes test*
- Hazardous materials test**

Triple trailers

- General knowledge test
- Combination vehicles test
- Air brakes test*
- Hazardous materials test**

Tractor-trailer

- Subject to interpretation

CDL may not be required for "first move." Towing from scene of mishap.

CDL required for "second move." Towing to distant location

Tow truck with heavy vehicle in tow

- General knowledge test
- Combination vehicles test
- Tank vehicles test
- Air brakes test*
- Hazardous materials test**

Straight (van) truck with cargo tank trailer

- General knowledge test
- Air brakes test*
- Hazardous materials test**
- Tank vehicles test (If tank holds 1,000 gallons or more

Straight truck with portable tank

A tank not permanently attached to vehicle is classed as a portable tank

** If placards are required   * If so equipped

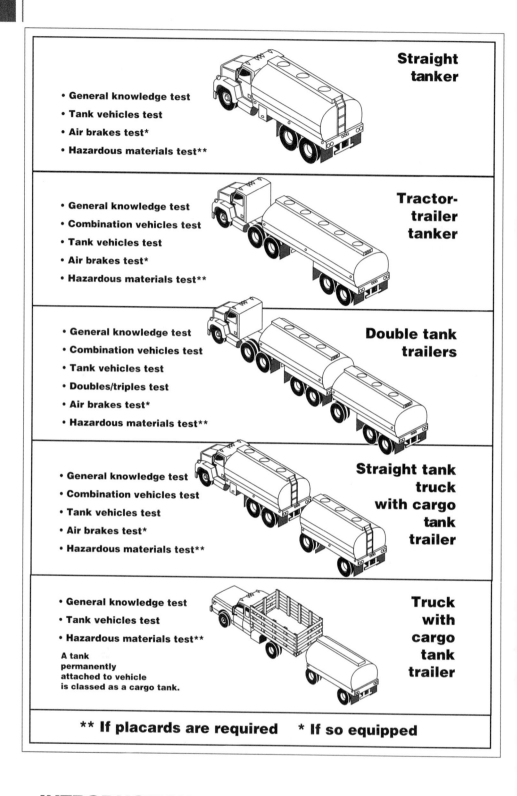

- General knowledge test
- Tank vehicles test
- Air brakes test*
- Hazardous materials test**

Straight tanker

- General knowledge test
- Combination vehicles test
- Tank vehicles test
- Air brakes test*
- Hazardous materials test**

Tractor-trailer tanker

- General knowledge test
- Combination vehicles test
- Tank vehicles test
- Doubles/triples test
- Air brakes test*
- Hazardous materials test**

Double tank trailers

- General knowledge test
- Combination vehicles test
- Tank vehicles test
- Air brakes test*
- Hazardous materials test**

Straight tank truck with cargo tank trailer

- General knowledge test
- Tank vehicles test
- Hazardous materials test**

A tank
permanently
attached to vehicle
is classed as a cargo tank.

Truck with cargo tank trailer

** If placards are required   * If so equipped

INTRODUCTION

As a professional driver, you should be aware that commercial driver licensing procedures have changed. In the past, states have been allowed to regulate and license operators of commercial vehicles under their own guidelines. But now, states must follow a new set of national minimum standards for licensing and testing commercial drivers. The national standards, set by the federal government, establish a new **commercial driver's license (CDL).** Since these are minimum standards, your state can make stricter rules for getting your CDL. You will need to read and study your state's commercial driver handbook to pass the required tests. You can also buy special test study books, videos, and audiotapes from Delmar Learning.

You can help yourself by becoming familiar with the CDL facts on the following pages. They are based on the minimum federal standards, but they apply to all states.

THE LAW

On October 26, 1986 the **Commercial Motor Vehicle Safety Act** was signed into law, requiring each state to meet the same minimum standards for commercial driver licensing. Federal standards require commercial vehicle drivers to test for a CDL. You must have a CDL to operate any of the following commercial motor vehicles (CMVs):

- A single vehicle with a gross vehicle weight rating (GVWR) of more than 26,000 pounds, as assigned by the manufacturer
- A trailer with a GVWR of more than 10,000 pounds if the gross combination weight rating is more than 26,000 pounds
- A vehicle designed to transport more than 15 persons, including the driver
- Any size vehicle requiring hazardous materials placards

Your state may have stricter definitions of CMVs. California, for example, defines a bus as any vehicle designed to transport 10 or more passengers, including the driver.

You cannot have more than one license, that is, licenses from more than one state. If you break this rule, a court may fine you up to $5,000 or put you in jail. Keep your home state license and return any others.

If you are an experienced commercial driver and have a safe driving record, you may not need to take the skills test to get your CDL. Check with your driver licensing authorities.

If you are employed as a commercial vehicle driver, you must tell your employer within 30 days of a conviction for any traffic violation (except parking). This must be done no matter what type of vehicle you were driving, even if you were driving your own car.

You must notify your motor vehicle licensing agency within 30 days if you are convicted in any other state of any traffic violation (except parking). This is true no matter what type of vehicle you were driving.

If you are employed as a commercial vehicle driver, you must notify your employer if your license is suspended, revoked, or canceled, or if you are disqualified from driving.

If you are employed as a commercial vehicle driver, you must give your employer information on all driving jobs you have held for the past 10 years. You must also do this when you apply for a commercial driving job.

No one can drive a CMV without a CDL. A court may fine you up to $5,000 or put you in jail if you drive a CMV without a CDL.

Your employer cannot let you drive a CMV if you have more than one license or if your CDL is suspended or revoked. A court may fine the employer up to $5,000 or put him or her in jail if they break this rule.

All states will be connected to one computerized system to share information about CDL drivers. The states will check on drivers' accident records and be sure that drivers do not have more than one CDL.

You will lose your CDL for at least 1 year for a first offense if you drive a CMV under the influence of alcohol or a controlled substance (e.g., illegal drugs), if you leave the scene of an accident involving your CMV, or if you used a CMV to commit a felony. If the offense occurs while you are operating a CMV that is placarded for hazardous materials, you will lose your CDL for at least 3 years. You will lose your CDL for life for a second offense. You will also lose your CDL for life if you use a CMV to commit a felony involving controlled substances.

You will lose your CDL: for at least 60 days if you have committed two serious traffic violations within a 3-year period in a CMV or for at least 120 days for three serious traffic violations (involving any vehicle) within a 3-year period. Serious traffic violations are excessive speeding, reckless driving, or traffic offenses committed in a CMV where there is a fatality.

If you drive after drinking any amount of alcohol, you are driving under the influence of alcohol. You will lose your CDL for 1 year for your first offense. You will lose it for life for your second offense.

These rules will improve highway safety for you and all highway users. Your state may have additional rules that you must obey.

New disqualifying offenses include driving a CMV with a suspended or revoked CDL and causing a fatality through negligent driving in either a CMV or a passenger vehicle.

States failing to comply with FMCSA's guidelines on issuing licenses and maintaining proper legal databases will risk losing federal funding as well as the right to issue CDLs. If this occurs, drivers operating in that state will be forced to go to another state to get a nonresident CDL.

The new CDL rules include the following specific directives:

- Seven new provisions in the regulation address the following: disqualification for driving while suspended, disqualified, or causing a fatality; emergency disqualification of drivers posing an imminent hazard; expanded definition of serious traffic violations; extended driver record check; new notification requirements; masking prohibition; and disqualification for violations obtained while driving a noncommercial motor vehicle.

- The Motor Carrier Safety Improvement Act of 1999 requires the agency to withhold Motor Carrier Safety Assistance Program grant funds from the states if they do not comply with the regulation.

- A new masking prohibition does not prevent a conviction from appearing on a driver's record and requires making conviction information available to authorized parties.

- Applicants for an initial CDL and those transferring or renewing a CDL must provide state driver licensing agency personnel with the name of all states where previously licensed for the past 10 years to drive any type of motor vehicle, allowing state officials to obtain an applicant's complete driving record. The final rule limits this record check to CDL drivers initially renewing their license after the effective date of this rule making.

- States must maintain a CDL driver history record noting an individual's convictions for state or local motor vehicle traffic control laws while operating any type of motor vehicle. Information on these convictions and other licensing actions must be kept a minimum of 3 years. Disqualifying offenses range from 3 years to life.

- The FMCSA may prohibit a state from issuing, renewing, transferring, or upgrading CDLs if the agency determined the state is in substantial noncompliance with the CDL licensing and sanctioning requirements.

- The new rule specifies that applicants must pass both a knowledge and a skills test to obtain a new school bus endorsement. The regulation requires the FMCSA to create a new endorsement that CDL holders must obtain to operate a school bus.

- Under the new regulation, a driver may apply for a CDL from another state if the state he or she lives in was decertified and if the other state to which he or she applies elects to issue that license. States are authorized but not required to issue nonresident CDLs to such drivers.

- States with a school bus licensing program meeting or exceeding FMCSA requirements may continue to license school bus drivers with that program. States have the option to not require applicants for the school bus endorsement to take the skills test when the applicant has experience driving a school bus and meets safety criteria.

- The regulations add these serious traffic violations: driving a CMV without obtaining a CDL, driving a CMV without a CDL in the driver's possession, and driving a CMV without the proper CDL and/or endorsement. Driver disqualification can result if a driver is convicted two or more times within a 3-year period.

- States must be connected to the Commercial Driver's License Program (CDLIS) and the National Driver Register (NDR) to exchange information about CMV drivers and traffic convictions and disqualifications. A state must check CDLIS, NDR, and the current state of licensure before a CDL can be issued, renewed, upgraded, or transferred to make sure the driver is not disqualified or has a license from more than one state. Employers, including motor carriers, are authorized users of CDLIS data and, therefore, have access to an employee's or an applicant's driving record.

- New notification requirements necessitate that states inform CDLIS and the state issuing the CDL no later than 10 days after disqualifying, revoking, suspending, or canceling a CDL or refusing to allow someone for at least 60 days to operate a CMV. Beginning 3 years after the final rule's effective date, notification of traffic violation convictions must occur within 30 days of the conviction. Six years after the final rule's effective date, notification of traffic violation convictions must occur within 10 days of the conviction.

- States whose CDL program may fail to meet compliance requirements but are making a "good-faith effort" to comply with the CDL requirements are eligible to receive emergency CDL grants.

- The FMCSA decided to merge all the CDL provisions into one final rule with one effective date because they were so closely related to one another.

CLASSES OF LICENSES AND ENDORSEMENTS

Class A CDL. Combination vehicles where the combined GVWR is 26,001 pounds or more and the GVWR of the vehicle(s) being towed is over 10,000 pounds.

Class B CDL. Single vehicles with GVWR of 26,001 pounds or more. These vehicles may also tow trailers with a GVWR of 10,000 pounds or less.

Class C CDL. Any vehicle with a GVWR less than 26,001 pounds if designed to carry 16 or more persons including the driver or transports hazardous materials requiring placards.

Endorsement T. Required when operating a double or triple trailer combination unit.

Endorsement P. Required when operating a passenger vehicle designed to carry 16 or more persons including the driver.

Endorsement N. Required when operating a tank vehicle designed to carry liquid in bulk or gases.

Endorsement H. Required when operating a vehicle carrying hazardous material requiring placarding. If the driver is operating a tanker carrying harzardous material, Endorsement X is needed.

Air brakes restriction. Restricts operators to vehicles without air brakes.

CDL KNOWLEDGE TESTS

You will also need to take one or more knowledge tests, depending on what class of license and what endorsements you need. The CDL knowledge tests include the following:

- **General Knowledge Test:** Taken by all applicants
- **Passenger Transport Test:** Taken by all bus driver applicants
- **Air Brakes Test:** Required if your vehicle has air brakes
- **Combination Vehicles Test:** Required if you want to drive combination vehicles
- **Hazardous Materials Test:** Required if you want to haul hazardous material or waste
- **Tanker Test:** Required if you want to haul liquids in bulk
- **Doubles/Triples Test:** Required if you want to pull double or triple trailers

All drivers must take the knowledge test(s). You may have to take from one to six written tests, depending on the endorsements requested. This requirement applies even if you presently hold a license.

CDL SKILLS TESTS

If you pass the required knowledge tests, you can take the CDL skills and performance tests. There are three types of CDL skills tests: the **Pretrip Inspection Test,** the **Basic Control Skills Test,** and the **Behind-the-Wheel Road Test.** You must take these tests in the type of vehicle for which you wish to be licensed.

The purpose of the Pretrip Inspection Test is to check if you know whether your vehicle is safe to drive. During the Pretrip Inspection Test, you will be asked to do a pretrip inspection of your vehicle and/or explain to the examiner what you would inspect and why. You must demonstrate that you have a predetermined or set routine for effectively conducting a pretrip inspection.

Your vehicle must be in satisfactory condition at the time of the pretrip test. All required equipment on your vehicle must be in place and in good working order. You must be able to demonstrate knowledge of your vehicle and its equipment.

For the Pretrip Inspection Test, the examiner will mark on a scoring form each item that you correctly inspect or explain. You and your vehicle must pass the pretrip inspection, or you will not be allowed to take the Behind-the-Wheel Road Test.

The Basic Control Skills Test evaluates your basic skills in controlling the vehicle. This test consists of various exercises marked out by lines, traffic cones, or other boundaries. The exercises may include moving the vehicle forward, backing, parking, and turning maneuvers.

The examiner will explain to you how each exercise should be done. You will be scored on how well you control the vehicle, how well you stay within the exercise boundaries, and how many pull-ups you make. (A pull-up is when you pull the vehicle forward in order to correct your position and continue the exercise.)

You must pass the Basic Control Skills Test if you intend to drive a Class A or Class B CMV. Your state may have you perform the Basic Control Skills Test exercises during the Road Test.

In some cases, when you apply for a Class A or Class B license, instead of taking a driving test, you may submit a certificate of driving. This certificate must be completed by your employer. The employer must be authorized by the state to issue such certificates. You can check with the state or your employer for more information on the Certificates of Driving Experience or Training.

The **Basic Control Skills Test** may include as many as seven test exercises:

- **Measured right turn:** You must drive forward and make a right turn around a cone, marker, or curb. Your right rear wheels should come as close as possible to the cone, marker, or curb without touching it.

- **Forward stop:** You drive forward between lines (alley) and stop as close as possible to a stop line at the end of the alley. The alley will be about 100 feet long and 12 feet wide. After you stop, the examiner will measure the distance between the bumper and the stop line.

- **Straight-line backing:** This exercise tests your ability to back straight without touching or crossing boundary lines in an alley. The alley will be about 100 feet long and 12 feet wide. The examiner will check if you touch or cross the boundaries. Pull-ups will also be counted as errors.

- **Alley dock:** This exercise involves backing into an alley stall from the sight (left) side to simulate docking. The examiner will watch for pull-ups and hitting or crossing boundary lines or markers. When you stop at the end of the exercise, the distance between the rear of your vehicle and the stop line or dock marker will be checked.

- **Parallel park (sight side):** For this exercise, you will park in a space that is on your left. The space you have to park in will be 10 feet longer than your vehicle. The examiner will look for pull-ups, hitting cones, and touching or crossing boundary lines. When you toot your horn at the end of the maneuver, the examiner will record the distance your vehicle is from the back, front, and curb lines.

- **Parallel park (blind side):** In this exercise, the parking space is on the right side of your vehicle. The routine is the same as the sight side parallel parking exercise.

- **Backward serpentine:** This exercise requires backing around cones or markers, beginning and ending with markers on the left side. The serpentine layout is a row of three cones. You are to back around the three cones in a serpentine or snake manner without striking the cones or markers. One correction or pull-up is usually allowed. In some tests, you may exit your vehicle to check your position.

Your state may require you to perform all seven of the skill exercises or only some of them. This will depend on the space available at the examination site and the type of vehicle you are driving. A failure on any part of the skills test may cause you to fail the complete test, or points may be deducted for each error. Make sure you know how the test will be scored before you attempt the exercises.

Once you have completed all other tests you are ready for the Behind-the-Wheel Road Test. This test is also known as the "drive test" and is the test where you show your ability to drive in traffic. In this test, you demonstrate your safe driving skills. The test drive is taken over a route chosen by the examiner. As you drive, you must follow the instructions and directions given by the examiner. You will need to take the road test in the type of vehicle for which you intend to be licensed. Since safety is of highest priority, if you cause an accident or do not obey a traffic law during the test, you may automatically fail the test.

The examiner will score you on how well you make turns, make lane changes, merge into traffic, and control your speed at certain places along the test route. You will also be scored on how well you signal, search for hazards, shift gears, use mirrors, control speed, and position your vehicle in your lane.

Like other CDL tests, your application fee generally entitles you to several attempts at passing the Road Test.

During the Road Test, you will drive over a test route that has been planned and set up in advance. The ideal test route would include the **scoring locations** described in the following list. The examiner will score certain driving performances at each location.

- **Left and right turns:** You will be asked to make turns at traffic lights, stop signs, and uncontrolled intersections. The turns will range from easy to somewhat difficult for heavy vehicles. You can expect to make from four to eight left turns and four to eight right turns.

- **City business streets:** This section will be a 1- to 2-mile-long, straight stretch in an urban business area. This test will contain uncontrolled intersections (no lights or stops) and controlled intersections. The traffic will be moderate. The section will require you to make lane changes somewhere along the route. This section will let you show how you cope with traffic in a typical business area.

- **Intersections:** These intersections may be located in the business area described. The test will include your driving through:
    - Two uncontrolled intersections. These are through intersections, not controlled by traffic lights or stop signs.
    - Two controlled intersections. These intersections are controlled by lights and signs. They are street corners where a stop may have to be made.

- **Railway crossings:** The test may include one uncontrolled crossing and one controlled crossing. The crossings should have enough sight distance so that you can look for oncoming trains. You must look left and right as you approach the crossing. Your head movement is the only way the examiner can tell if you have noticed the crossing and are searching for hazards.

- **Left and right curves:** This section includes two curves, one to the left and one to the right. The curves will be fairly tight. Tight curves are used so that a noticeable off-tracking situation is produced. (Off-tracking occurs when the rear wheels do not follow the same path as the front wheels.)

- **Two-lane rural or semirural road:** This section of the test will be about 2 miles long. If a rural road is not available in the test area, a street with few entrances and a higher speed limit will be used. This part of the test lets you show how you handle situations found on a two-lane rural road.

- **Freeway or expressway:** This is where you show your ability to handle freeway or expressway driving. The sections should start with a ramp entrance and end with a ramp exit. The section should be long enough for a heavy vehicle to do two lane changes. A section of multilane highway may be used if there is no freeway or expressway available.

- **Downgrade:** The grade should be steep enough and long enough to require you to gear down and brake. If a long grade is not available, a steep, short hill will probably be used.
- **Upgrade:** The grade should be steep enough and long enough to require gear changing to maintain your speed. The same grade may be used for both the upgrade and downgrade sections of the test.
- **Downgrade for stopping:** This is a grade where a bus or truck can be safely stopped and parked for a minute or so. The grade needs to be only steep enough to cause the vehicle to roll if you do not park properly. It only takes a gentle slope to cause a heavy vehicle to roll.
- **Upgrade for stopping:** This section checks your ability to safely park on an upgrade. The same grade used for the downgrade stop may be used for this part of the test.
- **Underpass or low clearance and bridge:** One underpass or low clearance and one bridge are used for this section. The underpass should have a posted clearance height. The bridge should have a posted weight limit. If an underpass or bridge is not available, the examiner will have you drive at places that have signs a heavy vehicle driver should heed. Examples of such signs are "No Commercial Vehicles after 11:00 P.M.," or "Bridge with 10 Ton Weight Limit in 5 Miles."
- **Before downgrade:** This is a flat section of road (1/4 mile long) where you are asked to go through the motions of driving down a steep grade. You will need to explain your actions. It may or may not be before a downgrade. If not, you are to pretend it is.
- **Other railway crossing:** When no actual railway crossing is available, a regular intersection may be used. You will be asked to pretend the intersection is a crossing. You must handle this as you would a real railway crossing. You will be scored as if you were driving at a real crossing.

As you can tell, these test route locations offer a wide variety of traffic situations. They also require you to perform certain driving tasks properly at each location. For instance, during each of four right turns, the examiner may grade your:

- Speed
- Position and lane usage
    - Starts in wrong lane
    - Ends in wrong lane
    - Swings too wide
    - Swings too short
- Mirror checks
- Signaling
- Canceling signal
- Gear changes
- Traffic checks

The Road Test course is planned so that certain tasks or maneuvers are scored only at selected locations during the test. You may make 10 right turns during the test drive, yet only four of the turns may be used as scoring locations. The examiner will not deduct points for a maneuver that is performed improperly if this occurs at a location other than the preselected location for the maneuver to be performed. There is one big exception: An error that is grounds for immediate failure will be scored anywhere along the test drive course.

Each state will have its own special **Grounds For Immediate Failure (GFIF)** rules. Make sure you know your state's GFIF rules before you take the test. The GFIF rules deal with serious errors. As soon as an error of this type is made, the test is stopped. Here is a list of errors that may be grounds for immediate failure:

- An accident during the test drive that involves any amount of property damage or personal injury.
- Refusal to perform any maneuver that is part of the test.
- Any dangerous action in which an accident is prevented by the actions of others, the examiner must help the test driver avoid an accident, the test driver drives over a curb or sidewalk and by doing so endangers others, the test driver creates a serious traffic hazard, such as driving the wrong way on a one-way street, driving on the wrong side of a two-way street, or stalling the vehicle in a busy intersection.
- The test driver commits one of the following:
    - Passes another vehicle that is stopped at a crosswalk while yielding to a pedestrian.
    - Passes a school bus, with its red lights flashing, while the bus is loading or unloading students.
    - Makes or starts to make a turn from the wrong lane under traffic conditions that create a dangerous situation. An example of this would be a left turn from the right-turn lane or a right turn from the left-turn lane. This could be on a two-way street with several lanes, or it could be on a one-way street.
    - Running through a red light or stop sign. This applies if the test driver has to be stopped from running the light or sign.
- The test driver is unable to properly operate vehicle equipment, or after a short distance on the test course, it becomes apparent that the test driver is dangerously inexperienced.

The national CDL system allows each state to make up its own tests and scoring systems. The national rules require the applicant to be able to perform certain skills, but the state may require more than the national rules. The applicant must successfully perform all the skills in the Road Test to achieve a passing score. There are a number of scoring systems a state can use.

Before you take your Road Test, make sure you know:

- How you will be scored
- What performances will be graded
- What makes up a passing score
- The grounds for immediate failure
- The rules for repeating the test in case you fail

EXCEPTIONS

There are exceptions to the national CDL rules. For instance, you may *not* have to take the Basic Control Skills Test and Road Test because of your CMV driving experience or good safety record. Who you work for or the type of work you do may free you from some CDL requirements. Your state is given leeway in deciding this. Check your state's CDL rules. You may qualify for an exemption or be an exception to the CDL rule.

Exemptions and exceptions to CDL testing do not apply for the knowledge tests. The knowledge test requirements apply to all commercial drivers—experienced and new drivers alike.

WHY SO MANY DIFFERENT TESTS?

It is easy to understand why there are three types of performance tests. Commercial drivers must be safe and skillful operators because of the safety issues involved and valuable cargo they haul. But what about all the written exams?

Only one written exam would be needed if all commercial drivers drove the same type of vehicle and hauled the same type of cargo. The different vehicles and many cargoes they haul require different knowledge and skills. The CDL tests were made to handle these differences.

The General Knowledge Test samples what every driver should know. That is why it is given to all drivers applying for a CDL. The other tests are specialized because they deal with different types of vehicles and cargoes. For example, drivers of vehicles with air brakes need to know about operating air brakes safely.

It would be unfair to ask all drivers to pass a test about air brakes when some drivers have vehicles without air brakes. The same types of arguments can be made for the other specialized tests. Another way of looking at the different tests is that each test result supports a decision about you. Results of the General Knowledge Test support the decision of whether you should be licensed at all. Results of the Tank Vehicles Test support a decision whether you should be permitted to drive a tanker and so forth.

PASSING SCORES

Here are the general rules set by the U.S. Department of Transportation (the federal agency in charge) on passing the CDL tests:

- You must correctly answer at least 80 percent of the questions on each knowledge test in order to pass the test.
- To get a passing score on the performance tests, you must show that you can perform all the required skills for your vehicle.
- Two factors decide if you receive an air brake restriction on your CDL: the score you receive on the air brake test questions and the type of vehicle you drive during the driving skills test.

Here is how the air brake restriction works:

- If you score less than 80 percent on the air brake test questions, you will receive an air brake restriction on your CDL. That means you can drive only vehicles without air brakes.
- If you take the driving skills test in a vehicle not equipped with air brakes, you will be restricted to driving vehicles without air brakes.

This restriction is now used by nearly all states. To avoid the restriction, take your driving skill test in a vehicle equipped with air brakes. The air brake restriction will be shown on your CDL.

For the driving skill test and restriction, air brakes mean any braking system that works fully or partly on the air brake principle.

Your state may have a separate air brake knowledge test. If it does not have the separate test, air brake questions will be found in the General Knowledge Test.

Your CDL is a **single license:** You hold only one license. There is no need for more than one license. In the past, you may have held an operator's license for your car and a chauffeur's license for your bus. When our national CDL system is fully in place, the chauffeur's license will no longer exist.

It is also a **classified license:** Your CDL authorizes you to operate a class of commercial motor vehicles. The CDL identifies the class of vehicle you are qualified to drive. To be issued a CDL, you must be tested in a vehicle like the one you will operate.

Finally, it is a **national license:** Your CDL is a single, classified license. The assignment of the CDL is based on a uniform set of rules issued by the federal government. Your CDL is issued by a state. Each state may have its own test system, but each state must meet a common set of standards. Because the standards are the same throughout the nation, the CDL is a national license.

Effective January 1, 2000, the **Motor Carrier Safety Improvement Act of 1999** accomplished two principal goals: (1) to establish the FMCSA and (2) to reduce the number and severity of large truck crashes through more commercial vehicle and driver inspections and carrier compliance laws, stronger enforcement, expedited completion of rules, sound research and effective CDL testing, record keeping and sanction.

The highest priority of the FMCSR is the assignment and maintenance of safety. Commercial driver's licensing does the following:

- Creates new 1-year qualifying offenses for driving a CMV with revoked, suspended, or canceled CDL or driving while disqualified and conviction for causing a fatality through the negligent or criminal operation of a CMV. Lifetime disqualification is required for multiple violations or conviction. Drivers may be disqualified for up to 30 days if their operation of a CMV would create an imminent hazard.

- Adds to the list of serious traffic violations for which a CDL holder can be disqualified: Driving a CMV without obtaining a CDL, driving a CMV without a CDL in possession, and driving without a required endorsement.

- States may not issue special licenses or permits to CDL holders.

- States are required to request a driver's record from another state that has issued the driver a license before issuing or renewing a CDL; include information on underlying violation when reporting disqualification, revocation, suspension, or cancellation of a CDL; include information on all violations of motor vehicle traffic control laws committed by CDL holders in the driver's record; and record all information on traffic violations received from other states on driver's record.

- Before issuing *any* CDLs, states must check the National Driver Register and the CDL information system.

- If a state is not complying with federal CDL requirements, the secretary must prohibit the state from processing and issuing CDLs and withhold Motor Carrier Safety and Assistance Program (MCSAP) funding increases until compliance is achieved.

Appendix A
Troubleshooting Guide

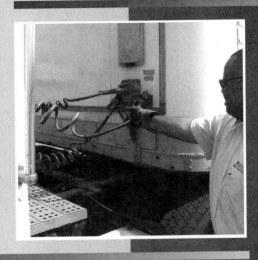

Find out your company's rules for drivers doing any type of repairs to their equipment. Find out what they expect of you. Follow your company's policy. Do *not* do any type of repair work unless you have been authorized to do so.

WARNING

Before you jack up a cab-over-engine tractor cab, make sure you have been properly trained to do so. Always use the safety so the cab will not fall on you. Make sure nothing is loose and will fall from the cab or sleeper and break the windshield when the cab is jacked over. Lower the cab back into position very carefully.

If You See . . .	System Affected	What to Look For	What to Do
1. Ammeter shows continuous maximum charge	Electrical	Short circuit in wiring	Disconnect battery terminal until short has been repaired
		Points in voltage regulator or cutout sticking	Have mechanic repair
2. Ammeter shows discharge with motor running	Electrical	Loose connection or short in wiring	Tighten connection
		Battery installed wrong	Have checked by a mechanic
		Burned out or improperly adjusted generator or alternator	Have replaced or repaired by mechanic
		Loose or broken alternator	Replace or tighten belt
3. High engine temperature	Cooling	Low water level	Shut off engine, allow to cool to normal, add water
		Frozen radiator	Cover radiator, run motor slowly, add water as needed
		Broken fan belt	Replace fan belt
		Slow water or oil circulation	Have checked and repaired by mechanic
		Defective fan clutch or shutters	Have checked and repaired by mechanic
		Blocked radiator	Have checked and repaired by mechanic
		Defective thermostat or radiator hose suction side	Have checked and repaired by mechanic
4. Coolant, oil, or fuel dripping	Cooling, lubricating, or fuel system	Check for source of leak	Have repaired by mechanic
5. Gauge reading out of proper range		Check the system that the gauge refers to	Have mechanic check gauge and appropriate system
6. Excessive exhaust smoke	Exhaust or turbo system	Air cleaner dirty	Clean filter
		Poor grade of fuel	
		Return fuel link blocked, bent, or squeezed together	Let mechanic check and repair
		Engine overfueled	
		Fuel pump malfunctioning	
		Pollution controls malfunctioning	Have checked and repaired by mechanic

If You See . . .	System Affected	What to Look For	What to Do
7. Black exhaust smoke	Engine, fuel system	Overrich mixture due to restricted air supply, poor fuel spray distribution, improperly adjusted fuel control racks, or overloading or lugging the engine	Clean or change filters, let mechanic check Shift to lower gear to keep engine speed up
8. White (sometimes gray) exhaust smoke	Engine, fuel system	Due to incomplete combustion in cold engine; should clear up when engine warms If it does not, look for misfiring due to worn injector spray holes, low cylinder compression, faulty cooling system, or low fuel volatility.	Have mechanic check
9. Blue exhaust smoke	Engine or fuel system	Due to the burning of large quantities of lubricating oil as a result of worn intake valve guides, poor oil control ring action, worn blower or turbo shaft seals, or overfilled oil bath air cleaner	Have mechanic check
10. Low pressure	Lubricating system	Oil has become diluted by fuel or coolant leaks High oil temperature Worn oil pump Wrong weight of oil for type of weather conditions Dirty filters Worn bearings Oil and filter needs changing Oil leak	Let mechanic check Let mechanic check Change oil Clean or replace Replace Change oil and filter Let mechanic check

If You Hear . . .	System Affected	What to Look For	What to Do
11. Metallic click in time with wheel revolutions	Suspension, wheels or tires	Wheel loose on axle Loose wheel or tire lugs Piece of metal in tire	Tighten axle nut Tighten lugs Remove metal or change tire
12. Dull thud in time with wheel revolutions	Wheels and tires	Flat tire Loose wheel or tire lugs Rock between duals	Change tire Tighten lugs Remove rock
13. Clanking noise in time with wheel	Tire on drive train system	Lock rim off tire Loose drive shaft	Change tire Have tightened by mechanic
14. Dull thud or loud rap in time with engine	Engine	Burned-out main or connecting rod bearing Piston slap	Shut off motor, contact garage for instructions

If You Hear . . .	System Affected	What to Look For	What to Do
15. Air escaping	Tires, air system, or braking system	Punctured or damaged tire Open petcock on air Air lines or fittings leaking Brake application or relay valve sticking Ice on brake valves	Change tire Close petcock Repair lines, tighten or change fittings Apply air to brakes several times Apply heat if you have been taught how to do this
16. Snap or click when starting from dead stop	Drive train system Fifth wheel	Loose universal joint bolts Excessive wear in universal joint or differential Worn or broken fifth-wheel lock Loose or broken mounting bolts	Tighten bolts Report to mechanic
17. Under floor noises	Drive train	Clutch trouble Bad throw-out bearing Bent drive shaft Broken teeth in transmission	Have mechanic check
18. Whine—harsh with high pitch	Drive train or engine system	Worn accessory drive gears Loose belts	Let mechanic check Tighten belts
19. Whine—short with high pitch	Engine	Ball bearing spinning in housing Generator or alternator malfunctioning Water pump malfunctioning	Have mechanic check Shut off engine immediately
20. Clicking sound in engine with loss of power, sluggishness, and overheating	Engine	Broken valve spring Worn timing gear	Have mechanic check

If You Feel . . .	System Affected	What to Look For	What to Do
21. Sudden loss of power	Brake, drive train, engine, or fuel system	Brakes dragging Clutch slipping Spark plug wire disconnected Overheated engine Vapor lock Blocked fuel filter Fuel pedal linkage failure	Have adjusted by mechanic Have adjusted by mechanic Replace wire Determine cause of overheating and correct it Let cool Change filter or have it changed Check linkage connectors
22. Engine surges	Fuel or engine system	Air in fuel system Worn gear on fuel pump Throttle linkage loose Low fuel supply Buffer screw not properly set	Have mechanic check

If You Feel . . .	System Affected	What to Look For	What to Do
23. Brakes grab	Braking system	Grease or brake lining	Have grease removed by mechanic
		Improperly adjusted brakes	Have readjusted by mechanic
24. Brakes do not hold	Braking system	Brakes out of adjustment	Have readjusted by mechanic
		Grease on linings	Have removed by mechanic
		Water or ice on linings	Drive short distance with hand brake set
		Low air pressure	Check for air leaks
		Air tanks full of oil or water	Bleed air tanks
		Master cylinder low on fluid	Fill master cylinder
		Worn brake linings	Have replaced by mechanic
		Hydraulic line broken	Repair or install new line
		Broken air line or fitting leaking	Repair or install new air line or fitting
25. Constant pull to right or left on steering	Tires, suspension, braking, or steering system	A soft tire	Repair or change it
		A broken spring	Drive carefully until it can be replaced or repaired
		One front brake tight	Adjust or have adjusted by mechanic
		Misadjusted tandem or front axle alignment	
26. Tractor does not want to come back straight after lane change or turn	Steering/ fifth wheel	Dry fifth wheel	Grease fifth wheel
27. Vibration in engine	Engine system	One or more cylinders not firing caused by defective spark plugs, shortened spark plug wires, or wires off spark plug	Change plugs or make necessary adjustments
		Sticky valve	Have repairs made by mechanic
		Broken valve	
		Blown cylinder head gasket	
		Vibration damper loose or worn	
		Unbalanced or damaged fan	
		Engine mounting loose or worn	
		Engine out of line in frame	
		Clutch out of balance	
		Drive line out of balance or line	
		Bad injectors	
		Air in fuel	

If You Feel . . .	System Affected	What to Look For	What to Do
28. Vibration in steering in time with rotation of wheels	Tire, wheel, or rim	Wheels out of balance Bubble on side of tire Broken lock rim on tire Bent wheels or rims Uneven tire wear caused by other defects Tire mounted on wheel incorrectly Loose wheel lugs, broken studs	Have adjustments made by mechanic Change tire Change tire Change tire Have defects corrected by mechanic Loosen tire lugs and tighten evenly Tighten lugs, have broken studs replaced
29. Gradual loss of power	Fuel or engine system	Fuel filter dirty or clogged Throttle linkage worn Air filter clogged Fuel pump gear worn Dirty air filter Cam lobes worn Faulty valve Jelling fuel Blocked or freezing fuel filter	Clean or replace Let mechanic check Clean filter Let mechanic check Clean or replace Clean or replace Let mechanic check Add antijell chemical to fuel Change fuel filter

If You Smell . . .	System Affected	What to Look For	What to Do
30. Burning rags	Drive train, engine, or brake system	Smoke or fire Overheated engine Clutch slipping (engine will race) Hot or dragging brakes Hand brake not released	Put out fire with fire extinguisher Repair or replace part causing overheating Have adjusted by mechanic Have adjusted by mechanic Release brake
31. Burning rubber	Brake system, tires, or electrical system	Tire on fire Hot or dragging brakes Short circuit in wiring Belt slipping or frozen pulley bearing	Extinguish immediately and remove from vehicle Have adjusted by mechanic Disconnect battery terminal Tighten or replace
32. Diesel fuel oil	Fuel system	Any leaks in system	Have repaired by mechanic
33. Burning oil (may also smell like burning rags)	Lubrication or engine system	Oil dripping on exhaust manifold or pipe Overheated engine	Find source of oil leak and wipe off excess oil Ascertain cause of overheating and repair or have repaired
34. Exhaust odor		Cracked manifold Loose connection in exhaust system Leaking muffler Improperly located tail pipe	Have repaired by mechanic Keep cab well ventilated until repairs have been made

Glossary

18-wheeler   the most familiar combination rig. The tractor has ten wheels and the semi-trailer has eight.

2-axle dolly   is attached to the trailer using the actual cargo. One end of the cargo rests on the dolly. The other end rests on the trailer.

2-axle float   has a flat bed frame with two rear axles and no landing gear. It is used mostly in oil fields for hauling drilling equipment, pipes, and so on.

2-axle jeep dolly   can be attached to the fifth wheel. The fifth wheel is between the tractor and trailer.

2-axle, double drop, low bed with outriggers   has a double-top frame and two rear axles. Outriggers are attached to each side of the trailer to support wider loads.

45-degree angle parking   an alley dock backing technique in which the rig is pulled forward at a 45-degree angle to the target, then backed in.

49 CFR Part 166   specification for hazardous materials that require special equipment or protection.

5-axle, removable gooseneck, low bed detachable, two axle dolly   this low bed frame has three rear trailer axles. A two-axle dolly is attached to the rear of the trailer.

A

Accelerator or accelerator pedal   located just under the steering wheel, you can operate this pedal with your right foot to control engine speed. Make sure there is no looseness or sticking.

Accident packet   given by most companies to drivers to help them handle their responsibilities at the scene of an accident. Packets usually contain basic instructions for handling the scene of an accident, a preliminary accident report or memo, and witness cards.

Agent   a person or company that acts as the official representative of another, such as a consignee's agent.

Air application pressure gauge   shows the amount of air pressure being applied to the brakes. When the brakes are not in use, the gauge will read zero psi.

Air blockage   when air cannot reach the brakes. This is usually caused by water freezing in the air system.

Air brake application gauge   indicates in psi the amount of air pressure used when the brake pedal is pushed.

Air brake system   in an air brake system, pressure is used to increase the braking force. The compressed air can multiply the force of mechanical braking many times.

Air filter element   keeps the air that flows through the vehicle clean and free of dirt particles.

Air intake system   delivers fresh air to the cylinders. An air cleaner removes dirt, dust, and water from the fresh air.

Air operated release   the device on a fifth wheel that allows you to release the locking mechanism on the sliding fifth wheel by moving the fifth-wheel release lever in the cab to the unlocked position.

Air pressure gauge   tells the amount of pressure in the tanks. The maximum pressure is around 120 psi. The air compressor will build whenever the pressure falls below 90 psi (pounds per square inch).

Air reservoir   provides air to your braking system. You should always bleed them each day to remove moisture.

Air starter   using another vehicle's air supply to charge your starter.

Air suspension   uses bags of air placed between the axle and frame.

Ammeter   a gauge on the instrument panel that shows the current output of the alternator. It indicates whether the alternator is being charged by the battery or is discharging.

Antilock brake system (ABS)   prevents the wheels from locking up by sensing the speed of each wheel electronically. The computer operated system can apply the brakes 3–5 times faster than pumping the brakes manually. ABS keeps the rig from moving outside its lane while coming to a stop.

Arrester beds   an escape ramp, 300–700 feet long, made of loose material (usually pea gravel).

Articulated vehicle   a rig that has several parts connected by joints.

Articulation   movement between two separate parts, such as a tractor and a trailer.

Atlas   consists of maps of states, major cities, and areas. Some atlases may also include the location of permanent scales, low underpasses, size and weight limits, fuel taxes, designated routes, and state laws for access to the designated highway system.

Automatic transmission   one that, when set for a certain speed range, will not exceed that speed and the engine automatically shifts through the gears until it reaches that speed.

Auxiliary brakes or speed retarders   devices that reduce the rig's speed without using the service brakes.

Auxiliary lights   include reflectors, marker lights, clearance lights, taillights, ID lights, and brake lights. When working, auxiliary lights make the rig visible to other highway users.

Auxiliary starter button   available on some cab-over-engine (COE) models. It lets you start the engine with the cab tilted.

Average speed formula   Average Speed = Distance ÷ Time.

Axle temperature gauge   shows the temperature of the lubricant in the front and rear drive axles. The normal reading is 150–200 degrees, but it can reach higher readings, up to 230–250 degrees for a short period of time.

Axle weight   the load each axle is supporting. It can either be checked with portable scales by adding the weight of the wheel or at a weigh station by driving each axle over the scale.

Axles   connect the wheels to the rest of the rig and support the weight of the vehicle and its cargo.

B

Baffle   a wall that has holes in it through which the liquid can flow in a tanker.

Bail-out area   places you can use to avoid a crash.

Battery   creates or receives and stores electrical energy.

Battery fluid   on some vehicles the fluid level in the batteries needs to be checked or maintained.

Belly mount trailer   a refrigerated trailer that has the refrigeration unit under the trailer.

Belted bias tires   have body cords that run across the tread at an angle.

Bias ply tires   have body cords running across the tire at an angle.

Bill of lading   a contract between a shipper and a carrier.

Binders   used to bind down loads on flatbed trailers. It is important to make sure that all cargo is packaged correctly.

Black ice   a thin layer of ice clear enough to let you see the road underneath.

Bleeding tar   tar in the roads that rises to the top, causing the road to be slippery.

Blind-side backing   backing toward the right (blind) side of the rig.

Blocking   pieces of wood nailed to the floor.

Blood alcohol content (BAC)   the amount of alcohol in the bloodstream. Determines the level of intoxication.

Blowout   when a tire suddenly loses air.

Braces and supports   Methods used to prevent loads from moving. Whether flatbed or drybox, a load must be blocked or braced to prevent movement on all sides.

Bracing   pieces cut to fit and nailed or otherwise secured.

Brake fade   occurs when the brakes overheat and lose their ability to stop the truck on a downgrade.

Brakes   used to stop the vehicle. Make sure that you maintain air pressure and don't have any leaks in brake lines. If the brakes are pulling, have them checked right away. Bad brakes are dangerous to you and other motorists.

Braking system   used to slow or stop the rig. The braking system uses service brakes, secondary brakes, and parking brakes.

B-train   is a rig with two semitrailers pulled by a tractor.

Bulkhead   a solid wall or steel divider that divides a large tank into smaller tanks.

Buttonhook turn   a right turn that allows you to clear the corner by proceeding straight ahead until the trailer tires clear the corner then turning right.

Bypass system   filters a small amount of the oil flow. It is normally used with the full flow system.

Cab   the part of the vehicle where the driver sits. Keep it clean so that papers and trash do not obstruct your view or fall under the clutch, brake, or accelerator.

Cable anti-jackknife devices   are mounted on the trailer and connected to the tractor. They keep the trailer and tractor in line.

Cabover engine tractor (COE)   has a flat face with the engine beneath the cab.

Camber   an alignment feature that is the amount the front wheels are tilted outward at the top. It is best for trucks to have positive camber.

Cargo doors   Doors at the back or side of trailer where cargo may be loaded or unloaded. All hinges should be secure and rust and damage free.

Cargo retainer bars   used to secure cargo and keep loose cargo from moving.

Cargo securement devices   tie-downs, chains, tarps, and other methods of securing cargo in a flatbed. During inspection, make sure there is no damage and that they can withstand 1 1/2 times any pressure from the load.

Carrier   an organization that hauls cargo by truck.

Carrier bearings   on trucks with a long wheel base, they join two drive shafts.

Carrier's time record   a record maintained by the carrier that records a driver's duty status.

Caster   an alignment feature that is the amount the axle kingpin is tilted backward at the top. It is measured in degrees. The axle should have a positive caster or tilt forward.

Centers for Disease Control (CDC)   agency to be notified if a cargo spill is a disease-causing agent.

Center of gravity   the point where weight acts as a force. Center of gravity affects the vehicle's stability.

Centrifugal filter   a type of bypass filter in which the oil enters the permanent housing, spins the filter at a high speed, forcing the dirt and particles out of the oil for more efficient cleaning of the oil.

Centrifugal force   the force that pushes objects away from the center of rotation. This force has the ability to push a vehicle off the road in a curve.

Chain control area   a highway area on which it is illegal to drive chains.

Charging circuit   produces electricity to keep the battery charged and run the electrical circuits which include battery, alternator or generator, voltage regulator, ammeter or voltmeter, electrical wires, and battery cables.

Checklist   list of parts of the vehicle to check or inspect.

Chemical Transportation Emergency Center (CHEMTREC)   tells emergency personnel what they need to know to take care of a chemical problem. It also helps make the proper notifications and supplies the emergency personnel with expert technical assistance.

Chock   a block, usually a piece of wood put in the front or back of a wheel to keep it from moving.

Circuit breaker breaks an electrical circuit during an overload.

Class A fire a fire in ordinary combustibles such as wood, paper, and cloth.

Class B fire a fire in flammable or combustible liquids and gases such as gasoline, diesel fuel, alcohol, paint, acetylene, hydrogen.

Class C fire a fire in live electrical equipment. You must put it out with something that does not conduct electricity. After the electricity is cut off, extinguishers suitable for Class A or Class B fires may be used.

Class D fire a fire in combustible metals such as magnesium and sodium. These fires can only be put out with special chemicals or powders.

Clutch connects or disconnects the engine from the rest of the power train.

Clutch brake stops the gears from turning. To engage it, push the clutch pedal all the way to the floor.

Clutch pedal used when you start the engine or shift the gears. It has three basic positions—disengaged, free play, and engaged.

COD shipments shipments in which the driver collects payment on delivery for freight or cargo and freight.

Combination bypass/full flow filter oil from the full flow filter goes to the bearings, and the oil from the bypass filter returns to the oil pan.

Combination ramp and arrester bed this escape ramp relies on loose surface material to stop a rig. It has a grade of 1.5%–6% and is 500–2,200 feet long.

Combination vehicle when you add a trailer to a tractor or a straight truck. It is also called a combination rig.

Combined axle weight the load of all axles (tandem or triple axles).

Commercial driver's license (CDL) required to operate commercial motorized vehicles.

Commercial motor vehicle (CMV) a motor vehicle or combination of motor vehicles used in commerce to transport passengers or property if the vehicle has a gross combination weight rating of 29,001 pounds or more inclusive of a towed unit with a gross vehicle weight rating of more than 10,000 pounds; or is designed to transport 15 or more passengers, including the driver.

Commercial Vehicle Safety Act of 1986 (CMVSA/86) was passed to make sure all CMV drivers were qualified.

Common carrier a motor carrier that offers its services to all individuals and businesses.

Compressor squeezes the air into a smaller space. This increases the force the air exerts.

Computerized idle timer a function of the engine's electronic controls, it will shut down the engine in a prescribed amount of time after the truck has come to a halt.

Connecting carrier any carrier that transports freight to an interchange location and then transfers the cargo to another company to continue the shipment.

Contract carrier a motor carrier that is under contract to customers to transport their freight. The contract sets the rates and other terms of service.

Controlled braking putting on the brakes with a steady pressure just short of wheel lockup.

Conventional converter dollies used to change semitrailers into full trailers. The dolly becomes the front axle of the trailer.

Conventional tractors have a smoother ride because the driver sits between the front wheels and the rear wheels. Its main drawback is a longer wheelbase, making it difficult to maneuver in tight spaces.

Converter dolly a set of wheels with a fifth wheel used to connect a tractor to a trailer or a trailer to a trailer.

Converter dolly axle Attaches to the front end of the trailer. This axle steers the second trailer in a set of doubles. The entire axle turns for steering.

Convex mirror a curved mirror that gives the driver a wide-angle view to the rear of the rig.

Coolant a fluid, usually water and antifreeze, that circulates within the system. Coolant helps keep the engine cool and should be checked according to your truck's operator manual.

Coolant filter   keeps the coolant system free of impurities.

Coolant level alarm   lights up when the coolant level starts dropping, indicating a probable leak.

Coolant temperature gauge   shows the temperature of the coolant in the engine block. The normal operating range is around 170–195 degrees.

Coolant temperature warning   lights up when the temperature is too high.

Cool-down   the period after stopping a rig but before turning off the engine.

Cooling system   keeps the temperature down in the engine.

Countersteering   turning sharply in one direction and then quickly turning back in the other direction.

Coupling   joining a tractor to a trailer.

Coupling device   device—called a converter gear or dolly—that makes it possible to attach one trailer to another or to a tractor. Check to make sure all parts are not damaged and are properly secured.

Coupling system   connects the tractor to the trailer.

Cranking circuit   sends electricity from the battery to a small starter motor.

Crosswind   wind-currents traveling from side to side—particularly dangerous on mountain roads.

Custom trailer and dolly for hauling large diameter and long items   has a drop frame and two rear axles.

Customer relations   how you, as a truck driver, get along with customers.

D

Dead axle   an axle that is not powered.

Defensive driving   driving to avoid or get out of problems that may be created by other drivers.

Deliver, or terminal, carrier   the carrier that delivers the shipment to the consignee.

Delivery receipt   a paper signed by the consignee or an agent of the consignee accepting the shipment from the driver. The driver keeps the receipt as proof of delivery.

Department of Motor Vehicles (DMV)   assists in making state laws and regulations for motor carriers.

Department of Transportation (DOT)   administers federal regulations and interstate trucking operations.

Detention time or demurrage   detaining a vehicle beyond a given time. Payment is made to the carrier when delivery is delayed.

Diesel engine   has fuel injectors to supply fuel to the cylinders. The air intake system supplies the air to the cylinders. It does not have a carburetor.

Diet   the food a person eats.

Differential   transfers driving power to the wheels through the drive axle shafts.

Differential warning   flashes when the interaxle differential is in the locked position.

Disc brakes   a modern disc brake system usually has a fixed disc attached to the inside of the wheel. To slow down or stop, the linings are squeezed against each side of the disc. This looks something like a wide-jawed vice closing quickly on a spinning disk. It creates the friction that slows or stops the rig.

Distance formula   Distance = Speed × Time.

Documentation   the papers that accompany shipments and provide an accurate record of the cargo. It also serves as a contract for the transportation services.

Double clutching   a method of shifting in which you shift to neutral, then shift to the desired gears to match the rpm.

Double drop frame   these are low beds that can haul heavy and oversized equipment without going over the height limits. Since these trailers are low to the ground they may have bottom clearance problems at railroad crossings, curbs, and large potholes.

Downgrade   a steep downward slant in the road, usually around mountains or hill country.

Downshifting   when the engine needs more power, moving down the gears increases engine power while giving up some speed.

Drag link   transfers movement from the Pitman arm to the left steering arm.

Drain cocks   drains moisture from the air brake system reservoirs; should be drained each day.

Drive shaft   is a steel shaft that runs from the transmission to the rear of the vehicle.

Drive train   takes the power generated by the engine and applies it to the tractor's rear wheels. As the wheels turn, the rig moves.

Drive wheel skid (Tractor jackknife)   a skid that occurs when the tractor drive wheels lose traction.

Driver awareness   a driver must be aware of his or her vehicle at all times and be constantly alert.

Driver image   the impression a truck driver makes on other people.

Driver reaction distance   the distance your rig travels during the time it takes to identify a hazard.

Driver's daily log, or driver's log   the most commonly used record of duty status for drivers.

Driver-side backing   backing toward the left (driver) side of the rig.

Driving time   all time spent at the controls of the rig. Written as a (D) on the log book.

Drum brakes   a metal cylinder that looks something like a drum that is bolted to each end of the axle. To stop the vehicle, the brake shoe linings are forced against the inside surface of the brake drums which creates the friction that slows or stops the rig.

Drum truck   hand truck used to carry drums. Never roll drums to load them.

Dry bulk tankers   used to haul dry bulk cargo. Dry bulk tankers have a high center of gravity that requires careful speed control, particularly on curves.

Duals   wheels with tires mounted in pairs on each end of the axle.

Dunnage   filler material such as sheets of plywood, padding, or inflatable bags used to fill voids in the load.

Dunnage and return   the weight of the dunnage will be listed on the bill of lading. If the shipper wishes it to be returned, this will be stated on the bill of lading.

E

Electric retarder   uses electromagnets to slow the rotors attached to the drive train. The driver turns it on or off with a switch in the cab.

Electrical system   provides electricity to power the charging, cranking, ignition, lighting and accessory circuits.

Emergency engine stop control   shuts down the engine. Use this control in emergency situations only. Many companies insist that it be reset by a mechanic after each use.

Emergency equipment   equipment needed during an emergency. For a CMV, the emergency equipment consists of a fire extinguisher, reflective emergency triangles, fuses if needed, tire change kit, accident notification kit, and a list of emergency numbers. It is also good to have extra food, drinking water, medicine, extra clothes and cold weather outerwear.

Emergency relay valve   relays air from the trailer air tank to the brake chambers. If there is a break in the lines between the tractor and trailer, the valve sends air from the trailer reservoir to the brake chambers.

Emergency stopping   stopping quickly while keeping the vehicle under control.

Emergency triangles   reflective triangles to be carried on all current commercial vehicles and required by law under FMCSR 393.95.

Employer–employee relations   how you, as a truck driver, get along with your employer.

Engine block   houses the pistons.

Engine brake   retarder alters valve timing and turns the engine into an air compressor. It can be operated by hand with a switch on the dash or automatically when the foot is removed from the accelerator pedal.

Engine compartment   area where engine is kept. Check to see that it has been properly serviced. Look for signs of damage or possible problems with the engine, steering mechanism, and suspension system.

Engine controls   start the engine and shut it down.

Engine oil temperature gauge   indicates the temperature of the engine oil. The normal operating temperature for engine oil is 180–225 degrees.

Engine shutdown   the period of time from stopping the rig until the engine is turned off. Shutting down an engine requires a cooling off period. This prevents damage if the engine has a turbo-charger.

Engine stop control knob   used in some diesel engines to shut off the engine. You pull the knob out and hold it until the engine stops.

En route inspection   a rig's control and instrument check while driving and a check of critical items at each stop.

Environment   the area around the rig that you must see, hear, feel, and sense when driving.

Environmental Protection Agency (EPA)   regulates hazardous materials.

Escape ramps   areas used to stop runaway rigs by either sinking the rig in loose gravel or sand or sending it up an incline. They are designed to stop a vehicle safely without injuring people or damaging the cargo.

Evasive steering   steering out of an emergency situation.

Exempt commodity carrier   carriers that haul commodities, intrastate or interstate, exempt from regulations, such as fresh fruit (except bananas) and vegetables.

Exercise   physical activity that elevates the heart rate, strengthens muscles and burns calories.

Exhaust brake   a retarder that keeps the exhaust gases from escaping which creates pressure that keeps the engine from increasing speed. It is controlled by an on/off switch in the cab or automatically by a switch on the accelerator or clutch pedal.

Exhaust pyrometer gauge   indicates the temperature of the gases in the exhaust manifold. Maximum safe operating temperatures may be shown on the pyrometer name plate or listed in the operator's manual.

Exhaust system   required on all motor vehicles and used to discharge gases created by the operation of the engine. These fumes could be deadly if they get into the cab or sleep berth. For safety, do not operate a vehicle with missing, loose, or broken exhaust pipes, mufflers, tailpipes, or vertical stacks.

Extreme driving conditions   hazardous conditions created by weather such as snow, rain, or ice, or by difficult terrain such as mountains.

F

Fan belt   a belt from the engine that drives the fan.

Fatigue   being very tired from overwork, stress, or lack of sleep.

Federal bridge formula   a formula used to figure permissible gross loads. It also requires minimum distances between the tractor and trailer axles.

Federal Motor Carrier Safety Regulations (FMCSR)   federal laws that regulate commercial vehicle operation.

Federal regulations for hazardous materials transport   federal laws that regulate the manner in which hazardous materials must be shipped.

Fender mirror   is mounted on the fender of a regular long nose tractor. Requires less eye movement and makes it easier to watch ahead of you. Wide angle fender mirrors let you see more when you are making right turns.

Field of view   the area that you can see either in front of you or behind you with your mirrors.

Field of vision   everything you can see (front and both sides) while looking straight ahead.

Fifth wheel   used to connect the trailer to the tractor. It should be properly lubricated, and there should be no worn or loose parts. Also check that there is not too much slack in the kingpin locking jaws.

Fifth wheel anti-jackknife device prevents a collision between the trailer and the cab. It is automatic and restricts the rotation of the kingpin.

Fire extinguishers used to put out fires, usually marked by a letter and symbol to indicate the classes of fires for which it can be used. Every truck or truck-tractor with a gross vehicle weight rating (GVWR) of 10,001 pounds or more must have a fire extinguisher.

First aid immediate and temporary care given to a victim until professional help arrives.

Fixed or stationary trailer tandem axle assembly is a tandem axle that is placed to get the best weight distribution between the tractor and the trailer, but cannot be moved. Weight adjustments between the tractor and the trailer are then made by moving, or shifting, the load inside the trailer.

Fixed-mount fifth wheel the fifth wheel that is secured in a fixed position behind the cab.

FMCSR 392.4 prohibits driving while under the influence of any dangerous drug. These drugs include: narcotics, morphine, heroin, codeine, and amphetamines.

FMCSR 397 regulations that deal with driving and parking vehicles with hazardous materials.

FMCSR 397.3 requires all vehicles carrying hazardous materials to comply with state and local restrictions on routes and parking.

FMCSR 397.5 the safe haven regulation that requires all vehicles carrying Class A or Class B explosives (Explosives 1.1 through 1.3) to be attended at all times.

FMCSR 397.9 controls the routes of hazmat carriers. Trips must be planned in the best interest of public safety.

FMCSR, Part 396, Inspection, Repair, and Maintenance of Motor Vehicles where you can find out-of-service regulations. By law you must know the requirements of FMCSR 396.9 (c), Motor Vehicle Declared Out-of-Service.

FMCSR 392.9 the part of the federal law that protects the driver by prohibiting driving a truck that is not loaded or secured properly.

Foot brake control valve (also called foot valve or treadle valve) this valve operates the service brakes on both the tractor and trailer.

Force of motion movement determined by the weight and speed of an object as it moves along.

For-hire carrier an organization that has as its primary business hauling cargo by truck.

Forklift used for loading pallets and heavy objects.

Four-axle, removable gooseneck, low bed with outriggers has a low bed frame, four rear trailer axles and a detachable gooseneck and outriggers for wide loads.

Four-way flashers two amber lights at front and two amber lights or red lights at rear of vehicle. These are usually the front and rear turn signal lights, equipped to do double duty as warning lights. Make sure they are clean.

Frame the metal infrastructure of any vehicle—creates the underpinnings to support the rest of the vehicle.

Frame rails steel beams that run the length of the tractor and trailer.

Frameless construction the exterior of the van or tank is the weight-carrying part instead of the frame.

Freight bills bills prepared by the carrier from the bill of lading that must be signed by the consignee before the cargo can be unloaded and indicate whether the charges are prepaid or COD.

Freight broker a person or company that arranges for transporting freight.

Freight forwarder a person who gathers small shipments from various shippers and puts them together into larger shipments. These shipments then may go to a break-bulk facility where they are broken down for delivery to the consignees.

Fuel filters clean the fuel as it goes from the entry tube of the tank, through the tank and fuel lines, and into the injectors. To keep containments out of the fuel system.

Fuel gauge shows how much fuel is in tanks. Since the gauge is not always accurate, a driver should check the tanks visually before each trip and at stopovers.

Fuel system regulates the amount of fuel that is sent to the engine and how often it is injected into the cylinders.

Fuel system heater keeps the fuel system from freezing.

Fuel tank holds the fuel.

Fuel tax a tax based on the number of miles driven in that state that is paid by the carrier to each state.

Full flow system all oil leaving the oil pump passes through an oil filter.

Full trailer is built so that no part of its weight rests upon the vehicle pulling and can fully support itself with its axles.

Fuse completes the electrical circuit and prevents overheating by breaking a circuit.

G

Gear box temperature gauge shows the temperature of the lubricant in the transmission. The normal reading is 150–200 degrees.

General knowledge test the written test all CDL applicants must take to see how much they know about the laws regulating the trucking industry.

Generators and alternators devices that recharge the battery when it loses electricity.

Glad hands connect the service and emergency air lines of the tractor to the trailer. The connections are secure when the glad hands lock.

Gooseneck used to rest the trailer on the ground to load heavy equipment.

Governor regulates the air flow to maintain the desired pressure. When the air pressure approaches 125 psi (pounds per square inch), the inlet valves open. They will close again when the pressure drops below 110 psi.

Gravity ramp escape ramp that has a loose material surface with a grade of 5%–43%.

Gross combination vehicle weight rating (GCVWR) the total weight of a tractor, trailer, and load.

Gross vehicle weight (GVW) the total weight of a straight truck and load.

Gross vehicle weight rating (GVWR) the total weight of a tractor and all trailers.

H

Hand truck used to carry small loads from the trailer to a storage area.

Handling brake Stopping the truck when the brakes fail.

Hazard any road condition or road user (driver, cyclist, pedestrian, or animal) that presents a possible danger to you or your rig.

Hazardous material material that may pose a risk to health, safety, and property while being transported.

Hazardous material shipping papers required and lists each item by the proper shipping name, hazard class, identification number, and packing group.

Hazardous materials endorsement an endorsement on a CDL that all drivers who transport hazardous materials must obtain.

Hazardous materials incident report a written report that must be filed within 15 days if there is an unintended release of hazardous materials.

Hazardous materials regulations standards set by the Research and Special Programs Administration (RSPA) Office of Hazardous Materials Transportation (OHMT) that regulate how hazardous materials are shipped.

Hazardous materials shipping paper A bill of lading that describes hazardous materials by the proper shipping name, hazard class, identification number, and the quantity being shipped. This form must be legible.

Hazardous waste manifest A form (EPA-8700-22) that describes hazardous waste and identifies the shipper, carrier, and destination by name and by the identification numbers assigned by the Environmental Protection Agency. The shipper prepares, dates, and signs the manifest. All carriers of the shipment must sign the paper. It must also be signed by the consignee. The driver keeps a copy.

Hazmat labels labels resembling small placards that are placed on packages near the proper shipping name and identification number.

Headerboard (Headache rack) protects the driver from the freight shifting or crushing him or her during a sudden stop and/or accident.

Headlights two white lights, one to the right and one to the left on the front of the tractor—required on buses, trucks and truck tractors. Used to illuminate the vehicle to help the driver see and help others see the vehicle. During an inspection, make sure they are clean and both high and low beams work.

Helper service a helper is to be provided for loading or unloading freight. The bill of lading specifies who will pay for the helper.

High center of gravity the bulk of the weight of the load is high off the ground.

Highway valve allows air from the hand valve to flow through the air line to put on only the trailer brakes.

HMR 177.810 requires drivers of vehicles containing hazardous materials to obey state and local laws for the use of tunnels.

Hours of service the amount of time you may spend on duty.

Household goods bill of lading used by moving companies for their shipments. This type of bill serves as a legal contract between the shipper and the carrier.

Hydraulic retarder a type of drive line retarder, mounted on the drive line between the engine and the fly wheel or between the transmission and drive axles that reduces speed by directing a flow of oil against the stator vanes. It can be turned on by hand with a lever in the cab or automatically by an accelerator switch on the floor.

Hydroplaning a road condition in which a thin film of water separates the tires from the road and the rig simply slides along on top of the water.

I

Identification (ID) number four-digit numbers used to identify all hazardous materials.

Idling letting the engine run while the rig is not moving.

Independent trailer brake (trolley valve) a hand valve that regulates the air flow to only the trailer unit and puts on the brakes. It is usually called the trolley valve and is normally on the right side of the steering column.

Individual wheel weight the load each wheel is supporting. It is usually checked by state or local officials with a portable scale.

Inner bridge the distance between the center of the rearmost tractor axle and the center of the leading trailer axle. Determines weight limits.

Inside delivery indicates the freight is to be delivered inside instead of unloaded at the curb.

Inspection routine list of steps you go through each time you inspect your vehicle so you do not forget a step.

Instruments and gauges make sure to check all instruments and gauges. In trucks with electronically controlled engines, the needles on all gauges will make a full sweep right after the engine is turned on to ensure all gauges are working.

Interaxle differential lock control locks and unlocks rear tandem axles. In the locked position, keeps the wheels from spinning. This position is used on slippery roads.

Interline carrier one that accepts or delivers shipments for only part of the trip. Another carrier either begins or completes the trip.

Internal combustion engine burns fuel within enclosed chambers called cylinders.

International Registration Plan (IRP) an agreement among the states and Canadian provinces for paying registration fees that are based on the percentage of miles operated in each state or province.

Interstate between states.

Interstate operating authority issued by the DOT.

Interstate routes these routes have separate opposing traffic, limited access, and bypass many small communities.

Intrastate within the state.

Invoice   a bill from the shipper that lists the goods, prices, and total due. This may be mailed to the consignee, or the driver may have to give it to the consignee if it is a COD shipment.

Irregular route   an irregular route describes long-distance transport between a combination of origin and destination points using any suitable route.

J

Jackknife   a type of accident in which the tractor and trailer turn to make a V-shape.

Jifflox converter dolly   used in the eastern U.S., it is hooked behind the axle of a single axle tractor. This converts it to a tandem axle tractor. The tractor then can pull a loaded trailer.

Jug handle turn   A right turn where you compensate for off-tracking by moving into another lane of traffic before entering the intersection. This type of turn is dangerous and sloppy.

Jump-starting   using another vehicle battery to start a dead battery. You should always remember to observe safety rules, prepare the truck, and properly hook up the jumper cables when working on the battery.

Just in Time (JIT) delivery system   a method of shipping that gets rid of the costly overhead of warehousing stock.

K

Kingpin   usually a 2" steel pin that is locked into the jaws of the fifth wheel to couple the tractor to the trailer.

L

Labels   for hazard class; look very much like small placards and should be placed near the proper shipping name and identification number.

Landing gear   on a trailer, used to support the load while it is not under a tractor.

Leaf spring suspension   narrow metal strips of varying lengths bolted together and attached to frame hangers.

Lift axle   can be raised off the pavement when loaded to reduce tire and axle wear. It is usually kept in the raised position.

Liquid cargo tankers   used to carry gasoline, asphalt, milk, juices, or liquefied gas. The smooth interior of the tanks and partial loads make driving very challenging. Drivers should accelerate slowly, avoid braking in turns, turn only at safe speeds.

Liquid surge   the wave action of the liquid cargo in a tanker.

Live axle   supports the vehicle weight, sends power to the wheels, and is hollow.

Livestock transport trailer   these trailers are either flat floor or double drop frame design. They are used to carry live animals. Live cargo shifts about and that changes the balance and stability. Drivers should drive at the speed that lets them keep the vehicle under control at all times. When braking, tap the brakes lightly to set the animals. Then slowly put on the brakes.

Local pickup and delivery   the driver operates in and around cities. He or she will usually be delivering freight to its final destination.

Local truck routes   many cities and towns have designated routes for trucks.

Long-distance transport   cargo is transported from a point of origin to one or more distant destinations.

Low air pressure warning alarm   sounds or lights up when there is low pressure in the air brake system.

Low pressure warning signal   tells the driver the air pressure has dropped below 60 psi. A red warning light will turn on, a buzzer will sound, or both will happen.

Lubrication system   distributes oil between the moving parts to keep them from rubbing together.

Lug lever   the device that unlocks locking lugs on a sliding tandem axle.

Lug tread   deep grooves in the tire shoulders that run perpendicular to the sidewalls. These tires are best for the drive wheels.

Lugging occurs when the driver fails to downshift when the engine speed starts to fall below the normal operating range. In this condition, the tractor produces too little power and lugs, or struggles.

M

Maintenance policy guidelines companies set up that tell drivers and mechanics what their responsibilities are in servicing and maintaining their vehicles.

Malfunction when a part of system does not work properly.

Managing your speed adjusting your speed for the road, weather, and traffic conditions.

Maneuver to change direction while moving.

Maneuverability the ability of the tractor-trailer to change direction while moving.

Manual release the device on a fifth wheel that allows you to release, or unlock, the sliding mechanism by pushing or pulling a release handle.

Manual transmission one that must be shifted by the driver through the different gears. A clutch must be used.

Meet and turn a type of relay run in which two drivers start toward each other from different points and meet at a chosen mid-point. At the meeting place, the drivers exchange complete units or only trailers. Then each driver goes back to his or her starting point.

Motor carrier (carrier) the person or company that is in the business of transporting goods.

Multiple axle assembly two or more dead axles together. They spread the rig's weight over more axles. This reduces the amount of weight on any one axle.

Multi-wheel low bed trailer with jeep dolly has a low bed frame and two rear trailer axles.

N

National network roadways that allow truck combinations to operate.

National Response Center helps coordinate the emergency forces in response to major chemical hazards.

National System of Interstate Highways also known as the Designated System or National Network. Consists of the interstates and many additional multi-lane, divided highways, such as the U.S. routes.

National Transportation Safety Board investigates accidents and offers solutions to prevent future accidents.

Nonsynchronized transmission one that does not have thin plates between the gears to assist in shifting. The driver must double-clutch.

Nose mount trailer a refrigerated trailer that has the refrigeration unit at the upper front of the trailer.

Nuclear Regulatory Commission (NRC) regulates hazardous materials.

O

Occupational Safety and Health Administration (OSHA) regulates hazardous materials.

Odometer shows how many miles or kilometers the rig has been driven.

Off-duty time illustrated as (OFF) on the log book. It is any time during which the driver is relieved of all on-duty time responsibilities.

Office of Hazardous Materials Transportation (OHMT) part of the Research and Special Programs Administration (RSPA) that classifies hazardous materials.

Office of Motor Carriers (OMC) part of the Federal Highway Administration (FHWA) that issues and enforces the Federal Motor Carrier Safety Regulations.

Off-road recovery using the roadside as an escape path and safely returning to the highway.

Off-tracking when the rear wheels of a tractor-trailer follow a different path than the front wheels while making a turn.

Oil filter   keeps the lubrication system free of impurities.

Oil level alarm   lights up when the oil level becomes too low for normal operation.

Oil pan   bolted to the bottom of the engine is a container, or reservoir.

Oil pressure gauge   indicates the oil pressure within the system. If pressure is lost, it means there is not enough lubrication in the system.

On-duty time   illustrated as (ON) in the log book; this is the time the driver begins work, or must be ready to go to work, until the time he or she is relieved from work of any kind.

One-way check valve   prevents air from flowing back into the compressor from the reservoirs.

Open dispatch   the driver goes from the point of origin to a distant point.

Order notify bill of lading   a bill of lading that permits the shipper to collect payment before the shipment reaches the destination. The driver must pick up the consignee's copy of the bill of lading before he or she delivers the shipment.

Order notify shipment   one in which payment for the goods is made when the driver gets a copy of the Order Notify Bill of Lading from the consignee.

Ordinary trailer axle   connects the trailer wheels to the trailer body.

Originating, or pickup, carrier   the carrier that first accepts the shipment from the shipper.

Outer bridge   the distance from the center of the steering axle to the center of the last axle in the combination. Determines weight limits.

Outriggers   used for extra support of wide loads.

Overdriving   driving at a speed that will not let you stop within your sight distance.

Overlength load   cargo that is longer than the legal limit permits.

Oversteering   turning the wheels beyond the intended path of travel or more sharply than the vehicle can handle.

Over-the-counter drugs   drugs that don't need a prescription, but still may have side effects like drowsiness that you should be aware of.

Over-the-road   cargo is hauled on regular routes. Drivers may be away for a week or more.

Overweight load   cargo that weighs more than the legal limit permits.

Overwidth load   cargo that is wider than the legal limit permits.

P

Packing slip   a detailed list of packed goods that is prepared by the shipper.

Pallet jacks   used for loading palletized cargo.

Parallel parking   parking in a straight line behind one vehicle and in front of another vehicle.

Parking brake   used when the vehicle is not running. To check that it is working, put on the brake and engage the transmission to see if it holds.

Parking brake control valve   a flip switch or push-pull knob that lets the driver put on the parking brake. Use this valve only when the vehicle is parked.

Parking brake system   is used to hold the rig in place when it is parked.

Peddle run   local pickup and delivery operation; the freight is usually hauled from the terminal to separate destinations in the nearby areas and freight is also picked up along the way and brought back to the terminal.

Pinion gear   At the rear end of the propeller shaft is a short shaft with a small gear at the end.

Pitman arm   connected to and moves the drag link.

Placards   10 3/4 inches square and turned upright on a point in a diamond shape. Federal laws specify when placards must be displayed on vehicles transporting hazardous materials.

Plane mirror   a flat mirror for seeing to the rear of the rig.

Point of reference   a stationary object that you spot or use as a target when you are driving.

Pole trailer   carries long, narrow cargo. A pole trailer can be telescoped, or made longer or shorter to fit the load. Cargo may be poles, timbers, logs, steel girders, or concrete beams. Be careful because you could have problems with visibility and location of the steering axle.

Port of entry   locations where the driver must stop and prove the carrier has authority to operate in the state.

Posted bridges   many bridges have special weight restrictions. Do not cross a bridge if your rig's weight is more than the weight that is posted. Some fines are as much as $10,000.

Post-trip inspection   a thorough check of the rig at the end of a trip.

Power skid   a skid that happens when the drive wheels spin and the rear of the tractor moves sideways.

Power steering   lets the driver control the tractor with less effort and stress.

Power steering fluid   makes the steering easier to turn and should be checked during regular maintenance.

Prepaid shipments   ones in which the transportation charges are paid at the shipping point.

Prescription drugs   are drugs that are prescribed by a doctor.

Pressure points   arteries that supply blood to the body.

Pre-trip inspection   a systematic parts and system check made before each trip.

Preventive maintenance   servicing that is done at regular intervals on a truck.

Primary vehicle controls   allow the driver to control the truck.

Principal place of business   the main office of the carrier where all records are kept.

Private carrier   an organization that uses trucks to transport its own goods in its own trucks.

Pro numbers   preprinted numbers on freight bills that are often used to identify the freight bill.

Progressive shifting   is shifting before you reach the maximum governed rpm.

PSI   pounds per square inch.

Public relations   how you, as a truck driver, get along with the public.

Pusher axle   non-driven axle mounted ahead of the drive axle.

Pusher tandem   the rear axle is powered (live) and the forward axle is not powered (dead). The forward axle must have a drop center so the drive shaft can be attached to the live axle.

Pyrometer   gauge that measures the temperature of exhaust gases.

Pyrometer warning   lights up when exhaust temperatures are too high.

Q

Quick release valve   allows the brakes to release swiftly. When you remove your foot from the brakes, air escapes from the chambers into the atmosphere.

R

Radial tires   the body ply cords run across the tire perpendicular to the tread.

Radiator cap   located at the top of the radiator. It keeps the coolant from overflowing.

Rear-view mirrors   mirrors used to see on the sides and behind the vehicle. Should be at the proper angle and clean.

Receiver/consignee   the person or company to whom the goods are being shipped or consigned.

Reflective triangle   warning device carried on big rigs that is placed to warn other drivers when the rig is stopped. It is usually bright orange with red borders.

Refrigerated trailer   used for hauling cargo that needs to be refrigerated.

Regular route   refers to line-haul transport between given origins and destinations using assigned highways.

Regular run   the driver operates between the same points on each trip and may or may not have a regular starting and finishing time for each period of driving.

Relaxation response   a relaxation technique that calms the mind, body, and spirit. The relaxation response helps combat the ill effects of stress.

Relay run   refers to a trip in which a driver drives for 10 hours and then goes off-duty as prescribed by the hours-of-service laws. Another driver takes the unit on to the next point. This cycle may be repeated several times as the truck is driven from origin to final destination by several different drivers.

Relay valve   makes up for brake lag on a long wheelbase vehicle.

Residential delivery   The bill of lading will specify the address and method of collecting payment if the shipment is to a residence.

Restricted routes   routes that you are not allowed to go on because the route is hazardous or prone to accidents.

Retention groove   a groove in the fifth wheel designed to retain lubrication for the ease of turning of the fifth wheel.

Rib tread   grooves in the tire tread that run parallel to the sidewalls. They are designed for highway speeds.

Rims   part of the wheel that holds the tire in place. To prevent excess wear, loss of air pressure, or loss of a tire, rims should not be dented or damaged and should be rust free.

Rocky Mountain double   larger than a standard double, but smaller than a turnpike double. The lead trailer is typically longer than the second trailer. Overall length is 80 to 100 feet.

Roll and rest   a single driver takes the truck from origin to destination.

Rolling traction   the friction occurring when one surface rolls over another.

Routine servicing   tasks that can be done by drivers, such as add fuel, oil, and coolant, or drain the moisture from the fuel and air systems.

S

Safe haven   an area approved in writing by local, state, or federal officials in which unattended vehicles carrying Class A or Class B explosives may be parked.

Safety valves   keep the air pressure from rising to a dangerous level.

Sand piles   mounds or ridges built high enough to drag the undercarriage of the rig.

Scanning   looking far ahead, just ahead of the rig, and on both sides.

Scene   the surroundings, or environment, in which the driver operates. It includes the road conditions, weather, scenery, people, animals, and other road users.

Scheduled preventive maintenance   servicing that is based upon time or mileage since the last scheduled maintenance.

Seat belt   safety harness that holds you in the seat. You should always put your seat belt on before you start the vehicle.

Secondary braking system   can slow or even stop the rig if the service brake system fails.

Secondary collision   a collision that results from either being involved in an accident or taking evasive action to avoid an emergency.

Secondary vehicle controls   do not affect the rig's power or movement but help the driver's vision, communication, comfort, and safety.

Security seals   seals shippers place on cargo containers that do not let the driver fully inspect the load.

Semi-automatic transmission   one that is essentially a manual transmission, but uses electronic controls to automate some of the gear changes.

Semitrailer   is the one most often used in a tractor-trailer combination. It has axles only at the rear of the trailer. The front of the trailer is supported by the tractor.

Service brake system   is normally used to slow down or stop the vehicle.

Shipper/consignor   the person or company who offers the goods for shipment.

Shock   happens whenever something reduces the flow of blood throughout the body and could kill a person. Keep the person warm and quiet.

Shock absorbers reduce the motion of the vehicle body as the wheels move over uneven surfaces.

Sight distance the objects you can see at night with your headlights. Your sight distance is limited to the range of your headlights.

Signal or identification lights truck lights on top, sides and back to identify it as a large vehicle. It is important for these lights to be clean, working, and the proper color.

Single drive axles found on the rear of the tractor.

Single drop frames these are low beds that can haul heavy and oversized equipment without going over the height limits. Since these trailers are low to the ground they may have bottom clearance problems at railroad crossings, curbs, and large potholes, but not as much of a problem as a double drop frame.

Skidding when the rig's tires lose grip or traction of the road.

Sleeper berth (SB) a berth in the tractor cab in which the driver can sleep. Its size and other specifications are determined by law.

Sleeper berth time time spent resting in an approved type of sleeper berth.

Sleeper operations the driver of a rig that has a sleeper berth can accumulate the required off-duty time in two periods as long as neither period is less than two hours.

Slides sliding assemblies for the fifth wheel and the tandem axle.

Sliding (adjustable) fifth wheel (slider) slides backward and forward. It can be locked into place to adapt to different loads. It greatly increases the flexibility of the total rig.

Sliding fifth wheels fifth wheels that are attached to sliding bracket assemblies and can be moved.

Sliding tandem used on semitrailers. Allows the trailer axles to be moved forward and backward on a track.

Sliding traction the friction occurring when one surface slides across another.

Sliding trailer tandem axle assembly is a tandem axle that allows the axle and suspension to slide, or move along, the frame rails of the trailer to make weight adjustments.

Smoothbore tank a tank that has no bulkheads or baffles.

Space management keeping a cushion of air around the rig at all times.

Spare tire additional tire used as a precaution in case something happens to the vehicle tires. Make sure they are properly secured, the right size, and inflated.

Speed the rate of motion of your rig.

Speeding driving faster than the legal or posted speed limit or driving too fast for the conditions.

Speedometer indicates road speed in miles and kilometers per hour and is required by law to work.

Splash guards (mud flaps) rubberized sheaths hanging behind the wheels that lessen the amount of water/mud kicked up in back of the trailer or truck. Make sure they are properly attached and not rubbing the wheels.

Splitter valve splits gears into direct or overdrive. This valve is controlled with a button on the top of the gear shift knob.

Spoke wheel made of two pieces. Difficult to balance and align the tires and rims. Make sure you check lug nuts often for tightness.

Stab braking first, apply the brakes fully. Then release the pedal partly when the wheels lock. Put on the brakes again when the wheels start to roll.

Standard double uses two semitrailers. The second trailer is converted into a full trailer by using a converter dolly.

Standard double rig a single axle tractor pulling a 28' semitrailer and a 28' trailer.

Starting routine steps used to start the engine.

Start-up the routine followed for starting an engine.

State primary routes within each state, these are the major routes.

Stationary fifth wheel a fifth wheel that is placed to get the best weight distribution between the tractor's steer axle and the drive axle(s) of a properly loaded trailer, and is fixed in that position.

Steering arm   the one on the right side attaches the tie rod to the wheels. The one on the left side is attached to the drag link.

Steering gear box   transfers the turning of the steering shaft to the Pitman arm.

Steering shaft   connects the steering wheel to the steering gear box.

Steering system   allows you to steer the vehicle and should not have more than 10 degrees of steering wheel play.

Steering wheel   connected to the steering shaft and controls the direction of the vehicle.

Steering wheel lash   the rebound of motion of the steering wheel after it has been turned its maximum rotations.

Storage and delay charges   an additional amount to be paid to the carrier if a delivery is postponed by the consignee or shipper or a shipment must be stored before it can be delivered. These terms are stated in the bill of lading.

Straight back parking   an alley dock backing technique in which the rig is pulled forward so that the rear is facing the target, then backed in.

Straight bill of lading   a contract that provides for delivery of a shipment to the consignee. The driver does not need to get a copy from the consignee when the goods are delivered.

Straight truck   a single unit truck with the engine, cab, and cargo compartment all on the same frame.

Stress   your body's response to difficulty, frustration, fatigue, or anger.

Suspension   springs used to support a vehicle and its axles. Failure can result in tragic results.

Suspension system   supports, distributes, and carries the weight of the truck.

Synchronized transmission   one that has thin plates between the gears called synchronizers. Allows shifting without double-clutching.

Systematic seeing   a driver's visual search pattern that helps him or her know what to look at, what to look for, and where to look.

T

Tachometer   Displays the engine speed in revolutions per minute (rpm). It is a guide to knowing when to shift gears. The tachometer helps you use the engine and transmission effectively during acceleration and deceleration.

Tag axle   non-driven axle mounted behind the drive axle.

Tag tandem   the forward axle is live and the rear axle is dead. The dead axle *tags* along behind the live axle.

Tailgate delivery   the freight is unloaded and delivered at the tailgate (the back of the truck).

Tailgating   following too close behind a vehicle.

Tandem axle tractor   a tractor with two axles.

Tandem axles   two axles that work together. There are three types of tandem axles.

Tank vehicles endorsement   an endorsement on a CDL that all drivers who transport liquids in bulk must obtain.

Tarp or tarpaulin   is used to cover most freight and tied down with rope, webbing or elastic hooks. To do its job properly it should be tightly secured.

Thermostat   a valve in the water jacket located at the point where the coolant leaves the engine. It opens to let the coolant go to the radiator for cooling after the engine temperature exceeds 180 degrees.

Through bill of lading   a bill of lading used for shipments transported by more than one carrier that has a fixed rate for the service of all of the carriers.

Tie rod   connects the front wheels together and adjusts their operating angle.

Tie-downs   chains, ropes, and other implements used to secure cargo. Cargo should have at least one tie-down for each 10 feet of cargo.

Tire chains   chain grids used on tires to provide additional traction on snowy, icy roadways. Tire chains are required during bad weather in some states.

Tire pressure   amount of air pressure enabling tires to support their maximum weight. Check the manufacturer's instructions for proper air pressure.

Tire slides   occur when the forces from weight and acceleration of the rig are greater than the tires' ability to maintain traction.

Tire tread   the part of the tire that makes contact with the road.

Tires   provide traction and reduce road vibration, transferring braking and driving force to the road. During inspection check tread depth, air pressure and general condition of the tires. Bald or worn tires can cause a blowout, hydroplaning, or make the vehicle hard to stop. Tires with low pressure make the rig hard to handle and cause unnecessary wear.

Toll roads   except for having to pay a toll, these roads are similar to the interstates.

Total stopping distance   the driver reaction distance plus the vehicle braking distance.

Traction   the contact between the tires and the road surface.

Tractor   pulls the trailer and drives the vehicle.

Tractor parking valve   a round blue knob you can push in to release the tractor parking brake.

Tractor protection system   secures the tractor's air pressure if the trailer would break away from the tractor and snap the air lines.

Tractor steering axle   supports and steers the front end of the tractor.

Trailer   the freight hauling part of the vehicle meant to be pulled by a tractor.

Trailer air supply valve (also called tractor protection valve)   in the open position, it provides air to the trailer brakes. In the closed position, it shuts off the air supply to the trailer.

Trailer brake control valve (also called hand valve, trolley valve, or independent trailer brake)   operates the service brakes on the trailer only.

Trailer emergency relay valve   used only in an emergency when the air supply is lost. If the air lines are crossed, the brakes will stay on.

Trailer hand valve brake   valve in the cab used to operate the service brake of the trailer. To check it, apply the brake and begin to drive. If the unit moves, you have a problem and should stop immediately.

Transmission   is a case, or box, of gears located behind the clutch. It adjusts the power generated by the engine so it provides the right speed and torque for the job.

Transportation charges   fees for transportation services.

Treadle valve (foot brake)   controls the air that operates the brakes.

Tri-drive axles   three axles in the same assembly. They are used where a load carrying advantage is needed.

Trip time formula   Trip Time = Distance ÷ Average Speed.

Triple trailers   are combination rigs that have three semitrailers pulled by a tractor.

Troubleshoot   search out the source of a problem and attempt to solve it.

Truck tractor   a vehicle used to pull one or more other vehicles, such as a semitrailer.

Turn signal lights   lights used to signal to other drivers that you are turning.

Turn-around   a driver travels for about five hours to a point destination and then returns to his or her home terminal. At the turn-around point, the driver might switch units or trailers for the return trip.

Turnpike double   a three-axle tractor pulling two tandem-axle semitrailers—nine axles in all. Turnpikes are most commonly used in the eastern states.

Twin-screws   the two drive axles of a tandem.

U

U.S. Coast Guard National Response Center   helps coordinate emergency forces in response to chemical hazards.

U.S. numbered routes   major through-routes. Those that parallel the interstates may be good alternatives in case of delays on the interstate.

Uncoupling   separating a tractor from a trailer.

Under the influence   refers to any driver operating under the influence of alcohol or drugs.

Uniform straight bill of lading   a contract that the parties cannot change. The goods must be delivered to the consignee or an authorized representative.

Universal joints (U-joints)   allow the cab to move in any direction and let the drive shaft change its angle of operation.

Unscheduled maintenance and repair   occurs when unexpected breakdowns or emergencies require immediate maintenance.

Upgrade   a steepening of the road, usually found around mountainous terrain or in the hill country; the opposite of a downgrade.

Upshifting   allows the rig to gain speed. Moving up the gears provides more speed but less power.

V

Variable load suspension axle (VLS)   allows adjustment of the weight carried by each axle. One type uses air or hydraulic suspension. The other type has springs.

Vehicle braking distance   the distance your rig travels from the time you apply pressure to the brake pedal until the rig stops.

Vehicle condition report (VCR)   a daily report filed with the supervisor by each driver that states the true condition of each truck he or she drove that day.

Visibility   your ability to see in front of you.

Vision   the ability to see, or sight.

Voltage regulator   controls the voltage produced by the alternator or generator. The regulator keeps the battery voltage from getting too high.

Voltmeter   gives an overview of the charging system. It tells the state of charge of the battery and whether the charging system is keeping up with the demands for electricity. During normal operation the meter needle should be between 13 and 14.5.

W

Warehouse receipt   a receipt kept by the driver to prove the shipment was unloaded at a warehouse.

Warm-up   the period of time after starting the engine but before moving the rig.

Weight distance tax   also called a mileage tax, ton-mile tax or axle tax. A tax paid by the carrier that is based on the annual ton mileage.

Weight distribution   the balancing of a load which is determined by the location of the fifth wheel.

Wheel load   the downward force of weight on a wheel.

Wheels   to be inspected with each trip, carries each tire, attached with lug nuts.

Index

TRUCKING

Tractor-Trailer Driver
Student Workbook

THOMSON

DELMAR LEARNING™

Australia   Canada   Mexico   Singapore   Spain   United Kingdom   United States

THOMSON

™

DELMAR LEARNING

Trucking: Tractor-Trailer Driver Student Workbook

Business Unit Executive Director:
Susan L. Simpfenderfer

Executive Production Manager:
Wendy A. Troeger

Executive Marketing Manager:
Donna J. Lewis

Developmental Editor:
Patricia Gillivan

Cover Design:
John Orozco

Channel Manager:
Wendy E. Mapstone

NOTICE TO THE READER

Contents

iv

Contents

CHAPTER ONE   AN INTRODUCTION TO TRUCKING

SUMMARY

This chapter begins your study and your understanding of the U.S. trucking industry and how it operates. You have become familiar with some of the agencies that regulate the transportation industry as well as the various types of carriers and how they operate under these regulations. You have also reviewed some of the differences among the various types of commercial motor vehicles on the highway today, and have learned some of the terms and acronyms (abbreviations) for various regulatory agencies as well as for terms related to the industry itself. Use this chapter as a foundation for your personal development as a professional driver—understanding the personal traits and values necessary to be a success behind the wheel and over the road.

LEARNING ACTIVITIES

Review Exercises

1. Name one advantage of the conventional tractor.

   _____

   _____

2. Name one disadvantage of the conventional tractor.

   _____

   _____

3. Name one advantage of the cab-over-engine tractor.

   _____

   _____

4. Name one disadvantage of the cab-over-engine tractor.

   _____

   _____

5. Name five types of tractor body styles.

   1. _____   4. _____

   2. _____   5. _____

   3. _____

6. Name six types of semitrailers.

   1. _____   4. _____

   2. _____   5. _____

   3. _____   6. _____

7. Name and describe each different type of truck-tractor.

   Name _____

   _____

   Name _____

   _____

   Name _____

   _____

8. Name and describe several types of tractor-trailer vehicles.

Name _____

_____

Name _____

_____

Name _____

_____

9. What do these terms mean?

Converter dolly _____

_____

Fifth wheel _____

_____

Duals _____

_____

Drive axle _____

_____

Tandem axle tractor _____

_____

Twin screws _____

_____

Turnpike double _____

_____

Semitrailer _____

_____

Full trailer _____

_____

Van body _____

_____

Combination vehicle _____

True/False Questions

If the statement is true, circle the T. If the statement is false, circle the F.

T   F   1. A tandem axle tractor has two rear axles.

T   F   2. A single-drive-axle tractor has one steering axle and one rear axle.

T   F   3. A tag axle is a rear axle that is powered.

T   F   4. A conventional tractor has the cab over the front wheels.

T   F   5. Two wheels with tires together on each side of the same axle are called duals.

T   F   6. A cab-over-engine tractor has a shorter wheel base than a conventional tractor.

T   F   7. A semitrailer can be made into a full trailer by using a twin screw.

T   F   8. The front of a semitrailer has no axle.

T F   9. A fifth wheel is a part of a device that connects a trailer to a tractor.

T F   10. A full trailer is completely supported by its own axles.

T F   11. A tag axle is a drive axle.

T F   12. A single-drive-axle tractor has a shorter wheelbase than a tandem axle
        tractor.

T F   13. A turnpike double is a tractor with three trailers.

T F   14. A tractor with dual rear axles is the only type of tractor that can be used
        to make a combination vehicle.

T F   15. Professional truck drivers understand they *are* the trucking industry in
        the eyes of the public.

CHAPTER TWO   CONTROL SYSTEMS

In this chapter, you have learned about the control systems for your rig. You now know where the readings should be for safe operation. As a professional driver concerned with safety, you understand the importance of wearing a seatbelt at all times. Warning devices were explained, as is the need to pay immediate attention to them if they should sound or light up.

Draw the needle at the correct setting for normal operation on each of the gauges and write the normal range on the line below the drawing.

Oil temperature

Normal range: _____

Coolant temperature

Normal range: _____

Air pressure

Normal range: _____

Oil pressure

Normal range: _____

Ammeter

Normal range: _____

Voltmeter

Normal range: _____

2.1

True/False Questions

If the question is true, circle the T. If the question is false, circle the F.

T F 1. The engine is started and shut down by the primary vehicle controls.

T F 2. Engine control switches allow the engine to start.

T F 3. Pushing the clutch pedal to the floor engages the clutch.

T F 4. Clutch brake has nothing to do with controlling the speed of the transmission input shaft.

T F 5. Manual transmissions typically have two ranges.

T F 6. The tractor protection valve controls the compressed air supply that actuates the trailer brakes.

T F 7. Engine brakes and retarders slow the rig without using the service brake system.

T F 8. When the air supply to the trailer is lost, the trailer emergency relay valve is activated.

T F 9. The interaxle differential lock control is used to prevent the wheels from spinning on slippery surfaces.

T F 10. The independent trailer brake operates the emergency brake on the tractor.

T F 11. Once you have begun your trip, you do not need to be concerned about the readings on the gauges and meters.

T F 12. The speedometer, odometer, tachometer, and fuel gauge are classed as basic instruments.

T F 13. The air pressure gauge inside the cab of the tractor measures the amount of air in the tires.

T F 14. The air pressure warning alarm will activate if the air pressure drops to 60 psi while you are driving.

T F 15. The coolant temperature gauge shows the temperature of the coolant in the engine block.

CHAPTER THREE HOURS OF SERVICE

SUMMARY

In this chapter, you have learned the importance of keeping a Daily Log accurately. The details of the on-duty and off-duty time requirements were explained. The penalties for both drivers and carriers if they break these laws were outlined. Finally, you have also learned that a neat and readable log is the result of a driver's professional attitude.

LEARNING ACTIVITIES

You are on a run from your home terminal in Los Angeles, California, to Amarillo, Texas, and then on to Wichita, Kansas. You are following the interstate highways all the way. You do not exceed the speed limit at any time. You have engine trouble in Kingman, Arizona, and must have repairs made to the truck. You also have a delay in Texas because of flooding and accidents. Fill in the Driver's Daily Log (see Figure 3-1) with all the necessary information.

True/False Questions

If the question is true, circle the T. If the question is false, circle the F.

T F 1. On-duty time may include other activities in addition to driving.

T F 2. All time spent in the tractor is considered driving time.

T F 3. In the event of bad weather, a driver is permitted, by law, to drive 2 extra hours to reach the original destination or a safe place to park the rig.

T F 4. The driver's log is the only method permitted by federal law to record a driver's duty status.

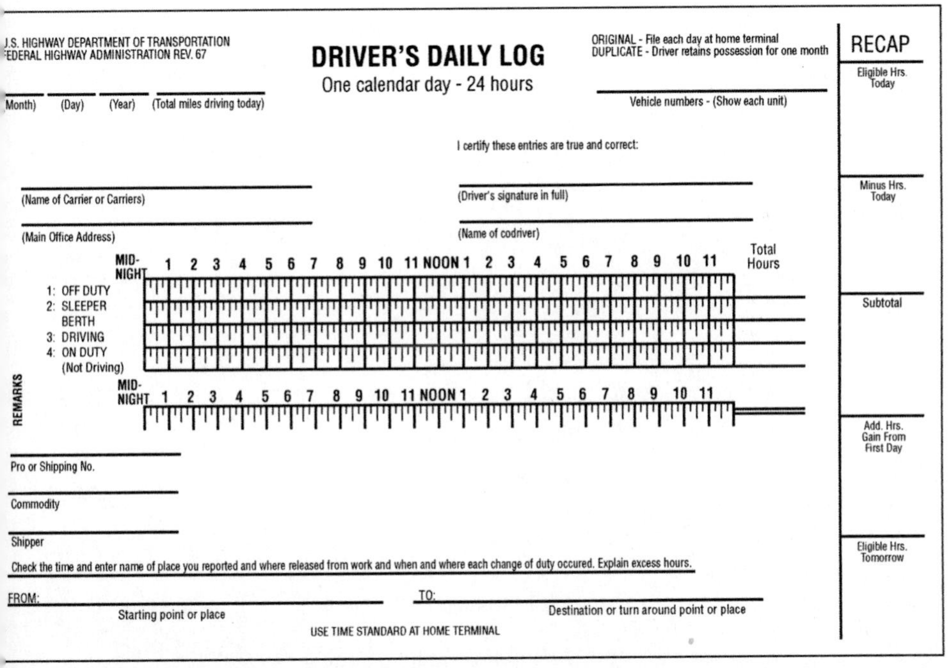
U.S. HIGHWAY DEPARTMENT OF TRANSPORTATION
FEDERAL HIGHWAY ADMINISTRATION REV. 67

DRIVER'S DAILY LOG
One calendar day - 24 hours

ORIGINAL - File each day at home terminal
DUPLICATE - Driver retains possession for one month

(Month) (Day) (Year) (Total miles driving today)

Vehicle numbers - (Show each unit)

I certify these entries are true and correct:

(Name of Carrier or Carriers)

(Driver's signature in full)

(Main Office Address)

(Name of codriver)

MID-NIGHT 1 2 3 4 5 6 7 8 9 10 11 NOON 1 2 3 4 5 6 7 8 9 10 11 Total Hours

1: OFF DUTY
2: SLEEPER BERTH
3: DRIVING
4: ON DUTY (Not Driving)

REMARKS

MID-NIGHT 1 2 3 4 5 6 7 8 9 10 11 NOON 1 2 3 4 5 6 7 8 9 10 11

Pro or Shipping No.

Commodity

Shipper

Check the time and enter name of place you reported and where released from work and when and where each change of duty occured. Explain excess hours.

FROM: Starting point or place

TO: Destination or turn around point or place

USE TIME STANDARD AT HOME TERMINAL

RECAP

Eligible Hrs. Today

Minus Hrs. Today

Subtotal

Add. Hrs. Gain From First Day

Eligible Hrs. Tomorrow

Figure **3-1** Driver's Daily Log *(continues)*.

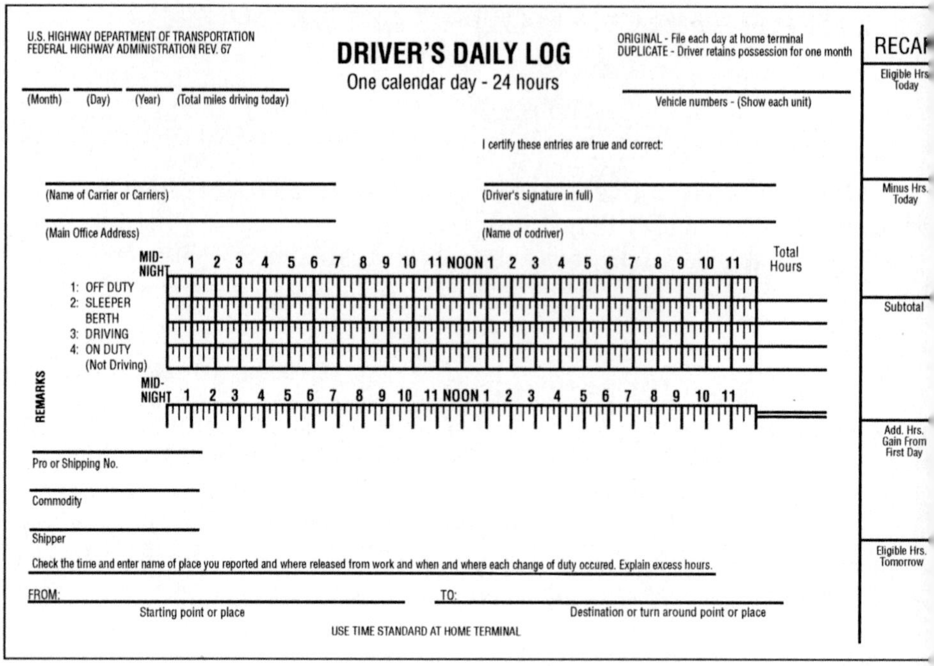

U.S. HIGHWAY DEPARTMENT OF TRANSPORTATION
FEDERAL HIGHWAY ADMINISTRATION REV. 67

DRIVER'S DAILY LOG
One calendar day - 24 hours

ORIGINAL - File each day at home terminal
DUPLICATE - Driver retains possession for one month

(Month) (Day) (Year) (Total miles driving today)

Vehicle numbers - (Show each unit)

I certify these entries are true and correct:

(Name of Carrier or Carriers)
(Driver's signature in full)
(Main Office Address)
(Name of codriver)

MID-NIGHT 1 2 3 4 5 6 7 8 9 10 11 NOON 1 2 3 4 5 6 7 8 9 10 11 Total Hours

1: OFF DUTY
2: SLEEPER BERTH
3: DRIVING
4: ON DUTY (Not Driving)

REMARKS

MID-NIGHT 1 2 3 4 5 6 7 8 9 10 11 NOON 1 2 3 4 5 6 7 8 9 10 11

Pro or Shipping No.
Commodity
Shipper

Check the time and enter name of place you reported and where released from work and when and where each change of duty occured. Explain excess hours.

FROM: Starting point or place
TO: Destination or turn around point or place

USE TIME STANDARD AT HOME TERMINAL

RECAP
Eligible Hrs. Today
Minus Hrs. Today
Subtotal
Add. Hrs. Gain From First Day
Eligible Hrs. Tomorrow

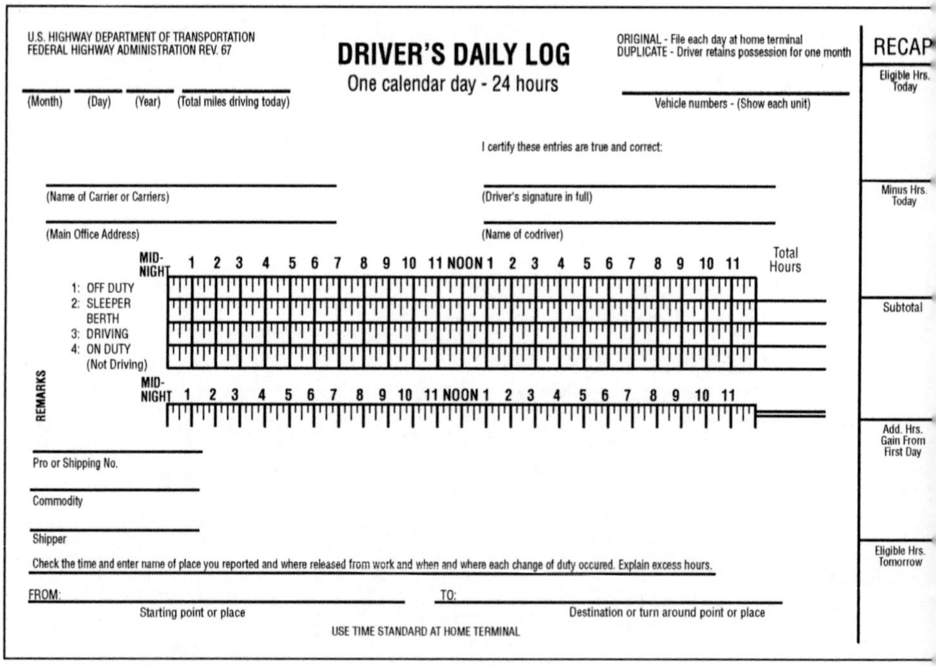

U.S. HIGHWAY DEPARTMENT OF TRANSPORTATION
FEDERAL HIGHWAY ADMINISTRATION REV. 67

DRIVER'S DAILY LOG
One calendar day - 24 hours

ORIGINAL - File each day at home terminal
DUPLICATE - Driver retains possession for one month

(Month) (Day) (Year) (Total miles driving today)

Vehicle numbers - (Show each unit)

I certify these entries are true and correct:

(Name of Carrier or Carriers)
(Driver's signature in full)
(Main Office Address)
(Name of codriver)

MID-NIGHT 1 2 3 4 5 6 7 8 9 10 11 NOON 1 2 3 4 5 6 7 8 9 10 11 Total Hours

1: OFF DUTY
2: SLEEPER BERTH
3: DRIVING
4: ON DUTY (Not Driving)

REMARKS

MID-NIGHT 1 2 3 4 5 6 7 8 9 10 11 NOON 1 2 3 4 5 6 7 8 9 10 11

Pro or Shipping No.
Commodity
Shipper

Check the time and enter name of place you reported and where released from work and when and where each change of duty occured. Explain excess hours.

FROM: Starting point or place
TO: Destination or turn around point or place

USE TIME STANDARD AT HOME TERMINAL

RECAP
Eligible Hrs. Today
Minus Hrs. Today
Subtotal
Add. Hrs. Gain From First Day
Eligible Hrs. Tomorrow

Figure **3-1** Driver's Daily Log *(continued)*.

T F 5. The carrier's time record may be used to record a driver's duty status when the driver operates within a 100-mile radius of the home terminal.

T F 6. The driver's log is the most commonly used record of duty status for tractor-trailer drivers.

T F 7. Federal rules require every carrier to make sure each driver records his or her duty status in duplicate.

T F 8. Only the driver is permitted to make entries in the daily log.

T F   9. Time spent sleeping on the seat or while sitting in the cab may be counted as sleeper berth time.

T F 10. All time spent at the controls of the tractor-trailer must be considered driving time.

T F 11. All of his or her daily logs for the previous 7-day period must be kept by the driver.

T F 12. A driver may be declared out of service by any agent of the FHWA if he or she has been on duty more than the maximum hours permitted.

T F 13. Drivers who make false entries on daily logs may be disciplined by their companies but not by other authorities.

T F 14. A neat and readable log is the result of a driver's professional attitude.

T F 15. As long as a driver updates his or her logbook on a monthly basis, he or she cannot be declared out of service.

CHAPTER FOUR   VEHICLE INSPECTION

Now that you have completed this chapter, you are able to describe ways to make a thorough and accurate pretrip inspection. You are also able to explain the importance of correcting malfunctions quickly. Because you have completed this chapter, you will have a working knowledge of federal and state regulations for inspections and can explain the procedures for en route and posttrip inspections.

Review Questions

1. Why is a vehicle safety inspection performed?

   _____

   _____

2. What are the three basic types of vehicle inspections? What is the purpose of each?

   _____

   _____

   _____

   _____

3. What are the four basic reasons for vehicle safety inspections? Briefly explain each.

   _____

   _____

   _____

   _____

4. Explain Federal Motor Carrier Safety Regulations (FMCSR), Parts 396.9 (Motor Vehicle Declared Out-of-Service), 392.9 (Secure Cargo Check), and 397.17 (Hazardous Material Tire Check).

   _____

   _____

   _____

   _____

   _____

5. Why is it important to have a step-by-step routine for a pretrip inspection?

   _____

   _____

6. Describe each of the seven steps that make up the "Seven-Step Pre-trip Inspection Procedure."

_____

_____

_____

_____

_____

_____

_____

_____

_____

7. What is a vehicle inspection report? Does the law require it?

_____

_____

_____

_____

8. What are the three basic points of a good inspection?

_____

_____

_____

_____

9. List five safety defects that are considered very dangerous.

_____

_____

_____

_____

_____

10. Why is it important to file a written vehicle condition report (VCR)?

_____

_____

_____

_____

Review Quiz, Part A—Problems

In column A are things that can occur because of a defect or malfunction. Column B shows a step in the pretrip inspection. Draw a line from the problem to the step in the inspection that might have told you there was a problem.

Column A	Column B
A problem you do not want to happen	**An inspection step that might have told you there was a problem**

1. Engine failed, and serious damage occurred as a result

2. Vehicle declared out of service because of defective steering

3. Pieces of cargo fell off trailer

4. A blowout in the right front tire made the rig run off the road

5. Brakes reacted too slowly, and the rig had an accident

A. Checked under front end of tractor for bent, worn, or missing parts

B. Checked tire pressure gauge and inspected tread wear

C. Conducted air pressure check of braking system

D. Looked under the vehicle hood and checked dash instruments

E. Inspected cargo

Review Quiz, Part B—Inspection Sequences

Listed here are the seven steps in a pretrip inspection. Put them in the best order (number them 1, 2, 3, 4, 5, 6, and 7).

_____ Shut off the engine. Secure the rig and check the high and low headlight beams and four-way flashers.

_____ Raise the cab or hood. Check the engine compartment.

_____ Start the engine. Check the instruments, controls, and emergency equipment.

_____ Walk toward the rig. Look it over for damage and fluid leaks.

_____ Do a walk-around inspection with the right turn signal on.

_____ Do a standing and rolling air brake system test and a last check of the instruments.

_____ Check the operation of the left turn signal and the stop lights.

Review Quiz, Part C—Federal Requirements

Put a T in front of the statements that are required by law.

As well as inspecting your rig to be sure it is safe to drive, federal laws say you must:

_____ Make out a Vehicle Condition Report (VCR) at the end of the day or tour of duty.

_____ Be able to repair any vehicle defect you identify.

_____ Inspect for hot tires and low pressure every 100 miles or 2 hours (whichever comes first) when pulling a cargo of hazardous material.

_____ Have a CB radio that works during a pretrip inspection.

_____ Review the previous VCR to determine if reported defects were corrected.

True/False Questions

Circle the T if the statement is true. Circle the F if the statement if false.

T F 1. The best way to check for loose lugs is to use a lug wrench.

T F 2. Low tire pressure, which makes the rig hard to handle, increases chances of a tire fire.

T F 3. To check steering wheel free play on a rig with power steering, the engine may be either on or off.

T F 4. On most rigs, the brake low-pressure alarm and/or light will go on when the air pressure drops to 80 psi.

T F 5. Rust around the lugs is most often a sign the lug nuts are loose.

T F 6. "*Thumping*" a tire with a tire iron to check for proper air pressure is a quick and accurate method.

T F 7. For a vehicle with a manual steering system and a 20-inch steering wheel, if steering wheel lash is more than 2 1/2 inches, the vehicle will be considered out of service.

T F 8. To check for air pressure loss in the brake system, watch the air pressure gauge while you put on the foot brake with the engine running.

T F 9. The proper way to inspect air tanks for oil is to open the petcocks and allow the tanks to drain.

T F 10. With the engine off, the air brake system fully charged, and the service brakes released, for a tractor the air pressure minute drop in 1 minute should be less than 2 psi.

T F 11. According to FMCSR 396, the steering wheel free play in a vehicle with power steering should not be more than 5 1/4 inches for a 20-inch steering wheel.

T F 12. According to FMCSR 392.9, you must stop to examine the cargo securing devices within 25 miles of the start of a trip.

T F 13. According to FMCSR 397.17, if you are hauling hazardous material and your vehicle has dual tires, you must stop and check the tires every 2 hours or 100 miles, whichever comes first.

T F 14. The tractor protection valve should automatically go from the *Normal* to the *Emergency* position when the air pressure drops to 60 psi.

T F 15. You must stop and do an en route walk-around safety inspection every 150 miles or every 3 hours, whichever comes first.

T F 16. For most clutches, normal free play is 2 to 3 inches.

Three-Axle Tractor With Two-Axle Trailer Pretrip Inspection Routine
Review Checklist

Use this checklist to review the items to be inspected on your rig. Do you know the check points for each of the items listed? If not, mark or check the item for further review.

Note: In Kansas, the preferred sequence for inspecting the rig is to start on the left side of the tractor and proceed along the left side of the trailer facing traffic, then inspect the rear of the trailer and proceed up the right side of the rig. Be sure to check with your state department of motor vehicles for the preferred sequence in your state.

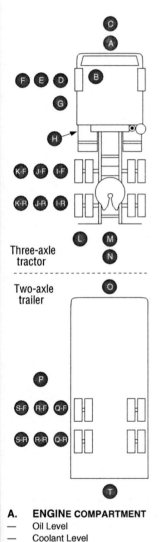

Three-axle tractor

Two-axle trailer

— Parking Brake
— Mirrors—Windshield
— Wipers
— Lighting Indicators
— Horn(s)
— Heater/Defroster
— Safety/Emergency Equipment

C.   FRONT OF TRACTOR
— Lights
— Steering Box
— Steering Linkage

D.   FRONT SUSPENSION
— Springs
— Spring Mounts
— Shock Absorber

E.   FRONT WHEEL
— Rim
— Tire
— Lug Nuts
— Hub Oil Seal

F.   FRONT BRAKE
— Slack Adjuster
— Chamber
— Hoses
— Drum

G.   DRIVER/FUEL AREA
— Door, Mirror
— Fuel Tank
— Leaks
— Battery/Battery Box

H.   UNDER TRACTOR
— Drive Shaft
— Exhaust System
— Frame

I-F. REAR WHEELS (FRONT AXLE)
— Rims
— Tires
— Axle Seals
— Lug Nuts
— Spacers

I-R. REAR WHEELS (REAR AXLE)
— Rims
— Tires
— Axle Seals
— Lug Nuts
— Spacers

A.   ENGINE COMPARTMENT
— Oil Level
— Coolant Level
— Power Steering Fluid
— Water Pump
— Alternator
— Air Compressor
— Any Leaks

B.   ENGINE START
— Clutch/Gearshift
— Air Buzzer Sounds
— Oil Pressure Builds
— Ammeter/Voltmeter
— Air Brake Check
— Steering Play

J-F. REAR SUSPENSION (FRONT AXLE)
— Springs
— Spring Mounts
— Torsion, Shocks
— Air Bags
— Torque Arm

J-R. REAR SUSPENSION (REAR AXLE)
— Springs
— Spring Mounts
— Torsion, Shocks
— Air Bags
— Torque Arm

K-F. REAR BRAKES (FRONT AXLE)
— Slack Adjuster
— Chamber
— Hoses
— Drums

K-R. REAR BRAKES (REAR AXLE)
— Slack Adjuster
— Chamber
— Hoses
— Drums

L.   COUPLING SYSTEM
— Mounting Bolts
— Safety Latch
— Platform/Catwalk
— Release Arm
— Kingpin/Apron
— Air/Electric Lines
— Locking Jaws
— Gap
— Guide Plate
— Fifth Wheel Plate

M.   SLIDING FIFTH WHEEL
— Locking Pins

N.   REAR OF TRACTOR
— Lights, Reflectors
— Signal/Brake Lights
— Splash Guards

O.   TRAILER FRONT
— Air/Electric Connect
— Header Board
— Lights, Reflectors

P.   SIDE OF TRAILER
— Landing Gear
— Lights, Reflectors
— Doors, Ties
— Frame
— Tandem Release

Q-F. WHEELS (FRONT AXLE)
— Rims
— Tires
— Axle Seals
— Lug Nuts
— Spacers

Q-R. WHEELS (REAR AXLE)
— Rims
— Tires
— Axle Seals
— Lug Nuts
— Spacers

R-F. SUSPENSION (FRONT AXLE)
— Springs
— Spring Mounts

R-R. SUSPENSION (REAR AXLE)
— Springs
— Spring Mounts

S-F. BRAKES (FRONT AXLE)
— Slack Adjuster
— Chamber
— Hoses
— Drums

S-R. BRAKES (REAR AXLE)
— Slack Adjuster
— Chamber
— Hoses
— Drums

T.   REAR OF TRAILER
— Lights, Reflectors
— Doors, Ties
— Splash Guards

SUMMARY

In this chapter, you have learned about most of the systems on a tractor-trailer. You have studied about the suspension, fuel, air intake and exhaust, lubrication, cooling, electrical steering, and coupling systems. You also now know where the frame, axles, wheels and their parts, engine, drivetrain, and the various brakes are located and how they operate.

Identify the Diagrams

LEARNING ACTIVITIES

Instructions: Write the name of the part on the line below the drawing. Tell its function on the lines beside the drawing.

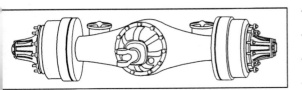

1. _____

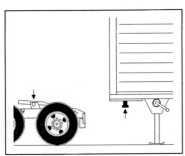

2. _____

3. _____

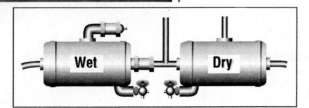

_____

_____

_____

_____

_____

4. _____

_____

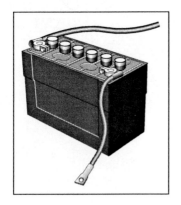

_____

_____

_____

_____

_____

_____

_____

5. _____

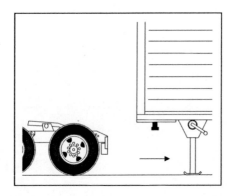

_____

_____

_____

_____

_____

6. _____   _____

True/False Questions

Circle the T if the statement is true. Circle the F if the statement is false.

T F   1. A tractor frame serves much the same purpose as the skeleton of the human body. It provides support for other parts of the system.

T F   2. The suspension system supports, distributes, and carries the weight of the truck.

T F   3. The only important difference between the front and rear tractor axles is the steering capability of the front axle.

T F 4. A lift axle, when in a lowered position, reduces the tire and axle wear on the other axles.

T F 5. Live axles are those that power the vehicle.

T F 6. Live axles are always on the road surface, while dead axles are retractable and may be raised above the ground surface.

T F 7. Trucks are powered by internal combustion engines.

T F 8. Diesel engines do not have a carburetor or spark plugs.

T F 9. Power from the engine turns the fifth wheel, which pulls the trailer.

T F 10. Fuel injectors can be ruined by a small speck of dirt.

T F 11. One disadvantage of diesel fuel is its tendency to form waxy crystals in cold temperatures.

T F 12. The air cleaner, which is an element of the air intake system, removes dirt, dust, and water.

T F 13. The most important function of the lubrication system is to distribute oil to reduce friction between the surfaces of engine parts.

T F 14. The lubrication system prevents loss of power and protects engine surfaces against corrosion.

T F 15. If it is necessary to add oil on a trip, any quality brand containing additives may be used.

T F 16. Damage from an overheated engine can generally be avoided by carefully monitoring lubrication and cooling system gauges.

T F 17. When the electrical system is working properly and not overtaxed, the battery provides electricity for starting the engine, and the alternator or generator provides for other electrical needs.

T F 18. The power train may be thought of as a series of parts that transfer the power generated by the engine to the drive wheels and road.

T F 19. By pushing in the clutch pedal, the driver can disconnect the engine from the rest of the power train. When the clutch pedal is released, the engine is connected to the rest of the power train again.

T F 20. The main purpose of transmission gears is to turn the torque of the drive shaft at right angles.

T F 21. The links at either end of the drive shaft are called universal joints because they can move up, down, or sideways as the tractor moves along the road.

T F 22. Rear wheels are able to turn at different speeds because of the rear universal joint.

T F 23. Tandem axles are able to carry greater loads than single-axle rigs.

T F 24. One advantage of all tandem axles is that they increase traction.

T F 25. The service brake system is used to reduce speed and stop the vehicle.

T F 26. The service system may include both disc and drum brakes, both of which are mechanical.

T F 27. With an air brake system, compressed air can multiply the force of mechanical brakes.

T F 28. An air brake system will work with disc brakes but not with drum brakes.

T F 29. Moisture should be drained from the air pressure system daily to protect against damage to the system.

T F 30. You must be careful and prevent the rig from rolling during the moisture draining process.

T F 31. If the low-pressure warning system (red light or buzzer) comes on, you should pull into the next convenient rest area and search for the cause.

T F 32. An antilock brake system helps keep the truck moving in a straight line during hard braking.

T F 33. Advice not to mix radial and bias-ply tires is a phony attempt to sell more tires.

T F 34. The most accurate reading of tire pressure will be achieved when the tires are cool.

T F 35. Overheated tires can result from a number of conditions, including underinflation, mixing tires of unequal size, and long-distance high-speed operation.

T F 36. The fifth wheel is one of the two main components of a tractor-trailer coupling system.

CHAPTER SIX   BASIC CONTROL

Now that you have completed this chapter, you understand and can explain routines for starting, warming up, cooling down, and shutting off four-cycle diesel engines. You are also able to test the trailer hookup, explain the proper way to put a rig into motion, and demonstrate the correct way to stop a rig. Because you have completed this chapter, you also can describe backing in a straight line, explain the correct procedures for turning right and turning left, and can define off-tracking.

Review Quiz, Part A

List the following steps in the correct order for starting up a two-cycle diesel engine. Each step is used only once, so you can cross it off as you list it.

A. Check the instruments for system malfunctions.

B. Depress the clutch pedal (prevents the starting motor from turning the transmission gears).

C. Turn on the switch-key.

D. Operate the starter. If the engine does not start in 15 to 20 seconds, turn off the starter. Allow it to cool for at least 1 minute, then try again.

E. Place the Stop and Emergency Stop controls in the Run position (if your rig has them).

F. Control the engine speed with the foot throttle until it is running smoothly.

G. Put on the parking brakes.

1. _____   2. _____   3. _____   4. _____

5. _____   6. _____   7. _____

Review Quiz, Part B

List the following steps in the correct order for starting up a four-cycle diesel engine. Each step is used only once, so you can cross it off as you list it.

A. Turn on the switch-key.

B. Crank for 3 or 4 seconds.

C. Close the throttle. Depress the clutch pedal.

D. Check the instruments.

E. Operate the starter.

F. Warm up the engine.

G. Put on the parking brake.

1. _____   2. _____   3. _____   4. _____

5. _____   6. _____   7. _____

True/False Questions

If the question is true, circle the T. If the question is false, circle the F.

T F   1. Pumping the throttle when starting is fuel efficient. It ensures that enough fuel will enter the engine for a smooth start.

T F   2. Some engines warm up better while being driven at slower speeds than while idling.

T F   3. Rapidly revving the engine wastes fuel.

T F   4. Engine warm-up is important because it aids lubrication, raises the coolant temperature, and builds up air pressure.

T F   5. Not warming up the engine can cause serious and costly damage.

T F   6. The steps in engine shutdown vary from one type of truck to another.

T F   7. In diesel engines, the cool-down is as important as the warm-up.

T F   8. Idling the engine can waste a lot of fuel.

T F   9. Idling is one method of cleaning fuel injectors.

T F 10. Once a driver has mastered the trailer hookup process, it becomes habit, and testing the hookup on later occasions becomes unnecessary.

T F 11. Putting the tractor-trailer in motion is a skill that can be mastered quickly by reading and memorizing the proper steps.

T F 12. Stopping a big rig smoothly is a skill that must be learned from practice.

T F 13. When attempting to back in a straight line, if the trailer gets bigger in the mirror, push the steering wheel toward the mirror.

T F 14. In turning a tractor-trailer, the rear wheels follow a shorter path than the front wheels.

T F 15. The longer the vehicle, the greater the off-tracking.

Diagrams

1. Draw the correct path a rig should take when taking a right curve.

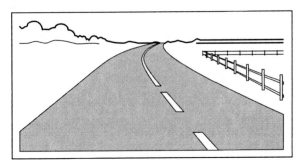

2. Draw the correct path a rig should take when taking a left curve.

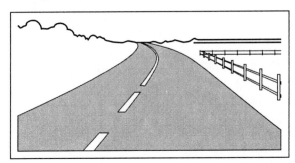

3. Draw the path the front wheels will take when the truck makes a left turn. Then draw the path the rear wheels will take in the turn. Label each path.

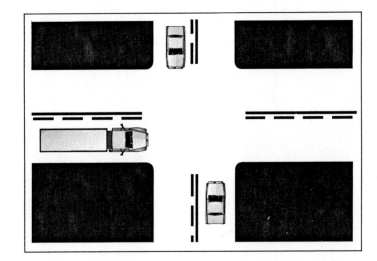

4. Draw the proper path for making a right turn.

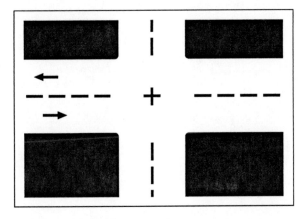

5. Draw the proper path for making a left turn.

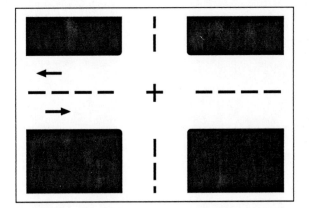

CHAPTER SEVEN SHIFTING

1. Know the shift pattern of the vehicle.
2. Start the rig in the lowest gear.
3. Use the clutch brake properly.
4. Upshift smoothly.
5. Downshift at the precise point and time required.
6. Use double clutching.
7. Avoid snapping or riding the clutch.
8. Use the tachometer and speedometer to time shifts.
9. Avoid lugging or revving the engine.
10. Do not force the transmission into gear.
11. Avoid overloading the rig.

True/False Questions

LEARNING ACTIVITIES

Circle the T if the statement is true. Circle the F if the statement is false.

T F 1. The clutch connects and disconnects the engine and transmission.

T F 2. Pushing down on the clutch pedal engages the engine.

T F 3. A standing vehicle requires more power to get it moving than to keep it moving once it is under way.

T F 4. Nonsynchronized transmissions require double clutching.

T F 5. Double clutching enables the driver to control engine rpms and the gear so the gears can be engaged smoothly.

T F 6. Double-clutching, though an obvious action, is not the main shifting event.

T F 7. Bringing the teeth of the driving gear and those of the driven gears to the same speed (synchronizing) requires special shifting skills.

T F 8. Nonsynchronized gears can be synchronized easily without double clutching.

T F 9. In double clutching, the driver disengages the clutch after shifting into neutral and accelerates to increase the tooth speed of the driving gear.

T F 10. When a vehicle with a nonsynchronized transmission is rolling in neutral, the driver must hunt, find, or hit a gear.

T F 11. The ability to find the synchronizing rpm under all possible shifting conditions is the major skill necessary in handling a nonsynchronized transmission.

T F 12. Controls differ for the many different transmissions, but all work on the principle of providing power and speed as needed for driving conditions.

CHAPTER EIGHT BACKING

SUMMARY

In this chapter you have learned the correct procedures for backing in a tractor-trailer safely and correctly. You also learned that tractor-trailer combinations have different backing characteristics from automobiles. How to proceed with alley dock backing and parallel parking were also explained.

LEARNING ACTIVITIES

Review Questions

1. How is backing a tractor-trailer different from backing a car?

   _____

   _____

2. When you want the trailer to move to the right, which way should you turn the steering wheel? Why?

3. You are attempting to back in a straight line and the trailer begins to drift to the left. Which way should you turn the steering wheel to correct the drift?

   _____

4. Explain what is meant by oversteering.

   _____

   _____

5. List the four general rules for backing safely. Give a brief explanation of each.

   _____

   _____

   _____

   _____

   _____

   _____

   _____

6. List and explain the four general backing rules.

   _____

   _____

   _____

   _____

   _____

   _____

   _____

7. What is the key to backing a tractor-trailer in a straight line?

   _____

8. What is the difference between sight-side backing and blind-side backing?

_____

_____

_____

9. Why is parallel parking a difficult maneuver?

_____

_____

_____

True/False Questions

If the statement is true, circle the T. If the statement is false, circle the F.

T   F   1. To correct a trailer drift when attempting to back straight, turn the top of the steering wheel toward the drift.

T   F   2. When backing into an alley, you can see best if you back toward the driver's side.

T   F   3. Before backing, check behind the vehicle by getting out of the cab.

T   F   4. When backing a tractor-trailer, the front tractor axle becomes the steering axle for the trailer.

T   F   5. Turning the steering wheel to the left when backing will force the rear of the trailer to the right.

T   F   6. Turning the top of the steering wheel to the right when backing will force the rear of the trailer to the left.

T   F   7. It is better to pull into an alley, cab first, so that you can back into the street when you leave.

CHAPTER NINE COUPLING AND UNCOUPLING

SUMMARY

In this chapter you have reviewed the steps to couple a trailer to a tractor and the steps necessary to uncouple the rig as well as the controls that must be used when coupling or uncoupling. How to test the connection was also demonstrated.

LEARNING ACTIVITIES

Review Questions

1. When preparing to couple, how should the tractor be placed in relation to the trailer?

   _____

   _____

2. Why is the height of the trailer nose an important part of the coupling process? What happens if it is too high? Too low?

   _____

   _____

   _____

3. What is the proper position for the fifth wheel before coupling?

   _____

   _____

4. Why is it dangerous to back under the trailer at an angle when coupling?

   _____

   _____

5. Name the two types of air lines found on a tractor-trailer air brake system.

   _____

6. List three ways the air lines may be coded. Why is it important to be able to tell them apart?

   _____

   _____

   _____

   _____

7. You have crawled under the trailer with a flashlight to inspect the coupling. What two steps do you take before checking the coupling?
   1._____ 2._____

   List three things you should look for.

   _____

   _____

   _____

8. As you lower the landing gear before uncoupling, you notice that one support touches the ground before the other. What does this tell you? What action, if any, should you take?

_____

_____

_____

_____

9. Why should you place the tractor protection valve in the emergency position before uncoupling?

_____

_____

_____

_____

10. What happens to blacktop when it gets hot?

_____

_____

_____

_____

Review Quiz, Part A

List the following steps in the correct order for coupling a tractor to a trailer. Each step is used only once, so you can cross them off as you list them.

A. Secure the tractor.   1. _____

B. Test the connection.   2. _____

C. Connect the air lines.   3. _____

D. Inspect the area, chock the wheels, and then place the
    tractor in front of the trailer.   4. _____

E. Release the tractor parking brake and put on the trailer
    brake.   5. _____

                                                                          6. _____
F. Raise the landing gear.
                                                                          7. _____
G. Inspect the fifth wheel.

H. Inspect the coupling.   8. _____

I. Check the trailer height.   9. _____

J. Back slowly until the fifth wheel just touches the trailer   10. _____
    pickup apron.
                                                                         11. _____
K. Put on parking brake. Exit cab.
                                                                         12. _____
L. Back slowly until the fifth wheel locks.

Review Quiz, Part B

List the following steps in the correct order for uncoupling a tractor from a trailer. Each step is used only once, so you can cross them off as you list them.

A. Lower the landing gear.
B. Place the tractor in line with the trailer.
C. Inspect the trailer supports.
D. Pull the tractor partly clear of the trailer.
E. Release the fifth-wheel latch.
F. Secure the tractor.
G. Disconnect and store the air lines and electrical cable.
H. Secure the vehicle.
I. Pull the tractor clear of the trailer.

1. _____
2. _____
3. _____
4. _____
5. _____
6. _____
7. _____
8. _____
9. _____

True-False Questions

If the statement is true, circle the T. If the statement is false, circle the F.

T F 1. When coupling a rig, the nose of the trailer should be slightly higher than the midpoint of the tractor's fifth wheel.

T F 2. When coupling, the tractor should be placed squarely in front of the trailer.

T F 3. When coupling, you should bring the upper fifth-wheel plate into contact with the lower trailer plate.

T F 4. Moving the tractor protection valve to the In position before coupling cuts off air pressure to the trailer.

T F 5. In the final coupling inspection, make sure you have a solid hookup. You must inspect it from the side of the trailer.

T F 6. To prepare for uncoupling, the tractor should be placed directly in line with the trailer.

T F 7. Moving the tractor protection valve to the emergency position before uncoupling cuts off air pressure to the trailer.

T F 8. To safely support the trailer, lower the landing gear with the crank until both supports touch the ground.

T F 9. For proper coupling to take place, the jaws of the fifth wheel must engage the head of the kingpin.

T F 10. For the brakes to work properly, the air lines must be connected properly.

CHAPTER TEN   VISUAL SEARCH

SUMMARY

In this chapter you have learned how to systematically search the environment around your tractor-trailer. You have learned the value of looking ahead and planning for hazards. You now know the correct methods of crossing an intersection and making lane changes. The differences in the reflected image in a plane mirror and a convex mirror were explained. You also learned how to adjust the mirrors for maximum visibility. Finally, you learned what you should look for when you check your mirrors.

Review Exercises

LEARNING ACTIVITIES

1. What is systematic seeing?

   _____

2. Explain the term "eye lead time." Why is it important?

   _____

   _____

3. List three ways a driver can benefit by looking ahead properly and maintaining enough visual lead time.

   _____

   _____

   _____

   _____

4. Why is it important to scan and search the area around your rig?

   _____

   _____

5. Explain what is meant by the left, right, left concept? Why does it make sense? Why is it important?

   _____

   _____

   _____

   _____

6. What are the two basic types of side mirrors?

   _____

   _____

7. Which type of side mirror provides the most accurate view of the rear of the trailer and roadway behind?

   _____

8. Which type of mirror provides the most accurate side close-ups?

   _____

9. Images will appear smaller and more distant than they really are in which type of mirror?

   _____

10. What is a fender mirror? How is it used? Is it commonly used on all tractors?
    _____

    _____

11. Explain the importance of mirror checks in lane changing.
    _____

    _____

12. How long should it take to check the right-side mirror? The left-side mirror? Why is the time it takes important?
    _____

    _____

13. Explain how to adjust the side mirrors.
    _____

    _____

    _____

    _____

Traffic Situations

Explain what traffic problem can occur in each of the traffic situations shown in the drawings. Write your solution to the problem. Be sure to include how to avoid such a problem if there is a way.

1. _____

   _____

   _____

   _____

   _____

   _____

   _____

   _____

2. _____

   _____

   _____

   _____

   _____

   _____

   _____

   _____

   _____

   _____

   _____

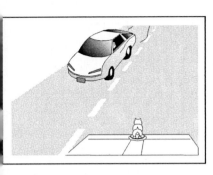

3. _____
_____
_____
_____
_____
_____
_____
_____

4. _____
_____
_____
_____
_____
_____
_____
_____
_____
_____
_____

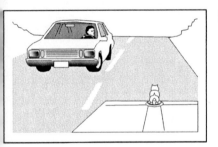

5. _____
_____
_____
_____
_____
_____
_____
_____

6. _____
_____
_____
_____
_____
_____
_____
_____

True/False Questions

Circle the T if the statement is true. Circle the F if the statement is false.

T   F   1. The image in a convex mirror will appear closer than it really is.

T   F   2. The image in a convex mirror will appear smaller than it really is.

T   F   3. In city driving, it is best to look ahead at least one full block.

T   F   4. You should establish an eye lead time by looking ahead 10 to 12 seconds.

T   F   5. At highway speeds, you should try to look ahead about 1/8 of a mile.

T   F   6. With the mirrors properly adjusted, a driver can see the same image in both the left and right mirror.

T   F   7. A plane (flat) side mirror gives an accurate view of the rear of the trailer and roadway behind.

T   F   8. For a close-up view of the side of the trailer, the image in a convex mirror is more accurate than the image in a plane or flat mirror.

T   F   9. Fender mirrors require less eye movement than side mirrors.

T   F   10. Properly checking the right-side mirror takes more time than checking the left-side mirror.

CHAPTER ELEVEN   COMMUNICATION

SUMMARY

In this chapter, you learned the importance of communicating with other road users. You also learned that communication is key to highway safety. The correct ways to signal a turn or lane change, slowing down, and overtaking another road user were explained. You also now know how to place warning devices correctly if you must stop your truck by the side of the road. Finally, you learned that truck drivers have a responsibility to continually communicate with the driving public as a whole.

Review Questions

LEARNING ACTIVITIES

1. What does communicating your intent mean? Why is it important?

   _____

   _____

2. What are the three special rules for signaling turns? Explain each.

   _____

   _____

   _____

   _____

   _____

   _____

   _____

3. Explain why the laws for signaling may not be enough in many cases to prevent accidents.

   _____

   _____

   _____

4. In addition to using your turn signals to communicate your intent to change lanes, what additional signal should you use? Why?

   _____

   _____

5. Any time you slow down suddenly, you should give some warning to the driver behind you. Tell of three situations in which this would apply.

   _____

   _____

   _____

6. If you are being slowed by hills or oversized cargo, what should you do?

   _____

   _____

7. Why is signaling others to pass you illegal and dangerous?

   _____

   _____

8. What does communicating your presence mean? Why is it important?

_____

_____

_____

9. What are three situations in which communicating your presence is necessary. Explain each.

_____

_____

_____

10. How long after you stop must you place warning devices, such as reflective triangles?

_____

_____

_____

11. What is road rage?

_____

_____

_____

Diagrams

Place reflective triangles in the correct places if a rig is stopped on an undivided highway. Be sure to tell how far away from the rig the triangle is.

Place reflective triangles in the correct places if a rig is stopped and there is something to block the view of oncoming drivers. Be sure to tell how far away from the rig the triangle is.

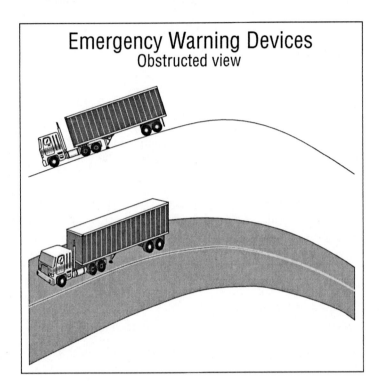

Place reflective triangles in the correct places if a rig is stopped on a divided highway. Be sure to tell how far away from the rig the triangle is.

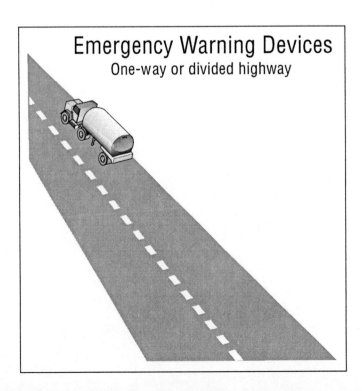

True/False Questions

If the question is true, circle the T. If the question is false, circle the F.

T F 1. The major reason for using turn signals is to obey the law.

T F 2. Turning on your turn signal is enough communication for every situation.

T F 3. Reducing speed unexpectedly can create problems for drivers following your rig.

T F 4. Emergency flashers are helpful in filling some communication needs but are of limited use in other situations.

T F 5. Helping others pass you by waving them on is both courteous and proper because it can help prevent long streams of slow-moving traffic behind you.

T F 6. Even though your vehicle is large in comparison to many others on the road, you should use special methods to let other highway users know of your presence.

T F 7. When stopping beside a well-traveled highway during daylight hours, your emergency flashers are enough warning for other drivers.

T F 8. For better safety at night, you should use flares or fusees in addition to the emergency flashers.

T F 9. Hills and curves present special communication problems when parking beside a roadway.

CHAPTER TWELVE   SPACE MANAGEMENT

SUMMARY

In this chapter, you learned the importance of managing the space around your tractor-trailer. There is space in front of it, behind it, to both the right and the left side, and above and below the vehicle. You also learned the types of hazards you may encounter if you do not manage these spaces correctly. You learned how to determine time and to turn it into distance, thus being able to decide if you are a safe distance from another road user. The types of road surfaces that may present a danger were described. Finally, you learned how to make both right and left turns correctly and to enter or cross traffic safely.

Review Questions

LEARNING ACTIVITIES

1. Of all the space around your vehicle, which is the most important? Why?

   _____

   _____

2. When driving a big rig, what is the general rule for how much space to have in front of the vehicle?

   _____

   _____

   _____

3. If you are driving a 60-foot rig at 55 mph on a clear day, how much following distance should you maintain?

   _____

   _____

   _____

4. What can you do to help keep enough space behind your vehicle?

   _____

   _____

   _____

5. Does the weight of your load affect the trailer's height? Explain.

   _____

   _____

   _____

6. When making a right turn, what should you do to make sure you have enough space?

   _____

   _____

   _____

7. Describe how to make a left turn in a tractor-trailer.

_____

_____

_____

8. When you are turning left and there is more than one turning lane, which lane should you use? Why?

_____

_____

9. You need a much larger gap to cross or enter traffic with a tractor-trailer than with an automobile. Why?

_____

_____

True/False Questions

Circle the T if the statement is true. Circle the F if the statement is false.

T F 1. Space management is keeping a cushion of air around your rig.

T F 2. Because bridges and overpasses have carefully posted heights, drivers of big rigs do not have to worry about hitting them.

T F 3. When we speak of space when driving, we are also talking about time.

T F 4. The most common cause of rear-ending another vehicle is following too closely.

T F 5. The space in front of your rig is the only area you need to be concerned with in managing the space around your rig.

T F 6. When making a right turn, one of the most dangerous things faced by the driver is striking a vehicle that tries to pass on the right during the turn.

T F 7. Left turns are safe because the driver has a good view of the space all around the rig.

T F 8. The only space that is constant and unchanging is the space under the rig.

Special Activity

Explain the reason for your answer to true/false statement number 3.

_____

_____

_____

_____

_____

_____

_____

_____

CHAPTER THIRTEEN   SPEED MANAGEMENT

SUMMARY

Now that you have completed this chapter, you have learned the critical importance of speed management. You understand and can explain the relationship of speed to stopping distance, hydroplaning, fuel economy, and accidents. You have also learned how speed affects your ability to control the rig. Because you have completed this chapter, you can now discuss the effect of speed on the rig's weight and center of gravity and loss of stability. You can also show how the driver's available sight distance and the road surface conditions affect choosing a safe speed.

LEARNING ACTIVITIES

Review Questions

1. What is speeding?

   _____

   _____

2. What are the two parts of stopping distance? Explain each.

   _____

   _____

   _____

3. Name two things besides speed that affect braking distance.

   _____

   _____

4. What is black ice?

   _____

5. What happens when your rig hydroplanes?

   _____

   _____

6. What are two things that can happen if you enter a curve too fast?

   _____

   _____

7. What is the best rule to follow about seeing and speed? Explain the rule and give an example.

   _____

   _____

   _____

8. What is a driver's field of vision?

   _____

   _____

9. How does speed affect your field of vision?

_____

_____

10. What is the safest speed when driving in traffic?

_____

_____

Case Study

This is an outline of a trip in which two drivers followed the same route for 1,000 miles.

Driver A

Drove as fast as possible

Driving time: 20 hours and 12 minutes

Braked 1,339 times

Overtook 2,004 vehicles

Four emergency stops

Driver B

Adhered to the speed limit

Driving time: 20 hours and 43 minutes

Braked 645 times

Overtook 645 vehicles

No emergency stops

Do these figures suggest anything about:

Time and speed?

_____

_____

Fuel economy and speed?

_____

_____

Safety and speed?

_____

_____

What could have happened by having to pass so many other vehicles?

_____

What possible damage to the rig could have happened?

_____

Why did the carrier possibly have to pay an extra cost for this trip?

_____

_____

For what traffic violations could the driver have been cited?

_____

_____

_____

True/False Questions

Circle the T if the statement is true. Circle the F if the statement is false.

T F 1. The total stopping distance is the perception distance plus the driver reaction distance plus the vehicle braking distance.

T F 2. Traction is created by the friction of the tires on the road.

T F 3. Hydroplaning occurs when your tires lose contact with the road, usually caused by water or slush on the highway.

T F 4. Your ability to steer your rig depends on the tires keeping a good grip on the road.

T F 5. Keeping the brakes applied in a curve is wise because it can cancel out the effects of a top-heavy load.

T F 6. Very little time can be saved by speeding on long trips.

T F 7. Your field of vision increases as you speed up.

T F 8. The safest speed in traffic is usually the same speed other vehicles are traveling.

T F 9. A person who drives according to the existing conditions and within the posted speed limits is managing speed properly.

T F 10. Your field of vision includes everything in front and on both sides that you can see.

CHAPTER FOURTEEN   NIGHT DRIVING

In this chapter, you have learned the many differences between driving during daylight hours and driving at night. You learned that inspection routines must be altered and that communication with other drivers must be done by signaling because you cannot have eye contact at night. You also learned that you must slow down so that you will be able to stop within the distance you can see ahead. The reasons for allowing more space around the tractor-trailer were explained. Finally, you learned that the changes while driving at night are made for safety. As a responsible professional truck driver, you want to create the safest road conditions possible for yourself and for other drivers.

Review Questions

1. What are the four driver factors affecting night driving?

   _____

   _____

   _____

   _____

2. What are the five road factors that affect the way you drive at night?

   _____

   _____

   _____

   _____

3. How far ahead will your low beam headlights project light?

   _____

4. Explain the phrase "overdriving your headlights."

   _____

   _____

5. The FMCSR says you must dim your headlights before meeting oncoming vehicles. When must you dim them? Why is this important to other drivers? To you?

   _____

   _____

   _____

6. How does wearing sunglasses during the day, when you must also drive that night, affect night vision?

   _____

   _____

7. In overtaking another vehicle, when should you dim your headlights? Why?

_____

_____

_____

8. What should you do to avoid being blinded by the headlights of oncoming vehicles?

_____

_____

9. Name two things you can do to improve your visibility when driving at night.

_____

_____

10. Why are signaling your presence and what you intend to do more important at night than during daylight hours?

_____

_____

11. How should following distance be adjusted at night?

_____

_____

12. Why should you drive at a lower speed at night?

_____

_____

True/False Questions

Circle the T if the statement is true. Circle the F if the statement is false.

T F   1. At night, low beam headlights let you see about 350 feet ahead of your rig.

T F   2. High-beam headlights let you see about 350 to 500 feet ahead of your rig.

T F   3. The FMCSR says you must dim your high beams 500 feet before meeting an oncoming vehicle.

T F   4. You should dim your headlights 200 feet before overtaking another vehicle.

T F   5. If your speed keeps you from stopping within the distance you can see ahead, you are overdriving your headlights.

For Discussion

Break into small groups of three to five people. Create a driving situation of about 100 miles that includes city, highway, and rural driving. List the conditions a driver may encounter, such as pedestrians, an accident, narrow streets, and so on. Describe how he or she may have to adjust for night driving. Do not leave out any small details when telling how the driver will have to react. Include the proper speed for each incident.

After you have created the situation and sent the driver through it, come back together as a class. Each group can then share with the others their situation and the driver's reaction to it. Ask each other questions. Share other possible solutions to the problems that were created.

CHAPTER FIFTEEN EXTREME DRIVING CONDITIONS

In this chapter, you learned that driving in adverse conditions differs greatly from driving in good weather or on good roads. You also learned that the inspection procedures in extreme driving conditions differ from a normal inspection. You learned how to become aware of possible bad weather conditions and what you should do when you encounter or anticipate them. You learned several methods of starting the truck's engine in cold weather and what to do if it will not start.

How to avoid skids was discussed as well as how to dry out the truck's brakes should they become wet. You also learned your responsibility should your rig become stuck and need to be towed. The hazards of driving in hot weather and the desert were explained. Finally, you learned that driving in the mountains takes special skills. Auxiliary braking systems, the best way to drive downgrades, and the use of escape ramps were illustrated and explained.

True/False Questions

If the question is true, circle the T. If the question is false, circle the F.

T F 1. Ice, snow, mud, salt, or dirt on your lights and reflectors can cut down how much you can see and how well others can see you.

T F 2. Reinforced chains are effective on glare ice.

T F 3. If you install tire chains correctly, you do not need to be concerned about them for the rest of the trip.

T F 4. Ether, while helpful for starting an engine in cold weather, can be dangerous to both the driver and the engine.

T F 5. The only major hazard of driving in extreme weather conditions is less traction.

T F 6. In snow, tires can lose as much as 80 percent of the normal traction.

T F 7. As the rig's speed increases, traction decreases.

T F 8. Skids can be caused by driving too fast and oversteering.

T F 9. Suddenly letting up on the accelerator can cause a skid.

T F 10. Once your brake pads or linings get wet, there is nothing you can do to dry them out.

T F 11. The best advice about a stuck vehicle is to avoid getting stuck.

T F 12. If you are stuck, a good way to get the rig loose is to rock it gently back and forth.

T F 13. If you need a tow truck, remember that the tow truck operator is a professional and should take charge of the operation.

T F 14. If your rig breaks down in bad weather, it is best to stay with it.

T F 15. If tire inflation pressure increases more than 15 psi, immediately let out some of the air before you drive again.

T F 16. Do not shift gears on downgrades.

T F 17. A major part of downhill braking should be done by the engine.

T F 18. Since escape ramps are for true emergencies, you should not use them until you have tried all other ways of bringing your truck under control.

T F 19. Speed retarders use the service brakes to reduce speed.

Discussion Questions

Divide the class into four groups. Have each group discuss one question. Then have the groups share their solutions to the problem with the class. After they have presented their solutions, give the question to the class for other possible solutions. Some of the class members may have actually had these experiences. Encourage them to share them with the class.

1. You are driving in the barren desert on a side road. You notice storm clouds on the horizon. Describe what can happen. Be sure to include why it can happen. What should you do? What would you do if there was no main highway close by?

2. Although only light snow was predicted when you began your trip, it has now turned into a blizzard. It is very important that your cargo reaches its destination as soon as possible. What should you do? Where should you go?

3. You have been broken down for 3 hours in the desert. What should you have been doing during those 3 hours? What are the dangers of the desert? What can you do to avoid them? Where should you go? What types of emergency supplies should you have? How can you get help?

4. You are going downhill on the Grapevine, a steep grade on I-5 between Los Angeles and Bakersfield. Describe how you should take the grade. What are the things you should be sure to do? What are the things you should never do? If you think your brakes are fading, what should you do? Describe the solution in detail.

CHAPTER SIXTEEN   HAZARD AWARENESS

SUMMARY

Blending with other roadway users depends on how well you can see and understand the road environment and the activities of other road users. The road environment includes the roadway, the curvature of the road, the surface condition of the road, and the immediate area around the road. You must watch for and interpret the intentions and actions of other road users. Watch for the clues to guide you and help pinpoint possible hazards. You should understand that driving is a "social" act. It is social because it involves you, everyone, and every object in your immediate environment. Your success as a professional driver will depend on how well you identify and interpret the potential hazards and how quickly you can react by adjusting your driving.

LEARNING ACTIVITIES

Commentary Driving and Hazard Perception

Commentary driving is making comments about what you see as you drive. During the on-street part of your instruction, you may be asked to try this exercise. It will help you identify hazards and let your instructor know what you are seeing and how you react to it.

In commentary driving, you do not discuss what you see at length. Your job is to see and identify any possible hazard. Use brief statements such as "car on right . . . could come in front of me." Such statements tell the instructor that you are aware of a possible hazard.

This simple example makes commentary driving sound quite easy. Depending on the situation, it may not be. Seeing and talking about *a car beside the road* is easy when it is the only thing you have to do. When you add other driving tasks, commenting can become very demanding.

Some people find it helpful to identify hazards out loud. Other people, including some instructors, do not like this method. Even though it may seem hard at first, you will find it will help you become a professional driver who is more aware of his or her road environment.

Guidelines for Commentary Driving

1. Identify in your mind any hazard (object, road condition, or road user) that is a possible threat to you. Identify and describe only those hazards to which you must be prepared to respond.

2. Describe the hazard in a few words. Tell what and where it is.
   Examples: "Child in the street on the left."
   "Yellow car on the right."
   "Pavement in the shade of that bridge."

3. Describe in a few words what makes the hazard.
   Examples: ". . . is looking the other way."
   ". . . is going to move backward."
   ". . . might be very slippery."

You do not have to describe how you are going to respond to the hazards.

4. In conflict (possible crash) situations, comment only on the object or vehicle in conflict with your vehicle. Do not bother to comment on the reason the conflict occurred.

Examples: ". . . car in my lane."

". . . bicyclist with back toward me in my lane."

". . . wind blowing debris across the road."

". . . cattle in unfenced field."

5. When the object, road condition, or person is not a hazard, say nothing.

Diagrams

What is the hazard in each drawing? Draw a circle around it. Comment and tell why it is a hazard on the lines below each drawing.

1. _____

_____

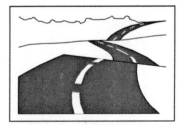

3. _____

_____

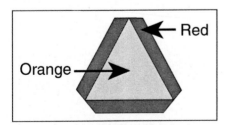

Red

Orange

2. _____

_____

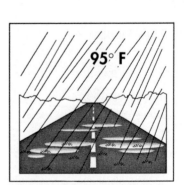

95° F

4. _____

_____

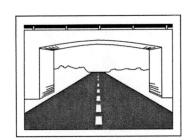

5. _____

_____

6. _____

_____

7. _____

_____

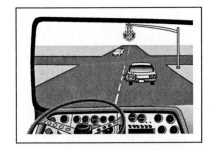

8. _____

_____

9. _____

_____

10. _____

_____

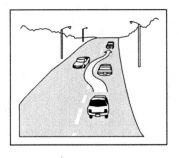

11. _____

_____

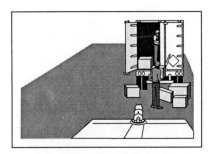

12. _____

_____

13. _____

_____

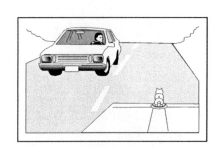

17. _____

_____

14. _____

_____

18. _____

_____

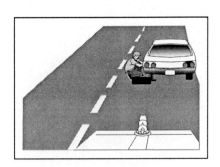

15. _____

_____

_____

19. _____

_____

16. _____

_____

20. _____

_____

21. _____

_____

22. _____

_____

True/False Questions

If the question is true, circle the T. If the question is false, circle the F.

T F 1. When it is hot, oil may rise to the surface of an asphalt road and make it slippery.

T F 2. If the road is properly banked on a curve, vehicles can maneuver that curve at a faster rate of speed.

T F 3. Since all expressway ramps are properly banked, you do not need to be concerned with your speed when entering a ramp.

T F 4. Since your rig is so large and heavy, wind is not likely to affect it.

T F 5. As long as you can see another vehicle, you may assume its driver sees you, too.

T F 6. You should be careful when driving near step vans, postal vehicles, and local delivery trucks.

T F 7. People in parked vehicles should always be considered hazards.

T F 8. Eye contact with other drivers is an important part of avoiding hazards.

T F 9. A vehicle carrying luggage on the roof or pulling a trailer is a clue to a hazard. Its driver may do something unexpected.

T F 10. Vehicles that travel slower than the speed of the other traffic are possible hazards.

T F 11. Some impatient drivers view all trucks as slow moving.

T F 12. An open window in cold weather may be a clue that the driver is under the influence.

T F 13. Drowsiness, like being under the influence, has a number of clues.

T F 14. Fortunately, the clues of intoxication and drowsiness are different.

T F 15. Head and body movement can give clues as to what a driver intends to do.

T F 16. Since most pedestrians and cyclists travel on the sidewalk, they are not likely to be hazards.

T F 17. Traffic merging, such as meeting at intersections, can be hazardous.

CHAPTER SEVENTEEN   EMERGENCY MANEUVERS

In this chapter, you learned how to avoid some of the common driving emergencies. You were shown how to steer evasively, how to recover when your rig goes off the road, and how best to stop in an emergency. You were also taught the reasons for brake failure and what to do when it occurs. Tire blowouts were described, as were the safest ways to deal with them.

Problem Solving: Emergencies

The emergency situations described here are examples of some of the problems that can develop during routine driving. The instructor will describe the conditions and then ask the class to discuss how to solve the emergency. He or she may also show you a visual. The class will review the correct procedures and suggest how the problem might have been avoided through safe driving practices. These include communication, speed and space management, and a careful search of the scene.

The correct procedures for avoiding each type of accident are found at the end of the chapter.

A. Oncoming Car Passing

You are traveling at 55 mph when an oncoming car tries to pass two vehicles. The lead car is a compact and was not seen at first by the driver, who is now committed to overtaking and passing both vehicles. A high curb runs along the right side of the road. Trees on the right are an additional hazard.

Name two things you should do.

1. _____

2. _____

3. Do not _____

4. Why? _____

B. Pedestrian in Street

You are traveling at 35 mph on a four-lane divided highway. A pedestrian runs into the road 75 feet in front of your rig. There is a low curb to your right. There is not enough time to brake.

1. What can you expect the pedestrian to do? _____

2. What is your best escape route? _____

3. Do not _____

4. Why? _____

C. Car Turning Left

While traveling at 40 mph, you see a car parked on the right moving out to cut across the road and make a left turn. There is not enough time to brake, and doing so will put you into a skid. There are no other vehicles parked on the right.

1. One good action is _____

2. Do not _____

3. Why? _____

D. Bicyclist

You are moving at 30 mph, and a bicyclist 75 feet ahead swerves in front of your right. There are no oncoming vehicles.

    Name three things you can do.

1. _____

2. _____

3. _____

E. Car Pulling Out

You are moving along a two-lane street with cars parked parallel to the curb. On the right side, a car pulls out about one car length ahead of you. There are no oncoming vehicles.

    Name two things you should do.

1. _____

2. _____

3. What might happen if you put on your brakes? _____

_____

F. Head-On Collision

While traveling at 55 mph on a two-lane road, an oncoming vehicle moves out of its lane and into your path. There are no obstructions on the right shoulder.

    Name two things you can do to encourage the other vehicle to return to its lane.

1. _____

2. _____

3. What else should you do? _____

G. Fallen Motorcyclist

You are moving at 45 mph and are being passed by an oncoming car. At the same time, a car is passing you on the right. There is a grassy shoulder on the right. A motorcycle rider falls down ahead of you.

Name two things you should do.

1. _____

2. _____

3. Why will you not honk the horn? _____

H. Ice Cream Truck

You are moving at 25 mph when an ice cream truck stops about 100 feet ahead because a child has run in front of it. A parked car and an oncoming car prevent evasive steering.

1. What should you do? _____

I. Cresting a Hill

While traveling on a two-lane highway at 50 mph, you go over the crest of a hill and see an oncoming car 150 feet ahead in your lane.
Name two things you can do to avoid a collision.

1. _____

2. _____

True/False Questions

If the statement is true, circle the T. If the statement is false, circle the F.

T F 1. When there is a hazard, it is usually easier to stop a rig than to steer around the hazard.

T F 2. When you must swerve off the right side of the road to avoid a collision, it is best if only the wheels on the right side of the rig leave the road.

T F 3. When you leave the road, you should return as soon as you have passed the hazard.

T F 4. You should avoid a head-on collision even if you must leave the road to do it.

T F 5. A driver usually has to train him- or herself to think of how to avoid an emergency rather than slamming on the brakes when the hazard appears.

T F 6. A rig can be stopped more quickly than it can be turned.

T F 7. The safest way to handle an emergency is to keep it from happening in the first place.

T F 8. Most emergencies occur because of mechanical failure.

T F 9. Speed management helps the driver handle possible emergencies.

T F 10. With knowledge and experience, you can usually stop your rig safely even though the brakes have failed.

Answers to Problem Solving: Emergencies

A. Oncoming Car Passing

1. *Reduce speed as much as possible.*
2. *Squeeze as far to the right of the road as possible.* Oncoming cars (those being overtaken and passed) will also squeeze to their right. This should result in an alley for the passing car.
3. Do not *try to climb the curb.*
4. Why? *Your rig can bounce back into the center of the road.*

B. Pedestrian in Street

1. *Continue, stop, or turn around and try to return to the side of the road.*
2. *The roadside to the right.* The curb can be easily mounted and there is plenty of open space beyond the curb.
3. Do not *use your horn.*
4. Why? *It can cause the pedestrian to turn back.*

C. Car Turning Left

1. *To angle to the right just far enough to pass behind the car.*
2. Do not *use the horn.*
3. Why? *It can frighten the other driver and cause him or her to stop and block your escape route.*

D. Bicyclist

1. *Slow down.*
2. *Keep as far behind the bicyclist as possible.*
3. *Sound your horn.* Sounding your horn should cause the cyclist to swerve back to the right. This will create space for you to move by on the left.

E. Car Pulling Out

1. *Swerve to the left.*
2. *Sound your horn.*
3. *Braking may cause a skid.* Sounding your horn may cause the driver pulling out to stop and reduce the amount of swerve you will need to make.

F. Head-On Collision

1. *Blast your horn.*
2. *Flash your headlights.*
3. *Swerve to the right.* When you swerve to the right, try to keep your left tires on the pavement. Concentrate on steering. After the oncoming vehicle has passed, let your rig come to a complete stop. When it is safe, pull back onto the highway.

G. Fallen Motorcyclist

1. *Brake hard.*
2. *Ease off the brakes and start swerving to the right.* Swerving to the right will force the car on your right to swerve to the right also. Sideswiping the passing car is better than hitting either the motorcyclist or the oncoming car.
3. *It will not communicate a definite message and may only confuse the other driver.*

H. Ice Cream Truck

1. *Brake to a stop.* You have enough room between you and the ice cream truck to stop. Use either controlled braking or stab braking.

I. Cresting a Hill

1. *Brake hard to slow down as much as you can.*
2. *Swerve to the right if the car does not return to its lane.* There is not enough room to brake to a stop but you should brake hard to reduce speed. If necessary, drive off the right side of the roadway. You have done everything possible to avoid a head-on collision in this situation.

CHAPTER EIGHTEEN SKID CONTROL AND RECOVERY

SUMMARY

In this chapter, you learned the types of skids and what can be done to prevent them. You also learned that there are ways to recover from each type of skid and prevent damage to your rig and injury to yourself or others. The conditions that cause skids were also discussed.

LEARNING ACTIVITIES

True/False Questions

If the question is true, circle the T. If the question is false, circle the F.

T F 1. The major cause of skids is a sudden change in speed or direction.

T F 2. Traction is the grip, or grab, between the tires and the pavement.

T F 3. The amount of traction determines how much control the driver has over the rig.

T F 4. The force of motion is controlled by the weight and speed of the rig.

T F 5. If the force of motion is greater than the traction of the tire on the pavement, the vehicle skids.

T F 6. When the wheels lock, the driver loses control of the rig.

T F 7. Locking the wheels decreases stopping distance.

T F 8. Drive-wheel skids occur when the amount of force applied to the drive wheels is more than the traction between the tires and the pavement.

T F 9. Accelerating too fast can cause a skid.

T F 10. When a vehicle turns, centrifugal force tends to pull it toward the center.

T F 11. It is easier to recover from a skid than to prevent it.

T F 12. A trailer jackknife is caused by overbraking or excessive speed while cornering.

T F 13. Overbraking can result from a mechanical brake problem.

T F 14. If you enter a curve too fast, traction may be overcome by centrifugal force.

T F 15. If you realize you are going too fast while in the curve, it is best to slam on your brakes to bring the rig under control.

T F 16. A tractor jackknife results when the tractor's drive wheels have more traction than the front wheels.

T F 17. A tractor jackknife can result from wheel lockup, overacceleration, or trailer override.

T F 18. If a tractor jackknifes, it is best to avoid overbraking, overaccelerating, or suddenly downshifting.

T F 19. During a front-wheel skid, the rig continues to move forward, but you cannot steer.

T F 20. Driving slower on wet pavement is vital if you want to prevent front-wheel skids.

T F 21. When wheels lock up, the movement of the rig is changed from rolling to sliding.

T F 22. The major cause for all-wheel skids is oversteering.

T F 23. The best way to prevent all-wheel skids is to avoid too much braking on slippery surfaces.

T F 24. Most skids happen when you overcontrol the rig (sudden changes in speed or direction).

T F 25. Skidding generally occurs on slippery surfaces because traction is easily lost.

T F 26. Fortunately, antijackknife devices prevent skidding.

T F 27. In a tractor jackknife, use corrective steering to put the tractor back on course.

T F 28. Antilock brakes use computerized braking.

T F 29. Stab braking is the preferred method to use with antilock brakes.

Name the Skid

Write the name of the skid and tell what happens in this kind of skid on the lines to the side of each drawing. Then tell how to prevent the skid.

1. _____

_____

_____

_____

_____

_____

_____

_____

_____

Line of travel

All wheels locked up and sliding

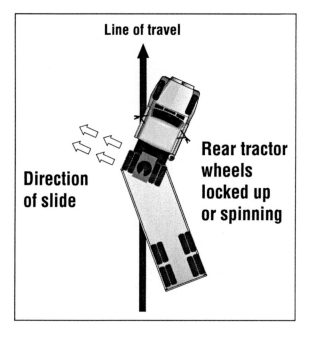

Line of travel

**Direction
of slide**

**Rear tractor
wheels
locked up
or spinning**

Line of travel

**Trailer
wheels
locked up
and sliding**

2. _____

_____

_____

_____

_____

_____

_____

3. _____

_____

_____

_____

_____

_____

_____

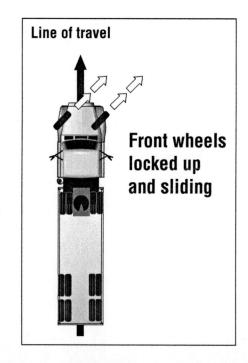

Line of travel

**Front wheels
locked up
and sliding**

4. _____

_____

_____

_____

_____

_____

_____

_____

_____

CHAPTER NINETEEN PASSIVE RAILROAD CROSSINGS

In conclusion, always check for traffic behind you and make sure they know your intentions. Use a pullout lane, if available. Turn on your flashers in traffic, if necessary. Choose an escape route in the event of a brake failure or unexpected problems or traffic tie-ups in front or behind you. While slowing or stopped, look carefully in each direction for approaching trains, moving your head and eyes to see around obstructions, such as mirrors, windshields, and pillars. If you drive a regular route, learn the highway rail-grade crossings on it and how your truck fits these crossings. When waiting for a train to pass, put on your emergency brakes so you will not move onto the track.

Before resuming travel: Make sure there is room on the other side of the track for the whole unit to clear the track, including your truck's overhang (and the 3-foot overhang of the train from the closest rail). If you stopped in a pullout lane, signal and pull back onto the road when there is a safe gap in traffic. Expect traffic in other lanes to pass you. Use the highest gear that will let you cross the track without shifting. If the red lights at the crossing begin to flash *after* you have started across the track, *keep going!* Lights should begin flashing at least 20 seconds before the train arrives. Look beyond the track to see if there is traffic congestion, a signal, or a stop sign. Is the containing area large enough to allow the truck to complete the crossing when stopped, allowing for your overhang and the train's 3-foot overhang? Check the crossing signals one final time before proceeding. Take time to cross safely.

Multiple Choice

(From "Can You Make the Grade" by Operation Lifesaver, Inc.)

Test yourself by answering the following questions:

Driving through a small town, you see a round, yellow sign with an "X" and the letters "RR."

_____ The round, yellow sign is called the (a) advance warning sign, (b) crossbuck, or (c) track sign.

_____ The round yellow sign tells you (a) there is a railroad yard nearby; (b) to slow down, you are approaching a railroad crossing; or (c) there is only one railroad track ahead.

As you get closer, you see a sign with the words "Railroad Crossing" on two crossed white boards.

_____ The sign is called the (a) advance warning sign, (b) crossbuck, or (c) track sign.

_____ It tells you (a) to hurry across the tracks; (b) there is only one railroad track ahead; or (c) to slow down, look, listen, and be prepared to yield to an approaching train.

You notice a smaller sign below the crossed white boards. On the small sign are the words "2 Tracks."

_____ The sign tells you (a) the road ahead crosses two tracks, (b) to expect trains approaching from either direction, or (c) both (a) and (b).

As you start driving over the tracks, you see the red lights begin to flash and the gate start to come down.

_____ This means (a) you tripped an emergency signaling device, (b) a train is approaching, or (c) someone is probably working on the signals.

_____ You should (a) keep going until you have cleared the tracks by at least 15 feet, (b) stop and abandon the vehicle, or (c) back up to get off the tracks.

_____ If your vehicle stalls on the tracks as a train approaches, (a) keep trying to start your vehicle until the train is really close, (b) stand next to your vehicle and wave at the locomotive engineer, or (c) get out of your vehicle *immediately* and move far away from the tracks at an angle in the direction of the approaching train.

The next day you encounter a "passive" railroad crossing without a gate or flashing red lights. Be very careful as you cross these tracks.

_____ It is very difficult to judge how far away a train is because (a) an optical illusion fools the eye in judging distance and speed, (b) you have not learned how, or (c) the train may unexpectedly speed up.

_____ After fully applying the brakes, a 100-car freight train traveling 55 miles per hour takes at least _____ to stop (a) 1/4 mile, (b) 1/2 mile, or (c) 1 mile.

_____ You cannot predict the arrival of a freight train at a crossing because (a) schedules are not published, (b) they do not keep regular schedules, or (c) published schedules may not be accurate.

True/False Questions

If the statement is true, circle the T. If the statement is false, circle the F.

T F 1. The names "railroad crossing," "highway–rail intersection," "crossing," and "highway–rail-grade crossing" all refer to the place where the highway crosses the train racks.

T F 2. The biggest factor in vehicle–train collisions is train speed.

T F 3. Light-rail trains carrying city passengers run more frequently than interstate freight or passenger trains.

T F 4. After fully applying the brakes, light-rail trains take only 100 feet to stop.

T F 5. On light-rail trains, the lights on the end cars tell you whether the train is approaching or leaving the crossing.

CHAPTER TWENTY   ACCIDENT PROCEDURES

SUMMARY

In this chapter, you learned how a driver should act if there is an accident: what information to be sure to obtain, what information you must give to others involved in the accident, and subjects you must not discuss. The requirements for hazardous material spills were outlined. The types of fires and ways of fighting them were also explained. You also learned there are different types of fire extinguishers and how they are used on different types of fires.

LEARNING ACTIVITIES

What to Do in an Emergency

1. Following are several different types of fires. On the lines corresponding to each drawing, identify the fire, tell how you would fight it and what you would use to put out the fire.

_____

_____

_____

_____

_____

_____

_____

_____

_____

_____

_____

_____

_____

_____

_____

_____

_____

_____

_____

_____

_____

_____

_____

_____

_____

_____

_____

_____

2. In the pictures shown here, draw reflective markers at the locations where they should be placed if the rig is stopped. Mark the distance they are from the truck.

Two-Lane or Undivided Highway

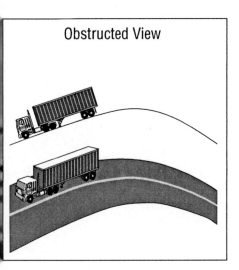

Obstructed View

One-Way or Divided Highway

3. You have been in an accident. You were driving in your correct lane. As you came over the crest of a hill, you sideswiped an oncoming car that had strayed into your lane. Draw a diagram of the accident using the instructions given in this chapter.

4. What four elements are necessary for a fire to continue burning?

A. _____ B. _____ C. _____ D. _____

5. What information should you collect from the other people involved in an accident?

_____

_____

_____

_____

_____

6. What information should you give to those involved?

_____

_____

_____

7. List the subjects you should not discuss if you are involved in an accident.

_____

_____

Discussion Topics

Discuss the following statements in class. Determine whether they are true or false. If they are false, give the correct answer. If they are true, explain why.

Most truck fires occur from failure in the exhaust system.

A bent or loose exhaust pipe may get too close to the gas tank or tires and cause a fire or explosion.

If an engine catches fire, you should raise the hood and smother the flames with an extinguisher.

True/False Questions

If the statement is true, circle the T. If the statement is false, circle the F.

T F 1. When there is an accident, it is the driver's responsibility to warn on-coming traffic to prevent further accidents.

T F 2. Fusees can be used for hand signals to warn of an accident scene.

T F 3. After stopping and protecting the scene, your first priority is to assist the injured.

T F 4. You should not try to do anything you are not adequately trained to do.

T F 5. When someone is injured and you want to help, it is important you know your limitations and the law.

T F 6. If a person is injured, your first effort should be to move him or her to a warm, calm place.

T F 7. Because accident scenes are usually hectic and disorganized, it is best if you wait to prepare a diagram of what happened until later when you can approach it calmly and without interruption.

T F   8. One use for accident reports is to aid in driver improvement and prevention of future accidents.

T F   9. An accident is judged preventable if there was at least one thing the driver could have done to prevent the accident and failed to do.

T F 10. If no one has stopped to help, you should drive by an accident where there are injuries without stopping to offer assistance.

T F 11. Your ability to assist is limited by how much you know about first aid and your skill in using it.

T F 12. You should not move an injured person even if there is danger from fire, heavy traffic, or some other serious threat.

T F 13. A fire can start and continue to burn only if heat, fuel, and oxygen are present or there is a chain reaction.

T F 14. If your rig catches fire and you are near a service station, you should pull in and get help at once.

T F 15. If a tire catches fire, you should keep using large amounts of water even after the flames are out.

CHAPTER TWENTY-ONE SLIDING FIFTH WHEELS AND TANDEM AXLES

SUMMARY

In this chapter, you have learned the reasons for sliding either the fifth wheel or the trailer tandem axles. You have also learned that doing this will change the distribution of weight as well as the overall length of the rig, ride, maneuverability, and off-tracking of the trailer wheels. The correct ways to slide the fifth wheel and the tandem axle assembly were explained and illustrated. Finally, you found there can be hazards if these procedures are not done correctly.

Review Questions

LEARNING ACTIVITIES

1. Who is responsible for the gross vehicle weight and the weight per axle of the tractor-trailer?

   _____

2. What is the purpose of the sliding fifth wheel?

   _____

   _____

3. Explain what happens to the weight per axle of the tractor when you move the fifth wheel forward toward the cab.

   _____

4. Explain what happens to the weight per axle of the trailer when you move the fifth wheel forward toward the cab.

   _____

5. Explain what happens to the weight per axle of the tractor when you move the fifth wheel rearward toward the trailer.

   _____

6. Explain what happens to the weight per axle of the trailer when you move the fifth wheel rearward toward the trailer.

   _____

7. What is the purpose of the sliding tandem axle?

   _____

   _____

8. Explain what happens to the weight per axle of the tractor when you move the sliding tandem axle forward toward the cab.

   _____

9. Explain what happens to the weight per axle of the tractor when you move the sliding tandem axle rearward toward the trailer.

   _____

10. Explain what happens to the weight per axle of the trailer when you move the sliding tandem axle rearward toward the trailer.

   _____

11. Will off-tracking increase or decrease when you move the fifth wheel rearward toward the trailer?

   _____

12. Will off-tracking increase or decrease when you move the sliding tandem axle forward toward the tractor?

   _____

13. Name the two types of locking devices that lock and unlock the sliding assembly.

   _____

   _____

14. What is the name of the locking device that locks and unlocks the trailer sliding axle?

   _____

15. How many locking lugs or pins are part of the sliding tandem axle? Where are they located?

   _____

16. What should you do if the sliding fifth wheel is binding?

   _____

17. What should you do if the sliding tandem axle is binding?

   _____

   _____

18. What four things will change when you move the fifth wheel?

   _____

19. What four things will change when you move the sliding tandem axle?

   _____

20. What should you check to make sure no damage occurs from the sliding fifth wheel?

   _____

21. What should you inspect on sliding tandems?

   _____

Review Quiz, Part A—Sliding Fifth Wheel

List the following steps in the correct order for sliding the fifth wheel. Each step is used only once, so you can cross off the steps as you use them.

   A. Remember you have just changed the rig's overall length.
   B. Set the tractor brakes and visually check that the fifth-wheel slider is properly locked into place.
   C. With the trailer brakes still set, gently tug or push against the trailer to seat the locking pins.

D. Set the trailer brakes using the hand valve or pulling the red trailer air supply valve.

E. Make sure the cab is properly coupled to the trailer.

F. Ease the tractor gently in the opposite direction from which you want to move the fifth wheel.

G. Place the fifth-wheel release in the locked position.

H. Release the tractor brake or parking brake system.

I. Place the fifth-wheel release in the unlocked position.

Sliding Fifth-Wheel Procedure

1. _____ 2. _____ 3. _____ 4. _____

5. _____ 6. _____ 7. _____ 8. _____

9. _____

Review Quiz, Part B—Sliding Tandem Axle

List the following steps in the correct order for sliding the tandem axle. Each step is used only once, so you can cross off the steps as you use them.

A. Ease the tractor gently in the opposite direction you want the sliding tandem axles to move.

B. Release the tractor brakes. With the trailer brakes still set, gently tug or push against the trailer to seat the locking lugs.

C. Inspect the trailer air supply lines for clearance under the trailer. Be sure they are not hanging down.

D. Reset your tractor brakes and look at all four lugs/pins to make sure they are firmly seated through the holes in the tandem axle slides.

E. Remember that you have just made changes to your tandem axle setting. This will affect the handling of the tractor-trailer.

F. Make sure the tractor is properly coupled to the trailer.

G. Lift and pull the lug (locking pin) control lever until the grooves slip into the sideways slot on the lever guide disengaging the locking lugs.

H. Release the lug/pin control lever. Place it into the locked position.

I. Release the tractor brakes by pushing in the yellow parking brake valve.

J. Set the tractor brakes.

K. Reset the tractor brakes by pulling out the yellow parking brake valve.

L. Set the trailer brakes by pulling out the red trailer air supply valve or pulling down the trailer brake hand valve.

M. Check to make sure all four lugs are retracted properly.

Sliding Tandem Axle Procedure

1. _____ 2. _____ 3. _____ 4. _____

5. _____ 6. _____ 7. _____ 8. _____

9. _____ 10. _____ 11. _____ 12. _____

13. _____

CHAPTER TWENTY-TWO   SPECIAL RIGS

SUMMARY

Many of the special rigs described in this section are dangerous in the hands of an untrained driver. All require special instruction and training. Most special rigs also require special permits and endorsements.

Identify These Vehicles

LEARNING ACTIVITIES

Write the correct name for each of the vehicles on the line below each drawing.

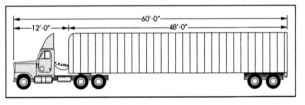

1. _____

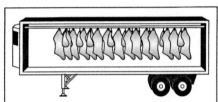

2. _____

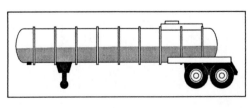

3. _____

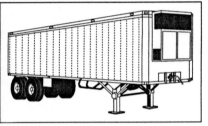

4. _____

5. _____

6. _____

7. _____

8. _____

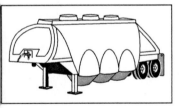

9. _____

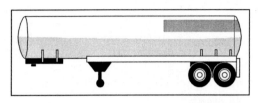

10. _____

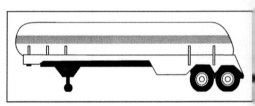

11. _____

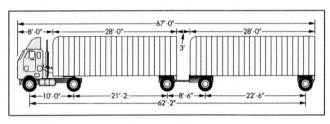

12. _____

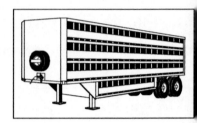

13. _____

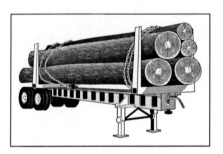

14. _____

15. _____

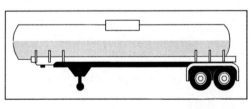

16. _____

Identification of Special Rigs

The best way to learn about special rigs is to watch them on the streets and highways. There are, as you now know, special rigs for many hauling needs. Carrying raw milk from the farm to a processing plant requires different equipment than would be used to haul new, boxed television sets to retail outlets.

Having read about many of the rigs, you can know and understand them better by seeing and identifying them. Discuss them with other learners or instructors. The purpose of this exercise is to identify special rigs during the on-road lessons.

Directions: As you see other tractor-trailers, look them over to see if they are special or different in any way. Point them out to the instructor. Describe what you see, what you think it was designed for, and any special handling features it requires. Ask questions.

This exercise, of course, should be done at a truck stop, not behind the wheel.

Field Trip

If time and a suitable site to visit are available, you might want to join other students in observing rigs at a manufacturing site or local transportation firm.

Contact the company you wish to visit, explain the purpose of your visit, number of visitors, and arrange for a time and length of stay. Ask for a company representative to accompany you. After the visit, one person from your group should write a letter of thanks to the host company.

True/False Questions

If the statement is true, circle the T. If the statement is false, circle the F.

T F 1. A special rig differs from the standard tractor that has a 48- to 53-foot dry weight trailer van and five axles and 18 wheels.

T F 2. A point of articulation is a joint or connecting link between two different parts of a rig.

T F 3. Special rigs do special hauling jobs.

T F 4. Refrigeration vans are sometimes called reefers.

T F 5. Rigs with a low center of gravity are easier to handle than those with a high center of gravity.

T F 6. Load stability problems occur when liquid is being transported.

T F 7. The center of gravity is higher in reefers hauling more than one level of hanging meat.

T F 8. Livestock is an unstable load because the animals can move around during a trip.

T F 9. When hauling dual trailers, the heavier trailer should be in front.

T F 10. Turnpike doubles and standard doubles are different names for the same rig.

T F 11. Tracking is more difficult with a set of doubles because you have more equipment following you around a curve.

T F 12. The difference between a reefer and semitrailer is that the reefer has a lower bed or cargo space.

T F 13. Drivers must avoid backing double or triple bottom rigs.

T F 14. Beware of bumps, potholes, and so on because the tops of the trailers can hit one another.

T F 15. Generally speaking, if you can handle one tractor-trailer combination, you have the skills necessary to handle any of the special rigs without additional instruction or training.

T F 16. Smooth steering is very important with a set of doubles because any jerking or whipping causes the second trailer to overreact.

T F 17. Rigs that haul bulldozers, cranes, and earth movers can have bottom clearance problems at railroad crossings, curbs, and large potholes.

T F 18. A surging load is dangerous because the shifting cargo weight can cause handling problems.

T F 19. When hauling cattle, hanging meat, or liquid cargo, vehicle speed is critical because of the possibility of shifting or surging cargo.

T F 20. Most special rigs require special permits and/or endorsements on the driver's CDL.

CHAPTER TWENTY-THREE   PREVENTIVE MAINTENANCE AND SERVICING

SUMMARY

In this chapter, you have learned what types of maintenance are needed for the various systems on your rig. You have learned that preventive maintenance keeps unscheduled or emergency maintenance to a minimum. The types of reports that you, as a driver, will be expected to fill out and turn in to your carrier were described. You also were taught how to do the basic, routine servicing expected of a driver, and you now know how to change a tire if an emergency arises.

LEARNING ACTIVITIES

Written Reports

Your instructor will give you a practice VCR. Below the letters "VCR," write what the letters stand for. Then fill out the report based on the information given to you by your instructor.

Danger Points

On the lines after each servicing procedure, tell why it can be dangerous.

1. Changing a tire

_____

_____

2. Changing an oil filter

_____

_____

3. Checking the battery

_____

_____

4. Changing the air filter element

_____

_____

5. Adjusting the brakes

_____

_____

Lab Exercise

For this exercise, you will need a truck or models of truck systems provided by your school. Divide into groups of three. Each group is given a part to be serviced or examined.

The first person is to have a paper with the correct steps to complete the servicing operation written on it. The second person is to actually perform the routine, explaining each step as it is done. The third person is to carefully watch the second person and correct any mistakes that are made. If the third person does not catch an error, the first person should read the correct step from the paper. The second person corrects his or her error and continues with the servicing.

When the servicing is complete, the three people change roles and repeat the routine. This continues until all three people can perform the servicing correctly. Then the group goes on to another system. This continues until all groups can correctly service each system.

True/False Questions

If the statement is true, circle the T. If the statement is false, circle the F.

T F   1. Future tractor-trailer drivers must know how to perform inspections and authorized maintenance and repairs.

T F   2. Once a student has learned the repairs presented in this lesson, he or she must always handle such repairs on a tractor-trailer.

T F   3. It is the driver's responsibility to ensure that the vehicle is safe to drive and will operate economically.

T F   4. Some carriers require drivers to perform certain routine maintenance tasks as part of their jobs.

T F   5. In some fleets, drivers cannot do any of the routine maintenance tasks.

T F   6. The FMCSR require drivers to perform a pretrip inspection and to review the last daily report (VCR) on the rig.

T F   7. Most drivers can safely remove a tire from the rim after they have been taught how.

T F   8. Most drivers have the skill to adjust tractor-trailer brakes because it is not hard to do.

T F   9. Brakes that are not properly adjusted can result in accidents.

T F 10. Air tanks should be drained only by a trained mechanic.

CHAPTER TWENTY-FOUR   RECOGNIZING AND REPORTING MALFUNCTIONS

In this chapter, you have learned the driver's responsibilities in maintaining and servicing his or her truck. You know there are some repairs a driver should let a trained mechanic perform. You also were taught how to troubleshoot and report on malfunctions. As a driver, you may have a truck that will not start, so you were shown safe and correct emergency starting procedures.

Troubleshooting Guide

The troubleshooting guide in Appendix A includes 33 symptoms that will help you search out, identify, and take proper action with mechanical problems. Use it to sharpen your skills in troubleshooting and know your responsibility as a driver.

True/False Questions

If the statement is true, circle the T. If the statement is false, circle the F.

T F   1. Few companies have a policy on what drivers may and may not do in the way of minor repairs and adjustments.

T F   2. If you find a mechanical problem, you should do only what you are qualified to do. Keep in mind company policy, safety, your rig, your load, and the well-being of yourself and others.

T F   3. Drivers and mechanics must work together to ensure the safe and economic operation of a rig.

T F   4. Though drivers are not mechanics, they should notice unusual noises and the need for abnormal handling of the vehicle.

T F   5. If you use your senses of sight, sound, feel, and smell to notice a defect before it develops into a breakdown, you may prevent costly repairs and accidents.

T F   6. One problem with detecting malfunctions early is that your truck may have to go into the shop. This will cause too much downtime.

T F   7. Finding problems early and repairing them leads to better operation and lower operating costs, which are good for everyone.

T F   8. If you are careless or do not pay attention, serious damage can disable your truck before the mechanic is aware a problem exists.

T F   9. If you find something wrong with your rig, you should fix it.

T F   10. You should report only the facts about the symptoms and what your troubleshooting has turned up.

T F   11. You should not try to repair brake problems. Leave them to a qualified mechanic.

T F 12. A good troubleshooter drives with a high degree of awareness.

T F 13. Good troubleshooters do not need to worry about company repair policies.

T F 14. One of the most important marks of a good troubleshooter is that he or she uses common sense.

T F 15. When you jump-start a dead battery, hook up one cable to the positive pole of the dead battery and the positive pole of the booster battery. Hook up the other cable to the negative pole of the dead battery and the negative pole of the booster battery.

CHAPTER TWENTY-FIVE HANDLING CARGO

SUMMARY

In this chapter, you learned why it is important to handle cargo properly. You have also learned what the driver's responsibilities are regarding various cargoes. You discovered there are laws that determine the way cargo is shipped and how it must be secured. You also know that certain types of cargo are hazardous materials and have their own rules for the way they must be shipped and the routes the driver can use. Weight limits and distribution of weight were also discussed.

LEARNING ACTIVITIES

In the following drawings, the cargo is *not* loaded correctly. On the lines beside each drawing, tell why it is not loaded properly and what may happen.

1. _____

_____

_____

_____

_____

2. _____

_____

_____

_____

_____

3. _____

_____

_____

_____

_____

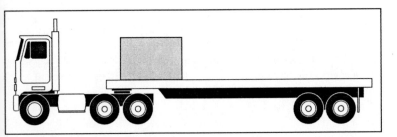

4. _____

_____

_____

_____

_____

True/False Questions

If the statement is true, circle the T. If the statement is false, circle the F.

T   F   1. The backbone of the trucking industry is the safe, efficient transport of products.

T   F   2. All over-the-road or long-haul drivers must personally load the cargo they haul or supervise the loading of trailers they pull.

T   F   3. All drivers are responsible for knowing and complying with federal, state, and local laws.

T   F   4. Federal regulations for protecting cargo from shifting or falling specify the methods for tie-down and blocking and bracing and how the vehicle is to be constructed.

T   F   5. Federal regulations require trailers to have headerboards between the cargo and the driver.

T   F   6. Federal laws set the standards for preventing movement of loose cargo.

T   F   7. Only chains may be used to secure cargo on a flatbed trailer.

T   F   8. There is only one reason for covering cargo, and that is to prevent dangerous spills.

T   F   9. Tying a tarp securely in the first place saves time because you will not have to check it again.

T   F   10. When a driver accepts freight for loading on a trailer, he or she becomes responsible for its safe delivery in good condition.

T   F   11. Any damage to freight, shortage or overage on count, or other discrepancies should be brought to the shipper's attention at once.

T   F   12. If a drum is too heavy to lift onto a drum truck, the only thing left to do is to roll it into place.

T   F   13. Hazardous materials should be handled and transported only by trained and qualified persons.

T   F   14. If you are employed by a carrier of hazardous materials, additional training and guidebooks must be provided.

T   F   15. Each hazard class has requirements for labeling and marking containers.

T   F   16. Hazardous material shipping papers must be within a driver's reach at all times and may be inspected by officials at any time.

T   F   17. Federal regulations require the engine to be shut off while refueling. The person filling the fuel tank must be in control of the nozzle or pump.

T   F   18. When hauling hazardous materials in a trailer that has dual wheels, the driver must stop the vehicle in a safe location and check all tires at least once every two hours or after 100 miles.

T   F   19. Shippers are required to place placards when they are needed.

T   F   20. When hazardous materials are loaded, the driver should check the regulations to determine placard requirements.

T   F   21. Overweight violations are often expensive and can affect a driver's professional record.

T   F   22. Distribution of weight on the tractor will have an effect on handling.

CHAPTER TWENTY-SIX CARGO DOCUMENTATION

SUMMARY

In this chapter, you have learned the importance of cargo documentation: bills of lading, freight bills, cargo manifest, invoices, packing slips, and hazardous material shipping papers. The responsibilities of both the shipper and the driver were explained. How to accept a load for shipment and the correct way to deliver it were described. The special requirements for loads of hazardous material were also explained.

LEARNING ACTIVITIES

Fill out the Form

In the form on page 26.2, put a check mark in each blank that must be filled out by the shipper before a driver can accept the shipment for transport.

Distributing Copies

You have a uniform straight bill of lading. There are three copies of the bill. Fill in the name of the person who gets the copy on the line beside the copy.

Copy 1 (original): _____

Copy 2 (shipping order): _____

Copy 3 (memorandum): _____

You have an order notify bill of lading. There are three copies. Fill in the color of the copy on the line beside the copy.

Copy 1 (original): _____

Copy 2 (shipping): _____

Copy 3 (memo): _____

Delivery of Freight

When you deliver freight, remember you are responsible for the shipment until it is accepted by the consignee. Put the following steps in the correct order by placing a number on the line beside the step. Put a 1 for the first step, 2 for the second step, etc.

_____ Check to be sure the entire consignment is delivered.

_____ Any differences, shortages, or changes in method of payment should be reported to your dispatcher or supervisor before you release the shipment to the consignee.

_____ Make sure the delivery is to the proper consignee.

_____ Collect COD payments before unloading the cargo.

_____ Obtain the correct signature on freight bills, bills of lading, receipts, or other documents before you unload the shipment.

_____ Obtain a properly signed order notify bill of lading before you unload the shipment.

(To be Printed on White Paper)

UNIFORM STRAIGHT BILL OF LADING
ORIGINAL-NOT NEGOTIABLE-Domestic

Shipper's No. _____
Agent's No. _____

_____ Carrier _____ (SCAC)

RECEIVED, subject to the classifications and tariffs in effect on the date of the issue of this Bill of Lading.

From _____ Date _____ , 19 _____

At _____ Street, _____ City, _____ County, _____ State _____

The property described below, in apparent good order, except as noted (contents and condition of contents of packages unknown) marked, consigned, and destined as shown below, which said company (the word company being understood throughout this contract as meaning any person or corporation in possession of the property under the contract) agrees to carry to its usual place of delivery at said destination, if on it's own railroad, water line, highway route or routes, or within the territory of its highway operations, otherwise to deliver to another carrier on the route to said destination. It is mutually agreed, as to each carrier of all or any of said property over all or any portion of said route to destination and as to each party at any time interested in all or any of said property, that every service to be performed hereunder shall be subject to all the conditions not prohibited by law, whether printed or written, herein contained, including the conditions on the back hereof, which are hereby agreed to by the shipper and accepted for himself and his assigns.

Consigned to _____

Destination _____ Street _____

City _____ County, _____ State _____ Zip _____

Routing _____

Delivering Carrier _____ Vehicle or Car Initial _____ No. _____

Collect On Delivery _____ and remit to:

_____

_____ Street _____ City _____ State

C.O.D. charge ⎫ Shipper ☐
to be paid by ⎭ Consignee ☐

No. Packages	Kind of Packages, Description of Articles, Special Marks, and Exceptions	*Weight (Subject to Correction)	Class or Rate	Check Column	Subject to Section 7 of conditions, if this shipment is to be delivered to the consignee without recourse on the consignor, the consignor shall sign the following statement: The carrier shall not make delivery of the shipment without payment of freight and all other lawful charges.
					(Signature of consignor)
					If charges are to be prepaid write or stamp here "To be Prepaid."
					Received $ _____ to apply in prepayment of the charges on the property described hereon.
					Agent or Cashier

*If the shipment moves between two ports by a carrier or by water, the law requires that the bill of lading shall state whether it is "Carrier's or shipper's weight."

Note -Where the rate is dependent on value, shippers are required to state specifically in writing the agreed or declared value of the property.

The agreed or declared value of the property is hereby specifically stated by the shipper to not be exceeding _____ per _____

Charges advanced:

$ _____

_____ Shipper _____ Agent

Per _____ Per _____

Permanent address of Shipper: Street, _____ City, _____ State _____

True/False Questions

If the statement is true, circle the T. If the statement is false, circle the F.

T F   1. A driver must completely understand the terms of all agreements in order to protect him- or herself against liability and personal expense.

T F   2. Surcharges on rates may include special services to be performed by the driver when the shipment is delivered.

T F   3. A bill of lading is a legally binding document that is regulated by federal law.

T F   4. Freight bills are prepared by the driver from the bill of lading.

T F   5. The driver must assure that shortages, overages, and damages are reported to the dispatcher.

T F   6. The driver's signature on the bill of lading means the driver and his or her company are legally responsible for fulfilling all terms and conditions of the contract.

T F   7. It is safe to take the word of a highly regarded shipper for the count and condition of the freight.

T F   8. Before signing a bill of lading for a shipment not loaded in your presence, you should inspect the load if possible.

T F   9. If the trailer is sealed with a security seal or cannot be visually inspected and quantities verified, a driver should note on the bill of lading "shipper's weight, load, and count."

T F 10. When a trailer has a security seal placed by the shipper, the driver should check the seal to be sure it is locked and the serial number matches the number on the bill of lading.

T F 11. Hazardous materials shipments require special preparation, handling, documentation, and communication of hazard.

T F 12. It is the driver's responsibility to properly label each package with the proper hazard class label.

T F 13. Placards are signs shaped like triangles that are similar in design to labels except for their large size.

T F 14. Only some of the more dangerous hazardous materials are identified by an assigned, four-digit identification number.

T F 15. Cargo tanks that have multiple compartments, or those used for hauling petroleum products, have special placarding requirements.

T F 16. Shipping papers must be made available for inspection by officials at any time.

CHAPTER TWENTY-SEVEN PERSONAL HEALTH AND SAFETY

SUMMARY

Anything that interferes with a driver's physical, mental, or emotional state can lead to poor performance. You have learned that drivers must stay away from drugs, use alcohol wisely, and practice safety at all times (Figure 27-1). A driver must also stay physically fit and eat the right foods. Trying to avoid the causes of stress also helps a driver do a better job.

LEARNING ACTIVITIES

True/False Questions

If the statement is true, circle the T. If the statement is false, circle the F.

T F 1. Good vision is one of the most important physical requirements for drivers.

T F 2. Although poor diet can cause a number of long-range physical problems, it has little or no short-term effect.

T F 3. Exercise, both on and off the job, is helpful for tractor-trailer drivers.

T F 4. Fatigue is the underlying cause of many accidents in the trucking industry.

T F 5. A fatigued driver loses some ability to judge and react well.

T F 6. Even though fatigue makes you physically weary, it does not cause drowsiness.

T F 7. Stress increases the chances of fatigue.

T F 8. The best way to deal with fatigue is to prevent it.

T F 9. Regarding fatigue, it is as important to know what not to do as well as what to do.

T F 10. Bringing fresh air into the cab is a sure way to keep from falling asleep.

T F 11. After you eat, the body's circulatory system works hard to digest food and makes the brain want to sleep or rest.

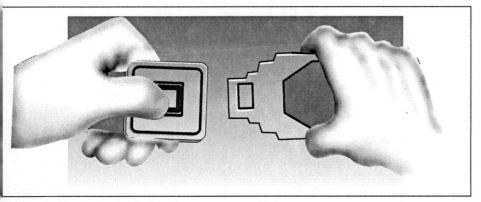

Figure **27-1** Always wear your seat belt.

T F 12. Short 20- to 30-minute naps can relieve a driver's need for sleep.

T F 13. Some people can drink alcohol and not be affected.

T F 14. If you eat a lot before drinking alcohol, you will not get drunk.

T F 15. Neither coffee nor fresh air will help a drinker sober up.

T F 16. A few beers affect a person in the same way as a few shots of whiskey.

T F 17. Like food, alcohol must be digested before it can be absorbed into the bloodstream.

T F 18. Alcohol builds in the bloodstream when it is absorbed faster than the drinker can get rid of it.

T F 19. The BAC is determined by the amount of alcohol consumed, the time it took to drink it, and the weight of the drinker.

T F 20. The first parts of the brain affected by alcohol are those that control judgment and inhibitions.

T F 21. After a few drinks, a person is usually more relaxed and can control his or her muscles better.

T F 22. A person's mood can make a difference in how much effect alcohol will have.

T F 23. The body requires about 1 hour to eliminate the alcohol in one drink.

T F 24. Time is the key to clearing the system of alcohol.

T F 25. FMCSR regulations say that no person shall drink any intoxicating beverage or be under the influence of alcohol within 4 hours of going on duty.

T F 26. Bennies and pep pills should be used by drivers to help them stay awake.

T F 27. If an item is sold over the counter, it is sure to be safe because pharmacies and drugstores are so carefully regulated.

T F 28. When a doctor prescribes a drug, you should ask if there are any side effects.

T F 29. Pep pills and bennies can increase alertness for only a short period of time and then may bring on fatigue.

T F 30. Drugs and alcohol should not be mixed.

T F 31. When used together, tranquilizers and alcohol can multiply their normal effect on the user.

T F 32. Many accidents and injuries happen while the trucker is working around the rig or with cargo.

T F 33. The height of the cab can be a danger to the driver.

T F 34. When getting in or getting out of the cab, a driver is safe as long as both feet are firmly planted on a secure surface.

T F 35. The coupling/uncoupling area can be dangerous because of grease and oil.

T F 36. When pulling down the back door of the trailer, many drivers have been injured because they grab for the strap and jump to the ground.

T F 37. Different types of trailers and cargoes present different kinds of hazards.

T F 38. One reason it is dangerous to work inside a van is because cargo can fall on a person who is climbing around.

T F 39. When two or more persons are lifting cargo, if one person cannot hold his or her share, the cargo should be dropped abruptly to avoid a back injury.

T F 40. When there is an emergency, how, where, and under what conditions you stop can make the difference between safety and serious problems.

T F 41. When checking tires for overheating, you should use the palm of the hand because it is more sensitive to heat levels.

T F 42. If live wires fall on your rig, you should get out of and away from the rig.

T F 43. You can best avoid hijacking and robbery by knowing and following company policy.

T F 44. Drivers who leave their rigs unsecured can be regarded as accomplices to crime and prosecuted.

T F 45. Driver error is the main cause of accidents.

T F 46. Job-related stress can increase chances for driver error.

T F 47. Poor health habits can increase stress levels and create problems for the driver.

T F 48. The number of calories needed per day for professional drivers is about 1,600 for a female and 2,000 for a male.

T F 49. A total exercise program consists of movement plus strength plus flexibility.

T F 50. It is important for the professional driver to minimize job stress whenever possible.

CHAPTER TWENTY-EIGHT   TRIP PLANNING

SUMMARY

In this chapter, you learned about the different kinds of trucking operations and how to plan for a trip. The different types of roads were explained. The permits that may be required were described. How to read maps, figure travel time and fuel consumption, plan for personal needs on a trip, and keep records was also explained. Legal weight and length limits and enforcement agencies for them were presented. You also learned that when you haul hazardous material, you will have special regulations to follow.

LEARNING ACTIVITIES

Trip Planning

Break into small groups. Using what you learned in this chapter, plan the following trips.

Trip #1

You are a delivery driver. You have goods to be delivered to 10 different locations in the same city. What must you plan for before beginning your deliveries? What actions must you take to be sure the consignee receives the right items on time?

Trip #2

You will be making an open dispatch run. Your point of origin is New Orleans, LA. Your destination is Houston, TX. At Houston, you are assigned a run to Dallas, TX. In Dallas, you pick up a load for Oklahoma City, OK. In Oklahoma City, your load is headed for Wichita, KS. In Wichita, you are given a load for Kansas City, MO. In Kansas City, the load is going to Tulsa, OK. In Tulsa, you are dispatched to St. Louis, MO. From St. Louis, you are sent to Batesville, MS. At Batesville, you pick up a load for New Orleans. The run is during the month of March.

1. For how many days should you plan?
2. What paperwork should you be able to produce at any given time?
3. What special permits might you need?
4. How much money should you bring along? What other alternatives do you have to carrying cash?
5. What type of weather may you encounter? At what points?
6. Where can you find information about weather conditions?
7. What type of clothing should you bring along?
8. What type of supplies should you bring?
9. Will you need any special maps?
10. Fill out a driver's log for the trip.
11. What information will you need to supply to your carrier about your trip?

Trip #3

You are carrying a load of radioactive material from White Sands, NM, to Huntsville, AL. The cargo is sealed. At an inspection point, the cargo's seal is broken so the load can be inspected. Plan your trip. List all permits needed. List all prohibited routes. What special care must you take? Fill out a driver's log for the trip. Will you need special maps?

Trip #4

You and another driver are assigned a run from Anacortes, WA, to Houma, LA. You will be hauling drilling equipment. Your load is classed as overweight. Your cab has a sleeper berth. The run is being made in November. Plan your trip. List all permits needed. List all clothing, supplies, and so on you should take. Will you need special maps? Fill out a driver's log for the trip. What information should your carrier give you before you begin the trip? What information should you supply to your carrier when you return?

Map Reading

For the following trips, find the best route. Tell what type of roads you will have to use. Note if there are any roads or bridges you cannot use. Will you need any special permits to make the run? What type of maps did you use to plan your route? How far did you travel? Your instructor may use different routes because there are more maps available for that run.

Trip #1

You pick up a load in Carbondale, PA. Your final destination is Youngstown, OH, with stops in Liberty, PA, and Ridgway, PA.

Trip #2

Your point of origin is Detroit, MI. Your destination is Traverse City, MI, with stops in Midland, MI; Big Rapids, MI; and Grayling, MI.

Trip #3

Your point of origin is Leadville, CO. Your final destination is Roswell, NM. You have stops in Aspen, CO; Gunnison, CO; Durango, CO; Shiprock, NM; Grants, NM; and Alamagordo, NM.

Trip #4

Your point of origin is Mountain Home, ID. Your final destination is Spirit River, Alberta, Canada. You have stops in Grangeville, ID; Missoula, MT; Coeur d'Alene, ID; Bonners Ferry, ID; Lethbridge, Alberta; Calgary, Alberta; Edmonton, Alberta; and Slave Lake, Alberta.

True/False Questions

If the statement is true, circle the T. If the statement is false, circle the F.

T F 1. In addition to being able to drive safely, a driver must be able to plan trips and read maps.

T F 2. Commercial truck drivers do not have to know the size and weight laws, how to register a CMV, how to get permits, or fuel tax requirements.

T F   3. Drivers should be able to find the approximate mileage from origin to destination.

T F   4. Drivers should know how to estimate trip time, fuel requirements, and personal financial needs.

T F   5. Drivers do not need to know which roads are prohibited. This is the job of the dispatcher.

T F   6. In all cases, the best routes for drivers to take are those using the U.S. numbered routes. These routes are always given priority in maintenance and repair.

T F   7. Only trucking company management is responsible for informing drivers of special weight restrictions on bridges.

T F   8. In areas where the speed limit is 55 mph drivers should be able to travel 575 miles in 10 hours without breaking the speed limit and hours-of-service regulations.

T F   9. Drivers or motor carriers may have to document runs to show they can be made without violations of the hours-of-service laws or speed limits.

T F 10. If a driver knows how much fuel the truck's tank can hold and the average fuel mileage, he or she can figure out the cruising range of the truck by multiplying the tank's capacity by the miles per gallon.

T F 11. Low tire pressure and prolonged idling can help improve fuel mileage.

T F 12. Drivers must carry a valid CDL and medical certificate while driving.

T F 13. Federal law allows drivers to have CDLs from many states.

T F 14. Logbooks and driver inspection reports must be completed only when the driver is hauling hazardous materials.

T F 15. At roadside inspections, inspectors do not have the authority to inspect the cargo.

T F 16. If a vehicle is put out of service at a roadside inspection, the driver may continue to operate the vehicle for another 100 miles before any correction or repair is made.

T F 17. Drivers should not be concerned with the weight of the vehicle or federal size and weight limits. These concerns are the responsibility of the company.

T F 18. If you haul hazardous materials, there are no special route restrictions or regulations that you need to know.

T F 19. If you are transporting class A or class B explosives (explosives 1.1–1.3), you must have a written trip plan. In some cases, the driver may prepare the plan for the company.

CHAPTER TWENTY-NINE PUBLIC RELATIONS AND EMPLOYER-EMPLOYEE RELATIONS

In this chapter, you have learned how a truck driver acts has much to do with how the public views the whole trucking industry. You have also learned how to present a good image. Ways to maintain good public relations were explained. You now know the minimum requirements for becoming a truck driver and how to obtain your CDL. Ways to find a job and handle an interview were also explained.

Role Playing

You are to take part in an interview for a job as a tractor-trailer driver. The instructor will set the scene by telling you how you found out about this job, what you know about it, and any other items of importance that have occurred before the interview.

Divide into groups of five. One person will act as the interviewer. The second person will act as the job applicant. The other three people will listen to the interview and offer comments after it is over. It is helpful if the listeners make notes as the interview progresses so nothing is overlooked. Rotate these roles until everyone has had a chance to play each character.

Then come back together and share with the class what you have learned from the experience. Decide what was the most helpful part in preparing for an actual interview. Each class member should have a chance to discuss the interview.

Good PR or Bad PR

Part A

The public's image of the trucking industry is determined, for the most part, by how their drivers act in a situation. Several common examples are given here. Discuss what a truck driver's reaction might be. Then determine if it is going to create good public relations or bad public relations. If the class decides the reaction was bad PR, discuss what should have been done to turn it into good PR.

1. You are driving on an interstate highway, and most of the traffic in the right two lanes are trucks. Traffic is heavy but is flowing at the speed limit. In your rearview mirror, you see this little sports car weaving in and out of traffic. You see it is a hazard for the big rigs. Suddenly it disappears into your blind spot. You are trying to anticipate what its next move will be when it whips around you, cutting you off as it zips into your lane. As the car passes you, the driver makes an obscene gesture. Your first thought is anger. After all, the sports car was a danger, and you were going as fast as the law allows.

2. You are in the second-from-the-right lane on an interstate highway. Traffic is heavy, so it is very difficult to change lanes. You notice that people in the lanes beside you are moving at a faster speed than you. One by one, the vehicles ahead of you change lanes. Then you see why. There is a slow-moving car ahead of you. As you become the first vehicle behind the car, you see the driver is an older person who is clutching the wheel, and the car has out-of-state plates. You decide to show the slow driver what a hazard he is, so you ride the car's bumper.

3. You are driving on a secondary road when you see a car stopped off to the side of the road. There are two small children inside. There is a woman standing beside the car waving frantically. What are your choices? What does company policy say? Should you stop and help? What other possibilities are there?

4. You are making local deliveries, and it has been a trying day. The roads out there are a zoo. You are sure every loony was on them. You have two deliveries left, and you will be glad to be able to go home. You try to deliver the shipment, but the owner of the company says he never ordered the merchandise. You check the shipping papers. They seem to be in order. You tell the consignee this information. He then launches into a tirade against your stupid company and the even more stupid drivers who obviously cannot read and so on. Your first impulse is to tell him what he can do with the shipment in no uncertain terms.

5. You come upon an accident shortly after it has happened. You are running behind schedule and really do not want to stop and help. You glance at the scene and see someone should at least warn oncoming traffic there is a problem here. What actions might the driver take? What should he or she do that would create good PR? What things should be avoided so there is no bad PR?

Part B

Have the class create additional situations and share normal reactions to them. Again, decide if the reaction is going to create good PR or bad PR. If it is bad PR, discuss how good PR could be produced instead.

Have the class bring in clippings from newspapers or magazines that tell of incidents involving trucks. Discuss the reasons for the incidents and possible public reaction to them.

True/False Questions

If the statement is true, circle the T. If the statement is false, circle the F.

T   F   1. How the public views the trucking industry influences laws that are passed related to the industry.

T   F   2. Many people have a poor image of the trucking industry.

T   F   3. Most conflicts between the public and the trucking industry occur in road-sharing situations.

T   F   4. All factors that affect the trucking industry's public image mean more when the public is a customer.

T   F   5. Those who wish to drive a tractor-trailer must be at least 20 years of age.

T   F   6. One important qualification for over-the-road driving is having a personality that suits the job.

T   F   7. No driver may be required to work in violation of federal, state, or local regulations.

T   F   8. Sometimes qualified drivers start out with a company as yard jockeys, freight handlers, or truck washers.

T F   9. The most important part of applying for a job is the list of references you give the employer.

T F 10. The interview is a good opportunity to brag about what you have done in the past.

T F 11. When being interviewed for a job, the candidate should answer questions but not ask the interviewer questions.

T F 12. The road test is a most important part of applying for a job.

T F 13. Even if you have a current valid doctor's certificate of a successful physical examination, you may be asked to take a physical exam given by a company appointed physician.

Glossary

18-wheeler the most familiar combination rig. The tractor has ten wheels and the semi-trailer has eight.

2-axle dolly is attached to the trailer using the actual cargo. One end of the cargo rests on the dolly. The other end rests on the trailer.

2-axle float has a flat bed frame with two rear axles and no landing gear. It is used mostly in oil fields for hauling drilling equipment, pipes, and so on.

2-axle jeep dolly can be attached to the fifth wheel. The fifth wheel is between the tractor and trailer.

2-axle, double drop, low bed with outriggers has a double-top frame and two rear axles. Outriggers are attached to each side of the trailer to support wider loads.

45-degree angle parking an alley dock backing technique in which the rig is pulled forward at a 45-degree angle to the target, then backed in.

49 CFR Part 166 specification for hazardous materials that require special equipment or protection.

5-axle, removable gooseneck, low bed detachable, two axle dolly this low bed frame has three rear trailer axles. A two-axle dolly is attached to the rear of the trailer.

A

Accelerator or accelerator pedal located just under the steering wheel, you can operate this pedal with your right foot to control engine speed. Make sure there is no looseness or sticking.

Accident packet given by most companies to drivers to help them handle their responsibilities at the scene of an accident. Packets usually contain basic instructions for handling the scene of an accident, a preliminary accident report or memo, and witness cards.

Agent a person or company that acts as the official representative of another, such as a consignee's agent.

Air application pressure gauge shows the amount of air pressure being applied to the brakes. When the brakes are not in use, the gauge will read zero psi.

Air blockage when air cannot reach the brakes. This is usually caused by water freezing in the air system.

Air brake application gauge indicates in psi the amount of air pressure used when the brake pedal is pushed.

Air brake system in an air brake system, pressure is used to increase the braking force. The compressed air can multiply the force of mechanical braking many times.

Air filter element keeps the air that flows through the vehicle clean and free of dirt particles.

Air intake system delivers fresh air to the cylinders. An air cleaner removes dirt, dust, and water from the fresh air.

Air operated release the device on a fifth wheel that allows you to release the locking mechanism on the sliding fifth wheel by moving the fifth-wheel release lever in the cab to the unlocked position.

Air pressure gauge tells the amount of pressure in the tanks. The maximum pressure is around 120 psi. The air compressor will build whenever the pressure falls below 90 psi (pounds per square inch).

Air reservoir provides air to your braking system. You should always bleed them each day to remove moisture.

Air starter using another vehicle's air supply to charge your starter.

Air suspension uses bags of air placed between the axle and frame.

Ammeter a gauge on the instrument panel that shows the current output of the alternator. It indicates whether the alternator is being charged by the battery or is discharging.

Antilock brake system (ABS) prevents the wheels from locking up by sensing the speed of each wheel electronically. The computer operated system can apply the brakes 3–5 times faster than pumping the brakes manually. ABS keeps the rig from moving outside its lane while coming to a stop.

Arrester beds an escape ramp, 300–700 feet long, made of loose material (usually pea gravel).

Articulated vehicle a rig that has several parts connected by joints.

Articulation movement between two separate parts, such as a tractor and a trailer.

Atlas consists of maps of states, major cities, and areas. Some atlases may also include the location of permanent scales, low underpasses, size and weight limits, fuel taxes, designated routes, and state laws for access to the designated highway system.

Automatic transmission one that, when set for a certain speed range, will not exceed that speed and the engine automatically shifts through the gears until it reaches that speed.

Auxiliary brakes or speed retarders devices that reduce the rig's speed without using the service brakes.

Auxiliary lights include reflectors, marker lights, clearance lights, taillights, ID lights, and brake lights. When working, auxiliary lights make the rig visible to other highway users.

Auxiliary starter button available on some cab-over-engine (COE) models. It lets you start the engine with the cab tilted.

Average speed formula Average Speed = Distance ÷ Time.

Axle temperature gauge shows the temperature of the lubricant in the front and rear drive axles. The normal reading is 150–200 degrees, but it can reach higher readings, up to 230–250 degrees for a short period of time.

Axle weight the load each axle is supporting. It can either be checked with portable scales by adding the weight of the wheel or at a weigh station by driving each axle over the scale.

Axles connect the wheels to the rest of the rig and support the weight of the vehicle and its cargo.

B

Baffle a wall that has holes in it through which the liquid can flow in a tanker.

Bail-out area places you can use to avoid a crash.

Battery creates or receives and stores electrical energy.

Battery fluid on some vehicles the fluid level in the batteries needs to be checked or maintained.

Belly mount trailer a refrigerated trailer that has the refrigeration unit under the trailer.

Belted bias tires have body cords that run across the tread at an angle.

Bias ply tires have body cords running across the tire at an angle.

Bill of lading a contract between a shipper and a carrier.

Binders used to bind down loads on flatbed trailers. It is important to make sure that all cargo is packaged correctly.

Black ice a thin layer of ice clear enough to let you see the road underneath.

Bleeding tar tar in the roads that rises to the top, causing the road to be slippery.

Blind-side backing backing toward the right (blind) side of the rig.

Blocking pieces of wood nailed to the floor.

Blood alcohol content (BAC) the amount of alcohol in the bloodstream. Determines the level of intoxication.

Blowout when a tire suddenly loses air.

Braces and supports   Methods used to prevent loads from moving. Whether flatbed or drybox, a load must be blocked or braced to prevent movement on all sides.

Bracing   pieces cut to fit and nailed or otherwise secured.

Brake fade   occurs when the brakes overheat and lose their ability to stop the truck on a downgrade.

Brakes   used to stop the vehicle. Make sure that you maintain air pressure and don't have any leaks in brake lines. If the brakes are pulling, have them checked right away. Bad brakes are dangerous to you and other motorists.

Braking system   used to slow or stop the rig. The braking system uses service brakes, secondary brakes, and parking brakes.

B-train   is a rig with two semitrailers pulled by a tractor.

Bulkhead   a solid wall or steel divider that divides a large tank into smaller tanks.

Buttonhook turn   a right turn that allows you to clear the corner by proceeding straight ahead until the trailer tires clear the corner then turning right.

Bypass system   filters a small amount of the oil flow. It is normally used with the full flow system.

C

Cab   the part of the vehicle where the driver sits. Keep it clean so that papers and trash do not obstruct your view or fall under the clutch, brake, or accelerator.

Cable anti-jackknife devices   are mounted on the trailer and connected to the tractor. They keep the trailer and tractor in line.

Cabover engine tractor (COE)   has a flat face with the engine beneath the cab.

Camber   an alignment feature that is the amount the front wheels are tilted outward at the top. It is best for trucks to have positive camber.

Cargo doors   Doors at the back or side of trailer where cargo may be loaded or unloaded. All hinges should be secure and rust and damage free.

Cargo retainer bars   used to secure cargo and keep loose cargo from moving.

Cargo securement devices   tie-downs, chains, tarps, and other methods of securing cargo in a flatbed. During inspection, make sure there is no damage and that they can withstand 1 1/2 times any pressure from the load.

Carrier   an organization that hauls cargo by truck.

Carrier bearings   on trucks with a long wheel base, they join two drive shafts.

Carrier's time record   a record maintained by the carrier that records a driver's duty status.

Caster   an alignment feature that is the amount the axle kingpin is tilted backward at the top. It is measured in degrees. The axle should have a positive caster or tilt forward.

Centers for Disease Control (CDC)   agency to be notified if a cargo spill is a disease-causing agent.

Center of gravity   the point where weight acts as a force. Center of gravity affects the vehicle's stability.

Centrifugal filter   a type of bypass filter in which the oil enters the permanent housing, spins the filter at a high speed, forcing the dirt and particles out of the oil for more efficient cleaning of the oil.

Centrifugal force   the force that pushes objects away from the center of rotation. This force has the ability to push a vehicle off the road in a curve.

Chain control area   a highway area on which it is illegal to drive chains.

Charging circuit   produces electricity to keep the battery charged and run the electrical circuits which include battery, alternator or generator, voltage regulator, ammeter or voltmeter, electrical wires, and battery cables.

Checklist   list of parts of the vehicle to check or inspect.

Chemical Transportation Emergency Center (CHEMTREC)   tells emergency personnel what they need to know to take care of a chemical problem. It also helps make the proper notifications and supplies the emergency personnel with expert technical assistance.

Chock   a block, usually a piece of wood put in the front or back of a wheel to keep it from moving.

Circuit breaker   breaks an electrical circuit during an overload.

Class A fire   a fire in ordinary combustibles such as wood, paper, and cloth.

Class B fire   a fire in flammable or combustible liquids and gases such as gasoline, diese fuel, alcohol, paint, acetylene, hydrogen.

Class C fire   a fire in live electrical equipment. You must put it out with something tha does not conduct electricity. After the electricity is cut off, extinguishers suitable for Class A or Class B fires may be used.

Class D fire   a fire in combustible metals such as magnesium and sodium. These fires can only be put out with special chemicals or powders.

Clutch   connects or disconnects the engine from the rest of the power train.

Clutch brake   stops the gears from turning. To engage it, push the clutch pedal all the way to the floor.

Clutch pedal   used when you start the engine or shift the gears. It has three basic positions— disengaged, free play, and engaged.

COD shipments   shipments in which the driver collects payment on delivery for freight or cargo and freight.

Combination bypass/full flow filter   oil from the full flow filter goes to the bearings, and the oil from the bypass filter returns to the oil pan.

Combination ramp and arrester bed   this escape ramp relies on loose surface materia to stop a rig. It has a grade of 1.5%–6% and is 500–2,200 feet long.

Combination vehicle   when you add a trailer to a tractor or a straight truck. It is also called a combination rig.

Combined axle weight   the load of all axles (tandem or triple axles).

Commercial driver's license (CDL)   required to operate commercial motorized vehicles.

Commercial motor vehicle (CMV)   a motor vehicle or combination of motor vehicles used in commerce to transport passengers or property if the vehicle has a gross combination weight rating of 29,001 pounds or more inclusive of a towed unit with a gross vehicle weight rating of more than 10,000 pounds; or is designed to transport 15 or more passengers, including the driver.

Commercial Vehicle Safety Act of 1986 (CMVSA/86)   was passed to make sure all CMV drivers were qualified.

Common carrier   a motor carrier that offers its services to all individuals and businesses.

Compressor   squeezes the air into a smaller space. This increases the force the air exerts.

Computerized idle timer   a function of the engine's electronic controls, it will shut down the engine in a prescribed amount of time after the truck has come to a halt.

Connecting carrier   any carrier that transports freight to an interchange location and then transfers the cargo to another company to continue the shipment.

Contract carrier   a motor carrier that is under contract to customers to transport their freight. The contract sets the rates and other terms of service.

Controlled braking   putting on the brakes with a steady pressure just short of wheel lockup.

Conventional converter dollies   used to change semitrailers into full trailers. The dolly becomes the front axle of the trailer.

Conventional tractors   have a smoother ride because the driver sits between the front wheels and the rear wheels. Its main drawback is a longer wheelbase, making it difficult to maneuver in tight spaces.

Converter dolly   a set of wheels with a fifth wheel used to connect a tractor to a trailer or a trailer to a trailer.

Converter dolly axle   Attaches to the front end of the trailer. This axle steers the second trailer in a set of doubles. The entire axle turns for steering.

Convex mirror   a curved mirror that gives the driver a wide-angle view to the rear of the rig.

Coolant   a fluid, usually water and antifreeze, that circulates within the system. Coolant helps keep the engine cool and should be checked according to your truck's operator manual.

Coolant filter   keeps the coolant system free of impurities.

Coolant level alarm   lights up when the coolant level starts dropping, indicating a probable leak.

Coolant temperature gauge   shows the temperature of the coolant in the engine block. The normal operating range is around 170–195 degrees.

Coolant temperature warning   lights up when the temperature is too high.

Cool-down   the period after stopping a rig but before turning off the engine.

Cooling system   keeps the temperature down in the engine.

Countersteering   turning sharply in one direction and then quickly turning back in the other direction.

Coupling   joining a tractor to a trailer.

Coupling device   device—called a converter gear or dolly—that makes it possible to attach one trailer to another or to a tractor. Check to make sure all parts are not damaged and are properly secured.

Coupling system   connects the tractor to the trailer.

Cranking circuit   sends electricity from the battery to a small starter motor.

Crosswind   wind-currents traveling from side to side—particularly dangerous on mountain roads.

Custom trailer and dolly for hauling large diameter and long items   has a drop frame and two rear axles.

Customer relations   how you, as a truck driver, get along with customers.

D

Dead axle   an axle that is not powered.

Defensive driving   driving to avoid or get out of problems that may be created by other drivers.

Deliver, or terminal, carrier   the carrier that delivers the shipment to the consignee.

Delivery receipt   a paper signed by the consignee or an agent of the consignee accepting the shipment from the driver. The driver keeps the receipt as proof of delivery.

Department of Motor Vehicles (DMV)   assists in making state laws and regulations for motor carriers.

Department of Transportation (DOT)   administers federal regulations and interstate trucking operations.

Detention time or demurrage   detaining a vehicle beyond a given time. Payment is made to the carrier when delivery is delayed.

Diesel engine   has fuel injectors to supply fuel to the cylinders. The air intake system supplies the air to the cylinders. It does not have a carburetor.

Diet   the food a person eats.

Differential   transfers driving power to the wheels through the drive axle shafts.

Differential warning   flashes when the interaxle differential is in the locked position.

Disc brakes   a modern disc brake system usually has a fixed disc attached to the inside of the wheel. To slow down or stop, the linings are squeezed against each side of the disc. This looks something like a wide-jawed vice closing quickly on a spinning disk. It creates the friction that slows or stops the rig.

Distance formula   Distance = Speed × Time.

Documentation   the papers that accompany shipments and provide an accurate record of the cargo. It also serves as a contract for the transportation services.

Double clutching   a method of shifting in which you shift to neutral, then shift to the desired gears to match the rpm.

Double drop frame   these are low beds that can haul heavy and oversized equipment without going over the height limits. Since these trailers are low to the ground they may have bottom clearance problems at railroad crossings, curbs, and large potholes.

Downgrade   a steep downward slant in the road, usually around mountains or hill country.

Downshifting   when the engine needs more power, moving down the gears increases engine power while giving up some speed.

Drag link   transfers movement from the Pitman arm to the left steering arm.

Drain cocks   drains moisture from the air brake system reservoirs; should be drained each day.

Drive shaft   is a steel shaft that runs from the transmission to the rear of the vehicle.

Drive train   takes the power generated by the engine and applies it to the tractor's rear wheels. As the wheels turn, the rig moves.

Drive wheel skid (Tractor jackknife)   a skid that occurs when the tractor drive wheels lose traction.

Driver awareness   a driver must be aware of his or her vehicle at all times and be constantly alert.

Driver image   the impression a truck driver makes on other people.

Driver reaction distance   the distance your rig travels during the time it takes to identify a hazard.

Driver's daily log, or driver's log   the most commonly used record of duty status for drivers.

Driver-side backing   backing toward the left (driver) side of the rig.

Driving time   all time spent at the controls of the rig. Written as a (D) on the log book.

Drum brakes   a metal cylinder that looks something like a drum that is bolted to each end of the axle. To stop the vehicle, the brake shoe linings are forced against the inside surface of the brake drums which creates the friction that slows or stops the rig.

Drum truck   hand truck used to carry drums. Never roll drums to load them.

Dry bulk tankers   used to haul dry bulk cargo. Dry bulk tankers have a high center of gravity that requires careful speed control, particularly on curves.

Duals   wheels with tires mounted in pairs on each end of the axle.

Dunnage   filler material such as sheets of plywood, padding, or inflatable bags used to fill voids in the load.

Dunnage and return   the weight of the dunnage will be listed on the bill of lading. If the shipper wishes it to be returned, this will be stated on the bill of lading.

E

Electric retarder   uses electromagnets to slow the rotors attached to the drive train. The driver turns it on or off with a switch in the cab.

Electrical system   provides electricity to power the charging, cranking, ignition, lighting and accessory circuits.

Emergency engine stop control   shuts down the engine. Use this control in emergency situations only. Many companies insist that it be reset by a mechanic after each use.

Emergency equipment   equipment needed during an emergency. For a CMV, the emergency equipment consists of a fire extinguisher, reflective emergency triangles, fuses if needed, tire change kit, accident notification kit, and a list of emergency numbers. It is also good to have extra food, drinking water, medicine, extra clothes and cold weather outerwear.

Emergency relay valve   relays air from the trailer air tank to the brake chambers. If there is a break in the lines between the tractor and trailer, the valve sends air from the trailer reservoir to the brake chambers.

Emergency stopping   stopping quickly while keeping the vehicle under control.

Emergency triangles   reflective triangles to be carried on all current commercial vehicles and required by law under FMCSR 393.95.

Employer–employee relations   how you, as a truck driver, get along with your employer.

Engine block   houses the pistons.

Engine brake   retarder alters valve timing and turns the engine into an air compressor. It can be operated by hand with a switch on the dash or automatically when the foot is removed from the accelerator pedal.

Engine compartment   area where engine is kept. Check to see that it has been properly serviced. Look for signs of damage or possible problems with the engine, steering mechanism, and suspension system.

Engine controls   start the engine and shut it down.

Engine oil temperature gauge   indicates the temperature of the engine oil. The normal operating temperature for engine oil is 180–225 degrees.

Engine shutdown   the period of time from stopping the rig until the engine is turned off. Shutting down an engine requires a cooling off period. This prevents damage if the engine has a turbo-charger.

Engine stop control knob   used in some diesel engines to shut off the engine. You pull the knob out and hold it until the engine stops.

En route inspection   a rig's control and instrument check while driving and a check of critical items at each stop.

Environment   the area around the rig that you must see, hear, feel, and sense when driving.

Environmental Protection Agency (EPA)   regulates hazardous materials.

Escape ramps   areas used to stop runaway rigs by either sinking the rig in loose gravel or sand or sending it up an incline. They are designed to stop a vehicle safely without injuring people or damaging the cargo.

Evasive steering   steering out of an emergency situation.

Exempt commodity carrier   carriers that haul commodities, intrastate or interstate, exempt from regulations, such as fresh fruit (except bananas) and vegetables.

Exercise   physical activity that elevates the heart rate, strengthens muscles and burns calories.

Exhaust brake   a retarder that keeps the exhaust gases from escaping which creates pressure that keeps the engine from increasing speed. It is controlled by an on/off switch in the cab or automatically by a switch on the accelerator or clutch pedal.

Exhaust pyrometer gauge   indicates the temperature of the gases in the exhaust manifold. Maximum safe operating temperatures may be shown on the pyrometer name plate or listed in the operator's manual.

Exhaust system   required on all motor vehicles and used to discharge gases created by the operation of the engine. These fumes could be deadly if they get into the cab or sleep berth. For safety, do not operate a vehicle with missing, loose, or broken exhaust pipes, mufflers, tailpipes, or vertical stacks.

Extreme driving conditions   hazardous conditions created by weather such as snow, rain, or ice, or by difficult terrain such as mountains.

F

Fan belt   a belt from the engine that drives the fan.

Fatigue   being very tired from overwork, stress, or lack of sleep.

Federal bridge formula   a formula used to figure permissible gross loads. It also requires minimum distances between the tractor and trailer axles.

Federal Motor Carrier Safety Regulations (FMCSR)   federal laws that regulate commercial vehicle operation.

Federal regulations for hazardous materials transport   federal laws that regulate the manner in which hazardous materials must be shipped.

Fender mirror   is mounted on the fender of a regular long nose tractor. Requires less eye movement and makes it easier to watch ahead of you. Wide angle fender mirrors let you see more when you are making right turns.

Field of view   the area that you can see either in front of you or behind you with your mirrors.

Field of vision   everything you can see (front and both sides) while looking straight ahead.

Fifth wheel   used to connect the trailer to the tractor. It should be properly lubricated, and there should be no worn or loose parts. Also check that there is not too much slack in the kingpin locking jaws.

Fifth wheel anti-jackknife device   prevents a collision between the trailer and the cab. It is automatic and restricts the rotation of the kingpin.

Fire extinguishers   used to put out fires, usually marked by a letter and symbol to indicate the classes of fires for which it can be used. Every truck or truck-tractor with a gross vehicle weight rating (GVWR) of 10,001 pounds or more must have a fire extinguisher.

First aid   immediate and temporary care given to a victim until professional help arrives.

Fixed or stationary trailer tandem axle assembly   is a tandem axle that is placed to get the best weight distribution between the tractor and the trailer, but cannot be moved. Weight adjustments between the tractor and the trailer are then made by moving, or shifting, the load inside the trailer.

Fixed-mount fifth wheel   the fifth wheel that is secured in a fixed position behind the cab.

FMCSR 392.4   prohibits driving while under the influence of any dangerous drug. These drugs include: narcotics, morphine, heroin, codeine, and amphetamines.

FMCSR 397   regulations that deal with driving and parking vehicles with hazardous materials.

FMCSR 397.3   requires all vehicles carrying hazardous materials to comply with state and local restrictions on routes and parking.

FMCSR 397.5   the safe haven regulation that requires all vehicles carrying Class A or Class B explosives (Explosives 1.1 through 1.3) to be attended at all times.

FMCSR 397.9   controls the routes of hazmat carriers. Trips must be planned in the best interest of public safety.

FMCSR, Part 396, Inspection, Repair, and Maintenance of Motor Vehicles   where you can find out-of-service regulations. By law you must know the requirements of FMCSR 396.9 (c), Motor Vehicle Declared Out-of-Service.

FMCSR 392.9   the part of the federal law that protects the driver by prohibiting driving a truck that is not loaded or secured properly.

Foot brake control valve (also called foot valve or treadle valve)   this valve operates the service brakes on both the tractor and trailer.

Force of motion   movement determined by the weight and speed of an object as it moves along.

For-hire carrier   an organization that has as its primary business hauling cargo by truck.

Forklift   used for loading pallets and heavy objects.

Four-axle, removable gooseneck, low bed with outriggers   has a low bed frame, four rear trailer axles and a detachable gooseneck and outriggers for wide loads.

Four-way flashers   two amber lights at front and two amber lights or red lights at rear of vehicle. These are usually the front and rear turn signal lights, equipped to do double duty as warning lights. Make sure they are clean.

Frame   the metal infrastructure of any vehicle—creates the underpinnings to support the rest of the vehicle.

Frame rails   steel beams that run the length of the tractor and trailer.

Frameless construction   the exterior of the van or tank is the weight-carrying part instead of the frame.

Freight bills   bills prepared by the carrier from the bill of lading that must be signed by the consignee before the cargo can be unloaded and indicate whether the charges are prepaid or COD.

Freight broker   a person or company that arranges for transporting freight.

Freight forwarder   a person who gathers small shipments from various shippers and puts them together into larger shipments. These shipments then may go to a break-bulk facility where they are broken down for delivery to the consignees.

Fuel filters   clean the fuel as it goes from the entry tube of the tank, through the tank and fuel lines, and into the injectors. To keep containments out of the fuel system.

Fuel gauge   shows how much fuel is in tanks. Since the gauge is not always accurate, a driver should check the tanks visually before each trip and at stopovers.

Fuel system   regulates the amount of fuel that is sent to the engine and how often it is injected into the cylinders.

Fuel system heater   keeps the fuel system from freezing.

Fuel tank   holds the fuel.

Fuel tax   a tax based on the number of miles driven in that state that is paid by the carrier to each state.

Full flow system   all oil leaving the oil pump passes through an oil filter.

Full trailer   is built so that no part of its weight rests upon the vehicle pulling and can fully support itself with its axles.

Fuse   completes the electrical circuit and prevents overheating by breaking a circuit.

G

Gear box temperature gauge   shows the temperature of the lubricant in the transmission. The normal reading is 150–200 degrees.

General knowledge test   the written test all CDL applicants must take to see how much they know about the laws regulating the trucking industry.

Generators and alternators   devices that recharge the battery when it loses electricity.

Glad hands   connect the service and emergency air lines of the tractor to the trailer. The connections are secure when the glad hands lock.

Gooseneck   used to rest the trailer on the ground to load heavy equipment.

Governor   regulates the air flow to maintain the desired pressure. When the air pressure approaches 125 psi (pounds per square inch), the inlet valves open. They will close again when the pressure drops below 110 psi.

Gravity ramp   escape ramp that has a loose material surface with a grade of 5%–43%.

Gross combination vehicle weight rating (GCVWR)   the total weight of a tractor, trailer, and load.

Gross vehicle weight (GVW)   the total weight of a straight truck and load.

Gross vehicle weight rating (GVWR)   the total weight of a tractor and all trailers.

H

Hand truck   used to carry small loads from the trailer to a storage area.

Handling brake   Stopping the truck when the brakes fail.

Hazard   any road condition or road user (driver, cyclist, pedestrian, or animal) that presents a possible danger to you or your rig.

Hazardous material   material that may pose a risk to health, safety, and property while being transported.

Hazardous material shipping papers   required and lists each item by the proper shipping name, hazard class, identification number, and packing group.

Hazardous materials endorsement   an endorsement on a CDL that all drivers who transport hazardous materials must obtain.

Hazardous materials incident report   a written report that must be filed within 15 days if there is an unintended release of hazardous materials.

Hazardous materials regulations   standards set by the Research and Special Programs Administration (RSPA) Office of Hazardous Materials Transportation (OHMT) that regulate how hazardous materials are shipped.

Hazardous materials shipping paper   A bill of lading that describes hazardous materials by the proper shipping name, hazard class, identification number, and the quantity being shipped. This form must be legible.

Hazardous waste manifest   A form (EPA-8700-22) that describes hazardous waste and identifies the shipper, carrier, and destination by name and by the identification numbers assigned by the Environmental Protection Agency. The shipper prepares, dates, and signs the manifest. All carriers of the shipment must sign the paper. It must also be signed by the consignee. The driver keeps a copy.

Hazmat labels labels resembling small placards that are placed on packages near the proper shipping name and identification number.

Headerboard (Headache rack) protects the driver from the freight shifting or crushing him or her during a sudden stop and/or accident.

Headlights two white lights, one to the right and one to the left on the front of the tractor—required on buses, trucks and truck tractors. Used to illuminate the vehicle to help the driver see and help others see the vehicle. During an inspection, make sure they are clean and both high and low beams work.

Helper service a helper is to be provided for loading or unloading freight. The bill of lading specifies who will pay for the helper.

High center of gravity the bulk of the weight of the load is high off the ground.

Highway valve allows air from the hand valve to flow through the air line to put on only the trailer brakes.

HMR 177.810 requires drivers of vehicles containing hazardous materials to obey state and local laws for the use of tunnels.

Hours of service the amount of time you may spend on duty.

Household goods bill of lading used by moving companies for their shipments. This type of bill serves as a legal contract between the shipper and the carrier.

Hydraulic retarder a type of drive line retarder, mounted on the drive line between the engine and the fly wheel or between the transmission and drive axles that reduces speed by directing a flow of oil against the stator vanes. It can be turned on by hand with a lever in the cab or automatically by an accelerator switch on the floor.

Hydroplaning a road condition in which a thin film of water separates the tires from the road and the rig simply slides along on top of the water.

I

Identification (ID) number four-digit numbers used to identify all hazardous materials.

Idling letting the engine run while the rig is not moving.

Independent trailer brake (trolley valve) a hand valve that regulates the air flow to only the trailer unit and puts on the brakes. It is usually called the trolley valve and is normally on the right side of the steering column.

Individual wheel weight the load each wheel is supporting. It is usually checked by state or local officials with a portable scale.

Inner bridge the distance between the center of the rearmost tractor axle and the center of the leading trailer axle. Determines weight limits.

Inside delivery indicates the freight is to be delivered inside instead of unloaded at the curb.

Inspection routine list of steps you go through each time you inspect your vehicle so you do not forget a step.

Instruments and gauges make sure to check all instruments and gauges. In trucks with electronically controlled engines, the needles on all gauges will make a full sweep right after the engine is turned on to ensure all gauges are working.

Interaxle differential lock control locks and unlocks rear tandem axles. In the locked position, keeps the wheels from spinning. This position is used on slippery roads.

Interline carrier one that accepts or delivers shipments for only part of the trip. Another carrier either begins or completes the trip.

Internal combustion engine burns fuel within enclosed chambers called cylinders.

International Registration Plan (IRP) an agreement among the states and Canadian provinces for paying registration fees that are based on the percentage of miles operated in each state or province.

Interstate between states.

Interstate operating authority issued by the DOT.

Interstate routes these routes have separate opposing traffic, limited access, and bypass many small communities.

Intrastate within the state.

Invoice   a bill from the shipper that lists the goods, prices, and total due. This may be mailed to the consignee, or the driver may have to give it to the consignee if it is a COD shipment.

Irregular route   an irregular route describes long-distance transport between a combination of origin and destination points using any suitable route.

J

Jackknife   a type of accident in which the tractor and trailer turn to make a V-shape.

Jifflox converter dolly   used in the eastern U.S., it is hooked behind the axle of a single axle tractor. This converts it to a tandem axle tractor. The tractor then can pull a loaded trailer.

Jug handle turn   A right turn where you compensate for off-tracking by moving into another lane of traffic before entering the intersection. This type of turn is dangerous and sloppy.

Jump-starting   using another vehicle battery to start a dead battery. You should always remember to observe safety rules, prepare the truck, and properly hook up the jumper cables when working on the battery.

Just in Time (JIT) delivery system   a method of shipping that gets rid of the costly overhead of warehousing stock.

K

Kingpin   usually a 2" steel pin that is locked into the jaws of the fifth wheel to couple the tractor to the trailer.

L

Labels   for hazard class; look very much like small placards and should be placed near the proper shipping name and identification number.

Landing gear   on a trailer, used to support the load while it is not under a tractor.

Leaf spring suspension   narrow metal strips of varying lengths bolted together and attached to frame hangers.

Lift axle   can be raised off the pavement when loaded to reduce tire and axle wear. It is usually kept in the raised position.

Liquid cargo tankers   used to carry gasoline, asphalt, milk, juices, or liquefied gas. The smooth interior of the tanks and partial loads make driving very challenging. Drivers should accelerate slowly, avoid braking in turns, turn only at safe speeds.

Liquid surge   the wave action of the liquid cargo in a tanker.

Live axle   supports the vehicle weight, sends power to the wheels, and is hollow.

Livestock transport trailer   these trailers are either flat floor or double drop frame design. They are used to carry live animals. Live cargo shifts about and that changes the balance and stability. Drivers should drive at the speed that lets them keep the vehicle under control at all times. When braking, tap the brakes lightly to set the animals. Then slowly put on the brakes.

Local pickup and delivery   the driver operates in and around cities. He or she will usually be delivering freight to its final destination.

Local truck routes   many cities and towns have designated routes for trucks.

Long-distance transport   cargo is transported from a point of origin to one or more distant destinations.

Low air pressure warning alarm   sounds or lights up when there is low pressure in the air brake system.

Low pressure warning signal   tells the driver the air pressure has dropped below 60 psi. A red warning light will turn on, a buzzer will sound, or both will happen.

Lubrication system   distributes oil between the moving parts to keep them from rubbing together.

Lug lever   the device that unlocks locking lugs on a sliding tandem axle.

Lug tread   deep grooves in the tire shoulders that run perpendicular to the sidewalls. These tires are best for the drive wheels.

Lugging   occurs when the driver fails to downshift when the engine speed starts to fall below the normal operating range. In this condition, the tractor produces too little power and lugs, or struggles.

M

Maintenance policy   guidelines companies set up that tell drivers and mechanics what their responsibilities are in servicing and maintaining their vehicles.

Malfunction   when a part of system does not work properly.

Managing your speed   adjusting your speed for the road, weather, and traffic conditions.

Maneuver   to change direction while moving.

Maneuverability   the ability of the tractor-trailer to change direction while moving.

Manual release   the device on a fifth wheel that allows you to release, or unlock, the sliding mechanism by pushing or pulling a release handle.

Manual transmission   one that must be shifted by the driver through the different gears. A clutch must be used.

Meet and turn   a type of relay run in which two drivers start toward each other from different points and meet at a chosen mid-point. At the meeting place, the drivers exchange complete units or only trailers. Then each driver goes back to his or her starting point.

Motor carrier (carrier)   the person or company that is in the business of transporting goods.

Multiple axle assembly   two or more dead axles together. They spread the rig's weight over more axles. This reduces the amount of weight on any one axle.

Multi-wheel low bed trailer with jeep dolly   has a low bed frame and two rear trailer axles.

N

National network   roadways that allow truck combinations to operate.

National Response Center   helps coordinate the emergency forces in response to major chemical hazards.

National System of Interstate Highways   also known as the Designated System or National Network. Consists of the interstates and many additional multi-lane, divided highways, such as the U.S. routes.

National Transportation Safety Board   investigates accidents and offers solutions to prevent future accidents.

Nonsynchronized transmission   one that does not have thin plates between the gears to assist in shifting. The driver must double-clutch.

Nose mount trailer   a refrigerated trailer that has the refrigeration unit at the upper front of the trailer.

Nuclear Regulatory Commission (NRC)   regulates hazardous materials.

O

Occupational Safety and Health Administration (OSHA)   regulates hazardous materials.

Odometer   shows how many miles or kilometers the rig has been driven.

Off-duty time   illustrated as (OFF) on the log book. It is any time during which the driver is relieved of all on-duty time responsibilities.

Office of Hazardous Materials Transportation (OHMT)   part of the Research and Special Programs Administration (RSPA) that classifies hazardous materials.

Office of Motor Carriers (OMC)   part of the Federal Highway Administration (FHWA) that issues and enforces the Federal Motor Carrier Safety Regulations.

Off-road recovery   using the roadside as an escape path and safely returning to the highway.

Off-tracking   when the rear wheels of a tractor-trailer follow a different path than the front wheels while making a turn.

Oil filter   keeps the lubrication system free of impurities.

Oil level alarm   lights up when the oil level becomes too low for normal operation.

Oil pan   bolted to the bottom of the engine is a container, or reservoir.

Oil pressure gauge   indicates the oil pressure within the system. If pressure is lost, it means there is not enough lubrication in the system.

On-duty time   illustrated as (ON) in the log book; this is the time the driver begins work, or must be ready to go to work, until the time he or she is relieved from work of any kind.

One-way check valve   prevents air from flowing back into the compressor from the reservoirs.

Open dispatch   the driver goes from the point of origin to a distant point.

Order notify bill of lading   a bill of lading that permits the shipper to collect payment before the shipment reaches the destination. The driver must pick up the consignee's copy of the bill of lading before he or she delivers the shipment.

Order notify shipment   one in which payment for the goods is made when the driver gets a copy of the Order Notify Bill of Lading from the consignee.

Ordinary trailer axle   connects the trailer wheels to the trailer body.

Originating, or pickup, carrier   the carrier that first accepts the shipment from the shipper.

Outer bridge   the distance from the center of the steering axle to the center of the last axle in the combination. Determines weight limits.

Outriggers   used for extra support of wide loads.

Overdriving   driving at a speed that will not let you stop within your sight distance.

Overlength load   cargo that is longer than the legal limit permits.

Oversteering   turning the wheels beyond the intended path of travel or more sharply than the vehicle can handle.

Over-the-counter drugs   drugs that don't need a prescription, but still may have side effects like drowsiness that you should be aware of.

Over-the-road   cargo is hauled on regular routes. Drivers may be away for a week or more.

Overweight load   cargo that weighs more than the legal limit permits.

Overwidth load   cargo that is wider than the legal limit permits.

P

Packing slip   a detailed list of packed goods that is prepared by the shipper.

Pallet jacks   used for loading palletized cargo.

Parallel parking   parking in a straight line behind one vehicle and in front of another vehicle.

Parking brake   used when the vehicle is not running. To check that it is working, put on the brake and engage the transmission to see if it holds.

Parking brake control valve   a flip switch or push-pull knob that lets the driver put on the parking brake. Use this valve only when the vehicle is parked.

Parking brake system   is used to hold the rig in place when it is parked.

Peddle run   local pickup and delivery operation; the freight is usually hauled from the terminal to separate destinations in the nearby areas and freight is also picked up along the way and brought back to the terminal.

Pinion gear   At the rear end of the propeller shaft is a short shaft with a small gear at the end.

Pitman arm   connected to and moves the drag link.

Placards   10 3/4 inches square and turned upright on a point in a diamond shape. Federal laws specify when placards must be displayed on vehicles transporting hazardous materials.

Plane mirror   a flat mirror for seeing to the rear of the rig.

Point of reference   a stationary object that you spot or use as a target when you are driving.

Pole trailer   carries long, narrow cargo. A pole trailer can be telescoped, or made longer or shorter to fit the load. Cargo may be poles, timbers, logs, steel girders, or concrete beams. Be careful because you could have problems with visibility and location of the steering axle.

Port of entry   locations where the driver must stop and prove the carrier has authority to operate in the state.

Posted bridges   many bridges have special weight restrictions. Do not cross a bridge if your rig's weight is more than the weight that is posted. Some fines are as much as $10,000.

Post-trip inspection   a thorough check of the rig at the end of a trip.

Power skid   a skid that happens when the drive wheels spin and the rear of the tractor moves sideways.

Power steering   lets the driver control the tractor with less effort and stress.

Power steering fluid   makes the steering easier to turn and should be checked during regular maintenance.

Prepaid shipments   ones in which the transportation charges are paid at the shipping point.

Prescription drugs   are drugs that are prescribed by a doctor.

Pressure points   arteries that supply blood to the body.

Pre-trip inspection   a systematic parts and system check made before each trip.

Preventive maintenance   servicing that is done at regular intervals on a truck.

Primary vehicle controls   allow the driver to control the truck.

Principal place of business   the main office of the carrier where all records are kept.

Private carrier   an organization that uses trucks to transport its own goods in its own trucks.

Pro numbers   preprinted numbers on freight bills that are often used to identify the freight bill.

Progressive shifting   is shifting before you reach the maximum governed rpm.

PSI   pounds per square inch.

Public relations   how you, as a truck driver, get along with the public.

Pusher axle   non-driven axle mounted ahead of the drive axle.

Pusher tandem   the rear axle is powered (live) and the forward axle is not powered (dead). The forward axle must have a drop center so the drive shaft can be attached to the live axle.

Pyrometer   gauge that measures the temperature of exhaust gases.

Pyrometer warning   lights up when exhaust temperatures are too high.

Q

Quick release valve   allows the brakes to release swiftly. When you remove your foot from the brakes, air escapes from the chambers into the atmosphere.

R

Radial tires   the body ply cords run across the tire perpendicular to the tread.

Radiator cap   located at the top of the radiator. It keeps the coolant from overflowing.

Rear-view mirrors   mirrors used to see on the sides and behind the vehicle. Should be at the proper angle and clean.

Receiver/consignee   the person or company to whom the goods are being shipped or consigned.

Reflective triangle   warning device carried on big rigs that is placed to warn other drivers when the rig is stopped. It is usually bright orange with red borders.

Refrigerated trailer   used for hauling cargo that needs to be refrigerated.

Regular route   refers to line-haul transport between given origins and destinations using assigned highways.

Regular run   the driver operates between the same points on each trip and may or may not have a regular starting and finishing time for each period of driving.

Relaxation response a relaxation technique that calms the mind, body, and spirit. The relaxation response helps combat the ill effects of stress.

Relay run refers to a trip in which a driver drives for 10 hours and then goes off-duty as prescribed by the hours-of-service laws. Another driver takes the unit on to the next point. This cycle may be repeated several times as the truck is driven from origin to final destination by several different drivers.

Relay valve makes up for brake lag on a long wheelbase vehicle.

Residential delivery The bill of lading will specify the address and method of collecting payment if the shipment is to a residence.

Restricted routes routes that you are not allowed to go on because the route is hazardous or prone to accidents.

Retention groove a groove in the fifth wheel designed to retain lubrication for the ease of turning of the fifth wheel.

Rib tread grooves in the tire tread that run parallel to the sidewalls. They are designed for highway speeds.

Rims part of the wheel that holds the tire in place. To prevent excess wear, loss of air pressure, or loss of a tire, rims should not be dented or damaged and should be rust free.

Rocky Mountain double larger than a standard double, but smaller than a turnpike double. The lead trailer is typically longer than the second trailer. Overall length is 80 to 100 feet.

Roll and rest a single driver takes the truck from origin to destination.

Rolling traction the friction occurring when one surface rolls over another.

Routine servicing tasks that can be done by drivers, such as add fuel, oil, and coolant, or drain the moisture from the fuel and air systems.

S

Safe haven an area approved in writing by local, state, or federal officials in which unattended vehicles carrying Class A or Class B explosives may be parked.

Safety valves keep the air pressure from rising to a dangerous level.

Sand piles mounds or ridges built high enough to drag the undercarriage of the rig.

Scanning looking far ahead, just ahead of the rig, and on both sides.

Scene the surroundings, or environment, in which the driver operates. It includes the road conditions, weather, scenery, people, animals, and other road users.

Scheduled preventive maintenance servicing that is based upon time or mileage since the last scheduled maintenance.

Seat belt safety harness that holds you in the seat. You should always put your seat belt on before you start the vehicle.

Secondary braking system can slow or even stop the rig if the service brake system fails.

Secondary collision a collision that results from either being involved in an accident or taking evasive action to avoid an emergency.

Secondary vehicle controls do not affect the rig's power or movement but help the driver's vision, communication, comfort, and safety.

Security seals seals shippers place on cargo containers that do not let the driver fully inspect the load.

Semi-automatic transmission one that is essentially a manual transmission, but uses electronic controls to automate some of the gear changes.

Semitrailer is the one most often used in a tractor-trailer combination. It has axles only at the rear of the trailer. The front of the trailer is supported by the tractor.

Service brake system is normally used to slow down or stop the vehicle.

Shipper/consignor the person or company who offers the goods for shipment.

Shock happens whenever something reduces the flow of blood throughout the body and could kill a person. Keep the person warm and quiet.

Shock absorbers   reduce the motion of the vehicle body as the wheels move over uneven surfaces.

Sight distance   the objects you can see at night with your headlights. Your sight distance is limited to the range of your headlights.

Signal or identification lights   truck lights on top, sides and back to identify it as a large vehicle. It is important for these lights to be clean, working, and the proper color.

Single drive axles   found on the rear of the tractor.

Single drop frames   these are low beds that can haul heavy and oversized equipment without going over the height limits. Since these trailers are low to the ground they may have bottom clearance problems at railroad crossings, curbs, and large potholes, but not as much of a problem as a double drop frame.

Skidding   when the rig's tires lose grip or traction of the road.

Sleeper berth (SB)   a berth in the tractor cab in which the driver can sleep. Its size and other specifications are determined by law.

Sleeper berth time   time spent resting in an approved type of sleeper berth.

Sleeper operations   the driver of a rig that has a sleeper berth can accumulate the required off-duty time in two periods as long as neither period is less than two hours.

Slides   sliding assemblies for the fifth wheel and the tandem axle.

Sliding (adjustable) fifth wheel (slider)   slides backward and forward. It can be locked into place to adapt to different loads. It greatly increases the flexibility of the total rig.

Sliding fifth wheels   fifth wheels that are attached to sliding bracket assemblies and can be moved.

Sliding tandem   used on semitrailers. Allows the trailer axles to be moved forward and backward on a track.

Sliding traction   the friction occurring when one surface slides across another.

Sliding trailer tandem axle assembly   is a tandem axle that allows the axle and suspension to slide, or move along, the frame rails of the trailer to make weight adjustments.

Smoothbore tank   a tank that has no bulkheads or baffles.

Space management   keeping a cushion of air around the rig at all times.

Spare tire   additional tire used as a precaution in case something happens to the vehicle tires. Make sure they are properly secured, the right size, and inflated.

Speed   the rate of motion of your rig.

Speeding   driving faster than the legal or posted speed limit or driving too fast for the conditions.

Speedometer   indicates road speed in miles and kilometers per hour and is required by law to work.

Splash guards (mud flaps)   rubberized sheaths hanging behind the wheels that lessen the amount of water/mud kicked up in back of the trailer or truck. Make sure they are properly attached and not rubbing the wheels.

Splitter valve   splits gears into direct or overdrive. This valve is controlled with a button on the top of the gear shift knob.

Spoke wheel   made of two pieces. Difficult to balance and align the tires and rims. Make sure you check lug nuts often for tightness.

Stab braking   first, apply the brakes fully. Then release the pedal partly when the wheels lock. Put on the brakes again when the wheels start to roll.

Standard double   uses two semitrailers. The second trailer is converted into a full trailer by using a converter dolly.

Standard double rig   a single axle tractor pulling a 28' semitrailer and a 28' trailer.

Starting routine   steps used to start the engine.

Start-up   the routine followed for starting an engine.

State primary routes   within each state, these are the major routes.

Stationary fifth wheel   a fifth wheel that is placed to get the best weight distribution between the tractor's steer axle and the drive axle(s) of a properly loaded trailer, and is fixed in that position.

G.17

Glossary

Steering arm   the one on the right side attaches the tie rod to the wheels. The one on the left side is attached to the drag link.

Steering gear box   transfers the turning of the steering shaft to the Pitman arm.

Steering shaft   connects the steering wheel to the steering gear box.

Steering system   allows you to steer the vehicle and should not have more than 10 degrees of steering wheel play.

Steering wheel   connected to the steering shaft and controls the direction of the vehicle.

Steering wheel lash   the rebound of motion of the steering wheel after it has been turned its maximum rotations.

Storage and delay charges   an additional amount to be paid to the carrier if a delivery is postponed by the consignee or shipper or a shipment must be stored before it can be delivered. These terms are stated in the bill of lading.

Straight back parking   an alley dock backing technique in which the rig is pulled forward so that the rear is facing the target, then backed in.

Straight bill of lading   a contract that provides for delivery of a shipment to the consignee. The driver does not need to get a copy from the consignee when the goods are delivered.

Straight truck   a single unit truck with the engine, cab, and cargo compartment all on the same frame.

Stress   your body's response to difficulty, frustration, fatigue, or anger.

Suspension   springs used to support a vehicle and its axles. Failure can result in tragic results.

Suspension system   supports, distributes, and carries the weight of the truck.

Synchronized transmission   one that has thin plates between the gears called synchronizers. Allows shifting without double-clutching.

Systematic seeing   a driver's visual search pattern that helps him or her know what to look at, what to look for, and where to look.

T

Tachometer   Displays the engine speed in revolutions per minute (rpm). It is a guide to knowing when to shift gears. The tachometer helps you use the engine and transmission effectively during acceleration and deceleration.

Tag axle   non-driven axle mounted behind the drive axle.

Tag tandem   the forward axle is live and the rear axle is dead. The dead axle *tags* along behind the live axle.

Tailgate delivery   the freight is unloaded and delivered at the tailgate (the back of the truck).

Tailgating   following too close behind a vehicle.

Tandem axle tractor   a tractor with two axles.

Tandem axles   two axles that work together. There are three types of tandem axles.

Tank vehicles endorsement   an endorsement on a CDL that all drivers who transport liquids in bulk must obtain.

Tarp or tarpaulin   is used to cover most freight and tied down with rope, webbing or elastic hooks. To do its job properly it should be tightly secured.

Thermostat   a valve in the water jacket located at the point where the coolant leaves the engine. It opens to let the coolant go to the radiator for cooling after the engine temperature exceeds 180 degrees.

Through bill of lading   a bill of lading used for shipments transported by more than one carrier that has a fixed rate for the service of all of the carriers.

Tie rod   connects the front wheels together and adjusts their operating angle.

Tie-downs   chains, ropes, and other implements used to secure cargo. Cargo should have at least one tie-down for each 10 feet of cargo.

Tire chains   chain grids used on tires to provide additional traction on snowy, icy roadways. Tire chains are required during bad weather in some states.

Tire pressure   amount of air pressure enabling tires to support their maximum weight. Check the manufacturer's instructions for proper air pressure.

Tire slides   occur when the forces from weight and acceleration of the rig are greater than the tires' ability to maintain traction.

Tire tread   the part of the tire that makes contact with the road.

Tires   provide traction and reduce road vibration, transferring braking and driving force to the road. During inspection check tread depth, air pressure and general condition of the tires. Bald or worn tires can cause a blowout, hydroplaning, or make the vehicle hard to stop. Tires with low pressure make the rig hard to handle and cause unnecessary wear.

Toll roads   except for having to pay a toll, these roads are similar to the interstates.

Total stopping distance   the driver reaction distance plus the vehicle braking distance.

Traction   the contact between the tires and the road surface.

Tractor   pulls the trailer and drives the vehicle.

Tractor parking valve   a round blue knob you can push in to release the tractor parking brake.

Tractor protection system   secures the tractor's air pressure if the trailer would break away from the tractor and snap the air lines.

Tractor steering axle   supports and steers the front end of the tractor.

Trailer   the freight hauling part of the vehicle meant to be pulled by a tractor.

Trailer air supply valve (also called tractor protection valve)   in the open position, it provides air to the trailer brakes. In the closed position, it shuts off the air supply to the trailer.

Trailer brake control valve (also called hand valve, trolley valve, or independent trailer brake)   operates the service brakes on the trailer only.

Trailer emergency relay valve   used only in an emergency when the air supply is lost. If the air lines are crossed, the brakes will stay on.

Trailer hand valve brake   valve in the cab used to operate the service brake of the trailer. To check it, apply the brake and begin to drive. If the unit moves, you have a problem and should stop immediately.

Transmission   is a case, or box, of gears located behind the clutch. It adjusts the power generated by the engine so it provides the right speed and torque for the job.

Transportation charges   fees for transportation services.

Treadle valve (foot brake)   controls the air that operates the brakes.

Tri-drive axles   three axles in the same assembly. They are used where a load carrying advantage is needed.

Trip time formula   Trip Time = Distance ÷ Average Speed.

Triple trailers   are combination rigs that have three semitrailers pulled by a tractor.

Troubleshoot   search out the source of a problem and attempt to solve it.

Truck tractor   a vehicle used to pull one or more other vehicles, such as a semitrailer.

Turn signal lights   lights used to signal to other drivers that you are turning.

Turn-around   a driver travels for about five hours to a point destination and then returns to his or her home terminal. At the turn-around point, the driver might switch units or trailers for the return trip.

Turnpike double   a three-axle tractor pulling two tandem-axle semitrailers—nine axles in all. Turnpikes are most commonly used in the eastern states.

Twin-screws   the two drive axles of a tandem.

U

U.S. Coast Guard National Response Center   helps coordinate emergency forces in response to chemical hazards.

U.S. numbered routes   major through-routes. Those that parallel the interstates may be good alternatives in case of delays on the interstate.

Uncoupling   separating a tractor from a trailer.

Under the influence   refers to any driver operating under the influence of alcohol or drugs.

Uniform straight bill of lading   a contract that the parties cannot change. The goods must be delivered to the consignee or an authorized representative.

Universal joints (U-joints)   allow the cab to move in any direction and let the drive shaft change its angle of operation.

Unscheduled maintenance and repair   occurs when unexpected breakdowns or emergencies require immediate maintenance.

Upgrade   a steepening of the road, usually found around mountainous terrain or in the hill country; the opposite of a downgrade.

Upshifting   allows the rig to gain speed. Moving up the gears provides more speed but less power.

V

Variable load suspension axle (VLS)   allows adjustment of the weight carried by each axle. One type uses air or hydraulic suspension. The other type has springs.

Vehicle braking distance   the distance your rig travels from the time you apply pressure to the brake pedal until the rig stops.

Vehicle condition report (VCR)   a daily report filed with the supervisor by each driver that states the true condition of each truck he or she drove that day.

Visibility   your ability to see in front of you.

Vision   the ability to see, or sight.

Voltage regulator   controls the voltage produced by the alternator or generator. The regulator keeps the battery voltage from getting too high.

Voltmeter   gives an overview of the charging system. It tells the state of charge of the battery and whether the charging system is keeping up with the demands for electricity. During normal operation the meter needle should be between 13 and 14.5.

W

Warehouse receipt   a receipt kept by the driver to prove the shipment was unloaded at a warehouse.

Warm-up   the period of time after starting the engine but before moving the rig.

Weight distance tax   also called a mileage tax, ton-mile tax or axle tax. A tax paid by the carrier that is based on the annual ton mileage.

Weight distribution   the balancing of a load which is determined by the location of the fifth wheel.

Wheel load   the downward force of weight on a wheel.

Wheels   to be inspected with each trip, carries each tire, attached with lug nuts.